Brief Contents

Contents

consumer behaviour

EDITION 3

LEON SCHIFFMAN | DAVID BEDNALL | ARON O'CASS | ANGELA PALADINO | LESLIE KANUK

To my dearest ones, Liz, Tim and Rob, and to my colleagues and students—a heartfelt thanks – DB

To my wife Karen and children Jessie, Karlee, Tonia, Jared and Lydia for their support and encouragement. A special thanks to my Mum (Julee) and Gran (May) who have encouraged me to work hard – AO

To my family for their endless encouragement and support – AP

Pearson Education Australia
Unit 4, Level 2
14 Aquatic Drive
Frenchs Forest NSW 2086

www.pearsoned.com.au

Senior Acquisitions Editor: Sonia Wilson
Senior Project Editor: Carolyn Robson
Editorial Coordinator: Liz Male
Copy Editor: Carolyn Leslie
Proofreader: Ron Buck
Permissions Coordinator: Louise Burke
Cover and internal design by designBITE
Cover image supplied by Getty Images
Typeset by Midland Typesetters, Maryborough, Vic.

Printed in China

2 3 4 5 09 08 07 06 05

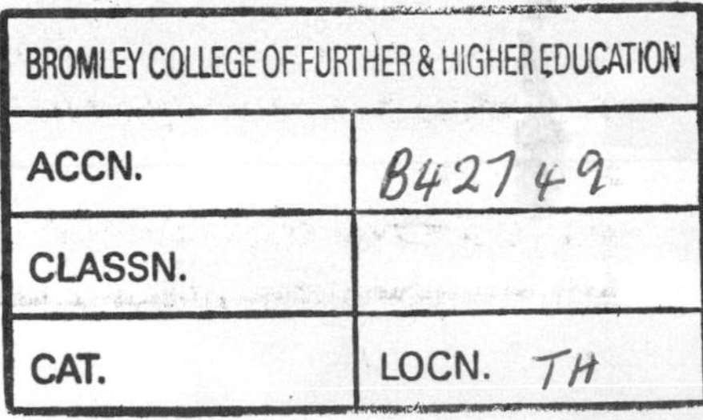

National Library of Australia
Cataloguing-in-Publication Data

Consumer behaviour.

3rd ed.
Includes index.
ISBN 1 74103 163 X.

1. Consumer behavior. 2. Motivation research (Marketing).
3. Marketing. I. Schiffman, Leon G.

658.8342

An imprint of Pearson Education Australia (a division of Pearson Australia Group Pty Ltd)

How to use this book

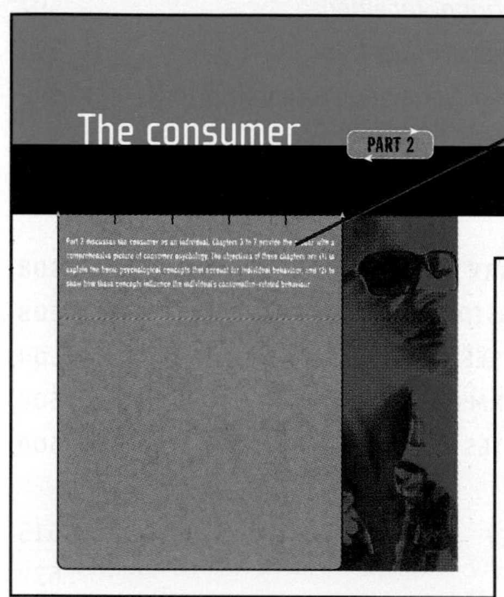

Part opener

Each part opens with a concise summary of the section's main focus and a breakdown of the chapters pertaining to it. A model of consumer decision making follows, with the related section highlighted for usability.

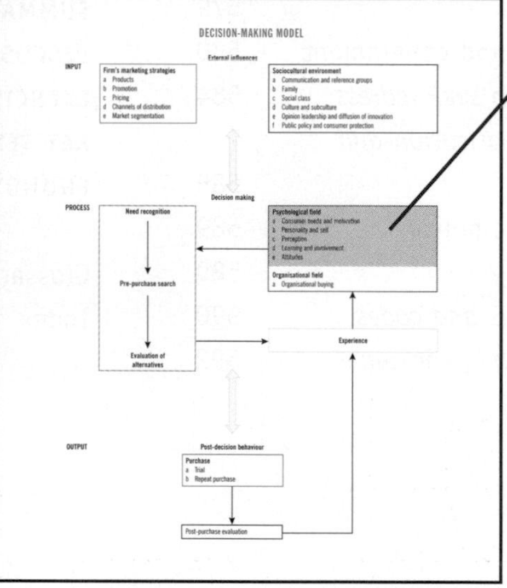

CHAPTER 12
Subcultural aspects of consumer behaviour
WHO SAID MEN CAN'T MULTI-TASK
NIVEA MEN
Source: Courtesy of Foote Cone & Belding.

Culture has a potent influence on all consumer behaviour. Individuals are brought up to follow the beliefs, values and customs of their society and to avoid behaviour that is frowned upon or considered taboo. In addition to cultural segmentation, marketers have begun to segment the larger society into smaller subgroups (subcultures) that identify themselves as members of these groups and who share similar customs and ways of behaving. These subcultures provide important marketing opportunities for astute marketing strategists.

Our discussion of subcultures, therefore, has a narrower focus than the discussion of culture. Instead of examining the dominant beliefs, values and customs that exist within an entire society, this chapter explores the marketing opportunities created by the existence of certain beliefs, values and customs specific to subcultural groups within society. These subcultural divisions are based on a variety of sociocultural and demographic variables, such as ethnicity, religion, race, age, gender, sexual preference and working status. In the Australian and New Zealand context, it must be understood that the *small size* of many subcultural markets may make fine-grained marketing segmentation impractical. However, unless marketers consider subcultural segments, they could:

- miss viable niche markets, particularly those with their own media;
- alienate significant numbers of customers in the subcultures;
- miss opportunities to use subcultural channels for distribution and marketing.

What is a subculture?

A subculture can be thought of as a distinct cultural group that exists as an identifiable segment within a larger, more complex multicultural society.[1] The members of a specific subculture possess beliefs, values and customs that set them apart from other members of the same society. In addition, they adhere to most of the dominant cultural beliefs, values and behavioural patterns of the larger society. We define **subculture**, then, as *a distinct cultural group that exists as an identifiable segment within a larger, more complex society.*

Thus the cultural profile of a society or nation can be viewed as a composite of four distinct elements:

1. the unique beliefs, values, and customs subscribed to by members of specific subcultures;
2. the central or core cultural themes that are shared by most of the population, regardless of specific subcultural memberships;
3. language used; and
4. self-identification.

FIGURE 12.1 Relationship between culture and subcultures

Subcultural traits of ESB Australians | Dominant cultural traits of Australians | Subcultural traits of NESB Australians

Figure 12.1 presents a model of the relationship between two subcultural groups—people with English-speaking background (ESB) and those with non-English-speaking backgrounds (NESB)—and the larger culture. As the figure depicts, each subculture has its own unique traits, yet both groups share the dominant traits of the overall Australian culture.[2] In this way, Australia is considered to be a **culturally diverse society**.

Let us look at it another way. Each Australian is in large part a product of the 'Australian way of life'. However, at the same time, each Australian is a member of various subcultures. For example, an 18-year-old girl may simultaneously be of Vietnamese origin, from a

404 PART 3 Consumers in their social and cultural settings

Chapter overview

Each chapter opens with a powerful colour advertisement, along with a topic overview.

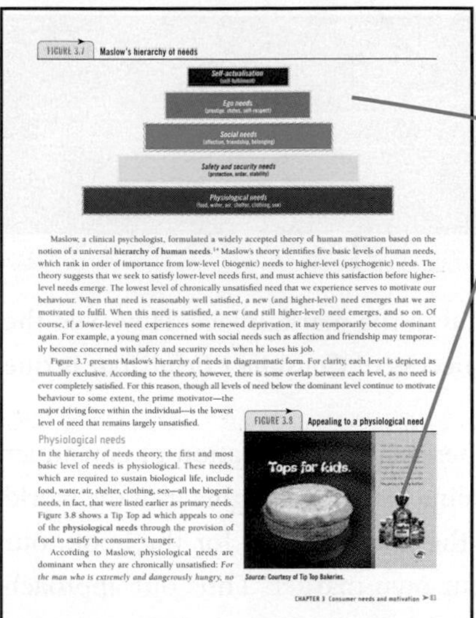

Colour figures, advertisements and illustrations

Throughout each chapter, key concepts, statistics and useful examples are presented with strong colour visual material.

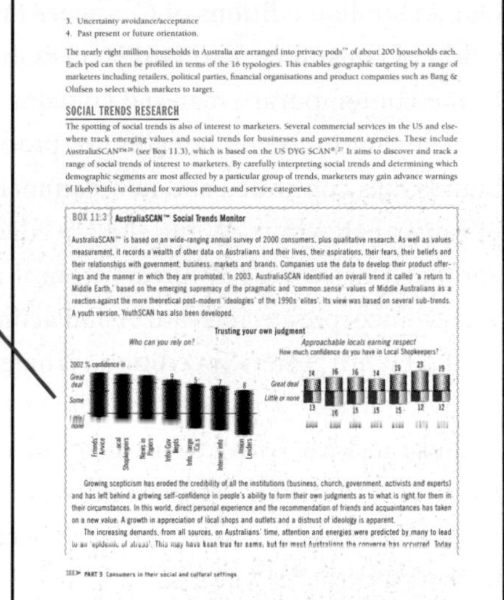

Boxes and tables

Statistics and findings are presented in clear tables. Research and business examples are shown in boxes with supporting colour graphs and illustrations.

End-of-chapter material

Each chapter contains a chapter summary, key terms and references.

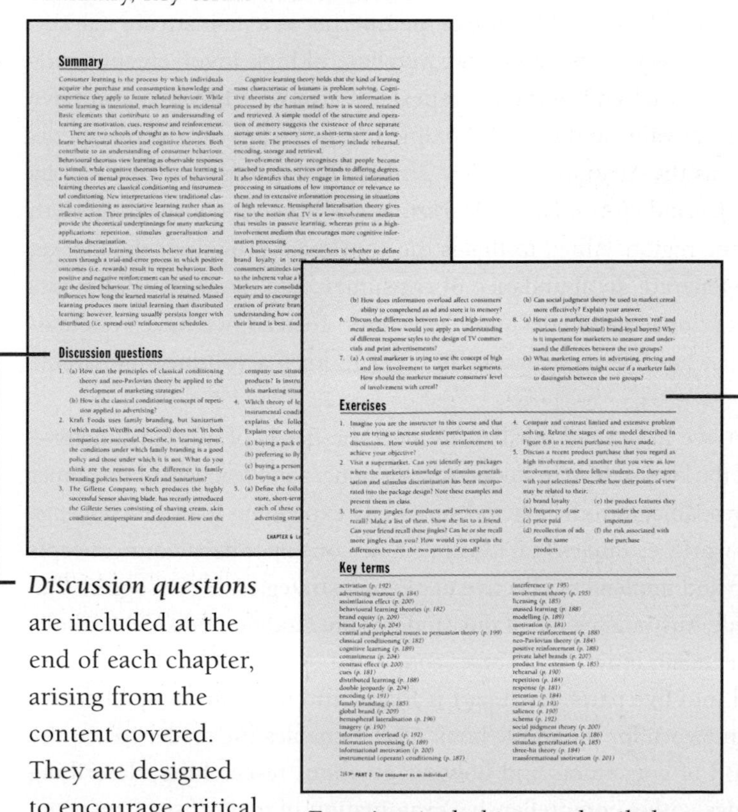

Discussion questions are included at the end of each chapter, arising from the content covered. They are designed to encourage critical thinking and discussion.

Exercises include more detailed scenarios and questions, which promote active participation and the application of personal experience.

Case study

Challenging case studies are included at the end of every chapter, ranging from theory-based to company-specific. Each case invites reflection and analysis and is followed by a set of questions.

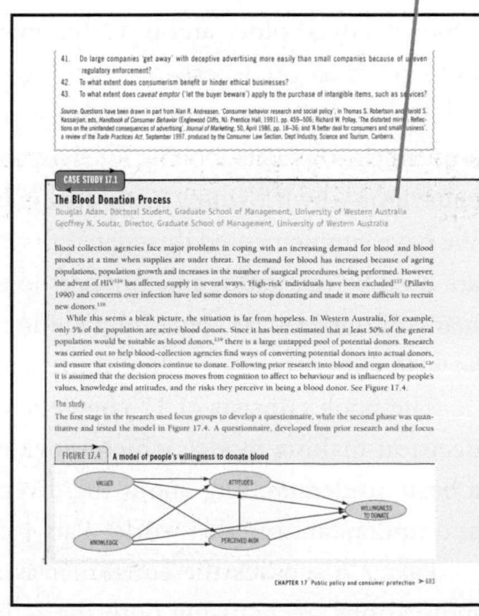

Preface

Our Australian editions of *Consumer Behaviour* have proven very successful in the marketplace. However, the world of consumer marketing moves on relentlessly and part of the past success of *Consumer Behaviour* is due to the contemporary material contained with the text.

The continuous innovation of products and brands, along with the increasing globalisation of consumer brands, has continued and new commercial and academic studies are revealing amazing insights into the world of buyer behaviour. While the US edition of this text provides some of the base material for the book, our approach has diverged further from it as we seek to meet the needs of our own market. Thus our approach was to incorporate relevant Asia-Pacific content and unique case studies into the basic framework provided by the eighth American edition. Where relevant, we also included material from European and other sources to give our text a more international focus. We have included a chapter on organisational buyer behaviour because it deals with key areas of the economy where marketers can have great influence. Public policy also has a decisive effect on the ability of marketers to reach buyers and we have updated and strengthened our material in this key area. We have been ruthless in eliminating unnecessary chapters and in pruning others to focus on the key issues.

Forces that have shaped the new edition include the embedded use of the Internet as a mainstream marketing channel and a realisation that buyer behaviour is not only about the purchase of high involvement goods and services, but is also about the everyday, habitual and mundane aspects of a buyer's life. We also have noticed a greater emphasis on the management of value and plentiful online resources full of advertisements and case study material. Through bodies such as the Australia and New Zealand Marketing Academy and its *Australasian Marketing Journal*, as well as the *Journal of Asia Pacific Marketing*, we have seen a steady growth in high quality and insightful research from the region. Allied to this is the continued growth of the market research and data mining industries, which generate an abundance of consumer data. Such developments could have led us to produce a twin-DVD encyclopaedia of consumer behaviour. Instead, we have systematically removed older and outdated material that has lost its relevance in order to keep a volume comparable in focus to its predecessor.

As true believers in the marketing concept, we have tried our best to meet the needs of our consumers—academic researchers looking for an overview of the latest research; students, practitioners and teachers of consumer behaviour—by providing a text that is highly readable, introducing and succinctly explaining relevant concepts. We have supplemented this material with 'real-world' examples that illustrate how consumer behaviour concepts are used by marketing practitioners to develop and implement effective marketing strategies. We recognise that many of our readers come from cultures outside Australia. Some of our students are studying outside Australia as well, either through online courses or in Australian university courses conducted outside Australia.

The book consists of 17 chapters, divided into five parts. Each part is linked through our comprehensive decision-making model, which provides a framework for the whole book. Part 1 enables the reader to acquire a basic understanding about the diverse world of consumers and how we go about researching, describing and understanding this world. Part 1 concludes with a comprehensive examination of market segmentation.

Part 2 discusses the consumer as an individual. It begins with an exploration of consumer needs and motivations, recognising both the rational and emotional bases of many consumer actions. A discussion of personality and the self-concept follows. A comprehensive examination of the impact of consumer perception on marketing strategies includes a discussion of product positioning, followed by new material on pricing and the perception of value. The discussion of consumer learning then focuses on both limited and extensive information processing, including an evaluation of involvement theory and its applications to marketing practice. Part 2 concludes with an in-depth examination of consumer attitudes.

Part 3 is concerned with the social and cultural dimensions of consumer behaviour. It begins with a discussion of two key social influences on buyer behaviour: marketing communication and reference groups. This is followed by an examination of new family role orientations and changing family lifestyles. It then examines consumers from the perspective of social status and culture, showing how values, beliefs, language and customs shape consumer behaviour. We have completely revised the material in this area and included extended discussion and research into important subcultural groups such as indigenous Australians.

Part 4 explores various aspects of consumer decision making. It begins with a more detailed discussion of decision making itself. It describes how consumers make product decisions, and offers the reader a simple model of consumer decision making that ties together the psychological, social and cultural concepts examined throughout the book. This is followed by an analysis of opinion leadership and its role in the diffusion of innovations. Part 4 concludes with a chapter on organisational buyer behaviour—sadly neglected in other texts but responsible for at least half of all buying.

Part 5 addresses the role of buyer behaviour in our society. The true marketing concept involves an exchange between parties which benefits both of them. At times, this exchange is unfair or unequal and here the role of consumerism and systems of regulation, self-regulation and customer charters must be considered.

Rather than merely summarising the research of others, we have also reported original research in our case studies and looked to identify areas where more research is required, particularly in public policy relating to consumer behaviour. We believe this third edition will prove a valuable tool for both academicians and students alike. May you grow old ever learning new things!

Acknowledgments

Of the many people who have been enormously helpful in the preparation of this third Australian edition of *Consumer Behaviour*, we are especially grateful to our own consumers—the graduate and undergraduate students of consumer behaviour and their lecturers. We would, however, particularly like to thank our colleagues and friends: Elizabeth Bednall, Elizabeth Cowley (our previous co-author who continues to publish widely in the area), Peter Wagstaff, Ian Walker, Kimble Montagu, Stewart Adam, Harmen Oppewal, Colin Jevons, Mike Ewing, Karen O'Cass, Debbie Grace, Deborah Griffin, Margo Poole, Rosa Paladino and Nick Parkington. Special thanks to Liem Viet Ngo who provided much help in compiling the various information for this edition—his assistance is greatly appreciated.

Our thanks go to the following reviewers, who provided useful comments during the development of the manuscript: Angela Bakonyi, University of South Australia; Gordon Brooks, Macquarie University; Dr Rob Hecker, University of Tasmania; Rajeev Kamineni, Bond University; Steve Kelly, Southern Cross University; Gretchen Larsen, University of Otago, New Zealand; Teresa Davis, University of Sydney; Jennifer Beckman-Wong, University of Western Sydney.

We greatly appreciate the contributions of the following case study authors: Douglas Adam, University of Western Australia; Jennifer Beckman-Wong, University of Western Sydney; Les Carlson, Clemson University, USA; Kenneth Chan, Deakin University; Clare D'Souza, La Trobe University; Michael Edwardson, Victoria University; Debra Grace, Griffith University, Gold Coast; Deborah Griffin, Griffith University, Gold Coast; Dimitri Kapelianis, University of Witwatersrand, South Africa; Suzette Major, University of Waikato, NZ; Nick

Parkington, University of Melbourne; Michael Polonksy, Victoria University; Margo Poole, University of Newcastle; Andrea Prothero, University of Dublin; Jenny Rindfleish, University of New England; Geoffrey Soutar, University of Western Australia; Gillian Sullivan Mort, University of Queensland; Mark Uncles, University of NSW; Jay Weerawardena, University of Queensland.

We gratefully acknowledge information and assistance provided by William Burlace and Michele Levine of Roy Morgan Research, Sol Lebovic of Newspoll Market Research, Kenneth Chan of ACNielsen International, Sheba Nandkeoylar and Melissa Chaw of ETCOM, Charles Xuareb of XAX, Colin Benjamin of the Horizons Network, John Elsworth of Holden Ltd and Jane Martin of QUIT Victoria.

Our thanks go to all the people at Pearson Education Australia who aided and supported us in the editorial, permissions and production processes. Without the consistent encouragement and support of Sonia Wilson, Liz Male, Carolyn Robson, Louise Burke, Marji Backer, Paul Petrulis and Carolyn Leslie, we would never have produced this third edition.

To the many other friends, colleagues and students who have not been specifically named, but have provided us with information, support and encouragement, please be assured that we thank you.

David Bednall, Deakin University
Aron O'Cass, University of Newcastle
Angela Paladino, University of Melbourne

➤ About the Australian authors

Dr David Bednall is an Associate Professor in the Bowater School of Management and Marketing at Deakin University. He has previously held senior positions at Telstra, Newspoll Market Research, Australia Post, the Australian Institute of Multicultural Affairs, Monash University and the Australian Broadcasting Tribunal. He is a Registered Psychologist in the State of Victoria and a Fellow of the Market Research Society of Australia. His PhD is in communication from La Trobe University. He is widely published in the areas of consumer behaviour and the market research industry.

Professor Aron O'Cass is Chair of Marketing in the Faculty of Business and Law at the University of Newcastle (Newcastle Graduate School of Business). He has a Bachelor of Commerce majoring in Marketing, a Master of Business majoring in Marketing and a PhD in Marketing. He has published extensively in journals such as the *Journal of Business Research*, *Journal of Advertising*, *Journal of Services Marketing*, *Psychology & Marketing*, *European Journal of Marketing*, *Journal of Product & Brand Management*, *Journal of Economic Psychology* and *Journal of Nonprofit and Public Sector Marketing*. His research interests include: consumer behaviour and branding, particularly consumer brand associations, cross-cultural consumer behaviour, web retail behaviour and brand development and political marketing. He has also studied and published in the areas of international marketing and political marketing.

Dr Angela Paladino is a lecturer in the Department of Management at the University of Melbourne. She has a PhD in strategic marketing and management from the University of Melbourne. She has received the Chancellor's Medal for Excellence in a PhD thesis at the University of Melbourne and has also received the Dean's Award for Teaching Excellence. Her articles have appeared in publications from the American Marketing Academy, Academy of Marketing Science, European Marketing Academy, Australia and New Zealand Marketing Academy and Strategic Management Society. She is also a fellow in each of these organisations. Angela teaches in consumer behaviour and also actively researches in the area. Her research interests include consumer behaviour, environmental marketing and strategic marketing issues.

PART 1

Introduction

Part 1 provides the background and foundation for a comprehensive understanding of consumer behaviour.

Chapter 1 introduces the study of consumer behaviour, its development, and the role of consumer research. It introduces a simple model of consumer decision making and concludes with a discussion of customer value, satisfaction and retention from a consumer behaviour perspective.

Chapter 2 presents a comprehensive examination of market segmentation and demonstrates how consumer behaviour variables provide both the conceptual framework and the strategic direction for the practical segmentation of markets.

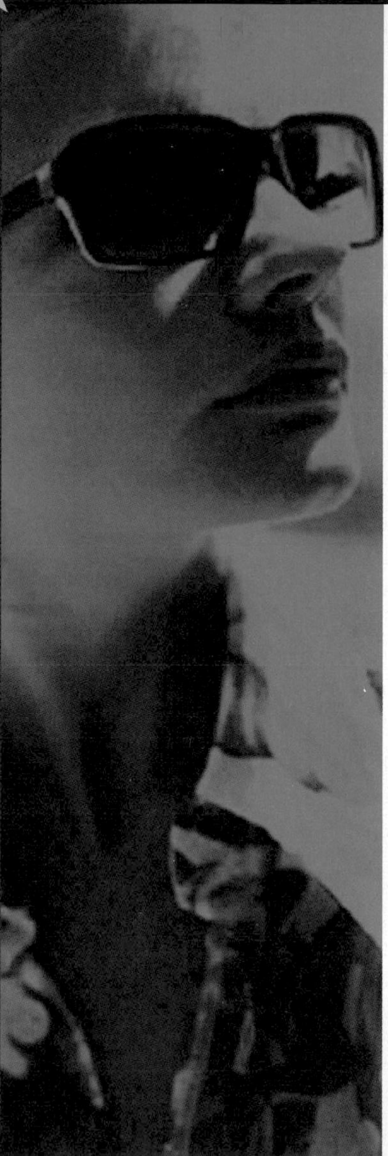

DECISION-MAKING MODEL

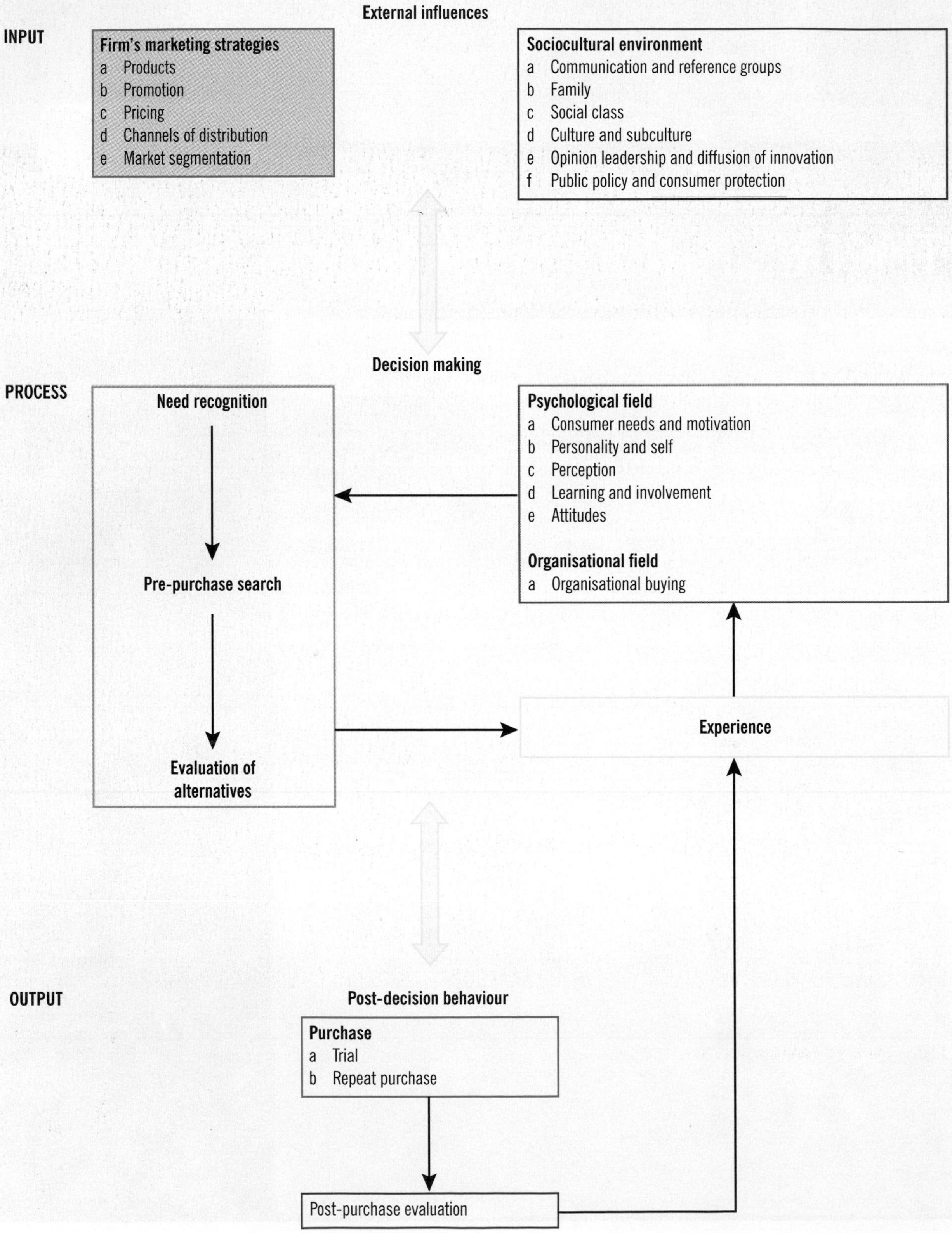

INPUT

External influences

Firm's marketing strategies
a Products
b Promotion
c Pricing
d Channels of distribution
e Market segmentation

Sociocultural environment
a Communication and reference groups
b Family
c Social class
d Culture and subculture
e Opinion leadership and diffusion of innovation
f Public policy and consumer protection

PROCESS

Decision making

Need recognition

Pre-purchase search

Evaluation of alternatives

Psychological field
a Consumer needs and motivation
b Personality and self
c Perception
d Learning and involvement
e Attitudes

Organisational field
a Organisational buying

Experience

OUTPUT

Post-decision behaviour

Purchase
a Trial
b Repeat purchase

Post-purchase evaluation

The foundations of consumer behaviour

enter the world of evoke

be free...

fragrances for every mood

meet your friends in the chit-chat room at www.evoke.net.au

OzGREEN cares for our rivers and water. Evoke does too. That's why we support them. After all, what could be more important in life than clean water! So get involved – Youth LEAD, membership, loads more at www.ozgreen.org.au

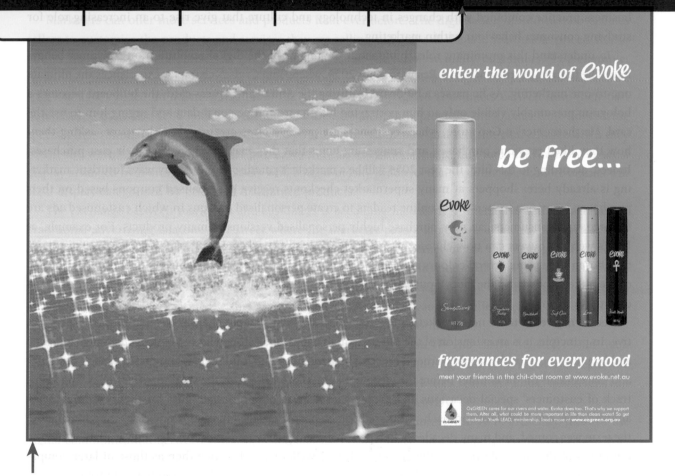

Source: Courtesy of Evoke Body Sprays.

FIGURE 1.1 Converse brand advertisement also depicting brand website

Source: Courtesy of Converse Australia.

supermarket scanners that keep track of households' purchases and instantly provide personalised coupons at the checkout counter and telephone devices that enable us to identify telemarketers automatically. The digital revolution of the marketplace and its impact on consumer behaviour present many challenges for today's marketers.

With the continual social, technological and economic changes in society, the profusion of goods and services offered and the freedom of choice available, we may wonder how marketers actually identify suitable target markets and reach them. How do they know which people to target, where to reach them, and what message would be most effective? The answer, of course, is consumer research. Recognising the diversity within society, consumer researchers seek to identify the many similarities and differences that exist among consumers, wherever they may be. For example, all individuals have the same kinds of biological needs, no matter where they are born. These include the need for food, water, and shelter from the elements. All individuals also acquire and develop needs after they are born. The environment and the culture in which we live, our education and the experiences we have shape these needs. For example, if we are brought up in a culture that values exercise and physical fitness, we might make a point of jogging every day before work or school. If we experience a euphoric 'high' after jogging, we may acquire the 'need' to jog daily in order to maintain a sense of well-being. The interesting thing about acquired needs is that there are usually many people who experience the same needs, despite the individual nature of such needs. Remember, even if you feel you're 'one in a million', there may be thousands of people who are similar to you in many ways.

No matter what our educational, political or social background, one of the few common denominators among us all is that we are, above all, consumers. We all consume food, clothing, shelter, transportation, vacations, entertainment, services, and even ideas on a regular basis. The decisions we make about our consumption behaviour affect the demand for basic raw materials, transportation, production, banking; they affect the employment of workers and the allocation and deployment of resources, the success of some industries and the failure of others. Thus, consumer behaviour is an integral factor in the ebb and flow of all business.

➤ What is consumer behaviour?

The answers to the myriad questions being raised regarding the impact of new technologies and changes in the social and cultural dynamics of society are presently unknown, but the source from which they will evolve is clear. That source is consumer behaviour. **Consumer behaviour** is defined as the behaviour that consumers display in seeking, purchasing, using, evaluating and disposing of products and services that they expect will satisfy their personal needs. Consumer behaviour includes how consumers think (their mental decisions) and feel, and the physical actions that result from those decisions. Although some social scientists limit their definition of 'behaviour' to observable actions, it is apparent that the reasons and decisions behind the actions involved in individuals (and consumer) behaviour are as important to study as the actions themselves. Therefore, as a research area, consumer behaviour is the study of how individuals make decisions to spend their available resources (money, time and effort) on products and services.

People engage in activities for many purposes other than consumption but, when acting as a customer, individuals have just one goal in mind—to obtain goods and services that meet their needs and wants. All consumers face varying problems associated with acquiring products to sustain life and provide for some comforts. Because solutions to these problems are vital to the existence of most people, and the economic well-being of all, they are usually not taken lightly. The consumer must make specific types of decisions in order to obtain desired products or services. The process is complex, as decisions must be made about what, why, how, when, where, and how often to buy an item.

Take bottled water as an example. This has become a multimillion-dollar industry. A study of consumption behaviour in this area would investigate what kinds of consumers buy bottled water, why they buy it, when they buy it, where they buy it, and how often they buy it. The study might find that, among some consumers, the growing use of bottled water is tied to concerns with health and fitness, and convenience and usage situations as shown in the copy for Figure 1.2: 'Moves with you'. It might find that brand images of domestic brands of bottled water differ from imported brands, and that different brands are purchased for varying occasions by consumers. Insights such as these make it easier for bottlers and marketers to select target markets and develop appropriate marketing strategies.

By contrast, a more durable product such as the PDA would have a very different target market. What kinds of consumers buy PDAs? What features do they look for? What benefits do they seek? How much are they willing to pay? How many will wait for prices to come down? The answers to these questions can be found through consumer research, and would provide PDA manufacturers and retailers with important input for product scheduling, design modification and marketing strategies.

FIGURE 1.2 Bottled water ad targeting convenience aspect of the brand

Source: Courtesy of The Coca-Cola Company. Trade marks of The Coca-Cola Company are used with permission. The Coca-Cola Company is not the producer of this guide, nor does it endorse the contents.

PERSONAL CONSUMERS AND ORGANISATIONAL CONSUMERS

The term 'consumer' is often used to describe two different kinds of consuming entities: the personal consumer and the organisational consumer. The **personal consumer** buys goods and services for his or her own use (e.g. clothes, food or music), for the use of the whole household (dinner set), for another member of the household (a toothbrush) or as a gift for a friend (a CD or a book). In all these contexts, the goods are bought for final use by individuals who are referred to as 'end-users' or 'ultimate consumers' as shown in Figure 1.3 (page 10).

The second category of consumer, the **organisational consumer**, includes profit and non-profit businesses, public sector agencies (local, State and national) and institutions (schools, churches, prisons), all of which buy products, equipment and services in order to run their organisations. Manufacturing companies must buy the raw materials and other components to manufacture and sell their products; service companies must buy the equipment necessary to render the services they sell; government agencies must buy the office products needed to operate agencies; and institutions must buy the materials they need to maintain themselves and their markets as shown in Figure 1.4 (page 10) targeting the organisational consumer.

Despite the importance of both categories of consumers—individuals and organisations—this book focuses primarily on individual consumers who purchase for their own use or for household use. (Chapter 16 examines organisational buyer behaviour.) **End-use consumption** is perhaps the most pervasive type of consumer behaviour, since it involves everyone in the role of either buyer or consumer, or both.

BUYERS AND USERS (CONSUMERS)

The person who purchases a product is not always the user of the product, or the only user of the product. Nor is the purchaser necessarily the person who makes the purchase decision or pays for the product. The marketplace activities of individuals entail three functions, or roles, as part of the processes involved in consumer behaviour. The three functions are: the **consumer**, the person who consumes or uses the product or service; the **buyer**, the person who undertakes the activities to procure or obtain the product or service; and the **payer**, the person who provides the money or other object of value to obtain the product or service. A mother may buy toys for her children (who are the users); she may buy food for dinner (and consume it along with other family members) or she may buy cosmetics (and be the only user). She may buy a magazine that one of her teenagers requested, or rent a video that her husband wants to watch, or she and her husband together may buy a car that they select and purchase together. Figures 1.5, 1.6 and 1.7 (pages 11 and 14) show different advertisements appealing to buyer, payer and consumer.

Marketers must decide whom to target their marketing at: the buyer, the payer or the user. For some products or services, they must identify the person who is most likely to influence the decision. For example, as people live longer, they often become dependent on the advice and counsel of their children or other caregivers. Should a retirement community advertise to the elderly or to their middle-aged children? Should an emergency response system be targeted to elderly parents or to their concerned children? Some marketers believe that the buyer of the product is the best prospect, others believe it is the user of the product, while still others play it safe by directing their promotional efforts to both buyers and users. For example, some toy manufacturers advertise their products on children's television shows to reach the users, others advertise in parenting magazines to reach the buyers, and others run dual campaigns designed to reach both children and their parents. (The various influences on family consumer behaviour are discussed in detail in Chapter 9.)

Although this book focuses on how and why consumers make decisions to buy goods and services, consumer behaviour research goes far beyond these facets of consumer behaviour. It also considers the uses consumers make of the goods they buy, and their subsequent evaluations. For example, a woman may feel regret or dissatisfaction with her choice of a car. Perhaps she had to forgo an overseas holiday in order to pay for the car, or maybe it has had continuing mechanical problems. In such a situation she may communicate her dissatisfaction to a friend, and so influence the friend's next car purchase. Or, she may vow to friends and family members never to buy the same make or model again, in turn affecting their future decisions. These possible consequences of consu[illegible]nifications for car marketers, who have to build post-pur[illegible]

In addition to stud[illegible]d their post-purchase evaluations, consumer researchers [illegible]ir once-new purchases when they are finished with them[illegible], do they store it, throw it away or give it away, sell it, ren[illegible]ually do with their obsolete mobile phones and notebook[illegible]t to marketers, as they must match production to the fre[illegible]It is also important to society as a whole, as solid waste[illegible]em that marketers must address in their development of[illegible]sufficient response to the problem. Many manufacturers [illegible]ll in new products, because remanufacturing is often ch[illegible]

➤ Consumer behaviour as an academic discipline and an applied field

The early focus of consumer research was more managerial, with marketing managers wanting to know the specific causes of behaviours consumers undertook. They also wanted to know how people receive, store and use consumption-related information so that they could design marketing strategies to influence consumption decisions. They regarded the consumer behaviour discipline as an applied marketing science: if they could predict consumer behaviour, they could influence it. The ability to understand and influence consumers is deeply rooted in **consumer research**. Consumer research describes the process and tools used to study consumer behaviour. Broadly speaking, there are two theoretical perspectives that guide the development of consumer research methodology: the positivist approach and the interpretivist approach. **Positivists** tend to be objective and empirical, to seek causes for behaviour, and to conduct research studies that can be generalised to larger populations. Consumer research designed to provide data to be used for strategic managerial decisions falls into this category. The research done by **interpretivists**, on the other hand, tends to be qualitative and based on small samples. Although they tend to view each consumption situation as unique and nonpredictable, interpretivists seek to find common patterns of operative values, meanings, and behaviour across consumption situations.

Given the interdisciplinary background in which the consumer behaviour discipline is rooted, it is not surprising that academics from a variety of fields, including marketing, have become interested in the study of consumer behaviour, not necessarily from a managerial or applied perspective, but simply to better understand the consumer.

CONSUMER BEHAVIOUR AS AN INTERDISCIPLINARY SCIENCE

The study of consumer behaviour as a separate marketing discipline began when marketers realised that consumers did not always act or react as economic theory suggested they would. By 'economic theory' we mean the traditional economic concept of decision making, where the maximisation of economic utility or satisfaction is considered to be rational. This explanation failed to recognise the difference between the reason for a decision and the outcome. The economic concept of utility maximisation also implies that physical and emotional motives are two different things. Despite the periodic 'me too' approach to fads and fashions, many consumers rebelled at using the identical products that everyone else used. Instead, they preferred differentiated products that they felt reflected their own special needs, personalities and lifestyles.

FIGURE 1.3 Targeting the individual–family (end) consumer for the motor vehicle

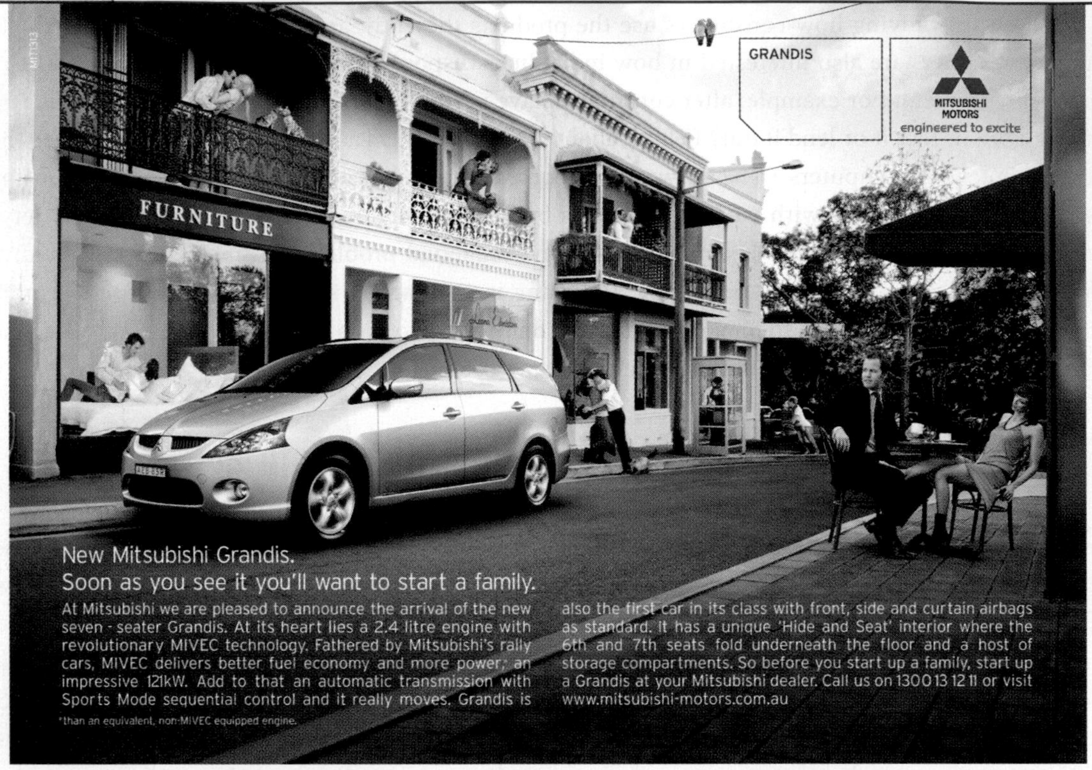

FURNITURE
GRANDIS
MITSUBISHI MOTORS
engineered to excite
New Mitsubishi Grandis.
Soon as you see it you'll want to start a family.
At Mitsubishi we are pleased to announce the arrival of the new seven - seater Grandis. At its heart lies a 2.4 litre engine with revolutionary MIVEC technology. Fathered by Mitsubishi's rally cars, MIVEC delivers better fuel economy and more power; an impressive 121kW. Add to that an automatic transmission with Sports Mode sequential control and it really moves. Grandis is also the first car in its class with front, side and curtain airbags as standard. It has a unique 'Hide and Seat' interior where the 6th and 7th seats fold underneath the floor and a host of storage compartments. So before you start up a family, start up a Grandis at your Mitsubishi dealer. Call us on 1300 13 12 11 or visit www.mitsubishi-motors.com.au
*than an equivalent, non-MIVEC equipped engine.

Source: Courtesy of Mitsubishi Motors Australia Ltd.

FIGURE 1.4 Targeting the organisational consumer for the motor vehicle

typical, only in the country a year and already it's getting all the jobs.
PREGIO
Good reliable workers are always in demand. So it's no surprise that after only one year in the country, the 1.25 tonne Pregio Diesel Van is already Number 2 in its class and the K2700 1.5 tonne tilt cab truck is Number 1^. Both have a gutsy 2.7 litre diesel engine with rear wheel drive for better load stability. And creature comforts like air, CD, power windows and remote central locking. Plus roadside assistance and a courtesy vehicle program† for added reassurance. All for an amazingly low $22,500*. Call Kia now on 1800 600 010 or visit www.kia.com.au to test drive the best valued fully spec'd van and light truck in Australia.
start something
KIA

Source: Courtesy of Kia.

Other factors that have contributed to an increasing focus on consumer behaviour are the accelerated rate of new product developments, the **consumer movement**, public policy and environmental concerns, non-profit marketing, and the development of international and global markets. Consumer behaviour as a field of study embraces numerous concepts and models derived from other areas such as psychology, sociology, social psychology, cultural anthropology and economics. Hence, consumer behaviour is an interdisciplinary science. These various disciplines are outlined below to reflect how they contribute to the field of consumer behaviour.

Psychology

Psychology is the study of the individual. It includes the study of motivation, perception, attitudes, personality and learning patterns. All these factors are integral to an understanding of consumer behaviour. They enable us to understand the various consumption

FIGURE 1.5 Targeting the buyer

Source: Courtesy of Wyeth Consumer Healthcare.

FIGURE 1.6 Targeting the payer

Source: Courtesy of Noni B Limited.

needs of individuals, their actions and reactions in response to different products and product messages, and the way personality characteristics and previous experiences affect their product choices.

Sociology

Sociology is the study of groups. Group behaviour describes the actions of individuals in groups, which often differ from the actions of individuals operating on their own. The influence of group memberships, family structure and social class on consumer behaviour is relevant to the study of consumer segments in the marketplace.

Social psychology

Social psychology is an amalgam of sociology and psychology. It is the study of how an individual operates in a group. The study of consumer behaviour is not only the study of how groups operate in terms of market behaviour; it is also the study of how individuals are influenced in their personal consumption behaviour by those whose opinions they respect such as their peers, their reference groups, their families and opinion leaders.

Cultural anthropology

Cultural anthropology is the study of human beings in society. It traces the development of the core beliefs, values and customs that are passed down to individuals from their parents and grandparents and influence their purchase and consumption behaviour. It also includes the study of subcultures (subgroups within the larger society), and lends itself to a comparison of consumers of different nationalities with diverse cultures and customs.

Economics

An important component of the study of economics is the study of consumers: how they spend their funds, how they evaluate alternatives, and how they make decisions to maximise satisfaction. Many early theories concerning consumer behaviour were based on economic theory. This theory postulates that individuals act rationally to maximise their utilities (i.e. their satisfaction) in the purchase of goods and services. More recent consumer studies have indicated that individuals often act less than rationally (i.e. emotionally) to fulfil their psychological needs.

The interdisciplinary nature of consumer behaviour is perhaps its greatest strength; it serves to integrate existing knowledge from other fields into a comprehensive body of knowledge about individuals in their consumption roles. Thus, despite the fact that the study of consumer behaviour is a relatively recent phenomenon, it has its foundations in scientific thought and evidence that has emerged from many years of research by scientists specialising in the study of human behaviour.

As in any science, consumer behaviour theories must be tested, and either supported or rejected, before conclusions can be generalised as principles applicable to marketing practice. Consumer behaviour research enables marketers to carve out new **market segments** based on variables that emerge as important discriminators among consumers for a specific product or product category. Consumer research is undertaken by various marketing organisations and constituted bodies such as the Market Research Society of Australia and a plethora of private marketing research firms such as Roy Morgan Research, Pacific Micromarketing and others.

Consumer researchers need a clear understanding of the marketing problem before they can start to design research to assist marketers. Fundamentally, researchers should ask the right questions. Once researchers understand the key decisions their marketing clients need to make, they can design research that addresses the needs of the marketer. They do this by considering what information the marketer will need to make reliable decisions. Thus, consumer research is used to gain a better understanding of consumption behaviour, to identify and locate appropriate target markets, and to learn their media habits. It is used to identify both felt and unfelt (latent) needs, to learn how consumers perceive products and brands and stores, what their attitudes are before and after promotional campaigns, and how and why they make their consumption decisions.

Consumer research provides the basis for the development of new product and service concepts to meet targeted consumer needs. It also enables the marketers to build consumer 'meaning' into the product or service by discovering which attributes are most important to the target market and integrating them into the product or service design. For example, Figure 1.8 (page 14) shows OsteoEze identifying the key attributes and benefits that consumer of such a product would be seeking. Market research does not *guarantee* correct decision-making, but it considerably *improves the chances* of this happening.

The field of consumer behaviour has taken on an increasingly significant role in marketing, to the point where it has become the backbone of most programs of marketing study. As students of consumer behaviour moved into marketing management positions in industry, they took with them a knowledge and appreciation of consumer behaviour principles as an applied science, opening up new opportunities in areas of needed research. At the same time, new journals were established to report on such research (see *Journal of Consumer Research*, *Psychology & Marketing*, and *Journal of Consumer Behaviour* as examples of journals focusing on consumer behaviour research), and new professional associations organised to provide forums for the dissemination of consumer research findings (see the Association for Consumer Research as an example of a body focusing on consumer research). The field of consumer behaviour has become a discipline in its own right, buttressed by a strong and growing body of research and the development of consumer behaviour models. Consumer researchers have discovered that consumers are just as likely to purchase impulsively, and to be influenced not only by family and friends, advertisers and role models, but by mood, situation and emotion. All these factors combine to form a comprehensive model of consumer behaviour that reflects both cognitive and emotional aspects of consumer decision making.

A simplified model of consumer decision making

The decision-making stage can be seen as three distinct but interlocking stages: the input stage, the process stage and the output stage. These stages are depicted in a simplified model of consumer decision making seen in Figure 1.10 (page 15). The input stage influences the consumer's recognition of a product need and consists of two major sources of information: the firm's marketing efforts (the product itself, the price, its promotion and where it is sold) and the external sociological influences on the consumer (family, friends, neighbours, other informal and non-commercial sources, social class, and subcultural and cultural memberships). The cumulative impact of each firm's marketing efforts, the influence of family, friends and neighbours, and society's existing code of behaviour are all inputs that are likely to affect what consumers purchase and how they use what they buy. For example, Figure 1.9 shows the Subaru Liberty RX advertisement providing detailed information on the product attributes, its price and website details as decision inputs for consumers.

The process stage of the model focuses on how consumers make decisions. The psychological factors inherent in each individual (motivation, perception, learning, personality and attitudes) affect how the external inputs from the input stage influence the consumer's recognition of a need, pre-purchase search for information and evaluation of alternatives. The experience gained through evaluation of alternatives in turn affects the consumer's existing psychological attributes.

The output stage of the consumer decision-making model consists of two closely related post-decision activities: purchase and post-purchase evaluation. Purchase behaviour for a low-priced, non-durable product (e.g. shampoo or batteries) may be influenced by a manufacturer's coupon and may actually be a trial purchase: if the consumer is satisfied, he or she may repeat the purchase. The trial is the exploratory phase of purchase behaviour in which the consumer evaluates the product (brand) through direct use. A repeat purchase usually signifies product (or brand) adoption. For a relatively high-priced, durable product such as a notebook computer (relatively durable because of the rapid obsolescence), the purchase is more likely to signify adoption.

The consumer decision-making process is examined more in depth in Part 4, where it ties together in greater detail the psychological and sociocultural concepts explored throughout the text.

WHY MARKETERS STUDY CONSUMER BEHAVIOUR

Consumer preferences are in many ways constantly evolving, and even in industrial markets, where needs for goods and services are more homogeneous than in consumer markets, buyers often exhibit diversified preferences and less predictable purchase behaviour. Thus, marketers require a better understanding of consumer behaviour. To meet the needs of specific groups of consumers more effectively, customer-oriented organisations have developed a process of market segmentation, which divides their total potential markets into smaller, homogeneous segments for which they are able to design specific marketing strategies (products, pricing, distribution and promotion). Such strategies can be seen, for example, when different promotional techniques are used to vary the image of a firm's products (and services) so consumers perceive them as more convincingly fulfilling their specific needs. That is the specific needs of a firm's target segments—a process now known as positioning.

The pace of technology is a significant catalyst for the introduction of new products, many of which (some experts estimate over 80%) prove to be marketing disasters. To counter this problem, good marketers have made

FIGURE 1.7 **Targeting the consumer**

Source: Courtesy of Nokia Australia.

FIGURE 1.8 **Herron OsteoEze brand targeting key brand attributes**

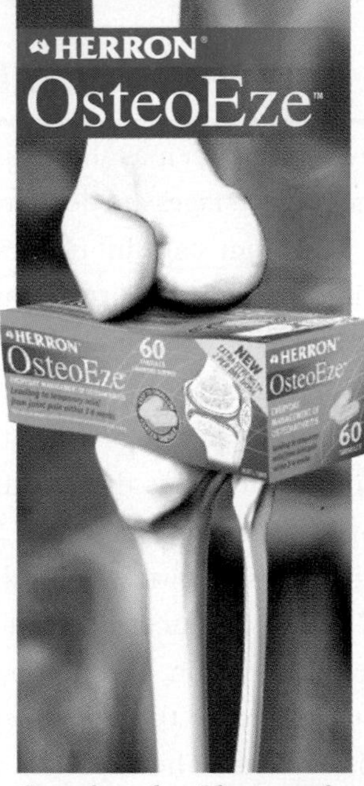

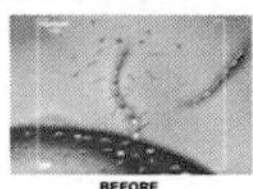

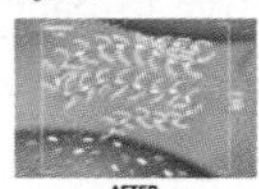

ORDER FROM YOUR LOCAL ALLIED PHARMACY SALES BROKER					
NSW	QLD	SA	TAS	VIC	WA
Tel: (02) 9804 0111	Tel: (07) 3875 2922	Tel: (08) 8354 2755	Tel: (03) 6376 2277	Tel: (03) 9761 0570	Tel: (08) 9451 3299
Fax: (02) 9804 0333	Fax: (07) 3875 2401	Fax: (08) 8354 2766	Fax: (03) 6376 2278	Fax: (03) 9762 7973	Fax: (08) 9451 3699

Source: Courtesy of Herron Pharmaceuticals.

FIGURE 1.9 **Subaru Liberty RX advertisement showing detailed information on features and price**

Source: Courtesy of Mark Llewellynn, c/o Blueprint Production and Management.

FIGURE 1.10 A simplified model of consumer decision making

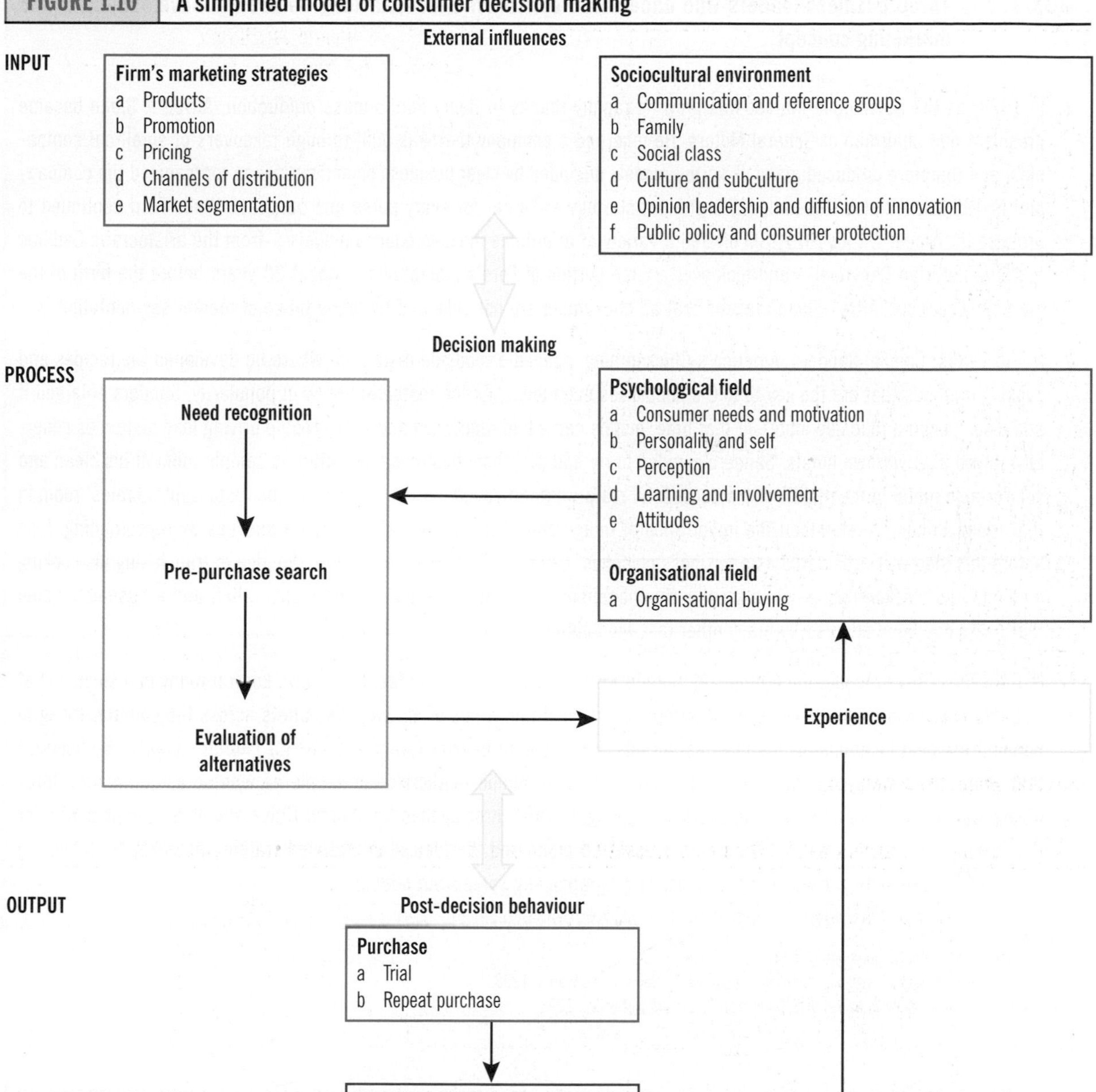

a determined effort to learn more about consumers (their needs, preferences and changing lifestyles) to guide the development of new products to fulfil unsatisfied needs. Box 1.1 provides three examples of business leaders who understood that identifying and satisfying consumer needs were the keys to marketing success.

Shorter product life cycles

Many product categories are driven by specific product life cycles and shorter life cycles have come about because of the fast pace of new product introductions and changes in technology. Many product life cycles are increasingly compressed as products are modified, improved or replaced by new and substitute products. This in turn requires a steady inflow of new product ideas to satisfy the needs (felt or unfelt) of consumers.

BOX 1.1 **Three business leaders who understood consumer behaviour long before the development of the marketing concept**

1. In 1923, as the automobile market was growing rapidly thanks to Henry Ford's mass production, Alfred P. Sloan became president and chairman of General Motors. He inherited a company that was built through takeovers of small car companies, and therefore produced many ill-sorted models unguided by clear business objectives. Sloan reorganised the company and in 1924 articulated the company's product strategy as 'a car for every purse and purpose'. While Ford continued to produce the Model T until 1927, GM offered a variety of affordable mass-produced models—from the aristocratic Cadillac to the proletarian Chevrolet—and took over a large portion of Ford's market share. About 30 years before the birth of the marketing concept, Alfred Sloan realised that all consumers are not alike and the importance of market segmentation.[a]
2. In the 1930s, Colonel Sanders, America's Chicken King, opened a roadside restaurant where he developed the recipes and cooking methods that are the key to KFC's successes even today. As the restaurant grew in popularity, Sanders enlarged it and also opened a roadside motel. At that time, motels had a bad reputation and 'nice' people driving long distances generally stayed at downtown hotels. Sanders decided to try and overcome this image by putting a sample room of his clean and comfortable motel in the middle of his successful restaurant, and even put the entrance to the restaurant's ladies' room in that room. Sanders understood the importance of image and of turning an offering into a success by repositioning, long before this idea was articulated as a business objective. Later on, Sanders came up with the idea of franchising his cooking methods and chicken recipe, while keeping the ingredients of the recipe a secret, and founded KFC and a businees model that has since been adopted by many other fast-food chains.[b]
3. In the 1950s, Ray Kroc met the brothers McDonald who pioneered the idea of fast food as we know it today in a single outlet in California and became their partner. Ray Kroc envisioned thousands of McDonald's outlets across the country. Trying to pinpoint the best locations for the new restaurants, Kroc used to fly over towns and look for church steeples. He believed that where there were churches there were good American families—the kind of people he wanted as customers. Intuitively, Kroc understood and practised market targeting. In 1961, Kroc opened Hamburger University as a training centre for the company's franchisees and their employees, and pioneered the idea of centralised training as a key to delivering standardised products across a large number of geographically spread-out outlets.[c]

Sources:

[a] <www.gm.com/company/corp_info/history>.
[b] Colonel Sanders, *America's Chicken King*, VHS Tape, A&E Television Networks, 1998.
[c] Ray Kroc, *Fast Food McMillionaire*, VHS Tape, A&E Television Networks, 1998.

Consumer research also provides the necessary insights to develop and place appropriate advertisements and other promotional materials to entice consumers to try new products or upgrade their existing ones.

Environmental concerns

Increased public concern about environmental deterioration and resource shortages have made both marketers and public policy makers aware of the potentially negative impact of products such as cooking oils, aerosol sprays and disposable bottles. Consumer research has revealed that many consumers are socially concerned, and favour products that have been modified to meet environmental concerns (e.g. recycled paper products, biodegradable cleansers and packaging), creating a growth in green marketing (which is discussed more fully in Chapter 17). This also extends to companies supporting environmental issues and groups. For example, the product advertised in Figure 1.11 shows that the marketer has aligned itself with an environmental group and is concerned about the cleanliness of our waterways.

FIGURE 1.11 **The brand is aligned with an environmental issue**

Source: **Courtesy of Evoke Body Sprays.**

Consumer protection and public policy concerns

An understanding of consumer behaviour can also aid in the development of public policy that protects consumers. Much effort has been devoted by consumer researchers, marketers and consumer advocates to identify sources of consumer confusion and deception, to discover how consumers perceive and interpret various marketing stimuli (e.g. promotional appeals, package labels, prices and warranties). Consumer research has provided the basis for a number of recommendations concerning consumer and trade practices legislation. In conjunction with the response to the lobbying power of specific consumer protection groups, policy makers at local, State and Federal levels have become more aware of their responsibilities to protect consumer interests and the well-being of their constituents. At the State level, consumer affairs departments, and at the Federal level, the Australian Competition and Consumer Commission (ACCC), monitor industry trade practices, advertising and pricing practices (visit <www.accc.gov.au>). For example, a 2003 court ruling from a case between the ACCC and the Commonwealth Bank required the bank to place corrective television and in-branch corrective advertising about misleading advertising for its home loans under the Cricket Home Loan Campaign, which ran from 22 November 2001 to 27 January 2002.

Growth of services marketing

As Australia develops a very strong service-oriented economy, it has become apparent to many service providers that marketing their offering is more difficult. Services cannot be tested in advance of purchase, nor is quality consistent over time. Services are also 'perishable' in the sense that they are lost forever to the marketer if not consumed at the scheduled time (e.g. the revenues lost from flying a half-empty plane or airing a television show without the full complement of commercials can never be recouped). Not only do service providers need to market, but they realise that knowledge of consumer needs and interests is essential to the development of effective marketing strategies.

Not-for-profit/social marketing

Organisations in the public and private non-profit sectors recognise the need to use marketing strategies to target specific groups or markets. For example, regional private schools and public universities have developed marketing campaigns to attract students; museums dependent on public support develop marketing programs to enlist private contributions and to encourage attendance. Such non-profit organisations use consumer research to gain a better understanding of their target market and thus develop more effective marketing strategies. Such marketing to specific segments is seen in Figure 1.12 (page 20), showing an advertisement by Kids Help Line showing a non-profit counselling service available for children.

Growth of global marketing

Australian companies increasingly recognise the need to market globally in order to increase sales and achieve economies of scale, to not only grow, but also (for some) to survive longer-term. In an effort to reduce the balance of trade deficit, the Federal Government has encouraged small and medium-sized companies to export their products, to assist in generating additional revenues for sustainable long-term economic growth. A major stumbling block to international markets has been the general lack of understanding of the different cultural needs, practices and consumption habits in foreign markets. Australian marketers are now beginning to realise the importance of international (cross-country, cross-cultural) consumer research so that they can tailor their marketing mix strategies to suit the needs of international consumer markets (see Chapter 13 for a further discussion).

➤ The application of consumer behaviour principles to marketing management

To operate successfully, organisations must have an explicit—rather than implicit—understanding of the factors that influence (encourage or discourage) consumers' behaviour (to buy or not to buy). They have to know why they buy, what needs they are trying to satisfy, and what influences consumers' product choices in order to design persuasive marketing strategies.

DEVELOPMENT OF THE MARKETING CONCEPT

While seen as an interdisciplinary field, consumer behaviour is rooted in the marketing concept, a marketing philosophy that evolved in the late 1950s, together with other philosophical approaches—the production concept, the product concept, the selling concept, the marketing concept and the societal marketing concept. For example, during the aftermath of World War II, marketers of many product types found they could sell almost any quantity of goods they could produce to consumers who had gone without while the nation's manufacturing facilities were dedicated to the production of war material. The marketing objective implicit in the production orientation was cheap, efficient production and intensive distribution. A production orientation is a feasible marketing strategy when demand exceeds supply, and when consumers are more interested in obtaining the product than they are in its specific features. In countries such as Australia and the United States, keen automobile consumers sometimes waited months (up to 6–12) for delivery of a new car after World War II. When a dealer notified a consumer that a new car was available, the consumer grabbed it, regardless of whether it was the style or colour originally ordered. Whenever demand exceeds supply, a production orientation can work. Consumers will buy what's available, rather than wait for what they really want. Australian consumers responded to the impetus of post-war reconstruction and the country promoted its manufacturing and produced a range of consumables to meet the demands of the post-war baby boom.

When goods and services become more readily available and competition intensifies, some marketers adopt a product orientation. The assumption underlying the product orientation is that consumers will buy the product that offers them the highest quality, the best performance and the most features. A product orientation leads a company to strive constantly to improve the quality of its product offering, with a result often referred to as marketing myopia (i.e. a focus on the product rather than on the consumer need it presumes to satisfy). A marketer in love with his or her product may improve it far beyond its worth to the consumer, passing the cost of unneeded quality or special features through to the final consumer. For example, sewing machines today come with an enormous number of special accessories (buttonholers, embroidery disks, hem attachments) that most people never use, but which are built into the price of the machine. Some VCRs can be programmed to record eight shows over a 28-day period, and many mobile phones record and transmit audio and visual material. These features are rarely used by most consumers, but built into the price of the product. Sometimes product improvements are technology-driven rather than a response to consumer needs. In highly competitive markets, companies may continue to develop new models and add features in the hope of attracting buyers.

Companies that switch to a selling orientation change their primary focus from improving the product to selling the product. Many companies exert a tremendous 'hard sell' on consumers in order to move goods they unilaterally decide to produce. The implicit assumption in the selling orientation is that consumers are unlikely to buy a product unless they are actively and aggressively persuaded to do so. The problem with a selling orientation is that it does not take consumer satisfaction into account. If consumers are induced to buy a product they don't want nor need, their unhappiness is likely to be communicated by negative word-of-mouth, which may dissuade other potential consumers. The kinds of goods and services that are possible candidates for a selling orientation are unsought goods, such as life insurance and encyclopaedias, and non-profit marketing activities like fund-raising and political campaigns. Even in these cases, if the product (or service or political candidate) does not fulfil a consumer need, it is unlikely that a repeat purchase (or donation or vote) will be forthcoming.

In the early 1950s, many marketers began to realise that they could sell more goods, more easily, if they produced only those goods they knew consumers would buy. Instead of trying to persuade customers to buy what the firm had already produced, marketing-oriented firms endeavoured to produce only what they had first determined consumers would buy. Consumer needs became the marketing-oriented firm's primary focus. This consumer-oriented marketing philosophy, introduced by General Electric in the mid-1950s, became known as the **marketing concept**. The key assumption underlying the marketing concept is that, to be successful, a company must determine the needs and wants of specific target markets and deliver the desired satisfaction better than the competition. While the selling concept focused on the needs of the seller, the marketing concept focuses on the needs of the buyer.

The adoption of the marketing concept by many Australian businesses has provided the impetus for the study of consumer behaviour. To identify unsatisfied consumer needs, companies had to engage in extensive marketing research. In so doing, they discovered that consumers were highly complex individuals, subject to a variety of psychological and social needs quite apart from their survival needs. They discovered that the

FIGURE 1.12 **Non-profit organisation supported by prominent company**

KEEP OUT
Tell your children it's OK to talk to strangers.
KIDS HELP LINE
Sometimes it's important for kids to talk to people other than their friends or family about their problems. So thankfully we're here. Kids Help Line provides a free 24-hour professional counselling service that is anonymous and confidential. Our counsellors are always available to listen to any child's problem, no matter how small or how embarrassing, all they have to do is call us on 1800 55 1800 or go to kidshelponline.com.au
Optus is proud to help kids connect to Kids Help Line.
Just say the word 'yes'
OPTUS
OPT1933/T

Source: **Courtesy of Optus.**

needs and priorities of different consumer segments differed dramatically. They also discovered that in order to design new products and marketing strategies that would fulfil consumer needs, they had to study consumers and their consumption behaviour in depth. Thus, market segmentation and the marketing concept laid the groundwork for the application of consumer behaviour principles to marketing strategy.

THE SOCIETAL MARKETING CONCEPT

Given the fact that business prospers when society prospers, many people believe that all of us, businesses as well as individuals, would be better off if social responsibility were an integral component of every marketing decision. Indeed, in an era of environmental deterioration, poverty, homelessness, drug addiction, gambling addiction, AIDS, gun misuse and countless other societal problems, the marketing concept as we know it (identifying and fulfilling the needs of target audiences) is sometimes inappropriate. This is particularly true in situations where the means for need satisfaction (the product or service), can be harmful to the individual or to society.

A reassessment of the traditional marketing concept suggests that a more appropriate conceptualisation for the times in which we live would balance the needs of society with the needs of the individual and the organisation. The **societal marketing concept** sees all marketers adhering to principles of social responsibility in the marketing of their goods and services; that is, they must endeavour to satisfy the needs and wants of their target markets in ways that preserve and enhance the well-being of consumers and society as a whole. Thus, a restructured definition of the marketing concept calls on marketers to fulfil the needs of the target audience in ways that improve society as a whole while also fulfilling the objectives of the organisation.[3] According to advocates of the societal marketing concept, fast-food restaurants would not sell hamburgers, or French fries, or pies that are high in fat and starch and low in nutrients, despite strong consumer acceptance of these products. Nor would marketers advertise alcoholic beverages to young people, or use young models or professional athletes in liquor advertisements, because they often serve as role models for the young.

A serious deterrent to the widespread implementation of the societal marketing concept is the tendency for most business managers to embrace a short-run orientation towards increased market share, quick profits and stock market consideration for public companies. This is understandable in light of the fact that managerial performance is usually evaluated on the basis of short-term results. When personal advancement depends on quick profits, marketing decisions tend to be based on anticipated short-term economic results. The societal concept in some people's minds may conflict with accountability measured in the short-term. The societal marketing concept necessarily requires a long-term perspective. It recognises that all companies would be better off in a stronger, healthier society, and that companies that incorporate ethical behaviour and social responsibility in all their business dealings will attract and maintain loyal consumer support over the long term.

SEGMENTATION, TARGETING, AND POSITIONING

The focus of the marketing concept is consumer needs. At the same time, recognising the high degree of diversity among us, consumer researchers seek to identify the many similarities—or constants—that exist among the peoples of the world. In this context, we all have similar kinds of biological needs, no matter where we are born—the needs for food, for water, for air, and for shelter from the elements. We also develop needs after we are born, and these needs are shaped by the environment and the culture in which we live, by our education, and by our experiences. The interesting thing about acquired needs is that there are usually many people who develop the same needs. This commonality of need or interest constitutes a market segment, enabling the marketer to target consumers with specifically designed products and/or promotional appeals that satisfy the needs of that segment. The marketer must also adapt the image of its product (i.e. 'position' it), so that each market segment perceives the product as better fulfilling its specific needs than competitive products. The three elements of this strategic framework are market segmentation, targeting, and positioning.

Market segmentation is the process of dividing a market into subsets of consumers with common needs or characteristics. The variables and methods used to form such subsets are detailed in Chapter 2. Because most companies have limited resources, few companies can pursue all of the market segments identified. Market targeting is selecting one or more of the segments identified for the company to pursue.

Positioning is developing a distinct image for the product or service in the mind of the consumer, an image that will differentiate the offering from competing ones and squarely communicate to consumers that the particular product or service will fulfil their needs better than competing brands. Successful positioning centres around two key principles: first, communicating the benefits that the product will provide rather than the product's features. As one marketing sage pointed out: '. . . consumers do not buy drill bits—they buy ways to make holes.' Second, because there are many similar products in almost any marketplace, an effective positioning strategy must develop and communicate a 'unique selling proposition'—a distinct benefit or point of difference—for the product or service. In fact, most of the new products introduced by marketers (including new forms of existing products such as new flavours, sizes, etc.) fail to capture a significant market share and are discontinued because they are perceived by consumers as 'me too' products lacking a unique image or benefit. The concepts and tools of positioning are explored further in Chapter 6.

THE MARKETING MIX

The marketing mix consists of a company's service and/or product offerings to consumers and the methods and tools it selects to accomplish the exchange. The marketing mix consists of four elements:

1. the product or service (i.e. the features, designs, brands, and packaging offered, along with postpurchase benefits such as warranties and return policies);
2. the price (the list price, including discounts, allowances, and payment methods);
3. the place (the distribution of the product or service through specific store and nonstore outlets);
4. promotion (the advertising, sales promotion, public relations, and sales efforts designed to build awareness of and demand for the product or service).

Box 1.2 depicts the implementation of the elements of the marketing concept by the Rollerblade company.

CUSTOMER VALUE, SATISFACTION, AND RETENTION

Since its emergence in the 1950s, many companies have very successfully adopted the marketing concept. The result has been more products, in more sizes, models, versions, and packages, offered to more precisely targeted (and often smaller) target markets. This has resulted in an increasingly competitive marketplace. In

BOX 1.2 | Rollerblade: Effective implementation of the marketing concept

Less than two decades ago, in-line skates were an off-season training tool for hockey players. In the mid-1980s, Rollerblade developed marketing strategies that positioned in-line skating as a new sport. The company sold in-line skates to bicycle and conventional skate rental stores in two trend-setting places: Miami Beach, Florida, and Venice Beach, California. A new form of recreational sport that appeals to many age groups and social classes was born. Backed by aggressive marketing and public relations, the popularity of the new sport soared and was quickly integrated into the mainstream. As competition appeared, Rollerblade continued to lead the market with such innovations as breathable shoe liners, buckle closure systems, and female-specific skates. Today the company holds several hundred patented innovations.

The company's product line illustrates the utilisation of segmentation, targeting, and positioning strategies. The company targets five segments and offers models that provide different benefits to the members of each segment:

1. Men can choose among models designed for expert, intermediate, or demanding skaters, and among such benefits as style, technological innovation, and performance.
2. Women are targeted with similar choices as men.
3. There are several models for kids.
4. Street and park skaters can choose among models focused on durability, performance, or attention to detail.
5. Race skaters are targeted with a model offering high-tech features and top performance.

The models offered to men, women, and kids include brakes, whereas the models offered to street, park, and race skaters do not.

Rollerblade's entire marketing mix stems from its core product. In addition to the in-line skates, the company sells helmets, skate bags, and wrist, elbow, and knee protectors. The skates are priced along a range varying from very expensive models offered to aggressive skaters who look for maximum performance, to value-oriented skaters, to recreational skaters. The products are distributed in a variety of outlets—both domestic and overseas—in a way that reflects the market segments targeted and the skate models' prices. The company advertises its products in the mass media, issues frequent press releases as part of its public relations, and promotes its products through athletic and event sponsorships, as well as its 'Skate School'.

The company's website also includes features that encourage skaters to revisit, such as a list of places to skate (arranged by state), a dealer locator, skating tips, tips for people who wish to take up the sport, and suggestions on skating safety. These features show that Rollerblade has a thorough understanding of customer retention as well as social responsibility.

Source: Developed from material available at <www.rollerblade.com>.

the 1990s, the digital revolution enabled many marketers to offer even more products and services and distribute them more widely, while reducing the costs and barriers of entering many industries. It has accelerated the rate at which new competitors enter markets and also has speeded up the rate at which successful segmentation, targeting, and positioning approaches must be updated or changed, as they are imitated or made obsolete by the offerings of new business rivals.

Savvy marketers today realise that in order to outperform competitors they must achieve the full profit potential from each and every customer. They must make the customer the core of the company's organisational culture, across all departments and functions, and ensure that each and every employee views any exchange with a customer as part of a customer relationship, not as a transaction. The three drivers of successful relationships between marketers and customers are customer value, high levels of customer satisfaction, and building a structure for customer retention.

Providing customer value

Customer value is defined as the ratio between the customer's perceived benefits (economic, functional and psychological) and the resources (monetary, time, effort and psychological) used to obtain those benefits. Perceived value is relative and subjective. For example, diners at an exclusive French restaurant, where a meal with beverages may cost up to $100 per person, may expect unique and delicious food, immaculate service, and beautiful decor. Some diners may receive even more than they had expected and will leave the restaurant feeling that the experience was worth the money and other resources expended (such as a month-long wait for a reservation). Other diners may go with expectations so high that they leave the restaurant disappointed. On the other hand, many millions of customers each year visit thousands of McDonald's restaurants, in scores of countries around the globe, where they purchase standard, inexpensive meals from franchise owners and employees systematically trained by the McDonald's Corporation to deliver the company's four core standards: quality, service, cleanliness, and value. Customers flock to McDonald's outlets repeatedly because the restaurants are uniform, customers know what to expect, and they feel that they are getting value for the resources they expend.

Developing a value proposition (a term rapidly replacing the popular business phrase 'unique selling proposition') is the core of successful positioning. For example, Lexus claims to deliver to its buyers quality, zero defects in manufacturing, and superior and personal postpurchase service. Dell's value proposition for personal computer users consists of customised systems speedily assembled and sold at economical prices (visit <www.dell.com> and read their commitment to customers showing their value philosophy). Figure 1.9 showed an example of a company identifying within its advertising specific value claims. Subaru identifies value in both the price of the car and the extras 'exclusive features' for only $990.

Customer satisfaction

Customer satisfaction is the individual's perception of the performance of the product or service in relation to his or her expectations. As noted earlier, customers will have drastically different expectations of an expensive French restaurant and a McDonald's, although both are part of the restaurant industry. The concept of customer satisfaction is a function of customer expectations. A customer whose experience falls below expectations (e.g. used dishes not cleared quickly enough at an expensive restaurant or cold fries served at a McDonald's) will be dissatisfied. Diners whose experiences match expectations will be satisfied. And customers whose expectations are exceeded (e.g. by small samples of delicious food 'from the Chef' served between courses at the expensive restaurant, or a well-designed play area for children at a McDonald's outlet) will be very satisfied or delighted.

A widely quoted study by Thomas Jones and W. Earl Sasser, Jr linked levels of customer satisfaction with customer behaviour and identified several types of customers: completely satisfied customers who are either loyalists who keep purchasing, or apostles whose experiences exceed their expectations and who provide very positive word of mouth about the company to others; 'defectors' who feel neutral or merely satisfied and are likely to stop doing business with the company; consumer 'terrorists' who have had negative experiences with the company and who spread negative word of mouth; 'hostages' who are unhappy customers who stay with the company because of a monopolistic environment or low prices and who are difficult and costly to deal with because of their frequent complaints; and mercenaries who are very satisfied customers but who have no real loyalty to the company and may defect because of a lower price elsewhere or on impulse, defying the satisfaction–loyalty rationale. The researchers propose that companies should strive to create apostles, raise the satisfaction of defectors and turn them into loyalists, avoid having terrorists or hostages, and reduce the number of mercenaries.[4]

Customer retention

The overall objective of providing value to customers continuously and more effectively than the competition is to have highly satisfied (even delighted) customers. This strategy of customer retention makes it in the best interest of customers to stay with the company rather than switch to another firm. In almost all business situations, it is more expensive to win new customers than to keep existing ones. Studies have shown that small reductions in customer defections produce significant increases in profits because:

1. loyal customers buy more products;
2. loyal customers are less price sensitive and pay less attention to competitors' advertising;
3. servicing existing customers, who are familiar with the firm's offerings and processes, is cheaper; and
4. loyal customers spread positive word of mouth and refer other customers.

Furthermore, marketing efforts aimed at attracting new customers are expensive; indeed, in saturated markets, it may be impossible to find new customers. Today the Internet and digital marketer–consumer interactions are ideal tools for tailoring products and services to the specific needs of consumers (often termed one-to-one marketing), offering them more value through increased customer intimacy and keeping the customers returning to the company.[5]

Marketers who designate increasing customer retention rates as a strategic corporate goal must also recognise that all customers are not equal. Sophisticated marketers build selective relationships with customers, based on where customers rank in terms of profitability, rather than merely strive 'to retain customers'. A customer retention–savvy company closely monitors its customers' consumption volume and patterns, establishes tiers of customers according to their profitability levels, and develops distinct strategies toward each group of customers. For example, some stockbrokers program their phones to recognise the phone numbers of high-volume traders to ensure that their calls receive priority. Customers who have purchased and registered several of a company's products should receive extensive and expedited customer support. On the other hand, a bank's less profitable customers who, say, make little use of their credit cards or maintain the minimum balance needed to receive free chequebook facilities should not have penalties waived for bounced cheques or late payments. Some companies also identify customer groups that are unlikely to purchase more if pursued more aggressively; such customers are often discouraged from staying with the company or even 'fired' as customers.

Classifying customers according to profitability levels goes beyond traditional segmentation methods that subdivide consumers on the basis of demographic, sociocultural, or behavioural characteristics. Customer profitability-focused marketing tracks costs and revenues of individual customers and then categorises them into tiers based on consumption behaviours that are specific to the company's offerings. Such a strategy is probably the most effective way to utilise the knowledge of consumer behaviour. For example, a recent study advocates using a 'customer pyramid' where customers are grouped into four tiers:

1. the platinum tier includes heavy users who are not price sensitive and who are willing to try new offerings;
2. the gold tier consists of customers who are heavy users but not as profitable because they are more price sensitive than those in the higher tier, ask for more discounts, and are likely to buy from several providers;
3. the iron tier consists of customers whose spending volume and profitability do not merit special treatment from the company;

TABLE 1.1 The traditional marketing concept versus value- and retention-focused marketing

The traditional marketing concept	Value- and retention-focused marketing
Make only what you can sell instead of trying to sell what you make.	Use technology that enables customers to customise what you make.
Do not focus on the product; focus on the need that it satisfies.	Focus on the product's perceived value, as well as the need that it satisfies.
Market products and services that match customers' needs better than competitors' offerings.	Utilise an understanding of customer needs to develop offerings that customers perceive as more valuable than competitors' offerings.
Research consumer needs and characteristics.	Research the levels of profit associated with various consumer needs and characteristics.
Understand the purchase behaviour process and the influences on consumer behaviour.	Understand consumer behaviour in relation to the company's product.
Realise that each customer transaction is a discrete sale.	Make each customer transaction part of an ongoing relationship with the customer.
Segment the market based on customers' geographic, demographic, psychological, sociocultural, lifestyle, and product-usage related characteristics.	Use hybrid segmentation that combines the traditional segmentation bases with data on the customer's purchase levels and patterns of use of the company's products.
Target large groups of customers that share common characteristics with messages transmitted through mass media.	Invest in technologies that enable you to send one-to-one promotional messages via digital channels.
Use one-way promotions whose effectiveness is measured through sales data or marketing surveys.	Use interactive communications in which messages to customers are tailored according to their responses to previous communications.
Create loyalty programs based on the volume purchased.	Create customer tiers based on both volume and consumption patterns.
Encourage customers to stay with the company and buy more.	Make it very unattractive for your customers to switch to a competitor and encourage them to purchase 'better'—in a manner that will raise the company's profitability levels.
Determine marketing budgets on the basis of the numbers of customers you are trying to reach.	Base your marketing budget on the 'lifetime value' of typical customers in each of the targeted segments compared with the resources needed to acquire them as customers.
Conduct customer satisfaction surveys and present the results to management.	Conduct customer satisfaction surveys that include a component which studies the customer's word of mouth about the company, and use the results immediately to enhance customer relationships.
Create customer trust and loyalty to the company and high levels of customer satisfaction.	Create customer intimacy and bonds with completely satisfied, 'delighted' customers.

Source: **Joseph Wisenblit, 'Beyond the marketing concept: From "make only what you can sell" to "let customers customize what you make"', Working Paper, May 2002, The Stillman School of Business, Seton Hall University, South Orange, NJ.**

4. the lead tier includes customers who actually cost the company money because they claim more attention than is merited by their spending, tie up company resources, and spread negative word of mouth.

The authors of the study urge companies to develop distinct marketing responses for each group.[6]

A corporate philosophy centred on customer value, satisfaction, and retention evolves from the marketing concept and also unfolds new dimensions of marketing. Table 1.1 on the previous page compares traditional marketing with perceived value and retention marketing.

Summary

The study of consumer behaviour enables marketers to understand and predict consumer behaviour in the marketplace; it is concerned not only with what consumers buy but also with why, when, where, how, and how often they buy it. Consumer behaviour is defined as the behaviour that consumers display when searching for, purchasing, using, evaluating and disposing of products, services and ideas that they expect will satisfy their needs. Consumer behaviour is interdisciplinary, and is based on concepts and theories about people that have been developed by scientists in such diverse disciplines as psychology, sociology, social psychology, cultural anthropology and economics. Our society is a study in diversity—diversity among consumers, marketers, retailers, advertising media, cultures and customs; but there are also many similarities among consumers. Segmenting target audiences on the basis of similarities makes it possible for marketers to design marketing strategies with which their target consumers identify.

The study of consumer behaviour enables marketers to understand and predict consumer behaviour in the marketplace; it is concerned not only with what consumers buy, but also with why they buy, when they buy, where they will buy, how they buy, and how often they buy. To answer such questions marketers utilise consumer research from a positivistic or interpretive viewpoint, and various methodologies (e.g. scanner data, surveys or interviews) to study consumer behaviour; it takes place at every phase of the consumption process: before, during and after the purchase.

Consumer behaviour has become an integral part of strategic market planning. The belief that ethics and social responsibility should also be integral components of every marketing decision is embodied in a revised marketing concept—the societal marketing concept—which calls on marketers to fulfil the needs of their target markets in ways that improve society as a whole.

Discussion questions

1. Describe the relationship between consumer behaviour and the marketing concept.
2. Discuss the differences involved in marketing personal computers to home use consumers and organisational consumers.
3. You are the brand manager of a new line of light-weight digital cameras. Describe how an understanding of consumer behaviour is useful to you in terms of market segmentation strategy.
4. Is it ethical for marketers to promote expensive sneakers to inner-city youth? Explain your answer.
5. Compare the marketing concept with the societal marketing concept. Do you think marketers should adopt the societal marketing concept? In which industries does the immediate adoption of the societal marketing concept appear to be necessary?
6. Apply each of the two models depicted in Table 1.3 (i.e. traditional marketing and value and retention marketing) to the marketing of mobile phone services. You may want to incorporate into your answer your own and your peers' experiences in selecting mobile phone providers.

Exercises

1. (a) Select a product you bought that has features you never use. Which of the business orientations discussed in the text may have guided the development of this product? Explain.
   (b) Select a product, brand or service that you bought or used because it was particularly suitable to your needs. Would you say that the development of this product or service was guided by the marketing concept? If so, how?
2. Find an advertisement for a new product. Identify the psychological, sociological and cultural factors that may influence consumers' decisions regarding the purchase of this product. In your opinion, will this product succeed or fail in the marketplace? Explain your answer.
3. Give an example of what you believe to be an unethical marketing practice. How can this practice be stopped through government regulation? Can the industry stop this practice? If so, how?

Key terms

buyer *(p. 8)*
consumer *(p. 8)*
consumer behaviour *(p. 6)*
consumer movement *(p. 10)*
consumer research *(p. 9)*
end-use consumption *(p. 8)*
interpretivist *(p. 9)*
market segment *(p. 12)*
market segmentation *(p. 21)*
marketing concept *(p. 19)*
organisational consumer *(p. 8)*
payer *(p. 8)*
personal consumer *(p. 7)*
positioning *(p. 21)*
positivist *(p. 9)*
societal marketing concept *(p. 20)*

Endnotes

1. Peter F. Drucker, *The Practice of Management* (New York: Harper and Row, 1954).
2. See, for example, Claudia H. Deutsch, 'Second time around and around: Remanufacturing is gaining ground in corporate America', *New York Times*, 14 July 1998, p. C1.
3 Philip Kotler, *Marketing Management—Analysis, Planning and Control*, 8th edn (Englewood Cliffs, NJ: Prentice Hall, 1994).
4. Thomas O. Jones and W. Earl Sasser, Jr, 'Why satisfied customers defect', *Harvard Business Review*, November–December 1995, pp. 88–99.
5. Frederick F. Reichheld and W. Earl Sasser, Jr, 'Zero defections: Quality comes to services', *Harvard Business Review*, September–October 1990, pp. 105–111; Michael Treacy and Fred Wiersema, 'Customer intimacy and other value disciplines', *Harvard Business Review*, January–February 1993, pp. 84–93; Bob Mueller, 'Keeping your customers from defecting', *Beyond Computing*, April 1999, pp. 30–31.
6. Valerie A. Zeithaml, Roland T. Rust, and Katherine N. Lemon, 'The customer pyramid: Creating and serving profitable customers', *California Management Review*, Summer 2001, pp. 118–142.

CHAPTER 2

Market segmentation

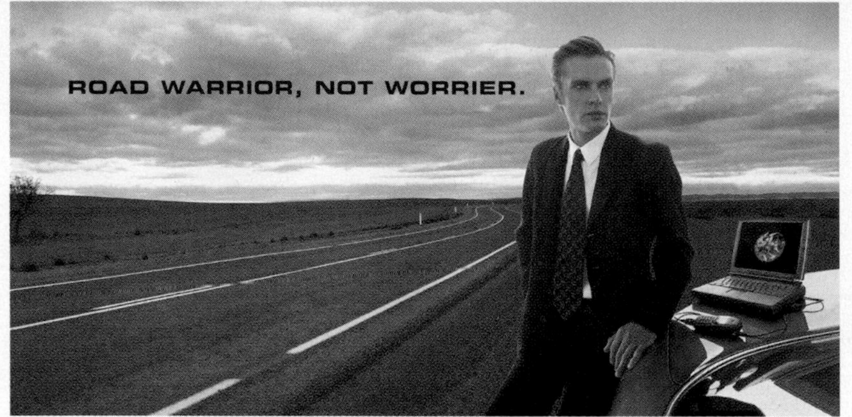
ROAD WARRIOR, NOT WORRIER.

THE GLOBALPULSE SOFTWARE MODEM.
NO PC CARD. NO LAND-LINE.
NO BATTERY DRAINAGE. NO LIMITS.

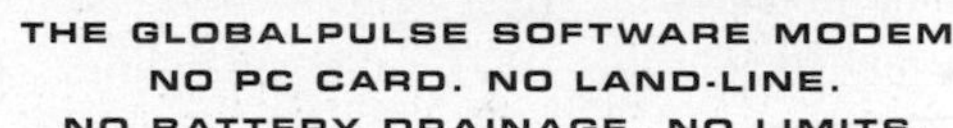
NOW COMPATIBLE WITH 3COM
PALM III, IIIX AND PALM V.

NO PC CARD REQUIRED.
MULTIPLE PLATFORM SUPPORT.

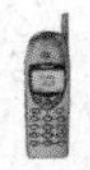

CONNECTS DIRECTLY TO GSM MOBILE PHONE.

TRUE GLOBAL ROAMING.

When you're working on the road, the last thing you need is a flat - flat battery that is.

Now, no matter where you are, you can keep your finger on the pulse for longer with TDK's GlobalPulse software modem.

GlobalPulse lets you use your GSM mobile phone to send data and facsimiles, or access the internet without the need for expensive, battery-draining PC Card hardware.

This revolutionary integrated software solution operates under Win95/98, NT/WinCE and is compatible with 3Com Palm III, IIIX and Palm V, as well as IBM's Workpad. It is designed to complement all your favourite existing communications packages such as e-mail and web browsers.

GlobalPulse supports the market leading phones from Nokia and Ericsson (Palm only) and can be readily upgraded to take advantage of new GSM features as they become available.

Priced from $199.00 RRP. including tax. For further details, call TDK on 1800 651 917. For more information on the entire range of TDK products, visit our web site at www.tdk.com.au.

TDK®
TDK DOES AMAZING THINGS TO MY SYSTEM

Source: Courtesy of TDK (Australia) Pty Ltd.

The nature of the Australian (and the global) marketplace makes market segmentation an attractive, viable and potentially profitable strategy. Organisations that sell to consumers (markets) recognise that they cannot appeal to all individuals (in those markets)—or at least not in the same way. Buyers are too numerous, too widely scattered and too varied in their needs and purchase methods. Such factors necessitate the need to segment markets. The necessary criteria for successful segmentation are a large enough population with sufficient money to spend (general affluence) and sufficient diversity to be capable of being partitioned (or grouped) into sizeable homogeneous segments on the basis of demographic, psychological, behavioural or other meaningful criteria. The presence of these conditions makes the Australian marketplace attractive to both Australian and global marketers.

When marketers provide a range of offerings to meet diverse consumer needs, consumers are ultimately more satisfied. Thus, market segmentation is a positive activity for both marketers and consumers alike.

➤ What is market segmentation?

Market segmentation is the process of dividing a market into distinct subsets of consumers with common needs or characteristics and selecting one or more segments to target with a distinct marketing strategy. Market segmentation, literally, means separating the total group of potential buyers (market, from the Latin verb *mercor*, to buy) into two or more subgroups (segments, from the Latin *seco*, I cut) using specific **segmentation criteria** (such as being measurable, accessible, substantial and congruent).

It is common practice when pursuing segmentation as a strategy to select one or more segments to target with a distinct marketing mix, once the market has been segmented. Companies vary in their ability to serve different (or multiple) segments of a market. So, rather than trying to compete in an entire market, sometimes against superior competitors, each company must identify the parts of the market that it can serve best (and better than the competition). Before the widespread adoption of market segmentation, the prevailing way of doing business with consumers was through **mass marketing**—that is, offering the same product and marketing mix to all consumers. The essence of this mass strategy was encapsulated by Ferdinand Porsche, who developed the original concept for a 'people's car', the Volkswagen, in 1934. The 'VW beetle', as it became known, was a mass-produced car that had a single configuration in its early model (see Figure 2.1). An earlier example of this mass strategy is seen in the marketing approach of Henry Ford and the Model T (see <www.ford.com>).

If all consumers were alike—having the same needs, wants, desires, and the same backgrounds, education and experience—mass (undifferentiated) marketing would be a logical strategy. Its primary advantage is that it costs less: it needs only one advertising campaign, one marketing strategy and, usually, only one standardised product. Today's companies are moving away from mass marketing and product-variety marketing towards target marketing. **Targeting** can help sellers find their marketing opportunities more efficiently. Instead of spreading their marketing efforts, sellers can develop the right product for each target market and adjust their prices, distribution channels and advertising to reach the target market efficiently. With the increasing fragmentation of Australian mass

FIGURE 2.1 Early Volkswagen (1930s): a mass-produced undifferentiated vehicle

Source: Courtesy of Volkswagen Group Australia.

markets into hundreds of micromarkets, each having different lifestyles with different requirements, target marketing is increasingly taking the form of **micromarketing**.

Some companies, primarily those that deal in agricultural products or very basic manufactured goods, successfully follow a mass-marketing strategy. Other marketers, however, see major drawbacks in an undifferentiated marketing approach. When trying to sell the same product to every prospective customer with a single advertising campaign, the marketer must portray its product as a means for satisfying a common or generic need, and often ends up appealing to no one. A washing machine may fulfil a widespread need to wash clothes, but a standard-size washing machine may be too big for a person who lives alone and too small for a family of six. Also, a motor vehicle may fulfil a widespread need to provide transportation, but a large six cylinder saloon may be too big for a single person who lives alone and too small for a family of six. Without market differentiation, both the single person and the family of six would have to make do with the same model (of washing machine or car) and, as we all know, 'making do' is a far cry from being satisfied.

The strategy of segmentation allows organisations to avoid head-on competition in the marketplace by differentiating their offerings, not just on the basis of price, but also through styling, packaging, promotional appeals, method of distribution and superior service. To accomplish this the marketer must decide on a specific marketing mix—that is, a specific product, price, channel and/or promotional appeal for each distinct segment. Marketers have found that the costs of segmentation (undertaking consumer research, shorter production runs, differentiated promotional campaigns) are usually more than offset by increased sales. In most cases, consumers readily accept the passed-on increases in costs for products that more closely satisfy their specific needs.

Market segmentation is just the first step in a three-phase marketing strategy (segmenting/targeting/positioning or STP). After segmenting the market into homogeneous clusters, the marketer must then select one or more segments to target with a specific marketing-mix strategy. The third step is to position the product so that it is perceived by each target market as satisfying its needs better than other competitive offerings.

WHO USES MARKET SEGMENTATION?

Because the strategy of market segmentation benefits both sides of the marketplace, marketers of consumer goods are eager practitioners. A consumer-oriented approach to marketing requires developing product strategies based on known consumer needs. It is obvious that marketers cannot allocate resources according to the needs of one individual. Therefore, some criterion for aggregating consumers is required; the most logical one is similarity in needs. For example, consider two diverse product categories—cars and running shoes. Toyota (see <www.toyota.com>) targets its Celica, with its sporty styling, minimal rear seat and small boot, to young singles; and its Camry, a much larger car, at the family car buyer needing a roomier vehicle. New Balance Athletic Shoes (see <www.newbalance.com>) targets its shoes to different segments, including usage segments of running, walking and cross-training athletes, and also gender-based segments targeting specific shoes to male and female segments (see <www.newbalance.com>). Most if not all consumer goods manufacturers apply some form of segmentation to markets. For example, Schwarzkopf segment their markets using different strategies and, as shown in Figure 2.2 (page 32), Schwarzkopf targets different usage or benefit segments for its hair gel products.

Segmentation frequently provides a marketer with the opportunity to expand a market (or enter a new one) by satisfying more effectively the specific needs or wants of particular consumers. Swatch, for example, has employed market segmentation to expand its offerings of inexpensive and fashionable watches for men and women. Today, the company (which distributes its watches through department stores and jewellers) markets a wide range of wristwatches designed to cater to the interests and lifestyles of different segments of consumers as shown in Figure 2.3 (page 32). While Swatch still offers consumers conservative watches to wear to work, and funky watches for leisure use, it now also features several distinctive lines: scuba or diving watches for the sports-minded, chronographic watches with stopwatches and other techno-features for wristwatch enthusiasts, limited edition watches for Swatch collectors (there is even a worldwide Swatch collectors' club), and children's watches for toddlers first learning to tell the time (see <www.swatch.com>).

Market segmentation has also been adopted by retailers. David Jones and Myer target the upscale market and their stores carry the higher-priced high-fashion clothing and other consumer goods sought by more affluent consumers. Big W and Kmart target blue-collar consumers looking for economy and practicality, who would react to a David Jones shirt priced at $200 with total disbelief. Other retailers, such as Target, have more recently tried to reposition themselves to capture a wider market and be seen to offer a broader and more stylish product range. David Jones, through extensive TV promotions featuring one of their high-profile female staff, has sought to communicate a message that would reposition it as a retailer that not only provides quality for the upper income target market, but also emphasises competitive prices; this ultimately attracts a wider range of consumers. Country Road seems to target upscale consumers who prefer a more casual and relaxed style of dress. The young parents who are seen as their target market are reached through a chain of Country Road stores. Another great example is Gap, Inc operating in countries such as the US, UK, Japan, France, Canada and Germany. Gap (see <www.gap.com>) targets different age, income, and lifestyle segments in a diversity of retail outlets. Gap and Super Gap stores are designed to attract a wide age range of consumers who seek a casual and relaxed style of dress. Gap targets upscale consumers through its Banana Republic stores (see <www.bananarepublic.com>) and somewhat downscale customers with its Old Navy Clothing Company stores (see <www.oldnavy.com>). It targets young parents (who are also likely to be Gap or Banana Republic shoppers) with its Baby Gap and Gap Kids stores.[1] Gap is mindful of catering to the needs of specific market components and acknowledging their unique or particular buying patterns.

Industrial manufacturers also segment their markets, as does the non-profit sector. Organisations such as Lifeline (see <www.lifeline.org.au>) frequently focus their fund-raising efforts on specific donor groups. Some opera companies and sporting clubs such as football and rugby league clubs such as the Broncos (see <www.broncos.com.au>) segment their subscribers and members on the basis of benefits sought and have succeeded in increasing attendance through specialised promotional appeals.

➤ How market segmentation operates

Segmentation studies are designed to discover the needs and wants of specific groups of consumers, so that specialised goods and services can be developed and promoted to satisfy their needs. Many new products have been developed to fill gaps in the marketplace revealed by segmentation research. For example, Bayer, makers of One-A-Day vitamins, has developed a variety of products that are designed to appeal directly to different age and gender market segments in terms of their specific vitamin requirements. Nyal, too, has developed a range of cough mixtures for different segments of the market as shown in Figure 2.4 (page 33).

Segmentation studies are also used to guide the redesign or repositioning of existing products or the addition of a new market segment. Not only must new products be positioned, but existing products must often be repositioned. Often, the basis for a repositioning strategy is the identification of a new market segment, changing consumer needs, stagnant or declining sales. **Repositioning** is accomplished by changing the promotional appeal, the distribution strategy or the price. For example, Cadbury repositioned its Schweppes ginger ale brand from a mixer for alcoholic drinks to a soft drink by refocusing its product mix (with more emphasis on flavoured ginger ales, such as raspberry ginger ale), its advertising and its packaging.[2] For Cadbury, this was a particularly important strategy, given the declining consumption of liquor in general, and mixed drinks in particular.

FIGURE 2.2 Haircare products for the Schwarzkopf brand targeting different benefits sought by consumers

Source: Courtesy of Schwarzkopf and Henkel.

FIGURE 2.3 Distinctive advertisement by Swatch targeting male consumers

Source: Courtesy of Swatch.

Repositioning can also be seen, for example, with the manufacturers of women's hygiene products (tampons and sanitary pads) who have over many years targeted the adult women users of this product. Now there is a concerted effort to target younger (teenage) users (see Figure 2.5, page 40) with advertisements appearing in magazines such as *Dolly* and *Girlfriend.* Their campaigns appeal to younger users by dealing with the topic in a humorous manner. In past campaigns they have used ads with, for example, a surfboard displayed along with the brand and package with copy such as 'The only time you need a surfboard is when you're surfing', an appeal that many younger female users find removes the stigma from the product.

A marketer has to try different segmentation variables in order to find the best way to view the market structure. For example, with increased consumer interest in health and natural foods, frozen yoghurt can be repositioned as an ice-cream substitute for use all day or, with the addition of extra fruit, redesigned to be perceived as a natural food. The Sanitarium company, makers of Weet-Bix, have promoted the cereal as an all-day food, 'too good to put away after breakfast'.

In addition to filling product gaps, segmentation research is used by marketers to identify the most appropriate media in which to place advertisements. Almost all media vehicles—from TV and radio stations to newspapers and magazines—use segmentation research to determine the characteristics of their audience and then publicise their findings in order to attract advertisers seeking similar audiences. For example, the magazines *New Idea* and *Good Medicine* are used by Mortein to advertise its Mortein Ultra Low Allergenic Fly & Insect Killer, targeted at females, who are the main purchasers of this product and readers of these two magazines.

Companies such as ACNielsen and Roy Morgan Research publicise the characteristics of TV and radio audiences and this data is used by TV and radio stations to attract potential advertisers. For example, ACNielsen conducted research into the makeup of the regional Australian TV audience and found that 57.2% of people were less than 40 years old, 71.1% of grocery buyers were female with an average age of 48 years, and 34.3% of homes had children aged 0 to 15.[3] Roy Morgan, a major Australian research company, conducts studies into readership characteristics for newspapers and magazines and makes the data available to the media and possible advertisers. Table 2.1 provides an indication of this type of data with the Roy Morgan readership profiles for the magazine *Cosmopolitan*. Using these facts, *Cosmopolitan* is able to target potential advertisers more effectively. It can identify its readers' characteristics and match them with the target markets of advertisers. The advertisers are also better able to select magazines with similar characteristics to their identified target market. For example, Table 2.1 shows key demographic and psychographic characteristics of the magazine readers. For example, the major segments are females aged in the 18–24 years age grouping and those who work full-time.

FIGURE 2.4 **Nyal advertisement identifying various benefits and demographics of users**

Source: Courtesy of ICN Pharmaceuticals.

Bases for segmentation

The first step in developing a segmentation strategy is to select the most appropriate base(s) on which to segment the market. Nine major categories of consumer characteristics provide the most common bases for market segmentation—geographic factors, demographic factors, psychological characteristics, psychographic (lifestyle) characteristics, sociocultural variables, user-related characteristics, user-situation and benefits sought, plus hybrid segmentation forms such as demographic/psychographic profiles, geodemographic factors and values and lifestyles. Hybrid segmentation formats each use a combination of several segmentation bases to create rich and comprehensive profiles of particular consumer segments (e.g. a specific age range, income, lifestyle and profession). Table 2.2 (page 35) breaks down these categories into specific variables and gives examples for each. The following section discusses each of these segmentation bases; several psychological and sociocultural segmentation variables are examined in greater depth in Parts 2 and 3 of this book.

DEMOGRAPHIC SEGMENTATION

Demography refers to the identifiable and measurable statistics of a population. Demographic characteristics, such as age, sex, marital status, income, occupation and education, are often used as the basis for market segmentation. Demographics help to locate a target market, whereas psychological and sociocultural characteristics help describe how its members think and feel. Demographic information is often the most accessible

TABLE 2.1 Selected demographic/psychographic characteristics of *Cosmopolitan* magazine readers

Demographics	
Gender	
Men	21.70%
Women	78.30%
Age	
17 & under	21.54%
18–24	37.51%
25–34	20.01%
35–49	13.99%
Total 50 and over	6.94%
Education	
Up to Grade 10 high school	29.86%
5th form/Leaving/Year 11	8.46%
Grade 12 or tech.	21.99%
Some/now at university	17.41%
Have diploma or degree	22.29%
Employment status	
Full-time	32.69%
Part-time	28.16%
Home duties	6.81%
Don't work	2.87%
Looking for work (full-time or part-time)	9.78%
Retired	2.25%
Students	17.44%
Occupation	
Professional/manager	8.99%
Farm owner	0.17%
White collar workers	30.58%
Skilled workers	4.35%
Others (incl. semi/unskilled)	16.76%
Income of respondent	
Under $15 000	50.12%
$15 000 to $19 999	8.56%
$20 000 to $29 999	14.33%
$30 000 to $39 999	11.88%
$40 000 to $49 999	6.73%
TOTAL $50 000 or more	8.38%
Home ownership	
Own home	29.00%
Paying off	29.88%
Rent	38.90%
Other/not stated	2.22%

Psychographics	
Travel	
Member of Qantas Club	2.93%
Member of other airport club lounge	1.11%
Air travel overseas last 12 months	15.82%
Air travel within interstate last 12 months	33.42%
Business decisions in last 12 months	
Personal computer	3.39%
Computer software	1.47%
Insurance for a business, etc.	1.16%
Organised conferences or training seminars	1.08%
Home activities done in the last 12 months	
Built a house/flat	1.36%
Spent over $5000 renovating/extending home	11.23%
Used a power tool around home	37.91%
Purchase decisions	
Bought goods using PC	12.81%
Bought goods over phone	7.49%
Bought goods via mail	12.45%
Bought goods on interest free terms	5.88%
Bought goods on lay-by	28.11%
Hobbies and activities	
Went to an art gallery, museum, or antique exhibition	20.39%
Casino or RSL/leagues or other club	40.62%
Amusement park or theme park or zoo	19.29%
Worked in the garden	39.92%
Watched sport on TV	87.05%
Went to professional sports events	13.36%
Played a sport	36.58%
Did some formal exercise (e.g. gym, aerobics, running, cycling, etc.)	53.50%
Went to a short course, seminar, convention or public lecture	19.72%

Source: Roy Morgan Single Source Australia: April 2003–March 2004.

TABLE 2.2 Market segmentation bases and selected variables

Segmentation base	Selected segmentation variables
Geographic segmentation	
State	New South Wales, Queensland, Western Australia, Victoria, South Australia, Tasmania
Region	Capital cities, regional cities, towns, rural
Location	Inner-city, suburban, outer-urban, rural
Housing density	High density, medium density, low density
Climate	Hot, humid, cold, wet
Demographic segmentation	
Age	Under 12, 12–17, 18–34, 35–49, 50–64, 65–74, 75+
Sex	Male, female
Marital status	Single, married, divorced, living together, widowed
Income	\$0–\$12 000, \$12 001–\$20 000, \$20 001–\$30 000, \$30 001–\$40 000, \$40 001–\$60 000, \$60 001 and over
Education	Primary school or less, some secondary, completed secondary, tertiary, postgraduate
Occupation	Professional, white-collar, blue-collar, agricultural or labourer
Psychological segmentation	
Needs-motivation	Shelter, safety, security, affection, sense of self-worth
Personality	Extrovert, introvert, sensing, feeling, intuitive
Risk perception	Low risk, moderate risk, high risk
Involvement	Low involvement, high involvement
Attitudes	Positive, negative or neutral
Psychographic	
Psychographic (lifestyle)	Basic needs, Look at me, True conservatism
Sociocultural segmentation	
Culture	Australian, Italian, Greek, Chinese, Vietnamese
Subculture	Asian, Indigenous Australian, Irish Australian
Religion	Jewish, Catholic, Protestant, Muslim, other
Race/Ethnicity	Aboriginal, English-speaking background, non-English-speaking background
Social class	Lower, middle, upper
Family life cycle	Singles, young marrieds, empty nesters
Use-related segmentation	
Usage rate	Heavy users, medium users, light users, non-users
Awareness status	Unaware, aware, interested, enthusiastic
Brand loyalty	Strong, some, none
Use-situational segmentation	
Time	Leisure, work, morning, night
Objective	Personal use, gift, snack, fun, achievement
Location	Home, work, friend's home, in-store, near-home
Person	Self, family members, friends, boss, peer

(continues)

Segmentation base	Selected segmentation variables
Benefit segmentation	Convenience, social acceptance, long-lasting, prestige, economy, value-for-money
Hybrid segmentation	
Demographic/psychographic	Combination of demographies and psychographic profiles of consumers
Geodemographics	Established investors, welfare dependants, outback Australia
VALS™	Actualiser, fulfilled, believer, achiever, striver, experiencer, maker, struggler

TABLE 2.3 **Demographic profiles of male grocery buyers versus female grocery buyers**

	Male grocery buyers	Female grocery buyers
Total number (in '000s)	3045	6506
Size of household		
• 1 person	20.53%	12.77%
• 2+ persons	79.47%	87.23%
Number of children		
• none	77.89%	62.98%
• 1	9.83%	14.64%
• 2	7.45%	14.41%
• 3+	4.82%	7.97%
Employed	61.88%	50.53%
Full-time	50.79%	26.25%
Part-time	11.09%	24.29%
Average age	47.52	47.97
Average household income	$57 070	$57 180

Source: **Roy Morgan Single Source Australia: April 2003–March 2004.**

and cost-effective way to identify a target market. Indeed, most secondary data, including census data, is expressed in demographic terms. Demographics are easier to measure than other segmentation variables; they are invariably included in psychographic and sociocultural studies because they add meaning to the findings. It is on this basis that **demographic segmentation** seems to be one of the most popular ways to segment customer groups. Table 2.3 shows demographic profiles of male and female grocery buyers. Particularly notable are differences in household size, number of children and employment status.

Even when market segments are first defined using other bases, such as personality or behaviour, their demographic characteristics must be known in order to assess the size of the target market and to reach it efficiently. For example, it is not enough to know that a certain percentage of a target market are avid golfers; it's much more meaningful to know that a percentage of the people identified as golfers are males between the ages of 30 and 40, and have an average income of, say, $60 000. Most media develop demographic profiles of their audiences and use them in addition to their editorial focus to attract advertisers with matching consumer profiles.

The major disadvantage of demographic segmentation is that it tends to be one-dimensional and does not differentiate among brands. For example, demographics can provide information on the potential for usage of a product (e.g. aftershave lotion or milk) but not on why a particular brand is used, or exactly who uses it. Such information is more likely to be learned from *psychographic* studies, or the cross-correlation of several demographic variables (such as depicted in Table 2.1). Demographics are often used in combination to fine-tune a market segment; they are also used to form composite variables (e.g. demographic and psychographic variables combine to form a composite variable) to measure such sociocultural constructs as family life cycle and social class (which are discussed in Chapters 9 and 10).

Demographic variables reveal ongoing trends that signal business opportunities to marketers, such as shifts in age, gender and income distribution. For example, demographic studies show that the over-55 population has a much greater proportion of disposable income than younger consumers. This factor alone makes consumers aged over 55 an important market for products and services that they might buy for themselves (luxury items) or for their adult children who are more likely to be facing major purchase decisions (such as home ownership) with fewer financial resources, or their grandchildren.

Age

A consumer's age is often a strong determinant of their product choices and consumption practices. Product needs often vary with age and many marketers are able to segment their market based on age. For example, while adults of all ages join health clubs primarily to 'improve or maintain their health', there are other interesting motivations that set adult-age segments apart with regard to joining a health club. Specifically, it appears that younger adults (those 18–34 years of age) join health clubs in part because they desire to 'look good', those who are between 35 and 54 years of age join to 'deal with stress', and those who are 55 and over join for 'medial-physical therapy'.[4] Also, Nyal has segmented the market for its cough-relief medicine on the basis of age (see Figure 2.4), with a flavoured version for infants, Children's Syrup for children aged 2 to 12, Adult Liquid for adults, and Senior DX for consumers over 50. Senior DX is carefully tailored to its target market: it contains no sugar, alcohol or antihistamine and has no decongestant properties (which can interfere with medication for hypertension, cardiovascular disease, diabetes, etc.); it also has an easy-to-open cap, easy-to-read packaging, easy-to-grip bottle and a wide-mouthed dosage cup. Tixylix is another successful brand of cough syrup that is targeted to the child market. Because of such age-related motivational differences, marketers have found age to be a particularly useful demographic variable for market segmentation.

Marketing communication plays a major role in product **positioning** or repositioning. Marketers can expand their markets by tailoring their messages to new consumer segments on the basis of research that identifies sought-after benefits by specific age groups. For example, as mentioned before, female hygiene manufacturers, such as Libra (see <www.libragirl.com.au>), or Carefree and Stayfree made by Johnson & Johnson which have been very successful in capturing a large share of the adult market for their feminine hygiene products, now target younger users. Using television commercials and magazine ads for their brands, the campaign applied an interesting approach with taglines such as 'The only time you need a surfboard is when you're surfing' and 'Designed just for ex-boyfriends'. Instead of an educational campaign, the advertisements suggest a humorous side to the product. Figure 2.5 (page 40) appeals to young female users via humour, a notion that many teenagers find appealing. Age has become an important factor in the marketing of many products, even those traditionally targeting image-conscious consumers, such as liquor and perfume.

Age is also used by radio stations as a segmentation criterion. As a result of competitive rivalry to maintain ratings, many radio stations have sought to distinguish themselves by targeting a particular market segment of listeners according to age. Magazines also target specific age groups. For example *Cosmopolitan* as shown in Table 2.1 clearly has a larger readership in the 18–24 and 25–34 age groups. Some magazines target the older market (i.e. those whose children have finished school or university, their houses are paid off and they are at the peak of their earnings curve).

A recently suggested segmentation approach is to group individuals into cohorts. Consumer cohorts are individuals born during the same period of time who grow and travel through life together, experiencing similar events as they grow up. The classification of consumers into cohorts is based largely on life experiences and the age bands that accompany such experiences. Such experiences that can define a cohort may include a depression, a war or a specific time period such as the 60s or 70s. Often we label such cohorts, giving them names such as baby boomers or generation X.

Baby boomers (i.e. those born in Australia between 1946 and 1964) are a special cohort (or group) in that, until 1987, they had never been faced with a major recession. They had largely sailed through life, consuming happily, creating new markets and radically changing the face of marketing (they like the extended trading hours now offered by supermarkets and other shopping centres). Smart marketers know that, to reach this market, they must deliver a straightforward sales pitch that lets them make up their own minds. Product quality, price, convenience and service are still important but, as they rush through life and ignore most marketing messages, information has become just as important.

Several contradictions characterise this age group. While many earn large incomes, others are former managers who have become victims of corporate restructuring and downsizing. Boomers see themselves as more adventurous and worldly than their parents; but they realise that financial security is more elusive today than when their parents retired. They are now realising that they must spend their money carefully and demand real value for their money. Of course, different consumers in this group are interested in different products:

- those who have older parents are interested in health-care services and retirement villages
- those who have come to parenthood late in life are interested in child-care services, educational toys and videos, and tutoring services
- white-collar workers who have started their own business are interested in computers, fax machines and mobile phones.

Selling products to the boomer market and older consumers in Australia has never been a strong point with advertising and marketing agencies. Many simply ignore these segments, focusing on the once all-powerful 25–35 age group, despite the fact that the baby boomers are one of the largest segments of Australia's total population grouped by age.

An important issue concerning age, especially chronological age, is that it implies a number of underlying forces. In particular, demographers have drawn an important distinction between **age effects** (occurrences due to chronological age) and **cohort effects** (occurrences due to growing up during a specific time period). Examples of the age effect are the heightened interest in leisure travel that often occurs when people (single and married) reach their late fifties or early sixties, and an interest in learning to play golf. While people of all ages learn to play golf, it is particularly prevalent among people in their fifties.

In contrast, the nature of cohort effects is captured by the idea that people hold onto the interests they grew up to appreciate. If 10 years from now it is found that many rock and roll fans are over 60, it would not be because they have suddenly altered their music tastes, but because baby boomers who grew up with rock and roll have become older.[5] It is important for marketers to be aware of the distinction between age effects and cohort effects; the first stresses the impact of ageing, while the other reflects the influence of the period in which people are born and the experiences they shared with others of the same age.

Defining market segments in strictly chronological terms can sometimes be stereotypical and misleading, particularly because many consumers have a *perceived* age (i.e. cognitive age) about 10 to 15 years younger than their *chronological* age. A useful segmentation approach can be to characterise older consumers in terms of their cognitive age rather than their actual chronological age. In particular, the 'new-age elderly' have been identified as a leading-edge consumer segment that is driven primarily by cognitive rather than chronological age factors. A glimpse at 'new-age elderly' consumer profiles in Chapter 12 provides an interesting portrait of contemporary older consumers.

Sex

Gender is frequently used as a distinguishing segmentation variable. For many products and services, markets have long been segmented by either female or male, due to differences in needs and/or social roles of female and male consumers. Women have traditionally been the main users of such products as hair colouring and cosmetics, and men the users of tools and shaving preparations. However, sex roles have blurred, and gender is no longer as accurate as it once was in distinguishing consumers in some product categories. For example, men have become users of skin care and hair products, and women are buying household repair tools, traditionally seen as a male-oriented domain. It is becoming increasingly common to see magazine and TV advertisements that depict men and women in roles traditionally occupied by the opposite sex. For example, many ads reflect the expanded child-nurturing roles of young fathers in today's society (the Australian Dairy Corporation butter commercials with the father cooking and serving dinner to the kids is an example of gender role reversal).

Much of the change in sex roles has come about because of the continued growth in the number of dual-income households (see Chapter 10) and the rise in single parent families. Many product categories are impacted on by the increased number of women in the workforce. One consequence for marketers is that women are not as readily accessible through traditional media as they once were. Because working women do not have much time to watch TV or listen to the radio, many advertisers now emphasise magazines in their media schedules, especially those specifically aimed at working women (e.g. *Working Mother*, *New Woman*, *Cosmopolitan*, *Marie Claire*). Direct marketers also have been targeting time-pressured working women who use merchandise catalogues, telesales 1800 numbers, and Internet sites as ways of shopping for personal clothing and accessories, as well as many household and family needs.

Recent research has shown that men and women differ in terms of the way they look at their Internet usage. Specifically, men tend to 'click on' a website because they are 'information hungry,' whereas women click because 'they expect communications media to entertain and educate.'[6] Table 2.4 presents additional male and female differences when it comes to using the Internet and compares some key usage situations and favourite Internet materials for men versus women.

Women are the critical family influencers or decision makers for many products and services used by other family members. For instance, women frequently purchase underwear, razor blades and shaving cream for their husbands and sons. Women also influence the purchase of products consumed jointly by household members. For example, United States research suggests that women critically affect the decision to install a pool in the backyard; while the decision to purchase a pool tends to involve the whole family, women typically argue in favour of the purchase while men argue against it. The net outcome is that the core target market for swimming pools consists of women aged between 24 and 45, usually well educated and members of upscale households.[7]

Women form an important segment in the newsprint and magazine industry. The number of magazines increased in the late 1990s, while actual readership slowed dramatically, reversing the sales growth of the early 1990s.[8] There is growing specialisation of magazines. For example, in the late 1990s *Minx* entered the Australian market, targeting the 18–35 age female market, with features on sex, fashion and lifestyle. *Minx*'s philosophy included 'Be glad to be a woman . . . we got off the *Titanic* first'. More recently ACP (Australian

FIGURE 2.5 Carefree brand targeting young female users via humour and important benefit (comfort)

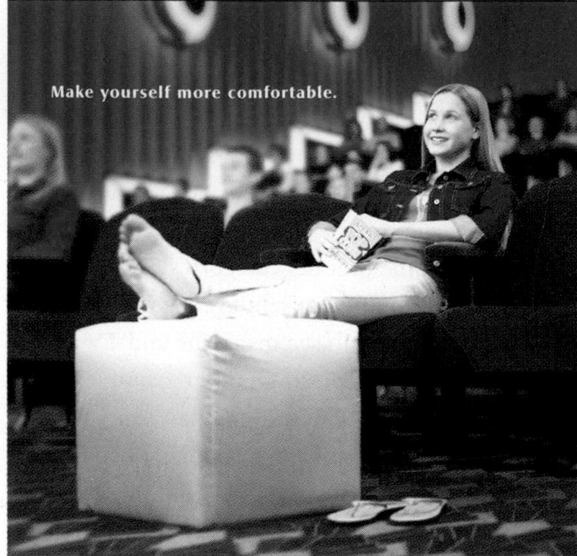
Make yourself more comfortable.

Even if you haven't tried using a tampon yet, you've probably thought about it.

After all, it means you can go swimming, wear anything you want and, best of all, forget you've even got your period. So there's plenty of upsides.

But what about the downsides? Like putting it in for the first time? Well there's really nothing to worry about. Honestly.

It may feel a bit odd actually inserting it for the first time but Carefree® Slim tampons have a unique Silk Ease™ cover that makes them so silky smooth, no other tampon is more comfortable to insert and remove.

The trick is just to relax and follow the instructions that come with each box of Carefree® Slims.

Once the tampon is in you won't even feel it at all. But you will feel completely protected knowing it has tiny pores which direct fluid inside the tampon where it is absorbed.

In fact, Carefree® Slims with the Silk Ease™ cover give you all the protection you need, in a tampon that's very gentle on your body.

Now that's a very comforting thought.

Carefree

Source: **Reproduced with permission from Johnson & Johnson Pacific.**

Consolidated Press) published *Shop Til You Drop* targeted at the 16–39 age group of women, 'who just love to shop'.[9] Women have new images of themselves and they no longer want to be locked into a second-class status (dependents/innocents) or portrayed as sexual appendages. Women want to be seen as strong and independent (Nike's 'Just do it' worldwide campaign portrays women in a positive light, getting on with life, being strong and successful); or they want to be presented with images that appeal to their values.

Those women who we might label as 'thirty-something' appear to differ from women in their twenties and forties. This age group of women has become a force to be reckoned with, as they are increasingly committed to autonomy and self-styled success. Australian women in their thirties have very different attitudes and aspirations to women in their twenties and forties, and on this basis marketers have to take them seriously as an important demographic group. These women are taking more interest in their careers and their finances, increasingly becoming more financially fluid, wielding significant purchasing power. They have changed their shopping habits since their twenties, are now more inclined to look

TABLE 2.4 Male and female segments of Internet users

	Key usage situation	Favourite Internet materials
Female Segments		
Social Sally	Making friends	Chat and personal Web page
New Age Crusader	Fighting for causes	Books and government information
Cautious Mum	Nurturing children	Cooking and medical facts
Playful Pretender	Role playing	Chat and games
Master Producer	Job productivity	White pages and government information
Male Segments		
Bits and Bytes	Computers and hobbies	Investments, discovery, software
Practical Pete	Personal productivity	Investments, company listings
Viking Gamer	Competing and winning	Games, chat, software
Sensitive Sam	Helping family and friends	Investments, government information
World Citizen	Connecting with world	Discovery, software, investments

Source: **Scott Smith and David Whitlark, 'Men and women online: What makes them click,' *Marketing Research*, Summer 2001, p. 22. Reprinted with permission from the American Marketing Association.**

for quality over price, read labels more, buy Australian, and seek environmentally friendly products. Women are now buying their own cars and jewellery, and there has been a gradual increase in men doing the supermarket shopping.

With around one in three marriages currently ending in divorce and just over 60% of women now working, the classic role model of 'mother/homemaker/domestic' is fast disappearing. Children are growing up with new images of the home and with a different definition of the distribution of tasks that were historically based on gender roles. While the women's lives may not be that different, the way in which they see themselves can vary enormously. The differences are attitudinal and are reflected in what they look for in brands, in advertising and in their media consumption. They relate to different advertising approaches to how women see themselves and their relationships with their families and others.

While the Australian population is considerably smaller, the trend is similar to the United States. Australian households are becoming more diverse in size and structure, and recognition of the female and male homemaker profile is an important reference for supermarkets and other retail outlets.

Marital status

Marketers have also discovered the benefits of targeting specific marital status groupings, such as singles, single parents, and dual-income married couples. For example, singles, especially one-person households with incomes greater than $35 000, comprise a market segment that tends to be above average in the use of products not traditionally associated with supermarkets (e.g. liqueurs, books, imported coffee) and below average in their consumption of traditional supermarket products (e.g. tomato sauce, peanut butter, mayonnaise). Such insights can be useful for a supermarket operating in a neighbourhood of one-person households in deciding the merchandise mix for the store. Some marketers target one-person households with single-serve prepared foods (e.g. Continental Cup-a-Soup, McCain dinner for one). The theme 'Are you looking after yourself?' is one successfully targeted to single people who, living by themselves, are perceived as not meeting their dietary needs. (The family, as a consuming unit, is discussed in greater detail in Chapter 9.)

Income, education and occupation

Income has long been an important variable for distinguishing market segments. Marketers commonly use income as a segmentation criterion, because they feel it is a strong indicator of the ability (or inability) to pay for a product (or brand) or a specific model of a product. The average household spending on goods and services in the 1993–94 period was $602 per week; yet there is a significant difference between the lowest income quintile spending $303 per week and the highest quintile spending $994 on average. This amount has changed considerably from the 1993–94 period, increasing to $699 in the 1998–1999 period, and the low income group increased to $466.20 and highest income quintile to $1155.90 in the 1998–99 period.[10] Studying the expenditure across this five-year period indicates an increase of approximately 16%, with major increases in spending in areas such as transportation increasing by 26%, and food and non-alcoholic beverages up 14%.

The major problem with segmenting the market on the basis of income alone is that income only indicates the presence (or absence) of the ability to pay for a product, whereas the actual choice may be based on personal lifestyle, taste and values—variables largely determined by occupation and education. Income is often combined with other demographic variable(s) to define the target market(s) more accurately. For instance, high income has been combined with age to identify the newly-recognised affluent elderly segment; it has also been combined with age and occupational status to produce the so-called yuppie segment, the most sought-after subgroup of the baby boomer market. Figure 2.6 (page 44) shows an ad for TDK, suggesting how well it suits the fast, 'on the go' lifestyle of affluent young professionals (Road Warrior).

Education, occupation and income tend to be closely correlated in almost a cause-and-effect relationship. High-level occupations that produce high incomes usually require advanced educational training. Individuals with little education rarely qualify for high-level jobs. Because of the interrelationship among these three variables (education, occupation and income), they are often combined into a composite index of social class (described in detail in Chapter 10), which reflects a person's values, attitudes, tastes and lifestyle more accurately. For example, a doctor and a plumbing contractor earning the same income but with different educational backgrounds are likely to spend their money in different ways. One may drive a BMW, the other a Holden Commodore HSV ClubSport or Holden Monaro. One may be an opera buff, the other a football follower. Importantly, for marketers of certain types of goods, income alone does not sufficiently differentiate a target market.

GEOGRAPHIC SEGMENTATION

In **geographic segmentation**, the market is divided by *location*. The theory behind this strategy is that people who live in the same area share some similar needs and wants, and that these needs and wants differ from those of people living in other areas. However, some marketing theorists and marketing practitioners believe that worldwide satellite television transmission and global communication networks have erased all regional boundaries, and that geographic segmentation should be replaced by a single global marketing strategy. Other marketers are going in the opposite direction and developing highly regionalist marketing strategies—localising their efforts to fit the needs of individual regions, cities and even suburbs. For example, in the United States, companies such as Campbell's Soups have been known to reorganise entire marketing operations by segmenting the domestic market into specific regions. Sales managers have the autonomy to develop advertising and promotional campaigns geared to local market needs and conditions, using a range of local media. They work closely with local retailers on displays and promotions and report on the micromarketing strategy. Coca-Cola has also—aside from its global advertising orientation—launched micromarketing campaigns in specific countries and regions.

While this trend is not as strong in Australia, due to the fact that the Australian market is substantially smaller, Australian marketers do notice some factors of notable contrast among various states, cities and regional centres. For example, certain food products and/or varieties sell better in one region than in others. Other regional differences can be accounted for by climate. The sunbelt regions of Queensland and Western Australia represent better opportunities for selling swimsuits and in-ground pools than do the alpine regions of New South Wales and Victoria, where home heating systems and overcoats are likely to be better sellers. In addition to regional and climatic differences, market researchers have found that product usage frequently differs among major cities. Table 2.5 provides a sample of Australian states, regions and

TABLE 2.5 Micromarketing at the geographic level

	7-Up %	McDonald's %
State		
NSW	37.59	37.33
Victoria	26.79	26.55
Queensland	18.13	18.91
Western Australia	9.73	8.04
Region		
Capital cities	76.24	63.54
Country areas	23.76	36.46
Cities		
Sydney	31.10	22.87
Melbourne	21.80	19.44
Brisbane	10.35	8.96
Perth	7.90	6.44

Source: **Roy Morgan Single Source Australia: April 2003–March 2004.**

cities (capital city versus country area) and corresponding consumption rates of the brands 7-Up Lemonade and McDonald's showing some interesting differences in consumption across the geographic identifiers.

Different purchasing patterns exist among the major suburbs of large cities, small towns and rural Australia where, for example, different types of household furnishings and leisure products are sold. Even within a large metropolitan area, people living in the inner city will buy different types of home furnishings and leisure goods to those living in the suburbs. Convertible sofa beds or couches and appliances that aren't too large are more likely to be bought by inner-city dwellers, whereas homeowners dispersed in the outer suburbs or country areas will be able to accommodate a large barbecue, outdoor setting, lawn-mower and lawn-edgers.

Geographic segmentation is a useful strategy for many marketers. It is relatively easy to find geographic-based differences for many products; in addition, geographic segments can be reached easily via local media, including newspapers, TV and radio, and regional editions of magazines.

PSYCHOLOGICAL SEGMENTATION

Psychological characteristics refer to the intrinsic qualities of the individual consumer. Consumer segmentation strategies are often based on specific psychological variables. For instance, consumers may be segmented in terms of their needs and motivations, personality, perceptions, learning, level of involvement, or attitudes. (Part 2 examines more fully the wide range of psychological variables that influence consumer decision making and consumption behaviour.)

PSYCHOGRAPHIC SEGMENTATION

Marketing practitioners are increasingly utilising psychographic research, which is closely aligned with psychological research, especially personality and attitude measurement. This form of applied consumer research (also commonly referred to as *lifestyle analysis)* has proven to be a valuable marketing tool that helps identify promising consumer segments that are likely to be responsive to specific marketing messages. For example, the promotion of such products as Colgate-Palmolive's Lux soap, Jack Daniels whiskey, Telstra's phone services, KFC fast food, Nescafé coffee and Dewar's White Label Scotch is based on psychographic research that captures insights and creates profiles of the consumers being targeted.[11]

In their most common form, **psychographic segmentation** studies employ a battery of statements designed to identify relevant aspects of a consumer's personality, buying motives, interests, attitudes, beliefs and values. The psychographic profile of a consumer segment can be thought of as a composite of consumers' measured activities, interests and opinions (often referred to as **AIOs**). As an approach to constructing consumer psychographic profiles, AIOs research seeks consumers' responses to a large number of statements that measure *activities* (how the consumer or family spends time—e.g. working, taking holidays, bushwalking), *interests* (the consumer's or family's preferences and priorities—e.g. home, fashion, food) and *opinions* (how the consumer feels about a wide variety of events and issues—politics, social issues, the state of education, the future). Table 2.6 presents a portion of a **psychographic inventory** from a recently designed study of 'techno-road-warriors', business people who spend a high percentage of their working week on the road, equipped with notebook computers, pagers, mobile phones and electronic organisers (as depicted in Figure 2.6).

Table 2.7 (page 45) presents a hypothetical psychographic profile of a techno-road-warrior. The appeal of psychographic research lies in the frequently vivid and practical profiles of consumer segments that it can produce (which will be illustrated later in this chapter).

In a psychographic research study, consumers are usually asked to reveal their own personal (individual) or their family's (household's) reactions to a variety of statements. For example, if Gillette decided to evaluate the target market for its successful Sensor razor in terms of psychographic characteristics, it might use the

FIGURE 2.6 **Road Warrior—Occupation-based segment for TDK product**

Source: Courtesy of TDK (Australia) Pty Ltd.

following statements to capture individual and family predispositions toward the Sensor razor system.

Personal statements

- I'm a demanding person.
- For me, seeking perfection in what I do is really not important.
- When I wake up in the morning, my appearance is uppermost on my mind.
- When it comes to the way I dress, I'm not particularly fashion-conscious.

Family statements

- 'Good' grooming is important to all members of my family.
- Members of my family frequently comment on how good I look after I shave.
- We are a particularly good-looking family.
- We are more likely to try new products than most of our friends and neighbours.
- I imagine that we buy and use more grooming products than other people we know.

Respondents are asked to evaluate such statements in terms of their degree of agreement (e.g. strongly

TABLE 2.6 **Portion of an AIO inventory used to identify 'techno-road-warriors'**

Instructions: *Please read each statement and place an 'x' in the box that* ***best*** *indicates how strongly you* ***agree*** *or* ***disagree*** *with the statement.*

	Agree completely						Disagree completely
• I feel that my life is moving faster and faster, sometimes just too fast.	[1]	[2]	[3]	[4]	[5]	[6]	[7]
• If I consider the 'pluses' and 'minuses', technology has been good for me.	[1]	[2]	[3]	[4]	[5]	[6]	[7]
• I find that I have to pull myself away from email.	[1]	[2]	[3]	[4]	[5]	[6]	[7]
• Given my lifestyle, I have more of a shortage of time than money.	[1]	[2]	[3]	[4]	[5]	[6]	[7]
• I like the benefits of the Internet, but I often don't have the time to take advantage of them.	[1]	[2]	[3]	[4]	[5]	[6]	[7]
• I am generally open to considering new practices and new technology	[1]	[2]	[3]	[4]	[5]	[6]	[7]

TABLE 2.7 **Hypothetical psychographic profile of the 'techno-road-warrior'**

- Goes on the Internet 6-plus times a week
- Sends and/or receives 15 or more email messages a week
- Regularly visits websites to gather information and/or to comparison shop
- Often buys personal items via 1800 numbers and/or over the Internet
- May trade stocks and/or make travel reservations over the Internet
- Earns $100 000 or more a year
- Belongs to several reward programs (e.g. frequent flyer programs, hotel programs, rent-a-car programs)

agree, agree, disagree, strongly disagree). For some statements, the respondent may be asked to indicate the degree of importance (e.g. very important, slightly important, unimportant).

In addition to reflecting either personal or family activities, interests and opinions, psychographic statements can be designed to be either general or product-specific. In a psychographic study of a specific product category, consumer researchers are likely to include both general and product-specific statements. For example, a study aimed at examining the practice of including snacks (e.g. a Mars bar or muesli bar) in children's lunches might include such *general* statements as these:

- My children could eat the same thing for lunch every day.
- My children are always telling me what their friends' mothers make them for lunch.
- My children prepare their own school lunches most of the time.

It might also include such *product-specific* statements as:

- When I was a child, my mother regularly gave me a snack as part of my school lunch.
- When choosing a lunchtime snack for my children, I select it as if I'm selecting food.

Both types of statements supply valuable insights into consumer attitudes. However, while the general statements focus on broader perceptions, preferences and attitudes, the product-specific statements pertain directly to the product and its use. Using TV viewership as an illustration, Table 2.8 provides examples of the four major types of psychographic statements discussed in this section.

TABLE 2.8 **Classification of different types of psychographic statements for a TV viewership study**

	Individual/Personal	Family/Household
General	'I'm the kind of person who hangs out at home a lot.'	'We really must be couch potatoes; we're always staying home.'
	'Give me a good reason, and I'll have a party.'	'We'll buy anything that will bring the family together.'
Product-specific	'My idea of a good evening is to stay at home and relax in front of the TV.'	'We have real limits as to how much TV we allow ourselves to watch.'
	'I can watch 10 hours of TV and not know it.'	'We eat our meals as a family while watching TV.'

(The discussion of psychographic segmentation is continued in the latter half of this chapter, where we consider how psychographic and demographic variables are combined to create descriptive profiles of consumer segments.)

SOCIOCULTURAL SEGMENTATION

Sociocultural segmentation variables (i.e. group and cultural) provide further bases for market segmentation. For example, consumer markets have been successfully subdivided into segments on the basis of stage in the family life cycle, social class, core cultural values, subcultural memberships and cross-cultural affiliation.

Family life cycle

Family life cycle segmentation is based on the premise that many families pass through similar phases in their formation, growth and final dissolution. At each phase, the family unit needs different products and product styles. Young single people, for example, need basic furniture for their first flat, while their parents, finally free of childrearing, often refurnish their homes with more elaborate pieces. Family life cycle is a composite variable based explicitly on marital and family status, but implicitly including relative age, income and employment status. Each stage in the family life cycle (singles, young marrieds, parenthood, post-parenthood and dissolution) represents an important target segment to a variety of marketers. (Chapter 9 discusses the family life cycle in greater depth and looks at the family and its consumer characteristics in more detail.)

Social class

Social class (or relative status in the community) can be used as a base for market segmentation It is usually 'measured' by a weighted index of several demographic variables, such as education, occupation and income (as discussed in the section on demographic segmentation). The concept of social class implies a hierarchy in which individuals in the same class generally have the same degree of status, while members of other classes have either higher or lower status. Studies have shown that consumers in different social classes vary in terms of values, product preferences and buying habits. Many major banks, investment companies and airlines, for example, offer a variety of different levels of service to people of different social classes (e.g. private banking services and first class air travel to upper class). Figure 2.7 (page 48) illustrates how class can be used as an appeal, by identifying that the brand of flooring appeals to all walks of life. (Chapter 10 discusses social class in detail.)

Culture, subculture and cross-cultural affiliation

Some marketers have found it useful to segment their domestic and international markets on the basis of cultural heritage, since members of the same culture tend to share common values, beliefs and customs. Marketers who use cultural segmentation stress specific, widely held cultural values with which they hope consumers will identify. For example, in Australia, most consumers would identify with the values of freedom of choice, mateship and individuality. Cultural segmentation is particularly useful in international marketing, but it is important for the marketer to understand fully the beliefs, values and customs of the countries in which the product is being marketed (i.e. the cross-cultural context; see Chapter 13).

Within the larger culture, distinct subgroups (*subcultures*) are often united by certain experiences, values or beliefs that make effective market segments. These groupings could be based on a specific demographic characteristic (e.g. race, religion, ethnicity or age) or lifestyle characteristics (working women, golfers). In Australia, important subcultural market segments include Greek-Australians, Italian-Australians, Asian-Australians (including Vietnamese-Australians) and the elderly. For example, advertisers use a variety of Italian-language and English-language print and broadcast media, through which they target the lucrative Italian market. Similarly, the appreciation of 50-plus consumers as a growth subcultural market segment has encouraged marketers to develop new products and reposition old products (and services) specifically for this market.

Hotels and retail stores offer special discounts to elderly consumers (e.g. with Senior Citizens Card); many personal-care products and health products are formulated especially for the over-50 market; and a variety of magazines target mature adults.

Often, a product must be altered or reformulated in some way for it to do well in several cultures. For example, Nestlé, a Swiss company that sells coffee worldwide, makes a strong brew for the Italian market and a weaker coffee for the Australian market. Sometimes, it is merely custom that divides cultural segments. Greetings cards, sold without verses in Europe, are usually sold with verses in Australia. Culturally distinct segments can be marketing prospects for the same product, but it may be necessary to reach them with different promotional appeals. For example, bicycles might be promoted as an efficient means of transportation in Asia and as a health and fitness product in Australia.

International marketers who base their products and promotional campaigns on the results of cross-cultural studies are more likely to succeed in specific ethnic markets than those who use a standardised marketing approach. For example, Parker Brothers, the manufacturer of Monopoly, has introduced a Russian version of the board game in Russia. Appropriate changes have been made on the board (e.g. instead of Pall Mall, players land on Arbat, a pedestrian mall in Moscow) as the standard board would have been meaningless to the Russian market. All references to stocks, which are not sold in the former Soviet Union, have been changed to bonds. The familiar Monopoly tokens remain the same, but a Russian bear token has been added.

With some product types, companies cannot always advertise abroad as they do in Australia. In Germany, toy soldiers can only be shown on TV if they are unarmed and seated in jeeps rather than in tanks. Germany also bans the use of comparative advertising and competitive claims. In Austria, children cannot be used in commercials; enterprising marketers have used dwarfs or animated drawings to represent children.[12] Television ads aimed at minors are regulated by the European Union's Television Broadcasting Directive of 1989, which states that television ads should not directly exhort juveniles to buy a product or service by exploiting their inexperience or credulity. (Chapters 11, 12 and 13 examine cultural, subcultural and cross-cultural bases of market segmentation in greater detail.)

USE-RELATED SEGMENTATION

Use-related segmentation is a popular and effective form of segmentation that categorises consumers in terms of product, brand or service usage characteristics, such as rate of usage, awareness, level and degree of brand loyalty.

Rate of usage

Rate of usage segmentation differentiates among heavy users, medium users, light users and non-users of a specific product, service or brand. For example, research has consistently indicated that 25–35% of beer drinkers account for more than 70% of all beer consumed. For this reason, most marketers prefer to target campaigns to the heavy users, rather than spend considerably more money trying to attract light users. This also explains the successful targeting of light beer to heavy drinkers on the basis that it is less filling (and thus can be consumed in greater quantities) than regular beer.

Marketers of a wide variety of products have found that a relatively small group of heavy users account for a disproportionately large percentage of product usage; targeting these heavy users has become the basis of their marketing strategies. Other marketers take note of the gaps in market coverage for light and medium users, and profitably target these segments. Usage rate has been a segmentation criterion for many mobile phone operators who offer plans according to usage.

Marketers also consider the *current* versus the *future* potential of consumer segmentation when setting marketing strategy. For example, many banks might deliberately not target university students or aged pensioners as a primary market because they view them as a high-use, low-profit segment (minimal deposits). Other

FIGURE 2.7 **Amtico brand identifies key images of elegance and copy 'for all walks of life' appealing to class**

Amtico
Beautiful, Durable Flooring for all Walks of Life

Source: Courtesy of Amtico.

bankers see university students as a very attractive long-term market (potentially higher than average incomes, and likely buyers of homes, cars and boats), and do their best to attract them as clients before graduation. Because current university students have the potential to become future heavy users, they are an attractive market.

Non-users represent a special challenge and marketers have to decide whether non-users are a potentially worthwhile segment, or whether the resources needed to convert them into users (i.e. enlarging the market) can be better spent in trying to lure present users away from competitive products (i.e. increasing their own market share).

Awareness level

Awareness level encompasses the notion of consumer awareness, interest level or buyer readiness. Marketers have to determine whether potential consumers are aware of the product, interested in the product, or need to be informed about the product. Figure 2.8 refers to the promotional campaign for lamb as a healthy alternative to other, more fatty foods. Although Australian consumers have long been aware of lamb as a major food, the campaign aimed to regenerate interest by portraying lamb as a food with low fat content, which could be prepared quickly and in ways other than the traditional roast. Such awareness- and use-related segmentation approaches have also been used by the Australian Dairy Corporation to promote dairy products.

Brand loyalty

Sometimes brand loyalty is used as the basis for segmentation. Marketers often try to identify the characteristics of their brand-loyal consumers so that they can direct their promotional efforts to people with similar characteristics in the larger population. Other marketers target consumers who show no brand loyalty (i.e. '*brand switchers*'), in the belief that such people represent greater market potential than consumers who are loyal to competing brands. Brand switchers or non-brand-loyal consumers also suggest a different type of marketing mix to the marketing practitioner (low price, consumer 'deals', point-of-sale displays, etc.). Almost by definition, consumer innovators—often a prime target for new products—tend not to be brand loyal.

Increasingly, marketers stimulate and reward brand loyalty by offering special benefits to consistent or frequent customers. Such frequent usage or relationship programs often take the form of a membership 'club' (e.g. Qantas Frequent Flyer, or FlyBuys). Relationship programs tend to provide special accommodation and services, as well as free extras, to keep these frequent customers loyal and happy. This segmentation approach identifies the purchase patterns of consumers and develops strategies targeted at either loyal users to keep them loyal, or switchers to attract them to the marketer's brand.

FIGURE 2.8 **Lamb ad designed to create awareness and interest**

Where's the bone?

Where's the Trim Lamb recipe?

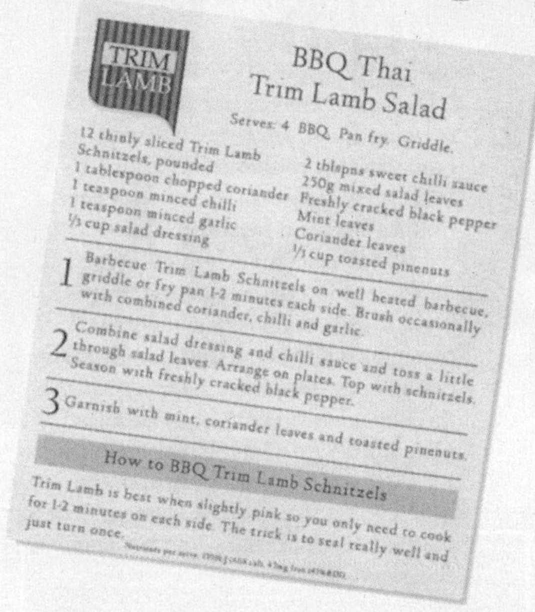

Where's the fat?

Source: **Courtesy of Meat and Livestock Australia.**

USER-SITUATION SEGMENTATION

Marketers recognise that the occasion or situation often determines what consumers will purchase or consume. For this reason, they sometimes focus on the usage situation as a segmentation variable. The following three statements reveal the potential of **user-situation segmentation**.

- 'When I'm on vacation, I always enjoy a hearty breakfast.'
- 'When I'm away on business, I stay at a Hilton Hotel; when I travel with my family, I stay at a Flag Inn.'
- 'I always send my mother flowers on her birthday.'

Under other circumstances, in other situations and on other occasions, the consumer might make different choices. Some situational factors that might influence a purchase or consumption choice include whether it is a weekday or weekend (e.g. going to a movie); whether there is sufficient time (e.g. use of regular mail or express mail); whether it is a gift for a friend, parent or boss or a self-gift (a reward to oneself).

Some marketers try to instil the notion of the suitability of certain products in certain situations; others try to break customary consumer habits. In an effort to challenge the customary usage of coffee as a breakfast and mid-morning adult drink, a US company test-marketed Jolt Cola (which is high in caffeine) as a 'wake-up' and mid-morning drink, as a replacement for coffee.

Many products are promoted for special usage occasions. The greeting card industry, for example, stresses special cards for a variety of occasions, which seem to be increasing almost daily (Secretaries' Day, etc.). The florist and confectionery industries promote their products for Valentine's Day and Mother's Day; the diamond

FIGURE 2.9 Advertisement targeting specific brand appeal for usage occasion

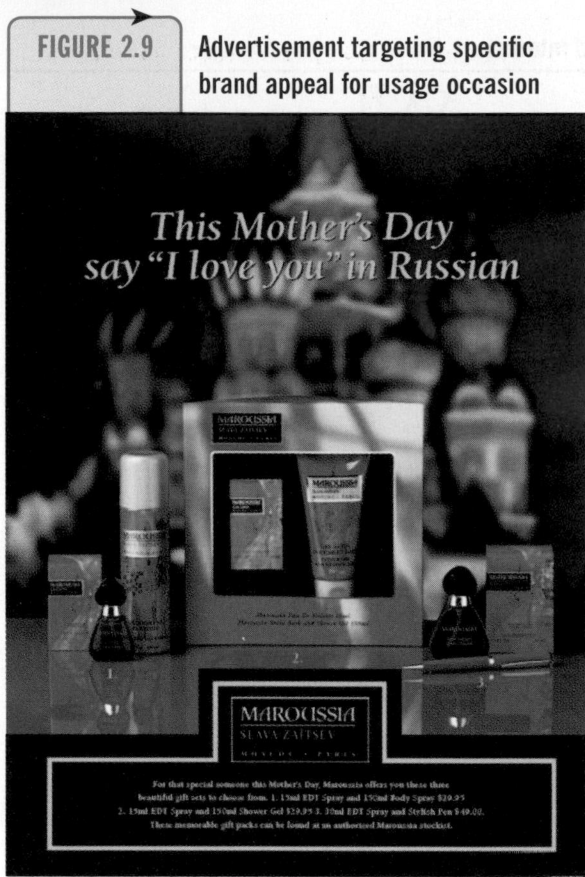

Source: Courtesy of L'Oreal Australia.

industry promotes diamond rings as an engagement symbol; the watch and pen industries promote their products as graduation gifts. Research evidence suggests that particular usage situations are viable bases for segmentation. For example, Orlando Wyndham promoted their Maison brand of drink as a stylish drink, suitable for celebration and party situations; the headline and copy target the occasion—'Celebrate in style'. Usage can also be seen in the advertisement shown in Figure 2.9 identifying the usage occasion as a gift for Mother's Day. *Business Review Weekly* and *Financial Review* clearly target corporate businesspeople who use newspapers to keep informed about business issues. In a somewhat similar fashion, *Reader's Digest* targets different segments with special editions of its flagship magazine that are designed to meet audience interests and the focus of potential advertisers more precisely.

Time pressure is a component of the usage situation. Consumers in a rush are less likely to visit a major shopping centre, but will select some other type of convenience store where they feel they can get in and out quickly. The airlines' pricing structure is based on time pressure: travel that is booked close to the departure date is priced at the top of the scale, while travel booked far in advance is usually priced much lower. This is evidenced in the Frequent Flyer program run by Qantas and other airlines (see <www.qantas.com.au>). This situational pricing policy tends to reflect the reality that holiday travel is optional, and the price-sensitive leisure market segment is willing to plan ahead to obtain lower fares.

BENEFIT SEGMENTATION

Marketing managers often attempt to isolate the one particular benefit that they should communicate to consumers. **Benefit (or needs based) segmentation** requires finding the major benefits people look for in the product class, the kinds of people who look for each benefit and the brands that deliver each benefit. Examples of benefits that are commonly used include health benefits (Vaalia yoghurt), a sense of 'doing good' (World Vision Australia), financial security (AXA), relief of dry skin (Vaseline Intensive Care), elimination of household odours (Glen 20), relief of arthritis (Blackmores: see Figure 2.10), pain relief (Naprogesic: see Figure 2.11), comfort (Rockport shoes) and safety (Volvo). In effect this process is based on the view of understanding the needs of the end user.

Changing lifestyles play a major role in determining the product benefits that are important to consumers, and provide marketers with opportunities for new products and services. For example, the microwave oven was the perfect solution to the needs of dual-income households, where neither partner has time for lengthy meal preparation. Food marketers offer busy families the benefits of breakfast products that require only seconds to prepare (e.g. Kellogg's Pop Tarts) or dinner that is quick and easy (McCain Combo meals).

FIGURE 2.10 Benefit segment and benefit-based appeal

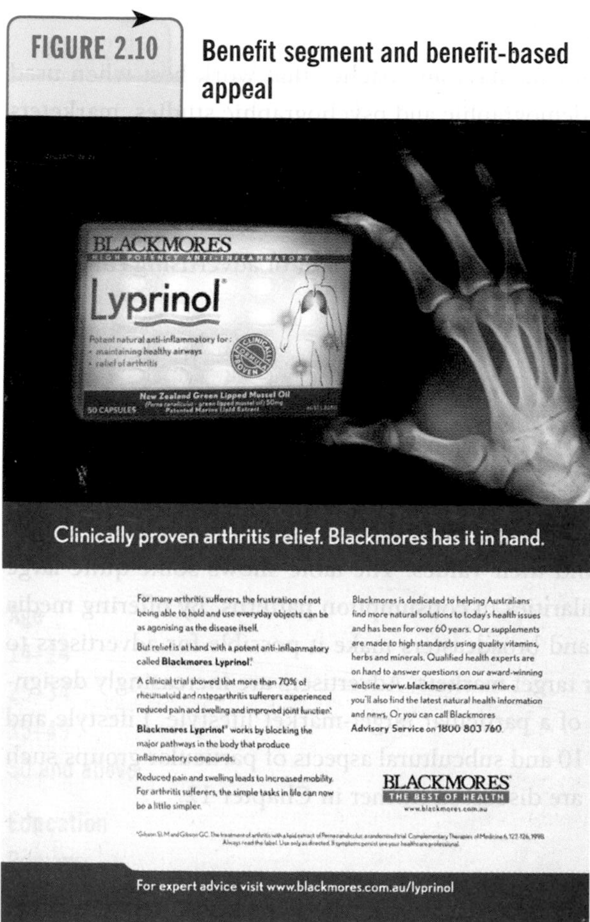

Source: Courtesy of Blackmores®.

FIGURE 2.11 Identifying key brand benefit uses

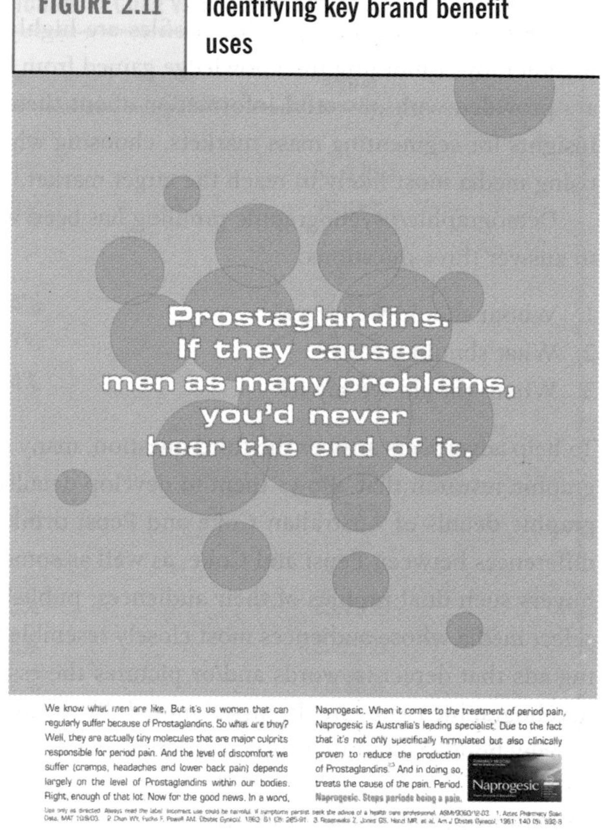

Source: Courtesy of Roche Products Pty Limited.

Benefit segmentation can be used to position various brands within the same product category.[13] The classic case of successful benefit segmentation is the market for toothpaste. Close-up, with a social appeal that stresses bright teeth, is targeted to young people; Aim is targeted to parents as a good-tasting toothpaste that will encourage children to brush longer; Colgate Tartar Control is targeted towards adults as a means of removing tartar (a cosmetic benefit) and plaque (a health benefit).

Benefit segmentation is used not only to find a niche for new products, but also to reposition established products. In a changing society concerned with sexually transmitted disease, condom manufacturers are now targeting women by means of aggressive advertising campaigns stressing disease prevention. They are also packaging condoms in pastel-coloured boxes and stocking them on open shelves in the feminine hygiene sections of pharmacies and supermarkets to make them easy to buy.

HYBRID SEGMENTATION APPROACHES

Marketers commonly segment markets by combining several segmentation variables, rather than relying on a single segmentation method. This section examines three hybrid segmentation approaches that provide marketers with richer and more accurately defined consumer segments than can be derived from using a single segmentation variable—demographic/psychographic profiles, geodemographics, and values and lifestyles hybrid segmentation approaches.

market segments include identification, sufficiency, stability and accessibility.

Once an organisation has identified promising target markets, it must decide whether to pursue several segments (differentiated marketing) or just one segment (concentrated marketing). It then develops a positioning strategy for each targeted segment. In certain instances, a company might decide to follow a countersegmentation strategy in which it combines two or more segments into one larger segment.

Discussion questions

1. What is market segmentation? How is the practice of market segmentation related to the marketing concept?
2. How are market segmentation, targeting and positioning interrelated? Illustrate how these three concepts can be used to develop a marketing strategy for a product of your choice.
3. Discuss the advantages and disadvantages of using demographics as a basis for segmentation. Can demographics and psychographics be used together to segment markets? Illustrate your answer with a specific example.
4. Many marketers have found that a relatively small group of heavy users accounts for a disproportionately large amount of the total product consumed. What are the advantages and disadvantages of targeting these heavy users?
5. Under which circumstances and for what types of products should a marketer segment the market on the basis of:
   (a) awareness status;
   (b) brand loyalty;
   (c) use-situation?
6. Some marketers consider benefit segmentation as the segmentation approach most consistent with the marketing concept. Do you agree or disagree with this view? Why?
7. Club Med is a prominent company in the vacation and travel industry. Describe how the company could use demographics and psychographics to identify TV shows and magazines in which to place its advertisements.
8. How can a marketer use the VALS2™ segmentation profiles to develop an advertising campaign for a chain of health clubs? Which segments should be targeted? How should the health club be positioned to each of these segments?
9. For each of the following products, identify the segmentation base that you consider best for targeting consumers.
   (a) coffee
   (b) soups
   (c) home exercise equipment
   (d) mobile telephones
   (e) non-fat frozen yoghurt.
   Explain your choices.
10. Apply the criteria for effective segmentation to marketing a product of your choice to university students.

Exercises

1. Select a product and brand that you use frequently and list the benefits you receive from using it. Without disclosing your list, ask a fellow student who uses a different brand in this product category (preferably a friend of the opposite sex) to make a similar list for his or her brand. Compare the two lists and identify the implications for using benefit segmentation to market the two brands.
2. Does your lifestyle differ significantly from your parents' lifestyle? If so, how are the two lifestyles different? What factors cause these differences?
3. Do you anticipate any major changes in your lifestyle in the next five years? If so, into which VALS2™ segment are you likely to belong five years from now? Explain.
4. The owners of a local health food restaurant have asked you to prepare a psychographic profile of families living in the community surrounding the restaurant's location. Construct a 10-question psychographic inventory appropriate for segmenting families on the basis of their dining-out preferences.
5. Find three print advertisements that you believe are targeted at a particular psychographic segment. How effective do you think each ad is in terms of achieving its objective? Why?

Key terms

age effects *(p. 38)*
AIOs (activities, interests, opinions) *(p. 43)*
benefit (or needs based) segmentation *(p. 50)*
cohort effects *(p. 38)*
concentrated marketing *(p. 60)*
countersegmentation *(p. 61)*
demographic segmentation *(p. 36)*
differentiated marketing *(p. 60)*
geodemographic segmentation *(p. 52)*
geographic segmentation *(p. 42)*
market segmentation *(p. 29)*
mass marketing *(p. 29)*
micromarketing *(p. 30)*
positioning *(p. 37)*
psychographic inventory *(p. 43)*
psychographic segmentation *(p. 43)*
repositioning *(p. 31)*
segmentation criteria *(p. 29)*
sociocultural segmentation variables *(p. 46)*
targeting *(p. 29)*
use-related segmentation *(p. 47)*
user-situation segmentation *(p. 49)*
VALS2™ *(p. 54)*

Endnotes

1. Nina Munk, 'Gap gets it', *Fortune*, 3 August 1998, pp. 68–82.
2. Alison Fahey, 'Schweppes mixes its message', *Brandweek*, 1 February 1993, p. 3.
3. ACNielsen Regional Television Facts 1998.
4. Martin G. Letscher, 'Sports fads and trends', *American Demographics*, June 1997, p. 54.
5. Charles D. Schewe and Stephanie M. Noble, 'Market segmentation by cohorts: The value and validity of cohorts in Amercia and abroad', *Journal of Marketing Management*, 16 (1–3), 2000, pp. 129–142 and Geoffrey Meridith and Charles Schewe, 'The power of cohorts', *American Demographics*, December 1994, pp. 22–31.
6. Scott Smith and David Whitlark, 'Men and women online: What makes them click?', *Marketing Research*, Summer 2001, pp. 20–25.
7. 'Pegging buyers by their gender', *New York Times*, 13 September 1992, p. 1D.
8. Paula Bombara, 'Mass mags rise', *B&T Weekly*, 26 November 1999, pp. 12, 14.
9. Jacinta Koch, 'New mags take gloss off oldies', *Courier-Mail*, 5 February 2000, p. 17; *Shop Til You Drop* (June 2004) <www.acp.com.au/magazines/wlifestyle/shoptilyoudrop>.
10. Australian Bureau of Statistics, *Household Characteristics. 1993–94 Household Expenditure Survey. Australia* (Canberra: ABS, 1996, Catalogue No. 6531.0), p. 1, and Australian Bureau of Statistics, *Household Expenditure Survey: Australia User Guide 1988–99* (Canberra: ABS, 2000, Catalogue No. 6527.0).
11. Lisa Mitchell, 'Welcome to the soap-opera world of advertising', *Age Green Guide*, 15 August 1996, pp. 10–11. Nestlé screened 10 Nescafé commercials based on 'The story of Roy and Gillian' between 1992 and 1996.
12. Peter Applebome, 'Setting the table for kids' cuisine', *New York Times*, 19 March 1989, p. D4.
13. For an interesting article contrasting several important forms of segmentation, see Joel S. Dubow, 'Occasion-based versus user-based benefit segmentation: A case study', *Journal of Advertising Research*, March/April 1992, pp. 11–18.
14. *VALS2: Your Marketing Edge for the 1990s*, Menlo Park, CA: SRI International, Values and Lifestyle [VALS] Program.
15. Janet Hoek, Philip Gendall and Don Esslemont, 'Market segmentation: A search for the Holy Grail?', *Journal of Marketing Practice: Applied Marketing Science*, 2(1), 1996, pp. 25–34; Kathy Hammond, A.S.C. Ehrenberg and G.J. Goodhardt, 'Market segmentation for competitive brands', *European Journal of Marketing*, 30(12), 1996, pp. 39–49.

The consumer as an individual

PART 2

Part 2 discusses the consumer as an individual. Chapters 3 to 7 provide the reader with a comprehensive picture of consumer psychology. The objectives of these chapters are (1) to explain the basic psychological concepts that account for individual behaviour, and (2) to show how these concepts influence the individual's consumption-related behaviour.

DECISION-MAKING MODEL

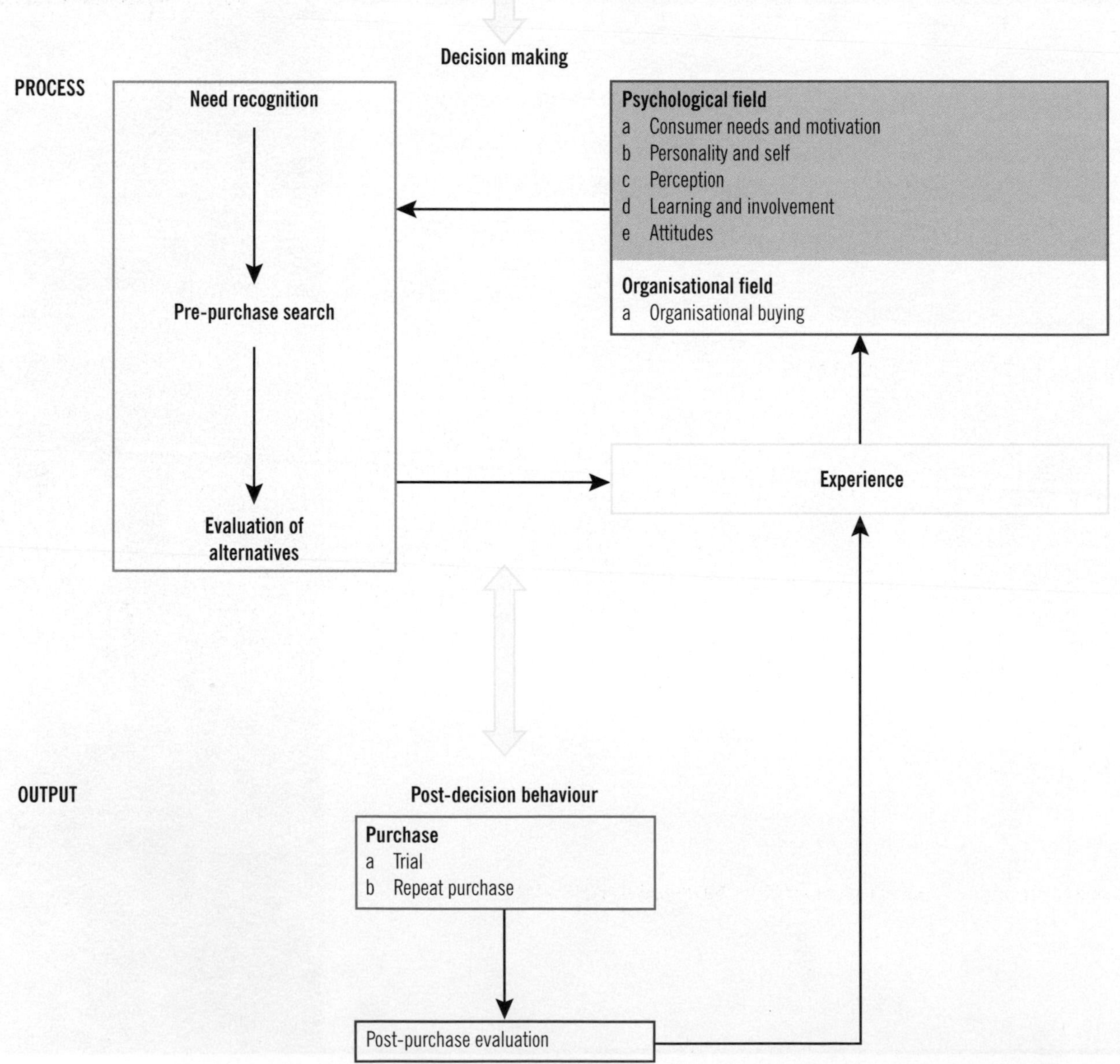

CHAPTER 3

Consumer needs and motivation

FROM CITY TO SURF AT THE FLICK OF A SWITCH.
Nissan Pathfinder is equipped with one of the most advanced four-wheel drive systems in the world. ALL MODE 4x4.
It means you can select the optimum driving mode at the flick of a switch. No stopping. No messing about.
On-road, you may select 2WD, off-road 4WD high and, should you find yourself running into something more challenging, you can choose 4WD low.
Or choose auto and the car automatically selects between 2WD and 4WD high to best suit conditions.
But it's not just about high technology.
The powerful 3.3 litre V6 boasts a whole host of luxury features. The ST comes with air conditioning, alloy wheels, ABS brakes, dual airbags, CD player, power windows, electric mirrors and cruise control. The top of the line Ti has leather seat trim, an in-dash 6-stacker CD, climate control air conditioning, electric sunroof, roof bars and fog lamps.
So, whether you're racing around in the city, or just fancy a run to the coast, you can be shore, sorry, sure that you're in a first class cabin.
www.nissan.com.au
PATHFINDER
SHIFT_the future
NISSAN

Source: **Reproduced with kind permission of Nissan Motor Co. (Australia) Pty Ltd.**

We all seek different pleasures and spend our money in different ways. One woman may spend her Christmas bonus on a new set of golf clubs; her neighbour may spend hers on a new suit. Diversity in consumer behaviour does not surprise us. We have been brought up to believe that the differences among people are what makes life interesting. However, underlying similarities operate across most types of people and serve to explain and clarify consumption behaviour. Psychologists and consumer behaviourists agree that most people tend to experience the same kinds of needs and motives; they simply express these motives in different ways. For this reason, an understanding of human motives is very important to marketers; it enables them to understand, and predict, human behaviour in the marketplace.

Human needs or, in this case, consumer needs, are the basis of all modern marketing. Needs are the essence of the marketing concept. The key to a company's survival, profitability and growth in a highly competitive marketing environment is its ability to identify and satisfy unfulfilled consumer needs better and sooner than the competition.

Marketers do not create needs, though in some instances they may make consumers more keenly aware of unfelt needs. Successful marketers define their markets in terms of the needs they presume to satisfy, rather than in terms of the products they sell. This is a *market-oriented*, rather than a *production-oriented*, approach to marketing. A market orientation focuses on the needs of the buyer; a production orientation focuses on the needs of the seller. The marketing concept implies that the manufacturer will make only what it knows people will buy; a production orientation implies that the manufacturer will try to sell what it decides to make.

Marketers who base their offerings on recognition of consumer needs find a ready market for their products. The popularity of weekend markets in Australia is grounded in their appeal to consumers' *needs for flavour, quality and freshness*, needs that too often are not met by large food marketers who focus on appearance and convenience. The increased emphasis on more flexible banking and financial services such as the increased use of ATM facilities, the Internet, and the ability to withdraw funds when using EFTPOS, are effective ways to satisfy the needs of the consumer.

Savvy companies define their missions in terms of the consumer needs they satisfy rather than the products they produce and sell. Consumers' basic needs do not change but the products that satisfy them do. Thus, a corporate focus on making products that will satisfy consumers' needs ensures that the company stays in the forefront of the search for new and effective solutions. By doing so, such companies are likely to survive and grow despite strong competition or adverse economic conditions. On the other hand, companies that define themselves in terms of the products they make may suffer or even go out of business when their products are replaced by competitive offerings that better satisfy the same need.

This chapter discusses the basic needs that operate in most people to motivate behaviour. It explores the influence such needs have on consumption behaviour. Later chapters in Part 2 explain why and how these basic human motives are expressed in so many diverse ways.

➤ What is motivation?

Motivation can be described as the driving force within individuals that impels them to action. This driving force is produced by a state of tension, which exists as the result of an unfulfilled need. Individuals strive, both consciously and subconsciously, to reduce this tension through behaviour that they anticipate will fulfil their needs and thus relieve them of the stress they feel. The specific goals they elect and the patterns of action they undertake to achieve their goals are the result of individual thinking and learning. Figure 3.1 presents a model of the motivational process. It portrays motivation as a state of need-induced tension that drives an individual to engage in behaviour that he or she expects will gratify a need, and thus reduce the tension.

FIGURE 3.1 **Model of the motivation process**

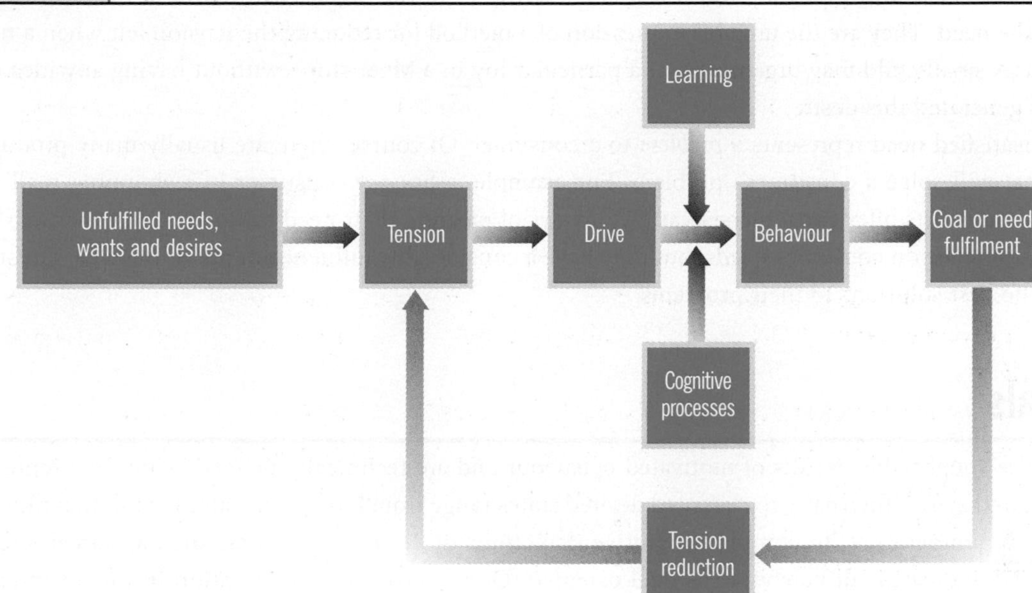

Whether gratification is actually achieved depends on the course of action being pursued. If a secondary school girl expects to become a great tennis player by wearing the same brand of runners that Venus Williams wears, she is likely to be disappointed; if she takes tennis lessons and practises diligently, she may succeed.

The specific courses of action that consumers pursue, and their specific goals, are selected on the basis of their thinking processes (i.e. cognition) and previous learning. For that reason, marketers who understand motivational theory attempt to influence the consumers' cognitive processes.

Needs

We use the term 'need' when referring to any human requirement. Every individual has needs; they underlie all human action: some are innate, others are acquired. Innate needs are physiological (i.e. biogenic); they include the needs for food, water, air, clothing, shelter and sex. Biogenic needs are considered *primary needs* or motives because they are needed to sustain biological life.

Acquired needs are needs that we learn in response to our culture or environment. They may include the need for self-esteem, prestige, affection, power or learning. Because acquired needs are generally psychological (i.e. psychogenic), they are considered *secondary needs or motives*. They result from the individual's subjective psychological state and from relationships with others. Psychological needs arise from the need for recognition, esteem and belonging.

A need becomes a motive when it is aroused to a sufficient level of intensity. For example, all individuals need shelter from the elements; thus, when people find themselves without shelter, they are motivated to find some. A newly-transferred executive has a primary need to find a place to live but the kind of residence she rents or buys may be the result of secondary needs. She may seek a place in which she can entertain large groups of people (and fulfil social needs); she may want to live in an exclusive community in order to impress friends and family (and fulfil ego needs). So the house an individual purchases fulfils both a primary need for shelter and secondary needs for a large, prestigious living space.

People may be unaware of the primary and even the secondary needs underlying their actions, but are usually quite clear about what they *want*. Wants usually refer to the object or experience that will result in satisfying the need. They are the tangible expression of a method for reducing the tension felt when a need is unsatisfied. A small child may urgently want a particular toy in a Myer store, without having any idea of the needs that generated this desire.

Any unsatisfied need represents a *problem* to a consumer. Of course, there are usually many products or services that will solve a consumer's problem. For example, a hungry consumer in a shopping mall needs food, and food courts offer consumers a variety of ways of meeting their need for food. Consumer marketers have little influence on consumer needs, but they have a considerable influence in providing what consumers regard as the best solutions to their problems.

Goals

Goals are the sought-after results of motivated behaviour and are technically defined as internal representations of desired states. Internally represented desired states range from biological states for internal processes, such as body temperature, to complex cognitive depictions of desired outcomes, such as career success.[1] As Figure 3.1 indicates, all behaviour is goal-oriented. Our discussion of motivation in this chapter is in part concerned with **generic goals**—that is, the general classes or categories of goals that consumers select to fulfil their needs. Marketers are even more concerned with consumers' **product-specific goals**—that is, the specifically branded or labelled products they select to fulfil their needs. For example, the Thomas J. Lipton Company wants consumers to view iced tea as a good way to quench summer thirst (i.e. as a generic goal). However, it is more interested in having consumers view Lipton's iced tea as the best way to quench summer thirst (i.e. as a product-specific goal). As trade association advertising indicates, marketers recognise the importance of promoting both types of goals. The Australian Dairy Association uses the advertising slogan 'Milk—Legendary Stuff', while Pura, a member of the Association, advertises its own brand of milk. Marketers who support their industry trade associations recognise the importance of promoting both generic and product-specific goals.

FIGURE 3.2 Achieving physical appearance-related goals by use of a cream

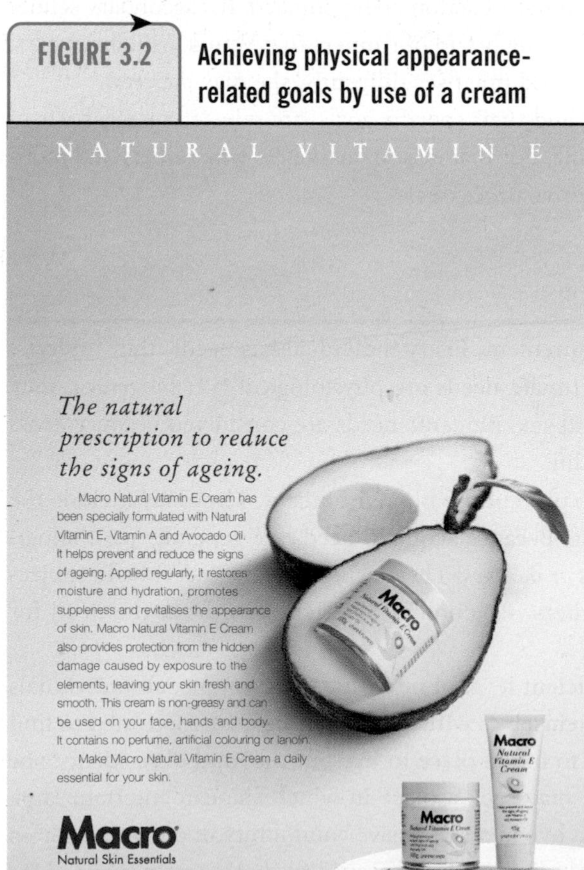

NATURAL VITAMIN E
The natural prescription to reduce the signs of ageing.
Macro Natural Vitamin E Cream has been specially formulated with Natural Vitamin E, Vitamin A and Avocado Oil. It helps prevent and reduce the signs of ageing. Applied regularly, it restores moisture and hydration, promotes suppleness and revitalises the appearance of skin. Macro Natural Vitamin E Cream also provides protection from the hidden damage caused by exposure to the elements, leaving your skin fresh and smooth. This cream is non-greasy and can be used on your face, hands and body. It contains no perfume, artificial colouring or lanolin.
Make Macro Natural Vitamin E Cream a daily essential for your skin.
Macro
Natural Skin Essentials
Macro
Macro
Natural Vitamin E Cream

Source: Courtesy of Wyeth Consumer Healthcare.

Means-end analysis is another way to view the needs-goals paradigm.[2] Individuals set desired *ends* (goals) on the basis of their personal values, and they select *means* (or behaviours) that they believe will help them achieve their desired ends. Take the personal value of *good health*. An individual may see certain behaviours (exercise, proper nutrition, cleanliness) as the means to achieving good health. A marketer of specific products within the 'means' product category (exercise equipment, low-fat foods, antibacterial soaps) would be wise to persuade people who are concerned with the goal of good health to use its product and, specifically, its brand to achieve that goal.[3] The marketer is trying to convert the generic goal into a product-specific goal. Figure 3.2 (page 72) depicts an ad that portrays the use of a Vitamin E cream as a means to achieve several physical appearance-related goals.

THE SELECTION OF GOALS

People have many needs, and for any given need there are many different and appropriate goals. The goals selected by individuals depend on their personal experiences, physical capacity, prevailing cultural norms and values, and the goal's accessibility in the physical and social environment. For example, a young woman may wish to get a deep and even tan and may envision spending time in the sun as a way to achieve her goal. However, if her dermatologist advises her to avoid direct exposure to the sun, she may settle for a self-tanning product instead. The goal object has to be both socially acceptable and physically accessible. If cosmetic companies did not offer effective alternatives to tanning in the sun, our young woman would have to either ignore the advice of her dermatologist or select a substitute goal, such as untanned (but undamaged) youthful-looking skin.

Our perception of ourselves also serves to influence the specific goals we select. The products we own, would like to own, or would not like to own are often perceived in terms of how closely they reflect (are congruent with) our **self-image**. A product that is perceived as matching our self-image has a greater probability of being selected than one that is not. Thus, a man who perceives himself as young and sophisticated may drive a Porsche; a woman who perceives herself as rich and conservative may drive a Mercedes. The types of houses we live in, the cars we drive, the clothes we wear, the very foods we eat—these specific goal objects are often chosen because they symbolically reflect our self-image while satisfying specific needs. (The relationship of self-concept to product choice is explained more fully in Chapters 4 and 5.)

INTERDEPENDENCE OF NEEDS AND GOALS

Needs and goals are interdependent; neither exists without the other. However, people are often not as aware of their needs as they are of their goals. For example, a teenager may not be consciously aware of her social needs but may join a photography club to meet new friends. A local politician may not consciously be aware of a power need but may regularly run for public office. A woman may not recognise her achievement needs but may strive to have the most successful real estate office in town.

Individuals are usually somewhat more aware of their physiological needs than they are of their psychological needs. Most people know when they are hungry or thirsty or cold, and they take appropriate steps to satisfy these needs. The same people may not consciously be aware of their needs for acceptance, self-esteem or status. They may, however, subconsciously engage in behaviour that satisfies these psychological (acquired) needs.

➤ Positive and negative motivation

Motivation can be positive or negative in direction. We may feel a driving force towards some object or condition, or a driving force away from some object or condition. For example, a person may be impelled towards a restaurant to fulfil a hunger need and away from motorcycle transportation to fulfil a safety need. Some psychologists refer to positive drives as needs, wants, or desires and to negative drives as fears or aversions. However, although positive and negative motivational forces seem to differ dramatically in terms of physical (and sometimes emotional) activity, they are basically similar in that both serve to initiate and sustain human behaviour. For this reason, researchers often refer to both kinds of drives or motives as needs, wants, and desires. Some theorists distinguish wants from needs by defining wants as product-specific needs. Others differentiate between desires, on the one hand, and needs and wants on the other. Thus, there is no uniformly accepted distinction among needs, wants, and desires.

Needs, wants, or desires may create goals that can be positive or negative. A positive goal is one towards which behaviour is directed, and thus is often referred to as an **approach object**. A negative goal is one from which behaviour is directed away, and thus is sometimes referred to as an **avoidance object**. Since both approach and avoidance goals can be considered objects of motivated behaviour, most researchers refer to both simply as goals. Consider this example. A middle-aged woman may have a positive goal of fitness (approach object) and so she joins a health club to work out regularly. Her husband may have a negative goal of getting fat (avoidance object), and so he joins a bushwalking club to maintain his shape. In the former case, the wife joins a health club to help her achieve her positive goal, health and fitness; in the latter case, her husband's action is designed to avoid a negative goal, a bloated figure. The product featured in Figure 3.3 (page 76) offers users a positive goal and approach object (**positive motivation**), whereas the ad in Figure 3.4 (page 76) depicts an avoidance object (**negative motivation**).

Sometimes people become motivationally aroused by a threat to, or elimination of, a behavioural freedom (e.g. the freedom to make a product choice without undue influence from a retailer). This motivational state is called *psychological reactance* and is usually manifested by a negative consumer response.[4] When the Coca-Cola company changed its traditional formula and introduced 'New Coke', many people reacted negatively to the fact that their 'freedom to choose' had been taken away, and refused to buy New Coke. Coca-Cola management responded to this unexpected psychological reaction by reintroducing the original formula as 'Classic Coke' and gradually developing additional versions of the product (for example, Vanilla Coke and Cherry Coke).

Rational versus emotional motives

Some consumer behaviourists distinguish between so-called **rational motives** and **emotional** (or non-rational) **motives**. They use the term 'rationality' in the traditional economic sense, which assumes that consumers behave rationally when they carefully consider all alternatives and choose those that give them the greatest utility. In a marketing context, rationality implies that consumers select goals based on totally objective criteria, such as size, weight, price, or kilometres per litre. Emotional motives imply the selection of goals according to personal or subjective criteria (e.g. pride, fear, or the desire for individuality, affection or status).

The assumption underlying this distinction is that subjective or emotional criteria do not maximise utility or satisfaction. However, it is reasonable to assume that consumers always attempt to select alternatives that, in their view, serve to maximise satisfaction. Obviously, the assessment of satisfaction is a very personal process, based on the individual's own need structure as well as on past behavioural and social (or learned) experiences. What may appear irrational to an outside observer may be perfectly rational in the context of the consumer's own psychological field. For example, a product purchased to enhance self-image (such as a fragrance) is a perfectly rational form of consumer behaviour. Emotional motives can also be used when rational motives do not result in a decision.[5]

The dynamic nature of motivation

Motivation is a highly dynamic construct that is constantly changing in reaction to life experiences. Our needs and goals are always growing and changing in response to our physical condition, environment, interactions with others, and experiences. As we attain our goals, we develop new ones. If we do not attain our goals, we continue to strive for old goals, or develop substitute goals. Some of the reasons why needs-driven human activity never ceases include the following:

- Existing needs are never completely satisfied; they continually induce activity designed to attain or maintain fulfilment.
- As needs become satisfied, new and higher-order needs emerge to be fulfilled.
- People who achieve their goals set new and higher goals for themselves. The Australian Defence Force's marketing campaigns promote the benefits of career options available to graduates by suggesting that as people successfully complete stages in their career, they will move on to higher goal achievement.

NEEDS ARE NEVER FULLY SATISFIED

Most human needs are never permanently or fully satisfied. For example, at regular intervals, people experience hunger needs that must be satisfied. Most people regularly seek companionship and approval from others to satisfy their social needs. Even more complex psychological needs are rarely satisfied. For example, a woman may partially or temporarily satisfy a power need by serving on the local council, but this small taste of power may not completely satisfy her need, and so she may run for successively higher public offices. In this instance, temporary goal achievement does not adequately satisfy the need for power, and the individual strives harder in an effort to satisfy the need more fully.

NEW NEEDS EMERGE AS OLD NEEDS ARE SATISFIED

Some motivational theorists believe that a hierarchy of needs exists and that new, higher-order needs emerge as lower-order needs are fulfilled.[6] For example, a man who has largely satisfied his basic physiological needs may turn his efforts to achieving acceptance among his new neighbours by joining their political club and supporting their candidates. Having achieved such acceptance, he may then seek recognition by giving lavish parties or making large charitable contributions.

Marketers must stay attuned to changing needs. Car manufacturers who stress the prestige value of their products may fail to recognise that many consumers now look elsewhere to satisfy needs for prestige—for example, through charitable gift-giving or taking expensive trips overseas. For this reason, manufacturers of prestige cars might do better if they stressed other needs satisfaction (e.g. family enjoyment or safety) as reasons for buying a new model. Marketers must be attuned to changing needs. For example, the Mercedes-Benz ad shown in Figure 3.5 (page 77) portrays three different car models corresponding to an individual's needs as he or she matures.

SUCCESS AND FAILURE INFLUENCE GOALS

Researchers have explored the nature of the goals that individuals set for themselves.[7] In general, they have concluded that those who successfully achieve their goals usually set new and higher goals for themselves; that is, they raise their **level of aspiration**. This is probably due to the fact that they become more confident of their ability to reach higher goals. Conversely, those who do not reach their goals sometimes lower their level of aspiration. Thus, goal selection is often a function of success or failure. For example, a Year 12 student who is not accepted into medicine may try instead to enter dentistry; failing that, she may train to be a pharmacist.

The nature and persistence of an individual's behaviour are often influenced by expectations of success or failure in reaching certain goals. Those expectations, in turn, are often based on past experience. A person who takes good photographs with an inexpensive camera may be motivated to buy a more sophisticated camera in the belief that it will enable him to take even better photographs. In this way, he may eventually upgrade his camera by several hundred dollars. On the other hand, a person who cannot take good pictures is just as

FIGURE 3.3 Appealing to consumers using positive motivation

Source: Reproduced with the permission of Johnson & Johnson Pacific.

FIGURE 3.4 Appealing to consumers using negative motivation

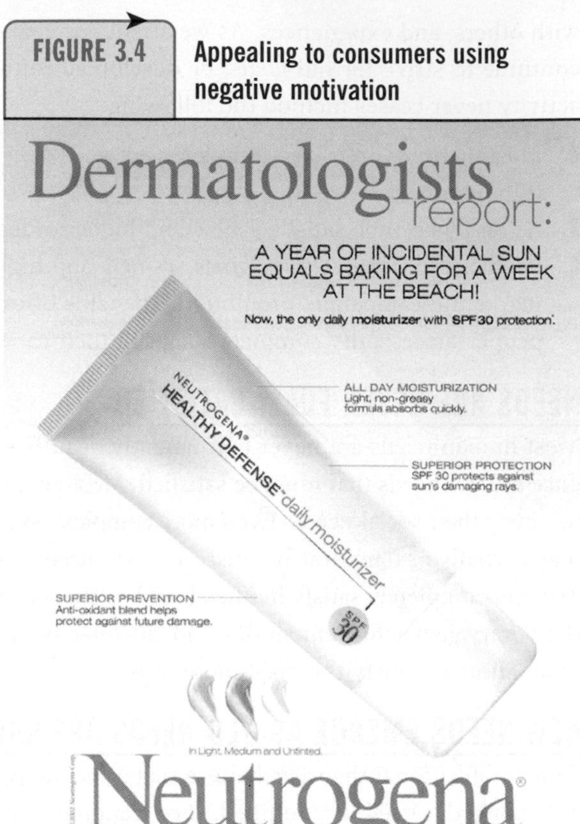

Source: Reproduced with the permission of Johnson & Johnson Pacific.

likely to keep the same camera and may even lose all interest in photography. How the reaction to success or failure to achieve goals in the past will affect goal setting depends on the consumer's personality, need for achievement (discussed later in this chapter) and monetary incentives.[8]

These effects of success and failure on goal selection have strategy implications for the marketer. Goals should be reasonably attainable. Advertisements should not promise more than the product will deliver. Even a good product will not be repurchased if it fails to live up to expectations. A disappointed consumer is likely to regard such a product with even less satisfaction than its objective performance warrants. Advertisers who create unrealistic expectations for their products are likely to cause dissatisfaction among consumers. Similarly, a consumer is likely to regard a mediocre product with greater satisfaction than it warrants if its performance exceeds her expectations.

SUBSTITUTE GOALS

When, for one reason or another, we cannot attain a particular goal or type of goal that we anticipate will satisfy certain needs, our behaviour may be directed to a **substitute goal**. Although the substitute goal may not be as satisfactory as the primary goal, it may be sufficient to dispel uncomfortable tension. Continued deprivation of a primary goal may result in the substitute goal assuming primary-goal status. A man who has stopped drinking whole milk because he is dieting may actually begin to prefer skimmed milk. A woman who cannot afford a Mercedes may convince herself that a Ford Fairmont has an image she clearly prefers. Of course, in this instance, the substitute goal may be a defensive reaction to frustration.

Frustration

Failure to achieve a goal often results in feelings of **frustration**. At one time or another, everyone has experienced the frustration that comes from the inability to attain a goal. The barrier that prevents attainment of a goal may be personal to the individual (i.e. a physical or financial limitation; or a psychological barrier such as conflicting goals) or it can be an obstacle in the physical or social environment. Regardless of the cause, individuals react differently to frustrating situations. Some people are adaptive and manage to cope by finding their way round the obstacle or, if that fails, by selecting a substitute goal. Others are less adaptive and may regard their inability to achieve a goal as a personal failure and experience feelings of anxiety. Such people are likely to adopt a defence mechanism to protect their egos from feelings of inadequacy.

FIGURE 3.5 Product alternatives for changing consumer needs

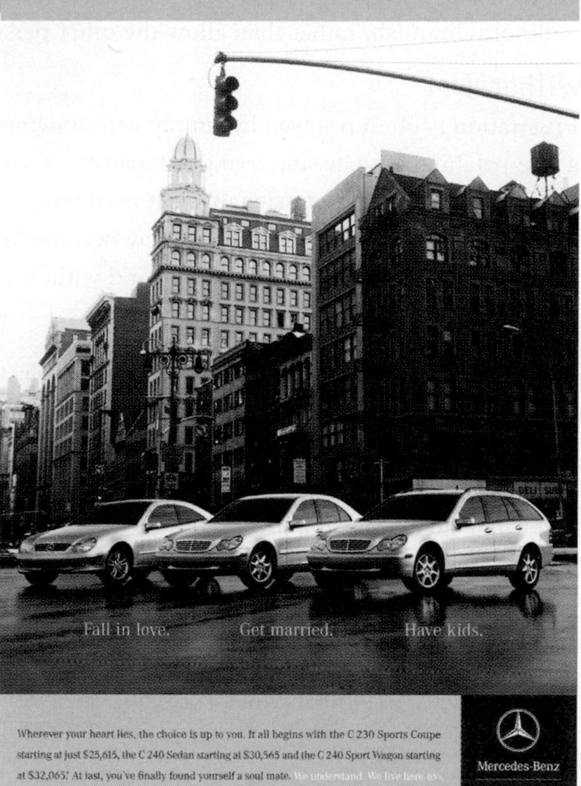

Source: Courtesy of DaimlerChrysler Australia Pacific.

DEFENCE MECHANISMS

People who cannot cope with frustration often mentally redefine the frustrating situation in order to protect their self-image and defend their self-esteem. For example, a young woman may yearn for an imported leather coat she cannot afford. The coping individual may select a less expensive cloth coat with a leather collar. The person who cannot cope may react with anger towards her boss for not paying her enough money to buy leather, or she may decide that wearing the skin of animals is a barbaric custom in which she will not participate. These two possibilities are examples, respectively, of aggression and **rationalisation**, **defence mechanisms** which people sometimes adopt to protect their egos from feelings of failure when they do not attain their goals. Other defence mechanisms include regression, withdrawal, projection, autism, escapism, identification and repression.

Aggression

Individuals who experience frustration may resort to aggressive behaviour in attempting to protect their self-esteem. This was aptly illustrated by two British yachtsmen who, disappointed at their poor showing in a sailing competition, burned their boat and swam ashore. Frustrated consumers have boycotted manufacturers in an effort to improve product quality, and boycotted retailers in an attempt to have prices lowered.

Rationalisation

Sometimes individuals redefine a frustrating situation by inventing plausible reasons for not being able to attain their goals. Or they may decide that the goal really wasn't worth pursuing. Rationalisations are not deliberate lies, since the individual is not fully aware of the cognitive distortion that arises as a result of the frustrating situation. Thus, a consumer who cannot quit smoking may convince herself she is smoking less if she switches to low-tar cigarettes.

Regression

Sometimes people react to frustrating situations with childish or immature behaviour. A shopper attending a bargain sale, for example, may fight over merchandise and resort to tearing a garment that another shopper will not relinquish, rather than allow the other person to have it.

Withdrawal

Frustration is often resolved by simply withdrawing from the situation. A consumer who has difficulty using a tyre-patching kit may stop trying to repair tyres. He may rationalise his withdrawal by deciding that it is safer to buy new tyres or professionally refit used tyres than to repair them himself. Similarly, a consumer considering the adoption of a new product may become frustrated in the purchase process by distribution problems or lack of technological compatability and withdraw from the market.[9]

Projection

People may redefine a frustrating situation by projecting blame for their own failures and inabilities onto other objects or persons. Thus, the golfer who misses a stroke may blame his caddy, the ball or the golf club; the driver who has a car accident may blame the other driver, the road conditions or the car itself. This external attribution often leads the consumer to blame the marketer for a faulty product when it is the ability of the consumer that is causing the frustration.

Autism

Autism, or autistic thinking, refers to thinking that is almost completely dominated by needs and emotions, with little effort made to relate to reality. Such daydreaming, or fantasising, enables the individual to attain imaginary gratification of unfulfilled needs. A person who is completely monogamous may daydream about having affairs.

Escapism

Escapism occurs when people seek to live out a fantasy to help them get away from reality and enjoy the luxury of indulging in a different lifestyle. See the Nissan ad in Figure 3.6 (page 80).

Identification

Sometimes people resolve their feelings of frustration by subconsciously identifying with other people or situations they consider relevant. Marketers have long recognised the importance of this defence mechanism and often use it as the basis for advertising appeals. That is why 'slice-of-life' commercials and advertisements are so popular. Such advertisements usually portray a stereotypical situation in which an individual experiences frustration and then overcomes the problem that caused the frustration by using the advertised product. If viewers can identify with the frustrating situation, they may very likely adopt the proposed solution and buy the product advertised.

For example, a man who has difficulty attracting a woman he likes may decide to use the same mouthwash or shampoo or deodorant that 'worked' for the man in the commercial. Interestingly enough, use of the product may increase his self-confidence sufficiently to enable him to achieve his goal.

Repression

Another way that individuals avoid the tension arising from frustration is by repressing the unsatisfied need. Thus, individuals may force the need out of their conscious awareness. Sometimes repressed needs manifest themselves indirectly. A couple who cannot have children may surround themselves with plants or pets. The wife may become a teacher or work in a library; the husband may do volunteer work in a boys' club. The manifestation of repressed needs in a socially acceptable form is called **sublimation**, another type of defence mechanism.

This listing of defence mechanisms is far from exhaustive. People have virtually limitless ways of redefining frustrating situations in order to protect their self-esteem from the anxieties that result from experiencing failure. Based on their early experiences, individuals tend to develop their own characteristic ways of handling frustration. Marketers often consider this fact in their selection of advertising appeals and construct advertisements that portray a person resolving a particular frustration through the use of the advertised product. For example, a flour manufacturer may convince consumers that baking failures were caused by the ingredients they used, rather than the ineptness of their efforts. (See also attribution theory in Chapter 7.)

MULTIPLICITY OF NEEDS

A consumer's behaviour often fulfils more than one need. In fact, it is more likely that specific goals are selected because they fulfil several needs. We buy clothing for protection and for a certain degree of modesty. In addition, our clothing fulfils a wide range of personal and social needs, such as acceptance or ego needs. Usually, however, there is one overriding (i.e. prepotent) need that initiates behaviour. For example, a man may stop smoking because he wants to rid himself of a chronic cough; he may also be concerned about cancer. In addition, his girlfriend may be 'turned off' by the smell of cigarette smoke. If the cumulative amount of tension produced by these three reasons is sufficiently strong, he will stop smoking. However, just one of the reasons (e.g. his girlfriend's influence) may serve as the triggering mechanism. That one would be called the **prepotent need**.

A consumer may also be faced with a situation in which more than one need is activated, but where the needs actually conflict. Jack, a university student, is athletic and concerned about fitness and health. He uses his success in athletics to fulfil his need for achievement. He also needs the social acceptance of his friends at university. Will Jack drink and smoke? It depends on which need is activated—the need for social acceptance or the need for success/achievement. The situation, the events prior to the moment, and the degree to which each of these needs has been satisfied recently will all play a part in determining which need will dominate.

NEEDS AND GOALS VARY AMONG INDIVIDUALS

One cannot accurately infer motives from behaviour. People with different needs may seek fulfilment through selection of the same goals, while people with the same needs may seek fulfilment through different goals. Consider the following examples. Five people who are active in a consumer advocacy organisation may each belong for a different reason. The first may be genuinely concerned with protecting consumer interests; the second may be concerned about an increase in counterfeit merchandise; the third may seek social contacts from organisational meetings; the fourth may enjoy the power of directing a large group; and the fifth may enjoy the status provided by membership in a powerful organisation.

Similarly, five people may be driven by the same need (e.g. an ego need) to seek fulfilment in different ways. The first may seek advancement and recognition through a professional career; the second may become active in an organisation such as the Australian Institute of Management (AIM); the third may join a health club; the fourth may take professional dance lessons; and the fifth may seek attention at school council meetings.

Arousal of motives

Most of our specific needs are dormant much of the time. The arousal of any particular set of needs at a specific point in time may be caused by internal stimuli found in our physiological condition, or in our emotional or cognitive processes, or by external stimuli in the environment. For the most part, purchases will not be made unless we experience a need and are activated to satisfy it. Unsatisfied needs create a state of tension.

FIGURE 3.6 **An ad offering a way to aspire to escape**

FROM CITY TO SURF AT THE FLICK OF A SWITCH.
Nissan Pathfinder is equipped with one of the most advanced four-wheel drive systems in the world. ALL MODE 4x4.
It means you can select the optimum driving mode at the flick of a switch. No stopping. No messing about.
On-road, you may select 2WD, off-road 4WD high and, should you find yourself running into something more challenging, you can choose 4WD low.
Or choose auto and the car automatically selects between 2WD and 4WD high to best suit conditions.
But it's not just about high technology.
The powerful 3.3 litre V6 boasts a whole host of luxury features. The ST comes with air conditioning, alloy wheels, ABS brakes, dual airbags, CD player, power windows, electric mirrors and cruise control. The top of the line Ti has leather seat trim, an in-dash 6-stacker CD, climate control air conditioning, electric sunroof, roof bars and fog lamps.
So, whether you're racing around in the city, or just fancy a run to the coast, you can be shore, sorry, sure that you're in a first class cabin.
www.nissan.com.au
PATHFINDER

SHIFT_the future
NISSAN

Source: **Reproduced with kind permission of Nissan Motor Co. (Australia) Pty Ltd.**

PHYSIOLOGICAL AROUSAL

Bodily needs at any specific moment are rooted in our physiological condition at that moment. A drop in blood sugar level, or stomach contractions, will trigger awareness of a hunger need. A decrease in body temperature will induce shivering, which makes us aware of the need for warmth. An increase in body temperature will induce sweating which makes us aware of a need for cooling.[10] Most of these physiological cues are involuntary, but they arouse related needs that cause uncomfortable tensions until they are satisfied. For example, a shivering man may turn up the heat in his home to relieve his discomfort; he may also make a mental note to buy flannel pyjamas. Research suggests that television programs can generate physiological arousal, which affects the impact of ensuing commercials.[11]

EMOTIONAL AROUSAL

Thinking or daydreaming sometimes results in the arousal or stimulation of latent needs. People who are bored or frustrated in attempts to achieve their goals often engage in daydreaming (autistic thinking), in which they imagine themselves in all sorts of desirable situations. These thoughts tend to arouse dormant needs, which may produce uncomfortable tensions that 'push' them into goal-oriented behaviour. A young woman who dreams of becoming a business tycoon may enrol in business school. A young man who wants to play professional AFL football may identify with a league player and use the products he endorses commercially.

COGNITIVE AROUSAL

Sometimes random thoughts or a personal achievement can lead to a cognitive awareness of needs. An advertisement that provokes memories of home might trigger instant recognition of the need to speak with someone special. This is the basis for many telephone company campaigns that stress their low rates for international and interstate long-distance calls.

ENVIRONMENTAL AROUSAL

The set of needs activated at a particular time are often determined by specific cues in the environment. Without these cues, the needs would remain dormant. For example, the evening news, the sight or smell of freshly baked bread, fast-food TV commercials, the children's return from school—all these may arouse the 'need' for food. In such cases, modification of the environment may be necessary in order to reduce the arousal of hunger.

A most potent form of situational cue is the goal object itself. A couple may experience an overwhelming need for a dishwasher when they see their neighbour's new appliance; a person may suddenly experience a need for a new car when passing a dealer's display window. Sometimes an advertisement or other environmental cue produces a psychological imbalance in the viewer's mind. For example, a couple who are concerned about the problem of rubbish and landfill areas may see an advertisement for a mulcher and compost unit. The ad may make them so unhappy with the current disposal of waste at their own home, and at their parents' homes, that they experience severe tension until they buy a garbage-reduction unit for themselves and one each for both sets of parents. In a research study investigating the influence of cues in a grocery environment on unplanned purchasing, exposure to in-store cues triggered need recognition.[12]

When people live in a complex and highly varied environment, they experience many opportunities for need arousal. Conversely, when their environment is poor or deprived, fewer needs are activated. This explains why television has had such a mixed effect on the lives of the unemployed and pensioners. It exposes them to lifestyles and expensive products they would not otherwise see, and awakens wants and desires they have little opportunity or even hope of attaining. Thus, while it enriches their lives, television may also serve to frustrate people and sometimes results in the adoption of antisocial defence mechanisms such as aggression.

There are two opposing philosophies concerned with the arousal of human motives. The *behaviourist* school considers motivation to be a mechanical process; behaviour is seen as the response to a stimulus, and elements of conscious thought are ignored. An extreme example of this **stimulus-response theory** of motivation is the impulse buyer, who reacts mainly to external stimuli in the buying situation. The cognitive control of such consumers is limited; they do not act, but *react* to stimuli in the marketplace.[13] The *cognitive* school believes that all behaviour is directed at goal achievement. Needs and past experiences are reasoned, categorised, and transformed into attitudes and beliefs that act as predispositions to behaviour. These predispositions are aimed at helping the individual satisfy needs, and they determine the direction that people take to achieve this satisfaction.

Types and systems of needs

For many years, psychologists and others interested in human behaviour have attempted to develop exhaustive lists of human needs and motives. Most lists of human needs tend to be diverse in content as well as in length. Although there is little disagreement about specific physiological needs, there is considerable disagreement about specific psychological (i.e. psychogenic) needs.

In 1938, the psychologist Henry Murray prepared a detailed list of 28 psychogenic needs which have served as the basic constructs for a number of widely used personality tests (e.g. the Edwards Personal Preference Schedule). Murray believed that everyone has the same basic set of needs, but that individuals differ in their priority ranking of these needs. Murray's basic needs include many motives that are assumed to play an important role in consumer behaviour, such as acquisition, achievement, recognition and exhibition (see Table 3.1).

Lists of human motives are often too long to be of practical use to marketers. The most useful kind of list is a limited one in which needs are sufficiently generic in title to subsume more detailed human needs. While some psychologists have suggested that people have different need priorities based on their personalities, their

TABLE 3.1 **Murray's list of psychogenic needs**

Needs associated with inanimate objects
Acquisition
Conservancy
Order
Retention
Construction
Needs that reflect ambition, power, accomplishment and prestige
Superiority
Achievement
Recognition
Exhibition
Inviolacy (inviolate attitude)
Infavoidance (to avoid shame, failure, humiliation, ridicule)
Defendance (defensive attitude)
Counteraction (counteractive attitude)
Needs concerned with human power
Dominance
Deference
Similance (suggestible attitude)
Autonomy
Contrarience (to act differently from others)
Sado-masochistic needs
Aggression
Abasement
Needs concerned with affection between people
Affiliation
Rejection
Nurturance (to nourish, aid or protect the helpless)
Succorance (to seek aid, protection or sympathy)
Play
Needs concerned with social intercourse (the needs to ask and tell)
Cognizance (inquiring attitude)
Exposition (expositive attitude)

Source: **Adapted from Henry A. Murray, 'Types of human needs', in David C. McClelland, *Studies in Motivation* (New York: Appleton-Century-Crofts, 1995), pp. 63–66.**

experiences, their environments, and so forth, others believe that most human beings experience the same basic needs, to which they assign a similar priority ranking.

HIERARCHY OF NEEDS

One of the most well-known theories of human motivation was developed by Abraham Maslow. His theory can be applied to interpreting how consumer goods and services can be perceived as satisfying different levels of needs of consumers.

FIGURE 3.7 Maslow's hierarchy of needs

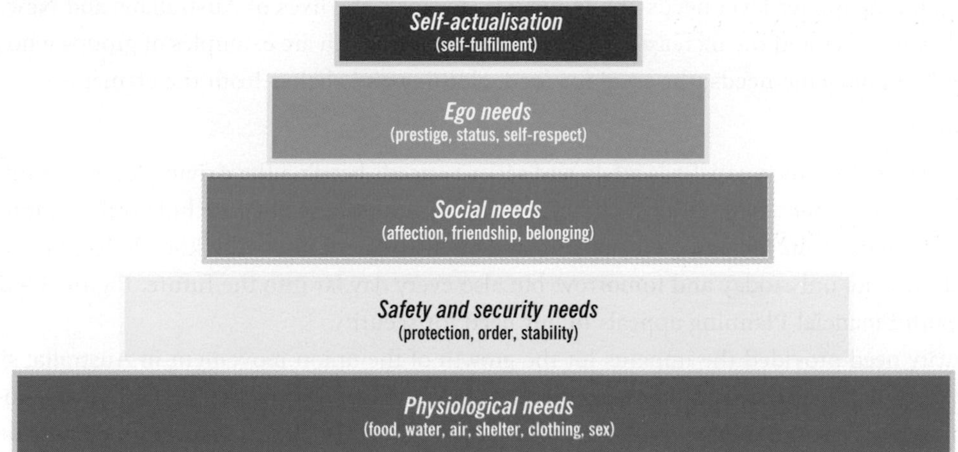

Maslow, a clinical psychologist, formulated a widely accepted theory of human motivation based on the notion of a universal **hierarchy of human needs**.[14] Maslow's theory identifies five basic levels of human needs, which rank in order of importance from low-level (biogenic) needs to higher-level (psychogenic) needs. The theory suggests that we seek to satisfy lower-level needs first, and must achieve this satisfaction before higher-level needs emerge. The lowest level of chronically unsatisfied need that we experience serves to motivate our behaviour. When that need is reasonably well satisfied, a new (and higher-level) need emerges that we are motivated to fulfil. When this need is satisfied, a new (and still higher-level) need emerges, and so on. Of course, if a lower-level need experiences some renewed deprivation, it may temporarily become dominant again. For example, a young man concerned with social needs such as affection and friendship may temporarily become concerned with safety and security needs when he loses his job.

Figure 3.7 presents Maslow's hierarchy of needs in diagrammatic form. For clarity, each level is depicted as mutually exclusive. According to the theory, however, there is some overlap between each level, as no need is ever completely satisfied. For this reason, though all levels of need below the dominant level continue to motivate behaviour to some extent, the prime motivator—the major driving force within the individual—is the lowest level of need that remains largely unsatisfied.

FIGURE 3.8 Appealing to a physiological need

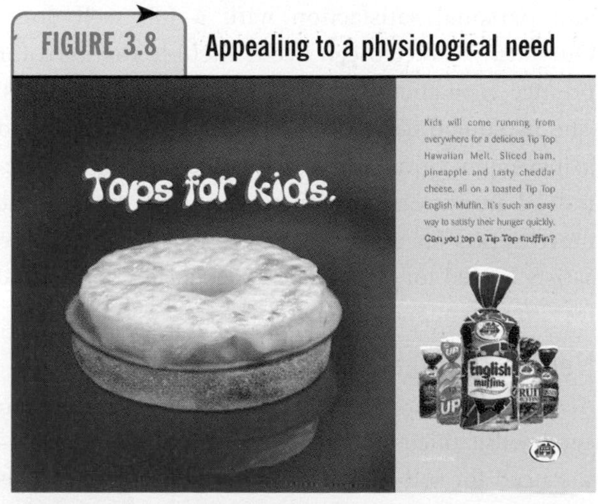

Source: Courtesy of Tip Top Bakeries.

Physiological needs

In the hierarchy of needs theory, the first and most basic level of needs is physiological. These needs, which are required to sustain biological life, include food, water, air, shelter, clothing, sex—all the biogenic needs, in fact, that were listed earlier as primary needs. Figure 3.8 shows a Tip Top ad which appeals to one of the **physiological needs** through the provision of food to satisfy the consumer's hunger.

According to Maslow, physiological needs are dominant when they are chronically unsatisfied: *For the man who is extremely and dangerously hungry, no other interest exists but food. He dreams food, he remembers food, he thinks about food, he emotes only about food, he perceives only food and he wants only food.*[15] For many people in this country, the biogenic needs are generally satisfied and the higher-level needs are dominant. However, the lives of Australians and New Zealanders who are on low incomes and the increased numbers of homeless youth are examples of groups who are focused almost entirely on biogenic needs: the need for food, clothing and shelter from the elements.

Safety needs

After the first level of needs is satisfied, safety and security needs become the driving force behind our behaviour. These needs are concerned with much more than physical safety. They include order, stability, routine, familiarity, control over our life and environment, and a sense of certainty—the knowledge, for example, that we will eat dinner not only today and tomorrow, but also every day far into the future. Figure 3.9 depicts how Commonwealth Financial Planning appeals to our need for security.

The security need provided the impetus for the growth of the union movement in Australia, since unions provide members with the security of knowing that their employment does not depend on the day-to-day whims of their employers. The social welfare programs enacted by Australia (e.g. social security, unemployment benefits, Medicare) have traditionally provided some degree of security to society. Savings accounts, insurance policies, education and vocational training are means by which we personally satisfy the need for security.

Social needs

The third level of Maslow's hierarchy includes such needs as love, affection, belonging and acceptance. People seek warm and satisfying human relationships with other people and are motivated by love for their families and friends, and even pets. Because of the importance of social motives in our society, advertisers often emphasise this appeal in their advertisements.

Ego needs

When our social needs are more or less satisfied, the fourth level of Maslow's hierarchy becomes operative. This level is concerned with ego needs. These needs can take either an inward or an outward orientation, or both. Inwardly directed ego needs reflect our need for self-acceptance, self-esteem, success, independence, and personal satisfaction with a job well done. Outwardly directed ego needs include the need for prestige, reputation, status and recognition from others. The presumed desire to 'show off' one's success and achievement through material possessions is a reflection of an outwardly-oriented ego need. One of the motivations for attending the performing arts is to satisfy a need for status, more specifically the need to feel important and influential.[16]

Need for self-actualisation

According to Maslow, most people do not satisfy their ego needs sufficiently ever to move to the fifth level—the need for self-actualisation (self-fulfilment). This need refers to our desire to reach our full potential—

FIGURE 3.9 Appealing to consumers' security needs

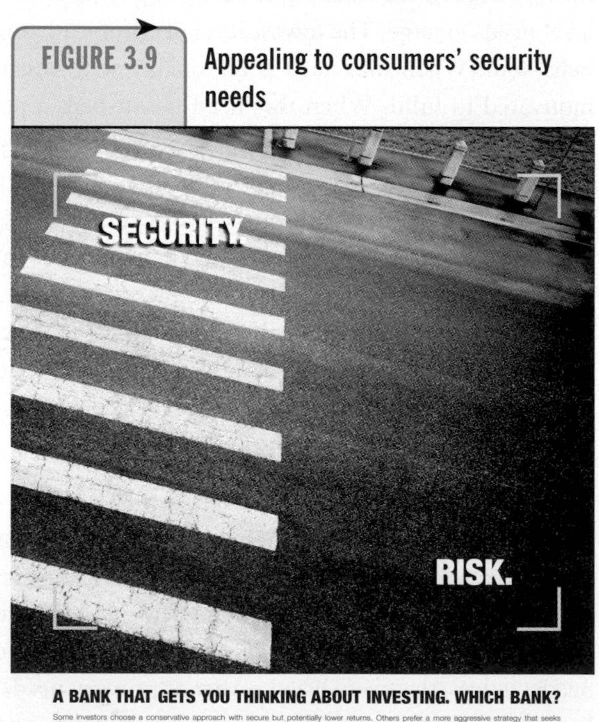

Source: Image supplied courtesy of Commonwealth Bank of Australia.

to become everything we are capable of becoming. In Maslow's words, 'What a man can be, he must be'.[17] This need is expressed in different ways by different people. A young man may desire to be the best athlete he possibly can and work single-mindedly for years to become the best in his sport. An artist may need to express herself on canvas; a business executive may try to build an empire. Maslow noted that the self-actualisation need is not necessarily a creative urge, but in people with some capacity for creativity it is likely to take that form. Advertisements for art lessons, banking services, and even for new graduate recruitment often try to appeal to the self-actualisation need. Various workplace conditions appeal to a number of elements in Maslow's hierarchy. For instance, challenging work and a sense of accomplishment appeal to esteem and self-actualisation needs, respectively.[18] Some of our largest companies use motivation-based promotion to encourage their highly paid employees to look beyond their pay cheques to find gratification and self-fulfilment in the workplace—to view their jobs as the way to become 'all they can be.'

In summary, the hierarchy of needs theory postulates a five-level hierarchy of prepotent human needs. Higher-order needs become the driving force behind human behaviour as lower-level needs are satisfied. The theory says, in effect, that *dis*satisfaction—not satisfaction—motivates behaviour.

AN EVALUATION OF THE NEEDS HIERARCHY

The needs hierarchy has received wide acceptance in many social disciplines because it appears to reflect the assumed or inferred motivations of many people in our society. The five levels of need postulated by the hierarchy are sufficiently generic to encompass most lists of individual needs. Some critics, however, maintain that Maslow's concepts are too general. To say that hunger and the desire for self-esteem are similar, in that both are needs, is to obscure the urgent, involuntary nature of the former and the largely conscious, voluntary nature of the latter. The main problem with the theory is that it cannot be tested empirically; there is no way of measuring precisely how satisfied one need is before the next higher need becomes operative. The needs hierarchy is reasonably universal in that different societies and cultures, including Australia, New Zealand and Asia, will have different levels of development when matched according to Maslow's hierarchical model. Factors such as the socioeconomic situation will influence the emphasis that Australian and New Zealand consumers place on physiological-need fulfilment versus ego-need fulfilment. While Maslow's hierarchy is popular, it has been criticised, among other things, for not taking account of heroic and altruistic behaviour, as other theories can do. Another criticism of the hierarchy is its limited applicability to predicting specific behaviours.[19] Consumers are continually being influenced by motives that they have 'passed' in the hierarchy. In Australia and New Zealand, where most people have satisfied their physiological and safety needs, security needs are still used effectively to motivate our decisions (refer to the Commonwealth Financial Planning ad in Figure 3.9). Although the model allows for the influence of motives that may not be the dominant ones, the fluctuation in position in the hierarchy makes it difficult to predict a consumer's dominant motivation at any given time.

Despite these criticisms, Maslow's hierarchy can be a useful tool for understanding consumer motivations and is readily adaptable to marketing strategy, primarily because consumer goods often serve to satisfy each of the need levels. For example, we buy houses, food and clothing to satisfy physiological needs; we buy insurance and radial tyres and vocational training to satisfy safety and security needs. Almost all personal care products (cosmetics, toothpaste, shaving cream) are bought to satisfy social needs. Luxury products such as jewels or big cars are often bought to fulfil ego needs, and university training and banking services are sold as ways to achieve self-fulfilment. Maslow's needs hierarchy has been called an 'emotional trigger' that enables marketers to communicate with their target audiences on a personal, meaningful level that goes beyond product benefits.[20]

The hierarchy offers a useful, comprehensive framework for marketers trying to develop appropriate advertising appeals for their products. It is adaptable in two ways: first, it enables marketers to focus their advertising appeals on a need level that is likely to be shared by a large segment of the prospective audience; second, it facilitates product positioning.

Segmentation applications

The needs hierarchy is often used as the basis for market segmentation, as specific advertising appeals are directed to individuals on one or more need levels. For example, soft drink ads directed to teenagers often stress a social appeal by showing a group of young people sharing good times as well as the advertised product.

Research in the United States, sponsored by the National Spa and Pool Institute, found that women and men had different motivations concerning these products. Women saw the purchase of a pool as an enhancement of family life (the social need), but were concerned about the safety of their small children (the safety need). Thus, pool advertisements tended to stress the supervision of children, health and family enjoyment, targeted primarily to women. The study found that men were more interested in spas than pools, so spa commercials began to stress a more intimate message: relaxation, privacy, time together.[21] In Australia research has not perhaps focused on these types of product usage situations by comparing male and female responses, but there are many examples of messages promoting safety needs, from toy products to cars. Social needs are exemplified by families enjoying holidays together. Hence, market segmentation can be derived from the needs hierarchy.

Positioning applications

Another way to utilise the hierarchy is for positioning products—that is, deciding how the product should be perceived by prospective consumers (see Chapter 5). The key to positioning is to find a niche (an unsatisfied need) that is not occupied by a competing product or brand. This application of the needs hierarchy relies on the notion that no need is ever fully satisfied, that it will continue to be motivating to some degree. Safety, for example, is a continuing need. Figure 3.10 depicts an ad for the Mercedes S-Class, with the emphasis on safety in the slogan 'S-Class with Pre-Safe. The first car with protective reflexes'.

Most manufacturers of luxury cars use status appeals ('Impress your friends'), self-actualising appeals ('You deserve the very best') or even social appeals ('The whole family can ride in luxurious comfort'). To find a unique position among its luxury competitors, some car companies have used a safety appeal in advertisements directed at high-income executives ('When your wife is driving the two children home on a dark and stormy night, you can relax if she's driving the Mercedes').

Versatility of the needs hierarchy

One way to illustrate the usefulness of the needs hierarchy in designing promotional programs is to show how workable appeals for a single product can be developed from each level. Consider, for example, the potential promotional appeals for home exercise equipment. An appeal to physiological needs would show how the home exercise unit can improve body tone and health; a safety appeal would demonstrate how safe the equipment is for home (and solo) use. A social appeal might show how much fun it can be to exercise with a friend, or even how having a streamlined body can encourage social encounters. Self-esteem is easily demonstrated through a narcissistic appeal such as 'Be proud of your body'. Finally, an appeal to self-actualisation may suggest to career couples that they deserve the convenience and luxury of home exercise after a long and challenging work day.

A TRIO OF NEEDS

Some psychologists believe in the existence of a trio of basic needs: the needs for power, affiliation and achievement. Each can be subsumed within Maslow's needs hierarchy but, considered individually, they have a unique relevance to consumer motivation.

FIGURE 3.10 **Ad emphasising safety needs**

S-Class with Pre-Safe. The first car with protective reflexes.

Source: Courtesy of DaimlerChrysler Australia Pacific.

The **power need** relates to our desire to control our environment. It includes the need to control other people and various objects. This need appears to be closely related to the ego need, in that many individuals experience increased self-enhancement when they exercise power over objects or people. A number of products, such as cars, lend themselves to promises of power or superiority for users. The need to control one's environment can be subsumed under Maslow's safety need.

Affiliation is a well-known and well-researched social motive that has far-reaching influence on consumer behaviour. The **affiliation need** suggests that behaviour is highly influenced by the desire for friendship, acceptance and belonging. People with high affiliation needs tend to have a strong social dependence on others. They often select goods they feel will meet with the approval of friends. People who go to craft fairs or garage sales, teenagers who hang out at shopping malls, car buffs who congregate at automobile shows, often do so more for the satisfaction of being with others than to make a purchase. This need is very similar to Maslow's social need.

A considerable number of research studies have focused on the **achievement need**.[22] Individuals with a strong need for achievement often regard personal accomplishment as an end in itself. The achievement need is closely related to both the ego needs and the self-actualisation needs. People with a high need for achievement have certain traits that make them open to relevant appeals. They are more self-confident, and enjoy taking calculated risks. They research their environment actively, and are very interested in feedback. Their interest in monetary rewards or profits is due mainly to the feedback that money provides as to how they are doing. People with high achievement needs like situations in which they can take personal responsibility for finding solutions.[23] They prefer activities that allow self-evaluation[24] and respond positively to feedback concerning their own competence.[25] High-achievement is a useful promotional strategy for many products and services targeted to educated and affluent consumers.

One study showed that the dominant needs may be related to an individual's career progress. The study found that achievement was a dominant need for MBA students and Air Force officers. The need for power was dominant for partners in an accounting firm, and the need for affiliation was dominant among high school students, first-year cadets at the Air Force Academy and undergraduate accounting students. Such findings imply that different promotional approaches should be targeted at consumers according to their occupational progress.[26]

In summary, individuals with specific psychological needs tend to be receptive to advertising appeals directed at those needs. They also tend to be receptive to certain kinds of products. Thus, awareness of such needs provides marketers with additional bases on which to segment their markets.

The measurement of motives

How are motives identified? How are they measured? How do researchers know which motives are responsible for certain kinds of behaviour? These are difficult questions to answer because motives are hypothetical **constructs**—that is, they cannot be seen or touched, handled, smelled or otherwise tangibly observed. For this reason, no one measurement method can be considered a reliable index. Instead, researchers usually rely on a combination of observation (and inference), self-reports and projective techniques, used in tandem to try to establish the presence and/or the strength of various motives.

The identification and measurement of human motives is an inexact process. Some psychologists are concerned that most measurement techniques do not meet the crucial test criteria of **validity** and **reliability**. (Validity ensures that the test measures what it purports to measure; reliability refers to the consistency with which the test measures what it does measure.)

The findings of projective research methods are highly dependent on the analyst; they focus not on the data themselves, but on what the analyst thinks they imply. Therefore, many consumer behaviourists are reluctant to rely on projective techniques alone. However, by using a combination of assessments (i.e. triangulation) based on behavioural data (observation), subjective data (self-reports) and projective techniques, many consumer researchers feel more confident of achieving valid insights into consumer motivations than they would by using any one technique alone. Though some marketers are concerned that such research does not produce hard numbers that objectively 'prove' a point under investigation, others are convinced that qualitative studies can be just as revealing as quantitative studies. However, there is a clear need for improved methodological procedures for measuring human motives.

Motivational research

The term **motivational research**, which should logically include all types of research into human motives, is generally used to refer to qualitative research designed to uncover the consumer's subconscious or hidden motivations. Operating on the premise that consumers are not always aware of the reasons for their actions, motivational research attempts to discover underlying feelings, attitudes and emotions concerning product, service or brand use.

DEVELOPMENT OF MOTIVATIONAL RESEARCH

Sigmund Freud's **psychoanalytic theory of personality** (discussed in greater detail in Chapter 4) provided the basis for the development of motivational research. This theory was built on the premise that unconscious needs or drives—especially biological and sexual drives—are at the heart of human motivation and personality. Freud constructed his theory from patients' recollections of early childhood experiences, analysis of their dreams, and the specific nature of their mental and physical adjustment problems.

In the 1950s, Dr Ernest Dichter, formerly a psychoanalyst in Vienna, adapted Freud's psychoanalytical techniques to the study of consumer buying habits. Marketing research up to this time had focused on what consumers did (i.e. quantitative, descriptive studies) rather than on why they did it. Marketers were quickly fascinated by the glib, entertaining and usually surprising explanations offered for consumer behaviour, especially since many of these explanations had their origins in sex. For example, marketers were told that cigarettes and Lifesaver lollies were bought because of their sexual symbolism, that men regarded cars as surrogate mistresses, and that women baked cakes to fulfil their reproductive yearnings (of course this sex-stereotyping would be questioned by modern marketing).[27] Over time, advertising agencies have recruited psychologists to conduct motivational research studies and consumer research groups. Box 3.1 presents four product profiles developed by Dichter and their applications to contemporary products.

By the early 1960s, marketers were realising that motivational research had some drawbacks. Because of the intensive nature of qualitative research, samples were necessarily small; thus, there was concern about generalising findings to the total market. Also, marketers soon realised that the analysis of projective tests and depth interviews was highly subjective. The same data given to three different analysts could produce three different reports, each offering its own explanation of the consumer behaviour examined. Critics noted that many of the projective tests that were used had originally been developed for clinical purposes, rather than for studies of marketing or consumer behaviour. (One of the basic criteria for test development is that tests be developed and validated for the specific purpose and the specific audience from which information is desired.) Other consumer theorists had noted additional inconsistencies in applying Freudian theory to the study of consumer behaviour: first, psychoanalytic theory was structured specifically for use with disturbed

BOX 3.1 Dichter's research: Selected product personality profiles and current applications

Baking Dichter described *baking* as an expression of femininity and motherhood, evoking nostalgic memories of delicious odours pervading the house when the mother was baking. He said that when baking a cake, a woman is subconsciously and symbolically going through the act of giving birth, and the most fertile moment occurs when the baked product is pulled from the oven. Dichter also maintained that when a woman bakes a cake for a man, she is offering him a symbol of fertility.[a] The Betty Crocker image was based on this profile.

Automobiles According to Dichter, the car allows consumers to convert their subconscious urges to destroy and their fear of death—two key forces in the human psyche—into reality. For example, the expression 'step on it' stems from the desire to feel power, and the phrase 'I just missed that car by inches' reflects the desire to play with danger. Based on this view, Dichter advised Esso (now Exxon) to tap into consumers' aggressive motives for driving cars in promoting the superiority of its gasoline product. The slogan 'Put a tiger in your tank' was developed as a result of his advice.[b]

Dichter also maintained that cars have personalities, and that people become attached to their cars and view them as companions rather than objects. This notion stands behind his views that a man views a convertible as a mistress and a sedan as his wife.

Dolls Dolls play an important part in the socialisation of children and are universally accepted as an essential toy for girls. Parents choose dolls that have the kind of characteristics they want their children to have, and the doll is an object for both the parents and the children to enjoy. When Mattel introduced Barbie in 1959, the company hired Dichter as a consultant. His research indicated that while girls liked the doll, their mothers detested the doll's perfect bodily proportions and Teutonic appearance. Dichter advised Mattel to market the doll as a teenage fashion model, reflecting the mother's desire for a daughter's proper and fashionable appearance. The advertising themes used subtly told mothers that it is better for their daughters to appear attractive to men rather than nondescript.[c]

Ice cream Dichter described ice cream as an effortless food that does not have to be chewed and that melts in your mouth, a sign of abundance, an almost orgiastic kind of food that people eat as if they want it to run down their chins. Accordingly, he recommended that ice cream packaging should be round, with illustrations that run around the box panel, suggesting unlimited quantity.

Sources: [a]Ernest Dichter, *Handbook of Consumer Motivations* (New York: McGraw-Hill Book Company, 1964); Jack Hitt, 'Does the smell of coffee brewing remind you of your mother?', *New York Times Magazine*, 7 May 2000, pp. 6, 71. [b]Phil Patton, 'Here come the car shrinks', *Fortune*, 18 March 2002, 145(6), p. 187. [c]Barbara Lippert, 'B-Ball Barbie,' *Adweek*, 9 November 1998, 35(45), p. 26.

people, while consumer behaviourists were interested in explaining the behaviour of 'typical' consumers. Second, Freudian theory was developed in an entirely different social context (19th-century Vienna), while motivational research was introduced in the 1950s in postwar America.[28]

Finally, many motivational researchers imputed highly complex reasons to rather prosaic consumer purchases. Marketers began to question their recommendations (e.g. Is it better to sell a man a pair of braces as a means of holding up his pants or as a 'reaction to castration anxiety'? Is it easier to persuade a woman to buy a garden hose to water her lawn or as a symbol of the 'futility of genital competition for the female'?). Motivational researchers often came up with sexual explanations for the most mundane activities. For example, an ad showing a hostess behind a beverage table filled with large bottles of soft drinks was once commended by a leading motivational researcher for its 'clever use of phallic symbolism'.[29]

MOTIVATIONAL RESEARCH TODAY

Despite these criticisms, motivational research is still regarded as an important tool by marketers who want to gain deeper insights into the reasons behind consumer behaviour than conventional marketing research techniques can yield. There is new and compelling evidence that the unconscious is the site of a far larger portion of mental life than even Freud envisioned. Research studies show that the unconscious mind may understand and respond to non-verbal symbols, form emotional responses and guide actions, largely independent of conscious awareness.[30] The science of **semiotics** is concerned with the conscious and subconscious meanings of non-verbal symbols to consumers.[31] Box 3.2 lists some psychological meanings ascribed to current advertising symbols.

Since motivational research often reveals unsuspected consumer motivations concerning product or brand usage, its principal use is in the development of new ideas for promotional campaigns, ideas that can penetrate the consumer's conscious awareness by appealing to unrecognised needs. Thus, manufacturers of house paint were able to persuade consumers in Minnesota to try pastel colours on the exteriors of their homes after researchers discovered a latent 'colour hunger' among people living in that grey, wintry climate.[32] In another example, researchers attempted to discover why women bought traditional roach sprays rather than a brand packaged in little plastic trays. To do this, they asked women to draw pictures of roaches and write stories about

BOX 3.2 Psychological symbolism in advertising

Teddy bear	A symbol of tamed aggression (Perfect image for a fabric softener that 'tames' the rough texture of clothing.)
Penguins	Symbolise coolness, refreshment and friendliness (Used in Diet Coke commercials to connote, subconsciously, these qualities.)
A male back	Can be perceived as 'rudely giving the consumer the cold shoulder' (Grey Flannel cologne removed this non-verbal from its ads.)
A male in a rugged, outdoor situation	Symbolises a 'lone wolf' (Schick uses this symbol to suggest the underlying message 'to be touched and loved and be a lover'.)

Source: Based on Ronald Alsop, 'Agencies scrutinize their ads for psychological symbolism', *Wall Street Journal*, 11 June 1987, p. 27. Dow Jones & Company, Inc.

their sketches. The study found that, for many of their respondents, roaches symbolised men who had left them feeling poor and powerless. The women reported that spraying the roaches and 'watching them squirm and die' allowed them to express their hostility toward men and gave them feelings of greater control.[33] Analysing these results enables the marketer to obtain a greater understanding of consumer purchase behaviours.

Motivational research also provides marketers with a basic orientation for new product categories and enables them to explore consumer reactions to ideas and advertising copy at an early stage, so that costly errors can be avoided. Furthermore, it gives marketers basic insights which enable them to design structured, quantitative marketing research studies—studies to be conducted on larger, more representative samples of consumers.

In addition, motivational research analyses often suggest new ways for marketers to present their products to the public. For example, in using figure sketches to determine consumers' differing perceptions of American Express Gold card and Green card holders, researchers found that the Gold card user was perceived as a 'couch potato' in front of a TV set. Based on this and other research, American Express decided to market the Gold card as 'a symbol of responsibility for people who have control over their lives and finances'.[34]

Although motivational research continues to be a useful tool for many marketers who want to know the actual reasons underlying consumer behaviour, it is no longer considered the only method for uncovering human motivation. It remains just one of a variety of research techniques available to the consumer researcher.

CASE STUDY 3.1

Colluding with Creativity: The Experience of Auckland Theatre Company

Dr Suzette Major, Department of Screen & Media Studies, University of Waikato, Hamilton, New Zealand

In the fast-paced lives we lead, with the constant strains of work and home, the need for leisure and entertainment is imperative. Leisure and entertainment services provide consumers with the opportunity to relax and escape from the pressures of everyday trials and tribulations. Creative industries in New Zealand are growing rapidly, to the point that they are now recognised by government and industry as being vital to the nation's economic and social well-being. One such sector within the creative industries is live theatre. And at the forefront of live theatre productions in New Zealand is Auckland Theatre Company (ATC). This company offers the public a variety of theatrical productions that allow consumers to relax, socialise and immerse themselves in the magical world of creativity.

ATC was established in 1992 and has swiftly risen to become one of New Zealand's most dynamic upmarket arts organisations. ATC offers a range of plays from New Zealand and overseas, including works that are new and classic, dramatic, comedic and musical. The number of productions per season has steadily increased from two plays in its first year of operation, to 10 plays being showcased in 2002. In 2003, the number of productions dropped to seven, to allow for the national tour of *The Vagina Monologues*. In that year, ATC took *The Vagina Monologues* to 12 centres throughout New Zealand. The growing success of ATC is evident in their large customer base, with more than 100 000 people now attending an ATC production each year.

So why do people attend a live theatre performance? Beyond the simple explanation of meeting consumers' need for a creative experience, lie multifaceted and complex reasons. For some, ATC's productions provide a space for social interaction, since performances take place in a social setting. Whether people are on a date, or catching up with an old friend, with their parents, or spending quality time with their partner, attending a performance is as much about socialising, as it is about fulfilling the need for experiencing creative expression. As explained by ATC Marketing Manager, Helen Bartle, 'attending a performance is a social activity. It's a chance for people to get together with family and friends'. This means that the experience of ATC rarely finishes as the curtain falls. Rather, the performance can spark lively conversation and debate among audience members. In this way, ATC's offerings can fulfil not only social needs, but also provide intellectual stimulation.

While the exact figures of individual attendees versus group attendees are unknown, ATC recognises the social nature of their offering. And with this awareness comes the ability to address the social needs of their consumers. For example, ATC encourages people to attend performances in groups by offering group discounts. ATC is also looking at bringing groups of elderly together, by marketing a production as a package to retirement villages. The package includes transport to and from a Sunday matinee performance and offers a group discount.

Within this social environment, psychological needs for status and prestige can also be satisfied. Attending a performance can be as much about 'being seen' as seeing the performance. It is no surprise that ATC booklets can be found on the coffee tables of the culturally educated. To be artistically aware and supportive is seen as a respectable and desirable attribute. ATC again recognises the prestigious nature of their offering and designs marketing strategies that appeal to this consumer need. For example, the subscription booklet for ATC leads with the statement, 'Be part of New Zealand's leading theatre company'.

Indeed, this sense of belonging to a prestigious group of 'arts supporters' is particularly evident in the high number of subscribers. At ATC, on average 25–30% of a season is booked in advance by subscribers. This is a significant figure, not only for financial reasons, but also for marketing purposes. As explained by Helen Bartle, 'subscribers tend to be loyal ambassadors of the company'.

People aspire to become ATC subscribers. Theatre is seen as a 'high-art' form, and theatre subscribers tend to fall within the higher socio-economic bracket. To be part of this exclusive group is enviable. As part of emphasising this exclusive nature of being a subscriber, ATC offers exclusive subscriber benefits. One such benefit is the subscriber briefing. These evenings provide the opportunity to meet cast and crew involved with the play and to see how the production is put together. Such direct involvement provides ATC with immediate feedback on its current play, as well as generating new concepts for future productions. From the consumers' standpoint, their privileged access 'behind the scenes' helps cultivate a sense of belonging to a prestige group of arts consumers. Membership to such a group is a way of fulfilling ego needs for prestige and status.

Consumers' need for safety and security is also recognised by ATC. One way of meeting these needs is by offering a Sunday matinee. As explained by Helen Bartle, 'people often feel more comfortable going out during the day'. This is particularly evident for elderly consumers. In Helen Bartle's experience, the front-of-house staff are also crucial for creating a safe and enjoyable environment. Many ATC productions are held at the Maidment Theatre where the customer service is superb.

Part of feeling safe and secure when attending an ATC production also lies in the ease to which the consumer can park and physically get to the theatre. This is an area that causes some concern. ATC is a non-venue based theatre company, which means they rely on venues for staging their productions which are outside of their control. Maidment Theatre is such an example. While the physical space of the theatre is excellent, and the customer service is outstanding, the location of this theatre can create accessibility difficulties. Helen Bartle recognises this as a downfall: 'we are aware that some subscribers have not renewed their membership because of this issue. It can be difficult to find a park in the centre of the city. And this can affect the overall enjoyment of attending an ATC production'. In addressing this safety issue, ATC is considering alternative ways of reaching the audience. The national tour of *The Vagina Monologues* for example, where the production was taken to various locations, provides an opportunity for ATC consumers to access the play in more convenient locations.

Another motivating factor for attending an ATC performance relates to the need for escapism and entertainment. While watching a performance, consumers have the chance to leave their worldly concerns behind, and simply be entertained for two brief hours. Unlike tangible products that perform utilitarian benefits, theatre feeds people's creativity and offers consumers the chance to experience artistic and creative expression. Through the performances, ATC consumers can experience tension, passion, humour, joy and humility. The various plays can be educational, entertaining and intellectually stimulating. As citizens living in the 'age of creativity', such experiences can be inspiring.

Part of the reason for the success of ATC lies in their ability to recognise and address the safety, social, ego and self-actualisation needs of their consumers. Through emphasising the prestigious nature of their offering (in particular to subscribers), encouraging social interaction through group bookings, offering Sunday matinees, touring productions, and delivering creative and inspirational performances, ATC has reached an inevitable position in the theatre sector. Their brand—ATC—is now standalone. Whenever an ATC production is advertised, consumers know it will be a quality performance. And in attending that performance, customers know their safety, social, egoistic and self-actualisation needs will be met through a totally satisfying theatre experience.

Note: Many thanks to Helen Bartle, Marketing Manager, Auckland Theatre Company, for her valuable assistance in putting this case study together.

Case Study Questions

1. Discuss how the experience of ATC relates to Maslow's hierarchy of needs.
2. Bartle's explanation for why people attend ATC's productions is based on informal conversations with audience members, rather than formal motivational research. What benefits would Bartle gain from conducting motivational research with ATC customers?
3. Bartle lists various reasons why consumers attend ATC productions, including the satisfaction of social, egoistic and self-actualisation needs. These needs could also be met through other products outside the live theatre industry. List and discuss other products that could satisfy these consumer needs.
4. A current trend facing contemporary organisations is 'the spontaneous consumer'. This consumer behaviour phenomenon is evident in the increasing number of people who live busy, unpredictable lives and make quick day-to-day decisions rather than planning activities well in advance. What impact could this trend have on ATC and what measures could ATC take to accommodate the 'spontaneous consumer'?
5. Bartle has chosen a series of black and white photographic images to promote ATC's product. What other marketing strategies could Bartle employ to emphasise how ATC satisfies social, egoistic and self-actualisation needs?

Summary

Motivation is the driving force within individuals that impels them to action. This driving force is produced by a state of uncomfortable tension, which exists as the result of an unfulfilled need. We all have needs, wants and desires. The drive to reduce need-induced tension results in behaviour that we anticipate will satisfy needs and thus bring about a more comfortable state.

All behaviour is goal-oriented. Goals are the sought-after results of motivated behaviour. The form or direction that behaviour takes—the goal that is selected—is a result of thinking processes (cognition) and previous learning. There are two types of goals: generic and product-specific. A generic goal is a general category of goal that may fulfil a certain need; a product-specific goal is a specifically branded or labelled product that the individual sees as a way to fulfil a need.

Innate needs—those we are born with—are primarily physiological (biogenic); they include all the factors required to sustain physical life (e.g. food, water, clothing, shelter, sex).

Acquired needs—those we develop after birth—are primarily psychological (psychogenic); they include esteem, fear, love and acceptance. For any given need, there are many different and appropriate goals. The specific goal selected depends on the individual's experiences and physical capacity, prevailing cultural norms and values, and the goal's accessibility in the physical and social environment.

Needs and goals are interdependent and change in response to our physical condition, environment, interaction with other people and experiences. As needs become satisfied, new, higher-order needs emerge that must be fulfilled.

Failure to achieve a goal often results in feelings of frustration. Individuals react to frustration in two ways: they may cope by finding a way round the obstacle that prohibits goal attainment, or by finding a substitute goal; or they may adopt a defence mechanism that enables them to protect their self-esteem. Defence mechanisms include aggression, regression, rationalisation, withdrawal, projection, autism, identification and repression.

Motives cannot easily be inferred from consumer behaviour. People with different needs may seek fulfilment through selection of the same goals; people with the same needs may seek fulfilment through different goals.

Although some psychologists have suggested that individuals have different need priorities, others believe that most human beings experience the same basic needs, to which they assign a similar priority ranking. Maslow's hierarchy of needs theory proposes five levels of prepotent human needs: physiological needs, safety needs, social needs, ego needs and self-actualisation needs. A trio of other needs widely used in consumer appeals comprises the needs for power, affiliation and achievement.

There are three commonly used methods for identifying and 'measuring' human motives: observation and inference, subjective reports, and projective techniques. None of these methods is completely reliable by itself, so researchers often use a combination of two or three techniques to assess the presence or strength of consumer motives.

Motivational research is qualitative research designed to delve below the consumer's level of conscious awareness. Despite some shortcomings, motivational research has proved to be of great value to marketers concerned with developing new ideas and new copy appeals.

Discussion questions

1. (a) Marketers don't create needs; needs pre-exist marketers. Discuss this statement.
   (b) Can marketing efforts change consumers' needs? Why or why not?
2. Consumers have both innate and acquired needs. Give examples of each kind of need and show how the same purchase can serve to fulfil either or both kinds of needs.
3. Specify the innate and/or acquired needs that would be useful bases for developing promotional strategies for:
   (a) air-bags in cars
   (b) vitamins
   (c) a Harley-Davidson motorcycle
   (d) recruiting university graduates to work for a company in the energy field.
4. Why are consumers' needs and goals constantly changing? What factors influence the formation of new goals?
5. How can marketers use consumers' failures to achieve goals in developing advertisements for products and services?
6. Most human needs are dormant much of the time. What factors cause their arousal? Give examples of personal care products which are designed to arouse latent consumer needs.
7. For each situation listed in question 3, select one level from Maslow's hierarchy of human needs that could be

used to segment the market and position the product (or company). Explain your choices. What are the advantages and/or disadvantages of using Maslow's hierarchy in segmentation and positioning?

8. (a) What is motivational research?
   (b) What are its strengths and weaknesses?
   (c) How did Ernest Dichter apply Freudian theory to consumer behaviour?
   (d) How was motivational research used in the 1950s?
   (e) How do marketers use the technique today?

Exercises

1. You are a member of an advertising team assembled to develop a promotional campaign for a new running shoe. Develop three slogans for this campaign, each based on one of the levels in Maslow's needs hierarchy.
2. Find an advertisement that depicts a defence mechanism. Present it in class and discuss its effectiveness.
3. Choose three magazine advertisements for different consumer goods. Carefully review Murray's list of human needs (Table 3.1). Through the advertising appeal used, identify which need(s) each product is presumed to satisfy.
4. Explain briefly the needs for power, affiliation and achievement. Find three advertisements for different products that are designed to appeal to these needs.

Key terms

achievement need *(p. 87)*
acquired needs *(p. 71)*
affiliation need *(p. 87)*
approach object *(p. 74)*
avoidance object *(p. 74)*
constructs *(p. 88)*
defence mechanism *(p. 77)*
emotional motives *(p. 74)*
frustration *(p. 77)*
generic goals *(p. 72)*
hierarchy of human needs *(p. 83)*
level of aspiration *(p. 75)*
motivation *(p. 70)*
motivational research *(p. 88)*
negative motivation *(p. 74)*
physiological needs *(p. 83)*
positive motivation *(p. 74)*
power need *(p. 87)*
prepotent need *(p. 79)*
product-specific goals *(p. 72)*
psychoanalytic theory of personality *(p. 88)*
rational motives *(p. 74)*
rationalisation *(p. 77)*
reliability *(p. 88)*
self-image *(p. 73)*
semiotics *(p. 90)*
stimulus-response theory *(p. 81)*
sublimation *(p. 78)*
substitute goal *(p. 76)*
validity *(p. 88)*

Endnotes

1. James T. Austin and Jeffrey B. Vancouver, 'Goal constructs in psychology: Structure, process and content', *Psychological Bulletin*, 120(3), 1996, pp. 338–375.
2. Jonathan Gutman, 'A means-end chain model based on consumer categorization processes', *Journal of Marketing*, 46, Spring 1982, pp. 60–72.
3. Jeffrey F. Durgee, Gina Colarelli O'Connor and Robert W. Veryzer, 'Observations: Translating values into product wants', *Journal of Advertising Research*, 36(6), Nov/Dec 1996, pp. 90–100.
4. Jack W. Brehm, 'Psychological reactance: Theory and applications', *Advances in Consumer Research*, 16, Association for Consumer Research, 1989, pp. 72–75.
5. Jon Elster, 'Emotions and economic theory', *Journal of Economic Literature*, 36(1), 1998, pp. 47–74.
6. See Abraham H. Maslow, 'A theory of human motivation', *Psychological Review*, 50, 1943, pp. 370–396; and Abraham H. Maslow, *Motivation and Personality* (New York: Harper & Row, 1954); and Abraham H. Maslow, *Toward a Psychology of Being* (New York: Van Nostrand

Reinhold, 1968), pp. 189–215.

7. A number of studies have focused on human levels of aspiration. See, for example, Kurt Lewin et al., 'Level of aspiration', in J. McV. Hunt, *Personality and Behavior Disorders* (New York: Ronald Press, 1944); and Howard Garland, 'Goal levels and task performance, a compelling replication of some compelling results', *Journal of Applied Psychology*, 67, 1982, pp. 245–248; and Edwin A. Locke, Elizabeth Frederick, Cynthia Lee and Philip Bobko, 'Effect of self efficacy, goals and task strategies on task performance', *Journal of Applied Psychology*, 69(2), 1984, pp. 241–251; and Edwin A. Locke, Elizabeth Frederick, Elizabeth Buckner and Philip Bobko, 'Effect of previously assigned goals on self-set goals and performance', *Journal of Applied Psychology*, 72(2), 1987, pp. 204–211; and John R. Hollenbeck and Howard J. Klein, 'Goal commitment and the goal-setting process: Problems, prospects and proposals for future research', *Journal of Applied Psychology*, 2, 1987, pp. 212–220.
8. Donald J. Campbell, 'Determinates of choice of goal difficulty level: A review of situational and personality influences', *Journal of Occupational Psychology*, 55(2), 1982, pp. 79–95.
9. Richard P. Bagozzi and Kyu-Hyun Lee, 'Consumer resistance to, and acceptance of, innovations', *Advances in Consumer Research*, 26, 1999, pp. 218–225.
10. Arnold Trehub, *The Cognitive Brain* (Cambridge, MA: The MIT Press, 1991).
11. Surendra N. Singh and Gilbert A. Churchill Jr, 'Arousal and advertising effectiveness', *Journal of Advertising*, 16(1), 1987, pp. 4–10.
12. Easwar S. Iyer, 'Unplanned purchasing: Knowledge of shopping environment and time pressure', *Journal of Retailing*, 65(1), 1989, pp. 40–57.
13. Peter Weinberg and Wolfgang Gottwald, 'Impulsive consumer buying as a result of emotions', *Journal of Business Research*, 10, 1982, p. 43.
14. Maslow, 'A theory of human motivation', op. cit.
15. Ibid., p. 380.
16. Howard E. Tinsley and Barbara D. Eldredge, 'Psychological benefits of leisure participation: A taxonomy of leisure activities based on their need-gratifying properties', *Journal of Counseling Psychology*, 42(2), April 1995, pp. 123–132.
17. Maslow, op. cit. p. 380.
18. Pat Kelley, 'Revisiting Maslow', *Workspan*, 45(5), May 2002, p. 50.
19. Fredrick Hertzberg, 'Retrospective comment', in Howard A. Thompson (ed.), *The Great Writings in Marketing* (Plymouth: Commerce, 1976), pp. 180–181.
20. Rudy Schrocer, 'Maslow's hierarchy of needs as a framework for identifying emotional triggers', *Marketing Review*, 46(5), February 1991, pp. 26, 28.
21. 'Pegging buyers by their gender', *New York Times*, 12 September 1992, p. F10.
22. See, for example, David C. McClelland, *Studies in Motivation* (New York: Appleton-Century-Crofts, 1955). Australian psychologist Norman Feather has conducted many studies of the value Australians place on achievement. For example, see N. Feather, 'Devaluing achievement within a culture: Measuring the cultural cringe', *Australian Journal of Psychology*, 45(3), 1993, pp. 182–188.
23. David C. McClelland, 'Business drive and national achievement', *Harvard Business Review*, July/August 1962, p. 99; and 'Achievement motivation can be developed', *Harvard Business Review*, November/December 1965, pp. 5–24, 178; and Abraham K. Korman, *The Psychology of Motivation* (Englewood Cliffs, NJ: Prentice Hall, 1974), p. 190.
24. A.G. Greenwald, 'Ego task analysis: An integration of research on ego-involvement and self awareness', in A. H. Hastorf and A. M. Isen (eds), *Cognitive Social Psychology* (New York: Elsevier North Holland, 1982), pp. 109–147.
25. Judith M. Harackiewicz, Carol Sansone and George Manderlink, 'Competence, achievement orientation, and intrinsic motivation: A process analysis', *Journal of Personality and Social Psychology*, 48, 1985, pp. 493–508.
26. Michael J. Stahl and Adrian M. Harrell, 'Evaluation and validation of a behavioral decision theory management approach to achievement, power, and affiliation', *Journal of Applied Psychology*, 67, 1982, pp. 744–751.
27. For additional reports of motivational research findings, see Ernest Dichter, *A Strategy of Desire* (Garden City, NY: Doubleday, 1960); Vance Packard, *The Hidden Persuaders* (New York: Pocket Books, 1957); and Pierre Martineau, *Motivation in Advertising* (New York: McGraw-Hill, 1957).
28. Jeff B. Murray and Deborah J. Evers, 'Theory borrowing and reflectivity in interdisciplinary fields', *Advances in Consumer Research*, 16, 1988, pp. 647–652.
29. Leslie Kanuk, 'Emotional persuasion in print advertising', Master's thesis, City College of New York, 1964.

30. Daniel Goleman, 'New view of mind gives unconscious an expanded role', *New York Times*, 7 February 1984, pp. C1–2.
31. Ronald Alsop, 'Agencies scrutinize their ads for psychological symbolism', *Wall Street Journal*, 11 June 1987, p. 27. See also David Mick, 'Consumer research and semiotics: Exploring the morphology of signs, symbols and significance', *Journal of Consumer Research*, 13, September 1986, pp. 196–213.
32. Ernest Dichter, 'Interpretative versus descriptive research' in Jagdesh Sheth, *Research in Marketing* 1 (Greenwich, CT: JAI Press, 1979), p. 72.
33. Daniel Goleman, 'New view of mind gives unconscious an expanded role,' *New York Times*, 7 February 1984, pp. C1–2.
34. Paula Drillman, quoted in Ronald Alsop, 'Advertisers put consumers on the couch', *Wall Street Journal*, 13 May 1988, p. 21.

Consumer personality and self-concept

IT'S NOT YOUR CAR.
IT'S NOT YOUR FRIENDS.
IT'S NOT YOUR JOB.

IT'S YOUR WATCH THAT
TELLS MOST ABOUT WHO YOU ARE.

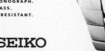

ARCTURA
KINETIC
CHRONOGRAPH

SNL001P $1200.
KINETIC CHRONOGRAPH.
SAPPHIRE GLASS.
100M WATER RESISTANT.

SEIKO

seiko.com.au

Source: Courtesy of Seiko Australia Pty Ltd.

Marketers have long tried to appeal to consumers in terms of their personality characteristics. They have intuitively felt that what consumers purchase, and when and how they consume, are likely to be influenced by personality factors. For this reason, advertisers and marketers have frequently depicted behaviours characteristic of specific personality traits or characteristics in their marketing and advertising messages. Advertising of alcoholic drinks such as Bundaberg Rum, Strongbow Cider and Victoria Bitter (VB) beer appeal to the sense of sociability and social interaction, whereas fragrances such as *Obsession* by Calvin Klein promote sexual appeal and individualism.

This chapter focuses on the relationship between an individual's *personality* and their behaviour as a consumer. It examines what personality is, how it influences our behaviour, particularly as consumers, and how it interrelates with other consumer behaviour concepts. It reviews several major personality theories and describes how they have stimulated marketing interest in the study of personality. The chapter also explores how the *self-concept* and *self-image as approaches to personality* influence consumer behaviour.

➤ What is personality?

The study of **personality** has been approached in a variety of ways. Some theorists have emphasised the dual influence of heredity and early childhood experiences on the development of personality; others have stressed broader social and environmental influences and the fact that personalities develop continuously over time. Some view personality as a unified whole, while others focus on specific traits. The variation in viewpoints makes it difficult to arrive at a single unambiguous definition. However, we propose that it is the inner psychological characteristics that both determine and reflect how a consumer responds to the environment, consistently influencing the way they respond. The emphasis in this definition is on *inner characteristics*—those specific traits that distinguish one individual from other individuals. An individual's personality is dynamic in nature and needs to be considered in relation to personal motivations and interactions with the surrounding environment.[1] Recently, the following definition was proposed and, as is the case with other definitions, it highlights the fact that it is our personality *combined* with the manner in which it interacts with the environment that influences our behaviour. Personality is:

> *The unique, dynamic organisation of characteristics of a particular person, physical and psychological, which influence behaviour and responses to the social and physical environment. Of these characteristics, some will be entirely unique to the specific person (i.e. memories, habits, mannerisms) and others will be shared with a few, many or all other people.*[2]

As discussed later in this chapter, the deeply ingrained (inner) characteristics that we call personality are likely to influence consumers' choices of products, stores and even holidays; they also affect how the consumer responds to an organisation's communication efforts. Therefore, the identification of specific personality characteristics associated with consumer behaviour may be useful in the development of an organisation's marketing strategies.

THE NATURE OF PERSONALITY

In the study of personality, three distinct properties are of central importance:

1. personality reflects individual differences;
2. personality is consistent and enduring; and
3. personality can change.

Personality reflects individual differences

Because the inner characteristics that constitute an individual's personality are a unique combination of factors, no two people are exactly alike. Nevertheless, many individuals tend to be similar in terms of a single (or limited set) personality characteristic. For instance, many people can be described as 'high' in sociability, or extroverted (the degree of interest they display in social or group activities), while others can be described as 'low' in sociability or introverted. Personality is a useful consumer behaviour concept because it enables us to categorise people into different groups on the basis of a single or limited set of traits. If each person were different in *all* respects, it would be impossible to group consumers into segments; and there would be little reason to develop standardised products and promotional campaigns.

Personality is consistent and enduring

An individual's personality is commonly thought to be both consistent and enduring. Both qualities are essential if marketers are to explain or predict consumer behaviour in terms of personality. The nature of personality suggests that it is unreasonable for marketers to attempt to change consumers' personalities to conform to certain products. They may, however, identify which personality characteristics influence specific consumer responses, and attempt to appeal to relevant traits inherent in their target group of consumers.

Personality can change

Although personality tends to be consistent and enduring, it may still change under certain circumstances. For instance, an individual's personality may be altered by major life events, such as the birth of a child, the death of a loved one, a divorce, or a significant career promotion. An individual's personality changes not only in response to abrupt events but also as part of a gradual maturing process and learning through life events.

There is also evidence that personality stereotypes may change over time. More specifically, it is felt that men's personality has generally remained relatively constant over the past 50 years, however women's personality has seemed to become increasingly more masculine and should continue to do so over the next 50 years. This prediction indicates a convergence in the personality characteristics of men and women.[3] The reason for this shift is that women have been moving into occupations that have traditionally been dominated by men and, therefore, have been associated with masculine personality attributes. For example, women now appear in senior managerial positions in organisations, they have taken on roles in trades once the sole domain of men (motor mechanics, electrical and plumbing, bricklaying etc.) and they undertake household tasks once the province of men.

➤ Theories of personality

Within the context of consumer behaviour three streams of research and theoretical development have contributed much to our understanding of personality and its usefulness in marketing. The following discussion examines Freudian theory, neo-Freudian personality theory and trait theory because of the role they play in the study of the relationship between consumer behaviour and personality.

FREUDIAN THEORY

Sigmund Freud's **psychoanalytic theory of personality** is the cornerstone of modern psychology. This theory was built on the premise that unconscious needs or drives, especially sexual and other biological drives, are at the heart of human motivation and personality. Freud constructed his theory on the basis of patients' recollections of early childhood experiences, analysis of their dreams, and the specific nature of their mental and physical adjustment problems.

Based on his analyses, Freud proposed that the human personality consists of three interacting systems—the **id**, the **superego** and the **ego**. The id was conceptualised as a 'warehouse' of primitive and impulsive drives—basic physiological needs such as thirst, hunger and sex—for which the individual seeks immediate satisfaction without concern for the specific means of satisfaction. The id operates on the *pleasure principle*, it acts to avoid pain and maximise immediate pleasure. The Interflora Flowerline advertisement shown in Figure 4.1 depicts a seemingly impulsive act of 'letting loose', expression of the primitive drives of id, whilst the advertisement in Figure 4.2 operates on the pleasure principle.

In contrast to the id, the superego is conceptualised as the individual's internal expression of society's moral and ethical codes of conduct. The superego defines what is right and good by internalising the values of society. The superego's role is to see that the individual satisfies needs in a socially acceptable fashion. Thus, the superego is a kind of 'brake' that restrains or inhibits the impulsive forces of the id.

Finally, the ego is the individual's conscious control. It functions as an internal monitor that attempts to balance the impulsive demands of the id and the sociocultural constraints of the superego. Through learning and experience, the ego develops the individual's capabilities of realistic thinking. Figure 4.3 represents the interrelationship among the three interacting systems. There are situations where the ego is not able to resolve the conflict between the id and the superego. In these cases, a *defence mechanism* is used to reduce the tension brought on by the lack of compromise. Two examples of defence mechanisms are *repression* and *projection*. Repression is a kind of selective forgetting. The individual blocks out some aspects of the conflict in order that the conflict no longer exists. For example, if two students are trying to decide whether to take a vacation during the Easter break instead of studying, they may selectively repress some of the promises they made to their parents about the marks they would achieve this semester. The repression of their promises reduces the workload for the semester, and effectively eliminates the conflict between working and going on holiday. Projection occurs when unacceptable feelings generated by the id are projected onto another person or group. The criticisms that individuals make of others are often a reflection of their own undesirable urges.

Stages of personality development

In addition to specifying a structure for personality, Freud emphasised that our personality is formed as we pass through five distinct stages of infant and childhood development—the oral, anal, phallic, latent and genital stages. Freud labelled four of these stages of development to conform to the area of the body on which he believed the child's sexual instincts are focused at the time.

Oral stage The infant first experiences social contact with the outside world through the mouth (e.g. eating, drinking, sucking). A crisis develops at the end of this stage when the child is weaned from the mother's breast or from the bottle.

Anal stage During this stage, the child's primary source of pleasure is the process of elimination. A second crisis develops at the end of this stage when parents try to toilet train the child.

Phallic stage The child experiences self-oriented sexual pleasure during this phase with discovery of the sex organs. A third crisis occurs when the child experiences sexual desire for the parent of the opposite sex. How the child resolves this crisis affects later relationships with people of the opposite sex and with authority figures.

Latency stage Freud believed that the sexual instincts of the child lie dormant from about age five until the beginning of adolescence.

Genital stage At adolescence, the individual develops a sexual interest in people of the opposite sex, beyond self-oriented love and love for parents.

According to Freud, an adult's personality is determined by how well they deal with the crises that are experienced while passing through each of these stages (particularly the first three). For instance, if a child's

FIGURE 4.1 An example of id-driven impulsive behaviour

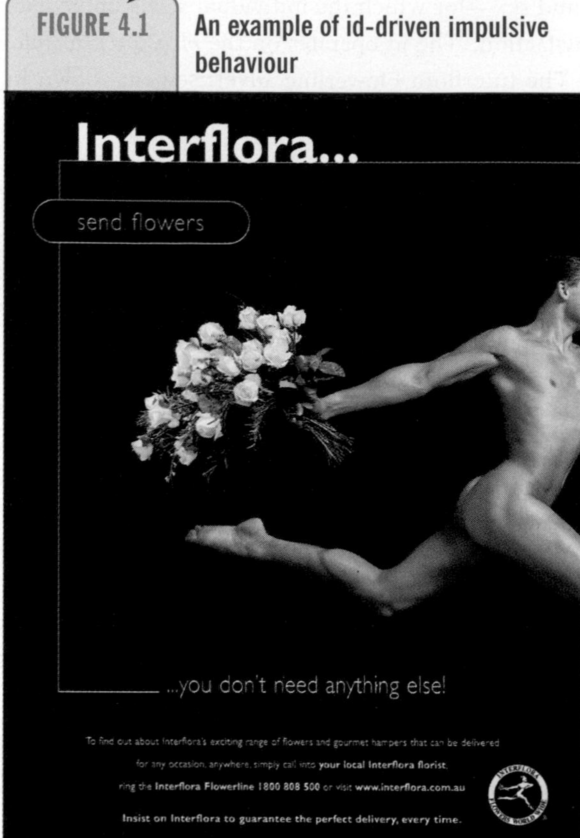

Source: Courtesy of Interflora. © Interflora Australia.

FIGURE 4.2 Emphasises the pleasure benefit from Passion Pink Venus

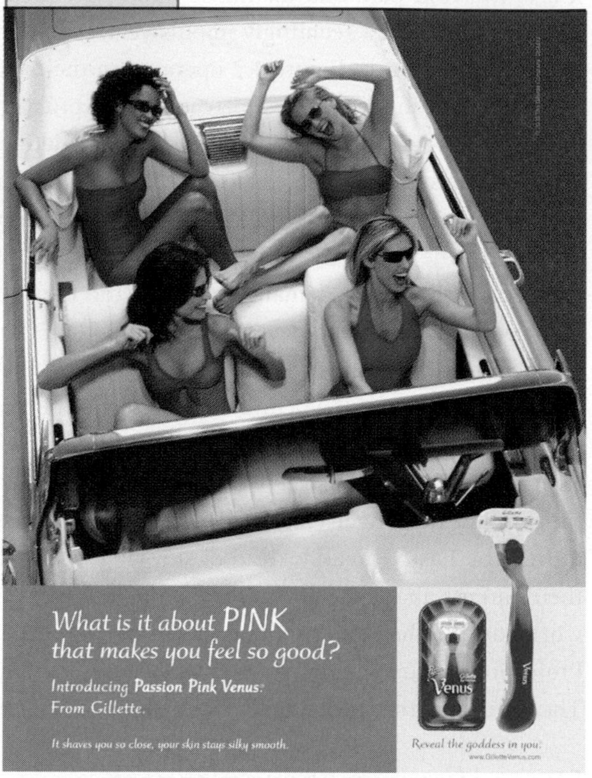

Source: Thanks to Gillette for Women Venus Passion.

FIGURE 4.3 The interrelationships among the id, superego and ego

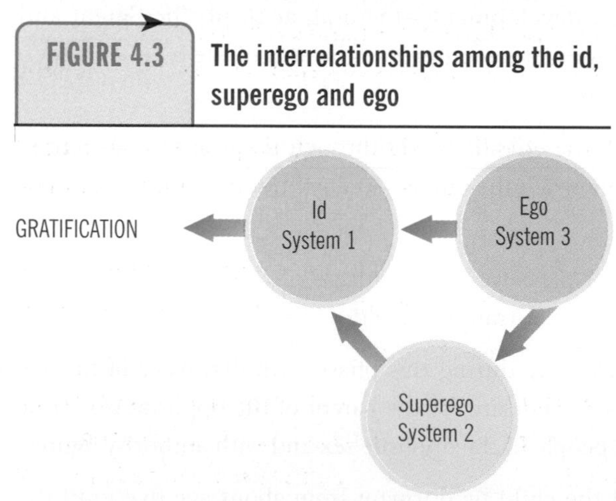

oral needs are not adequately satisfied at the first stage of development, the person may become fixated at this stage and, as an adult, display a personality that includes such traits as dependence and excessive oral activity (e.g. smoking and gum chewing). If an individual is fixated at the *anal* stage, the adult personality may display other traits, such as an excessive need for neatness.

Marketing applications of Freudian theory

Researchers who apply Freud's psychoanalytic theory to the study of consumer personality tend to stress the idea that human drives are largely unconscious, and that consumers are primarily unaware of their true reasons for buying what they buy. These researchers tend to focus on consumer purchases and/or consumption situations, treating them as a reflection and extension of the consumer's own personality. In other words, our appearance and possessions—how well-groomed we are, what we wear, carry and display—are taken to reflect our personality. Table 4.1 presents the results of a study of 19 000 consumers that examined the link between snack food perceptions and selected personality traits.[4] The findings of the research reveal, for example, that potato chips are associated with being

TABLE 4.1 Snack foods and personality traits

Snack food	Personality traits
Potato chips	Ambitious, successful, high achiever, impatient with less than the best.
Tortilla chips	Perfectionist, high expectations, punctual, conservative, responsible.
Pretzels	Lively, easily bored with same old routine, flirtatious, intuitive, may overcommit to projects.
Snack crackers	Rational, logical, contemplative, shy, prefers time alone.
Cheese curls	Conscientious, principled, proper, fair, may appear rigid but has great integrity, plans ahead, loves order.
Nuts	Easygoing, empathetic, understanding, calm, even-tempered.
Popcorn	Takes charge, pitches in often, modest, self-confident but not a show-off.
Meat snacks	Gregarious, generous, trustworthy, tends to be overly trusting.

Source: **Alan Hirsch, MD, *What Flavor is Your Personality? Discover Who You Are by Looking at What You Eat* (Naperville, IL, Sourcebooks, 2001). Used with permission of Sourcebooks. © 2001, Alan Hirsch, MD.**

ambitious, successful, a high achiever and impatient with less than the best, whereas popcorn seems to be related to a personality that takes charge, often pitches in, is modest and self-confident but not a show-off. (The relationship between how consumers see the products or brands they use, and how they see themselves, is considered later in the chapter as part of the discussion on self and self-images.)

NEO-FREUDIAN PERSONALITY THEORY

Several of Freud's colleagues disagreed with his contention that personality is primarily instinctual and sexual in nature. Instead, these neo-Freudians believed that social relationships are fundamental to the formation and development of personality. For instance, Alfred Adler viewed human beings as seeking to attain various rational goals, which he called 'style of life'. He also emphasised the individual's efforts to overcome feelings of inferiority (i.e. by striving for superiority).

Harry Stack Sullivan, another neo-Freudian, stressed that people continuously attempt to establish significant and rewarding relationships with others. He was particularly concerned with the individual's efforts to reduce tensions, such as anxiety.

Like Sullivan, Karen Horney was also interested in anxiety. She focused on the impact of child–parent relationships and the individual's desire to conquer feelings of anxiety. Horney proposed that individuals be classified into three personality groups: compliant, aggressive, and detached.[5]

- Compliant individuals are those who move toward others (they desire to be loved, wanted, and appreciated).
- Aggressive individuals are those who move against others (they desire to excel and win admiration).
- Detached individuals are those who move away from others (they desire independence, self-reliance, self-sufficiency, and individualism or freedom from obligations).

A personality test based on Horney's theory, Interpersonal Orientation: The CAD Scale (known as CAD), has been developed and tested within the context of consumer behaviour.[6] The initial CAD research uncovered a number of tentative relationships between college students' scores and their product and brand usage patterns. For example, highly compliant students were found to prefer name-brand products such as Bayer aspirin (see brand at <www.bayer.com>); students classified as aggressive showed a preference for Old Spice deodorant (see brand at <www.oldspice.com>) over other brands (seemingly because of its masculine appeal); and highly detached students proved to be heavy tea drinkers (possibly reflecting their desire not to conform). More recent research has found that children who scored high in self-reliance—who preferred to do things independently of others (i.e. detached personalities)—were less likely to be brand loyal and were more likely to try different brands.[7]

Many marketers intuitively use some of these neo-Freudian theories. For example, marketers who position their products or services as providing an opportunity to belong or to be appreciated by others in a group or social setting would seem to be guided by Horney's characterisation of the compliant individual. Figure 4.4 (page 106) shows an ad for Telstra that captures the personality factor related to the desire to be admired and have friends envy you with its emphasis on body copy that states: 'The phone will make your friends jealous. Free text lets you rub it in.' The aggressive individual needs to be the focus of attention and be admired.

TRAIT THEORY

A **trait** is defined as '. . . any distinguishing, relatively enduring way in which one individual differs from another'[8] but has also been described as a tendency to respond (either in thought or action) in a similar fashion over time and situations.[9] **Trait theory** is primarily *quantitative* or *empirical*: focusing on the identification and measurement of personality in terms of specific psychological characteristics. Trait theorists believe that a personality can be understood by studying the pattern of traits within an individual. Accordingly, they are concerned with the construction of personality tests (or inventories) that pinpoint individual differences in terms of specific traits. Trait theories attempt to describe individuals in terms of their predispositions on a bank of adjectives. Essentially, a consumer's personality would be described in terms of a particular combination of traits. Trait theory constitutes a major departure from the predominantly *qualitative* approaches that typify the Freudian and neo-Freudian approaches (e.g. personal observation, self-reported experiences, dream analysis, projective techniques).

This approach assumes that we have many dimensions to our personalities, but some people possess such dimensions more strongly or weakly than others. That is they have 'more' or 'less' of each trait than others. Trait theory does not try to provide a single label for each personality type. Instead, it provides information about a number of personality traits that make up the personality of the individual. Trait theories have endeavoured to overcome the limitations of the type theories by focusing on individual differences, strengths and weaknesses. Such traits provide marketers with a better understanding of how consumers respond to marketing stimuli. For example, some traits are associated with consumers' interactions with marketing environments and others on consumption objects.

One of the most influential of the trait theories is the 'Big Five' model. This model was originally derived from analyses of natural-language terms people use to describe themselves and others. These terms, after factor analysis, can be explained by a narrower set of dimensions. Each of the five dimensions is represented by six, more specific, scales that measure facets of the dimension. The dimensions and their facets are as follows.

- *Neuroticism*—the tendency to experience negative effects such as fear, sadness, embarassment, anger, guilt and disgust. A low score on this dimension indicates emotional stability characterised by calmness, and an even-tempered, relaxed nature. The facets of neuroticism are: anxiety, angry hostility, depression, self-consciousness, impulsiveness and vulnerability.
- *Extroversion*—the tendency to interact with the world. Individuals tending towards extroversion enjoy excitement and stimulation; they are upbeat, energetic and optimistic; they like people and prefer large groups and gatherings. A low score on this dimension indicates introversion. Introverts tend to be reserved

and independent, and prefer to spend time alone. The facets of extroversion are: warmth, gregariousness, assertiveness, activity, excitement-seeking and positive emotions.

- *Openness to experience*—the tendency to seek a variety of experiences, to entertain novel ideas and unconventional values, and to experience both positive and negative emotions more keenly. A high score on this dimension is associated with an active imagination, preference for variety, intellectual curiosity and an independence of judgment. A low score on this dimension indicates a conservative outlook, a desire for the familiar and the conventional. The facets of openness to experience are: fantasy, aesthetics, feelings, actions, ideas and values.
- *Agreeableness*—the tendency to move towards people and act kindly towards them. A high score on this dimension is associated with altruism, an eagerness to help people, cooperativeness and a belief that others will be equally helpful in return. A low score indicates the tendency to be antagonistic, egocentric, competitive and sceptical of others' intentions. The facets of agreeableness are: trust, straightforwardness, altruism, compliance, modesty and tender-mindedness.
- *Conscientiousness*—the tendency to control impulses and pursue goals. A high score on this dimension is associated with an individual who is purposeful, strong-willed, punctual, reliable and determined. A low score on this dimension indicates a tendency to be lackadaisical in working towards goals. The facets of conscientiousness are: competence, order, dutifulness, achievement-striving and self-discipline.

These traits may be inherited, imprinted by early childhood experience, or modified by disease or psychological intervention; but at any given time they define an individual's potential and direction. These traits have been incorporated into a larger and more elaborate model of personality, the *five-factor model*[10] illustrated in Figure 4.5. The traits, or *basic tendencies*, affect *characteristic adaptations* such as skills, habits and attitudes. Characteristic adaptations are concrete manifestations of traits or basic tendencies. For instance, a person who tends to be extroverted is more likely to develop skills that facilitate socialising, such as learning to dance. A person who tends to be disagreeable will cultivate cynical attitudes.[11] *Self-concept* is a component of characteristic adaptations and is discussed in more detail later in this chapter. Characteristic adaptations and *external influences*, such as cultural norms, affect a consumer's behaviour, or *objective biography*. If the individual who tends to be extroverted is also open to experience, that person not only learns to dance, but frequents dance parties. The behaviour is the outcome variable that market researchers often try to predict. All the five factors—basic tendencies, characteristic adaptations, self-concept, objective biography and external influences—are related to dynamic processes. The *dynamic processes* represent development and change due to experience. This reflects the notion that personality is a dynamic entity, not static, which is a significant divergence from Freud's approach.

The 'Big Five' model has been used to understand a consumer's propensity to engage in certain activities. Research supports the notion that consumer motives for exercising can be explained by the 'Big Five'. For instance, those high in extroversion and conscientiousness were more likely to engage in exercise. Those high in neuroticism were likely to exercise for body image and weight control motives. Those high in extroversion were motivated by the social aspect of exercise. Those high in conscientiousness were motivated by health and fitness concerns. Those high in openness to experience were motivated by stress relief and the potential for fun.[12]

Selected **single-trait personality tests** (which measure just one trait, such as self-confidence) are increasingly being developed specifically for use in consumer behaviour and marketing. As we see in the sections that follow, these personality scales measure such traits as *consumer innovativeness* (how receptive a person is to new experiences), *consumer susceptibility to interpersonal influence* (how consumers respond to social influence), *self-monitoring* (the degree an individual is sentitive to their environment and adjusts or modifies behaviour accordingly) and *consumer ethnocentrism* (consumers' likelihood to accept or reject foreign-made

FIGURE 4.4 Telstra advertisement emphasising key personality factors

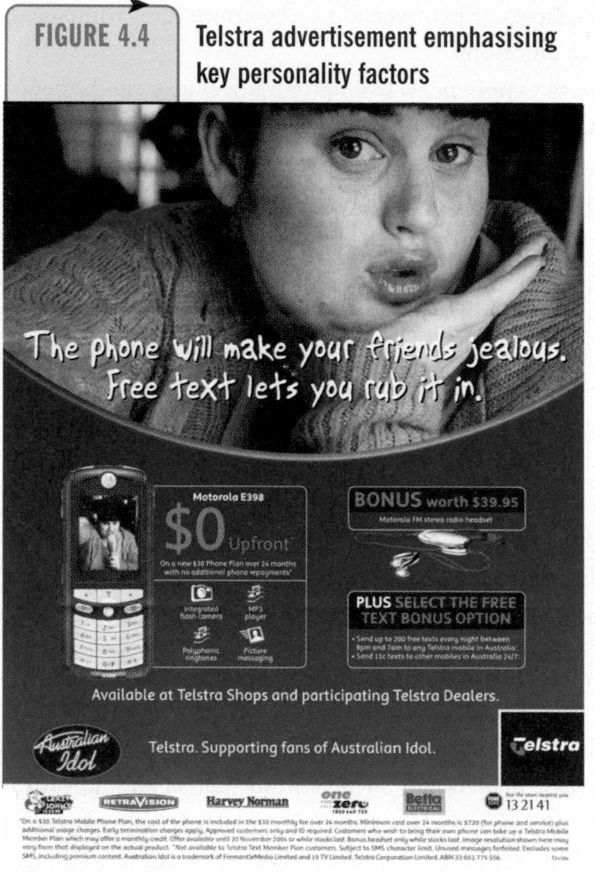

Source: Courtesy of Telstra.

products).[13] Recent research using a scale of romanticism and classicism found that consumers with a more romantic temperament (sensitive, imaginative and emotional) tend to prefer more risky vacations. Consumers with a more classic temperament (purposeful, rational and controlled) tend to prefer safer, more traditional types of vacation.[14] Such research indicates a valid use of personality to market products. In general, consumer marketers should regard personality as one of the influences on behaviour, linked to decision making where the situation and material circumstances allow a choice. For example, a consumer's personality might impel him to buy a particular two-seater, luxury sportscar. The fact that the consumer has three children and a spouse to carry around and has little money to spend will constrain the actual choice. In contrast, faced with a range of available rides at Dreamworld amusement park, the same consumer's choice may be deeply affected by personality factors. The criticism of the trait approach to personality has led to the view that for the approach to be useful to marketers, the consumer characteristics selected should be closely identified in terms of their specific relevance to some aspect of consumer behaviour.

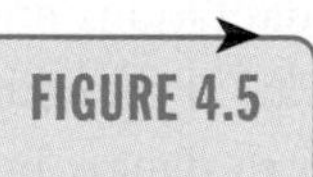

FIGURE 4.5 A five-factor theory of personality, with examples of specific content and arrows indicating the direction of major causal pathways mediated by dynamic processes

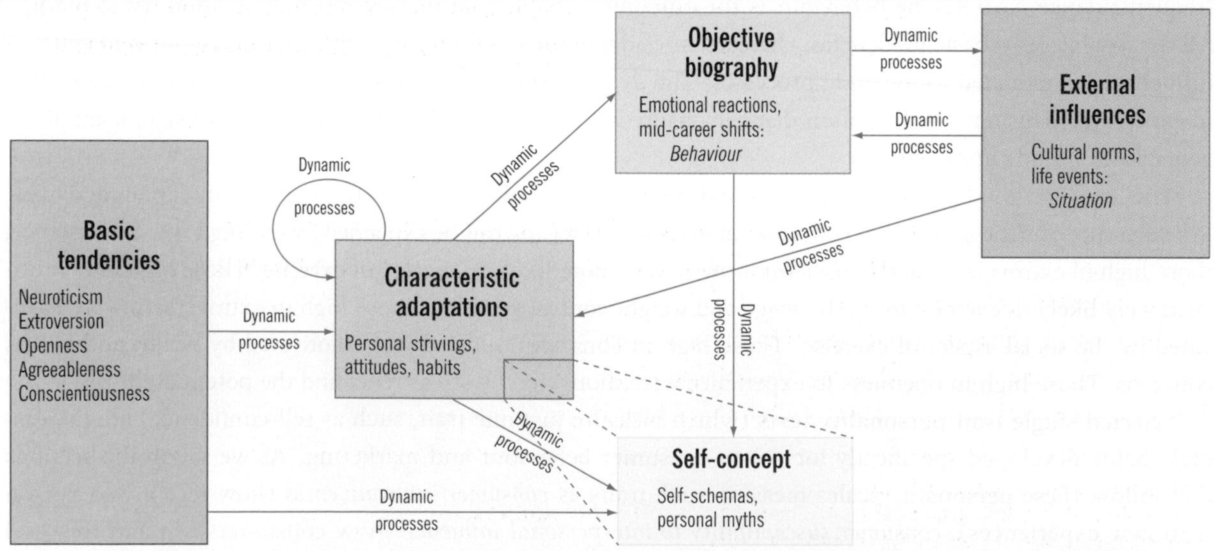

Source: Adapted from Robert R. McCrae and Paul T. Costa Jr, 'Toward a new generation of personality theories: Theoretical contexts for the five-factor model', in Jerry S. Wiggins (ed.), *The five-factor model of personality: Theoretical perspectives* (New York: Guilford Press, 1996), pp. 51–87.

Personality and consumer behaviour

Marketers are interested in understanding how personality influences consumption behaviour, because such knowledge enables them to understand consumers better, and more appropriately segment and target those consumers who are likely to respond positively to their product or service communications. This section examines some specific personality traits that influence specific behaviours and as such are useful to marketers for a better understanding of consumer behaviour.

CONSUMER INNOVATIVENESS

Marketing practitioners must learn all they can about those consumers who are likely to try new products, services or practices, for the market response of such innovators is often crucial to the ultimate success of a new product or service.

Personality traits that have proved useful in differentiating between consumer innovators and non-innovators include: consumer innovativeness, dogmatism, social character, optimum stimulation level and variety seeking. (Chapter 15 examines additional characteristics that distinguish between consumer innovators and non-innovators.)

How receptive consumers are to new products, new services or new practices is quite important to both consumers and marketers, for both can benefit from the right innovation. Consumer researchers have endeavoured to develop measurement instruments to gauge the level of **consumer innovativeness**, because such personality-trait measures provide insights into the nature and boundaries of a consumer's willingness to innovate.[15] Table 4.2 presents a six-item measure of consumer innovativeness that is specially designed to be flexible in terms of the boundaries or domain being studied (e.g. *broad product category*: music; *subproduct category*: rock music; *type*: new rock group). (The important topic of consumer innovativeness is examined in greater detail in Chapter 15.)

CONSUMER DOGMATISM

Dogmatism is a personality trait that measures the degree of rigidity we display towards the unfamiliar or towards information that is contrary to our own established beliefs.[16] A person who is highly dogmatic approaches the unfamiliar defensively and with considerable discomfort and uncertainty. At the other end of the spectrum, someone who is low in dogmatism will readily consider unfamiliar or opposing beliefs.

TABLE 4.2 A consumer innovativeness scale[a]

- In general, I am among the last in my circle of friends to buy a new (rock album[b]) when it appears.
- If I heard that a new (rock album) was available in the store, I would be interested enough to buy it.
- Compared to my friends, I own few (rock albums).[c]
- In general, I am the last in my circle of friends to know the (titles of the latest rock albums).[c]
- I will buy a new (rock album), even if I haven't heard it yet.
- I know the names of new (rock acts) before other people do.

[a] Measured on a 5-point 'agreement' scale.
[b] The product category and related wording are altered to fit the purpose of the researcher.
[c] These items are negatively worded and are scored inversely.

Source: Ronald E. Goldsmith and Charles F. Hofacker, 'Measuring consumer innovativeness', *Journal of the Academy of Marketing Science*, 19, 1991, p. 212. Copyright © 1991 Academy of Marketing Science.

Consumers who are low in dogmatism (open-minded) are more likely to prefer innovative products to established or traditional alternatives. In contrast, highly dogmatic (closed-minded) consumers are more likely to choose established products. It is likely that highly dogmatic consumers will be more accepting of ads for new products or services that contain an *authoritative* appeal. To this end, marketers have employed celebrities and experts in their new-product advertising to make it easier for potentially reluctant consumers (non-innovators) to accept the innovation. In contrast, low-dogmatic consumers (who are frequently high in innovativeness) seem to be more receptive to messages that stress factual differences and product benefits.

CONSUMER SOCIAL CHARACTER

The personality trait known as **social character** has its origins in sociological research, which focuses on the identification and classification of individuals into distinct sociocultural types.[17] As used in consumer psychology, social character is a personality trait that ranges on a continuum from inner-directness to other-directness. Available evidence indicates that **inner-directed consumers** tend to rely on their own inner values or standards in evaluating new products and are likely to be consumer innovators. Conversely, **other-directed consumers** tend to look to others for direction on what is 'right' or 'wrong'; thus, they are less likely to be consumer innovators.

Inner-directed and other-directed consumers may also be attracted to different types of promotional messages. Inner-directed people seem to prefer ads that stress product features and personal benefits (enabling them to use their own values and standards in evaluating products), while other-directed people seem to prefer ads that feature a social environment or social acceptance (in keeping with their tendency to look to others for direction). Thus, other-directed individuals may be more easily influenced because of their natural inclination to go beyond the content of an ad and think in terms of likely social approval of a potential purchase.

NEED FOR UNIQUENESS

We all know people who seek to be unique. For these people conformity to others' expectations or standards, either in appearance or in their possessions, is something to be avoided. Moreover, we would expect that it is easier to express or act uniquely if one does not have to pay a price in the form of others' criticism. Supporting this perspective, a recent study of consumers' need for uniqueness (NFU) explored the circumstances under which high NFU individuals do (and do not) make unconventional (i.e. unique) choices. The research revealed that when consumers are asked to explain their choices, but are not concerned about being criticised by others, they are more receptive to making unique choices.[18] Seeing the importance of NFU, other consumer researchers have developed an inventory to measure the trait within the context of consumer behaviour. Table 4.3 presents a sample of items drawn from the inventory.

CONSUMER SUSCEPTIBILITY TO INTERPERSONAL INFLUENCE

A consumer's susceptibility to interpersonal influence (CSII) has been shown to effect consumer behaviour. Consumer susceptibility to interpersonal influence is defined as the need to identify with or enhance one's image in the opinion of others, the willingness to conform to the expectations of others and the tendency to learn by observing others or seeking information from others.[19] As such, CSII is argued to have an influence on information processing, attitude development and purchase behaviour, and as a general trait, it seems that people who have a tendency to conform in one area will exhibit similar tendencies in others. For example, recent studies have shown as strong tendency for those who are higher in CSII to perceive some brands as being higher in status.[20] This shows that those who are susceptible to interpersonal influence use specific brands to either fit into their social groups or stand out. The influence of CSII has also been shown in the context of

TABLE 4.3 **Sample items from a consumers' need for uniqueness scale***

- I collect unusual products as a way of telling people I'm different.
- When dressing, I have sometimes dared to be different in ways that others are likely to disapprove.
- When products or brands I like become extremely popular, I lose interest in them.
- As far as I'm concerned, when it comes to the products I buy and the situations in which I use them, customs and rules are made to be broken.
- I have sometimes purchased unusual products or brands as a way to create a more distinctive personal image.
- I sometimes look for one-of-a-kind products or brands so that I create a style that is all my own.
- I avoid products or brands that have already been accepted and purchased by the average consumer.

*** This inventory is measured on a 5-point Likert scale ranging from 'strongly agree' to 'strongly disagree'.**

***Source*: Kelly Tepper Tian, William O. Bearden, and Gary L. Hunter, 'Consumers' need for uniqueness: Scale development and validation', *Journal of Consumer Research*, 28, June 2001, pp. 50–66. Reprinted by permission of The University of Chicago Press.**

social issues. However, as a personality trait the influence across issues varies. For example, CSII seems to influence young people's involvement and attitudes towards anti-smoking, but not excessive drinking.[21] By identifying a target market's susceptibility to interpersonal influence, a marketer can create persuasive communications that identify the product or brand's value in helping the individual to fit to their social groups. CSII is generally measured using similar items to that shown in Table 4.4 with higher scores implying greater susceptibility.

OPTIMUM STIMULATION LEVEL

Some people seem to prefer a simple, uncluttered and calm existence, while others prefer an environment crammed with novel, complex and unusual experiences. Consumer research has examined how such variations in need for stimulation may be influenced by selected personality traits, and how, in turn, specific stimulation levels may be related to consumer behaviour.[22] So far, this research has linked high **optimum stimulation levels** (OSL) with more willingness to take risks, try new products, be innovative, seek purchase-related information and accept new retail facilities.

TABLE 4.4 **Example items from the consumer susceptibility to interpersonal influence (CSII)***

- I often consult other people to help choose the best alternative available from within a product class.
- If I want to be like someone, I often try to buy the same brands they buy.
- It is important that others like the products and brands I buy.
- To make sure I buy the right product or brand, I often observe what others are buying and using.
- I often identify with other people by purchasing the same products and brands they purchase.
- If I have little experience with a product, I often ask my friends about the product
- When buying products and brands, I generally purchase those products and brands that I think others will approve of.
- I like to know what products and brands are likely to make good impressions on other people.

*** Scores are based on a bipolar, 7-place rating scale ranging from strongly agree to strongly disagree.**

***Source*: William O. Bearden, Richard G. Netemeyer and Jesse E. Teel, 'Consumer susceptibility to interpersonal influence', *Journal of Consumer Research*, 15, March 1989, pp. 473–481. Reprinted by permission of The University of Chicago Press.**

OSL also seems to reflect a person's desired level of lifestyle stimulation.[23] For instance, if consumers' actual lifestyles are equivalent to their OSL scores, then they are likely to be quite satisfied. On the other hand, if their lifestyles are understimulated (i.e. their OSL is greater than current reality), they are likely to be bored; if their lifestyles are overstimulated (i.e. their OSL is lower than current reality), they are likely to seek rest or relief. This suggests that the relationship between consumers' lifestyles and their OSL is likely to influence their choice of products or services, and how they manage and spend their time. For instance, a person who feels bored (an understimulated consumer) is likely to be attracted to a vacation that offers a great deal of activity and excitement. In contrast, a person who feels overwhelmed (an overstimulated consumer) is likely to seek a quiet, isolated, relaxing, and rejuvenating vacation.

Consumers requiring higher levels of stimulation might be expected to respond favourably to products, service environments and promotional campaigns that stress more, rather than less, risk or excitement. The reverse would be true for consumers seeking lower levels of stimulation.

VARIETY SEEKING

A personality-driven trait quite similar to OSL is **variety seeking**. There appears to be several different types of variety seeking:

- *exploratory purchase behaviour* (e.g. switching brands to experience new and possibly better alternatives);
- *vicarious exploration* (e.g. where the consumer secures information about a new or different alternative, and then contemplates or even daydreams about the option);
- *use innovativeness* (e.g. where the consumer uses an already adopted product in a new or novel way).[24]

The third form of variety seeking—use innovativeness—is particularly relevant to technological products (such as home electronics products, where some models offer an abundance of features and functions, while others contain only a few essential features or functions). For example, researchers found that consumers with higher variety-seeking scores bought calculators with more features than consumers with lower variety-seeking scores.[25]

Research indicates that the consumer innovator differs from the non-innovator in terms of personality orientation. A knowledge of these personality differences should help marketers select target segments for new products and design distinctive promotional strategies for specific segments.

COGNITIVE PERSONALITY FACTORS

Consumer researchers have been increasingly interested in how cognitive personality factors influence various aspects of consumer behaviour. In particular two **cognitive personality traits**—*visualisers vs verbalisers* and *need for cognition*—have shown signs of being useful in understanding selected aspects of consumer behaviour.[26]

Visualisers vs verbalisers

One highly promising area of cognitive personality research classifies consumers as **visualisers** (consumers who prefer visual information and products that stress the visual, such as membership in a videotape cassette club) or **verbalisers** (consumers who prefer written or verbal information and products, such as membership in book clubs or audiotape clubs). Some marketers stress strong visual dimensions to attract visualisers, such as the Pepsi advertisement in Figure 4.6, while others feature a detailed description or point-by-point explanation to attract verbalisers.

Need for cognition

Another promising cognitive personality characteristic is **need for cognition (NFC)**, which measures a person's craving for or enjoyment of thinking. Available research indicates that consumers who are *high* in NFC are more

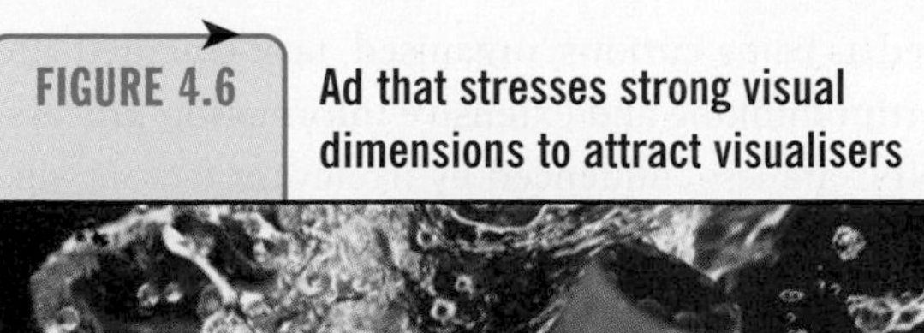

FIGURE 4.6 Ad that stresses strong visual dimensions to attract visualisers

Source: Courtesy of PepsiCo Australia Holdings.

likely to be responsive to the part of an ad that is rich in product-related information or description, and unresponsive to the contextual or peripheral aspects of the ad, such as the presence of a celebrity endorser.[27] In contrast, those consumers who are relatively *low* in NFC are more likely to be attracted to the background or peripheral aspects of an ad, such as an attractive model or well-known celebrity. (See also the discussion on central and peripheral routes to persuasion in Chapters 6 and 7.) Other research suggests that consumers who are high in NFC are more likely to be partial to cool colours (e.g. blue and green) than those who are low in NFC.[28] If substantiated by future research, such insights should provide advertisers with valuable guidelines for creating advertising messages and supporting art (including colour) that appeals to particular target consumers' need for cognition.

Need for cognition (NFC) is defined as an individual's tendency to desire, engage in and enjoy effortful cognition. Specific measures have been developed to identify this trait and, as shown in Table 4.5, they tap into the desire or propensity to engage in higher levels of thinking. Consumers with low NFC appear to process information differently to those with high NFC who are more inclined to form an attitude about an attitude object by relying on easily processable peripheral cues such as humour, boldface slogans or an attractive endorser. Consumers with *high NFC* are more likely to process all product information to arrive at a final consumption decision. Thus, the manner in which information is processed can be determined by an individual's level of NFC. Those with high NFC are motivated to engage in more extensive processing of issue-relevant information and elaboration is high. With this, the central route to persuasion is followed and only those elements that form an objective opinion are influential in making a decision. Conversely, when an individual lacks motivation to process issue-relevant information, as is the case with low NFC, there is minimal elaboration and peripheral cues that are not relevant to forming a reasoned opinion are used.[29]

Individuals with high NFC take considerable time and effort to seek out and carefully scrutinise information[30] and high NFC is associated with the desire to pay greater attention to information and enjoyment in

TABLE 4.5 Example items from a need for cognition (NFC) measure*

- I enjoy a task that involves coming up with new solutions to a problem.
- I prefer a task that is intellectual and difficult to one that does not require much thought.

*** The measure is 10-item scale adapted from Cacioppo and Petty's (1982) 34-item measure.**

***Source*: E. M. Perse, 'Predicting attention to local television news: Need for cognition and motives for viewing', *Communications Reports,* 5(1), 1992, pp. 40–50.**

undertaking complex tasks. Such individuals are characterised as being curious, organised, task-oriented and purposeful in their actions; being motivated to engage in effortful thinking and extensive information processing. When interpreting information, consumers with high NFC are less influenced by irrelevant factors, disregarding non-essential information and attending to the essence of the communication. High NFC is also associated with an individual's willingness to consider new ideas and a sounder self-concept.[31] On the other hand, individuals with low NFC are unmotivated to attend to issue-relevant elements of communications. They tend to depend on, and are more susceptible to easily processable peripheral cues, such as the attractiveness of the person conveying the information, music or the humorous tone of a message.[32] Hence, consumers with low NFC are more likely to be influenced by peripheral cues that they find enjoyable rather than issue-relevant information.[33]

Locus of control

Locus of control (LOC) proposes that some individuals believe that they can control the outcomes by their own actions and personal abilities, others feel that external forces such as fate, luck or chance control their destiny. Those who believe they have personal control are said to have an *internal LOC* while those who feel that their destiny is controlled by other circumstances have an *external LOC*. Measures of LOC identify the tendency to attribute causes and outcomes as shown in Table 4.6. Research has found that those with an internal LOC engage in greater and more complex information search, using various media for their information, while those with external LOC tend to believe more in the 'stability of the marketplace',[34] and so prefer to rely more on information gained in the past. Externals also find advertisements more credible and believe that sales are a signal of quality.

Locus of control can be used to understand where consumers prefer to shop. For example, do they prefer to shop in traditional shopping malls or online via the Web? Traits also help explain information seeking behaviours and perceptions of advertising. It also appears that those with an internal LOC are more likely to be drawn to the Internet in general because they would enjoy using technology that allows them to have a great deal of personal control.[35] Furthermore, people who are mall browsers often feel that they 'do not have enough control over their lives' which would indicate that they are possibly individuals with an external LOC.[36] Because internal LOC is associated with a belief in personal abilities, as well as problem-directed thinking[37] and engagement in greater and more complex information-search, it could be argued that consumers with an

TABLE 4.6 **Example items from a locus of control measure***

- It isn't wise to plan ahead.
- When things go right it's good luck.
- What will happen will happen anyway.
- Success is mostly getting a good break.
- What will be will be.
- Life is a gamble.
- I have little influence over things.

*** Measure is based on an adapted version of the short form of James' Internal-External Locus of Control Scale (1957), with lower score implying internal locus of control and higher score external locus of control. The scale is a 7-item measure of the poles from strongly agree to strongly disagree.**

***Source*: Aron O'Cass, 'Electoral choice: The effect of voter control and involvement on satisfaction and voting stability', *Journal of Political Marketing*, 3(1), 2004, pp. 61–85.**

internal LOC may be drawn to a shopping environment that offers a high level of information. Here they have the opportunity to undertake information search relying only on their own abilities and skills. This would be in keeping with the online shopping environment. Conversely, consumers with an external LOC may prefer the stability of the mall environment where they can rely on past experiences, sales people and other shoppers to assist them. It could be argued that here, the environment is filled with atmospherics rather than descriptive information and the shopper does not need to engage in complex information search.[38]

Self-monitoring

Self-monitoring (SM) recognises that some individuals are more aware of external environmental cues and will adjust their behaviour in a manner that they believe will be more socially appropriate. Those who have this tendency to monitor the environment and modify their behaviour are referred to as *high self-monitors* while those who are less sensitive to external cues are *low self-monitors*. Measures of SM tap into this aspect by identifying the sensitivity and ability components as shown in Table 4.7. Self-monitoring has also been examined in the context of consumption of specific product types. Importantly, the degree to which consumers possess SM characteristics may be reflected in product and brand choices because of differences in orientations and concerns for prestige and appearance. To better understand high and low self-monitors, imagine sitting at a bar where one customer is intent on talking about the contents and taste of her drink while another is far more concerned with what other people may think of her brand-choice of alcohol. The first customer has little regard for what other people might think of her favourite brand of beer, let alone how she happens to look, while the other is far more concerned about the brand's image, what it portrays to other customers and whether or not she has worn the right clothes for the occasion. The former is an example of a low SM and

TABLE 4.7 **Self-monitoring measure***

Ability factor

- In social situations, I have the ability to alter my behaviour if I feel that something else is called for.
- I have the ability to control the way I come across to people, depending on the impression I wish to give them.
- When I feel that the image I am portraying isn't working, I can readily change it to something that does.
- I have trouble changing my behaviour to suit different people and different situations.**
- I have found that I can adjust my behaviour to meet the requirements of any situation in which I find myself.
- Once I know what a situation calls for, it's easy for me to regulate my actions accordingly.

Sensitivity factor

- I am often able to read people's true emotions correctly (through their eyes).
- In conversations, I am sensitive to even the slightest change in the facial expression of the person with whom I am conversing.
- My powers of intuition are quite good when it comes to understanding the emotions and motives of others.
- I can usually tell when others consider a joke to be in bad taste, even though they may laugh convincingly.
- I can usually tell when I've said something inappropriate by reading it in the listener's eyes.
- If someone is lying to me, I usually know it at once from that person's manner of expression.

* Scale based on 6-point strongly agree to strongly disagree, with higher scores indicating higher self-monitoring tendencies.
** Reverse scored items.

Source: Aron O'Cass, 'A psychometric evaluation of a revised version of the Lennox and Wolfe revised self-monitoring scale', *Psychology and Marketing,* 17(5), 2000, pp. 397–419. Copyright © This material is used by permission of John Wiley & Sons, Inc.

the latter, a high SM. High SMs are preoccupied with what others may think of their appearance and actions. They are able to readily interpret interpersonal or situational cues and then respond by changing their behaviour. Low SMs have little concern with either their physical or social environment and, at times, might even avoid situations where they may be required to change their self-image.[39]

Low SMs are relatively insensitive to social cues and often seek goods that offer functionality over style, while high SMs could be thought of as actors on a stage, continually changing their persona to fit the role they believe they are expected to play, and using products to fit in. High SMs have been found to exhibit very different attitudes towards branded and unbranded clothing, believing that an unbranded product must be lower in quality and should be rejected as unacceptable, whereas low SMs seek functional attributes over brand names. High SMs are more influenced by images in advertisements and tend to give socially-based arguments for product purchases, while low SMs make their judgment on the quality of argument offered and give utilitarian-based arguments for purchase decisions, and they generally believe that they have less control over the marketplace and feel somewhat alienated from marketplace events. High SMs may also feel the necessity to browse so that they remain aware of any changes in clothing brands and fashion trends that they may need as props to portray a particular image.[40] When studying specific product types, self-monitoring has been shown to influence consumers' motives for consumption. For example, self-monitoring influences consumers' behaviour related to fashion clothing because it is associated with the degree of interest in maintaining a front through fashion clothing as it can be used as a prop to convey an image of the individual to other people. High self-monitors appeared to have a strong concern for their appearance and image (social-symbolic approval) and a strong emphasis on getting sensory pleasure out of fashion clothing. They appear to be aware of the impressions or messages that fashion clothing sends to others about them and, as such, motives such as social approval are a strong driver for a high self-monitor's choices in fashion clothing. It appears that the direct relationship between self-monitoring and involvement in fashion clothing is very weak, but self-monitoring has an indirect relationship with fashion clothing involvement via specific motives (i.e. symbolic).[41]

Uncertainty orientation

Uncertainty orientation (UO) relates to information seeking and makes a distinction between individuals who actively seek clarity and information about themselves and the environment in which they find themselves (*uncertainty-oriented*), and those who prefer to maintain things as they are, not seeking new information or situations which only causes a sense of confusion (*certainty-oriented*). Those who are *uncertainty-oriented* (UO) are motivated to resolve uncertainty, predisposed to systematically process information during uncertain situations, and possess a discovery-oriented cognitive style.[42] On the other hand, those who are *certainty-oriented* (CO) are more attuned to, and comfortable in handling familiar and safe situations, and for this reason do not deal well with uncertainty. UO individuals actively seek and value new information and continually challenge themselves with new ideas while those who are CO prefer to stay with the status quo within a predictable environment. Those who are UO are open to new ideas, seeking to learn about and understand the world around them. UO individuals have been found to be motivated by diagnostic tasks while those who are CO are more motivated by non-diagnostic tasks.[43] Uncertainty orientation appears to be valuable to marketers in explaining individual differences in consumer information search as well as possibly other consumer processes.

When considering this personality trait and, for example, shopping environments, it would appear that those who are CO will seek an environment that is relatively predictable and one they know well, while new, unknown environments would be avoided. Conversely, those who are UO would actively seek and explore a new environment, particularly where they would have the opportunity to then systematically process information. Thus, it would appear that those who are UO may well find the environment offered online both challenging and sequentially diagnostic. Here they are able to continually seek new information and ideas to resolve uncertainty. The information they acquire can then be systematically processed.[44] Typical items used to measure UO are:

- I believe it is important for us to challenge our beliefs.
- If I do not understand something, I find out about it.

Cognitive personality theory has also been used to predict the identity of opinion leaders by Aron O'Cass (one of this book's authors).[45] Research found that cognitively differentiated individuals (people with more complex views about the world in which they live) were more likely to be opinion leaders. Personality traits are increasingly being studied in the context of a wide variety of consumer behaviour activities, from product purchases to shopping environment preferences. For example, examining consumers' need for cognition, uncertainty orientation, self-monitoring and locus of control regarding the shopping environment preferences of consumers it was found that consumers who are higher SMs, have a greater external LOC, are more CO and have a lower NFC prefer the mall environment. On the other hand, consumers who are lower SMs, have more of an internal LOC, are more UO and higher NFC are drawn to the online environment.[46]

FROM CONSUMER MATERIALISM TO COMPULSIVE CONSUMPTION

Consumer researchers have become increasingly interested in exploring several interrelated consumption and possession traits. These traits range from consumer materialism, to fixated consumption behaviour, to compulsive consumer behaviour.

Consumer materialism

Materialism (or people being materialistic) is a topic frequently appearing in newspapers, magazines and on TV (e.g. 'Australians are very materialistic' 'Australians over-consume') and in everyday conversations between friends ('He's so materialistic!'). Materialism, as a personality-like trait, distinguishes those individuals who regard possessions as essential to their identities and lives, from those for whom possessions are secondary or less important. Researchers testing a measure of materialism have found some general support for the following characteristics of materialistic people:

- They especially value acquiring and showing off possessions.
- They are particularly self-centred and selfish.
- They seek a lifestyle full of possessions (i.e. they desire to have lots of things rather than a simple uncluttered lifestyle).
- Their many possessions do not give them greater personal satisfaction (i.e. possessions do not lead to greater happiness).[47]

Table 4.8 presents sample items from a materialism scale, capturing the dimensions of acquisition centrality, success and happiness.

Fixated consumption behaviour

Somewhere between being materialistic and being compulsive or addictive with respect to buying or possessing objects is the notion of being *fixated* with regard to consuming or possessing. Like materialism, **fixated consumption behaviour** is within the realm of normal and socially acceptable behaviour (i.e. fixated consumers do not keep their objects or purchases of interest a secret; rather, they frequently display them, and their

TABLE 4.8 Measure of consumer materialism*

Acquisition centrality

- The things I own aren't all that important to me.**
- Buying things gives me a lot of pleasure.
- I like a lot of luxury in my life.
- It is important to me to have really nice things (possessions).

Possession defining success

- I admire people who own expensive possessions (such as homes, cars and clothes).
- I don't place much emphasis on the amount of material possessions people own as a sign of success.**
- The things I own say a lot about how well I'm doing in life.
- I like to own things that impress people.
- I don't pay much attention to the material objects people own.**

Acquisition as the pursuit of happiness

- I have all the things I really need to enjoy life.**
- My life would be better if I owned certain things that I don't currently have.
- I'd be happier if I could afford to buy more things (possessions).
- It sometimes bothers me quite a bit that I can't afford to buy all the things I'd like.

*** Measure based on a 6-point Likert scale from strongly agree to strongly disagree.**
**** Reverse scored items.**

***Source*: Aron O'Cass, 'Consumer self-monitoring, materialism and involvement in fashion clothing', *Australasian Marketing Journal*, 9(1), 2001, pp. 46–60.**

involvement is openly shared with others who have a similar interest). Fixated consumers typically possess the following characteristics:

- A deep (possibly passionate) interest in a particular object or product category.
- A willingness to go to considerable lengths to secure additional examples of the object or product category of interest.
- The dedication of a considerable amount of discretionary time and money to searching out the object or product.[48]

This profile of the fixated consumer describes many collectors or hobbyists (e.g. coin, stamp or antique collectors, vintage wristwatch or fountain pen collectors). Research exploring the dynamics of the fixated consumer (in this case, coin collectors) revealed that, for fixated consumers, there is not only enduring involvement in the object category itself, but a considerable amount of involvement in the *process of acquiring* the object (sometimes referred to as the 'hunt').[49]

Compulsive consumption behaviour

Unlike materialism and fixated consumption, **compulsive consumption** lies within the realm of abnormal behaviour. Consumers who are compulsive have an addiction; in some respects they are out of control, and their actions may have damaging consequences to themselves and those around them. Examples of compulsive consumption problems are uncontrollable gambling, drug addiction, alcoholism, and various food and eating disorders.[50] To control, or possibly eliminate, such compulsive problems generally requires some type of therapy or clinical treatment.

There have been some research efforts to develop a screener inventory to pinpoint compulsive consumption.[51] Consumer research into compulsive consumption behaviour would not only benefit those who are personally suffering from this consumption disorder, but would also give marketers a better understanding of the so-called 'normal' consumer.

CONSUMER ETHNOCENTRISM: RESPONSES TO FOREIGN-MADE PRODUCTS

In an effort to distinguish between consumer segments that are likely to be receptive to foreign-made products and those that are not, researchers have developed and tested a **consumer ethnocentrism** scale called CETSCALE as shown in Table 4.9.[52] The CETSCALE results have been encouraging in terms of identifying consumers with a predisposition to accept (or reject) foreign-made products. Consumers who are highly ethnocentric are likely to feel that it is inappropriate or wrong to purchase foreign-made products because of the economic impact on the domestic economy; non-ethnocentric consumers tend to evaluate foreign-made products more objectively for their extrinsic characteristics.

Thus, domestic marketers can attract ethnocentric consumers by stressing a nationalistic theme in their promotional appeals (e.g. 'Made in Australia' or 'Made in America'), since this segment is predisposed to buy products made in their native land. The appeal to Australian made can be seen in Figure 4.7 for the Australian Made campaign which advertises 'Buying Australian Made'.

Marketers should also be aware of the possibility that a 'Made in Australia' distinction may not incite the consumer preference directed purchase. According to a 1993 study by Australian Preference Marketing, 46% of

TABLE 4.9 The consumer ethnocentrism scale—CETSCALE*

- Australian people should always buy Australian-made products instead of imports.
- Only those products that are unavailable in Australia should be imported.
- Buy Australian-made products. Keep Australia working.
- Australian products, first, last and foremost.
- Purchasing foreign-made products is un-Australian.
- It is not right to purchase foreign products, because it puts Australians out of jobs.
- A real Australian should always buy Australian-made products.
- We should purchase products manufactured in Australia instead of letting other countries get rich off us.
- It is always best to purchase Australian products.
- There should be very little trading or purchasing of goods from other countries unless out of necessity.
- Australians should not buy foreign products, because this hurts Australian business and causes unemployment.
- Curbs should be put on all imports.
- It may cost me in the long run, but I prefer to support Australian products.
- Foreigners should not be allowed to put their products in our markets.
- Foreign products should be taxed heavily to reduce their entry into Australia.
- We should buy from foreign countries only those products that we cannot obtain within our own country.
- Australian consumers who purchase products made in other countries are responsible for putting their fellow Australians out of work.

*Response format is a 7-point Likert-type scale (strongly agree = 7, strongly disagree = 1). Range of scores is from 17 to 119. Calculated from confirmatory factor analysis of data from 4-area study.

Source: Adapted from Terence A. Shimp and Subhash Sharma, 'Consumer ethnocentrism: Construction and validation of the CETSCALE', *Journal of Marketing Research*, 24, August 1987, p. 282. Reprinted with permission of the American Marketing Association.

the Australian respondents agreed that 'It is not worth it to me to pay more to buy Australian-made'. Therefore, if a special 'Made in Australia' marketing campaign is going to result in a marked increase in the product's cost, those marketers who lack an awareness of consumer behaviour may actually end up decreasing product sales.

In the same study, as many as 77% of the respondents indicated they 'would buy Australian' if the price was the same (depending on the type of product—i.e. food, clothing, cars, etc.). In the ad shown in Figure 4.8, Sunbeam Corporation Limited is banking on the 'Made in Australia' sentiment by marketing its traditional values and warm continued relationship with the Australian consumer. (Notice the Australian-made symbol in the lower left-hand corner of the ad.) In an advertisement for a brand of headache remedy, manufactured by Herron, consumers are informed that Australian-made is not good enough; Herron products are both Australian-made *and* Australian-owned.

Responses to foreign-made products

Table 4.10 presents a marketing mix strategy that can be used to manage country-of-origin effects. Specifically, if marketers determine that the potential customers in a particular country possess a positive image of products made in the country in which their products originate, the marketers may be able to create a marketing mix strategy that follows options in the positive column. In contrast, if marketers assess that the potential customers in a particular country possess a negative image of products made in the country in which their products originate, the marketers might be wise to elect a marketing mix strategy that follows options in the negative column.

FIGURE 4.7 **Emphasising buying Australian made**

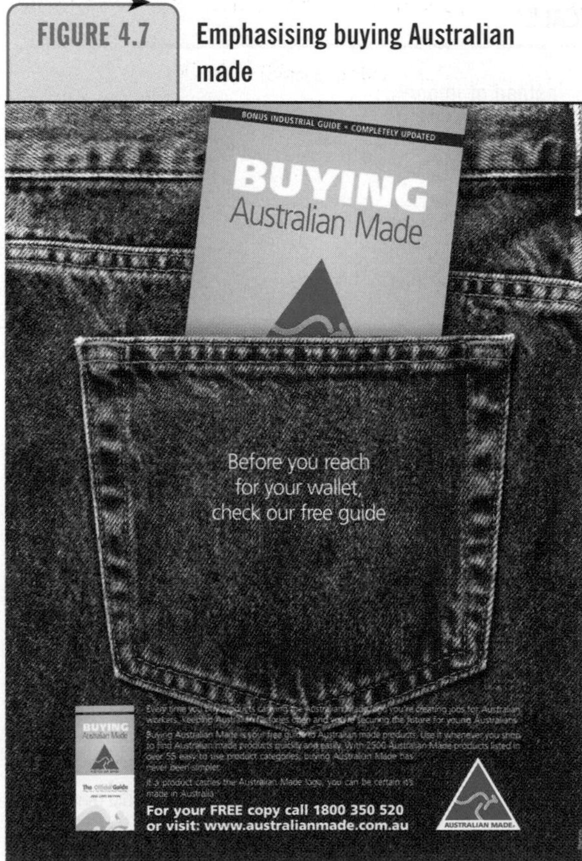

Source: Courtesy of Australian Made Campaign.

FIGURE 4.8 **Ad that employs an ethnocentric appeal**

Source: Courtesy of Sunbeam Corporation Limited.

TABLE 4.10 Strategies for managing country-of-origin effects

Marketing mix	Country image Positive	 Negative
Product	Emphasise 'Made In'	Emphasise brand name
Price	Premium price	Low price to attract value conscious
Place (channel of distribution)	Exclusive locations	Establish supply chain partners
Promotion	Country image Nation sponsored	Brand image Manufacturer sponsored

Source: Osman Mohamad, Zafar U. Ahmed, Earl D. Honeycutt, Jr and Taizoon Hyder Tyebkhan, 'Does "Made in..." matter to consumers? A Malaysian study of country of origin effect', *Multinational Business Review*, Fall 2000, p. 73.

Consumer self-concept

The notion of consumer self-concept has been the focus of extensive study for many years by consumer researchers. Self-concept is seen as the totality of the individual's thoughts and feelings in reference to themselves as an object. Importantly, the behaviour of consumers is often directed toward enhancing their self-concept through the consumption of products and services as symbols. Self-image has been considered a multidimensional construct, with various forms of the self, such as actual, ideal and social (among others).

Self and self-images

Consumers have a number of enduring images of themselves. These self-images, or perceptions of self, are very closely associated with personality, in that we tend to buy products and services, and patronise retailers, with images or 'personalities' that closely correspond to our own self-image. For example, the advertisement shown in Figure 4.9 identifies a clear appeal by Seiko to image by identifying 'It's not your car. It's not your friends. It's not your job. It's your watch that tells most about who you are.' The Seiko ad uses a basic appeal to self-image and its enhancement through key brands. In the five-factor model discussed earlier in this chapter, self-concept is one of the factors. Self-concept is influenced by the 'Big Five', the situation and the individual's history, and in turn influences behaviour. In this section, we examine the issue of one self or multiple selves, and explore the makeup of the self-image, the notion of the extended self, and the possibilities of altering the self-image.

FIGURE 4.9 Seiko appeal to image

IT'S NOT YOUR CAR.
IT'S NOT YOUR FRIENDS.
IT'S NOT YOUR JOB.
IT'S YOUR WATCH THAT
TELLS MOST ABOUT WHO YOU ARE.
ARCTURA
KINETIC
SEIKO
seiko.com.au

Source: Courtesy of Seiko Australia Pty Ltd.

ONE SELF OR MULTIPLE SELVES?

Historically, individual consumers have been thought to have 'a single self'—and to be interested in products and services that satisfy that single self. However, research indicates that it is more accurate to think of the consumer in terms of a **multiple self** or multiple selves.[53] The change in thinking reflects the understanding that a single consumer is likely to act quite differently with different people and in different situations. For instance, a person is likely to behave differently at a museum opening, at school, at work, with parents, and with friends at a night club. The healthy or normal person is likely to be a somewhat different person in each of these different situations or social roles. In fact, acting exactly the same in all situations or roles is likely to be a sign of an abnormal or unhealthy person.

An important ramification of having more than one self-image is that the traits activated in one self may not be as important in another self. In terms of consumer behaviour, the idea that an individual embodies a number of different 'selves' (i.e. has multiple self-images) suggests that marketers should target their products and services to consumers *within the context of a particular self.* (The notion of a consumer having multiple selves or multiple roles is consistent with the idea of use-situation segmentation discussed in Chapter 2.)

THE MAKEUP OF THE SELF-IMAGE

Despite our varying social roles, we all have an image of ourself as a certain kind of person, with certain traits, habits, possessions, relationships and ways of behaving. As with our personality, our self-image is unique, the outgrowth of our background and experience. We develop our self-image through interactions with other people: initially our parents, then other individuals or groups with whom we relate over the years.

Products and brands have symbolic value for us, and we evaluate them on the basis of their consistency (i.e. congruence) with our personal picture or image of ourself. Some products seem to match our self-image; others seem totally alien. It is generally held that consumers attempt to preserve or enhance their self-image by selecting products with 'images' or 'personalities' they believe are congruent with their own self-image, and avoiding products that are not.[54]

A variety of self-image constructs has been identified in the consumer behaviour literature. One popular model depicts four specific kinds of self-image:

1. **actual self-image** (i.e. how consumers in fact see themselves);
2. **ideal self-image** (i.e. how consumers would like to see themselves);
3. **social self-image** (i.e. how consumers feel others see them);
4. **ideal social self-image** (i.e. how consumers would like others to see them).[55]

Other research has identified a fifth type of self-image, **expected self-image** (i.e. how consumers expect to see themselves at some specified future time). The expected self-image is somewhere between the actual and ideal self-images. It is somewhat like a future-oriented combination of 'what is' (the actual self-image) and what consumers 'would like to be' (the ideal self-image). Moreover, because the expected self-image provides consumers with a realistic opportunity to change the 'self', it is likely to be more valuable to marketers than the actual or ideal self-image as a guide for designing and promoting products.

In different contexts (i.e. in different situations and/or with respect to different products), consumers might select a different self-image to guide their attitudes or behaviour. For instance, for products that we consume privately, such as household products, consumers might be guided by their actual self-image. For socially-enhancing or socially-conspicuous products, they might be guided by their social self-image. When it comes to vacations, or even clothing, they might be guided by either ideal self-image or ideal social self-image.

The concept of self-image has strategic implications for marketers. For example, marketers can segment their markets on the basis of relevant consumer self-images, and then position their products or stores as symbols of such self-images. Such a strategy is consistent with the marketing concept, in that the marketer first assesses the needs of a consumer segment (with respect to both the product category and to an appropriate symbol of self-image) and then proceeds to develop and market a product or service that meets both criteria. Another approach is the assessment of the discrepancy or difference between a consumer's self-concept (self-images) and product or brand images. This approach has been used to study differences in the perceptions of eastern versus western brands of fashion clothing,[56] of individual characteristics, perceptions of a brand's status and self-image brand-image congruency.[57] Self-image product-image congruency has also been studied. Such studies indicate that the self-concept is important because different perceptions of the self influence purchase behaviour and decisions, and how and why consumers provide status to a brand as well as product usage to communicate their image to others. Some of the leading authorities on self-concept propose that consumer behaviour is, in part, determined by the congruence resulting from a psychological comparison involving the product-user image and the consumer's self-concept. We are now able to measure a consumer's self-concept and self-image product-image congruency. As shown in Table 4.11, self-concept can be measured via identifying particular

TABLE 4.11 **Examples of measures of self-concept and self-image product-image congruency**

Self-concept measure[a][b]

Please rate how you see yourself on the following descriptive word pairs by circling a number in each row closer to the word that describes you.

Rugged	1	2	3	4	5	6	7	Delicate
Exciting	1	2	3	4	5	6	7	Calm
Thrifty	1	2	3	4	5	6	7	Indulgent
Youthful	1	2	3	4	5	6	7	Mature
Formal	1	2	3	4	5	6	7	Informal
Colorless	1	2	3	4	5	6	7	Colorful

Global assessment of self-image product-image congruency

These items relate to the images you have of Calvin Klein clothing and your own self-image. Think for a moment about the way you actually see yourself (your actual self) and how you would ideally like to be (your ideal self). Then read each statement and respond to how you see Calvin Klein and how you see your actual self and your ideal self.

Calvin Klein's image is very similar to my **actual** image.

1 2 3 4 5 6

The brand's image and my **actual** image are quite similar.

1 2 3 4 5 6

Calvin Klein portrays an image very similar to the image I would **ideally** like to have or portray.

1 2 3 4 5 6

The image I would **ideally** like to have or portray and the image of Calvin Klein is quite similar.

1 2 3 4 5 6

[a] **The original scale had 20 items.**

Sources:

[b] **Adapted from Naresh Malhotra, 'A scale to measure self-concepts, person concepts and product concepts', *Journal of Marketing Research*, 8 November 1981, pp. 456–464.**

[c] **Adapted from Aron O'Cass and Kenny Lim, 'The influence of brand associations on brand preference and purchase intention: An Asian perspective on brand associations', *Journal of International Consumer Marketing*, 14(2/3), 2002, pp. 41–72.**

[d] **Aron O'Cass and Hmily Frost, 'Status brands and brand associations', *Australian New Zealand Marketing Academy Conference Proceedings*, Melbourne, 2002, (eds) Robin Shaw, Steward Adam and Heath McDonald, pp. 1381–1388.**

[e] **Aron O'Cass and Thomas Muller, 'A study of Australian materialistic values, product involvement and self-image/product-image congruency relationships for fashion clothing', *The Ninth Biennial World Marketing Congress*, Academy of Marketing Science, 1999, pp. 402–404.**

images individuals may hold of themselves. The original scale contains 20 items and can be used to assess self-concept and product-concept. Self-image product-image congruency can also be used to assess global images and study the discrepancy between self and products or brands. For example, Table 4.11 shows a more contemporary measure of self-image product-image congruency adapted from the work of Joseph Sirgy.

THE EXTENDED SELF

The relationship between consumers' self-images and their possessions (i.e. objects they call their own) is an exciting topic for consumer research. Specifically, consumers' possessions can be seen to define, confirm or extend their self-images. For instance, acquiring a desired or sought-after racing bicycle might serve to expand or enrich Mary's image or 'self'. Mary might now see herself as being more competitive, more fit and more successful, because she has added the bicycle to her inventory of self-enhancing possessions. Consumers have also been found to use products to help them through transitional periods in their life. When a consumer is going from high school to university there are some negative psychological consequences that accompany the transition. Consumers often use possessions from the past or new possessions that reflect the past to ease the transition.[58]

The above examples suggest that much human emotion can be connected to valued possessions. In such cases, possessions can be considered extensions of the self.[59] It has been proposed that possessions can extend the self in a number of ways:

- Actually, by allowing the person to do things that otherwise would be very difficult or impossible to accomplish (e.g. problem solving using a computer).
- Symbolically, by making the person feel better or 'bigger' (e.g. receiving an employee award for excellence or driving an expensive and 'sexy' car).
- By conferring status or rank (e.g. status among collectors of rare works of art because of the ownership of a particular masterpiece).
- By conferring feelings of immortality, by leaving valued possessions to young family members (this also has the potential of extending the recipients' 'selves').
- By conferring magical powers (e.g. a ring inherited from one's grandmother might be perceived as a magic amulet bestowing good luck when it is worn, or any good luck charm).[60]

The ad in Figure 4.10 for Brilliant Brunette™ appeals to aspects of the self-concept, focusing on the **extended self** with such copy as 'Expose your glamorous side, your stunning, luminous, Brunette Goddess side', which encourages the consumer to use the brand to communicate information about their self-concept. The ad in Figure 4.11 suggests that the brand can affect our confidence in self.

FIGURE 4.10 **Ad appealing to the extended self**

brilliant
brunette.
Expose your glamorous side.
Your stunning, luminous,
BRUNETTE GODDESS side.
Introducing Brilliant Brunette®
the first shampoo, conditioner and styling line just for brunettes
Be a little more stare-worthy. Illuminate your full range of brunette - amber to maple, chestnut to espresso - without changing the color that makes you a stunning brunette. Show off your highlights. Get multi-dimensional shine. Brilliant Brunette. Expose your goddess side.
www.johnfrieda.com
JOHN FRIEDA.
london · paris · new york

Source: Courtesy of Kao Brands.

ALTERING THE SELF

Sometimes consumers wish to change themselves—to become a different or 'improved' self. Clothing, grooming aids and all kinds of accessories (e.g. cosmetics, jewellery)

FIGURE 4.11 **Brand usage helps boost confidence in self**

Hirudoid is widely used to speed up the healing of bruises – up to 50% faster.

But the good news is that Hirudoid also has a beneficial effect on the appearance of scars. Studies have shown that Hirudoid softens scars, increases flexibility of the scar tissue, reduces redness and results in a better cosmetic appearance. You can look your best with Hirudoid, scientifically proven. Available in pharmacies and Priceline stores.

For a free sample please call 1800 653 373.

Always read the label. Use only as directed. If symptoms persist see your healthcare professional.
ASMI/9748-08/04
ambacommunications

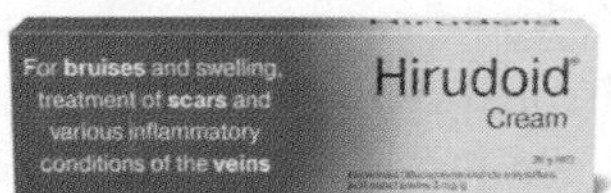

Accelerates your body's healing

Source: **Courtesy of Key Pharmaceuticals.**

offer consumers the opportunity to modify their appearance and thereby to alter their self-image. In using 'self-altering products', consumers are frequently attempting to express their individualism or uniqueness by creating a new self, maintaining the existing self (or preventing the loss of self) or extending the self (modifying or changing the self).

Altering one's self, particularly one's appearance or body parts, can be accomplished by cosmetics (see Figure 4.12), hair restyling or colouring, switching from eye glasses to contact lenses (or the reverse) or undergoing cosmetic surgery.[61] By using these options, it is possible to create a 'new' or 'improved' person. Some people also call upon image consultants to achieve an appropriate and mutually agreed upon self-image.[62] Image consultants provide clients with advice on such personal attributes as clothing, colour, presentation, appearance, posture, speaking and media skills.

FIGURE 4.12 **Altering one's self, particularly one's appearance or body parts, can be accomplished by cosmetics**

Source: **Courtesy of Avon.**

BRAND PERSONALITY

Whilst the focus above is on human personality, we often also talk in terms of brand personality. That inanimate objects such as brands can be associated with human characteristics is now quite widely accepted amongst consumer researchers. Consumers tend to ascribe various descriptive 'personality-like' traits or characteristics—the ingredients of brand personalities—to different brands in a wide variety of product categories. For instance, in the United Kingdom, Foster's brand is associated with Australia. According to those watching the beer industry, 'Australia is seen as "the land of sunshine and plenty" and the ideal place to live'. For UK consumers, Australia equals 'great attitude, great life, great beer'. Recent campaigns for Foster's have used Australian comedians Roy Slaven and HG Nelson to communicate 'the witty, optimistic "no worries" Australian attitude to life', and is not dissimilar to the use of original brand spokesman Paul Hogan who single-handedly invented the laid-back, blunt-speaking attitude.

Although human and brand personalities may have similar structures, they are formed differently. Human personality traits are inferred by a human's behaviour, physical characteristics, attitudes, beliefs and demographic characteristics.[63] Brand personality is inferred by the set of human characteristics typical of the user of the brand, or the brand's endorsers. The traits of the people associated with the brand are transferred to the brand.[64] **Brand personality** is also inferred by the advertising style, price, brand name or logo.[65] Research has identified that the 'Big Five' for the brand may differ from the 'Big Five' associated with human personality.[66] Brand personality can be explained by aspects such as sincerity, excitement, competence, sophistication and ruggedness. Recently, brand personality has been used to examine the preferences and purchase intentions of eastern and western brands of fashion clothing. It was found that brand personality of a fashion clothing brand could be explained by five broad personality characteristics including excitement, sincerity, sophistication, competence and ruggedness. The study also showed that the personality assigned to a brand was strongly related to preference and purchase intention of specific brands.[67]

Along these lines, marketers in the car industry have often chosen to market their product by positioning favourable personality traits within an image developed in advertisements. The car is portrayed, not as a car, but rather as an extension of the personality of the targeted consumer group. Maserati (Figure 4.13) uses the desirable personality trait of 'independence'. The ad challenges the consumer to 'Be your own knight in shining armour'. It is clear that Maserati is not trying to sell the consumer a car *per se*, but rather a desirable personality and identity.

FIGURE 4.13 **Maserati positions the desirable personality trait of 'independence'**

Source: Courtesy of Maserati.

CASE STUDY 4.1

Involvement, Self-Concept and Murdoch Magazines

Michael Edwardson, School of Marketing, Victoria University

Walk into any newsagency and you can't fail to be immediately struck by the hundreds of magazines on offer, everything from lifestyle, sport and recreation, business and investment, to fashion, entertainment, motoring and computers.

Each year sees the launch of new titles, targeted at seemingly more and more segmented audiences. Whilst some succeed over the long term, eventually becoming part of people's lives, others often fail within months, failing to attract circulation and advertising revenue. The experience that readers have with the magazine such as being 'relevant and useful', 'grabs me visually' or 'inspires me' is critically important.[68]

You may have your own favourite magazines that you subscribe to, buy each week or month, or that you regularly browse through at the newsagency.

Now imagine yourself as a brand manager or advertiser trying to make the decision about which magazine to advertise in. All of a sudden how people relate to the magazine becomes all-important. How do they read it? Do they skim through it? Do they read the advertisements as extensions of the editorial, or are the ads totally unconnected to the content of the stories?

At Murdoch Magazines, such questions have been central to the success of their publications. As publishers of some of the leading circulation titles in Australia: *Marie Claire*, *Better Homes and Gardens*, *Men's Health*, they are committed to increasing reader involvement with their magazines.

Involvement is a theoretical concept with which any student of consumer behaviour would be more than familiar. At Murdoch Magazines, however, involvement is more than just theory. It is central to the company vision and the strategy of their publications.

> *Our readers are hungry for information to make decisions—and most importantly they are ready to act on this information. What a powerful environment for advertisers! . . . Murdoch Magazines are therefore dedicated to service journalism. Service journalism is about building a strong magazine/reader relationship by helping consumers do things that, in one way or another enrich their lives—as opposed to magazines that primarily seek to entertain, provide light relief, pictures, gossip or unattainable dreams—Matt Handbury, Chairman, Murdoch Magazines*

Murdoch Magazines pays strong attention to ongoing research to assess their connection to the consumer. As part of their program of research they recently commissioned a consumer psychology study to explore in depth the whole platform of involvement.[69] This comprised a unique combination of consumer behaviour and the latest techniques from experimental social psychology.

This particular study was focused on assessing experimentally how involvement could be measured through the link between self-concept and the reader's magazine. If the magazine is indeed central to people's lives then it stands to reason that it should also be linked to a person's sense of self and hence the way they relate to the magazine.

Such questions involve not only understanding consumer and social psychology but also necessitate the use of valid and reliable procedures and measures.

The research team used a multi-method approach which comprised, amongst other techniques, two instruments: The Personal Involvement Inventory[70] and The Implicit Association Test.[71]

The Personal Involvement Inventory is a 20-item scale that is one of the most cited in the consumer behaviour literature.[72]

The Implicit Association Test is an exciting new technique in social cognition that measures implicit or unconscious associations through a reaction time task. You can visit the Implicit Association Test website at <https://implicit.harvard.edu/implicit> and read more about the technique, see other research studies and also conduct the test yourself. It is especially useful in testing for self-concept related associations.

In the research into magazine involvement, respondents were 78 female readers (25–44 years of age) who regularly read both *Better Homes and Gardens* and *Women's Weekly* (having bought three to four out of the last six issues). Half had a slight preference for *Women's Weekly* and half had a slight preference for *Better Homes and Gardens*. In other words they read both magazines regularly. It was a conservative test of the concepts because if anything the possibility of there being any differences was minimised. *Women's Weekly* was chosen as the comparison magazine as it is the highest circulation monthly women's magazine. *Better Homes and Gardens* is the circulation leader in the Lifestyle magazine category.

The methodology used a within-subjects repeated measures design. Respondents were recruited over the telephone and invited to attend a central location research session. They completed the computer based IAT test first and then moved on to the paper and pencil Involvement Inventory. They were 'blind' to the purpose of the research and the researchers were not present during the experimental procedure.

Although there were other tests used and many more relationships investigated, there were three key hypotheses that were tested:

1. Readers should have significantly higher involvement with *Better Homes and Gardens* than *Women's Weekly*, as measured by the Personal Involvement Inventory. This was not because they didn't like *Women's Weekly* or that it wasn't fun to read, but because *Better Homes and Gardens* was related more to taking action and doing things in one's life. Previous research had indicated that *Better Homes and Gardens* was read as a source for information whilst *Women's Weekly* was read more for entertainment/enjoyment.
2. Readers would have faster IAT reaction times for the association between their self-concept and *Better Homes and Gardens* than for their self-concept and *Women's Weekly*. This was because what people do to make their lives better is more related to their sense of self or their striving to express their ideal self-concept. The research team called this Identity Involvement. People should therefore be quicker overall at reacting to 'Me and *Better Homes and Gardens*' associations in the IAT test, and slower to reacting to 'Me and *Women's Weekly*'.
3. Faster IAT scores should be significantly associated with higher involvement scores. This is a fundamental test of the convergent validity of the two related constructs, and methodologies.

Let's look at the results.

Firstly which magazine were readers more involved with as measured by the Personal Involvement Inventory? Figure 4.14 below shows the 95% Confidence Intervals for the mean Involvement scale scores for both magazines.

FIGURE 4.14 Personal involvement scores: *Better Homes and Gardens* and *Women's Weekly*

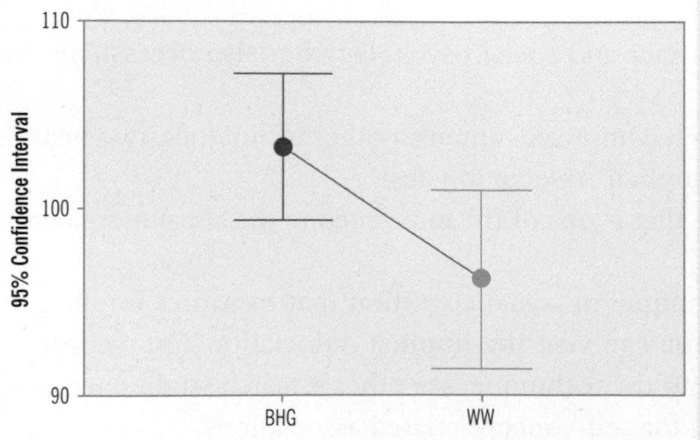

There was a significant difference (p = .025) between the mean scores for *Better Homes and Gardens* and *Women's Weekly*. The readers in the study enjoyed both magazines, yet they felt significantly more involved with *Better Homes and Gardens*.

Looking at the results of the Implicit Association Test we can see from Figure 4.15 that readers who preferred *Better Homes and Gardens* had significantly faster average response times for 'Me and *Better Homes and Gardens*' associations than they did for 'Me and *Women's Weekly*' (p = .038). These reaction times are measured in milliseconds. The readers who preferred *Women's Weekly* had faster response times for 'Me and *Women's Weekly*' than they did for 'Me and *Better Homes and Gardens*' as would be expected. The response times for *Better Homes and Gardens* were, however, faster overall as predicted.

Furthermore *Women's Weekly* preference readers did not distinguish between their preferred and non-preferred magazines as strongly as *Better Homes and Gardens* preference readers did. We can attribute this difference between the preference groups to the fact that BHG preference readers are more strongly *identity involved* with BHG.

FIGURE 4.15 IAT reaction time scores

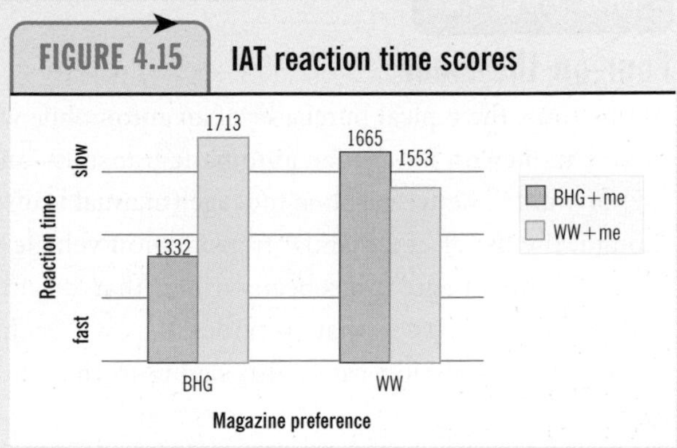

Note: Faster scores indicate closer associations.

The association between the IAT reaction times and the Involvement Inventory was (r = 0.32, p = .005) for *Women's Weekly* and (r = 0.35, p = .002) for *Better Homes and Gardens*. In other words people's implicit association between their self-concept and the magazine (identity involvement) was significantly related to their stated personal involvement with the magazine. Whilst the two methods measure two different constructs in quite different ways, they are obviously conceptually related.

Putting the Murdoch Magazines 'Involvement' platform to a scientific experimental consumer psychology test supported the foundation of their strategy of service journalism. Readers were more personally involved with *Better Homes and Gardens* and this involvement was reflected in their unconscious self-concept associations.

Further data collected in the complete project indicated that this stronger personal and identity involvement with *Better Homes and Gardens* also translated into spending more time reading the magazine and a greater likelihood of trying new ideas and purchasing from the magazine.

The research shows how the concepts derived in consumer behaviour research and the related discipline of social psychology have direct relevance to the real world of publishing. Next time you browse through those magazines in the newsagent or read the stories and look at the ads, think how involved its readers are. Think about how they read the editorial content and the advertisements and whether the editorial and ads connect to the reader's self-concept. It could be a crucial business decision to an advertiser.

The research team for the project: Michael Edwardson, School of Marketing, UNSW; Professor Ladd Wheeler, School of Psychology, UNSW; Dr Kipling Williams, School of Psychology, UNSW; Cassandra Govan, School of Psychology, UNSW; Deborah Davis, Strategic Consultant, Murdoch Magazines; Ada Giaquinto, Research Manager, Murdoch Magazines; Kate Maloney, Senior Researcher, Murdoch Magazines.

Special thanks to Professor Anthony Greenwald at Washington University for permission to use the IAT test, and Mark Day, Managing Director, Surveytalk for the fieldwork management.

Note: For further research into magazines and reader involvement visit the Magazine Publishers of Australia website at <www.magazines.org.au>.

Case Study Questions

1. Why should involvement be related to advertising in magazines? If you were an advertiser what would be the advantages of a service journalism based magazine?
2. What are some problems in explicit (paper and pencil) methods to measure self-concept and associations with it? What is the benefit of the IAT approach? (visit the website to learn more about it).
3. How would involvement and self-concept relate to advertising in other media?
4. What sorts of products and services advertising would be suited to entertainment-based magazines and why?
5. What sorts of magazines do you read and why? Which ones are you more involved with and which ones are more representative of who you are or who you would like to be?

CASE STUDY 4.2

Four-on-the-Floor

At one time, the typical purchaser of an automobile with a manual transmission was an individual who wanted to save money on his car (an automatic transmission can sometimes add more than $1000 to the price of the car) or wanted better gasoline mileage (manual transmissions usually offer slightly better gas mileage). Today, though, the buyer of a manual-transmission vehicle is most likely to be an affluent, college-educated male at least 45 years of age. It has been written that 'driving a stick shift reflects a preoccupation with authenticity and the unrefined . . . that provides its own cachet in our plastic, materalistic society'. The driver of a manual-transmission car is also saying to the world 'I would rather drive the car than have the car drive me.'

Research results also reveal that owners of cars with manual transmissions are more likely than the average US consumer to cook from scratch, do their own financial planning, and engage in 'solo' leisure activities, such as jogging and skiing. They also like to make their own bread and pasta and prefer buying foods that require more work (e.g. they brew coffee rather than spoon out instant coffee).

Source: Michael J. Weiss, 'Feel of the road,' *American Demographics*, March 2001, pp. 72–73.

Case Study Question

1. Considering the discussion of trait theory in Chapter 4, which traits do you believe owners of manual transmission vehicles might score higher or lower on than the general US population?

Summary

Personality may be described as an amalgam of the psychological characteristics that both determine and reflect how we respond to our environment. Although personality tends to be consistent and enduring, it may change abruptly in response to major life events, as well as gradually over time.

Three theories of personality are prominent in the study of consumer behaviour: Freudian theory, and neo-Freudian and trait theory. Freud's psychoanalytic theory provides the foundation for the study of motivational research, operating on the premise that human drives are largely unconscious in nature and serve to motivate many consumer actions.

Neo-Freudian theory focuses on personality types. Consumer researchers are interested in four pairs of personality types: sensing–intuiting, thinking–feeling, extroversion–introversion and judging–perceiving. Each pair of dimensions reflects two distinctly different personality characteristics which influence consumer responses to the world around them.

Trait theory is a major departure from the qualitative or subjective approach to personality measurement. It postulates that individuals possess innate psychological traits (neuroticism, extroversion, openness to experience, agreeableness and conscientiousness) to a greater or lesser degree, and that these traits can be measured by specially designed scales. Because personality inventories are simple to use and score, and can be self-administered, they are the preferred method for many researchers in the assessment of consumer personality.

Each individual has a perceived self-image (or multiple self-images) as a certain kind of person with certain traits, habits, possessions, relationships and ways of behaving. Consumers frequently attempt to preserve, enhance, alter or extend their self-image by purchasing products or services and shopping at stores believed to be consistent with the relevant self-image, and by avoiding products and stores that are not.

Discussion questions

1. Although no two individuals have identical personalities, how would you explain the fact that personality is sometimes used in consumer research to identify distinct and sizeable market segments?
2. Contrast the main characteristics of the following personality theories:
   (a) Freudian theory
   (b) Neo-Freudian theory
   (c) Trait theory.
   In your answer, illustrate how each theory is applied to the understanding of consumer behaviour.
3. Describe trait theory. Give five examples of how personality traits can be used in consumer research.
4. How can a marketer of cameras use the research findings that its target market consists primarily of (a) inner-directed or other-directed consumers, and (b) consumers who are high (or low) on innovativeness?
5. Describe the type of promotional message that would be most suitable for each of the following personality market segments and give an example of each:
   (a) highly dogmatic consumers
   (b) inner-directed consumers
   (c) consumers with high optimum stimulation levels
   (d) consumers with a high need for recognition
   (e) consumers who are visualisers vs consumers who are verbalisers.
6. Is there likely to be a difference in personality traits between individuals who readily purchase foreign-made products and those who prefer Australian-made products? How can marketers use the consumer ethnocentrism scale to segment consumers?
7. A marketer of health food is attempting to segment its market on the basis of Australian consumers' self-image. Describe the four types of consumer self-image and discuss which one(s) would be most effective for the stated purpose.

Exercises

1. How do your clothing preferences differ from those of your friends? What personality differences might explain why your preferences are different from those of other people?
2. Find three print advertisements based on Freudian personality theory. Discuss how Freudian concepts are used in these ads. Do any of the ads 'personify' a brand? If so, how?
3. Find three print ads based on trait theory. Discuss how traits are used in the ads.
4. Administer the items from the materialism scale (listed in Table 4.8) to two of your friends. In your view, are their consumption behaviours consistent with their scores on the scale? Why, or why not?

Key terms

actual self-image *(p. 120)*
brand personality *(p. 124)*
cognitive personality traits *(p. 110)*
compulsive consumption *(p. 116)*
consumer ethnocentrism *(p. 117)*
consumer innovativeness *(p. 107)*
dogmatism *(p. 107)*
ego *(p. 100)*
expected self-image *(p. 120)*
extended self *(p. 122)*
fixated consumption behaviour *(p. 115)*
id *(p. 100)*
ideal self-image *(p. 120)*
ideal social self-image *(p. 120)*
inner-directed consumers *(p. 108)*
materialism *(p. 115)*
multiple self *(p. 120)*
need for cognition *(p. 110)*
optimum stimulation levels (OSLs) *(p. 109)*
other-directed consumers *(p. 108)*
personality *(p. 99)*
psychoanalytic theory of personality *(p. 100)*
single-trait personality test *(p. 105)*
social character *(p. 108)*
social self-image *(p. 120)*
superego *(p. 100)*
trait *(p. 104)*
trait theory *(p. 104)*
variety seeking *(p. 110)*
verbalisers *(p. 110)*
visualisers *(p. 110)*

Endnotes

1. L. A Pervin, 'Personality: A view of the future based on a look at the past', *Journal of Research in Personality*, 30, 1996, pp. 309–318.
2. R. M. Liebert and L. L. Liebert, *Liebert and Spiegler's Personality Strategies and Issues*, 8th edn (Pacific Grove, CA: Brooks/Cole Publishing Company, 1998), p. 309.
3. Amanda B. Diekman and Alice H. Eagly, 'Stereotypes as dynamic constructs: Women and men of the past, present, and future', *Personality and Social Psychology Bulletin*, 26(10), October 2000, pp. 1171–1188.
4. Ellen Creager, 'Do snack foods such as nuts and popcorn affect romance?', *The Patriot-News*, Harrisburg, PA, 14 February 2001, p. E11.
5. For example, see Karen Horney, *The Neurotic Personality of Our Time* (New York: Norton, 1937).
6. Joel B. Cohen, 'An interpersonal orientation to the study of consumer behavior', *Journal of Marketing Research*, 6, August 1967, pp. 270–278; Arch G. Woodside and Ruth Andress, 'CAD eight years later', *Journal of the Academy of Marketing Science*, 3, Summer–Fall 1975, pp. 309–313; see also Jon P. Noerager, 'An assessment of CAD: A personality instrument developed specifically for marketing research', *Journal of Marketing Research*, 16, February 1979, pp. 53–59; and Pradeep K. Tyagi, 'Validation of the CAD instrument: A replication', *Advances in Consumer Research*, 10, eds Richard P. Bogazzio and Alice M. Tybout (Ann Arbor, MI: Association for Consumer Research, 1983), pp. 112–114.
7. Morton I. Jaffe, 'Brand-loyalty/variety-seeking and the consumer's personality: Comparing children and young adults', in *Proceedings of the Society for Consumer Psychology*, eds Scott B. MacKenzie and Douglas M. Stayman (La Jolla, CA: American Psychological Association, 1995), pp. 144–151.
8. J. P Gilford, *Personality* (New York: McGraw-Hill, 1959), p .6.
9. E. J. Phares, *Introduction to Personality,* 3rd edn (New York: Harper Collins, 1991).
10. Paul T. Costa and Robert R. McCrae, 'Normal personality assessment in clinical practice: The NEO Personality Inventory', *Psychological Assessment,* 4, 1992, pp. 5–13.
11. Robert R. McCrae and Paul T. Costa Jr, 'Toward a new generation of personality theories: Theoretical contexts for the five-factor model', in Jerry S. Wiggins (ed.), *The Five-Factor Model of Personality: Theoretical Perspectives* (New York: Guilford Press, 1996), pp. 51–87.
12. Kerry Courneya and Laura-Ann Hellsten, 'Personality correlates of exercise behavior, motives, barriers and preferences: An application of the five-factor model', *Personality and Individual Differences*, 24(5), pp. 625–633.
13. Ronald E. Goldsmith and Charles F. Hofacker, 'Measuring consumer innovativeness', *Journal of the Academy of Marketing Science*, 19, 1991, pp. 209–221; William O. Bearden, Richard G. Netemeyer and Jesse E. Teel, 'Further validation of the consumer susceptibility to interpersonal influence scale', in Marvin E. Goldberg, Gerald Gorn and Richard W. Pollay (eds), *Advances in Consumer Research*, 17 (Provo, UT: Association for Consumer Research, 1990), pp. 770–776; Russell W. Belk, 'Three scales to measure constructs related to materialism: Reliability, validity, and relationships to measures of happiness', in Thomas C. Kinnear (ed.), *Advances in Consumer Research*, 11 (Ann Arbor: Association for Consumer Research, 1984); and Terence A. Shimp and Subash Sharma, 'Consumer ethnocentrism: Construction and validation of the CETSCALE', *Journal of Marketing Research*, 24, August 1987, pp. 280–289.
14. Morris Holbrook and Thomas Olney, 'Romanticism and wanderlust: An effect of personality on consumer preferences', *Psychology and Marketing*, 12(3), 1995, pp. 207–222.
15. See also: Suresh Subramanian and Robert A. Mittelstaedt, 'Conceptualizing innovativeness as a consumer trait: Consequences and alternatives', in Mary C. Gilly, F. Robert Dwyer et al. (eds), *1991 AMA Educator's Proceedings* (Chicago: American Marketing Association, 1991), pp. 352–360; and 'Reconceptualizing and measuring consumer innovativeness', in Robert P. Leone, V. Kumor et al. (eds), *1992 AMA Educator's Proceedings* (Chicago: American Marketing Association, 1992), pp. 300–307.
16. Milton Rokeach, *The Open and Closed Mind* (New York: Basic Books, 1960).
17. David Riesman, *The Lonely Crowd* (New Haven: Yale University Press, 1950).
18. Itamar Simonson and Stephen M. Nowlis, 'The role of explanations and need for uniqueness in consumer decision making: Unconventional choices based on reasons', *Journal of Consumer Research*, 27, June 2000, pp. 49–68.
19. William O. Bearden, Richard G. Netemeyer and Jesse E. Teel, 'Consumer susceptibility to interpersonal influ-

ence', *Journal of Consumer Research*, 15, March 1989, pp. 473–481.

20. Aron O'Cass and Hmily Frost, 'Status Consciousness and fashion consumption', *Australian New Zealand Marketing Academy Conference Proceedings*, Melbourne 2002, (eds) Robin Shaw, Steward Adam and Heath McDonald, pp. 3371–3378.
21. Deborah Griffin and Aron O'Cass, 'Antecedents of attitudes toward social issues and intention to comply', *Australian New Zealand Marketing Academy Conference Proceedings*, Melbourne 2002, (eds) Robin Shaw, Steward Adam and Heath McDonald, pp. 441–449.
22. P. S. Raju, 'Optimum stimulation level: Its relationship to personality, demographics, and exploratory behavior', *Journal of Consumer Research*, 7, December 1980, pp. 272–282; Leigh McAlister and Edgar Pessemier, 'Variety seeking behavior: An interdisciplinary review', *Journal of Consumer Research*, 9, December 1982, pp. 311–322; Edgar Pessemier and Moshe Handelsman, 'Temporal variety in consumer behavior', *Journal of Marketing Research*, 21, November 1984, pp. 435–444; Erich A. Joachimsthaler and John L. Lastovicka, 'Optimal stimulation level—exploratory behavior models', *Journal of Consumer Research*, 11, December 1984, pp. 830–835; Elizabeth C. Hirschman, 'Experience seeking: A subjectivist perspective of consumption', *Journal of Business Research*, 12, 1984, pp. 115–136; and Jan-Benedict E. M. Steenkamp and Hans Baumgartner, 'The role of optimum stimulation level in exploratory consumer behavior', *Journal of Consumer Research*, 19, December 1992, p. 434.
23. Russell G. Wahlers and Michael J. Etzel, 'A consumer response to incongruity between optimal stimulation and lifestyle satisfaction', in Elizabeth C. Hirschman and Morris B. Holbrook (eds), *Advances in Consumer Research*, 12 (Provo, UT: Association for Consumer Research, 1985), pp. 97–101.
24. Elizabeth C. Hirschman, 'Innovativeness, novelty seeking and consumer creativity', *Journal of Consumer Research*, 7, 1980, pp. 283–295; and Wayne Hoyer and Nancy M. Ridgway, 'Variety seeking as an explanation for exploratory purchase behavior: A theoretical model', *Advances in Consumer Research*, 11 (Provo, UT: Association for Consumer Research, 1990), pp. 114–119.
25. S. Ram and Hyung-Shik Jung, 'How does variety seeking affect product usage?', in Jon M. Hawes and George B. Gilsan (eds), *Developments in Marketing Science*, 10 (Akron, OH: Academy of Marketing Science, 1987), pp. 85–89.
26. Morris B. Holbrook et al., 'Play as a consumption experience: The roles of emotions, performance, and personality in the enjoyment of games', *Journal of Consumer Research*, 11, September 1984, pp. 728–739; and Morris B. Holbrook, 'Aims, concepts, and methods for representation of individual differences in esthetic responses to design features', *Journal of Consumer Research*, 13, December 1986, pp. 337–347.
27. Richard Petty et al., 'Personality and ad effectiveness: Exploring the utility of need for cognition', in Michael Houston (ed.), *Advances in Consumer Research*, 15, (Provo, UT: Association for Consumer Research, 1988), pp. 209–212.
28. Ayn E. Crowley and Wayne D. Hoyer, 'The relationship between need for cognition and other individual difference variables: A two-dimensional framework', in Thomas K. Srull (ed.), *Advances in Consumer Research*, 16 (Provo, UT: Association for Consumer Research, 1989), pp. 37–43.
29. Y. Zhang and R. Buda, 'Moderating effects of need for cognition on responses to positively versus negatively framed advertising messages', *Journal of Advertising*, 28(2), 1999, pp. 1–16.
30. C. J. Sadowski and H. E. Cogburn, 'Need for cognition in the big-five factor', *Journal of Psychology*, 131(3), 1997, pp. 307–312.
31. M. Geuens and P. De Pelsmacker, 'Need for cognition and the moderating role of the intensity of warm and humorous advertising appeals', *Asia Pacific Advances in Consumer Research*, 3, 1998, pp. 74–80; and Y. Zhang and R. Buda, op cit.
32. Sadowski and Cogburn, op. cit.
33. N. Srinivasan and S. Tikoo, 'Effect of locus of control on information search behavior', *Advances in Consumer Research*, 19, 1992, pp. 498–504.
34. P. Wallace, *The Psychology of the Internet* (Cambridge, UK: Cambridge University Press, 1999).
35. G. R. Jarobe and C. D. McDaniel, 'A profile of browsers in regional shopping malls', *Academy of Marketing Science*, 15(1), 1987, pp. 46–53.
36. E. Ferguson, 'A facet and factor analysis of typical intellectual engagement (TIE): Associations with locus of control and the five factor model of personality', *Social Behavior and Personality*, 27(6), 1999, pp. 545–556.
37. M. Poole and A. O'Cass, *Consumer Personality Differences Between Mall and Online Shopping Environments*. Paper presented at the World Marketing Congress:

Marketing Across Borders and Boundaries: Understanding Cross-Functional and Inter-Disciplinary Interfaces Within an Increasingly Global Environment, Perth, Australia, 2003, pp. 4–8.

38. M. K. Hogg, A. J. Cox and K. Keeling, 'The impact of self-monitoring on image congruence and product/brand evaluation', *European Journal of Marketing*, 34(5/6), 2000, pp. 641–666.
39. Aron O'Cass, 'A psychometric evaluation of a revised version of the Lennox and Wolfe revised self-monitoring Scale', *Psychology and Marketing*, 17(5), 2000, pp. 397–419.
40. A. O'Cass, 'Consumer self-monitoring, materialism and involvement in fashion clothing', *Australasian Marketing Journal*, 9(1), 2000, pp. 46–60.
41. G. Hodson and R.M. Sorrentino, 'Uncertainty orientation and the big five personality structure', *Journal of Research in Personality*, 33, 1999, pp. 253–261.
42. R. M. Sorrentino and C. Roney, 'Uncertainty orientation, achievement-related motivations, and task diagnosticity as determinants of task performance', *Social Cognition*, 4, 1986, pp. 420–436.
43. M. Poole and A. O'Cass, *Consumer Personality Differences Between Mall and Online Shopping Environments*. Paper presented at the World Marketing Congress: Marketing Across Borders and Boundaries: Understanding Cross-Functional and Inter-Disciplinary Interfaces Within an Increasingly Global Environment, Perth, Australia, 2003, pp. 4–8.
44. Joel N. Greene, Richard E. Plank and Leon G. Schiffman, 'Using cognitive personality theory to predict opinion leadership behavior', in Ken Grant and Ian Walker (eds), *Proceedings of the Seventh Bi-Annual World Marketing Congress*, Vol. VII-I, 6-83 to 6-92. See also G. A. Kelly, *The Psychology of Personal Constructs* (New York: Norton, 1955).
45. Poole and O'Cass, op. cit.
46. Marsha L. Richins and Scott Dawson, 'A consumer values orientation for materialism and its measurement: Scale development and validation', *Journal of Consumer Research*, 19, December 1992, pp. 303–316.
47. Ronald J. Faber and Thomas C. O'Guinn, 'A clinical screener for compulsive buying', *Journal of Consumer Research*, 19, December 1992, pp. 459–469.
48. Ibid., p. 467.
49. Elizabeth C. Hirschman, 'The consciousness of addiction: Toward a general theory of compulsive consumption', *Journal of Consumer Research*, 19, September 1992, pp. 155–179.
50. Dan L. Sherrell, Alvin C. Burns and Melodie R. Phillips, 'Fixed consumption behavior: The case of enduring acquisition in a product category', in Robert L. King (ed.), *Developments in Marketing Science* (Richmond, VA: Academy of Marketing Science, 1991), pp. 36–40.
51. Terence A. Shimp and Subhash Sharma, 'Consumer ethnocentrism: Construction and validation of the CETSCALE', op. cit. (note 13); and Richard G. Netemeyer, Srinivas Durvaula and Donald R. Lichtenstein, 'A cross-national assessment of the reliability and validity of the CETSCALE', *Journal of Marketing Research*, 28, August 1991, pp. 320–327.
52. Hazel Markus and Paula Nurius, 'Possible selves', *American Psychologist*, 41, 1986, pp. 954–969.
53. For a detailed discussion of self-images and congruence, see M. Joseph Sirgy, 'Self-concept in consumer behavior: A critical review', *Journal of Consumer Research*, 9, December 1992, pp. 287–300; C.B. Claiborne and M. Joseph Sirgy, 'Self-image congruence as a model of consumer attitude formation and behavior: A conceptual review and guide for future research', in B. J. Dunlap (ed.), *Developments in Marketing Science*, 13 (Cullowhee, NC: Academy of Marketing Science, 1990), pp. 1–7; and J.S. Johar and M. Joseph Sirgy, 'Value-expressive versus utilitarian advertising appeals: When and why to use which appeal', *Journal of Advertising*, 20, September 1991, pp. 23–33.
54. Ibid.
55. Charles H. Noble and Beth A. Walker, 'Exploring the relationships among liminal transitions, symbolic consumption, and the extended self', *Psychology and Marketing*, 14(1), 1997, pp. 29–47.
56. Aron O'Cass and Kenny Lim, 'The influence of brand associations on brand preference and purchase intention: An Asian perspective on brand associations', *Journal of International Consumer Marketing*, 14(2/3), 2002, pp. 41–72.
57. Aron O'Cass and Hmily Frost, 'Status consciousness and fashion consumption', *Australian New Zealand Marketing Academy Conference Proceedings*, (eds) Robin Shaw, Steward Adam and Heath McDonald, Melbourne, 2002, pp. 3371–3378.
58. Charles H. Noble and Beth A. Walker, 'Exploring the relationships among liminal transitions, symbolic consumption, and the extended self', *Psychology and Marketing*, 14(1), 1997, pp. 29–47.

59. Russell W. Belk, 'Possessions and the extended self', *Journal of Consumer Research*, 15, September 1988, pp. 139–168.
60. Ibid.
61. John W. Schouten, 'Selves in transition: Symbolic consumption in personal rites of passage and identity reconstruction', *Journal of Consumer Research*, 17, March 1991, pp. 412–425; and Stacey M. Fabricant and Stephen J. Gould, 'Women's makeup careers: An interpretive study of color cosmetic use and "face value"', *Psychology & Marketing*, 10(6), 1993, pp. 531–548.
62. Joseph Z. Wisenblit, 'Person positioning: Empirical evidence and a paradigm', *Journal of Professional Services Marketing*, 4, 1989.
63. Bernadette Park, 'A method for studying the development of impressions of real people', *Journal of Personality and Social Psychology*, 51, 1986, pp. 907–917.
64. Grant McCracken, 'Who is the celebrity endorser? Cultural foundations of the endorsement process', *Journal of Consumer Research*, 16(3), 1989, pp. 310–321.
65. Rajeev Batra, Donald R. Lehmann and Dipinder Singh, 'The brand personality component of brand goodwill: Some antecedents and consequences', in David Aaker and Alexander Biel (eds), *Brand Equity and Advertising: Advertising's Role in Building Strong Brands* (Hillsdale, NJ: Lawrence Erlbaum Associates, 1993).
66. Jennifer Aaker, 'Dimensions of brand personality,' *Journal of Marketing Research*, 34(3), August 1997, pp. 347–356.
67. O'Cass and Lim, op. cit.
68. Edward C. Malthouse, Bobby J. Calder and Wayne P. Eadie, Conceptualizing and Measuring Magazine Reader Experiences, 11th Worldwide Readership Research Symposium, Boston, MA, 26–29 October 2003.
69. Kip Williams, Michael Edwardson, Ladd Wheeler and Cassandra Govan, Consumer Involvement can be Measured by the Implicit Association Test, Society for Consumer Psychology Winter Conference, February 2001 (Scottsdale, Arizona).
70. Judith L. Zaichowsky, 'Measuring the involvement construct', *Journal of Consumer Research*, 12, December 1985, pp. 341–352.
71. Anthony G. Greenwald, Debbie E. McGhee and Jordan L. K. Schwartz, 'Measuring individual differences in implicit cognition: The implicit association test', *Journal of Personality and Social Pyschology*, 74(6), 1998, pp. 1464–1480.
72. Banwari Mittal, 'A comparative analysis of four scales of consumer involvement', *Psychology & Marketing*, 12(7), 1985, pp. 663–682.

Consumer perception

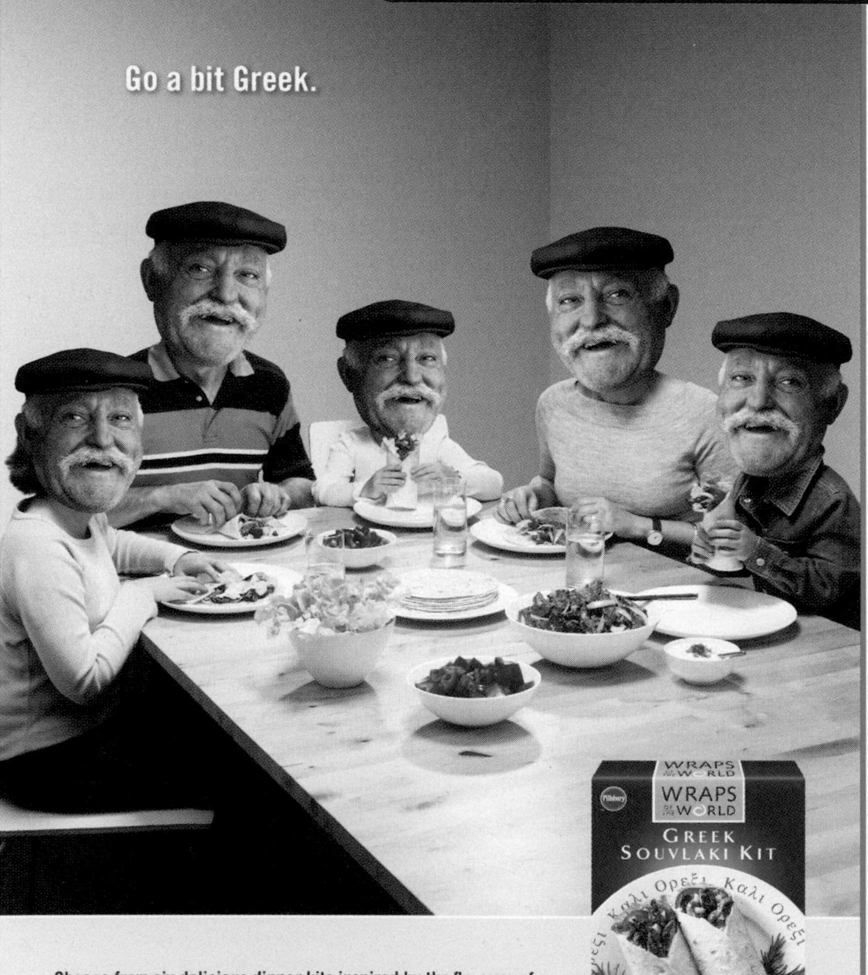

Go a bit Greek.
WRAPS OF THE WORLD
GREEK SOUVLAKI KIT
Choose from six delicious dinner kits inspired by the flavours of the world. Available in the Asian section of your supermarket.
A Taste for Adventure.

Source: © 2004 General Mills. Reproduced with permission of General Mills. Developed by George Patterson Partners.

As diverse individuals, we all tend to see the world in our own special way. Four people can view the same advertisement and react in entirely different ways. One person may barely notice yet another car ad on TV; another will watch with rapt attention because they have just bought this model; while a third will notice the safety features of the car; and the fourth only the pretty model driving the car. For each individual, the ad that was experienced was a personal phenomenon, based on that person's needs, wants, values and personal experiences. 'Reality' to each of us is merely our perception of what is 'out there', of what has taken place. We act and react on the basis of our perceptions, not on the basis of objective reality (i.e. reality as recorded by a camera).

Perception involves three vital processes of interest to marketers. The first is *sensation*, which defines the stimuli in our environment that we are capable of processing (e.g. is the advertising message too faint to hear?); the second is *selection* in terms of those stimuli (such as advertising) that we pay attention to; the third is *interpretation* in which we make sense of the stimuli we have processed (e.g. does that new brand appear to be high quality?).

➤ Elements of perception

Perception is defined as the *process by which an individual receives, selects and interprets stimuli to form a meaningful and coherent picture of the world.* A **stimulus** is any unit of input to any of the senses. The study of perception is largely the study of what we add to, or subtract from, raw sensory inputs to produce our own private picture of the world. Perception is so basic a function that we usually take it for granted without conscious examination of how it occurs.

SENSATION

Sensation is the immediate and direct response of the sensory organs to simple stimuli (an advertisement, a package, a brand name). **Sensory receptors** are the human organs (eyes, ears, nose, mouth and skin) that receive sensory inputs. Their sensory functions are to see, hear, smell, taste and feel movement. Examples of stimuli (i.e. sensory input) include products, packages, jingles, scent strips, brand names, advertisements and commercials. Human sensitivity refers to the experience of sensation. Sensitivity to stimuli varies with the quality of our sensory receptors (e.g. eyesight or hearing) and the amount or intensity of the stimuli to which we are exposed. For example, a blind person may have a more highly developed sense of hearing than the average sighted person and may be able to distinguish sounds that the average person cannot. Smell is the sense most closely linked to memory. For example, the disinfectant Pineocleen has a very evocative smell.

Sensation itself depends on energy change or differentiation of input. A perfectly bland or unchanging environment, regardless of the strength of the sensory input, provides little or no sensation at all. Thus, a person who lives on a busy street in inner Sydney would probably receive little or no sensation from the inputs of such noisy stimuli as rumbling trucks, the swoosh of cars and clatter of passing trains, since such sounds are so commonplace. One truck more or less would never be noticed. In situations where there is a great deal of sensory input, the senses do not detect small intensities or differences in input.

As sensory input decreases, however, our ability to detect changes in input or intensity increases, to the point that we attain maximum sensitivity under conditions of minimal stimulation. This accounts for the statement: 'It was so quiet I could hear a pin drop.' It also accounts for the increased attention given to a commercial that appears alone during a program break, or to a black-and-white advertisement in a magazine full of four-colour advertisements. This ability of the human organism to accommodate itself to varying levels of sensitivity as external conditions vary not only provides more sensitivity when it is needed, but also serves to protect us from damaging, disruptive or irrelevant bombardment when the input level is high.

THE ABSOLUTE THRESHOLD

The lowest level at which we can experience a sensation is called the **absolute threshold**. The point at which we can detect a difference between 'something' and 'nothing' is our absolute threshold for that stimulus. To illustrate, the distance at which a driver can first detect a specific advertising hoarding on the highway is based on that individual's absolute visual threshold. Two people riding together may first notice the hoarding at different distances; thus, they appear to have different absolute thresholds. Australian advertisers have experimented with very short TV commercials, some as short as one second, close to the absolute threshold in a cluttered environment.[1]

Under conditions of constant stimulation, such as driving through a 'corridor' of hoardings, the absolute threshold increases (i.e. the senses tend to become increasingly dulled). After an hour of driving past advertising hoardings, it is doubtful that any one of them will make much of an impression. Hence we often speak of 'getting used to' a hot bath, a cold shower, the bright sun, or even the smells and sounds of a Bangkok street. In the field of perception, the term **adaptation** refers specifically to 'getting used to' certain sensations, becoming accommodated to a certain level of stimulation.

Sensory adaptation is a problem experienced by many TV advertisers during special programming events, such as the Olympic games. For example, with many brilliantly executed commercials all competing with one another as well as with the Olympic games themselves for viewer attention, often no one commercial will stand out from all the rest. Advertisers use a variety of attention-seeking devices to attract attention, such as periods of silence,[2] loud noises and contrasting colours.[3] It is because of adaptation that advertisers tend to change their advertising campaigns regularly. They are concerned that consumers will get so used to their current print ads and TV commercials that they will no longer 'see' them; that is, the ads will no longer provide sufficient sensory input to be noted. For this reason, advertisers often try to vary the execution of their advertising to maintain impact. Australian research by Max Sutherland indicates that some advertisers have over-reacted to this problem, by having far too many executions and too few repetitions.[4]

In an effort to cut through the advertising clutter and ensure that consumers note their ads, some marketers try to increase sensory input. Table 5.1 shows some examples. Cadbury once bought all the advertising space (hoardings) at a railway station in Australia (Richmond, Victoria) to ensure that commuters would notice its Cherry Ripe ads. Some marketers seek unusual or technological media in which to place their advertisements in an effort to gain attention. Examples of such media include small monitors attached to shopping carts that feature actual brands in TV shows and in movies, individual TV screens (placed in the back of the seat ahead) on airplanes, and monitors integrated into the above-the-door floor indicators on elevators. Some have advertised their products on bus shelters; others have used parking meters and shopping trolleys; still others pay to have their products appear in movies, TV soaps or lifestyle programs. Fragrance marketers often include fragrance samples in their direct mail and magazine advertisements, while stores, particularly food stores, now pay particular attention to their smell environment. A stale-smelling fish shop or a scrumptious yeasty smell at a bakery both convey important quality messages. American researchers have shown that waiting times and time spent in-store appeared shorter in stores using an ambient scent.[5] A new-car spray gives used vehicles the smell of new plastic and carpeting. A 'fresh linen' scent has been added to a line of plastic garbage bags to make consumers feel 'healthy and clean'.[6] Some Australian market research companies, such as Colmar Brunton, specialise in *sensory research* aimed at systematic studies of how consumers process the sensory quality of services and products.

Companies often use a number of techniques to appeal to the consumer. Figure 5.1 (page 138) depicts the use of increased sensory input to support the product's advertising claim.

TABLE 5.1 **Advertisers' attempts to increase sensory input**

Magazine inserts

- Aramis introduced its new men's Havana fragrance using a scent strip.[a]
- In the US, Proctor & Gamble used a 'scratch and sniff' sticker in ads for Gain detergent to evoke the perception of sun-dried clothes.[b]
- Rolls-Royce put the aroma of leather upholstery on a scent strip in *Architectural Digest*.[b]
- Absolut vodka magazine advertisements contained microchips that played 'Jingle Bells' and 'Santa Claus is Coming to Town'.[c]
- Toyota bound 3-D spectacles into magazine ads for Corolla cars.[c]
- Revlon and Estée Lauder offer eye shadow and blusher samples bound into fashion magazines.[c]
- Proctor & Gamble included a sample of its line extension 'Pert Plus for Kids' within *Woman's Day*.[d]

Point-of-sale displays

- Kiwi developed a supermarket mini-terminal to give consumers information about shoe care.
- Major video stores show excerpts of videos for hire.
- In the US, Kraft used an electronic kiosk which responded to consumers' questions by printing out recipes that call for Kraft products, along with a discount coupon for Kraft ingredients. Nabisco used cereal displays which emitted the smell of fresh strawberries. Orville Redenbacher packaged popcorn in packets designed to resemble videos for sale in video libraries.[e]
- Interactive computers are programmed to give consumers advice about which do-it-yourself paint products to use.
- In-store videos give consumers the sense of what products will be like, in use.

Sources:

a. ***New Woman*, November 1994.**
b. **Michael deCourcy Hinds, 'Finding new ways to make smell sell', *New York Times*, 23 July 1988, p. 52.**
c. **Bernice Kanner, 'Special effects', *New York*, 19 September 1988, p. 28.**
d. **31 October 1994.**
e. **Bernice Kanner, 'Trolling in the aisles', *New York*, 16 January 1989, p. 12.**

THE DIFFERENTIAL THRESHOLD

The minimal difference that can be detected between two stimuli is called the **differential threshold**, or the **just noticeable difference (j.n.d.)**. A 19th-century German scientist, Ernst Weber, discovered that the just noticeable difference between two stimuli was not an absolute amount, but an amount relative to the intensity of the first stimulus. **Weber's law**, as it has come to be known, states that the stronger the initial stimulus, the greater the additional intensity needed for the second stimulus to be perceived as different.

For example, if the price of a car increased by $100, it would probably not be noticed (i.e. the increment would fall below the j.n.d. It may take an increase of $200 or more before a differential in price would be noticed. However, a $1 increase in the price of a litre of petrol would be noticed very quickly by consumers because it is a significant percentage of the initial (i.e. base) cost.

According to Weber's law, an additional level of stimulus equivalent to the j.n.d. must be added for the majority of people to perceive a difference between the resulting stimulus and the initial stimulus. Weber's law holds for all the senses (e.g. for sight and sound) and for almost all intensities.[7]

Let us say that a manufacturer of silver polish wishes to improve the product sufficiently to claim that it retards tarnish longer than the leading competitive brand. In a series of experiments, the company has determined that the j.n.d. for its present polish, which now gives a shine that lasts about 20 days, is five days, or 25% longer. That means that the shine given by the improved silver polish must last at least 25% longer than that of the

FIGURE 5.1 **Depicts the use of increased sensory input to support the product's advertising claim**

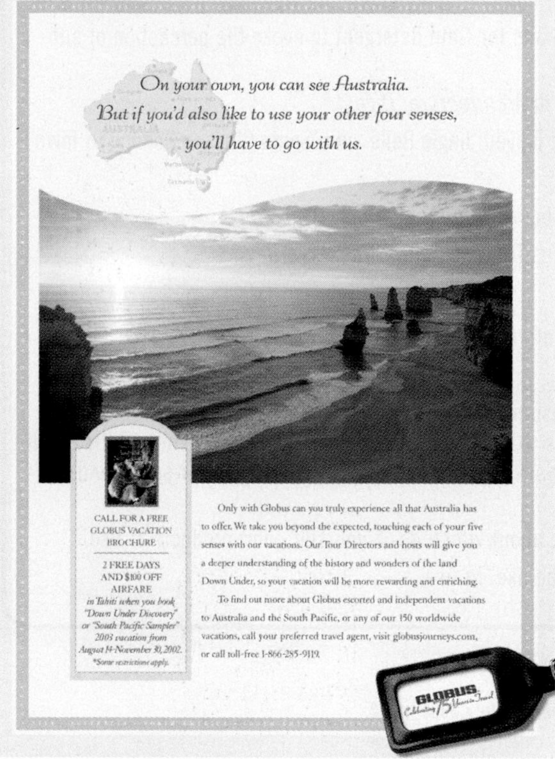

Source: Courtesy of Globus.

present polish if it is to be perceived by the majority of users as, in fact, improved. By finding this j.n.d. of five days, the company has isolated the minimum amount of time necessary to make its claim of 'lasts longer' believable to the majority of consumers. If the company had decided to make the silver polish effective for 40 days, it would have sacrificed a good deal of repeat purchase frequency. If it had decided to make the polish effective for 23 days (just three extra days of product life), its claim of 'lasts longer' would not be perceived as true by most consumers. Making the product improvement just equal to the j.n.d. thus becomes the most efficient decision that management can make.

The j.n.d. has other uses in setting prices. For example, discounts on fast-moving consumer goods (FMCG) are often *framed* as percentages rather than specific amounts (e.g. a 10% discount on a 60¢ item sounds bigger than a 6¢ saving). Similarly, price increases can be framed as small, insignificant changes (electricity price rises will cost the average family only an extra 25¢ a day, rather than $90 a year).

Marketing applications of the j.n.d.

Weber's law has important applications for marketing. Manufacturers and marketers endeavour to determine the relevant j.n.d. for their products for two very different reasons:

1. so that negative changes (e.g. reductions in product size, increases in product price, or reduced quality) are not readily discernible to the public (they remain below the j.n.d.);
2. so that product improvements (such as improved or updated packaging, larger size, lower price) are readily discernible to consumers without being wastefully extravagant (ie. they are at or just above the j.n.d.).

For example, because of rising costs, many manufacturers are faced with the choice of increasing prices or reducing the quantity of the product offered at the existing price. An Australian favourite, Cherry Ripe, has done both. Over the past 40 years, it has increased in price many times and altered its weight a number of times. Because a chocolate bar is relatively inexpensive to begin with, price increases are very noticeable, so decreasing the size of such a product to just under the j.n.d. is a simpler strategy for product producers.

Manufacturers who choose to reduce the quality of their products also try to ensure that product changes remain just under the point of noticeable difference. For example, when the price of coffee beans goes up, coffee processors often downgrade quality by using inferior beans, up to but not including the j.n.d., the point at which the consumer will notice a difference in taste. Another example: to meet current nutritional concerns, a number of food processors have adjusted their recipes to substitute unsaturated fats for the animal fats and coconut and palm oils previously used, with the intention of keeping any differences in taste under the j.n.d.

A number of well-known food companies have 'downsized' their packaging—that is, decreased the package size or even maintained the package size but decreased the contents. For example, in 1999 Australian producers of light beer reduced the contents of small bottles by 35–45 ml, while maintaining the price. Despite the fact that the adjusted quantity was listed on the package label, most consumers would be unlikely to notice it because the package size remained similar. (For further discussion of this issue, see Chapter 17.)

Marketers often want to update existing packaging without losing the ready recognition of consumers who have been exposed to years of cumulative advertising impact. In such cases, they usually make a number of small changes, each carefully designed to fall below the j.n.d., so that consumers will not perceive the brand to be different. For example, that great Australian product symbol, Redhead matches, has had four main redheads since the product was introduced in 1946, along with some hundreds of variations to interest collectors. As Figure 5.2 shows, the brand remains identifiable, though the redhead face and hairstyle changed to keep the matchbox contemporary.[8] The name 'Redhead' was originally coined to symbolise the red striking head of the match. Brand names often undergo a similar subtle transition to avoid customer alienation and remain contemporary. Figure 5.3 illustrates how Holden Ltd did this.

FIGURE 5.2 **Sequential changes in the Redhead symbol**

1946

1958

1971

1975

Source: Courtesy of Swedish Match Australia.

FIGURE 5.3 **Revitalised over time (around a core idea)**

1948

1974

HOLDEN

1994

Source: Courtesy of Holden Ltd.

Lexmark International, Inc., which bought the office supplies and equipment line from the International Business Machine Corporation in March 1991, agreed to relinquish the IBM name by 1996.[9] Recognising the need to build a brand image for Lexmark while they moved away from the well-known IBM name, Lexmark officials planned a four-stage campaign for phasing in the Lexmark name on products. As Figure 5.4 indicates, Stage 1 has only the IBM name; Stage 2 features the IBM name and downplays Lexmark; Stage 3 features the Lexmark name and downplays IBM; Stage 4 features only the Lexmark name.

In 1997, Pepsi in the United States updated its packaging. Its new cola cans were given a bright royal blue look, with the brand Pepsi in white lettering along the length of the can. However, to make sure the public perceived continuity, the initial packaging and ads used a lighter blue similar to that of the original can which was gradually intensified to the bright royal blue. An interesting example came when the US Coors Brewing Company changed its packaging *above* the j.n.d. by adding the words 'original draft' to the label on its Coors beer. The new label prompted hundreds of complaints from drinkers who believed the product itself had been changed, thus forcing the company to bring back the old label.[10] In Australia, Kraft realises it has little opportunity to make any change to the label of that Australian icon, Vegemite.

When it comes to product improvements, marketers very much want to meet or exceed the consumer's differential threshold; that is, they want consumers to perceive readily any improvements made in the original product. Marketers can use the j.n.d. to determine the amount of improvement they should make in their

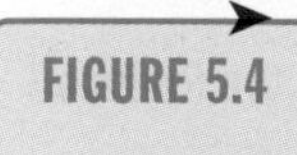

FIGURE 5.4 **Gradual change in brand below the j.n.d.**

Stage 1

Stage 2

Stage 3

Stage 4

Current logo

Source: Courtesy of Lexmark International Inc.

products. Less than the j.n.d. is wasted effort because the improvement will not be perceived; more than the j.n.d. may be wasteful because it will reduce the level of repeat sales or cost too much to develop.

On the other hand, when it comes to price increases, less than the j.n.d. is desirable because consumers are unlikely to notice it. Since many routinely purchased consumer goods are rather inexpensive, companies are reluctant to raise prices when their profit margins on these items are declining. Instead, many marketers decrease the product quantity included in the packages, while leaving the prices unchanged—thus, in effect, increasing the per unit price. The manufacturer of Huggies reduced the number of diapers in a package from 240 to 228 while maintaining the same price; PepsiCo reduced the weight of one snack food bag by 25 grams (and maintained the same price),[11] and Sanitarium reduced its Hi-Bran breakfast cereal from 1 kg to 750 g (and only marginally reduced the new price). The packages for these products remained virtually unchanged. Presumably, the decreases in the number of items or weight of these products reflect j.n.d.-focused research; the reductions in quantity were below most consumers' j.n.d. for these products.

Subliminal perception

In Chapter 3 we spoke of people being motivated 'below their level of conscious awareness'. People are also *stimulated* below their level of conscious awareness; that is, they can perceive stimuli without being consciously aware of the stimuli in question. The threshold for conscious awareness or conscious recognition appears to be higher than the absolute threshold for effective perception. Stimuli that are too weak or too brief to be consciously seen or heard may nevertheless be strong enough to be perceived by one or more receptor cells. This process is called **subliminal perception** because the stimulus is beneath the threshold, or 'limen', of awareness, though obviously not beneath the absolute threshold of the receptors involved. (Perception of stimuli that are above the level of conscious awareness is called **supraliminal perception**.)

Subliminal perception created a great furore in the late 1950s, when it was reported that consumers were being exposed to subliminal advertising messages that they were not aware of receiving. These messages purportedly were persuading people to buy goods and services without being aware of why they were motivated to do so. The effectiveness of so-called subliminal advertising was repeatedly tested at a drive-in movie in New Jersey, where the words 'eat popcorn' and 'drink Coca-Cola' were flashed on the screen during the movie.[12] Exposure times were so short that viewers were unaware of seeing a message. It was reported that, during the 6-week test period, popcorn sales increased by 58% and Coca-Cola sales by 18%. However, no scientific controls were used, and researchers were never able to replicate the results. Indeed, the cinema owner where the 'research' took place was later reported as saying the study was a fabrication.[13] This controversy prompted studies that gave some support to the notion that individuals could perceive below the level of their conscious awareness, but found no evidence that the subliminal stimulation influenced purchase intentions.[14]

Every decade or so, some incident seems to revive interest in the subject, despite a lack of any substantial evidence. Reviews of literature[15] in the mid-1990s suggested that research has followed two theoretical approaches. The first hypothesises that the constant repetition of very weak (i.e. sub-threshold) stimuli has an incremental effect that enables such stimuli to build response strength over many presentations. Some evidence does exist for the efficacy of this approach, but only under a limited set of circumstances that would be too expensive or impractical in an advertising context.[16] The second theory proposes that subliminal sexual stimuli arouse unconscious sexual motivations. This is the theory behind the use of *sexual embeds* in print advertising. **Embeds** were defined as disguised stimuli not readily recognised by readers, that are 'planted' in print advertisements to persuade consumers to buy the products. It was alleged, for example, that liquor advertisers try to increase the subconscious appeal of their products by embedding sexually suggestive symbols in ice cubes floating in a pictured drink. However, research showed no evidence that these methods worked.[17] Figure 5.5 contains a spoof sending up such an approach.

Several experiments into the effectiveness of subliminal messages in television commercials concluded that it would be very difficult to use the technique on television; that even if the messages had some influence, they would be far less effective than supraliminal messages and would probably interfere with consumers' processing of brand names.[18]

Many marketers and many consumers continue to believe that subliminal persuasion works.[19] Self-help audio cassettes are built on this premise. Consumers have been buying these tapes to the tune of millions of dollars a year in the belief that they can learn a foreign language, break a bad habit, improve their willpower or their memory, or take any of a thousand roads to self-improvement. The tapes play relaxing music (or the sound of ocean waves) and contain subliminal messages not perceptible to the ear but supposedly recognisable to the subconscious mind. Most of the tapes come with a written script of the subliminal messages (e.g. 'I chew slowly'; 'I eat less'; 'I am capable'; 'I act decisively').[20] Department stores incorporate subliminal messages in musical sound-tracks played on their public address systems to motivate employees and discourage shoplifting. Subliminal messages, such as 'I am honest', 'I won't steal', 'Stealing is dishonest', have been reported to bring about cuts in shoplifting and inventory shrinkage.[21]

In summary, while there is some evidence that subliminal stimuli may influence affective reactions, there is no evidence that subliminal stimulation can influence consumption motives or actions. As to sexual embeds, most researchers are of the opinion that 'What you see is what you get'; that is, a vivid imagination can see whatever it wants to see in just about any situation, including any illustration. That very much sums up the whole notion of perception: individuals see what they want to see (e.g. what they

FIGURE 5.5 **Borrowing from the subliminal message format to appeal to the consumer**

Source: Courtesy of American Association of Advertising Agencies.

are motivated to see) and what they expect to see. In general, it is hard enough to cut through the clutter of competing advertising without taking the considerable risk that your expensive advertising will not be noticed or understood.

In Australia, subliminal television advertising was originally banned.[22] It is now prohibited under the Commercial Television Industry Code of Practice, which prohibits the use of 'any technique which attempts to convey information to the viewer by transmitting messages below or near the threshold of normal awareness'.[23] (See also Chapter 17.)

The dynamics of perception

The preceding section explained how we receive sensations from stimuli in the outside environment, and how the human organism adapts to the level and intensity of sensory input. We now come to one of the major principles of perception: raw sensory input by itself does not produce or explain the coherent picture of the world that most adults possess.

Human beings are constantly bombarded with stimuli during every minute and every hour of every day. The sensory world is made up of an almost infinite number of discrete sensations which are constantly and subtly changing. According to the principles of sensation, such heavy intensity of stimulation should 'turn off' most individuals, who would subconsciously block the receipt of such a heavy bombardment of stimuli. Otherwise the billions of different stimuli to which we are constantly exposed might serve to confuse us totally and keep us perpetually disoriented in a constantly changing environment. However, neither of these consequences tends to occur, because perception is not a function of sensory input alone. Rather, perception is the result of two different kinds of inputs that interact to form the personal pictures, the perceptions, that each individual experiences.

One type of input is physical stimuli from the outside environment; the other type of input is provided by individuals themselves in the form of certain predispositions (e.g. expectations, motives and learning based on previous experience). The combination of these two very different kinds of inputs produces for each of us a very private, very personal picture of the world. Because each person is a unique individual, with unique experiences, wants, needs, wishes and expectations, it follows that each individual's perceptions are also unique. This explains why no two people see the world in precisely the same way.

We are very selective as to which stimuli we 'recognise'; we organise the stimuli we do recognise subconsciously according to widely held psychological principles, and we give meaning to such stimuli (i.e. we interpret them) subjectively in accordance with our needs, expectations and experiences. Let us examine in more detail each of these three aspects of perception: selection, organisation and interpretation of stimuli.

PERCEPTUAL SELECTION

Consumers subconsciously exercise a great deal of selectivity about which aspects of the environment—that is, the stimuli—they will perceive. An individual may look at some things, ignore others, and turn away from still others. In total, people actually receive—or perceive—only a small fraction of the stimuli to which they are exposed.

Consider, for example, shoppers in a supermarket. They may be exposed to over 20 000 products of different colours, sizes and shapes: to perhaps 100 people (looking, walking, searching, talking); to smells (from fruit, meat, disinfectant, people); to sounds within the store (cash registers ringing, Muzak, shopping trolleys rolling, air conditioners humming, and staff sweeping, mopping aisles, stocking shelves); to sounds from outside the store (planes passing, cars tooting, tyres squealing, children shouting, car doors slamming). Yet they manage on a regular basis to visit their local supermarket, select the items they need, pay for them with EFTPOS, use a FlyBuys card and leave, all within a relatively brief time, without losing their sanity or personal orientation to the world. This is because they exercise **selective perception**.

Which stimuli get selected depends on two major factors, in addition to the *nature of the stimulus itself:* the consumers' previous experience as it affects their expectations (what they are prepared, or 'set', to see) and their motives at the time (needs, desires, interests, and so on). Each of these factors can serve to increase or decrease the probability that the stimulus will be perceived.

Nature of the stimulus

Marketing stimuli include an enormous number of variables that affect the consumer's perception, such as the nature of the product, its physical attributes, package design, brand name, advertisements and commercials (including copy claims, choice and sex of model, positioning of model, size of ad and typography), position of a print ad or time of a commercial, and the editorial environment.

In general, contrast is one of the most attention-compelling attributes of a stimulus. Advertisers often use extreme attention-getting devices to achieve maximum contrast and thus penetrate the consumer's perceptual screen. For example, a growing number of magazines and newspapers are carrying ads that readers can unfold to reveal oversized, poster-like advertisements for products ranging from cosmetics to cars, because of the 'stopping power' of giant ads among more traditional sizes.[24]

However, advertising does not have to be unique to achieve a high degree of differentiation; it simply has to contrast with the environment in which it is run. The use of lots of white space in a print advertisement, the absence of sound in a commercial's opening scene, a 60-second commercial within a string of 15-second spots, all offer sufficient contrast from their environment to achieve differentiation and merit the consumer's attention. Figure 5.6 illustrates the attention-getting nature of white space in an advertisement.

In an effort to achieve contrast, advertisers are also using splashes of colour in black-and-white print ads to highlight the advertised product (see Figure 5.7, page 145, which highlights the Panadol brand).

With respect to packaging, astute marketers usually try to differentiate their packaging sufficiently to ensure rapid consumer perception, as the average package on the supermarket shelf has only a brief time to make an impression on the consumer. According to Max Sutherland, '56 per cent of all buying episodes fell into the category of "simple locating behaviour" '.[25] It is therefore important that every aspect of the package—name, shape, colour, label and copy—provides sufficient sensory stimulation to be noted and remembered. Hallmark Cards, Inc. has used a colour-coded system to help consumers find the greetings cards they want. General and humorous cards are grouped under a turquoise band, while new-baby cards are marked by

FIGURE 5.6 **Illustrates the attention-getting nature of white space in an advertisement**

Colour attracts.
LG's G7020 colour screen mobile. Stylishly designed, with superior polyphonic ring tones and a large, high definition colour screen. You may find you have more friends to call. For details see your Telstra store or visit www.lge.com.au
LG
Life's Good

Source: Courtesy of LG Electronics Australia Pty Ltd.

a mint-green band. Duracell batteries have introduced a similar system whereby different battery sizes are colour-coded to assist consumers in making their product selection. One distinct colour is assigned to identify each different battery size. For instance, AA batteries are coded yellow, AAA batteries are coded green, while D-sized batteries are coded purple.

Sometimes advertisers capitalise on the lack of contrast. A technique that has been used effectively in TV commercials is to position the commercial so close to the story line of a program that viewers are unaware they are watching an ad until they are well into it. In the case of children's programming, there are limitations on the use of this technique. TV stars or cartoon characters, such as Hi-Five, are prohibited from promoting products during children's shows in which they appear.

Advertisers are producing 30-minute commercials (called **infomercials**) that appear to the average viewer as documentaries, and thus command more attentive viewing than obvious commercials would receive. Advertisers are also running print ads (called **advertorials**) which so closely resemble editorial material that it has become increasingly difficult for readers to tell them apart. Restaurant reviews in suburban newspapers sometimes resemble advertisements.

Expectations

People usually see what they expect to see, and what they expect to see is usually based on familiarity, previous experience or preconditioned set. In a marketing context, people tend to perceive products and product attributes according to their own expectations. A man who has been told by his friends that a new brand of Scotch has a bitter taste will probably perceive the taste to be bitter; a teenager who attends a horror movie that has been billed as terrifying will probably find it so. On the other hand, stimuli that conflict sharply with expectations often receive more attention than those that conform to expectations. For example, Figure 5.8 attracts viewer attention because it shows multiple people with the same face, an image in sharp contrast to a person's expectation of what to see at the dinner table. For years, certain advertisers have used blatant sexuality in advertisements for products to which sex was not relevant. They believed such advertisements would attract a high degree of attention; however, such ads often defeated their purpose because readers tended to remember the sexual content (e.g. the girl), but not the product or brand. Nevertheless, advertisers continue to use erotic appeals in promoting a wide variety of products, from office furniture to jeans.

In services, expectations of quality will affect how a service is perceived. Marketers will seek to manage expectations so that customers are not dissatisfied. For example, a person buying a first-class airline seat will expect a larger seat, high levels of personal service and good food. A consumer in 'cattle class' will not expect such service, yet be satisfied with what they get. Occasionally, airlines may *exceed expectations* by providing an upgrade or some extra service, delighting their customers. Service providers need to be careful to control expectations. 'Extra' services, if frequently provided, will come to be expected and consumers may be dissatisfied when they are not provided.

Motives

People tend to perceive things they need or want; the stronger the need, the greater the tendency to ignore unrelated stimuli in the environment. A woman interested in a portable computer is more likely to notice and to read carefully ads for computer laptops than her neighbour, who doesn't use a computer. In general, there is a heightened awareness of stimuli that are relevant to our needs and interests, and a decreased awareness of stimuli that are irrelevant to those needs (see Figure 5.9, page 146). Our perceptual process simply attunes itself more closely to those elements of the environment that are important to us. Someone who is hungry looks for, and more readily perceives, restaurant signs; a sexually repressed person may perceive sexual symbolism where none exists.

FIGURE 5.7 **The use of black & white and colour attracts attention to highlight the advertised product**

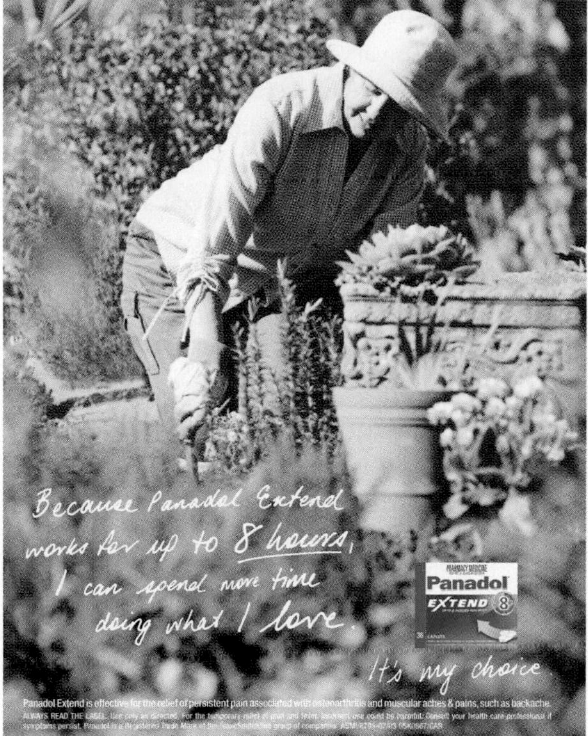

Source: Courtesy of GlaxoSmithKline Australia Pty Ltd.

FIGURE 5.8 **The unexpected attracts attention**

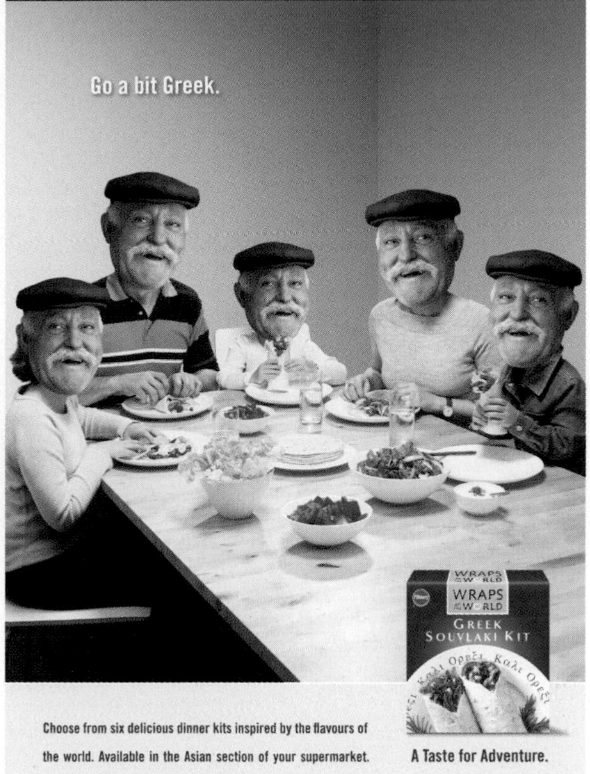

Source: © 2004 General Mills. Reproduced with permission of General Mills. Developed by George Patterson Partners.

Marketing managers recognise the efficiency of targeting their products to the perceived needs of consumers. In this way, they help to ensure that their products will be perceived by potential prospects. The identification of perceived consumer needs has a number of different applications. For example, marketers can determine through marketing research what consumers consider to be the ideal attributes of the product category, or what consumers perceive their needs to be in relation to the product category. The marketer can then segment the market on the basis of these needs and vary the product advertising so that consumers in each segment will perceive the product as meeting their own specific needs, wants and interests.

Important selective perception concepts

As the preceding discussion illustrates, the consumer's 'selection' of stimuli from the environment is based on the interaction of expectations and motives with the stimulus itself. These factors give rise to a number of important concepts concerning perception.

- **Selective exposure**. Consumers actively seek out messages they find pleasant or with which they are sympathetic, and actively avoid painful or threatening ones. Thus, heavy smokers avoid articles that link cigarette smoking to cancer. Instead, they note (and even quote) the relatively few articles that deny the relationship. Consumers also selectively expose themselves to advertisements that reassure them of the wisdom of their purchase decisions.
- **Selective attention**. Consumers exercise a great deal of selectivity in terms of the attention they give to commercial stimuli. They have a heightened awareness of the stimuli that meet their needs or interests

FIGURE 5.9 Needs trigger selective perception

ISN'T IT FUNNY HOW STEREO ADS ARE BORING UNTIL YOU WANT A STEREO?
We admit it. There are times when advertising isn't especially interesting.
For instance, stereo ads when you're not looking for a new stereo. Or insurance ads when you're not looking for a new insurance company. Or detergent ads when you're not looking for a new detergent.
But suppose your stereo breaks down. Or your insurance rates go up. Or your laundry comes out gray. All of a sudden, stereo ads, insurance ads and detergent ads start looking a lot more interesting.
It's one of the basic truths of advertising. We try to be entertaining, but that's not really our job. Our job is to help you make the right choices when you're in the market for any kind of product or service.
Of course, when you're not in the market, we recognize that advertising may seem beside the point. In that case, you're free to pretend it isn't there. In fact, you're free to ignore advertising for as long as you choose.
Right up until your stereo breaks down.
ADVERTISING.
ANOTHER WORD FOR FREEDOM OF CHOICE.
American Association of Advertising Agencies

Source: Courtesy of American Association of Advertising Agencies.

and a lower awareness of stimuli irrelevant to their needs. Thus, they are likely to note ads for products that would satisfy their needs or for stores with which they are familiar, and disregard those in which they have no interest. People also vary in terms of the kind of information they are interested in, and the form of message and type of medium they prefer. Some people are more interested in price, some in appearance, and some in social acceptability. Some people like complex, sophisticated messages; others like simple graphics.

- **Perceptual defence**. Although somewhat controversial, some psychologists continue to claim that people may subconsciously screen out stimuli that are important for them *not* to see, even though exposure has already taken place.[26] Furthermore, we may unconsciously distort information that is not consistent with our needs, values and beliefs. One way to combat perceptual defence is to vary and increase the amount of sensory input. For example, since most smokers no longer pay attention to the written warning labels on cigarette packs, Canada and Brazil now require tobacco firms to feature graphic health warnings on cigarette packaging. One such warning shows a damaged brain and warns about strokes, and another shows a limp cigarette and states that tobacco can cause impotence.[27] Similar graphic imagery is proposed for Australian cigarette packaging.[28]
- **Perceptual blocking.** Consumers protect themselves from being bombarded with stimuli by simply 'tuning out', blocking such stimuli from conscious awareness. Research shows that enormous amounts of advertising are screened out by consumers; they mentally tune out because of the visually overstimulating nature of the world in which we live.[29] This perceptual blocking-out is somewhat akin to the mechanical 'zapping' of commercials using the TV remote control.

PERCEPTUAL ORGANISATION

We do not experience the numerous stimuli we select from the environment as separate and discrete sensations; rather, we tend to organise them into groups and perceive them as unified wholes. Thus, the perceived characteristics of even the simplest stimulus are viewed as a function of the whole to which the stimulus appears to belong. This method of organisation simplifies life considerably for us.

The specific principles underlying **perceptual organisation** are often referred to by the name given to the school of psychology that first developed it, **Gestalt psychology**. (*Gestalt* in German means pattern or configuration.) Three of the most basic principles of perceptual organisation are figure and ground, grouping and closure.

Figure and ground

As noted earlier, stimuli that contrast with their environment are more likely to be noticed. A sound must be louder or softer, a colour brighter or paler. The simplest visual illustration consists of a **figure** on a **ground** (i.e. background). The figure is usually perceived clearly because, in contrast to its ground, it appears to be well defined, solid, and in the forefront. The ground, however, is usually perceived as indefinite, hazy and continuous. The common line that separates the figure and the ground is perceived as belonging to the figure rather than to the ground, which helps give the figure greater definition. Consider the stimulus of music. People can either 'bathe' in music or listen to music. In the first case, music is simply background to other activities; in the second, it is figure. Figure is more clearly perceived because it appears to be dominant; in contrast, ground appears to be subordinate and therefore less important.

People have a tendency to organise their perceptions into figure-and-ground relationships. However, learning affects which stimuli are perceived as figure and which as ground. We are all familiar with the reversible figure-ground pattern, such as the picture of the woman in Figure 5.10. How old would you say she was? Look again, very carefully. Depending on how you perceived figure and how you perceived ground, she can be either in her early twenties or her late seventies.

Like perceptual selection, perceptual organisation is affected by motives and by expectations based on experience. For example, how a reversible figure-ground pattern is perceived can be influenced by prior pleasant or painful associations with one or the other element in isolation. The consumer's physical state can also affect how he or she perceives reversible figure-ground illustrations. For example, a short time after the destruction of the World Trade Center on 11 September 2001 by hijacked airplanes, a university professor came across an ad for Lufthansa (Germany's national airline) that featured a flying plane, photographed from the ground up, between two glass high-rise buildings. Rather than focusing on the brand and the plane (i.e. the 'figure'), all the viewer could think about was the two tall glass towers in the background (i.e. the 'ground'), and the possibility of the jet crashing into them. When the professor presented the ad to her students, many expressed the same thoughts. Clearly, this figure–ground reversal was the outcome of the painful events that occurred on 11 September 2001.

FIGURE 5.10 Figure-ground reversal

Advertisers have to plan their advertisements carefully to make sure that the stimulus they want noted is seen as figure and not as ground. The musical background must not overwhelm the jingle; the background of an advertisement must not detract from the product. Some print advertisers often silhouette their products against a white background to make sure that the features they want noted are clearly perceived. Others use reverse lettering (white letters on a black background) to achieve **contrast**; however, they must be careful to avoid the problem of figure-ground reversal. Figure 5.11 shows an ad for Domestos that cleverly uses the figure-ground effect to highlight the product.

Marketers sometimes run advertisements that confuse the consumer because there is no clear indication of which is figure and which is ground. In some

FIGURE 5.11 **Use of figure and ground effect to highlight the product**

Domestos
ELIMINATES SMELLS AND BACTERIA FROM SPONGES.
Disinfect sponges and dishcloths regularly by soaking for 10 minutes in a dilute solution of Domestos. Then allow them to dry.
It's also a great way to disinfect your sink. Domestos is a powerful cleaner. Always read the label before use and follow the directions

Source: Used with the permission of Unilever Australasia.

Absolut vodka print ads, the figure is not very clearly delineated against its ground, but readers are conditioned to look for the shape of the Absolut bottle, which is usually cleverly hidden in the ad. The resulting audience participation produces more intense scrutiny. Figure 5.12 invites the reader to find the bottle in the ad. Sony adopts a similar technique in combination with the use of white space to highlight the product in a repetitive and symbolic manner in Figure 5.13, inviting the consumer to find the footprints (or 'walkman') in the advertisement.

Grouping

Individuals tend to group stimuli automatically so that they form a unified picture or impression. The perception of stimuli as groups or *chunks* of information, rather than as discrete bits of information, facilitates their memory and recall. **Grouping** can be used advantageously by marketers to imply certain desired meanings in connection with their products. For example, if an advertisement for coffee shows a young man and woman in a friendly, country town setting, the grouping of stimuli by proximity leads the consumer to associate the

FIGURE 5.12 **Consumers must work to distinguish the Absolut figure from the ground**

Source: Under permission by V&S Vin & Sprit AB (publ). Absolut country of Sweden vodka and logo, Absolut, Absolut bottle design and Absolut calligraphy are trademarks owned by V&S Vin & Sprit AB (publ). © 2004 V&S Vin & Sprit AB (publ).

drinking of coffee with romance, fine living and warmth.

Most of us can remember and repeat our telephone numbers because we automatically group them into chunks rather than ten separate numbers. For example, mobile phone numbers are typically grouped into one chunk of four followed by two chunks of three. We find it easy to hear the numbers if they are grouped in this expected way, but have difficulty when people use some other way of chunking information to give their number.

Closure

Individuals look for **closure**. They express this need by organising their perceptions so that they form a complete picture. If the pattern of stimuli to which they are exposed is incomplete, they tend to perceive it nevertheless as complete; that is, they consciously or subconsciously fill in the missing pieces. Thus, a circle with a section of its periphery missing will invariably be perceived as a circle and not as an arc. The need for closure is also seen in the tension an individual experiences when a task is incomplete, and the satisfaction and relief that come with its completion.

FIGURE 5.13 **Increasing audience participation to attract attention**

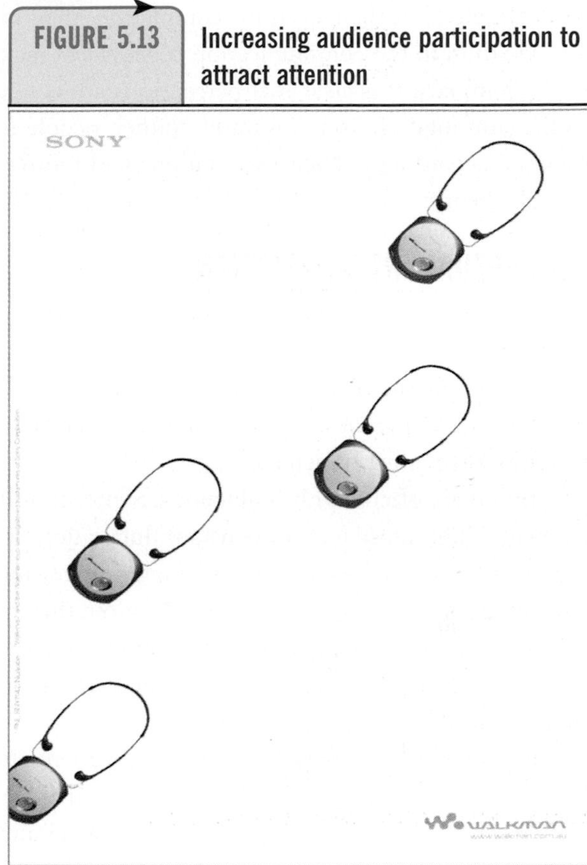

Source: Courtesy of Sony.

A classic study, reported in 1972, found that incomplete tasks may be remembered more readily than complete tasks. One explanation for this phenomenon is that the person who begins a task develops a need to complete it. If he or she is prevented from doing so, a state of tension is created that manifests itself in improved memory for the incomplete task (the Zeigernik effect). Hearing the beginning of a message leads to the development of a need to hear the rest of it, like waiting for the second shoe to drop.[30] The resulting tension leads to improvement in memory for that part of the message that has already been heard. One marketer reported several instances of 'concept closure', in which viewers reacted to background cues by 'filling in' more information than the commercial provided.[31] For example, a commercial for a US brand of bacon showed a close-up of bacon frying in an iron skillet while a voice-over in a deep cowboy twang said what fine bacon it was. Beneath the laid-back delivery was the sound of a harmonica playing a soft, mournful cowboy tune. A telephone survey conducted 24 hours later found that people remembered far more than the simple ad had shown them. One respondent recalled bacon frying on a campfire with cowboys sitting around; another recalled horses standing in the background and the light of the campfire reflecting on the faces of the cowboys eating bacon. The viewers filled in the story 'painted' by the background cues, in effect creating their own more effective, more memorable commercial.

The need for closure has some interesting implications for marketers. The presentation of an incomplete or incorrect advertising message 'begs' for completion or correction by consumers. The very act of completion and/or correction serves to involve them more deeply in the message itself. In a related vein, advertisers have discovered that they can achieve excellent results by using the soundtrack of a frequently shown television commercial on radio. Consumers who are familiar with the TV commercial perceive the audio track alone as incomplete; in their need for completion, they mentally play back the visual content as well. Consumer participation in the communication process can make it far more effective.

In summary, it is clear that perceptions are not equivalent to the raw sensory input of discrete stimuli or to the sum total of discrete stimuli. Rather, people tend to add to or subtract from stimuli to which they are exposed according to their expectations and motives, using generalised principles of organisation based on Gestalt theory.

PERCEPTUAL INTERPRETATION

The preceding discussion has emphasised that perception is a personal phenomenon. We exercise selectivity as to which stimuli we perceive, and organise these stimuli on the basis of certain psychological principles. The interpretation of stimuli is also uniquely individual, since it is based on what we expect to see in light of our previous experience, on the number of plausible explanations we can envisage, and on our motives and interests at the time of perception.

Stimuli are often highly ambiguous. Some stimuli are weak because of such factors as poor visibility, brief exposure, high noise level or constant fluctuation. Even stimuli that are strong tend to fluctuate dramatically because of such factors as different angles of viewing, varying distances and changing levels of illumination. Consumers usually attribute the sensory input they receive to sources they consider most likely to have caused the specific pattern of stimuli. Past experiences and social interactions may help to form certain expectations that provide categories or alternatives that we use in interpreting stimuli. The narrower our experience, the more limited the access to alternative categories.

When stimuli are highly ambiguous, we usually interpret them in such a way that they serve to fulfil personal needs, wishes, interests, and so on. It is this principle that provides the rationale for the projective tests discussed in Chapter 3. Such tests provide ambiguous stimuli (such as incomplete sentences, unclear pictures, untitled cartoons and ink blots) to respondents who are asked to interpret them. How a person describes a vague illustration, what meaning the individual ascribes to an ink blot, is a reflection not of the stimulus itself, but of the subject's own needs, wants and desires. Through the interpretation of ambiguous stimuli, respondents reveal a great deal about themselves.

How close our interpretations are to reality, then, depends on the clarity of the stimulus, our past experiences and our motives and interests at the time of perception.

Distorting influences (Perceptual distortion)

Individuals are subject to a number of influences that tend to distort their perceptions; some of these are discussed below.

Physical appearance People tend to attribute the qualities they associate with certain people to others who may resemble them, whether or not they consciously recognise the similarity. For this reason, the selection of models for advertisements can be a key element in their ultimate persuasiveness. Studies on physical appearance have found that attractive models are more persuasive and have a more positive influence on consumer attitudes and behaviour than average-looking models; attractive men are perceived as more successful businessmen than average-looking men. Some research suggests that models influence consumers' perceptions of physical attractiveness, and through comparisons, their own self-perceptions.[32] Recent research indicates that merely choosing a highly attractive model may not increase message effectiveness. One study revealed that highly attractive models are perceived as having more expertise regarding enhancing products (e.g. lipstick, perfume) but not regarding problem-solving products (e.g. products that correct beauty flaws such as acne or dandruff).[33] Therefore, advertisers must ensure that there is a rational match between the product advertised and the physical attributes of the model used to promote it.

Stereotypes We tend to carry 'pictures' in our minds of the meanings of various kinds of stimuli. These **stereotypes** serve as expectations of what specific situations or people or events will be like, and are important determinants of how such stimuli are subsequently perceived. For example, Megan Gale's Australian tourism ads for the Italian market build on various national stereotypes. Similarly, Paul Hogan's tourism ads for the American market built on these stereotypes, with a humorous Australian overtone. In another example, an ad for Benetton featured two men—one black and one white—handcuffed together. This was part of the 'united colors of Benetton' campaign promoting racial harmony. This advertisement produced a public outcry globally because people perceived it as depicting a white man arresting a black man.[34] Clearly, this perception was the result of stereotypes, since there was nothing in the ad to indicate that the white person was arresting the black person rather than the other way around.

Irrelevant cues When required to form a difficult perceptual judgment, consumers often respond to irrelevant stimuli. For example, many high-priced cars are purchased because of their colour, or luxury options like retractable headlights or leather upholstery, rather than on the basis of mechanical or technical superiority.

First impression First impressions tend to be lasting; yet, in forming such impressions, the perceiver does not yet know which stimuli are relevant, important or predictive of later behaviour. With great effect, a shampoo commercial used the line 'You'll never have a second chance to make a first impression'. Because first impressions are often lasting, introducing a new product before it has been perfected may prove fatal to its ultimate success, because subsequent information about its advantages, even if true, will often be negated by memory of its early failure.

Jumping to conclusions Many people jump to conclusions before examining all the relevant evidence. For example, the consumer may hear just the beginning of a commercial message and draw conclusions regarding the product or service being advertised on the basis of such limited information. For this reason, copywriters are careful to place their most persuasive arguments early in the ad. A recent study found that most consumers do not read the volume information on food labels. They also purchase packages that they believe contain greater volume, whether or not this is actually so. For example, consumers perceived elongated packaging to contain more volume than round packaging.[35] The study found a positive correlation between perceived product volume and consumption. Thus, the products inside packages that were perceived to hold more volume when purchased were also consumed faster after the purchase. Clearly, these findings have important implications for package design, advertising, and pricing.

Halo effect Historically, the **halo effect** has been used to describe situations in which the evaluation of a single object or person on a multitude of dimensions is based on the evaluation of just one or a few dimensions (e.g. a man is trustworthy, fine and noble because he looks you in the eye when he speaks). Consumer behaviourists broaden the notion of the halo effect to include the evaluation of multiple objects (e.g. a product line) on the basis of the evaluation of just one dimension (a brand name or a spokesperson).

Using this broader definition, marketers take advantage of the halo effect when they extend a brand name associated with one line of products to another. Building on the reputation it had gained in marketing inexpensive, reliable, disposable pens, BIC successfully introduced a line of disposable razors under the BIC name. Consumers bought the new BIC razor on the basis of their favourable evaluation of the BIC pen. (An extension of this phenomenon, stimulus generalisation, is discussed in Chapter 5.) The mushrooming field of licensing also makes use of the halo effect. Manufacturers and retailers hope to acquire instant recognition and status for their products by association with a well-known celebrity or designer name. Cosmetics marketers have used female stars like Elizabeth Hurley or Heather Locklear in their ads.

The reader may well ask how 'realistic' perception can be, given the many subjective influences on **perceptual interpretation**. It is somewhat reassuring to remember that previous experiences usually serve to resolve stimulus ambiguity in a realistic way and help in its interpretation. Only in situations of unusual or changing stimulus conditions do expectations lead to wrong interpretations.

Consumer imagery

Consumers have a number of enduring perceptions, or images, that are particularly relevant to the study of consumer behaviour. Chapter 4 discusses consumer self-images; this section examines consumers' perceived images of product categories, brands, retail stores and service and product producers.

Products and brands have symbolic value and we evaluate them on the basis of their consistency (i.e. congruence) with our personal picture of ourself. Some products seem to agree with our self-image; others do not. Consumers attempt to preserve or enhance their self-image by buying products they believe are congruent with that self-image and avoiding products that are not.[36]

POSITIONING AND REPOSITIONING PRODUCTS AND SERVICES

The image that a product or service has in the mind of the consumer—that is, its **positioning**—is probably more important to its ultimate success than its actual characteristics. Marketers try to differentiate their brands by stressing attributes they claim will fulfil the consumer's needs better than competing brands. They strive to create a positioning consistent with the relevant self-image of the targeted consumer segment. Most new products fail because they are perceived as 'me too' offerings that do not offer potential consumers any advantages or unique benefits over competitive products.

Marketers of different brands in the same category can effectively differentiate their offerings only if they stress the benefits that their brands provide rather than their products' physical features. The benefits featured in a product's positioning must reflect attributes that are important to and congruent with the perceptions of the targeted consumer segment.

Positioning strategy thus complements the company's segmentation strategy and selection of target markets. It conveys the concept, or meaning, of the product or service in terms of how it fulfils a consumer need. Different consumer meanings (i.e. product images) can be assigned to the same product (or service). Thus, it can be positioned differently to different audiences, or it can be repositioned to the same audience, without actually being physically changed. Successful positioning results in a distinctive brand image that consumers can rely on, affecting both consumer beliefs about brand characteristics and the price the consumer is willing to pay.[37] A positive brand image also leads to consumer loyalty, positive beliefs about brand value, and a willingness to search for the brand. A positive brand image also promotes consumer interest in future brand promotions and inoculates consumers against competitors' marketing activities. As markets become more crowded and services become more complex, a distinctive image is most important. Consumers may rely more on the image conveyed by the brand than on its actual attributes. This becomes particularly important for **credence** and **experience products** where the consumer is unable to evaluate them prior to use because of their intangible properties (e.g. health insurance). As a result of successful positioning strategy, consumers carry defined mental images of particular brands.[38]

The Guinness Import Company has an overall positioning strategy for its imported brand that creates a distinctive product image that places its beer 'above the fray' of competition. Stella Artois[39] with its outrageous print commercials, and Tooheys Dry with its distinctive advertising, established clear positioning for their brands. Foster's, with its worldwide sports promotion, has established an international image for the brand as well as pushing into major new markets such as China. It has also tried to position itself as an innovator in the market by introducing new products such as Empire, not just line extensions.[40] Worldwide beer producers have thus gone to considerable efforts to differentiate their products.

The major positioning strategies are discussed in the following five sections.

Umbrella positioning

This strategy entails creating an overall image of the company around which many products can be featured individually. This strategy is appropriate for very large corporations with diversified product lines. For example, McDonald's positioning approaches over the years include 'You deserve a break today at McDonald's', 'Nobody can do it like McDonald's can', and 'Good times, great taste'. Coca-Cola has produced similar positioning strategies with themes including 'You can't beat the feeling', 'Always Coca-Cola', 'Enjoy' and most recently 'Coca-Cola Real', helping to position the product over the past two decades.[41]

Positioning against the competition

Visa's past slogan 'We make American Express green with envy' is a good example of this strategy. The Hertz car rental company has run TV ads depicting other car rental companies as lacking in features that Hertz's outlets generally possess, such as proximity to passenger terminals at airports (e.g. 'Hertz? Not exactly'). Despite much legal wrangling, Duracell succeeded in its battle to advertise its slogan 'Duracell lasts up to 3 times longer than Eveready Super Heavy Duty (In AA, AAA, C and D sizes only)'. Herron has run a successful campaign against Panadol and most recently Nurofen with its latest campaigns positioning the brand and products as Australian owned and produced.[42]

Positioning based on a specific benefit

FedEx created its highly reliable service image with the slogan 'When it absolutely, positively has to be there overnight'. Maxwell House Coffee is 'good to the last drop'. Cadbury Chocolate has 'a glass and a half [of full cream dairy milk]'. These are examples of slogans that smartly and precisely depict key benefits of the brands they promote and have effectively positioned these brands in the minds of consumers. There are also many examples of products that failed because they were positioned to deliver a benefit that consumers either did not want or did not believe. For example, Gillette's 'For Oily Hair Only' shampoo failed because most consumers do not acknowledge that they have oily hair. Pepsi's 1992 'Pepsi Crystal' was a clear, 'natural' Pepsi that took away all the qualities, including the taste, that consumers liked about Pepsi's drink.[43] Effective depictions of a core benefit often include memorable imagery.

Finding an 'unowned' position

In highly competitive markets, finding a niche unfilled by other companies is challenging but not impossible. A clever approach in finding (or even creating) an 'unowned' position was Palmolive's claim to '. . . soften your hands as you do the dishes'; today, even though many people no longer wash dishes by hand, Palmolive positions its dishwashing liquid as 'tough on grease, soft on hands'. Herron Pharmaceuticals has also found a niche in the market place. In a market dominated by Panadol, Herron successfully built on the ethnocentric tendencies of consumers by consistently advertising its products as Australian owned and made, and contributing to the Australian economy.[44]

Filling several positions

Because unfilled gaps or 'unowned' perceptual positions present opportunities for competitors, sophisticated marketers create several distinct offerings, often in the form of different brands, to fill several identified niches. For example, among Foster's major brands, Crown Lager is positioned as the 'finest premium beer', Foster's Lager as the largest-selling 'king of beers', and Redback as the 'specialty' brew; the prices of the three brands reflect their images. Panadol's adult analgesic versions include a number of products for pain relief, such as Panadol, Panadeine and Panadeine Forte. Colgate-Palmolive, one of the largest producers of laundry detergents (which are actually commodity-like products, since the physical make-up of almost all detergents is largely identical) offers consumers such brands as Fab (deeply cleans, softly protects fabrics, and whitens and brightens clothes), Dynamo (for front loading washers), Cuddly (extra softness and freshness), Sard Wondersoap (for pre-treating need and shifting tough stains) and several other detergents.[45] It would be difficult for a manufacturer to penetrate the detergent market with a product that offers a benefit that is not already provided by a Colgate-Palmolive brand.

Product repositioning

Regardless of how well positioned a product appears to be, the marketer may be forced to reposition it in response to market events, such as a competitor cutting into the brand's market share or too many competitors stressing the same attribute. For example, rather than trying to meet the lower prices of high-quality private-label competition, some premium brand marketers have repositioned their brands to justify their higher prices, playing up brand attributes that had previously been ignored. David Jones presents a good example where it focused on attaining exclusive deals with fashion designers (e.g. Collette Dinnigan) and various suppliers (e.g. Witchery) to achieve a point of distinction from its closest competitor, Myer. To complement its service levels, store ambience and range of goods, exclusive offerings allowed David Jones to retain its loyal consumers and avoid price wars in the market place.[46]

Firms often adopt a **repositioning** strategy in order to boost the appeal of their products. Case Study 5.1 shows how WD-40 in Australia successfully repositioned its product, increasing both awareness and sales. Coca-Cola entered the millennium by repositioning its flagship product as a 'unique taste sensation' and a 'sparkle on your tongue'.[47] Volvo has also sought to reposition its vehicles by adopting the controversial 'bloody Volvo driver' campaign. While the critics were sceptical about the campaign claiming that it would offend and alienate its most loyal drivers,[48] the campaign has increased awareness of the Volvo brand, changed consumer attitudes and perceptions, appealed to non-traditional and younger potential Volvo drivers and driven up sales.[49]

Another reason to reposition a product or service is to satisfy changing consumer preferences. For example, when health-oriented consumers began to avoid high-fat foods, many fast-food chains acted swiftly to reposition their images by offering salad bars and other health-oriented foods. Kentucky Fried Chicken changed its well-known corporate name to KFC in order to omit the dreaded word 'fried' from its advertising. Weight Watchers repositioned its line of frozen foods from 'dietetic' to 'healthy,' maintaining its diet-thin imagery while responding to a perceived shift in consumer values. McDonald's has most recently introduced its Salads Plus range in Australia with unprecedented success, appealing to the health-conscious and the older consumer.[50] As birthrates decline and consumers' preferences for more gentle and pure products emerge, Johnson & Johnson repositioned its baby lotion, powder, and shampoo as products for grown-ups. One of the most successful product repositioning is the promotion of bi-carbonate soda as a standard household item for cleanliness and purity by showing it used as a refrigerator deodoriser, toothpaste (when combined with water), household cleaner and cooking raising agent.

Perceptual mapping

The technique of **perceptual mapping** helps marketers to determine just how their products or services appear to consumers in relation to competitive brands, on one or more relevant characteristics.[51] It enables them to see gaps in the positioning of all brands in the product or service class, and to identify areas in which consumer needs are not being adequately met.

Figure 5.14 shows the outcome of such a study, based on Australian consumers.[52] From this research, a producer of iced coffee may discover that consumers perceive its product (DD) to be very similar to product

FIGURE 5.14 **Perceptual map for an Australian iced coffee study**

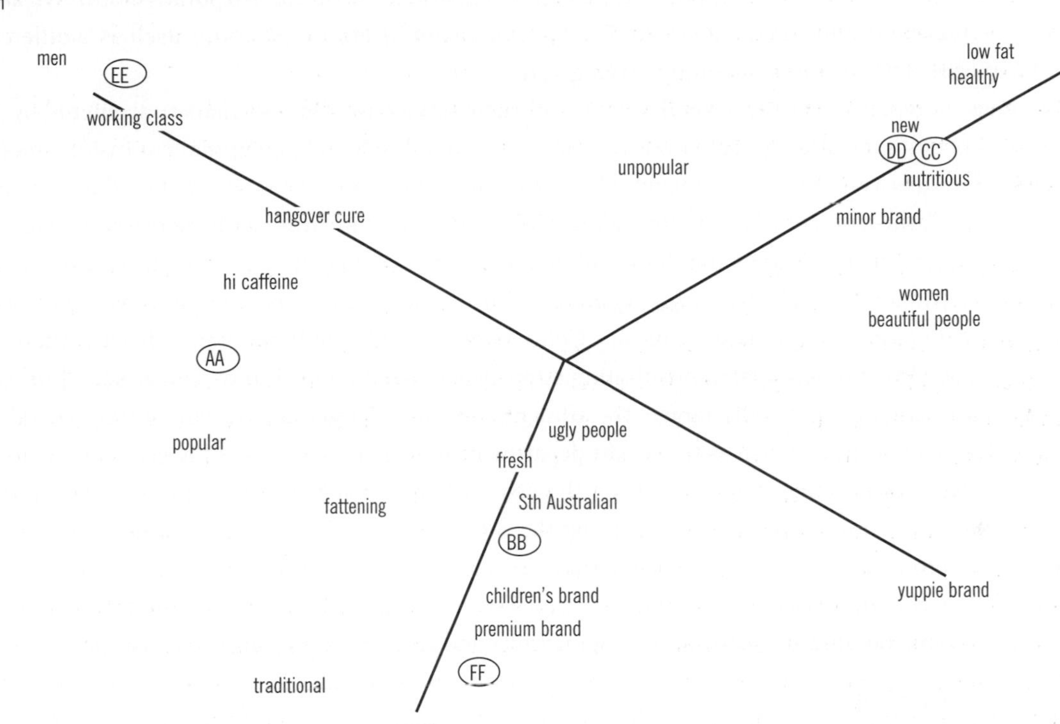

Source: **Rachel Kennedy, Christopher Riquier and Byron Sharp, 'Putting correspondence analysis to use with categorical data in market research', in Ken Grant and Ian Walker (eds),** ***Proceedings of the Seventh Bi-Annual World Marketing Congress*** **(Melbourne: Academy of Marketing Science, 1995), Vol. VII-III, 14-102 to 14-111. © 1995 Academy of Marketing Science.**

CC but a long way from AA, the brand leader. Repositioning the brand may be difficult. Although there are clear gaps, most of these were near to undesirable attributes, such as 'ugly people' or 'fattening'. A repositioned brand for 'women' and 'beautiful people' would be a possibility, through use of advertising. However, to be a large seller, the presentation should be aspirational in orientation, appealing to the larger part of the market.

Perceptual maps can be insightful snapshots of the market at a particular time. However, because of the analysis method used, many maps are not good at tracking changes.

The positioning of services

Compared with manufacturing firms, service marketers face several unique problems in positioning and promoting their offerings. These include service characteristics and the importance of the service environment.

Because services are intangible, *image* becomes a key factor in differentiating the service from its competition. Thus, the marketing objective is to enable the consumer to link a specific image with a specific brand name. The Commonwealth Bank logo, by Cato Design, is a clear attempt to brand the service. Many service marketers have developed strategies to provide customers with visual images and tangible reminders of their service offerings. These include painted delivery vehicles, restaurant matchbooks, packaged hotel soaps and shampoos, and a variety of other specialty items. Some financial companies try to associate their services with tangible objects. The MLC Company invites consumers to see their savings as a golden nest egg which the company will mind. AXA managed to establish its brand in place of the venerable (but weakened) National

Mutual brand—by emphasising its strength and sense of innovation. Many service companies feature real service employees in their ads (as tangible cues) and some use people-focused themes to differentiate themselves. For example, the Ritz-Carlton promotes its 'guest experience' with the corporate motto 'We are ladies and gentlemen serving ladies and gentlemen', The Marriott Sydney Harbour positions itself as 'a different kind of five star [with] staff who actually enjoy serving you'.

Sometimes, companies market several versions of their service to different market segments by using a differentiated positioning strategy. However, they must be careful to avoid perceptual confusion among their customers. The American Express Company offers its regular (green and the new blue) card to consumers as a short-term credit instrument and the prestigious Gold and Platinum cards, with increased services, to the affluent cardholder. Financial funds that target affluent consumers focus on estate planning, investments and trust funds to maintain an exclusive image; commercial banks stress cash machines and overdraft privileges to consumers with more modest financial means. Coles-Myer uses different brand names for its various department stores to achieve a differentiated positioning strategy and avoid confusion by consumers. For example, the Myer department store generally targets the affluent consumer, Target department stores generally focus on the middle-class consumer whereas the Kmart department store generally targets the consumer with limited financial means by positioning itself as 'cutting the cost of living'. Each of these brands targets a different segment, each with its own expectations regarding the service delivered. Although distinct brand names are important to all products or services, they are particularly crucial in marketing services due to the abstract and intangible nature of many services. For example, names such as Federal Express (later abbreviated to FedEx) is an excellent name because it is distinctive, memorable, and relevant to the service it features.

The service environment

The design of the service environment is an important aspect of service positioning strategy and sharply influences consumer impressions and consumer and employee behaviour.[53] The physical environment is particularly important in creating a favourable impression for such services as banks, retail stores and professional offices, because there are so few objective criteria by which consumers can judge the quality of the services they receive. The service environment conveys the *image* of the service provider, with whom the service is so closely linked. Thus, at David Jones stores there is an ambience of quality, but with the possible implication of higher prices.

One study of service environments identified the environmental variables of most importance to customers of banks. They included, in order:

1. *Privacy* (of both a visual and auditory nature), such as enclosed offices, transaction privacy, etc.
2. *Efficiency* and *convenience* (transaction areas that are easy to find, directional signs, etc.)
3. *Ambient background conditions* (temperature, lighting, noise, music)
4. *Social conditions* (the appearance of other people in the bank environment, such as bank customers and bank personnel)
5. *Aesthetics* (colour, style, use of materials, art works).[54]

Clearly, a favourable service environment creates the perception among consumers that the service itself will satisfy their needs more effectively.

➤ Perceived price

How consumers perceive price—both in terms of the actual amount to be sacrificed and the value to be gained—will affect how they evaluate what marketers offer them. If a price is regarded as unfair, cheap, expensive or trivial then purchase intentions will be greatly affected. Consumers will compare themselves with others and this may be a problem. For example, people sitting together in an aircraft may have paid a range of different prices (FlyBuys flyers for free, people on standby for a low fare and business people at full fare). Strategies that reduce price unfairness ultimately enhance perceived value.[55] Perceptions of price unfairness affect consumers' perceptions of product value and, ultimately, their willingness to patronise a store or a service. One study, focused on the special challenges of service industries in pricing intangible products, proposed three types of pricing strategies based on the customer's perception of the value provided by the purchase (see Table 5.2).

TABLE 5.2 Three pricing strategies focused on perceived value

Pricing strategy	Provides value by . . .	Implemented as . . .
Satisfaction-based pricing	Recognising and reducing customers' perceptions of uncertainty, which the intangible nature of services magnifies.	Service guarantees. Benefit-driven pricing. Flat-rate pricing.
Relationship pricing	Encouraging long-term relationships with the company that customers view as beneficial.	Long-term contracts. Price bundling.
Efficiency pricing	Sharing with customers the cost savings that the company has achieved by understanding, managing, and reducing the costs of providing the service.	Cost-leader pricing.

Source: **Leonard L. Berry and Yadav S. Manjit, 'Capture and communicate value in the pricing of services', *Sloan Management Review*, Summer 1996, pp. 41–51. Reproduced with permission.**

REFERENCE PRICE

Products advertised as 'on sale' tend to create enhanced consumer perceptions of savings and value. Different formats used in sales advertisements have differing impacts, based on consumer reference prices. A **reference price** is any price that a consumer uses as a basis for comparison in judging another price. Reference prices can be *external* or *internal*. Advertisers often try to frame (or depict) the normal price (*external reference price*) as being higher than the sale price, as in 'Red Spot Specials' at supermarkets. In contrast, *internal reference prices* are those learned or perceived by the consumer. They include those prices (or price range) retrieved by the consumer from memory. They form an internal standard that consumers can use to judge the value of the price offered and the credibility of any claim made. Advertised prices (both external reference and sale prices) affect consumer learning of internal reference prices.[56] For example, when petrol prices increased suddenly due to an OPEC-produced shortage of crude oil, consumers soon realised that the previous price range no longer applied and shifted their reference prices upwards.

Several studies have investigated the effects on consumer price perceptions of various types of advertised reference prices: implausible low, plausible low, plausible high and implausible high. *Implausible low* prices are 'too good to be true'. A brand new Porsche offered for $10 000 is an example: 'What's the catch?' the consumer may say. *Plausible low* prices are well within the range of acceptable prices; *plausible high* prices are near the outer limits of the range but not beyond the realm of believability. As long as the advertised reference price is within a given consumer's acceptable price range, it is considered plausible and *assimilated*. (See assimilation-contrast theory in Chapter 7.) If the advertised price is outside the range of acceptable prices (i.e. implausible), it will be *contrasted* and thus will not be perceived as a valid external reference point.[57] Findings show that an implausible high reference price can affect both consumer evaluations and the advertiser's image of credibility. By setting the reference price at the highest price recently offered for identical or comparable products, the advertiser can enhance consumer perceptions of value while minimising negative effects.

According to *acquisition-transaction utility theory*, two types of utility are associated with consumer purchases. *Acquisition utility* represents the consumer's perception of economic gain or loss associated with a purchase, and is a function of several cost elements. These include product utility, the price paid and sunk costs (including the cost of change). *Transaction utility* concerns the perceived pleasure or displeasure associated with the financial aspect of the purchase and is determined by the difference between the internal reference price and the purchase price.[58] For example, buying a new TV set at $600 when this is the internal reference price carries no transaction utility. Buying the same set at a discount will produce a positive utility, the 'consumer surplus' described by economists. Research indicates that transaction utility is significant only when the consumer is certain about consistency of quality.[59]

TENSILE AND OBJECTIVE PRICE CLAIMS

The words used to communicate price-related information give consumers cues that can affect their price perceptions. **Tensile price claims**, involving a range of possible discounts (e.g. 'save up to 60%', 'save 10–40%') are used to promote a range of price discounts for a product line, an entire department or even an entire store. In contrast to tensile cues, **objective price claims** provide a single discount level, such as 'save 25%'. Because of the broad range of sale merchandise covered by both types of claim, they can have a greater effect on purchasing and store traffic generation than a reference price advertisement for a single product.[60]

Consumer evaluations and shopping intentions are least favourable for advertisements stating the minimum discount level ('save 10% or more'). Ads that state a maximum discount level ('save up to 40%') either equal or *exceed* the effectiveness of ads stating a discount range ('save 10–40%'). When different levels of savings are advertised across a product line, the maximum discount level has been found to be most effective at influencing consumers' perceptions of savings. The *width* of a tensile claim also affects price perceptions. For broader discount ranges, tensile claims stating the maximum level of savings (e.g. 'up to 40% off') have more positive effects than those stating the minimum level (e.g. 'at least 10% off') or the entire savings range (e.g. '10–40% off'). For narrow discount ranges, those stating the maximum level of discount appeared no more effective than the minimum or range claims.[61]

In a related fashion, **bundle pricing** (the marketing of two or more products in a single package for a special price) can affect value perceptions. The additional savings offered directly on the bundle have a greater impact on perceived value than savings offered on the bundle's individual items.[62] Bundle pricing is commonly used with financial services, cars and mobile phone services. Consumers appear less sensitive to price when using credit cards (compared to cash). A related phenomenon is on-line sales where consumers appear less price-sensitive than they are in stores.[63]

PROSPECT THEORY

For most consumers, the value of various alternatives on offer is not obvious. As the above examples show, the information that consumers pay attention to and the manner of evaluation will affect perceived value. **Prospect theory** attempts to deal with these phenomena.[64] The fundamental point is that all transactions involve some form of risk and can be seen as a balance of losses (e.g. monetary sacrifice) and gains (e.g. value of products acquired). According to the theory, choices are evaluated in two stages. First, there is an *editing stage* where available information is simplified, with gains and losses assigned according to a reference point, usually the status quo. This process of assigning losses and gains is referred to as **framing**. Then there is an *evaluation* stage where the consumer works out which alternative involves the best value.

Marketers attempt to provide consumers with a frame to evaluate what they have on offer. For example, the 'beat the price rise' advertising ploy suggests to consumers that they will face a loss if they do not buy at the current price. Similarly, new car salespeople can often make more money selling accessories for new cars (e.g. protection strips, alloy wheels) than they do on the actual car. Here the loss (price paid) by the consumer is framed relative to the price of the car itself and seen as a small amount. Discounts are usually shown in proportional terms when the monetary value is small (e.g. '10% off') and in monetary terms when they are larger (e.g. 'reduced by $10'). A discount of $5 on a $20 calculator will be more highly valued than a $5 discount on the price of a $40 000 car. Framing suggests that gains and losses will have a greater impact when presented separately.[65] Assuming price rises are above the j.n.d., it is better to present them in aggregate, while gains should be presented individually.

In general, losses are more keenly felt than gains. Under conditions of gain, consumers tend to become risk-averse; under conditions of loss consumers tend to become risk-prone. Gambling behaviour may provide some of the clearest examples. When gamblers win, they become increasingly averse to risking all their winnings in a single bet. However, when they are losing they are more prone to gamble further to reverse their losses. If marketers can reframe their offer as a gain, consumers are more likely to accept it. While there has been some criticism of prospect theory,[66] it does point to the need for marketers to frame their offerings in a positive, though plausible, fashion and to consider consumers' evaluation of risk. (See also Chapter 14 where the role of perceived risk in decision making is discussed.)

PERCEIVED QUALITY

Consumers often judge the quality of a product or service on the basis of a variety of informational cues that they associate with the product. Some of these cues are intrinsic to the product (or service); others are extrinsic, such as price, store image, service environment, brand image and promotional message. Either singly or in composite, these **intrinsic** and **extrinsic cues** provide the basis for perceptions of product and service quality.

Perceived quality of products

Cues that are intrinsic concern physical characteristics of the product itself, such as size, colour, flavour and aroma.[67] In some cases, consumers use physical characteristics to judge product quality—for example, they may judge the flavour of ice-cream or cake by colour cues. Even the perceived quality of laundry detergents is affected by colour cues. That is why many detergents are blue, with the expectation that housewives will associate the colour with the 'blue bag' their grandmothers used to whiten and brighten their laundry. Consumers like to believe they base their product quality evaluations on intrinsic cues, because they can justify the resulting product decisions (either positive or negative) on the basis of 'rational' or 'objective' product choice. More often than not, however, the physical characteristics they use to judge quality have no intrinsic relationship to the product's quality. For example, though many consumers claim they buy a brand of beer because of its superior taste, they are often unable to identify that brand in blind taste tests. One study discovered that the colour of a powdered fruit drink product is a more important determinant than the label and the actual taste in determining the consumer's ability to identify the flavour correctly. The study's subjects perceived the purple or grape-coloured versions of the powdered product 'tart' in flavour and the orange-coloured version as 'flavorful, sweet, and refreshing'.[68]

In the absence of actual experience with a product, consumers often 'evaluate' quality on the basis of extrinsic cues, cues that are external to the product itself, such as its price, the image of the store(s) that carries it, or the image of the manufacturer or the country that produces it. *Consumer Reports* (the US equivalent of *Choice*) found that consumers often cannot differentiate among various cola beverages, and that their preferences are often based on such extrinsic cues as pricing, packaging, advertising and even peer pressure.[69]

Many consumers use country-of-origin stereotypes to evaluate products (e.g. 'German engineering is excellent' or 'Japanese cars are reliable'). Many consumers believe that a 'Made in Australia' label means a product is 'very good' and purchase of the good will positively contribute to the Australian economy. Figure 5.15 presents the findings of an Australian survey in which respondents were asked to evaluate the quality of clothing products based on their country of origin.[70] In general, Australian, New Zealand and British clothing was judged to be of higher quality than material from China and South-East Asia, though the gap was narrowing over time. This can be used to understand the success of Giordano International Limited, a clothing store originating from Hong Kong, which adopted a company name from Italian derivation to avoid the negative perception often attributed to clothing manufactured in Asia. There are many other examples that support the notion that Australian and New Zealand consumers are much more impressed with domestic clothing or foreign clothing from Europe than they are with clothing from China and South East Asia. Buy Australian campaigns seemed to have little impact here.

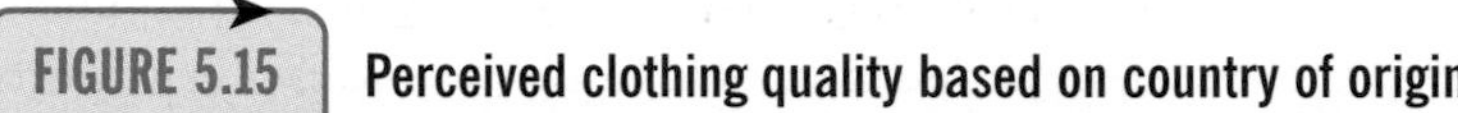

FIGURE 5.15 Perceived clothing quality based on country of origin

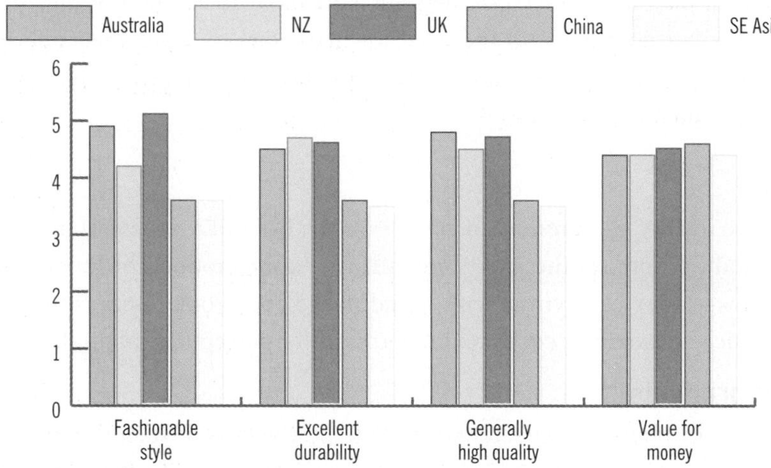

Source: Adapted from Muris Cicic, 'A longitudinal study of country-of-origin effect for the apparel industry in Australia', in Ken Grant and Ian Walker (eds), *Proceedings of the Seventh Bi-Annual World Marketing Congress* (Melbourne, Academy of Marketing Science, 1995), Vol. VII-I, 2-61 to 2-70. © 1995 Academy of Marketing Science.
Ratings were on a 7-point semantic differential scale. Only the 1994 data are shown.

Perceived quality of services

It is more difficult for consumers to evaluate the quality of services than the quality of goods. This is because of certain distinctive characteristics of services:

- their intangibility
- their variability
- the fact that they are simultaneously produced and consumed
- their perishability.

To overcome the fact that consumers are unable to compare services side-by-side as they do with products, consumers rely on **surrogate cues** (i.e. extrinsic cues that signal quality) to evaluate services. In evaluating a dentist's services, for example, the quality of the reception area and consulting room furnishings, the number of framed degrees on the wall, the pleasantness of the receptionist and the professionalism of the nurse all contribute to the consumer's overall evaluation of service quality.

Since the actual quality of the service can vary from day to day, from service employee to service employee, and from customer to customer (e.g. in food, in waiter service, in haircuts, even in classes taught by the same lecturer), marketers try to standardise their services in order to provide consistency of quality. The downside of service standardisation, unfortunately, may be the loss of customised services which many consumers value. In fact, some Australian consumers react unfavourably to standardisation, rejecting the 'Would you like fries with that?' approach to service.

Unlike products, which are first produced, then sold, then consumed, most services are first sold, then produced and consumed simultaneously. If a product is defective, it is likely that the factory's quality control inspectors will catch it before it ever reaches the consumer. However, since a 'defective' service is often consumed as it is being produced, there is little opportunity to correct it. A defective haircut is difficult to correct, just as a disagreement between two service employees in the presence of the customer creates a negative impression that is hard to eradicate.

Since services are normally perishable (i.e. they cannot be produced and stored), some marketers try to change demand patterns in order to 'distribute' the service more equally over time. Telstra and Optus, for instance, offer a discount on telephone calls placed after 6 p.m.; some restaurants offer a significantly less expensive 'early bird' dinner for consumers who come in before 6 p.m. During peak demand hours, the interactive quality of services often declines, because both the customer and the service provider are hurried and under stress. Without special effort by the marketer to ensure consistency of service during peak hours, service image will decline. Giving consumers something interesting to do while they are waiting for service can have a positive effect. Diners may be invited to study the menu while waiting for a table; patients can view informative videos in the doctor's waiting room.[71]

Over the past decade, a group of researchers have devoted themselves to the study of how consumers evaluate service quality. One approach takes the view that the service quality that a customer perceives is a function of the magnitude and direction of the gaps between the customer's expectations of service and the customer's assessment (perception) of the service actually delivered.[72] For example, when a holiday advertisement promises that Queensland is 'beautiful one day, perfect the next', consumers may be disappointed if their Whitsunday holiday is wet for most of their stay. Some companies have moved to exceed customer expectations, to 'delight' their customers. However, service marketers should be wary here. What is a delight on one occasion will be expected the next. Companies could drive themselves into debt by continually exceeding expectations, unless they can lower their costs or raise their prices. Of course, the expectations of a given service vary widely among different consumers of the same service. These expectations stem from word-of-mouth the consumer has heard about the service, their past experience, the promises made about the service in its ads and by its salespersons, the purchase alternatives available, and other situational factors.[73] Based on these factors, the sum total of a consumer's expectations of a service before receiving it is termed predicted service; services whose quality, as evaluated by the customer at the end of the service, significantly exceeds the predicted service are perceived as offerings of high quality and generate more customer satisfaction, increased probability of repeat purchase, and favourable word-of-mouth.[74]

It has been observed that people expect a service to live up to its best performance, but judge it against its worst. Thus, suburban trains are believed 'typically' to run late or to be unreliable, even though consumers know they can often run on time. Research studies often show that the actual service experienced was often not as poor as the customers feared.

A quality scale, called SERVQUAL, measures the gap between customers' expectations of services and their perceptions of the actual service delivered along the following five dimensions of service quality (reduced from 10 original dimensions)—tangibles, reliability, responsiveness, assurance and empathy.[75] Table 5.3 presents a description of these dimensions, which the researchers believe customers use in judging service quality. For example, although Federal Express provides the same core service as other couriers (the outcome dimension), it provides a superior process dimension through its advanced tracking system, which can provide customers with instant information about the status of their packages at any time between pickup and delivery. It also provides call centres with knowledgeable, well-trained, and polite employees who can readily answer customers' questions and handle problems. Thus, FedEx uses the process dimension as a method to exceed customers' expectations and has acquired the image of a company that has an important, customer-focused competitive advantage among the many companies providing the same core service.

Since its development, the SERVQUAL scale has been used in numerous studies, though not all its empirical findings correspond precisely to the five dimensions that the scale is designed to measure.[76] In addition, other researchers have questioned whether the 'gap' approach fully accounts for consumer perceptions of service quality and the changing nature of expectations.[77] For example, just because a bank lives up to expectation does not mean that consumers evaluate it positively.

Another scale to measure service quality, called SERVPERF, is based on consumer perceptions of performance.[78] The dimensions along which consumers evaluate service quality fall into two groups: the *outcome* dimension (which focuses on the reliable delivery of the core service) and the *process* dimension (which focuses on how the core service is delivered). The process dimension offers the service provider a significant opportunity to surpass customer expectations. For example, the National Australia Bank (NAB), while providing the same core service as other banks, deliberately set out to provide a superior process dimension in terms of opening new accounts. This was based on its streamlined computer and documentation systems. Thus the NAB used the process dimension to exceed customers' expectations, and acquire the image of a company that has an important, customer-focused competitive advantage among the many companies providing the same core service. Researchers have tried to integrate the concepts of *product quality* and *service quality* into an overall *transaction satisfaction index*, based on the idea that all products contain some service elements beyond their intrinsic qualities. Some of these may relate to satisfaction with the purchase occasion (such as the helpfulness and responsiveness of the salesperson). Figure 5.16 presents a simple model depicting this approach.[79] Consumers also evaluate how products function in use.[80] For example, a Web cam that is difficult to program has poor *usability*, an intangible aspect of products. One research model suggests that the consumer's overall satisfaction with the transaction is based on the evaluation of three components: service quality, product quality, and price.[81]

TABLE 5.3 SERVQUAL dimensions for measuring service quality

Reliability	Providing the service as promised, at the promised time and doing it right the first time; handling customer problems in a dependable manner and keeping customers informed.
Responsiveness	Prompt service, willingness to help customers, and readiness to respond to customer requests.
Assurance	Instilling confidence in customers and making them feel safe in their transactions; consistently courteous employees with the knowledge to answer customers' questions.
Empathy	Employees who deal with customers in a caring fashion and understand their needs; giving customers individual attention and having their best interests at heart.
Tangibility	Modern equipment, visually appealing facilities and materials related to the service, employees with professional appearance, and convenient operating hours.

Source: **A. Parasuraman, Valarie A. Zeithaml and Leonard L. Berry, 'Moving forward in service quality research: Measuring different customer-expectation levels, comparing alternative scales, and examining the performance-behavioral intentions link', *Report No. 94–114* (Marketing Science Institute, 1994).**

Perceptions of high service quality and high customer satisfaction lead to higher levels of purchase intentions and repeat buying. Research has shown that perceived service quality and perceived service satisfaction interact in complex ways to produce consumer intentions to repurchase.[82] Some theorists have related these factors to customer loyalty or defections to a competitor.[83] When either one is low, defections to a competitor are likely if consumers believe they have an effective choice. Figure 5.17 is a conceptual model depicting the behavioural and financial consequences of service quality as it affects the retention or defection of customers. Although there are many studies of customer evaluations of service quality, few studies have examined the relationship between such perceptions and future buying intentions. Even fewer studies have related customer evaluations to customer retention levels and, most importantly, to profitability. A recent study identified numerous aspects of the relationship between perceived service quality and profitability; these are yet to be explored.[84] Such research is very important because it will enable marketers to implement those service improvements that make customers more satisfied and at the same time increase company profits.

FIGURE 5.16 **Conceptual model of the components of transaction satisfaction**

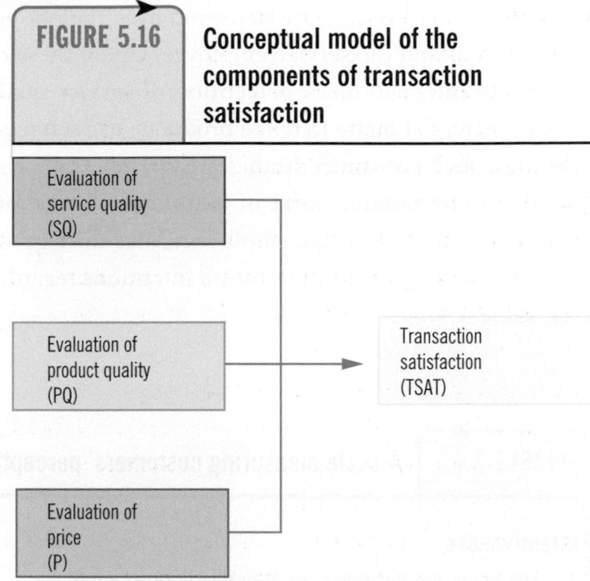

Source: A. Parasuraman, Valarie A, Zeithaml and Leonard L. Berry, 'Reassessment of expectations as a comparison standard in measuring service quality', *Journal of Marketing*, 58, January 1994, p. 121. Reprinted by permission of the American Marketing Association.

FIGURE 5.17 **Conceptual model of the behavioural and financial consequences of service quality**

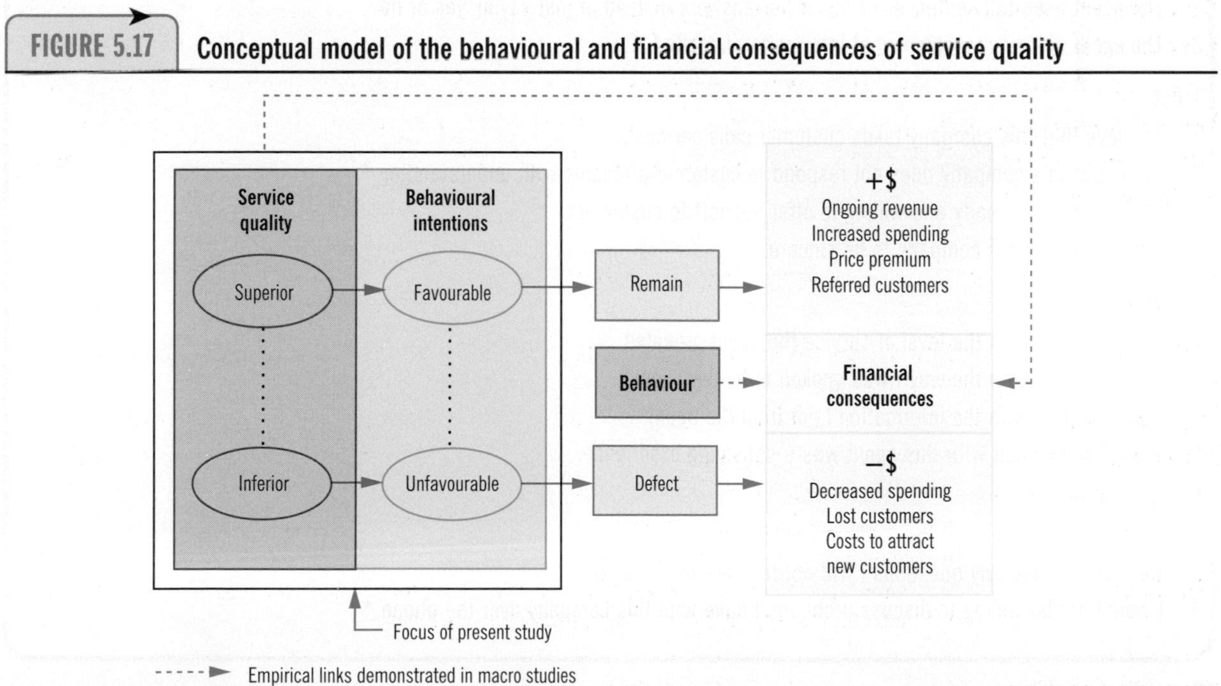

Source: Valarie A. Zeithaml, Leonard L. Berry and A. Parasuraman, 'The behavioral consequences of service quality', *Journal of Marketing*, 60, April 1996, p. 33. Reprinted by permission of the American Marketing Association.

Today many services are delivered over the phone or the Internet, without direct visual contact between the customer and the service employee. Under these conditions, it is more difficult to research the factors that determine the customer's perception of service quality. Because more and more companies, including the manufacturers of many tangible products, use service-focused selling points to promote and differentiate their offerings, such consumer studies are crucial. Call centres are a key point for customer access to the company and also an important source of customer information. One study analysed voice-to-voice encounters among customers and call-centre employees, and developed a scale that measures customers' perceptions of such service experiences and their future intentions regarding the company represented by the call centre contacted (see Table 5.4).

TABLE 5.4 **A scale measuring customers' perceptions of call-centre employees**

Attentiveness
1. The agent did not make an attentive impression.*
2. The agent used short, affirmative words and sounds to indicate that (s)he was really listening.

Perceptiveness
1. The agent asked for more details and extra information during the conversation.
2. The agent continually attempted to understand what I was saying.
3. The agent paraphrased what had been said adequately.

Responsiveness
1. The agent offered relevant information to the questions I asked.
2. The agent used full sentences in his or her answers instead of just saying yes or no.
3. The agent did not recognise what information I needed.*

Trust
1. I believe that this company takes customer calls seriously.
2. I feel that this company does not respond to customer problems with understanding.*
3. This company is ready and willing to offer support to customers.
4. I can count on this company to be sincere.

Satisfaction
1. I am satisfied with the level of service the agent provided.
2. I am satisfied with the way I was spoken to by the agent.
3. I am satisfied with the information I got from the agent.
4. The telephone call with this agent was a satisfying experience.

Call intention
1. I will very likely contact this company again.
2. Next time I have any questions I will not hesitate to call again.
3. I would not be willing to discuss problems I have with this company over the phone.*

***Negatively phrased item.**
Source: **Ko de Ruyter and Martin G. M. Wetzels, 'The impact of perceived listening behavior in voice-to-voice service encounters',** ***Journal of Service Research*****, February 2000, pp. 276–284, copyright © 2000 by Sage Publications, Inc. Reprinted by permission of Sage Publications, Inc.**

Price/quality relationship

Perceived value is often seen as a trade-off between perceived benefits and perceived sacrifice (monetary and non-monetary).[85] A number of research studies support the view that consumers rely on price as an indicator of product quality. Several studies have shown that consumers attribute different qualities to identical products that carry different price labels. The perception of value differs according to segment (such as age and income).[86] The success of frequent flyer programs may be attributed to the perceived value of a free airline ticket which to the airlines may carry an incremental cost.

Other studies suggest that consumers using a *price/quality* relationship are actually relying on a well-known (and hence more expensive) brand name as an indicator of quality, without actually relying on price per se.[87] A later study found out that consumers use price and brand to evaluate the prestige of the product but do not generally use these cues when they evaluate the product's performance.[88] Because price is so often considered to be an indicator of quality, some product advertisements deliberately emphasise a high price to underscore their claims of quality. One danger of sales pricing for retailers is that products with lower prices may be perceived as reduced quality. At the same time, when consumers evaluate more concrete attributes of a product, such as performance and durability, they rely less on the price and brand name as indicators of quality than when they evaluate the product's prestige and symbolic value.[89] For this reason, discount advertising needs to be accompanied by other information (branding, specific attributes) associated with quality to counter any negative perceptions.

When other cues are available to consumers (e.g. brand name or store image), they may be more influential than price in determining perceived quality. A study that investigated the effects of the extrinsic cues of price, brand and store information on consumers' perceptions of product quality found that price had a positive effect on product quality but a negative effect on perceived value and willingness to buy. Brand and store information also had a positive effect on perceived quality, but in addition had a positive effect on perceived value and willingness to buy.[90] Figure 5.18 presents a conceptual model of the effects of price, brand name and store name on perceived product value.

Consumers use price as a surrogate indicator of quality if they have little information to go on, or if they have little confidence in their own ability to make the choice on other grounds. When the consumer is familiar with a brand name or has experience with a product, price declines as a factor in product selection.

STORE IMAGE

Retail stores have images of their own that serve to influence the perceived quality of products they carry, as well as the decisions of consumers as to where to shop. A study of retail store image based on comparative pricing strategies found that consumers tend to perceive stores that offer a small discount on a large number of items (i.e. *frequency* of price advantage) as having lower prices overall than competing stores that offer larger discounts on a smaller number of products (*magnitude* of price advantage).[91] This finding has important implications for retailers' positioning strategies in this era of value-pricing (or everyday low pricing, which Bi-Lo, Franklins and to a degree Coles and Safeway (Woolworths) supermarkets have adopted. Kmart and Big W have pursued similar everyday low pricing initiatives for department stores). The research also showed that frequent advertising of price specials reinforces consumer beliefs about the competitiveness of a store's prices.[92]

The width of product assortment also affects retail store image. Grocery retailers may be reluctant to reduce the number of products they carry out of concern that perceptions of a smaller assortment will reduce the likelihood that consumers will shop in their stores.[93] At the same time shelf space is expensive, so stores need to encourage products with high stock turns, given tight retail margins.

FIGURE 5.18 Conceptual model of the effects of price, brand name and store name on perceived value

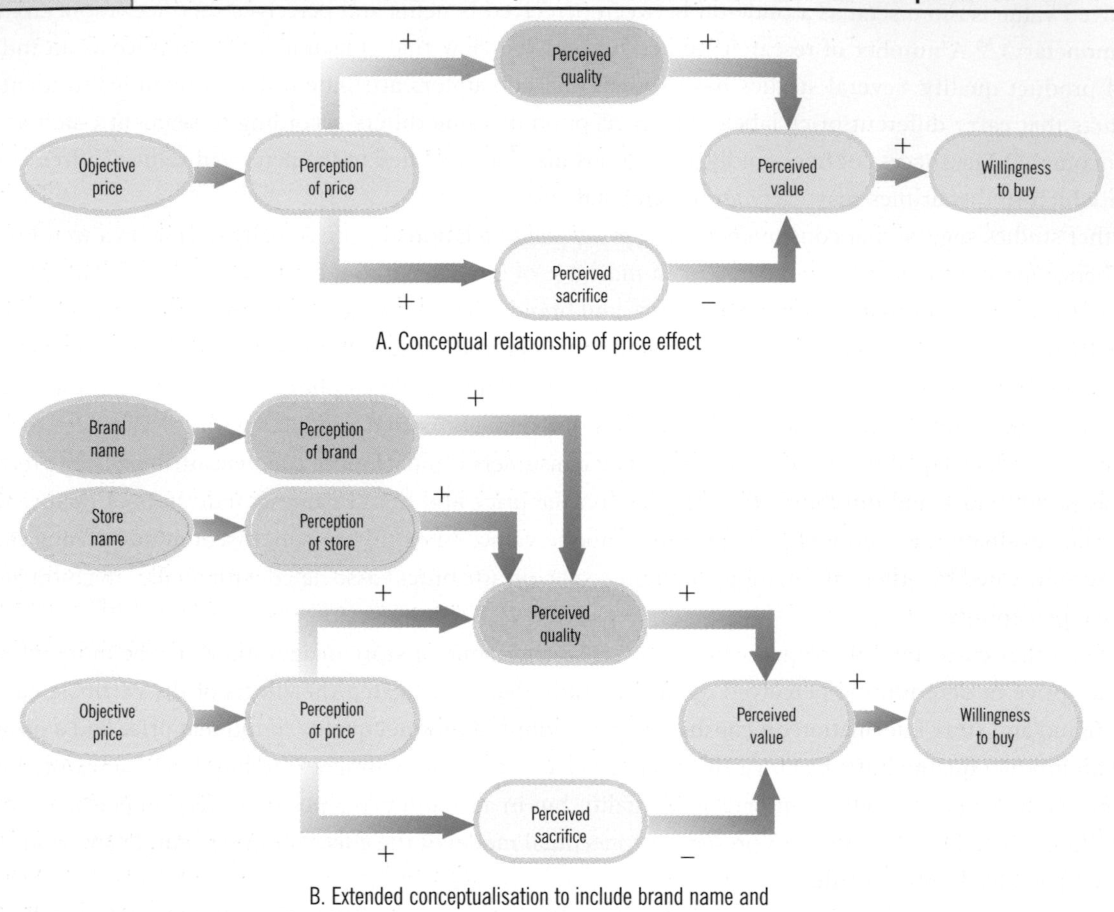

Source: **Wm B. Dodds, Kent B. Monroe and Dhruv Grewel, 'Effects of price, brand and store information on buyers' product evaluations', *Journal of Marketing Research*, 28, August 1991, p. 308. Reprinted by permission of the American Marketing Association.**

The type of product consumers wish to buy influences their selection of retail outlet; conversely, consumers' evaluation of a product is often influenced by the knowledge of where it was bought. A consumer wishing to buy an elegant table setting for a special occasion may go to a store with an elegant, high-status image, such as Georg Jensen in Sydney. Regardless of what she actually pays for the setting she selects (regular price or marked-down price), she will probably perceive its quality to be high. However, she may perceive the quality of the same setting to be much lower if she buys it in a discount store with a low-price image. Research has indicated that consumer perceptions of store quality were more heavily influenced by ambient factors (such as the number, type and behaviour of other customers and sales personnel) than they were by store design features.[94]

Most studies of the effects of extrinsic cues on perceived product quality have focused on just one variable, either price or store image. However, when a second extrinsic cue is available (e.g. price *and* store image), perceived quality is sometimes a function of the interaction of both cues on the consumer. For example, a study found that when brand and retailer images become associated, the less favourable image becomes enhanced at the expense of the more favourable image. Thus, when a low-priced store carries a brand with a high-priced image, the image of the store will improve, while the image of the brand will be adversely affected.[95]

For that reason, marketers of prestigious designer goods often try to control the outlets where these products are sold. Also, when upscale stores sell left-over expensive items to discount stores, they remove the designer labels from these goods as part of the agreements they have with the manufacturers of these products.

MANUFACTURER'S IMAGE

Consumer imagery extends beyond perceived price and store image to the producers themselves. Manufacturers who enjoy a favourable image generally find that their new products are accepted more readily than those of manufacturers who have a less favourable or a 'neutral' image. Pioneer brands (the first in the product category) tend to have favourable images, even when follower brands become available. Positive pioneer brand image is correlated with ideal self-image, helping to explain why pioneer brands may enjoy an advantage.[96] Some pioneer brands become so well known that they form the generic name for a category, such as Biro ballpoint pens and Thermos flasks.

Obviously, consumers have greater confidence that they will not be disappointed in a major name-brand product. Advertising plays an important role in establishing a favourable brand image. In the absence of other information about a new brand, people may use the amount of advertising as a signal of quality. Even products that are not new but are heavily advertised are often perceived as higher in quality than non-advertised brands.[97] 'As seen on television' is a claim to reassure consumers. Sometimes being a major and regular advertiser can cause consumers to regard the company and its products as staid or conservative. This has led some major companies to introduce entirely new brands positioned as independent and non-conformist products. Boutique beers produced by major brewers are an example.

Some major marketers introduce new products under the guise of supposedly smaller, pioneering (and presumably more forward-thinking) companies. The goal of this so-called stealth (or faux) parentage is to persuade consumers that the new brands are produced by independent, non-conformist free spirits, rather than by giant corporate entities. Companies sometimes use stealth parentage when they enter a product category totally unrelated to the one with which their corporate name has become synonymous. For example, when Disney Studios—a company with a wholesome, family-focused image—produces films that include violence and sex, it does so under the name Touchstone Pictures.

Today, companies are using advertising, exhibits and sponsorship of community events to enhance their image. While some marketers argue that product and service advertising do more to boost the corporate image than institutional (i.e. image) advertising, others see both types of advertising—product and institutional—as integral and complementary components of a total corporate communications program.

PERCEIVED RISK

Consumers must constantly make decisions regarding what products or services to buy and where to buy them. Because the outcomes (or consequences) of such decisions are often uncertain, the consumer perceives some degree of 'risk' in making a purchase decision. Perceived risk is defined as the uncertainty that consumers face when they cannot foresee the consequences of their purchase decisions. This definition highlights two relevant dimensions of perceived risk: uncertainty and consequences.

The degree of risk that consumers perceive and their own tolerance for risk taking are factors that influence their purchase strategies. It should be stressed that consumers are influenced by risks that they perceive, whether or not such risks actually exist. Risk that is not perceived—no matter how real or how dangerous—will not influence consumer behaviour. The major types of risks that consumers perceive when making product decisions include functional risk, physical risk, financial risk, social risk, psychological risk, and time risk (see Table 5.5). (Refer also to Chapter 14.)

TABLE 5.5 **Types of perceived risks**

Functional risk is the risk that the product will not perform as expected. ('Can the new PDA operate a full week without needing to be recharged?')

Physical risk is the risk to self and others that the product may pose. ('Is a mobile phone really safe, or does it emit harmful radiation?')

Financial risk is the risk that the product will not be worth its cost. ('Will a new and cheaper model of a plasma TV monitor become available six months from now?')

Social risk is the risk that a poor product choice may result in social embarrassment. ('Will my classmates laugh at my purple mohawk haircut?')

Psychological risk is the risk that a poor product choice will bruise the consumer's ego. ('Will I be embarrassed when I invite friends to listen to music on my five-year-old stereo?')

Time risk is the risk that the time spent in product search may be wasted if the product does not perform as expected. ('Will I have to go through the shopping effort all over again?')

Perception of risk varies

Consumer perception of risk varies, depending on the person, the product, the situation, and the culture. The amount of risk perceived depends on the specific consumer. Some consumers tend to perceive high degrees of risk in various consumption situations; others tend to perceive little risk. For example, studies of risk perception among adolescents have found that adolescents who engage in high-risk consumption activities (such as smoking or drug use) have lower perceived risk than those who do not engage in high-risk activities.[98] High-risk perceivers are often described as narrow categorisers because they limit their choices (e.g. product choices) to a few safe alternatives. They would rather exclude some perfectly good alternatives than chance a poor selection. Low-risk perceivers have been described as broad categorisers because they tend to make their choices from a much wider range of alternatives. They would rather risk a poor selection than limit the number of alternatives from which they can choose. One study concluded that risk preference may be a stable personality trait, with experience a mediating factor in risk perception.[99]

An individual's perception of risk varies with product categories. For example, consumers are likely to perceive a higher degree of risk (e.g. functional risk, financial risk, time risk) in the purchase of a plasma television set than in the purchase of an automobile. In addition to product-category perceived risk, researchers have identified product-specific perceived risk.[100] One study found that consumers perceive service decisions to be riskier than product decisions, particularly in terms of social risk, physical risk, and psychological risk.[101]

The degree of risk perceived by a consumer is also affected by the shopping situation (e.g. a traditional retail store, online (Internet), catalogue or direct-mail solicitations, or door-to-door sales). The sharp increase in mail-order catalogue and Internet sales in recent years suggests that on the basis of positive experiences and word-of-mouth, consumers now tend to perceive less risk in these shopping alternatives than they once did, despite their inability to physically inspect the merchandise before ordering. High-risk perceivers are unlikely to purchase items online despite the geometric expansion of online retailing. However, as they gain experience in online purchasing, it is likely that their levels of perceived risk regarding electronic buying will decline.

How consumers handle risk

Consumers characteristically develop their own strategies for reducing perceived risk. These risk-reduction strategies enable them to act with increased confidence when making product decisions, even though the consequences of such decisions remain somewhat uncertain. Some of the more common risk-reduction strategies are discussed in the following sections.

Consumers seek information Consumers seek information about the product and product category through word-of-mouth communication (from friends and family and from other people whose opinions they value), from salespeople, and from the general media. They spend more time thinking about their choice and search for more information about the product alternatives when they associate a high degree of risk with the purchase. This strategy is straightforward and logical because the more information the consumer has about the product and the product category, the more predictable the probable consequences and, thus, the lower the perceived risk.

Consumers are brand loyal Consumers avoid risk by remaining loyal to a brand with which they have been satisfied instead of purchasing new or untried brands. High-risk perceivers, for example, are more likely to be loyal to their old brands and less likely to purchase newly introduced products.

Consumers select by brand image When consumers have had no experience with a product, they tend to 'trust' a favoured or well-known brand name. Consumers often think well-known brands are better and are worth buying for the implied assurance of quality, dependability, performance, and service. Marketers' promotional efforts supplement the perceived quality of their products by helping to build and sustain a favourable brand image.

Consumers rely on store image If consumers have no other information about a product, they often trust the judgment of the merchandise buyers of a reputable store and depend on them to have made careful decisions in selecting products for resale. Store image also imparts the implication of product testing and the assurance of service, return privileges, and adjustment in case of dissatisfaction.

Consumers buy the most expensive model When in doubt, consumers often feel that the most expensive model is probably the best in terms of quality; that is, they equate price with quality. (The price/quality relationship was discussed earlier in this chapter.)

Consumers seek reassurance Consumers who are uncertain about the wisdom of a product choice seek reassurance through money-back guarantees, government and private laboratory test results, warranties, and prepurchase trial. For example, it is unlikely that anyone would buy a new model car without a test drive. Products that do not easily lend themselves to free or limited trial (such as a refrigerator) present a challenge to marketers.

The concept of perceived risk has major implications for the introduction of new products. Because high-risk perceivers are less likely to purchase new or innovative products than low-risk perceivers, it is important for marketers to provide such consumers with persuasive risk-reduction strategies, such as a well-known brand name (sometimes achieved through licensing), distribution through reputable retail outlets, informative advertising, publicity stories in the media, impartial test results, free samples, and money-back guarantees. Also, most stores that carry a number of different brands and models of the same product, as well as manufacturers of such diverse model lines, now offer online consumers quick and easy ways to generate side-by-side comparisons with detailed charts of the features of all the available models. It is likely that computer software and the Internet will play an increasingly important part in reducing the information-seeking burden of perceived risk.

CASE STUDY 5.1

WD-40: Changing Product Perceptions

David Bednall, Deakin University

As a brand name, WD-40 might conjure an image of a staid industrial product, bought and used mainly by men. In its earliest years of distribution in Australia, this was the case with this all-purpose lubricant, maintenance and cleaning product. Around 70% of sales came from automotive distribution. Unchanged in formulation and pack colours for 40 years, it had achieved high awareness in its target market in Australia.

In 1988, WD-40 (Australia) was established to take over the distribution and marketing of its product in Australia. The company, in association with its agency McMurtry, Sherbon, Vartan & Partners, developed a new marketing strategy. The company aimed to give WD-40 a small share of many, many markets, such as household cleaning, leisure, manufacturing, lubrication and maintenance products, in which it could compete. To help 'unposition' the product, the company avoided any element of the marketing mix that would narrowly define its usefulness. Its new slogan, 'WD-40—there's always another use', reflected this approach. This slogan has been used in every promotion for the last 11 years. So successful has it been that the American parent also adopted it and now uses it worldwide.

The natural extension of this approach was to widen its distribution, particularly in supermarkets and hardware stores. Telemarketing was also used to establish small retail accounts. By 1993, near 100% distribution in target retail outlets was achieved. Given the many uses of the product, the company was also able to achieve something rather unusual—multiple outlets in the one retail store. Since it had automotive, household cleaning and other applications, it was important that consumers could find it in the correct store locations. Thus the company sought shelf place in areas such as automotive products, gardening supplies and cleaning products. As sales increased, pricing was reduced. In February 1993, the company was able to take advantage of these increased sales and start local production. Price discounting of the 300 g can started to upset sales of the 150 g can, and so a 255 g can was introduced for non-automotive outlets.

More important still was the need to broaden the spread of users by increasing the number of women buyers so, in mid-1993, WD-40 commissioned qualitative research by the Stollznow company. This showed that women saw WD-40 as having a macho image, with little association with use inside the home. Mostly the women saw a role for WD-40 as a grease remover, lubricant and a loosener of 'knobs and nuts, particularly where they have been tightened too hard, probably by a man, or where the woman lacks strength or has arthritis'. The main competitors were existing household items, such as cooking oil and candlewax and, to some extent, Selley's Ezy Glide.

Significantly, the research concluded that there appeared to be 'opportunities to awaken women to the possibilities of eliminating the minor irritating problems around the home without waiting for a man to do it'. Price was less than expected, though the main 255 g size was judged too big. As a result, a smaller 60 g can was introduced. Although logo and colours could not be changed, the text was softened in appearance and the text on the can stressed within-home applications. The container featured a cartoon, 'WD-40's Houseful of Uses', which had proved successful in the qualitative research. A clip strip display was designed for the pack.

For stores that could not accept this display, a special presentation pack for the existing 150 g can was developed. Each can was printed with the slogan, 'No woman should be without me'—a direct quote from one woman in the research. A 'power wing' (V-shaped) display of 150 g cans was developed, which also incorporated the slogan.

WD-40 has been extensively advertised on metropolitan television (significantly featuring a woman doing the voice-overs) and in the national women's magazines *Women's Weekly* and *Family Circle*. The ads show an extended range of applications for WD-40. Radio has also been used nationally, and was boosted with a competition for family members. PR activities and a trade campaign complemented these activities.

Product trial has always been important to WD-40. A striking example came with the handing out of 100 000 sample cans at the 1992 AFL Grand Final by women in WD-40 outfits.

The Newspoll omnibus service has traced the development of WD-40 in the Australian market.

A national telephone survey of 1200 people found a positive impact on the usage of WD-40 among all adults. Similarly for women (based on a sample of 600), growth in awareness and use of the product has been strong throughout the 1990s.

This case study has some lessons for consumer marketers. A too narrow segmentation of the market, either in terms of target groups or usage segments, can lead marketers to underestimate potential sales. This should always be a consideration in Australia where the market is perhaps only 5% of the size of comparable US markets. In addition, it shows how a broader perceptual positioning can help the marketer access a larger market.

Case Study Questions

1. What other products on the Australian market are too narrowly positioned?
2. If you were a competitor to WD-40, what competitive positioning would you take?
3. Given WD-40's wider positioning, would it be wise to extend the WD-40 brand to other types of household products?

Summary

Perception is the process by which individuals select, organise and interpret stimuli, to form a meaningful and coherent picture of the world. Perception has strategy implications for marketers, because consumers make decisions based on what they perceive, rather than on the basis of objective reality.

The lowest level at which an individual can perceive a specific stimulus is called the absolute threshold. The minimal difference that can be perceived between two stimuli is called the differential threshold, or just noticeable difference (jnd). Most stimuli are perceived above the level of the consumer's conscious awareness; however, weak stimuli can be perceived below the level of conscious awareness (i.e. subliminally). Research does not support the contention that subliminal stimuli affect consumer buying decisions.

Consumers' selections of stimuli from the environment are based on the interaction of their expectations and motives with the stimulus itself. The principle of selective perception includes the following concepts: selective exposure, selective attention, perceptual defence and perceptual blocking. People usually perceive things they need or want, and block the perception of unnecessary, unfavourable or painful stimuli. Consumers organise their perceptions into unified wholes according to the principles of Gestalt psychology: figure and ground, grouping and closure.

The interpretation of stimuli is highly subjective. It is based on what consumers expect to see in light of their previous experience, on the number of plausible explanations they can envisage, on motives and interests at the time of perception, and on the clarity of the stimulus itself. Influences that tend to distort objective interpretation include physical appearance, stereotypes, halo effects, irrelevant cues, first impressions, and the tendency to jump to conclusions.

Just as individuals have a perceived self-image as a certain kind of person so, too, do products and brands have images (i.e. symbolic meanings) for the consumer. The perceived image of a product or service (i.e. its positioning) is probably more important to its ultimate success than its actual physical characteristics. Products and services that are perceived favourably have a much better chance of being purchased than products or services with unfavourable or neutral images.

Perceived value is based on monetary and non-monetary costs combined with perceptions of quality. Reference prices are used to evaluate pricing claims. Prices outside an acceptable range are likely to be rejected. Research suggests that the frame of reference for prices and how consumers evaluate competitive offers will strongly affect buyer behaviour.

Compared with manufacturing firms, service marketers face several unique problems in positioning and promoting their offerings, including the service environment and service characteristics (e.g. intangibility, variability, perishability, simultaneous production and consumption). Regardless of how well positioned a product or service appears to be, the marketer may be forced to reposition it in response to market events, such as new competitive strategies or changing consumer preferences.

Consumers often judge the quality of a product or service on the basis of a variety of informational cues: some are intrinsic to the product (e.g. colour, size, flavour, aroma) while others are extrinsic (e.g. price, store image, brand image, service environment). In the absence of direct experience or other information, consumers often rely on price as an indicator of quality. The images of retail stores influence the perceived quality of products they carry, as well as the decisions of consumers as to where to shop. Consumer imagery extends beyond perceived price and store image to the producers themselves. Manufacturers who enjoy a favourable image generally find that their new products are accepted more readily than those of manufacturers with less favourable or neutral images.

Discussion questions

1. How does sensory adaptation affect advertising comprehension? How can marketers overcome sensory adaptation and increase the likelihood that consumers will notice their ads?
2. Describe how manufacturers of chocolate bars can apply their knowledge of differential threshold to packages and prices during periods of:
   (a) rising ingredient costs
   (b) increasing competition
   (c) heightened consumer awareness regarding nutrition and ingredient labelling.
3. Does subliminal advertising work? Support your view. Assuming that some forms of subliminal persuasion can influence consumers, do you think the use of these techniques is ethical? Explain your answer.
4. How do advertisers use contrast to make sure their ads stand out? Can the lack of contrast between the ad and the medium in which it appears be used to increase the effectiveness of the ad? If so, how? What are the ethical considerations in employing such strategies?
5. Megan is a 29-year-old, single investment banker who lives in an apartment in a large city. After a particularly long and difficult workday, she relaxed in her apartment by reading through one business and two fashion magazines. When questioned by a researcher the next day, she could clearly recall two holiday ads and vaguely remembered one ad for a personal computer from among the nearly 100 ads she had seen in the three magazines. However, she could recount in detail the articles that she had read and even recalled the titles of articles she had not read. How can you explain this?
6. (a) Discuss the differences between the absolute threshold and the differential threshold.
   (b) What is consumer reality?
7. What are the implications of figure-ground relationships for print ads and for TV ads? How can the figure-ground construct help or interfere with the communication of advertising messages?
8. How is perceptual mapping used in consumer research? Why are marketers sometimes forced to reposition their products or services? Illustrate your answers with examples.
9. Why is it more difficult for consumers to evaluate the quality of services than the quality of products?
10. Discuss the roles of extrinsic cues and intrinsic cues in the perceived quality of:
    (a) wines
    (b) shampoo
    (c) restaurants
    (d) medical services
    (e) graduate education.
11. How can an advertiser best frame the value of a discount and of a price rise?

Exercises

1. Find five examples of print advertisements or packages that use stimulus factors to create attention. For each example, evaluate the effectiveness of the stimulus factors used. Also, identify the principles of perceptual organisation that are integrated into these ads.
2. Using Weber's law as a guideline, develop reasonable jnds for a sales price of a:
   (a) car
   (b) personal computer
   (c) pair of denim jeans
   (d) tube of toothpaste.
   Explain your choices.
3. What roles do actual product attributes and perceptions of attributes play in positioning a product? Find three different toothpaste advertisements which stress different product attributes and discuss whether the marketers have effectively positioned their products to communicate a specific image.
4. Construct a two-dimensional perceptual map of your university, using the two attributes that were most important to you in choosing that university rather than others in your area. Then, mark the position of your Faculty on the diagram relative to that of a Faculty in another university that you considered. Discuss the implications of this perceptual map for the student recruitment function of the university that you did not choose.
5. Conduct interviews with five of your fellow students in this class. On what dimensions do they evaluate this course? Which intrinsic and extrinsic cues do they use as indicators of quality? Do your observations support the concepts discussed in the chapter? Explain.
6. Select a restaurant where you have recently eaten. Analyse the atmosphere and physical environment of this service establishment. What image does the environment convey? Should the owner change anything to make the environment more appealing to customers? Do the people who eat there affect your evaluation of quality and value? Explain.

Key terms

absolute threshold *(p. 136)*
adaptation *(p. 136)*
advertorial *(p. 144)*
bundle pricing *(p. 158)*
closure *(p. 149)*
contrast *(p. 147)*
credence products *(p. 152)*
differential threshold *(p. 137)*
embeds *(p. 141)*
experience products *(p. 152)*
extrinsic cues *(p. 159)*
figure and ground *(p. 147)*
framing *(p. 158)*
Gestalt psychology *(p. 146)*
grouping *(p. 148)*
halo effect *(p. 151)*
infomercial *(p. 144)*
intrinsic cues *(p. 159)*
just noticeable difference (j.n.d.) *(p. 137)*
objective price claims *(p. 158)*
perceived quality *(p. 159)*
perception *(p. 135)*
perceptual blocking *(p. 146)*
perceptual defence *(p. 146)*
perceptual interpretation *(p. 152)*
perceptual mapping *(p. 154)*
perceptual organisation *(p. 146)*
positioning *(p. 152)*
prospect theory *(p. 158)*
reference price *(p. 157)*
repositioning *(p. 154)*
selective attention *(p. 145)*
selective exposure *(p. 145)*
selective perception *(p. 143)*
sensation *(p. 135)*
sensory receptors *(p. 135)*
stereotypes *(p. 151)*
stimulus *(p. 135)*
subliminal perception *(p. 140)*
supraliminal perception *(p. 140)*
surrogate cues *(p. 160)*
tensile price claims *(p. 158)*
Weber's law *(p. 137)*

Endnotes

1. Heather Jacobs, 'Ruski: Is one second enough?', *B&T Weekly*, 1 October 1999.
2. C. Douglas Olsen, 'Observations: Sounds of silence: Functions and use of silence in television advertising', *Journal of Advertising Research*, September–October 1994, pp. 89–95.
3. Sarah Brown, 'Category appraisals in Australasia', Paper presented to the Market Research Society of Australia, 1992.
4. Max Sutherland, *Advertising and the Mind of the Consumer: What Works, What Doesn't and Why* (Sydney: Allen & Unwin, 1993).
5. Eric R. Spangenberg, Ayn E. Cowley and Pamela W. Henderson, 'Improving the store environment: Do olfactory cues affect evaluations and behaviours?', *Journal of Marketing*, 60, April 1996, pp. 87–130. See also Isobel King, 'Dollars and scents', *Australian Professional Marketing*, May 1994, pp. 15–18.
6. N.R. Kleinfield, 'The smell of money', *New York Times*, 25 November 1992, p. B1.
7. Bernard Berelson and Gary A. Steiner, *Human Behavior: An Inventory of Scientific Findings* (New York: Harcourt, Brace & World, 1964), pp. 87–130.
8. For an American example, see 'Betty Crocker goes Yuppie', *Time*, 2 June 1986, p. 63.
9. Stuart Elliott, 'Another remarkable story of the brand-name lexicon', *New York Times*, 13 August 1992, p. D9.
10. 'Coors' new label is a bust with diehard beerhounds', *Marketing News*, 30 January 1988, p. 8.
11. Greg Winter, 'What keeps a bottom line healthy? Weight loss,' *New York Times*, 2 January 2001, p. 1
12. W. Bevan, 'Subliminal stimulation: A pervasive problem for psychology', *Psychological Bulletin*, 61(2), 1964, pp. 81–89.
13. W. Weir, 'Another look at subliminal "facts"', *Advertising Age*, 15 October 1984, p. 46.
14. Sharon E. Beatty and Del J. Hawkins, 'Subliminal stimulation: Some new data and interpretation', *Journal of Advertising*, 18(3), 1989, pp. 4–8. See also Max Sutherland (op. cit.), Chapter 3, 'Subliminal advertising: The biggest myth of all', where the results of 200 studies are reviewed.
15. Kathryn I. Theus, 'Subliminal advertising and the psychology of processing unconscious stimuli: A review of research', *Psychology and Marketing*, 11(3), May–June 1994, pp. 271–290. See also Dennis L. Rosen and Surenra N. Singh, 'An investigation of subliminal embed effect on multiple measures of advertising effectiveness', *Psychology and Marketing*, 9(2), March–April 1992, pp. 157–173.
16. Carl L. Witte, Madhavan Parthasarathy and James W. Gentry, 'Subliminal perception versus subliminal persuasion: A re-examination of the basic issues', *American Marketing Association*, Summer 1995, pp. 133–138.
17. Myron Gable, Henry T. Wilkens, Lynn Harris and Richard Feinberg, 'An evaluation of subliminally embedded sexual stimuli in graphics', *Journal of Advertising*, 16(1), 1987, pp. 26–31. See also Wilson Bryan Key, *Subliminal Seduction* (New York: New American Library, 1973) and Jack Haberstroh, *Ice Cube Sex: The Truth About Subliminal Advertising* (Notre Dame, IN: Cross Cultural Publications, 1994).
18. Kirk H. Smith and Martha Rogers, 'Effectiveness of subliminal messages in television commercials: Two experiments', *Journal of Applied Psychology*, 19(6), 1994, pp. 866–874.
19. Nicolas E. Synodinos, 'Subliminal stimulation: What does the public think about it?,' in James H. Leigh and Claude R. Martin Jr (eds), *Current Issues and Research in Advertising*, 11(1 and 2), 1988, pp. 157–187; and Martha Rogers and Kirk H. Smith, 'Public perceptions of subliminal advertising: Why practitioners shouldn't ignore this issue', *Journal of Advertising Research*, March–April 1993, pp. 10–18. See also Martha Rogers and Christine A. Seiler, 'The answer is no: A national survey of advertising practitioners and their clients about whether they use subliminal advertising', *Journal of Advertising Research*, March–April 1994, pp. 36–45.
20. 'Inaudible messages making a noise', *Insight*, 14 September 1987, pp. 44–45.
21. Mary Alice Crawford, 'A 50s technology enjoys a rebirth', *Security Management*, August 1985, pp. 54–56.
22. Australian Broadcasting Control Board, *Television Programme Standards*, Melbourne, 1970, 'Advertisements must be clearly recognisable as such and separate from the presentation of programme matter', p. 24.
23. Federation of Australian Commercial Television Stations (FACTS), *Commercial Television Industry Code of Practice* (Sydney: FACTS, April 1999), Section 1.8.

Stations are required to comply with this code under the *Broadcasting Services Act 1992*. See p. 5 of the Code.

24. Stuart Elliot, 'Fold-out print ads give marketers a poster's worth of space', *New York Times*, 12 August 1993, p. D19.
25. See Max Sutherland, op. cit., p. 17.
26. For a contrary view, see D.S. Holmes, 'The evidence for repression: An examination of sixty years of research', in Jerome L. Singer (ed.), *Repression and Dissociation: Implications for Personality Theory, Psychopathology and Health* (Chicago: University of Chicago Press, 1990).
27. Keith Naughton, 'Gross out, smoke out,' *Newsweek*, 25 March 2002, p. 9.
28. Commonwealth Department of Health and Aged Care, 'Review of health warnings on tobacco products in Australia', Discussion Paper (April), 2001. Commonwealth of Australia. Canberra: Australia.
29. See Max Sutherland, op. cit.
30. James T. Heimbach and Jacob Jacoby, 'The Zeigernik effect in advertising', in M. Venkatesan (ed.), *Proceedings of the Third Annual Conference,* Association for Consumer Research, 1972, pp. 746–758.
31. Julius Harburger, 'Concept closure', *Advertising Age,* 12 January 1987, p. 18.
32. Marsha L. Richins, 'Social comparison and the idealized images of advertising', *Journal of Consumer Research*, 18, June 1991, pp. 71–83. See also Mary C. Martin and James W. Gentry, 'Stuck in the model trap: The effect of beautiful models in ads on female preadolescents and adolescents', *Journal of Advertising Research*, 26(2), Summer 1997, pp. 19–33.
33. Amanda B. Bower and Stacy Landreth, 'Is beauty best? Highly versus normally attractive models in advertising', *Journal of Advertising*, 30(1), Spring 2001, pp. 1–12.
34. Kim Foltz, 'Campaign on harmony backfires on Benetton,' *New York Times*, 20 November 1989, p. D8.
35. Priya Raghubir and Aradhna Krishna, 'Vital dimensions in volume perception: Can the eye fool the stomach?' *Journal of Marketing Research*, August 1999, pp. 313–326.
36. Russell W. Belk, 'Possessions and the extended self', *Journal of Consumer Research*, 15, September 1988, pp. 139–168.
37. Ajay Kalra and Ronald C. Goodstein, 'The impact of advertising positioning strategies on consumer price sensitivity', *Journal of Marketing Research*, 35, May 1998, pp. 210–224.
38. Mary W. Sullivan, 'How brand names affect the demand for twin automobiles', *Journal of Marketing Research*, 35, May 1998, pp. 154–165.
39. Bob Garfield, 'Working-man's reward idea is given a perverse twist (beer commercial in Europe and New Zealand for Stella Artois from Amster Yard)', *Advertising Age International*, November 1999, p. 6.
40. Neil, Shoebridge 'The shock of the new', *Business Review Weekly,* 21 August 2003, p. 63.
41. This information was derived from the Coca-Cola Australia website: <www.coca-cola.com.au/about_advert.asp>.
42. Simon Lloyd, 'Green, gold and true blue', *Business Review Weekly,* 4 July 2002, p. 46.
43. Robert McMath and Thomas Forbes, *What Were They Thinking?* (New York: Time Business, Random House, 1998), pp. 28, 70.
44. Simon Lloyd, 'Green, gold and true blue', *Business Review Weekly,* 4 July 2002, p. 46.
45. This information was derived from the GlaxoSmith Klein website at: <www.gsk.com.au/gskinternet/publishing.nsf/content/products> and the Colgate-Palmolive website: <www.colgate.com/cp/corp.class/care-products> and product packaging (FAB).
46. Simon Lloyd, 'The big store brawl', *Business Review Weekly*, 28 October 2003, pp. 32–36.
47. Stuart Elliott and Constance Hays, 'Revamp with feeling for the real thing', *Age*, 2 November 1999, p. B5.
48. Neil Shoebridge, 'Bloody Volvo ads', *Business Review Weekly,* 9 October 2003.
49. Paul Gover, 'Bloody Volvos persist on TV', *Cars Guide, Herald-Sun Newspaper*, 28 November 2003.
50. Neil Shoebridge, 'The arches shine again', *Business Review Weekly,* 11 December 2003, p. 63.
51. John L. Aitchison, 'Brand mapping: Some practical issues', *Australian Marketing Researcher*, 9(1), 1985, pp. 5–31.
52. Rachel Kennedy, Christopher Riquier and Byron Sharp, 'Putting correspondence analysis to use with categorical data in market research', in Ken Grant and Ian Walker (eds), *Proceedings of the Seventh Bi-Annual World Marketing Congress* (Melbourne: Academy of Marketing Science 1995), Vol. VII-III, 14-102 to 14-111.
53. Mary Jo Bitner, 'Servicescapes: The impact of physical surroundings on customers and employees', *Journal of Marketing*, 56, 1992, pp. 57–71.

54. Julie Baker, Leonard L. Berry and A. Parasuraman, 'The marketing impact of branch facility design', *Journal of Retail Banking*, 10(2), 1988, pp. 33–42.
55. Marielza Martins and Kent B. Monroe, 'Perceived price fairness: A new look at an old construct', *Advances in Consumer Research*, 21, 1994, pp. 75–78.
56. Dhruv Grewal et al., 'The effects of price-comparison advertising on buyers' perceptions of acquisition value, transaction value, and behavioural intentions', *Journal of Marketing*, 62, April 1998, pp. 46–59.
57. Katharine Fraccastoro, Scot Burton and Abhijit Biswas, 'Effective use of advertisements promoting sales prices', *Journal of Consumer Marketing*, 10(1), 1993, pp. 61–79.
58. Ibid.
59. Joel E. Urbany et al., 'Transaction utility effects: When quality is uncertain', *Journal of the Academy of Marketing Science*, 25(1), Winter 1997, pp. 45–55.
60. Fraccastoro, Burton and Biswas, op. cit.
61. Abhijit Biswas and Scot Burton, 'Consumer perceptions of tensile price claims in advertisements: An assessment of claim types across different discount levels', *Journal of the Academy of Marketing Science*, 21(3), 1993, pp. 217–229.
62. Manjit S. Yadav and Kent B. Monroe, 'How buyers perceive savings in a bundle price: An examination of a bundles transaction value', *Journal of Marketing Research*, 30, August 1993, pp. 350–358.
63. Robert D. Hershey Jr, 'Information Age? Maybe not when it comes to prices', *New York Times*, 23 August 1998, p. D10.
64. Daniel Kahneman and Amos Tversky, 'Prospect theory: An analysis of decision under risk', *Econometrica*, 47(2), March 1979, pp. 263–291. See also Amos Tversky and Daniel Kahneman, 'Rational choice and the framing of decisions', *Journal of Business*, 59(4), pp. 251–278; Marc Jegers, 'Prospect theory and the risk-return relation: Some Belgian evidence', *Academy of Management Journal*, 34(1), 1991, pp. 215–225.
65. R. Thaler, 'Mental accounting and consumer choice', *Marketing Science*, 4, Summer 1985, pp. 199–214.
66. Mikhail Myagkov and Charles R. Plott, 'Exchange economics and loss exposure: Experiments exploring prospect theory and competitive equilibria in market environments', *American Economic Review*, December 1997, pp. 801–828.
67. Sarah Brown, 'Category Appraisals in Australasia', Paper presented at the 21st Annual Conference of the Market Research Society of Australia, Sydney, 1992; Isobel King, 'Dollars and scents', *Australian Professional Marketing*, May 1994, pp. 15–18; and Neil Shoebridge, 'Refreshed Listerine starts new assault', *Business Review Weekly*, 9 April 1993, pp. 70–71.
68. Lawrence L. Garber Jr, Eva M. Hyatt and Richard G. Starr Jr, 'The effects of food color on perceived flavor,' *Journal of Marketing Theory and Practice*, Fall 2000, pp. 59–72.
69. Michael J. McCarthy, 'Forget the ads: Cola is Cola, magazine finds', *Wall Street Journal*, 24 February 1991, p. B1.
70. Muris Cicic, 'A longitudinal study of country-of-origin effect for the apparel industry in Australia', in Ken Grant and Ian Walker (eds), *Proceedings of the Seventh Bi-Annual World Marketing Congress* (Melbourne: Academy of Marketing Science, 1995), Vol. VII-I, 2-61 to 2-70. See also Linda J. Morris, Kathy Kearney and Yvette Reisinger, 'Comparative perceptions of wool products: A comparative study of US and Australian consumers', in the same volume, 3-80 to 3-86. For some US data, see The Roper Organization, 'Consumer data', *Adweek's Marketing Week*, 20 August 1990, p. 10.
71. Shirley Taylor, 'Waiting for service: The relationship between delay and evaluations of service', *Journal of Marketing*, 58, April 1994, pp. 55–69; Michael K. Hui and David K Tse, 'What to tell consumers in waits of different lengths: An integrative model of service evaluation', *Journal of Marketing*, 60, April 1996, pp. 81–90.
72. Valarie A. Zeithaml, A. Parasuraman and Leonard L. Berry, *Delivering Quality Service: Balancing Customer Perceptions and Expectations* (New York: The Free Press, 1990).
73. Valarie A. Zeithaml, Leonard L. Berry and A. Parasuraman, 'The nature and determinants of customer expectation of service,' *Journal of the Academy of Marketing Science*, Winter 1993, pp. 1–12.
74. Ibid.
75. A. Parasuraman, Leonard L. Berry and Valarie A. Zeithaml, 'Refinement and reassessment of the SERVQUAL scale', *Journal of Retailing*, 67(4), 1991, pp. 420–450. See also James M. Carman, 'Consumer perceptions of service quality: An assessment of the SERVQUAL dimensions', *Journal of Retailing*, 66(1), 1990, pp. 33–55.
76. J. Joseph Cronin and Steven A. Taylor, 'Measuring service quality: A reexamination and extension', *Journal of Marketing*, 56, 1992, pp. 55–68.

77. J. Joseph Cronin Jr and Steven A. Taylor, 'SERVPERF versus SERVQUAL: Reconciling performance-based and perception-minus-expectations measurement of service quality', *Journal of Marketing*, 58, January 1994, pp. 125–131; see also William Boulding, Ajay Kalra, Richard Staelin and Valarie A. Zeithaml, 'A dynamic process model of service quality: From expectations to behavioural intentions', *Journal of Marketing Research*, 30, February 1993, pp. 7–27; and Kenneth Teas, 'Expectations as a comparison standard in measuring service quality: An assessment of a reassessment', *Journal of Marketing*, 58, January 1994, pp. 132–139.
78. Cronin and Taylor (1994), op. cit.
79. A. Parasuraman, Valarie A. Zeithaml and Leonard L. Berry, 'Reassessment of expectations as a comparison standard in measuring service quality: Implications for further research', *Journal of Marketing*, 58, January 1994, pp. 111–124.
80. Gitte Lindgaard, *Usability Testing and System Evaluation* (London: Chapman & Hall, 1994), p. 39.
81. A. Parasuraman, Valarie A. Zeithaml, and Leonard L. Berry, 'Reassessment of expectations as a comparison standard in measuring service quality: Implications for further research,' *Journal of Marketing*, 58, January 1994, pp. 111–124.
82. Steven A. Taylor, 'Assessing regression-based importance weights for quality perceptions and satisfaction judgements in the presence of higher order and/or interaction effects', *Journal of Retailing*, 73(1), 1997, pp. 135–59.
83. Valarie A. Zeithaml, Leonard L. Berry and A. Parasuraman, 'The behavioural consequences of service quality', *Journal of Marketing*, 60, April 1996, pp. 31–46. See also Valarie A. Zeithaml, 'Consumer perceptions of price, quality, and value: A means-end model and synthesis of evidence', *Journal of Marketing*, 52, July 1988, pp. 2–23.
84. Valarie A. Zeithaml, 'Service quality, profitability, and the economic worth of customers: What we know and what we need to learn', *Journal of the Academy of Marketing Science*, Winter 2000, pp. 67–85.
85. William B. Dodds, Kent B. Monroe and Dhruv Grewal, 'Effects of price, brand and store information on buyers' product evaluations', *Journal of Marketing Research*, 28, August 1991, pp. 307–319. See also Kent Monroe, *Pricing: Making Profitable Decisions*, 2nd edition (New York: McGraw-Hill, 1990); Robert J. Dolan and Herman Simon, *Power Pricing: How Managing Price Transforms the Bottom Line* (New York: The Free Press, 1996); and Tung-Zong Chang and Albert R. Wildt, 'Price, product information, and purchase intention: An empirical study', *Journal of the Academy of Marketing Science*, 22(1), 1994, pp. 16–27.
86. Indrajit Sinha and Wayne S. DeSasrbo, 'An integrated approach toward the spatial model of perceived customer value', *Journal of Marketing Research*, 35, May 1988, pp. 236–249.
87. Donald R. Liechtenstein, Nancy M. Ridgway and Richard G. Nitemeyer, 'Price perception and consumer shopping behavior: A field study', *Journal of Marketing Research*, 30, May 1993, p. 242.
88. Merrie Brucks and Valarie A. Zeithaml, 'Price and brand name as indicators of quality dimensions for consumer durables,' *Journal of the Academy of Marketing Science*, Summer 2000, pp. 359–374.
89. Ibid.
90. Dodds, Monroe and Grewal, op. cit. See also Noel Mark Lavenka, 'Measurement of consumers' perceptions of product quality, brand name and packaging: Candy bar comparisons by magnitude estimation', *Marketing Research*, 3(2), June 1991, pp. 38–45.
91. Joseph W. Alba, Susan M. Broniarczyk, Terrence A. Shimp and Joel E. Urbany, 'The influence of prior beliefs, frequency cues, and magnitude cues on consumers' perceptions of comparative price data', *Journal of Consumer Research*, 21, September 1994, pp. 219–235.
92. Ibid.
93. Susan M. Broniarczyk, Wayne D. Hoyer and Leigh McAlister, 'Consumers' perceptions of the assortment carried in a grocery category: The impact of item reduction', *Journal of Marketing Research*, 35, May 1998, pp. 166–176.
94. Julie Baker, Dhruv Grewal and A. Parasuraman, 'The influence of store environment on quality inferences and store image', *Journal of the Academy of Marketing Science*, 22(4), 1994, pp. 328–339.
95. Jacob Jacoby and David Mazursk, 'Linking brand and retailer images: Do the potential risks outweigh the potential benefits?', *Journal of Retailing*, 60, Summer 1984, pp. 105–122.
96. Frank H. Alpert and Michael A. Kamins, 'An empirical investigation of consumer memory, attitude and perceptions towards pioneer and follower brands', *Journal of Marketing*, 59, October 1995, pp. 34–45.

97. Ama Carmine, 'The effect of perceived advertising costs on brand perceptions', *Journal of Consumer Research*, 17, September 1990, pp. 160–171.
98. Herbert H. Severson, Paul Slovic, and Sarah Hampson, 'Adolescents' perception of risk: Understanding and preventing high risk behavior,' *Advances in Consumer Research*, 20, 1993, pp. 177–182.
99. Elke U. Weber and Richard A. Milliman, 'Perceived risk attitudes: Relating risk perception to risky choice', *Management Science*, 43(2), February 1997, pp. 123–144.
100. Grahame R. Dowling and Richard Staelin, 'A model of perceived risk and intended risk handling activity', *Journal of Consumer Research*, 21, June 1994, pp. 119–134.
101. Keith B. Murray and John L. Schlacter, 'The impact of services versus goods on consumers' assessment of perceived risk and variability', *Journal of the Academy of Marketing Science*, 18, Winter 1990, pp. 51–65.

CHAPTER 6

Learning and consumer involvement

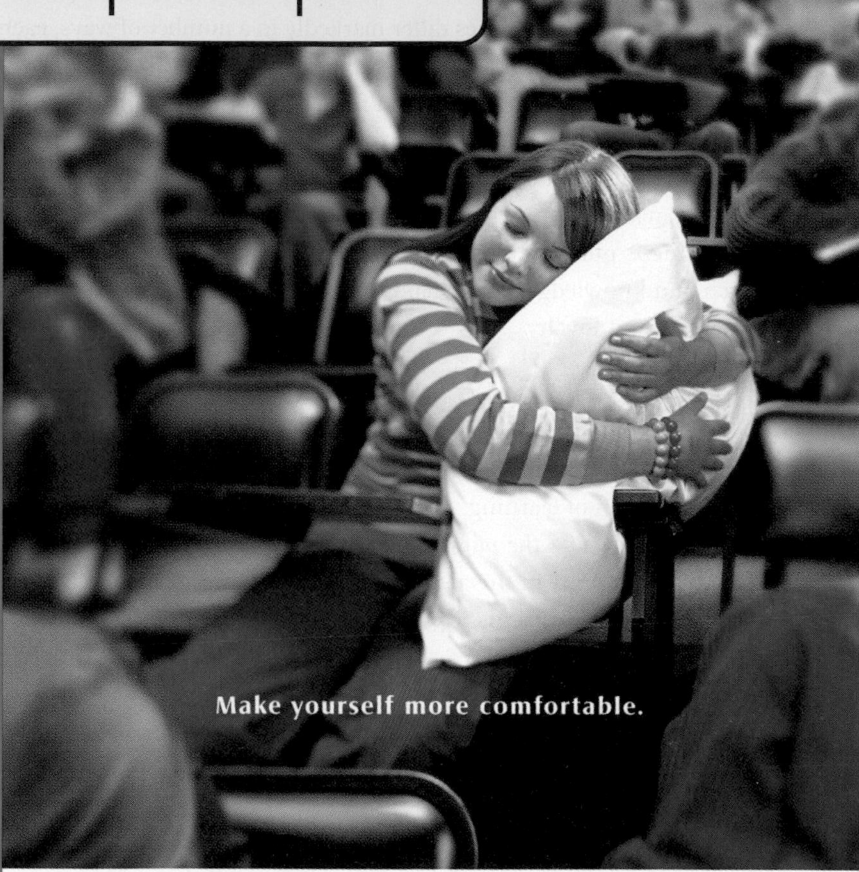

Source: **Reproduced with permission from Johnson & Johnson Pacific.**

How individuals learn and become involved with products is a matter of great interest and importance in consumer behaviour. Marketers are concerned with how consumers learn because they are interested in teaching consumers, in their roles as consumers, payers and buyers, about products, product attributes and potential benefits; about where to buy their products, how to use them, how to maintain them, even how to dispose of them. Marketing strategies are based on communicating with the consumer, directly through advertisements, and indirectly through product appearance, packaging, price and distribution channels. Marketers want their communications to be noticed, believed, remembered and recalled. For these reasons, they are interested in every aspect of the learning process.

Despite the fact that learning is pervasive in our lives, there is no single, universal theory of how people learn. Instead, there are two major schools of thought concerning the learning process: one consists of behavioural theories, the other of cognitive theories. Cognitive theorists view learning as a function of purely mental processes, while behavioural theorists focus almost exclusively on observable behaviours (responses) that occur as the result of exposure to stimuli.

In this chapter, we examine the two general categories of learning theory—behavioural theory and cognitive theory. Though these theories differ markedly in a number of ways, each theory offers insights to marketers on how to shape their messages to consumers in order to bring about desired purchase behaviour. We also discuss how consumers store, retain and retrieve information, how learning is measured, and how marketers use learning theories in their marketing strategies.

This chapter also examines consumer involvement. Involvement plays a key role in many aspects of consumer behaviour. Marketers are often concerned with their target market's (consumers) level of involvement in products, purchase decisions and advertising because of its influence on decision making, information search and knowledge. The chapter concludes with a discussion of an important aspect of learning and involvement, brand loyalty.

What is learning?

Since learning theorists do not agree on how learning takes place, it is difficult to come up with a generally acceptable definition of learning. From a marketing perspective, however, consumer learning is *the process by which individuals acquire the purchase and consumption knowledge and experience they apply to future related behaviour*. Several points in this definition are worth noting.

First, consumer learning is a process; that is, it continually evolves and changes as a result of newly-acquired knowledge (which may be gained from reading, or observation, or thinking) or from actual experience. Both newly-acquired knowledge and experiences serve as feedback to the individual and provide the basis for future behaviour in similar situations. The definition makes clear that learning results from acquired knowledge and experience. This qualification distinguishes learning from instinctive behaviour, such as suckling on the breast in infants.

The role of experience in learning does not mean that all learning is deliberately sought. Much learning is intentional—that is, it is acquired as the result of a careful search for information. But a great deal of learning is also incidental, acquired accidentally or without much effort. For example, some ads may induce learning (e.g. of brand names), even though the consumer's attention is elsewhere (on a magazine article rather than on the advertisement on the facing page). Other ads are sought out and carefully read by consumers contemplating an important decision.

The term 'learning' encompasses a wide range of learning, from simple, almost reflexive responses to the learning of abstract concepts and complex problem solving. Most learning theorists recognise the existence of different types of learning and explain the differences through the use of distinctive models of learning.

Despite their different viewpoints, learning theorists in general agree that, in order for learning to occur, certain basic elements must be present. The elements included in most learning theories are *motivation*, *cues*, *response* and *reinforcement*. These concepts are discussed first because they tend to recur in the theories discussed later in this chapter.

MOTIVATION

The concept of **motivation**, discussed in Chapter 3, is important to learning theory. Remember, motivation is based on needs and goals and it in effect acts as a catalyst for learning, with needs and goals serving as stimuli. For example, people who want to 'get in shape' are motivated to learn all they can about aerobics classes, weight training and jogging. They may seek information concerning the prices, quality and the resulting fitness levels associated with each of these activities. Conversely, individuals who are not interested in fitness are likely to ignore all information related to these activities. The goal object (an improved fitness level) simply has no relevance for them.

The degree of relevance (an aspect of involvement in the product or service) is critical to how motivated the consumer is to search for knowledge or information. Uncovering consumer motives is one of the prime tasks of marketers, who then try to teach 'motivated' consumer segments why their product will best fulfil the consumer's needs. (*Involvement theory*, as it has come to be known, will be discussed later in the chapter.)

CUES

If motives serve to stimulate learning, **cues** are the stimuli that give direction to those motives. An advertisement for a fitness club or a home fitness machine may serve as a cue for potential fitness enthusiasts, who may suddenly 'recognise' that using a home fitness machine is a simple way of improving their fitness level. The ad is the cue, or stimulus, that suggests a specific way to satisfy a salient motive. In the marketplace, price, styling, packaging, advertising and store displays all serve as cues to help consumers fulfil their needs in product-specific ways. For service marketers, tangible signals of quality, such as keeping arranged appointments, and providing stylish decor and well-groomed staff are essential.

Cues serve to direct consumer drives when they are consistent with consumer expectations. Marketers must be careful to provide cues that do not upset those expectations. For example, consumers expect advocates of a home fitness machine to be in excellent physical condition. Thus, the actors used to demonstrate the machine must appear to be in good shape. Each aspect of the marketing mix must reinforce the others if cues are to serve as the stimuli that guide consumer actions in the direction desired by the marketer.

RESPONSE

How individuals react to a drive or cue, how they behave, constitutes their **response**. Learning can occur even if responses are not overt. The car manufacturer who provides consistent cues to a consumer may not always succeed in stimulating a purchase, even if that individual is motivated to buy. However, if the manufacturer succeeds in forming a favourable image of a particular model in the consumer's mind, when the consumer is ready to buy, it is likely he or she will consider that make or model.

A response is not tied to a need in a one-to-one fashion. Indeed, as was discussed in Chapter 3, a need or motive may evoke a whole variety of responses. For example, there are many ways to respond to the need for physical exercise besides buying a home fitness machine. Cues provide some direction, but there are many cues competing for consumers' attention. The response they make depends heavily on previous learning; that, in turn, may depend on which responses were reinforced in the past.

REINFORCEMENT

Reinforcement increases the likelihood that a specific response will occur in the future as the result of particular cues or stimuli. If, after using the fitness machine for a few weeks, a consumer feels better physically, or is complimented on her appearance by her friends, she is more likely to continue using the machine and possibly to engage in other fitness-related activities. Clearly, through reinforcement, learning has taken place, since the use of the machine lived up to expectations. On the other hand, if working out at home had not resulted in an improved fitness level, the consumer would be less likely to continue using the machine or to buy any other product claiming to aid in improving fitness, despite extensive advertising or store display cues for the product.

With these basic principles, we can now discuss some well-known theories or models of how learning occurs.

Behavioural learning theories

Behavioural learning theories are sometimes referred to as *stimulus-response theories* because they are based on the premise that observable responses to specific external stimuli signal that learning has taken place. If people act (i.e. respond) in a predictable way to a known stimulus, they are said to have 'learned'. Behavioural theories are not so much concerned with the process of learning as they are with the inputs and outcomes of learning; that is, in the stimuli that are selected from the environment and the observable behaviours that result. Two behavioural theories with great relevance to marketing are *classical conditioning* and *instrumental* (or *operant*) *conditioning*.

CLASSICAL CONDITIONING

Early **classical conditioning** theorists regarded all organisms (both animal and human) as relatively passive entities that could be taught certain behaviours through repetition (or conditioning). In everyday speech, the word 'conditioning' has come to mean a kind of 'knee-jerk', or automatic, response to a situation built up through repeated exposure. If you feel tired every time you look at your textbooks, your reaction may be conditioned from years of late nights studying for exams.

Ivan Pavlov, a Russian physiologist, was the first to describe conditioning and to propose it as a general model of how learning occurs. According to Pavlovian theory, conditioned learning results when a stimulus that does not initially evoke a response is paired with another stimulus that elicits a known response until, eventually, it serves to produce the same response when used alone.

Pavlov demonstrated what he meant by conditioned learning in his studies with dogs. The dogs were hungry and highly motivated to eat. In his experiments, Pavlov sounded a bell (conditioned stimulus or CS) and then immediately applied a meat paste (unconditioned stimulus or US) to the dogs' tongues, which caused them to salivate (unconditioned response or UR). Learning (i.e. conditioning) had occurred when, after a sufficient number of repetitions of the bell sound, followed almost immediately by the food, the bell alone caused the dogs to salivate. The dogs associated the bell with the meat paste and, after a number of pairings, gave the same response (salivation) to the bell alone as they did to the meat paste. The unconditioned response (UR) to the meat paste became the conditioned response (CR) to the bell as depicted in Figure 6.1(a) which models this relationship.

An analogous situation would be one in which the smells of dinner cooking cause your mouth to water. If you usually listen to the evening news while waiting for dinner to be served, you would tend to associate the evening news with dinner, so that eventually the sound of the evening news alone might cause your mouth to water, even if dinner was not being prepared and even if you were not hungry as depicted in Figure 6.1(b) which shows this basic relationship.

In a consumer behaviour context, conditioned stimuli consist of consumption objects such as brands, products and retail stores, and the conditioned response would be purchases or store patronage. Unconditioned stimuli might consist of celebrity endorsers, sports figures and well-known consumption symbols.[1]

A new look at classical conditioning by learning theorists sees early Pavlovian theory as inadequately characterising the circumstances that produce the conditioned learning, the content of that learning, and the manner in which that learning influences behaviour. Later conditioning theory views classical conditioning as the learning of associations among events that allow the organism to anticipate and 'represent' its environment.[2] Thus, the relationship (i.e. contiguity) between the CS and the US (the bell and the meat paste) influenced the dogs' expectations, which in turn influenced their behaviour (salivation).

Classical conditioning is seen as cognitive associative learning through the acquisition of new knowledge about the world, rather than being a reflexive action through the acquisition of new reflexes. As such, the creation of a strong association between the conditioned stimulus and unconditioned stimulus—seen as optimal conditioning—commonly has five key features:

1. the CS precedes the US (called forward conditioning)
2. a CS and US that logically belong together
3. a CS that is novel and unfamiliar

FIGURE 6.1 Models of classical conditioning

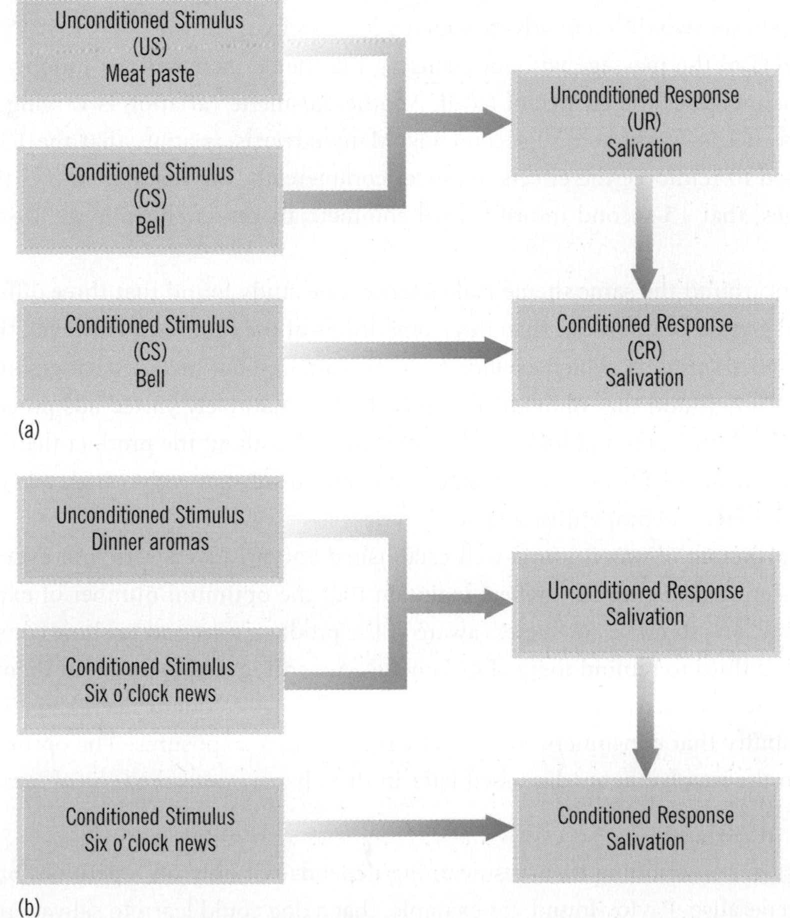

4. repeated pairing of CS and US
5. a US that is biologically or symbolically salient.

Recently, however, it has been suggested that conditioning can occur in an advertising context with no logical relationship between CS and US, and with as little as one repetition.[3]

Under **neo-Pavlovian theory**, consumers can be viewed as information seekers who use logical and perceptual relations among events, together with their own preconceptions, to form a sophisticated representation of the world.[4] Conditioning is the learning that results from exposure to relationships among events in the environment; such exposure creates expectations as to the structure of the environment.

Three basic concepts are fundamental to classical conditioning: *repetition*, *stimulus generalisation* and *stimulus discrimination*. Each of these concepts is important to an understanding of consumer behaviour.

Repetition

Repetition increases the strength of association between a conditioned stimulus and an unconditioned stimulus and by slowing the process of forgetting. The relationship between repetition and memory is a complex one. Evidence suggests that some overlearning, or repetition beyond what is necessary to learn, aids **retention**. However, with a greater number of repetitions, an individual can become satiated, and attention and retention will decline. Memory may no longer improve with repeated exposures. This phenomenon, called **advertising wearout**, can be decreased by varying the advertising message.[5]

Some marketers avoid wearout by adopting a variation strategy. This can be by for example repeating the same advertising theme, but varying the background, print type or spokesperson as depicted in Figure 6.2 (page 186) which shows two different advertisements for Carefree.

Changing aspects of the message without changing the theme increases the number of retrieval cues for the brand, and this increases the chance of recall. Another cosmetic variation is varying the ad length. Some campaigns have both 15-second and 30-second ads. Many advertisers argue that the 15-second commercial should only be used to reinforce the effects of longer commercials; but research shows this is only true with emotional messages, that 15-second informational commercials are as effective as 30-second informational commercials.[6]

Varying formats around the same theme makes sense: one study found that three different ads for a brand of liquor produced greater brand recall than three repetitions of the same ad.[7] However, there are other strategies, such as *substantive variation*, which exclude cosmetic variation but include changes in advertising content. A recent research study found that individuals exposed to substantively varied ads processed more information about the product attributes and had more positive thoughts about the product than those exposed to the cosmetic variation.[8] Attitudes formed as a result of exposure to substantively varied ads were also more resistant to change in the face of competitive attack.

Although the principle of repetition is well established among advertisers, not everyone agrees on how much repetition is enough. Some researchers maintain that the optimum number of exposures to an advertisement is just three: one to make consumers aware of the product; a second to show consumers the relevance of the product; and a third to remind them of its benefits. According to this **three-hit theory**, all other ad repetitions are wasted effort. Other researchers suggest that an average frequency of 11 to 12 airings is needed to increase the probability that consumers will actually receive three exposures. The optimum number of repetitions depends on the involvement (discussed later in this chapter) and the type of message strategy.

Stimulus generalisation

According to classical conditioning theorists, learning depends not only on repetition, but also on the ability of individuals to generalise. Pavlov found, for example, that a dog could learn to salivate not only to the sound of a bell, but also to the somewhat similar sound of jangling keys. If we were not capable of **stimulus generalisation**—that is, of making the same response to slightly different stimuli—not much learning would take place.

Stimulus generalisation explains why imitative 'me too' products succeed in the marketplace: consumers confuse them with the original product they have seen advertised. It also explains why manufacturers of private brands try to make their packaging resemble the national brand leaders. They are hoping that consumers will confuse their packages with the leading brand. Some brands are so valuable that similarly packaged or distributed products can result in millions of lost sales.[9] In Australia, an electronics company marketing televisions and microwave ovens under the brand name Palsonic uses a very similar font style to Panasonic, facilitating stimulus generalisation.

Product line, form and category extensions, the practice of adding related products to an already established brand, is another application of stimulus generalisation. Of the 20 000 or so new products introduced into the US market each year, about 80% are product or brand extensions.[10] That's because it's a lot cheaper to associate a new product with a known and trusted brand name than to try to develop a totally new brand. For a long time marketers have offered **product line extensions**, which included different sizes, different colours, even different flavours; but now they offer product form extensions (e.g. Figure 6.3 illustrates a product form extension: Omo liquid to Omo Sensitive liquid) and product category extensions (Cadbury chocolate bars to Cadbury chocolate biscuits and Cadbury ice-creams).

The success of this strategy depends on the relevance of the new product to the marketplace image of the brand name. For example, Mars Confectionery was able to move successfully from Snickers chocolate bars to Snickers ice-creams, but Arm & Hammer, the makers of bicarbonate of soda products, was unable in the United States to move from a refrigerator deodorant to a personal care deodorant. Product line extensions are no panacea for all marketing problems; indeed, many companies now see the need to rationalise their product lines to focus on the best-selling items.

A laboratory experiment found that the greater the similarity between the primary product and the brand extension, the greater the transfer of positive (or negative) evaluations to the new product. It also found that a brand's reputation for excellence in one product area may have a negative impact on consumer ratings of its new product in an unrelated product area.[11] Brand name extensions are used extensively in packaged goods marketing.

Family branding, the practice of marketing a whole line of company products under the same brand name, is another strategy that capitalises on the consumer's ability to generalise favourable brand associations from one product to the next. The Campbell's Soup Company, for example, continues to add new soup entrees to its product line under the Campbell's brand name, achieving ready acceptance for the new products from satisfied consumers of other Campbell's Soup products.

Licensing is another type of marketing strategy that operates on the principle of stimulus generalisation. The names of designers, celebrities and even cartoon characters are attached (i.e. 'rented') to a variety of products for a fee, enabling the manufacturers and marketers of such products to achieve instant recognition and implied quality for the licensed products. Some of the successful licensors include Pierre Cardin, Calvin Klein, Lacoste and Christian Dior, whose names appear on a wide variety of products, from sheets to shoes, luggage to perfume and shirts to watches. Versace has extended this principle licensing their name to be used as a hotel name on the Gold Coast. Licensing agreements earn Versace more than $900 million a year.[12]

The licensing of cartoon characters has also become big business. In fact, seeing how lucrative the licensing of its own cartoon characters had become, the Disney Corporation opened a chain of retail stores that sell a multitude of products, from schoolbags to t-shirts to beach towels, emblazoned with the names or pictures of the many well-known Disney characters.

FIGURE 6.2 Advertisements by Carefree varying the basic scene and keeping the theme the same

Source: Reproduced with permission from Johnson & Johnson Pacific.

FIGURE 6.3 Illustrates a product form extension

Source: Used with permission of Unilever Australia.

However, the increase in licensing has made counterfeiting a booming business, as counterfeiters add well-known licensor names to a variety of products without benefit of contract or quality control, and sell them as licensed goods. Counterfeiting has spread to many product categories, and a lot of counterfeit merchandise is virtually identical to the original and for the unwary or consumer with little knowledge virtually undectable. Fakes have appeared in many countries in the Asia–Pacific region, including Australia.

Stimulus discrimination

Stimulus discrimination is the opposite of stimulus generalisation, and results in the selection of a specific stimulus from among similar stimuli. The consumer's ability to discriminate among stimuli is the basis of positioning strategy, which seeks to establish a unique image for a brand in the consumer's mind.

Imitators want consumers to generalise their experience, but market leaders want to retain the top spot by persuading consumers to discriminate. It is often quite difficult to unseat a brand leader once stimulus discrimination has occurred. One explanation is that the leader is usually first in the market and has had a longer period to 'teach' consumers (through advertising and selling) to associate the brand name with the product. In short, it owns the market. Australians still talk of a Biro, Esky or Thermos because these brands were first on the market. And because of its strong association in the consumer's mind with computers, IBM was able to redirect the personal computer market when it first entered that market, despite its relatively late entry into the PC field. But, as the IBM experience shows, that is not enough to ensure longer-term market dominance.

In general, the longer the period of learning to associate a brand name with a product, the more likely the consumer is to discriminate, and the less likely to generalise the stimulus. In our overcommunicated society, a key to stimulus discrimination is effective positioning (see Chapter 5).

Evaluation of classical conditioning

The principles of classical conditioning provide the theoretical underpinnings for many marketing applications. Repetition, stimulus generalisation and stimulus discrimination are useful concepts in explaining how consumers learn to behave in the marketplace. However, they do not explain all the activities classified as consumer learning. Traditional classical conditioning assumed that consumers were passive beings who reacted with predictable responses to stimuli after a number of trials. Neo-Pavlovian theory views individuals as information seekers using logical and perceptual relationships among events, along with their own preconceptions, to form a sophisticated representation of their world.

While some of our purchase behaviour—for example, the purchase of branded convenience goods—may have been shaped to some extent by repeated advertising messages, other purchase behaviour results from evaluation of product alternatives. Our assessments of products are often based on the rewards we experience as the result of making specific purchases—in other words, from *instrumental conditioning*.

INSTRUMENTAL CONDITIONING

Like classical conditioning, **instrumental (operant) conditioning** requires a link between a stimulus and a response. However, in instrumental conditioning, the stimulus that provides an optimal response is learned. Instrumental learning theorists believe that learning occurs through a trial-and-error process, with habits formed as a result of rewards received for certain responses or behaviours. While classical conditioning is useful in explaining how consumers learn very simple kinds of behaviours, instrumental conditioning is more helpful in explaining complex, goal-directed activities.

The name closely associated with instrumental (operant) conditioning is that of the American psychologist B.F. Skinner. According to Skinner, most individual learning occurs in a controlled environment in which individuals are 'rewarded' for choosing an appropriate behaviour. In consumer behaviour terms, instrumental conditioning suggests that consumers learn by means of a trial-and-error process in which some purchase behaviours result in more favourable outcomes (i.e. rewards) than other purchase behaviours. A favourable experience is instrumental in teaching the individual to repeat a specific consumption behaviour.

Like Pavlov, Skinner developed his model of learning by working with animals. Animals such as rats and pigeons were placed in his 'Skinner box'; if they made appropriate movements (e.g. depressed levers or pecked keys) they received food (a positive reinforcement). Skinner and his many adherents have done amazing things with this simple learning model, including teaching pigeons to play ping-pong, to dance, and even to act as the guidance system in a missile. In a marketing context, the consumer who tries several brands and styles of jeans before finding a style that fits her figure (positive reinforcement) has engaged in instrumental learning. Presumably, the brand that fits best is the one she will continue to buy. The instrumental conditioning process is presented in Figure 6.4. It details the learning process of trying different brands and the various outcomes (responses) that accompany trying the different stimuli (brands).

FIGURE 6.4 A model of instrumental conditioning

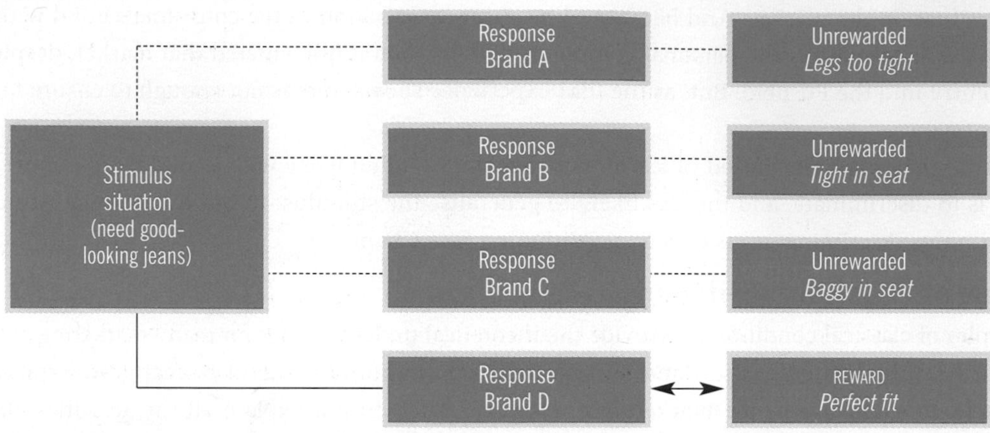

Positive and negative reinforcement

Skinner distinguished two types of reinforcement (or reward) that influence the chances that a response will be repeated. The first type, **positive reinforcement**, consists of events that strengthen the likelihood of a specific response. Using a shampoo that leaves your hair feeling silky and clean is likely to result in repetition of the shampoo purchase. **Negative reinforcement** is an unpleasant or negative outcome that also serves to encourage a specific behaviour. For example, an American Express ad that shows a pickpocket stealing a holiday-maker's wallet is likely to encourage consumers to buy travellers' cheques. Negative reinforcement should not be confused with punishment, which is designed to discourage behaviour. Parking tickets are not negative reinforcement: they are a form of 'punishment' designed to discourage drivers from parking illegally.

Fear appeals in ad messages are examples of negative reinforcement. Life insurance commercials, warning husbands that in the event of sudden death their wives will be left penniless widows, rely on negative reinforcement to encourage the purchase of life insurance. Marketers of headache remedies use negative reinforcement when they illustrate the unpleasant symptoms of an unrelieved headache, as do marketers of mouthwash when they show the loneliness suffered by someone with bad breath. In each of these cases the consumer is encouraged to avoid the negative consequences by buying the advertised product.

Forgetting and extinction

When a learned response is no longer reinforced, it diminishes to the point of *extinction*: that is, to the point at which the link between the stimulus and the expected reward is eliminated. If a consumer is no longer satisfied that her hair is silky smooth after using a brand of shampoo, the link between the stimulus (shampoo) and the response (silky smooth hair) is no longer reinforced. When behaviour is no longer reinforced, it is 'unlearned', which is different from forgetting. Forgetting is often related to the passage of time and is caused by lack of use, rather than lack of reinforcement. It is a process of decay. A consumer may not visit a previously favoured cafe for a long time and simply forget that he used to enjoy eating there.

Massed or distributed learning

Another important influence on consumer learning is timing. Should a learning schedule be spread over a period of time (**distributed learning**) or should it be 'bunched up' all at once (**massed learning**)? The question is an important one for advertisers planning a media schedule; while massed advertising produces more initial learning, a more dispersed schedule usually results in learning that persists longer. When advertisers want an immediate impact (e.g. to introduce a new product or to counter a competitor's blitz campaign), they generally use a massed schedule. However, when the goal is long-lasting repeat buying on a regular basis, a distributed schedule is preferable. Car makers use a combination of the two: they use concentrated (massed) advertising during the first few weeks of a new model's life, then distributed (drip-feed) advertising over the rest of the product life cycle, possibly punctuated by bursts of massed advertising.[13]

Evaluation of instrumental conditioning

Instrumental learning theory applies to many situations in which consumers learn about products, services and stores. For example, when Amanda O'Brien moved to Melbourne, she learned which stores carried the type of clothing she liked, at prices she could afford by shopping in a number of stores, and looking for the colours, sizes and styles she preferred at prices she was able to pay. Once she found a store that carried clothing that met her requirements, she tended to patronise that store to the exclusion of others. Every time she purchased a top or a dress there that she really liked, her store loyalty was rewarded (reinforced) and her store patronage (i.e. shopping behaviour) more likely to be repeated.

Critics of instrumental learning theory point out that a considerable amount of learning takes place in the absence of direct reinforcement, either positive or negative. We do not have to be arrested to know that we should obey the law. We learn a great deal through a process psychologists call **modelling** or observational learning (also called vicarious learning). We observe the behaviour of others, remember it and imitate it. Instrumental theorists argue that children learn in this way because they can imagine a reward and therefore imitate the behaviour that leads to it. But critics maintain that instrumentalists confuse learning and performance (behaviour). Both children and adults learn a great deal that they do not act upon.

Some researchers argue that because instrumental learning theory views behaviour as a result of environmental manipulation rather than cognitive processes, it is applicable only to products that have little personal relevance or importance to the consumer. Other marketers claim that instrumental learning theory is applicable to products of both high and low relevance to the consumer.[14] (The question of product relevance is discussed later in the chapter in connection with involvement theory.)

➤ Cognitive learning theory

Not all learning takes place as the result of repeated trials. A considerable amount of learning takes place as the result of consumer thinking and problem-solving. Sudden learning is also a reality. When confronted with a problem, we sometimes see the solution instantly. More often, however, we are likely to search for information on which to base a decision, and carefully evaluate what we learn in order to make the best decision possible for our purposes. Learning based on mental activity is called **cognitive learning**.

Cognitive learning theory holds that the kind of learning most characteristic of human beings is problem solving, which enables us to gain some control over our environment. Unlike behavioural learning theory, cognitive theory holds that learning involves complex mental processing of information. Instead of stressing the importance of repetition or the association of rewards with a specific response, cognitive theorists emphasise the role of motivation and mental processes in producing a desired response.

INFORMATION PROCESSING

Just as a computer processes information received as input, so too does the human mind process the information it receives as input. **Information processing** is related to both the consumer's cognitive ability and the complexity of the information to be processed. Consumers process product information by attributes, brands, comparisons between brands, or a combination of these factors. While the attributes included in the brand's message and the number of available alternatives influence the intensity of information processing, consumers with a higher cognitive ability apparently acquire more product information and are more capable of integrating information on several product attributes than consumers with less ability. Individuals also differ in terms of **imagery**—that is, in their ability to form mental images—and these differences influence their ability to recall information.[15] Individual differences in imagery processing can be measured with tests of imagery vividness (the ability to evoke clear images), processing style (preference for, and frequency of, visual versus verbal processing), and tests of daydream (fantasy) content and frequency.[16] Australian research has shown that one reason why some brands have low awareness is a lack of **salience**, or distinctiveness as a brand.[17]

The more experience consumers have with a product category, the greater their ability to make use of product information. Greater familiarity with the product category also increases cognitive ability and learning during a new purchase decision, particularly with regard to technical information.[18] This suggests that advertising of technical features and technical evaluations of products (e.g. by magazines such as *Choice* magazine) has greater impact on the purchase decisions of consumers who are already knowledgeable about the product category.

How consumers store, retain and retrieve information

Of central importance to the processing of information is human memory. A basic research concern of most cognitive scientists is discovering how information gets stored in memory, how it is retained and how it is retrieved.

The structure of memory Since information processing occurs in stages, it is generally believed that there are separate 'storehouses' in the memory where information is kept temporarily while waiting to be processed further: a sensory store, a short-term store and a long-term store.

- *Sensory store.* All data come to us through our senses; however, the image of a sensory input lasts for just a second or two in the mind's sensory store. For example, after staring at a TV image for a few seconds and then looking away, we retain an after-image. That after-image, though very short-lived, is packed with more information than we tend to use or process further. We subconsciously block out a great deal of information. For marketers this means that, although it is relatively easy to get information into the consumer's sensory store, it is difficult to make a lasting impression.
- *Short-term store.* The short-term store is the stage of real memory in which information is processed and held for just a brief period. Anyone who has ever looked up a number in a telephone book, only to forget it just before dialling, knows how briefly information lasts in short-term storage. If information in the short-term store undergoes the process known as *rehearsal*, it is then transferred to the long-term store. (**Rehearsal** can be defined as the silent, mental repetition of material.) The transfer process takes 2–10 seconds. If information is not rehearsed and transferred, it is lost in about 30 seconds or less. The amount of information that can be held in short-term storage is limited to four or five items. Through *chunking* of information, we can easily store more items, a fact exploited by Domino's pizza with its 131 888 phone number.
- *Long-term store.* In contrast to the short-term store, where information lasts only seconds, the long-term store retains information for relatively extended periods of time. Although it is possible to forget something a few minutes after the information has reached long-term storage, it is more common for data in long-term storage to last for days, weeks, even years. Almost all of us, for example, can remember the name of our first-grade teacher. Figure 6.5 depicts the transfer of information received by the sensory store, through the short-term store, to long-term storage.

FIGURE 6.5 Information processing and memory stores

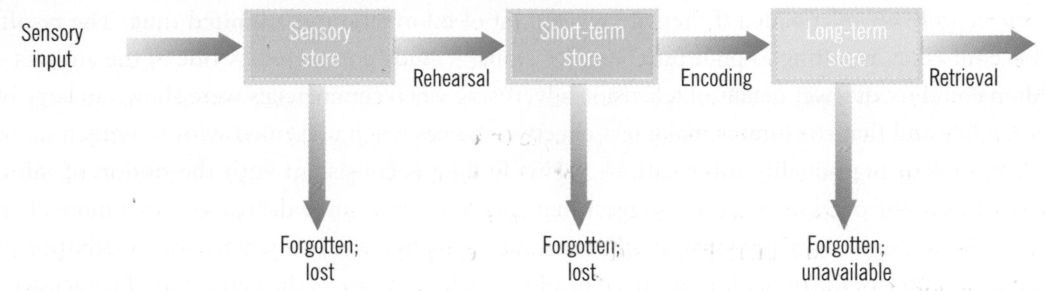

Rehearsal and encoding

How much information is available for delivery from the short-term store to the long-term store depends on the amount of rehearsal given to it. Failure to rehearse an input, either by repeating it or by relating it to other data, can cause fading and eventual loss of the information. Information can also be lost because of competition for attention. For example, if the short-term store receives a number of inputs simultaneously from the sensory store, its capacity may be reduced to only two or three pieces of information.

The purpose of rehearsal is to hold information in short-term storage long enough for encoding to take place. **Encoding** is the process by which we select and assign a word or visual image to represent a perceived object. Marketers, for example, help consumers encode brands by using brand symbols. The Commonwealth Bank uses the highly visual logo designed by Ken Cato and described by one wag as 'a Salada dipped in Vegemite'. (Actually, the symbol is a stylised version of the Southern Cross in the Bank's traditional colours.) The St George Bank also uses a visually memorable logo by incorporating a dragon. A memorable brand name, such as Uncle Tobys, can also aid in the consumer's encoding process.

'Learning' a picture takes less time than learning verbal information, but both types of presentation are important in forming an overall mental image. A print ad with both an illustration and body copy is more likely to be encoded and stored than an illustration without verbal information. A study that examined the effects of visual and verbal advertising found that when advertising copy and illustrations focus on different product attributes, the illustrations disproportionately influence consumer inferences.[19] Another study found that high-imagery copy was more likely to be recalled whether or not it was accompanied by an illustration, but that illustrations were important for audience recall when verbal imagery was low.[20] Not only visual cues add to the processing ability of consumers; other non-verbal elements such as music influence processing and memory. Research findings suggest that musical cues evoke even more responses involving images and visual associations than verbal cues.[21]

Researchers have found that the encoding of a commercial is related to the context of the TV program during which it is shown. Some parts of a program may require viewers to commit a larger portion of their cognitive resources to processing (e.g. a dramatic event versus a casual conversation). When viewers commit more cognitive resources to the program itself, they encode and store less of the information conveyed by a commercial. Thus, ads positioned in a dramatic program setting may be more effective with a relatively low level of elaboration.[22]

In relation to processing communications men and women exhibit different encoding of communication. For example, women have been found to be more likely than men to recall TV commercials portraying a social relationship theme. However, no differences seem to exist in the frequency of recall among men and women for commercials that focus on the product in isolation of people.[23]

Importantly, however when consumers are presented with too much information (called **information overload**), they may encounter difficulty in encoding and storing it all. It has been argued that consumers can become cognitively overloaded if they are given a lot of information in a limited time. The result of this overload is confusion, resulting in poor purchase decisions. A study conducted by one of the authors showed that children could recall fewer details of television advertising when commercials were shown in large blocks.[24] Other research found that consumers make less effective choices when presented with too much information (also with too much high-quality information).[25] This finding is consistent with the notion of information overload. Critics of the overload research suggest that choice accuracy only decreases when more alternatives are added to the decision; they demonstrate that accuracy actually increases when more attributive information is provided.[26] One of the difficulties in this type of research, however, is the definition of choice accuracy—or a 'good' decision.[27]

Retention of information by consumers is vital to marketers. Information doesn't just sit in a long-term storage, waiting to be retrieved. Instead, information is constantly being organised and reorganised as new links between chunks of information are forged. In fact, many information processing theorists view the long-term store as a network consisting of nodes (i.e. concepts) with links among them. Figure 6.6 is a representation of long-term storage of information about personal computers, showing nodes (e.g. models, monitors, manufacturers, modems, software, operating systems, printers) connected by links (e.g. for software: word processing, databases, graphics, games, spreadsheets). As we gain more knowledge of computers, we expand our network of relationships, and sometimes our search for additional information. This process is known as **activation**, which involves relating new data to old to make the material more meaningful. Our memory of the name of a product may also be activated by relating it to the spokesperson used in its advertising. The total package of associations brought to mind when a cue is activated is called a **schema**.

Product information stored in memory tends to be brand-based, and consumers interpret new information in a manner consistent with the way it is already organised.[28] Consumers are confronted with thousands of new products each year, and their information search often depends on how similar or dissimilar (discrepant) these products are to product categories already stored in memory. One study found that, at a moderate level of discrepancy, consumers are more likely to examine a relevant set of attributes in greater depth than search for new information on a broad range of attributes.[29]

Consumers are also able to recode what they have already encoded to include larger amounts of information (chunking). People who are new to a computer keyboard must type letter by letter. Those with more experience type in chunks of whole words or phrases. It is important for marketers to discover the groupings (chunks) of information that consumers can handle. Recall may be hampered if the chunks offered in an advertisement do not match those in the consumer's frame of reference. The degree of prior knowledge is an important consideration. Experts can take in more complex chunks of information. Thus, the amount and type of information in a computer ad can be much more detailed in a magazine such as *Australian Personal Computer*, *BYTE* (now only avaliable in Japan and Germany), or online magazines such as BYTE.com, than in a general interest magazine such as *Time*. Learning through advertisements is a common activity of consumers and one used often by marketers in a wide variety of product categories. Figure 6.7 (page 194) shows two ads stressing consumer learning for the same brand of paper towel. The visual is the same and the same information is being conveyed via different copy so that the consumer will learn the key features of the advertised brand.

Information is stored in long-term memory in two ways: episodically (i.e. by the order in which it is acquired) and semantically (according to significant concepts). Thus, we may remember having gone to a film last Saturday because of our ability to store data episodically, and we may remember the plot, the stars and the director because of our ability to store data semantically. Many learning theorists believe that memories

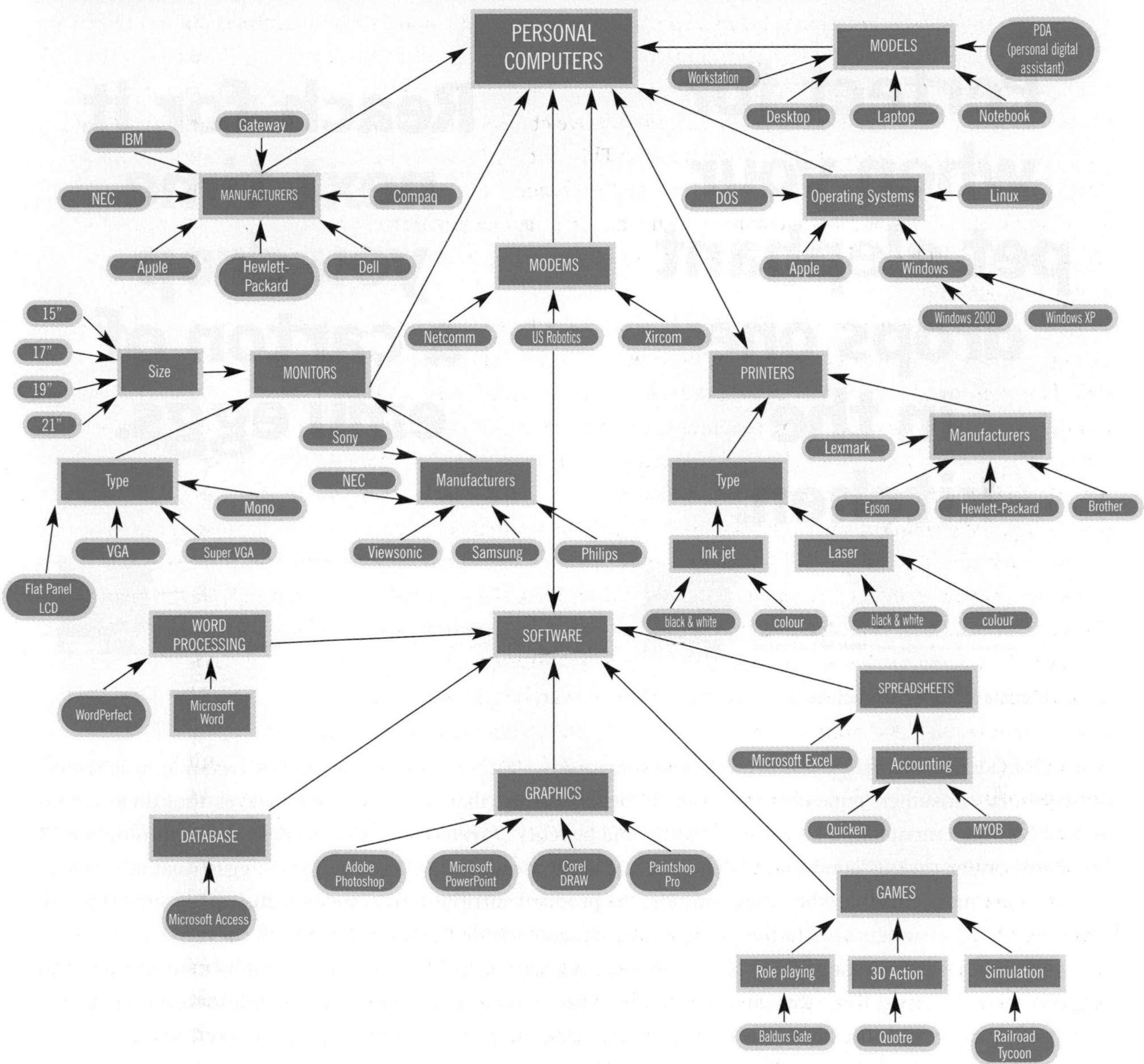

FIGURE 6.6 Conceptualisation of long-term storage of personal computer information

stored semantically are organised into frameworks by which we integrate new data with previous experience. Consumers with more knowledge, product experts, are more likely to integrate this information into frameworks than lower-knowledge consumers.[30] For information about a new model of fax machine to enter long-term memory, we would need to relate it to our previous experience with fax machines in terms of speed, print, quality, resolution, memory and automatic feeding qualities.

Information retrieval

Fundamentally, information **retrieval** is the process by which consumers recover information from long-term storage. Most people have had the experience of not being able to recollect something with which they are quite familiar. Information-processing theorists look on such forgetting as a failure of the retrieval system. There is

FIGURE 6.7 **Handee Ultra attempting to aid the consumer learning process**

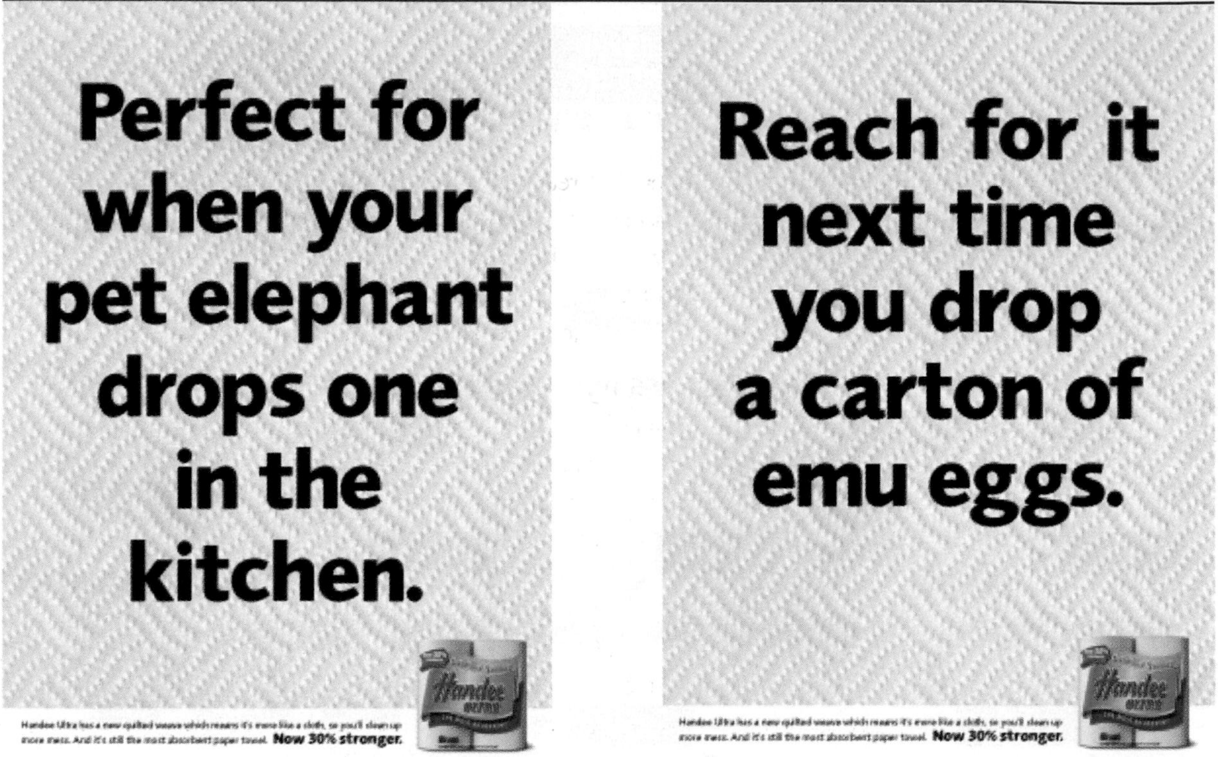

Perfect for when your pet elephant drops one in the kitchen.
Now 30% stronger.
Reach for it next time you drop a carton of emu eggs.
Now 30% stronger.

Source: Courtesy of SCA Hygiene Australasia.

research evidence that suggests retrieval from memory is a rather simple process. For example, it is widely believed that consumers remember the product's benefits rather than its attributes. However, they do not automatically form a mental link between attributes and benefits. Furthermore, they retrieve different numbers of attributes under various conditions.[31] The marketing implications of these findings suggest that advertising messages are most effective when they combine the product's attributes with the benefits (discovered through research) that consumers seek in the product, and clearly provide the linkage between the two.

Motivated consumers are likely to spend time interpreting and elaborating on information they find relevant to their needs; thus, they are likely to activate such relevant knowledge from long-term memory.[32] When consumers lack the ability to engage in extensive information processing, however, relatively low-level information may become influential, particularly when motivation is high.[33] When people retrieve information, they rarely search for negative information, though they do sometimes search for disconfirming information.[34]

The greater the number of competitive ads in a product category, the lower the recall of brand claims in a specific ad. These interference effects are caused by confusion with competing ads, and result in a failure to retrieve.[35] One study found that ads can act as retrieval cues for a competitive brand.[36] This was seen when consumers attributed the long-running and attention-getting television campaign featuring the Eveready Energizer Bunny to Eveready's competitor, Duracell.

Advertisements for competing brands or for other products made by the same manufacturer can lower the consumer's ability to remember advertised brand information. Such effects occur in response to even a small amount of advertising for similar products. Consumers can also forget brand information in response to interference, depending on previous experiences, prior knowledge of brand attribute information, and the amount of brand information available at the time of choice.[37] There are actually two kinds of **interference**. New learning can interfere with the retrieval of previously stored material, and old learning can interfere with the recall of recently learned material. With both kinds of interference, the problem is the similarity of old and new information. Advertising that creates a distinctive brand image can help consumers retain and retrieve the message more effectively.

There are times when a marketer would prefer that retrieval did not take place. This is particularly true when negative information or an unfounded rumour is publicised. In a laboratory simulation of the rumour that there were worms in McDonald's hamburgers, a refutational message that did not specifically mention the rumour was found to be more effective than a message that did. The refutational comment that specifically denied the existence of worms actually triggered the retrieval of the original rumour.[38]

Limited and extensive information processing

For a long time, consumer researchers believed that all consumers passed through a complex series of mental and behavioural stages in arriving at a purchase decision. These stages ranged from awareness (exposure to information), to evaluation (preference, attitude formation), to behaviour (purchase), to final evaluation (adoption or rejection). This same series of stages is often presented as the *consumer adoption process* (see Chapter 15).

A number of models have been developed over the years to express the same notion of sequential processing of information by consumers (see Figure 6.8). Initially, marketing theorists believed that such sequential, extensive and complex processing of information by consumers was applicable to all purchase decisions. However, on the basis of their own subjective experiences as consumers, some theorists began to realise that there were many purchase situations that simply did not call for extensive information processing and evaluation, that sometimes consumers simply went from awareness of a need to a routine purchase, without a whole lot of information search and mental evaluation. Such purchases were considered of minimal personal relevance as opposed to highly relevant search-oriented purchases. Purchases of minimal personal importance were called *low-involvement* purchases, and complex, search-oriented purchases were considered *high-involvement* purchases.

The following section describes the development of involvement theory and discusses its applications to marketing strategy.

INVOLVEMENT THEORY

Much of the early work on **involvement theory** focused on the tendency of individuals to make personal connections between their own life and the stimulus object (an ad or a brand). The focus was on the personal

FIGURE 6.8 Models of cognitive learning

Tricomponent model	Promotional model	Decision-making model	Innovation adoption model	Innovation decision process
Cognitive	Attention	Awareness Knowledge	Awareness	Knowledge
Affective	Interest Desire	Evaluation	Interest Evaluation	Persuasion
Conative	Action	Purchase Post-purchase evaluation	Trial Adoption	Decision Confirmation

CASE STUDY 6.1

The Pitfalls of Reinforcement of Customer Behaviour

Learning theory stresses that reinforcement is crucial in shaping future behaviour. Today, thanks to technology, service marketers can track past behaviour of customers more effectively than ever before and easily reward desirable behaviour. Thus, the records of highly profitable customers are given special codes designed to provide them with faster and better service when they contact the company, move them ahead of other customers in service queues, and provide them with upgrades and special discounts unknown and unavailable to other customers. Furthermore, since many companies share data about customers' transactions, customers are often assigned to 'reward tiers' before they even begin to do business with a given company because their buying potential has already been measured.

However, rewarding the best customers also means that 'lesser' patrons receive inferior service. For example, the calls of selected customers calling a brokerage company are answered within 15 seconds while other customers wait 10 minutes or more. At the websites of some banks, highly profitable customers have access to special links directing them to service agents and special phone lines while other customers never even see these links. At many financial institutions, service agents are permitted to grant fee waivers to highly profitable customers while other patrons have no negotiating power. In addition, the special treatment of selected customers also means that other customers pay more service fees.

Source: Diane Brady, 'Why service stinks,' *Business Week*, 23 October 2000, pp. 118–122, 124.

Case Study Questions

1. In the context of learning theory, what are the drawbacks of creating a reward system based entirely on measured past behaviour?
2. How can marketers create more effective reward systems designed to shape the future behaviour of less profitable customers?

CASE STUDY 6.2

Aroma Australia Pty Limited Goes to Japan

Professor Mark Uncles, University of New South Wales

Aroma Australia Pty Limited is contemplating a move into the Japanese market. Its instant coffee brand, *Caffeine Infusion*, has performed very well in Australasia and Singapore, and now the Japanese market holds the promise of even more lucrative sales. In preparation for this market entry, Aroma's marketing manager, Ken Ishiguro, is assembling a considerable amount of data about the instant coffee market in Japan. His goal is to obtain some background understanding of the market. He is not expecting the data to give him exact answers to the problems he faces nor tell him precisely how to enter the market—such issues will depend on alliances and partnerships with local distributors, cost and budgetary considerations, and so forth. He knows he will have to tackle these implementation issues once he feels more confident about entering the new market.

In assembling background data, Ken has acquired many market research reports. These reports include: attitude surveys among consumers in Tokyo shopping malls, in-depth interviews with coffee drinkers at their workplaces, brand research to see how local consumers will react to a name like *Caffeine Infusion*, studies in a Kyoto suburb to assess purchase intentions at various price points, etc. The results are very mixed—in fact, Ken is beginning to wonder whether the cultural differences between Japanese and Western consumers are so great that it will not be possible for Aroma to enter the market.

However, it now occurs to Ken that, while he has a wealth of data about consumer attitudes, beliefs and intentions, he has nothing on revealed behaviour. Yet, ultimately, it seems reasonable to assume that behavioural action on the part of consumers is going to be of the utmost importance. After all, behaviour is directly related to the measures used to assess Ken's performance—namely, sales and revenue. For this reason he decides to commission a market report from the Market Intelligence Corporation (MIC). The report comprises week-by-week buying records over a year for about 1000 households on a consumer panel in Tokyo and neighbouring prefectures.

Consultants working with MIC have compiled the data into tables in which are reported a number of measures of consumer behaviour for a variety of leading brands. Table 6.4 is an extract from the report. In this table the leading brands of instant coffee in Japan are listed, together with a few brand groupings. These are arranged in market-share order. Then, for each brand, measures are shown for penetration (per cent buying), average purchase frequency per buyer, average purchases of the product category per buyer of the brand, share of instant coffee requirements met by the brand, the per cent of buyers who are sole buyers ('100% loyals') and their average purchase frequency. In addition, Table 6.5 shows those who also buy competing brands (e.g. the per cent of those who bought Nesgold who also bought Nescafé, Maxim, etc.); this set of data refers to duplication of purchase.

The consultants have provided a number of predicted values for these measures as well. An extract is shown in Table 6.6. The predictions come from a model of consumer behaviour that was originally developed

TABLE 6.4 **Observed measures of buyer behaviour in the Japanese instant coffee market**

Brands arranged in market-share order

Japan Annual figures	Market share	Penetration (per cent buying)	Average purchase frequency per buyer	Average purchase frequency of the category per buyer	Share of category requirements (per cent)	Per cent of buyers who are sole buyers	Average purchase frequency per sole buyer
Any instant	100	73	6.5	—	—	—	—
Nesgold	39	50	3.7	7.3	51	26	3.3
Nescafé	22	27	3.9	8.7	35	19	4.5
Maxim	19	32	2.8	8.1	43	16	2.1
Minor brands	10	22	2.1	8.7	24	13	2.9
Maxwell House	8	15	2.4	9.8	20	8	1.6
Other Nestlé	1	3	1.9	9.3	19	6	2.5
Other General Foods brands	1	3	1.8	9.3	24	14	1.5
Average brand	14	22	2.7	8.7	31	15	2.6

and quantity of information on decision effectiveness', *Journal of Consumer Research*, 14, 1987, pp. 200–213.

26. See, for example, Jacob Jacoby, 'Perspectives on information overload', *Journal of Consumer Research*, 10, March 1984, pp. 432–435; and Thomas E. Muller, 'Buyer response to variations in product information load', *Journal of Applied Psychology*, 69, 1984, pp. 300–306.
27. Eric J. Johnson, Robert J. Meyer and Ghose Sanjoy, 'When choice models fail: Compensatory models in negatively correlated environments', *Journal of Marketing Research*, 26(3), August 1989, pp. 255–270.
28. Itamar Simonson, Joel Huber and John Payne, 'The relationship between prior brand knowledge and information acquisition order', *Journal of Consumer Research*, 14, 1988, pp. 566–578.
29. Julie L. Ozanne, Merrie Brucks and Dhruv Grewal, 'A study of information search behavior during the categorization of new products', *Journal of Consumer Research*, 18, 1992, pp. 452–463.
30. Elizabeth Cowley and Andrew A. Mitchell, 'The Moderating Effect of Product Knowledge on the Learning and Organization of Product Information', Working Paper, University of New South Wales, 2000.
31. Lorne Bozinoff and Victor J. Roth, 'Recall and recognition memory for product attributes and benefits', in Thomas C. Kinnear (ed.), *Advances in Consumer Research*, 11, 1984, pp. 348–352.
32. Kevin Lane Keller, 'Memory and evaluation effects in competitive advertising environments', *Journal of Consumer Research*, 17, 1991, pp. 463–476.
33. Carolyn L. Costley and Merrie Brucks, 'Selective recall and information use in consumer preferences', *Journal of Consumer Research*, 18, 1992, pp. 464–473.
34. Richard L. Celsi and Jerry C. Olson, 'The role of involvement in attention and comprehension processes', *Journal of Consumer Research*, 15, 1988, pp. 210–224.
35. Joseph W. Alba, Howard Marmorstein and Amitava Chattopadhyay, 'Transitions in preference over time: The effects of memory on message persuasiveness', *Journal of Marketing Research*, 29, 1992, pp. 406–416.
36. John H. Lingle, Janet M. Dukerich and Thomas M. Ostrom, 'Accessing information in memory-based impression judgments: Incongruity versus negativity in retrieval selectivity', *Journal of Personality and Social Psychology*, 44, 1983, pp. 262–272.
37. Raymond R. Burke and Thomas K. Srull, 'Competitive interference and consumer memory for advertising', *Journal of Consumer Research*, 15, 1988, pp. 55–68.
38. Alice M. Tybout, Bobby J. Calder and Brian Sternthal, 'Using information processing theory to design marketing strategies', *Journal of Marketing Research*, 18, 1981, pp. 73–79.
39. Herbert E. Krugman, 'The impact of television advertising: Learning without involvement', *Public Opinion Quarterly*, 29, 1965, pp. 349–356.
40. John L. Bradshaw, *Hemispheric Specialization and Psychological Function* (Chichester: John Wiley & Sons, 1989). See p. 209.
41. Banwari Mittal, 'Measuring purchase-decision involvement', *Psychology & Marketing*, 6, 1989, pp. 147–162. Aron O'Cass, 'An assessment of consumers' product, purchase decision, advertising and consumption involvement in fashion clothing', *Journal of Economic Psychology*, 21, 2000, pp. 545–576.
42. Aron O'Cass, 'An assessment of consumers' product, purchase decision, advertising and consumption involvement in fashion clothing', *Journal of Economic Psychology*, 21, 2000, pp. 545–576.
43. Ibid.
44. Mita Sujan, 'Consumer knowledge: Effects on evaluation strategies mediating consumer judgments', *Journal of Consumer Research*, 12(1), 1985, pp. 31–46.
45. Edward Rosbergen, Rik Pieters and Michel Wedel, 'Visual attention to advertising: A segment-level analysis', *Journal of Consumer Research*, 24(3), 1997, pp. 305–314.
46. Stephen Worchel, Virgina Andreoli and Joe Eason, 'Is the medium the message? A study of the effects of media, communicator, and message characteristics on attitude change', *Journal of Applied Social Psychology*, 5(2), 1975, pp. 157–172.
47. Krugman, op cit.; see also 'Brain wave measures of media involvement', *Journal of Advertising Research*, 11, 1971, pp. 3–10; and 'Memory without recall, exposure without perception', *Journal of Advertising Research*, Classics 1, 1982, pp. 80–85. For an Australian perspective, see Richard Silberstein, Susanna Agardy, Ben Ong and David Heath, *Electroencephalographic Responses of Children to Television* (Melbourne: Australian Broadcasting Tribunal, 1983).
48. Andrews, op. cit.
49. Richard L. Celsi and Jerry C. Olson, 'The role of involvement in attention and comprehension processes', *Journal of Consumer Research*, 15(2), 1988, pp. 210–224.
50. C. Whan Park, Henry Assael and Seoil Chaiy, 'Mediating effects of trial and learning on involvement-

associated characteristics', *The Journal of Consumer Marketing*, 4(3), 1987, pp. 25–34.

51. Paul McIntyre, 'Emotional involvement drives appeal', *B&T*, 11 February 1994, p. 7.
52. John T. Cacioppo, Richard E. Petty, Chuan Feng Kao and Regina Rodriguez, 'Central and peripheral routes to persuasion: An individual difference perspective', *Journal of Personality and Social Psychology*, 51(5), 1986, pp. 1032–1043; and John R. Rossiter, Larry Percy and Robert J. Donovan, 'A better advertising grid', *Journal of Advertising Research*, 31(5), 1991, pp. 11–20.
53. See, for example, Richard E. Petty and John T. Cacioppo, 'Issue involvement can increase or decrease persuasion by enhancing message-relevant cognitive responses', *Journal of Personality and Social Psychology*, 37, 1979, pp. 1915–1926; Cacioppo and Petty, 'The need for cognition', *Journal of Personality and Social Psychology*, 42, 1982, pp. 116–131; and Cacioppo, Petty and Katherine J. Morris, 'Effects of need for cognition on message evaluation, recall and persuasion', *Journal of Personality and Social Psychology*, 45, 1983, pp. 805–818.
54. Wayne D. Hoyer, 'An examination of consumer decision making for a common repeat purchase product', *Journal of Consumer Research*, 11, 1984, pp. 822–829.
55. Carl W. Sherif, Muzafer Sherif and Robert E. Nebergall, *Attitude and Attitude Change: The Social Judgement Involvement Approach* (Philadelphia: Saunders, 1965).
56. Paul W. Miniard, Peter R. Dickson and Kenneth R. Lord, 'Some central and peripheral thoughts on the routes to persuasion', in Michael Houston (ed.), *Advances in Consumer Research*, 15, 1988, pp. 204–208.
57. Muzafer Sherif and Carl I. Hovland, *Social Judgement Assimilation and Contrast Effects in Communication and Attitude Change* (New Haven, CT: Yale University Press, 1961); and Carolyn E. Sherif, Muzafer Sherif and R.W. Nebergall, *Attitude and Attitude Change: The Social Judgment-Involvement Approach* (Philadelphia: Saunders, 1965).
58. Mark B. Traylor, 'Product involvement and brand commitment', *Journal of Advertising Research*, 21, 1981, pp. 51–56.
59. These examples are adapted from John R. Rossiter and Omnia Holland, 'Cognitive response theory: Its transference from psychology to advertising research and some considerations for its application', in Ken Grant and Ian Walker (eds), *Proceedings of the Seventh Bi-Annual World Marketing Congress* (Melbourne: Academy of Marketing Science, 1995), Vol. VII-I, 2-102 to 2-109.
60. Nader T. Tavassoli, Clifford J. Schultz II and Gavan J. Fitzsimons, 'Program involvement: Are moderate levels best for ad memory and attitude toward the ad?', *Journal of Advertising Research*, 35(5), 1995, pp. 61–72.
61. Claire E. Norris and Andrew M. Colman, 'Context effects on recall and recognition of magazine advertisements', *Journal of Advertising*, 21(3), 1994, pp. 32–41.
62. Jong-Won Park and Manoi Hastak, 'Memory-based product judgments: Effects of involvement at encoding', *Journal of Consumer Research*, 21(3), 1994, pp. 534–547.
63. Scott A. Hawkins and Stephen J. Hoch, 'Low-involvement learning: Memory without evaluation', *Journal of Consumer Research*, 19(2), 1992, pp. 212–225.
64. Kenneth Schneider and William Rodgers, 'An importance subscale for the consumer involvement profile', *Advances in Consumer Research*, 23, (eds) Kim Corfman and John Lynch (Provo, Utah: Association for Consumer Research, 1996), pp. 249–254.
65. Simon Walls and David W. Schumann, 'Measuring the customer's perception of the bond between the customer and the company', *American Marketing Association Educators' Conference Proceedings* 12 (2001), pp. 388–400.
66. Liane A. Ringham, Lester W. Johnson and Claude P. Morton, 'Customer satisfaction and loyalty for a continuous consumer service', *Australasian Journal of Market Research*, 2(2), 1994, pp. 43–48; Ringham, Morton and Johnson, 'What do you reach for when almost everyone is satisfied?', Paper presented to the Market Research Society of Australia, Sydney, 1994; Chuck Chakrapani, 'Service quality: Techniques of research and measurement', Sydney: AMR: Quantum, 1992. See also Robert M. Morgan and Shelby D. Hunt, 'The commitment-trust theory of relationship marketing', *Journal of Marketing*, 58, July 1994, pp. 20–38.
67. For example, see the following articles in Thomas C. Kinnear (ed.), *Advances in Consumer Research*, 11, 1984: James A. Muncy and Shelby D. Hunt, 'Consumer involvement: Definitional issues and research directions', pp. 193–196; John H. Antil, 'Conceptualization and operationalization of involvement', pp. 203–209; and Michael L. Rothschild, 'Perspectives on involvement: Current problems and future directions', pp. 216–217.
68. Muncy and Hunt, in Kinnear (ed.), op. cit.
69. Judith L. Zaichkowsky, 'Conceptualizing involvement', *Journal of Advertising*, 15(2), 1986, pp. 4–34.
70. Antil, in Kinnear (ed.), op. cit.

71. David W. Finn, 'The integrated information response model', *Journal of Advertising*, 13, 1984, pp. 24–33.
72. Banwari Mittal and Myung Soo Lee, 'Separating brand choice involvement from product involvement via consumer involvement profiles', in Michael Houston (ed.), *Advances in Consumer Research*, 15, 1988, pp. 43–49.
73. Mark E. Slama and Armen Tashchian, 'Validating the SOR paradigm for consumer involvement with a convenience good', *Journal of the Academy of Marketing Science*, 15(1), 1987, pp. 36–45.
74. Robert N. Stone, 'The marketing characteristics of involvement', in Kinnear (ed.), op. cit., pp. 210–215.
75. Daniel L. Sherrell and Terence A. Shimp, 'Consumer involvement in a laboratory setting', in Bruce J. Walker et al. (eds), *An Assessment of Marketing Thought and Practice—Proceedings of the American Marketing Association Educators' Conference* 48 (Chicago: American Marketing Association, 1982), pp. 104–108.
76. Finn, 'The integrated information response model', op. cit.
77. Gilles Laurent and Jean-Noel Kapferer, 'Measuring consumer involvement profiles', *Journal of Marketing Research*, 22, 1985, pp. 41–53.
78. Jean-Noel Kapferer and Gilles Laurent, 'Consumer involvement profiles: A new practical approach to consumer involvement', *Journal of Advertising Research*, 25(6), December 1985/January 1986, pp. 48–56.
79. Antil, in Kinnear (ed.), op. cit.
80. Edward F. McQuarrie and J. Michael Munson, 'The Zaichkowsky personal involvement inventory: Modification and extension', in M. Wallendorf and P. F. Anderson (eds), *Advances in Consumer Research*, 14, 1987, pp. 36–40.
81. Michael Janofsky, 'Discount brands flex their muscles', *Wall Street Journal*, 9 March 1993, p. D1, and ACNielsen Grocery Report 2003, ACNielsen, August 2003, pp. 1–19.
82. 'Declining brand loyalty: More fiction than fact', *Marketing News*, 6 January 1984, p. 4.
83. Andrew Ehrenberg and Mark Uncles, 'Dirichlet-type markets: A review', University of New South Wales Working Paper Series, 1997.
84. Megan Jones, 'FlyBuys win on points in battle for retail trade', *Age*, 19 August 1995, p. 31.
85. For a discussion of the business strategy involved in such marketing schemes, see Adam M. Brandenburger and Barry J. Nalebuff, 'The right game: Using game theory to shape strategy', *Harvard Business Review*, 73(4), 1995, pp. 57–71.
86. Andy Biziorek, 'Desperately seeking loyalty', *Thomson's Business-to-Business Review*, October/November 1994, pp. 3–5; see also Paul McIntyre, 'Warning on loyalty programs, Keig', *B&T*, 22 April 1994, p. 11. For a US example, see Stuart Elliot, 'Consumer product marketers are using premiums and incentives as rewards for customers' loyalty', *New York Times*, 4 May 1993, p. D20. For a view on co-branded car/credit cards, see Steve Worthington, 'Flashing the plastic and moving the metal—where the credit card meets the automobile', in K. Grant and I. Walker (eds), *Proceedings of the Seventh Bi-Annual World Marketing Congress* (Melbourne: Academy of Marketing Science, 1995), Vol. VII-II, 8-60 to 8-66.
87. See also Crispell and Brandenburg, op. cit.
88. Jannie Hofmeyr, 'Patterns of commitment to products and brands' and Butch Rice, 'The new face of marketing', Papers reproduced by Yann Campbell (Hoare Wheeler, Melbourne: YCHW, 1995).
89. For Australian research in this area, see Ron Lane, 'Brand loyalty and brand equity: Implications for business strategy and brand management', in K. Grant and I. Walker (eds), *Proceedings of the Seventh Bi-Annual World Marketing Congress* (Melbourne: Academy of Marketing Science, 1995), Vol. VII-II, 13-61 to 13-70.
90. V. Kumar and Jaishankar Ganesh, 'State-of-the-art in brand equity research: What we know and what needs to be known', *Australasian Journal of Market Research*, 3(1), 1995, pp. 3–21.
91. Anne Kurts, 'Protecting your brand name', *Marketing*, September 1995, pp. 57–58.
92. Max Blackston, 'The qualitative dimension of brand equity', *Journal of Advertising Research*, 35(4), 1995, pp. 6–11.
93. See Crispell and Brandenburg, op. cit.
94. Stuart Elliot, 'P&G sacrifices White Cloud in battle of brands', *New York Times*, 6 May 1993, p. D1.
95. See Kumar and Ganesh, op. cit.
96. Kenneth N. Gilpin, 'Brands still easier to buy than create', *New York Times*, 14 September 1992, p. D1.
97. Stuart Elliot, 'Gillette is reinforcing its commitment to brands despite Wall Street', *New York Times*, 11 May 1993, p. D22.

The nature of consumer attitudes

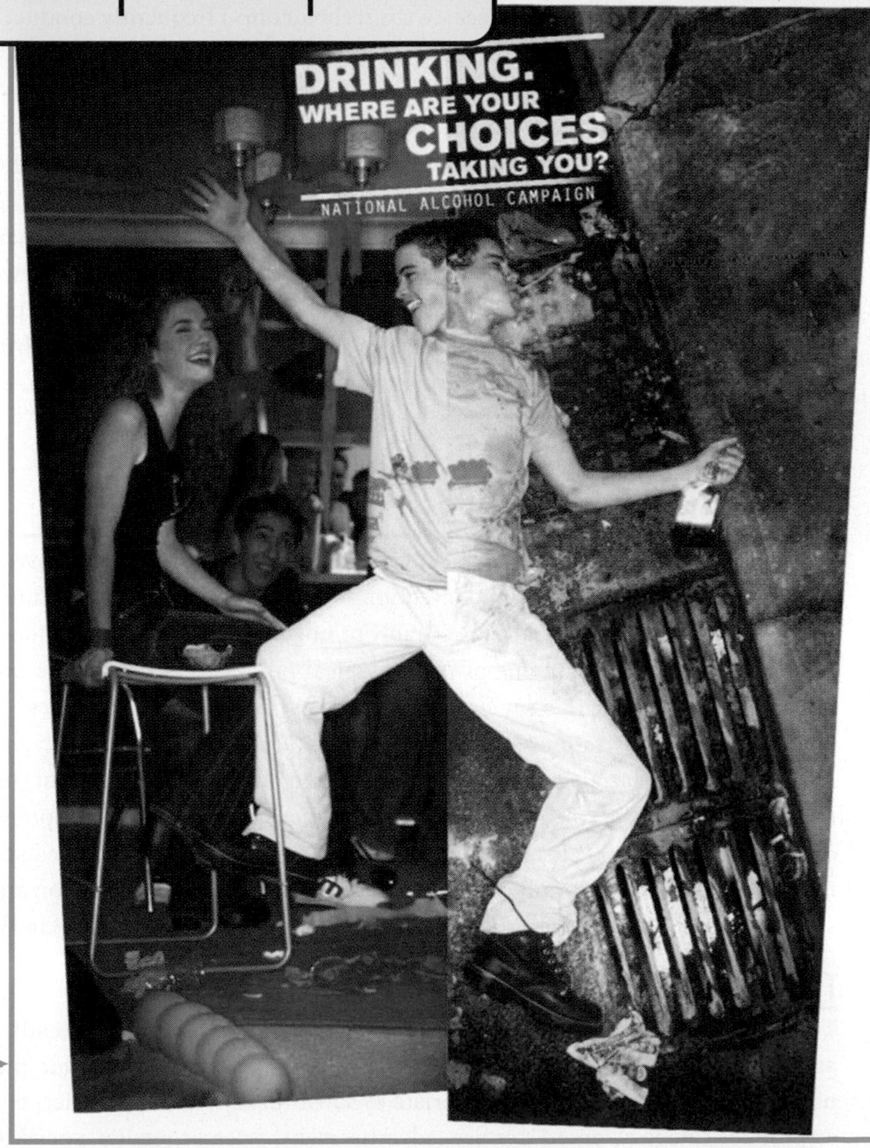

Source: Courtesy of the Australian Government's National Youth Alcohol Campaign.

Within consumer behaviour, an understanding of consumer attitudes is important. Consumers hold a vast number of attitudes towards products, services, issues, advertisements and retailers. Whenever we are asked whether we like or dislike a specific product type (e.g. cigarettes or alcohol) a specific brand (e.g. Pepsi), a service (e.g. Telstra), a particular retailer (e.g. Coles), an advertising theme (e.g. Decoré), we are being asked our **attitude** towards the object.

To get to the heart of what is driving consumers' behaviour, *attitude research* has been used to study a wide variety of strategic marketing questions. For example, attitude research is frequently undertaken to determine whether consumers will accept a proposed new product idea, to gauge why a firm's target audience has not reacted more favourably to its new promotional theme, or to learn how target customers are likely to react to a proposed change in the firm's packaging. For instance, there has been rapid growth in the sales of natural-ingredient bath, body and cosmetic products throughout the world. This trend seems linked to the idea that all things 'natural' are good, and that 'synthetic' is bad. Yet, in reality, the positive attitude towards 'natural' things is not based on any systematic evidence that natural cosmetics are in fact any safer or better for consumers. To further illustrate the importance of attitudes in marketing, major athletic shoe marketers such as Nike (see <www.nike.com>), or Reebok (see <www.reebok.com>) frequently conduct research among target consumers of the different types of athletic footwear products that they market. They seek attitudes of target consumers with respect to size, fit, comfort, and fashion elements of their footwear, as well as test reactions to potential new designs or functional features. They also regularly gauge reactions to their latest advertising and other marketing messages designed to form and change consumer attitudes. All these marketing activities are related to the important task of impacting consumers' attitudes.

This chapter examines the characteristics of attitudes, and particular attention is paid to a number of important models depicting the structure and composition of attitudes and how consumer researchers model the attitude–behaviour relationship. The chapter also examines some of the properties that have made attitudes fundamental to consumer researchers, as well as some of the common frustrations encountered in attitude research. Finally, the chapter focuses on the topics of attitude formation, and attitude change or persuasion used by marketers.

➤ What are attitudes?

A wide variety of consumer behaviours—including consistent purchase, recommendations to others, top rankings, beliefs, evaluations and intentions—are related to attitudes and influenced by attitudes. Attitudes as such reflect whether a person is favourably or unfavourably predisposed to some object (e.g. a brand, a service, a retail store). As an outcome of psychological processes, attitudes are not directly observable, but can be inferred from what people say or what they do. What, then, are attitudes? In a consumer behaviour context, an attitude is *a learned predisposition to respond (behave) in a consistently favourable or unfavourable way with respect to a given object*. Each part of this definition describes an important property of an attitude and is critical to understanding the role of attitudes in consumer behaviour. The key properties of attitudes are: the attitude object (the focal object) itself, that attitudes are learned, attitudes are predispositions (they reside in the mind), they have consistency (produce a consistent response) and have direction and intensity. Attitudes are in reality schema of an object (brand, social issues, person etc) consumers store in their long-term memory.

THE ATTITUDE OBJECT

The word 'object' in the context of attitudes should be interpreted broadly. In its place, we could substitute any one of many more specific concepts, such as issue, action, behaviour, practice, person or event. In context of consumer behaviour, it is appropriate to substitute specific consumer- or marketing-related concepts, such as product category, brand, service, advertisement, price or retailer, social issue or even person.

When conducting attitude research, we become even more specific. For example, if we were int ascertaining shoppers' attitudes towards various major mass merchandisers, our **attitude object** mi Target, Big W and Kmart; if we were examining consumer attitudes towards a number of major brands drink, our object might include Pepsi, Coca-Cola, Fanta and Solo.

ATTITUDES ARE LEARNED PREDISPOSITIONS

As indicated in the definition of attitudes adopted above they are *learned*. This means that the attitudes which are relevant to purchase and consumption behaviours are formed as a result of direct experience with the product or brand, information acquired from others, and exposure to mass media (e.g. advertising). It is important to remember that whilst attitudes may result in behaviour or be the result of behaviour, they are not synonymous with behaviour, but reflect either a favourable or an unfavourable evaluation of the attitude object. As a predisposition, attitudes have a motivational quality; that is, they propel the consumer towards a particular behaviour or repel them away from some object or behaviour.

ATTITUDES ARE TRANSFERABLE

Consumer attitudes play an important part in simplifying consumer decision making. One way that this occurs is by attitude transfer, where an attitude towards one situation can be applied to another. Although a consumer may receive thousands of stimuli, the attitude that he or she feels towards one purchase situation is often quite similiar to that felt towards another. For example, a person who is conservative in dress is likely to be conservative in the choice of a car, in eating habits, in recreation and in furniture. Thus, one attitude affects several purchase situations. It follows that product marketers may find clues about how a consumer purchases one product, a suit for instance, by observing that person's purchase of another product, shoes.

ATTITUDES HAVE CONSISTENCY

Consumer attitudes also possess another important characteristic in that they are generally *consistent* in the behaviour they reflect. However, despite their consistency, attitudes are not necessarily permanent (immovable); they do change. It is important to illustrate what we mean by **attitude consistency**. Normally, we expect consumers' behaviour to correspond with their attitudes. For example, if a male executive stated that he liked luxury motor vehicles, we expect that he would buy that particular type of car when next purchasing a motor vehicle. Similarly, if a colleague said she did not like German cars, we would not expect her to buy a German car. In other words, when consumers are free to act as they wish, we anticipate that their actions will be consistent with their attitudes. However, circumstances often preclude consistency between attitudes and behaviour. For example, the matter of affordability may intervene in the purchase of a luxury car. So we must consider possible situational influences on consumer attitudes and behaviour.

ATTITUDES OCCUR WITHIN A SITUATION

It is not immediately evident from our definition that attitudes occur within, and are affected by, the situation. *Situations* are events or circumstances that, at a certain point in time, may influence the attitude that will guide behaviour. A situation can cause consumers to behave in a manner that is seemingly inconsistent with their attitudes. For instance, let us assume that a consumer purchases a different brand of coffee each time their inventory runs low. Although this brand-switching may seem to reflect a negative attitude or dissatisfaction, it may actually have been influenced by a specific situation—for example, the need to economise. Although the consumer may have a strong preference for Moccona coffee, a tight budget may influence them to purchase whatever brand is on 'special' at the supermarket.

The opposite can also be true. If a consumer purchases a can of decaffeinated Coke each time her supply runs low, we may erroneously infer that they have a favourable attitude towards the taste of decaffeinated Coke. On the contrary, the consumer may dislike the taste of decaffeinated Coke, but may be following their doctor's suggestion that they reduce the amount of caffeine in their diet. Such a consumer therefore regards decaffeinated Coke favourably as a means of accomplishing this goal.

Indeed, people can have a variety of attitudes towards aspects of a particular behaviour. A man may feel it is suitable to eat lunch at McDonald's but may not consider it appropriate for dinner. In this case, McDonald's has its 'time and place', which functions as a *boundary* surrounding those situations when McDonald's is acceptable. However, if the individual is coming home late one night, feeling exhausted and hungry, and spots a McDonald's, he may just decide to have dinner there. The man does not prefer McDonald's as a 'place to have dinner', but convenience has become the more important objective.

Clearly, when measuring attitudes, it is important to consider the situation in which the behaviour takes place, or we can misinterpret the relationship between attitudes and behaviour.

Attitudes have a direction and intensity

Along with the other properties, attitudes also express a direction toward an object in the context of feeling favourable or unfavourable. The favourable/unfavourable nature of the attitude is often refered to as the attitude valance. Attitudes also possess an intensity about the object or reflect how strongly the attitude is held: The strength that the attitude is held with in relation to the focal object. As such, in a marketing context we might identify our segment has a very positive attitude toward a brand. This is a favourable predisposition that is intensely held.

Structural models of attitudes

Motivated by a desire to understand the relationship between attitudes and behaviour, psychologists have sought to construct models that capture the underlying dimensions of an attitude.[1] To this end, the focus has been on specifying more precisely the composition of an attitude and the relationships between the key components of attitudes. Whilst varied approaches to attitude development have been proposed four models of attitude have been useful to marketers. These include:

- the tricomponent attitude model
- multi-attribute attitude models
- trying-to-consume model
- attitude-toward-the-ad models.

Each model provides a somewhat different perspective on the number of component parts of an attitude, and how those parts are arranged or interrelated.

FIGURE 7.1 A simple representation of the tricomponent attitude model

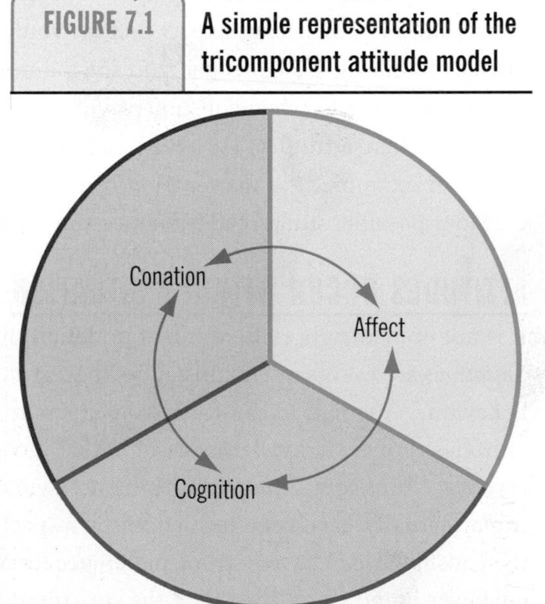

TRICOMPONENT ATTITUDE MODEL

According to the **tricomponent attitude model**, attitudes consist of three major components: a *cognitive* component, an *affective* component and a *conative* component (see Figure 7.1).

The cognitive component

The first component of the tricomponent attitude model consists of a person's **cognitions**: that is, the knowledge and perceptions that are acquired by a combination of direct experience with the attitude object and related information from various sources. This knowledge and the resulting perceptions frequently take the form of beliefs; that is, the consumer believes that the attitude object possesses various attributes and that specific behaviour will lead to specific outcomes.

These beliefs may also be referred to as expectations. Consumer perceptions and expectations are commonly studied in relation to customer satisfaction. Customer dissatisfaction is generally the result of met or unmet expectations (negative and positive). New Zealand universities have undertaken research studies aimed at understanding the expectations and perceptions of their students, specifically their international students.[2] The overall effect of the research has been increased student satisfaction, leading ultimately to the development of favourable attitudes among the international student body.

Let us look at the example of a female consumer, Lydia, and the beliefs she has about three pain-relieving, over-the-counter medicines. Each of them, Nurofen, Actiprofen and ACT-3, contains the same active ingredient, 200 mg of the chemical ibuprofen. Two of them are in tablet form, while ACT-3 is in the form of a liquid-filled capsule. Figure 7.2 illustrates just how complex a consumer's belief system can be, although it captures only a part of Lydia's belief system about the three brands. Lydia's belief system for all three brands consists of the same five basic attributes—relief from pain, relief from inflammation, speed of action, ease of swallowing and gentleness to the stomach.

However, Lydia has somewhat different beliefs about the brands for several of the attributes. Specifically, when it comes to speed of action, she regards the claim 'because it's liquid, it works fast' as a real plus for ACT-3. In contrast, she believes that Actiprofen is more effective for treating the 'pain associated with inflammation' because of the trouble the Actiprofen ads take to explain how inflammation produces the prostaglandins which aggravate the sensation of pain. Lydia prefers slightly Actiprofen and Nurofen over ACT-3 because their advertising graphically illustrates the pain of a headache. Nurofen is regarded as easier to swallow, a minor plus for Lydia. ACT-3 advertises that it is gentle on the stomach, but Lydia is not sure how this fits in with its effectiveness claim. Research that identifies such insights are useful in positioning a particular brand against competing brands (see the discussion of perceptual mapping in Chapter 5).

The affective component

A consumer's feelings about a particular product or brand constitute the **affective component** of an attitude. These feelings are primarily evaluative in nature. They capture an individual's overall assessment of the attitude

FIGURE 7.2 A consumer's belief system for three brands of pain-relief medicines

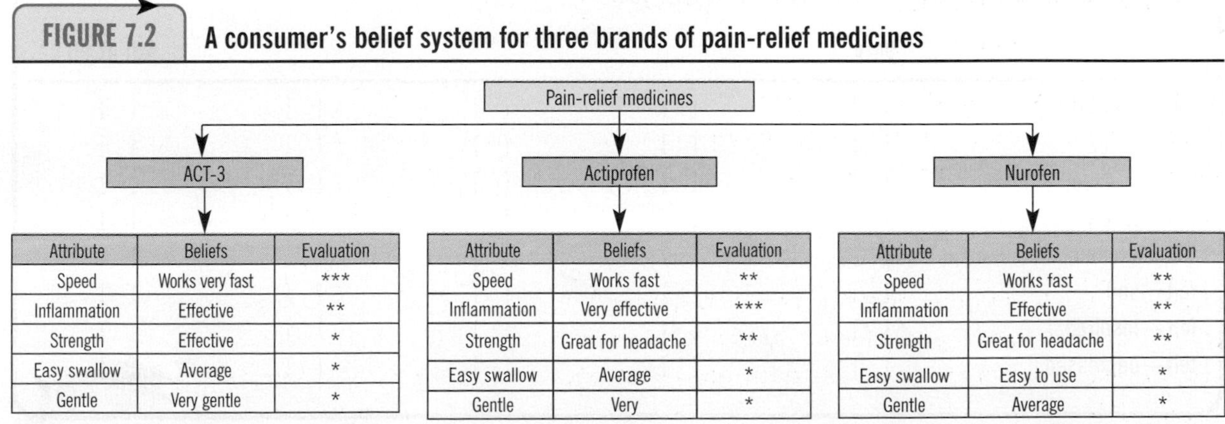

ACT-3

Attribute	Beliefs	Evaluation
Speed	Works very fast	***
Inflammation	Effective	**
Strength	Effective	*
Easy swallow	Average	*
Gentle	Very gentle	*

Actiprofen

Attribute	Beliefs	Evaluation
Speed	Works fast	**
Inflammation	Very effective	***
Strength	Great for headache	**
Easy swallow	Average	*
Gentle	Very	*

Nurofen

Attribute	Beliefs	Evaluation
Speed	Works fast	**
Inflammation	Effective	**
Strength	Great for headache	**
Easy swallow	Easy to use	*
Gentle	Average	*

object; that is, the extent to which the person rates the attitude object as favourable or unfavourable. To illustrate, Table 7.1 shows an evaluative (affective) scale of items that might be employed to assess air travellers' attitudes towards Virgin airlines.

Affect-laden experiences also manifest themselves as aroused feelings (e.g. happiness, sadness, shame, disgust, anger, distress, guilt, surprise). Research indicates that such emotional states may enhance or amplify positive or negative experiences, and that later recollections of such experiences may impact on what comes to mind and how the individual acts.[3] For instance, a young woman viewing a masterpiece in a leading art gallery is likely to be influenced by her emotional state at the time. If she is feeling particularly joyous, her positive response to the painting may be greatly amplified. The emotionally-enhanced response to the masterpiece, and the whole museum experience, may lead her to recall with great pleasure the day she spent at the gallery. It may also influence her to persuade friends and acquaintances to visit the same gallery, and to make the personal decision to revisit the gallery frequently.

In addition to utilising direct or global evaluative measures of an attitude object (e.g. from 'good' to 'bad,' or 'pleasant' to 'unpleasant', as depicted in Table 7.1), consumer researchers can also use a battery of affective response scales (i.e. measuring feelings and emotions) to construct a picture of consumers' overall feelings about a product, service or ad. Table 7.2 gives an example of a 5-point scale that measures affective responses towards Virgin airlines.

TABLE 7.1 Evaluative scale used to gauge travellers' attitudes towards Virgin airlines

Compared with other airlines, flying Virgin airlines is:

bad	(1)	(2)	(3)	(4)	(5)	(6)	(7)	good
negative	(1)	(2)	(3)	(4)	(5)	(6)	(7)	positive
unpleasant	(1)	(2)	(3)	(4)	(5)	(6)	(7)	pleasant
unappealing	(1)	(2)	(3)	(4)	(5)	(6)	(7)	appealing

TABLE 7.2 Measuring consumer feelings and emotions about a Virgin airlines flight

You have just flown from Sydney to Brisbane. We would appreciate it if you would identify how you felt during this flight. For each of the statements listed below, please place an 'X' in the box that corresponds with how you felt on the flight you have just made. (As an example, the first one has been done for you).

	Very				Not at all
I felt—relaxed	[ ]	[x]	[ ]	[ ]	[ ]
I felt—bored	[ ]	[ ]	[ ]	[ ]	[ ]
I felt—stressed	[ ]	[ ]	[ ]	[ ]	[ ]
I felt—lonely	[ ]	[ ]	[ ]	[ ]	[ ]
I felt—excited	[ ]	[ ]	[ ]	[ ]	[ ]
I felt—sad	[ ]	[ ]	[ ]	[ ]	[ ]
I felt—inspired	[ ]	[ ]	[ ]	[ ]	[ ]
I felt—depressed	[ ]	[ ]	[ ]	[ ]	[ ]

The conative component

Conation, the final component of the tricomponent attitude model, is concerned with the likelihood or tendency that an individual will undertake a specific action or behave in a particular way with regard to the attitude object. According to some interpretations, the conative component may include the actual behaviour itself.

In marketing and consumer research, the conative component is frequently treated as an expression of the consumer's intention to buy. Buyer intention scales are employed to assess the likelihood of a consumer purchasing a product or behaving in a certain way. Table 7.3 provides two examples of methods of measuring intention-to-buy.

TABLE 7.3 Two examples of intention-to-buy scales

- Which of the following statements best describes the chance that you will buy Absolut vodka during the next month?
  - ______ I definitely will buy a bottle
  - ______ I probably will buy a bottle
  - ______ I am uncertain whether I will buy a bottle
  - ______ I probably will not buy any
  - ______ I definitely will not buy any
- How likely are you to buy Absolut vodka during the next month?
  - ______ Very likely
  - ______ Likely
  - ______ Unlikely
  - ______ Very unlikely

Consistency between the three components

Although the three components are discussed separately, consumers strive for consistency among them. Certain cognitions give rise to certain feelings (or affect) and certain intentions. The consistency can be related to both the *valence* and the *intensity*. The valence refers to whether the thoughts, feelings and intentions are favourable or unfavourable. If experience leads to the modification of one component, some modification of the other components will occur. For instance, if the advertising for a Magnum Ego ice-cream bar produced positive beliefs and feelings, and the first experience with the ice-cream confirmed the thoughts and feelings, then the intention would also be positive. However, if over time the taste did not seem as pleasant as in the initial trials, consumers might alter their favourable beliefs about the combination of caramel and chocolate, and reduce the favourable intention to purchase.

The second aspect of consistency is the strength with which the thoughts, feelings and intentions are held. Attitude strength refers to the degree of commitment one feels towards a thought, feeling or intention. The three components are interdependent and, therefore, influence each other.

MULTI-ATTRIBUTE ATTITUDE MODELS

Multi-attribute attitude models appeal to both consumer researchers and marketing practitioners because they examine attitudes in terms of selected product attributes or beliefs. While there are many variations of this type of attitude model, those proposed by Martin Fishbein and his associates have stimulated the greatest amount of research interest.[4] We have selected three Fishbein models to consider here:

1. the attitude-toward-object model
2. the attitude-toward-behaviour model
3. the theory-of-reasoned-action model.

The attitude-toward-object model

The **attitude-toward-object model** is especially suitable for measuring attitudes towards a product or service category or specific brands (i.e. the object).[5] According to this model, a consumer's attitude towards a product, or specific brands of a product, is defined as a function of the presence (or absence) *and* evaluation of certain product-specific beliefs or product attributes. In other words, consumers have generally favourable attitudes towards those brands they believe have an adequate level of positive attributes, and unfavourable attitudes towards those brands they feel have an inadequate level of desired attributes or too many negative attributes. Table 7.4 presents two hypothetical consumer belief systems for Lipton herbal teas (one favourable and the other unfavourable).

The Fishbein attitude-toward-object model is usually depicted in the form of the following equation:

$$\text{Attitude}_0 = \sum_{i=1}^{n} b_i e_i$$

where

Attitude_0 is a separately assessed overall measure of affect for or against the attitude object (e.g. a product, brand, service, retail establishment)

b_i is the strength of the belief that the attitude object contains the *i*th attribute (e.g. the likelihood that the Gillette Sensor will give a closer shave)

e_i is the evaluative dimension associated with the *i*th attribute (e.g. how good or bad is a closer shave)

Σ indicates that there are *n* salient attributes over which the b_i and e_i combinations are summated.

One of the shortcomings of the model is that a positive evaluation for a brand does not always predict behaviour. For instance, a positive attitude towards BMW cars is not necessarily predictive of purchase behaviour.

Box 7.1 shows examples of the questions that might be used to measure the attitude-toward-object model.

The attitude-toward-behaviour model

The focus of Fishbein's **attitude-toward-behaviour model** is the individual's attitude towards behaving or acting with respect to an object, rather than the attitude towards the object itself. The appeal of the attitude-toward-behaviour model is that it seems to correspond more closely to actual behaviour than does the attitude-

TABLE 7.4 Two hypothetical consumer belief systems about Lipton herbal teas

- *Consumer 1* (mainly favourable)
  'Lipton herbal teas are worth the few additional cents.'
  'Lipton herbal teas are an adventure.'
  'Lipton herbal teas are never boring.'
  'Lipton herbal teas receive great comments from my guests.'
- *Consumer 2* (mainly unfavourable)
  'Lipton makes the best tea.'
  'I sometimes drink regular Lipton tea.'
  'Lipton herbal teas sound too fancy for my wallet.'
  'Anyway, I don't drink much tea; I'm a coffee person.'

BOX 7.1 An illustration of how attitude-toward-object is measured and calculated

$$A_0 = \sum_{i=1}^{n} b_i e_i$$

1. Background

This exhibit is designed to demonstrate how the Attitude-Toward-the-Object model might be used to measure and calculate consumers' attitudes with respect to three brands of fine wristwatches (i.e., Bulova, Concord and Omega) costing more than $600.00 each. For some sense of realism, assume that a consumer research firm is conducting a study of target consumers' attitudes toward expensive watches.

Based upon a series of focus groups with target consumers, the research firm identified the following five major attributes that tend to be used by consumers to assess fine watches:

(1) *Design/style:*
'Whether the watch has a distinctive look'

(2) *Status:*
'Whether the watch is easily recognised by others'

(3) *Accuracy:*
'Whether the watch keeps very good time'

(4) *Durability:*
'Whether the watch runs a long time without needing repairs'

(5) *Priced over $600.00:*
'Whether the watch is priced under $600.00'

2. Questions used to measure Attitude-Toward-the-Watches (i.e. the object)

The following are questions prepared by the consumer research firm to measure each of the component parts of the Attitude-Toward-the-Object model, in terms of the identified five major attributes:

(1) *The evaluative (e_i) component might be measured as follows:*

A watch that has a distinctive look is:
very good [+3] [+2] [+1] [0] [−1] [−2] [−3] very bad

A watch that is easily recognised by others is:
very good [+3] [+2] [+1] [0] [−1] [−2] [−3] very bad

The remaining three product attributes would also be measured on the same 7-point scale.

(2) *The belief (b_i) component might be measured as follows:*

How likely is a Bulova watch to have a distinctive look?
very likely [+3] [+2] [+1] [0] [−1] [−2] [−3] very unlikely

How likely is a Bulova watch to be easily recognised by others?
very likely [+3] [+2] [+1] [0] [−1] [−2] [−3] very unlikely

How likely is a Bulova watch to keep accurate time?
very likely [+3] [+2] [+1] [0] [−1] [−2] [−3] very unlikely

How likely is a Bulova watch to run a long time between repairs?
very likely [+3] [+2] [+1] [0] [−1] [−2] [−3] very unlikely

How likely is a Bulova watch to be priced under $600?
very likely [+3] [+2] [+1] [0] [−1] [−2] [−3] very unlikely

The same five belief-strength questions would be asked for the remaining two brands of watches. Given three brands of watches and five major attributes, a total of 15 belief-strength scales would be used.

3. Survey Research

The consumer research company next would conduct mall intercept interviews with 350 target market consumers who meet the client's demographic criteria (basically upscale consumers, with $75,000-plus incomes and professional-managerial occupations).

From the 350 completed questionnaires, an average response is determined for each belief (*b*) and evaluative (*e*) measure. A set of hypothetical summary results are presented below.

Hypothetical Findings for the Attitude-Toward-the-Object Analysis for Fine Watches
(Average Results)

Attribute	Evaluation (e_i)	Beliefs (b_i): Bulova		Concord		Omega	
	e	*b*	*be*	*b*	*be*	*b*	*be*
Design/style	+3	−2	−6	+1	+3	+2	+6
Status	+3	−2	−6	+1	+3	+1	+3
Accuracy	+1	+3	+3	+3	+3	+3	+3
Durability	+2	+1	+2	+1	+2	+3	+6
Priced over $600	+2	−2	−4	+2	+4	+3	+6
Total $\sum b_i e_i$ score			−11		+15		+24

4. Comments

The *design/style* attribute (e.g., 'Whether the watch has a distinctive look') and the *status* attribute (e.g., 'Whether the watch is easily recognised by others') are the two most important attributes (i.e., each with a +3 value). The fact that the *accuracy* attribute received only a +1 value does not mean that it is unimportant, but rather that consumers tended to assume that all three watches were accurate.

The Omega watch was assessed positively, with a total score of +24, followed by Concord with a +15, and Bulova trailing with a −11. The low score for Bulova might mean that consumers have a negative attitude about it. Alternatively, it may be that consumers feel that it is not a luxury watch (scoring negatively on three attributes: *design/style, status* and *priced over $600*). It is therefore possible that consumers do not see the Bulova in the same subgroup of watches as the Omega and the Concord.

While the Omega does very well (+24 out of a possible +33), the one area in which it has room to improve is *status*. If the Rolex watch was included in the analysis, it is likely that it would have done better than Omega with regard to status, since the Rolex is such a well recognized and admired watch.

The above comments represent just some of the strategic marketing thoughts that flow from the research findings, and illustrate the types of insights possible from such analyses.

toward-object model. For instance, knowing a consumer's attitude about the act of purchasing an $86 000 BMW car (i.e. the attitude towards the *behaviour*) reveals more about the potential act of purchasing than does simply knowing the consumer's attitude towards the car (i.e. the attitude towards the *object*). This seems logical, because the consumer might have a positive attitude towards the $86 000 car, but a negative attitude towards the possibility of being able to purchase such an expensive vehicle.

The attitude-toward-behaviour model is depicted by the following equation:[6]

$$\text{Attitude}_{(beh)} = \sum_{i=1}^{n} b_i e_i$$

where

$\text{Attitude}_{(beh)}$ is a separately assessed overall measure of affect for or against carrying out a specific action or behaviour (e.g. buying or preparing)

b_i is the strength of the belief that an *i*th specific action will lead to a specific outcome

e_i is an evaluation of the *i*th outcome

Σ indicates that there are *n* salient outcomes over which the b_i and e_i combinations are summated.

Box 7.2 (page 231) shows examples of the questions that might be used to measure the attitude-toward-behaviour model.

Theory-of-reasoned-action model

The **theory of reasoned action** builds on other research conducted by Fishbein and his associates. It represents a comprehensive integration of attitude components into a structure that is designed to lead to both better prediction and better explanations of behaviour. Like the basic tricomponent attitude model, the theory-of-reasoned-action model incorporates a cognitive component, an affective component and a conative component; however, these are arranged in a pattern different from that of the tricomponent model.

Figure 7.3 is a depiction of the theory of reasoned action. Examine it carefully. Working backwards from behaviour (e.g. the act of purchasing a particular service, product or brand), the model suggests that the best

FIGURE 7.3 **A simplified version of the theory of reasoned action**

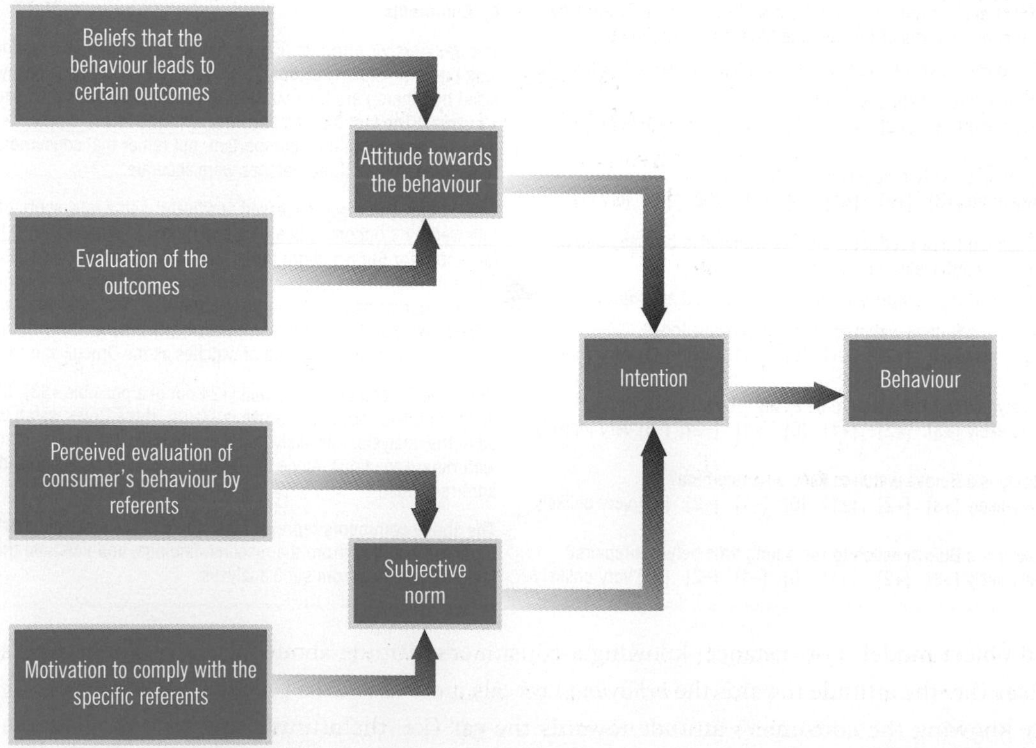

Source: **Adapted from Icek Ajzen and Martin Fishbein, *Understanding Attitudes and Predicting Social Behavior*, p. 84. © 1980. Adapted by permission of Pearson Education Inc., Upper Saddle River, NJ.**

BOX 7.2 An illustration of how attitude-toward-behaviour is measured

1. Direct measure of attitude-toward-behaviour (beh)

Buying a Bulova watch is

good [ ] [ ] [ ] [ ] [ ] [ ] [ ] bad
foolish [ ] [ ] [ ] [ ] [ ] [ ] [ ] wise
pleasant [ ] [ ] [ ] [ ] [ ] [ ] [ ] unpleasant
harmful [ ] [ ] [ ] [ ] [ ] [ ] [ ] beneficial
appealing [ ] [ ] [ ] [ ] [ ] [ ] [ ] unappealing

2. Indirect measure of attitude-toward-behaviour (beh)

(a) Examples of behavioural beliefs (b_i):

Buying a Bulova watch is
very likely [ ] [ ] [ ] [ ] [ ] [ ] [ ] very unlikely
to give me a distinctive-looking watch.

Buying a Bulova watch is
very likely [ ] [ ] [ ] [ ] [ ] [ ] [ ] very unlikely
to give me a watch that keeps accurate time.

Buying a Bulova watch is
very likely [ ] [ ] [ ] [ ] [ ] [ ] [ ] very unlikely
to give me a reliable watch.

Buying a Bulova watch is
very likely [ ] [ ] [ ] [ ] [ ] [ ] [ ] very unlikely
to give me a watch that my friends would like to own.

Buying a Bulova watch is
very likely [ ] [ ] [ ] [ ] [ ] [ ] [ ] very unlikely
to give me a watch that would cost more than $600.

The same five behavioural belief questions would be asked for the other two brands of watches. Given three brands of watches and five major attributes, a total of 15 behavioural-belief scales would be used.

(b) The evaluative (e_i) component might be measured as:

Buying a watch that gives me a distinctive look is
very good [ ] [ ] [ ] [ ] [ ] [ ] [ ] very bad

Buying a watch that keeps accurate time is
very good [ ] [ ] [ ] [ ] [ ] [ ] [ ] very bad

Buying a watch that is reliable is
very good [ ] [ ] [ ] [ ] [ ] [ ] [ ] very bad

Buying a watch that my friends would like to own is
very good [ ] [ ] [ ] [ ] [ ] [ ] [ ] very bad

Buying a watch that costs more than $600 is
very good [ ] [ ] [ ] [ ] [ ] [ ] [ ] very bad

predictor of behaviour is the intention to act. Thus, if consumer researchers were directly interested solely in predicting behaviour, they would measure intention (using an intention-to-act scale). However, if they were also interested in understanding the underlying factors that contribute to a consumer's intention to act in a particular situation, they would look behind intention and consider the factors that *led* to intention—that is, the consumer's attitude towards the behaviour and the subjective norm.

The consumer's attitude towards the behaviour can be directly measured as affect (i.e. a measure of overall favourability towards the purchase). Further, as with intention, we can get behind the attitude to its underlying dimensions (see the discussion of the attitude-toward-behaviour model).

In accordance with this expanded model, to understand intention we must also measure the subjective norm that influences an individual's intention to act. A **subjective norm** can be measured directly by assessing a consumer's feelings as to what relevant others (family, friends, flatmates, co-workers) would think of the action being contemplated; that is, would they look favourably or unfavourably on the anticipated action? As with an attitude, consumer researchers can get behind the subjective norm to the underlying factors that are likely to produce it. They accomplish this by assessing the normative beliefs that the individual attributes to relevant others, as well as the person's motivation to comply with each of the relevant others. For instance, in a recent study comparing different attitude models the subjective norm was measured by asking students to indicate whether the people important to them approve or disapprove of their intended behaviour.[7]

The above discussion and examples suggest that the theory of reasoned action is a series of interrelated attitude components (i.e. beliefs precede attitude and normative beliefs precede subjective norms; attitudes and subjective norms precede intention; and intention precedes actual behaviour).[8] Consistent with the theory of reasoned action, an attitude is not linked to behaviour as strongly or as directly as intention is linked to behaviour.

Why study attitudes at all, if intention is ultimately a better predictor of behaviour? The answer is simple: intention may be a better predictor, but it does not provide an adequate explanation of behaviour. If marketers want to understand why consumers act as they do, they require something more than a basically mechanical measure of what consumers expect to do (e.g. their buying intentions). Similarly, a measure of affect may be equivalent to an attitude; however, marketers usually want to know the underlying or salient attributes or beliefs that produce the specific effect (attitude). Box 7.3 illustrates the type of questions that might be used in applying the theory-of-reasoned-action model.

THEORY OF TRYING

Certain behaviours may be more difficult for individuals to achieve (e.g. quitting smoking or losing weight). The **theory of trying**[9] was developed to explain strivings to perform a behaviour or to reach a goal. In such cases, there are often personal impediments (trying to quit smoking when addicted to nicotine or trying to lose weight but loving desserts) and/or environmental impediments (many people you socialise with smoke or a dinner invitation where you have little control over the menu) that might prevent the desired action or outcome from occurring. There are two important differences between the theory of reasoned action and the theory of trying. First, when trying to achieve a difficult goal a triad of concerns becomes salient: trying and succeeding, trying and failing, and the process of striving. The attitudes towards success and failure influence intentions. Each of the three attitudes (i.e. towards success, towards failure and towards process) are determined by the summation of the 'product' of the **consequence likelihoods** (e.g. the chance that a person anticipates 'looking better from dieting') and **consequence evaluations** (e.g. how pleasant it would be for the person to 'look better').

The second difference between the two theories is that the theory of trying incorporates past behaviour. The model proposes that the *frequency of past trying* (i.e. the consumer's prior experience with trying) impacts on both intention-to-try and the act of trying; the *recency of past trying* (i.e. the consumer's most recent experience with trying) impacts solely on trying. The results of research into the model support the importance of these two factors in providing understanding and predictive accuracy of trying to consume. Box 7.4 (page 234) provides examples of the questions that might be employed to measure the variables that make up the theory of trying (as depicted in Figure 7.4, page 236).

BOX 7.3 | **An example of how the key elements in the theory of reasoned action model are measured**

1. Direct measure of intention to buy

Which of the following statements best describes the chance that you will buy a Bulova* watch during the next six months?

— I definitely will buy one
— I probably will buy one
— I am uncertain whether I will buy one
— I probably will not buy one
— I definitely will not buy one

2. Direct measure of attitude-toward-behaviour (beh)

(see measures in Box 7.2(1))

3. Indirect measure of attitude-toward-behaviour (beh)

(see measures in Box 7.2(2))

4. Direct measure of subjective norm

Most of the people who are important to me think I

should [ ] [ ] [ ] [ ] [ ] [ ] [ ] should not

buy myself a Bulova watch during the next six months.

5. Indirect measure of subjective norm

(a) *Normative belief*

My wife thinks I

should [ ] [ ] [ ] [ ] [ ]

buy myself a Bulova watch during the next six mor

My friends think I

should [ ] [ ] [ ] [ ] [ ]

buy myself a Bulova watch during the next six mo

(b) *Motivation to comply*

Typically, I like to do what my wife suggests that I

always [ ] [ ] [ ] [ ] [ ]

Typically, I like to do what my friends suggest that

always [ ] [ ] [ ] [ ] [

*Would also be asked for the two other brands of watches (i.

Published by Atlantic publishers & Distributors New Delhi 2006

ATTITUDE-TOWARD-THE-AD MODELS

In an effort to understand the influence of advertising on consumer attitudes towards particular products or brands, considerable attention has been paid to developing what has been referred to as **attitude-toward-the-ad models**.

Figure 7.5 (page 236) presents a schematic of some of the basic relationships described by an attitude-toward-the-ad model. As the model depicts, the consumer forms various feelings (affect) and judgments (cognition) as the result of exposure to an ad. These feelings and judgments in turn affect the consumer's attitude towards the ad and beliefs about the brand acquired from being exposed to the ad. Finally, the consumer's attitude towards the ad and beliefs about the product influence his or her attitude towards the brand.[10]

In assessing consumer attitudes towards an ad, researchers maintain that it is critical to distinguish between, and separately measure, *cognitive evaluations* of the ad (i.e. judgments about the ad such as whether it is

BOX 7.4 How the theory of trying is measured

Trying is assessed by a self-report measure in terms of past frequency, recency, beliefs and evaluations of consequences. Example: Trying to buy a house

A. Past frequency

During the past two years, I have looked for a house to buy

[1]	[2]	[3]	[4]	[5]	[6]
very many times	many times	several times	a couple of times	once	not at all

B. Recency

During the past six months, I have looked for a house to buy

_______ yes _______ no

C. Beliefs about consequent likelihoods are measured on a series of 7-point scales, using *extremely likely/extremely unlikely* as end-points.

1. Beliefs about trying and succeeding:
   a. I would feel very good about myself.
   b. My family would be very proud.
   c. My children would grow up in a better environment.
   d. My wife would be happier.
   e. My home life would be more enjoyable.
2. Beliefs about trying but failing:
   a. No bank would give me a mortgage.
   b. I won't have to worry about gardening chores.
   c. I would have more free time.
   d. My family would be disappointed in me.
3. Beliefs about the process itself:
   a. It's fun looking through other people's houses.
   b. Looking gives my wife and me something to do on weekends.
   c. Looking at houses I can't afford depresses me.
   d. It's hard to know how firm an asking price is.
   e. The agent is really working for the seller.

D. Evaluations of consequences are assessed on the same series of 7-point scales as beliefs, using *very satisfying/very unsatisfying* as end-points.

1. Trying and succeeding:
   a. I would feel very good about myself.
   b. My family would be very proud.
   c. My children would grow up in a better environment.
   d. My wife would be happier.
   e. My home life would be more enjoyable.
2. Trying but failing:
   a. No bank would give me a mortgage.
   b. I won't have to worry about gardening chores.
   c. I would have more free time.
   d. My family would be disappointed in me.

3. The process itself:
   a. It's fun looking through other people's houses.
   b. Looking gives my wife and me something to do on weekends.
   c. Looking at houses I can't afford depresses me.
   d. It's hard to know how firm an asking price is.
   e. The agent is really working for the seller.

Attitude toward trying is measured on a series of 7-point scales.

All things considered, looking for a house this past spring made me feel:

good	[1]	[2]	[3]	[4]	[5]	[6]	[7]	bad
frustrated	[1]	[2]	[3]	[4]	[5]	[6]	[7]	hopeful
happy	[1]	[2]	[3]	[4]	[5]	[6]	[7]	unhappy
satisfied	[1]	[2]	[3]	[4]	[5]	[6]	[7]	dissatisfied

1. Attitude toward trying and succeeding:
   a. Finding a house I can afford to buy would make me feel:

lucky	[1]	[2]	[3]	[4]	[5]	[6]	[7]	unlucky
richer	[1]	[2]	[3]	[4]	[5]	[6]	[7]	poorer

2. Attitude toward trying but failing:
   a. Not being able to find a house I can afford to buy would make me feel:

lucky	[1]	[2]	[3]	[4]	[5]	[6]	[7]	unlucky
richer	[1]	[2]	[3]	[4]	[5]	[6]	[7]	poorer

Expectations of success and failure are measured on a 7-point scale, using *extremely likely/extremely unlikely* as end-points. (Expectations represent the individual's perceived control over his or her lifestyle and/or environment.)

1. a. Assuming I *try* to find a house next autumn, it is:

extremely likely	[1]	[2]	[3]	[4]	[5]	[6]	[7]	extremely unlikely

   that I will actually find a house I can afford.

2. b. Assuming I *try* to find a house next autumn, it is:

Extremely likely	[1]	[2]	[3]	[4]	[5]	[6]	[7]	extremely unlikely

   that I can get a mortgage at a rate I can afford.

Subjective norms toward trying are measured on a 7-point scale, using *extremely likely/extremely unlikely* as end-points.

Most people who are important to me think that I should try to buy a house during the next year.

extremely likely	[1]	[2]	[3]	[4]	[5]	[6]	[7]	extremely unlikely

Source: Based on Richard P. Bagozzi and Paul R. Warshaw, 'Trying to consume', *Journal of Consumer Research*, 17, September 1990, p. 134. Reprinted by permission of The University of Chicago Press.

'humorous' or 'informative') and *affective responses* towards the ad (i.e. feelings experienced from exposure to the ad, including 'a sense of fear' or 'a smile' or 'laughter').[11] Box 7.5 (page 237) presents an example of how feelings or emotions (affective responses) and cognitive evaluations (judgments) have been measured within the context of studying attitudes towards an ad. Feelings appear to be properties of the individual, while evaluations tend to be properties of the ad. For instance, it has been found in research that people are more likely to agree on whether an ad is credible, than to agree on how the ad makes them feel.[12] Feelings are more affected by the similarity to other campaigns seen, the mood of the consumer[13] and the viewing environment.[14]

FIGURE 7.4 The theory of trying

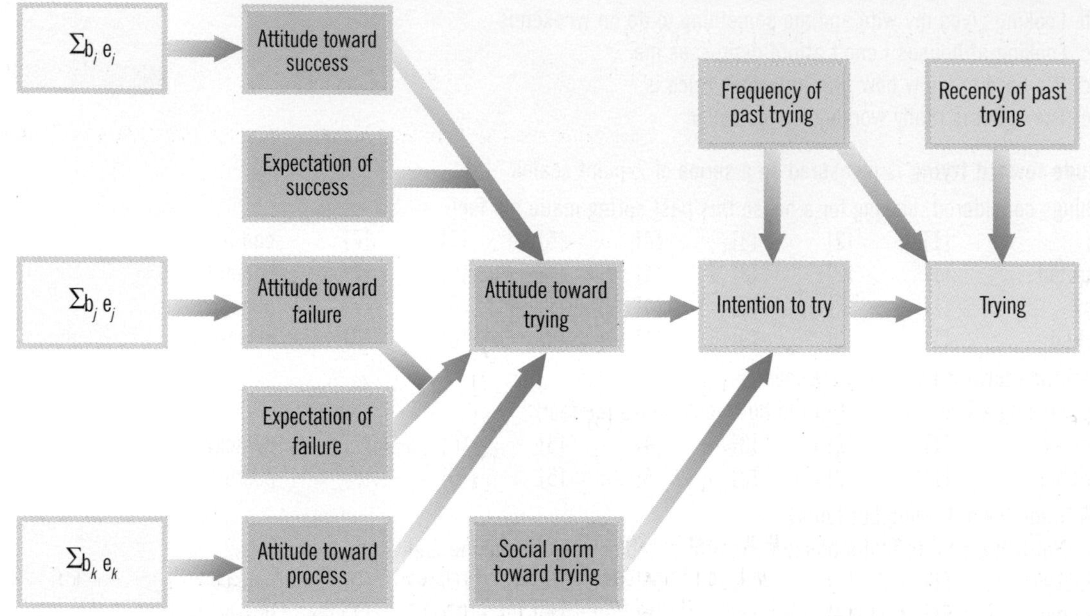

Source: **Richard P. Bagozzi and Paul R. Warshaw. 'Trying to consume', *Journal of Consumer Research*, 17, September 1990, p. 131. Reprinted by permission of The University of Chicago Press.**

Note: **Regarding the ∑be terms, the 'b's are consequence likelihoods, the 'e's are consequence evaluations; subscript i refers to consequences contingent on success; subscript j refers to consequences contingent on failure; subscript *k* refers to consequences associated with the process of trying, independent of success or failure considerations.**

FIGURE 7.5 A conception of the relationship among elements in an attitude-toward-the-ad model

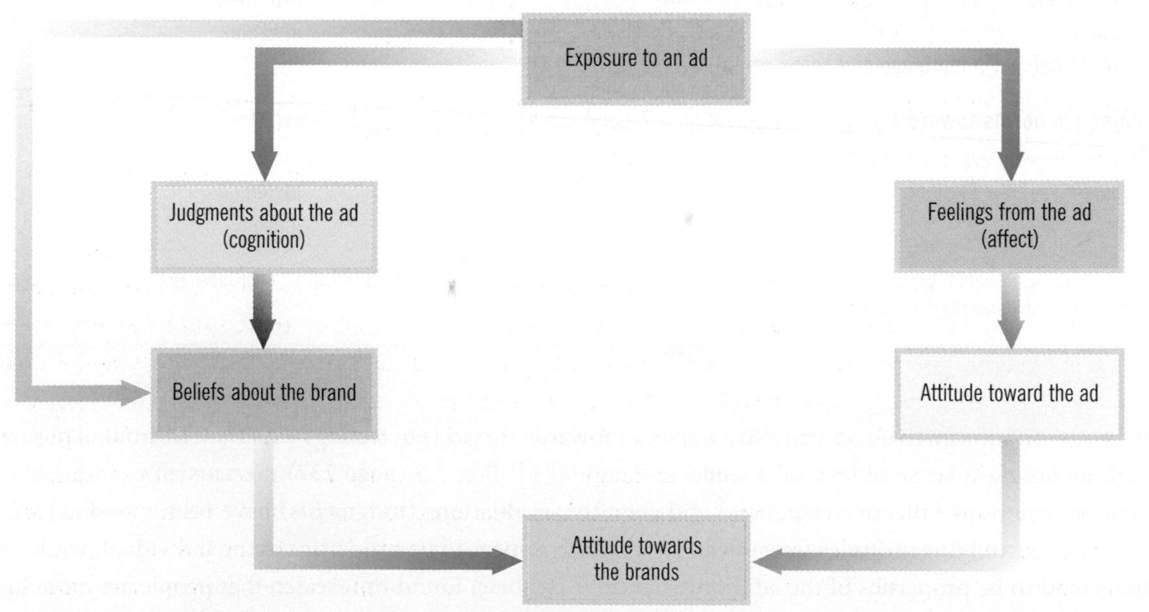

Source: **Inspired by and based in part on Julie A. Edell and Marian Chapman Burke, 'The power of feelings in understanding advertising effects', *Journal of Consumer Research*, 14, December 1987, p. 431. Published by The University of Chicago Press.**

BOX 7.5 Examples of how feelings and judgments are assessed in studies of attitudes towards advertisements

A. Gauging affective responses (feelings) to the ad

Instructions: 'We would like you to tell us how the ad you just saw made you feel. We are interested in your reactions to the ad, not how you would describe it . . .'

The following are samples of *feeling-items* that consumers would rank on a 5-point scale in terms of how well the word describes the consumer's feelings (5 = very strongly; 1 = not at all).

active	[1]	[2]	[3]	[4]	[5]
amused	[1]	[2]	[3]	[4]	[5]
carefree	[1]	[2]	[3]	[4]	[5]
creative	[1]	[2]	[3]	[4]	[5]
elated	[1]	[2]	[3]	[4]	[5]
joyous	[1]	[2]	[3]	[4]	[5]
inspired	[1]	[2]	[3]	[4]	[5]
sad	[1]	[2]	[3]	[4]	[5]
suspicious	[1]	[2]	[3]	[4]	[5]

B. Gauging cognitive evaluations (judgments) of the ad

Instructions: 'Now please tell us how well you think each of the words listed below describes the ad you have just seen ... Here we are interested in your thoughts about the ad, not about the brand or the product class.'

The following are samples of *judgment-items* that consumers would rank on a 5-point scale in terms of how well the word describes the ad (5 = extremely well; 1 = not at all well).

believable	[1]	[2]	[3]	[4]	[5]
exciting	[1]	[2]	[3]	[4]	[5]
humorous	[1]	[2]	[3]	[4]	[5]
interesting	[1]	[2]	[3]	[4]	[5]
phoney	[1]	[2]	[3]	[4]	[5]
tender	[1]	[2]	[3]	[4]	[5]
terrible	[1]	[2]	[3]	[4]	[5]
valuable	[1]	[2]	[3]	[4]	[5]

Source: Reprinted by permission from Marian Chapman Burke and Julie A. Edell, 'The impact of feelings on ad-based affect and cognition', *Journal of Marketing Research*, 16, February 1989, pp. 73–74. Published by the American Marketing Association. Reprinted by permission.

Consistent with Figure 7.5, research suggests that the feelings conveyed by an ad not only influence the attitude towards the ad itself, but also affect the consumer's evaluations of the brand and attitude towards the brand.[15] However, it also appears that the positive effect of a liked ad on the attitude towards a brand immediately after an ad exposure may dwindle after a delay of a week. This implies that immediately after an ad exposure there may be a heightened impact which wears off quite rapidly if purchase action is postponed or delayed.[16] Also, there is evidence that liking an ad does not compensate for what consumers believe is poor brand performance, nor does a disliked ad necessarily mean that the consumer would not select a brand that is felt to offer positive brand performance.[17] Such research is helping to create a better understanding of how consumers' attitudes towards specific ads influences their attitudes towards particular brands.

A great deal of research has investigated the role of mood and the processing of persuasive messages. A general finding in the mood and persuasion literature is that positive moods decrease central processing and negative moods decrease peripheral processing.[18] However, in a recent study, the researchers demonstrated that when the mood induced by a television program seen before and after an ad is negative the consumer continues to think about the program during the ads, while a consumer in a more positive mood is likely to focus on the ad.[19] The consumer in a positive mood processes the ad centrally and generates more positive thoughts about the ad. The consumer in a negative mood is more likely to process the ad peripherally and generate more negative thoughts about the ad.

A number of other interesting observations can be drawn from attitude-toward-the-ad research. Specifically, it appears that for a novel product (e.g. 'ice-cream for dogs'), the consumer's attitude towards the ad has a *stronger* impact on brand attitude and purchase intention than for a familiar product (e.g. traditional dog foods such as Pal or Chum).[20] This same research found that beliefs about a brand (brand cognition) resulting from ad exposure play a much stronger role in determining attitudes towards the brand for a familiar product. This research highlights the importance of considering the nature of the attitude object in assessing the potential impact of advertising exposure.

Still other research indicates that both positive and negative feelings towards ads tend to exist side by side, with both uniquely influencing an attitude.[21] This suggests the importance of assessing a wide variety of feelings when studying the influence of ad exposure.

Finally, research reveals that attitudes towards ads in general seem to have little impact on the attitude towards a specific ad; however, the attitude towards a specific type of advertising (e.g. comparative advertising) may have some impact on the attitude towards a specific ad.[22] If supported, these findings would establish that individuals who profess to 'hate' ads in general (or to 'love' advertising) would still be likely to form a unique attitude towards a specific ad (e.g. liking or disliking it). In the case of responses to a specific type of advertising, the implications are different. It appears, for instance, that if a consumer dislikes comparative advertising, a specific comparative ad (e.g. 'Pepsi is better than Coke') would be negatively influenced by the attitude towards comparative advertising in general.

Attitude formation

We must consider how people, especially young people, form their initial general attitudes towards 'things'. Consider consumer attitudes towards liquids they drink—water, soft drinks, milk, beer coffee and tea. On a more specific level, how do they form attitudes towards Mount Franklin spring water, Moccona coffee, Lipton tea, Pub Squash or Victoria Bitter beer? How do family members, friends, celebrities, mass media advertisements, even cultural memberships, influence the formation of their attitudes about consuming or not consuming each of these drinks? Why do some attitudes seem to persist indefinitely, while others change fairly often? The answers to such questions are of vital importance to marketers, for without knowing how attitudes are formed they are unable to understand or to influence consumer attitudes or behaviour in a desired way.

Beliefs and attitudes form in a number of ways. People often form positive attitudes towards products before buying them, but not always. Low-involvement purchase decisions concerning inconspicuous, low-risk products, such as those that fill the pantry each week or fortnight, are handled differently from those where self-perception might be affected by a poor decision, or where there is a high economic price to pay for a poor decision. In the case of the high-involvement purchase decision, there is a greater likelihood that consumers will need to have developed a positive attitude towards the product before they will consider a brand, let alone purchase it. In the case of low-involvement products, bought at a convenience store or supermarket without much thought, it is quite likely that a positive or negative attitude is developed *after* the purchase.

Our examination of attitude formation is divided into three areas: the learning of attitudes; the sources of influence on attitude formation; and the impact of personality on attitude formation.

HOW ATTITUDES ARE LEARNED

When we speak of the formation of an attitude, we refer to the shift from having no attitude towards a given object (e.g. a personal computer) to having some attitude towards it (e.g. a personal computer is a useful tool). This is also relevant to a shift from having a negative attitude toward an object to a positive attitude. To understand this shift (attitude formation) requires an appreciation of the basic learning processes involved. We focus briefly on how attitudes are learned by considering how the learning theories discussed in Chapter 6 relate to attitude formation.

Classical conditioning

Consumers often purchase new products that are associated with a favourably viewed brand name. Their favourable attitude towards the brand name, originally a neutral stimulus, may be the result of repeated satisfaction with other products produced by the same company. Using the classical conditioning (introduced in Chapter 6), the brand name is the unconditioned stimulus that, through associative learning and repetition, results in a favourable attitude (the *unconditioned response*). The idea of family branding is based on this form of attitude learning. For example, by giving a new blend of coffee the benefit of a well-known and respected family name, the Nestlé company is counting on an extension of the favourable attitudes already associated with the Nescafé brand name to the new Nescafé product. They are counting on stimulus generalisation from the brand name to the new product (see Figure 7.6).

Similarly, marketers who associate their new products with admired celebrities are trying to create a positive bond between the celebrity, who already enjoys a positive attitude, and the 'neutral' new product. The

FIGURE 7.6 Attitudes are formed through association with a favourable brand name

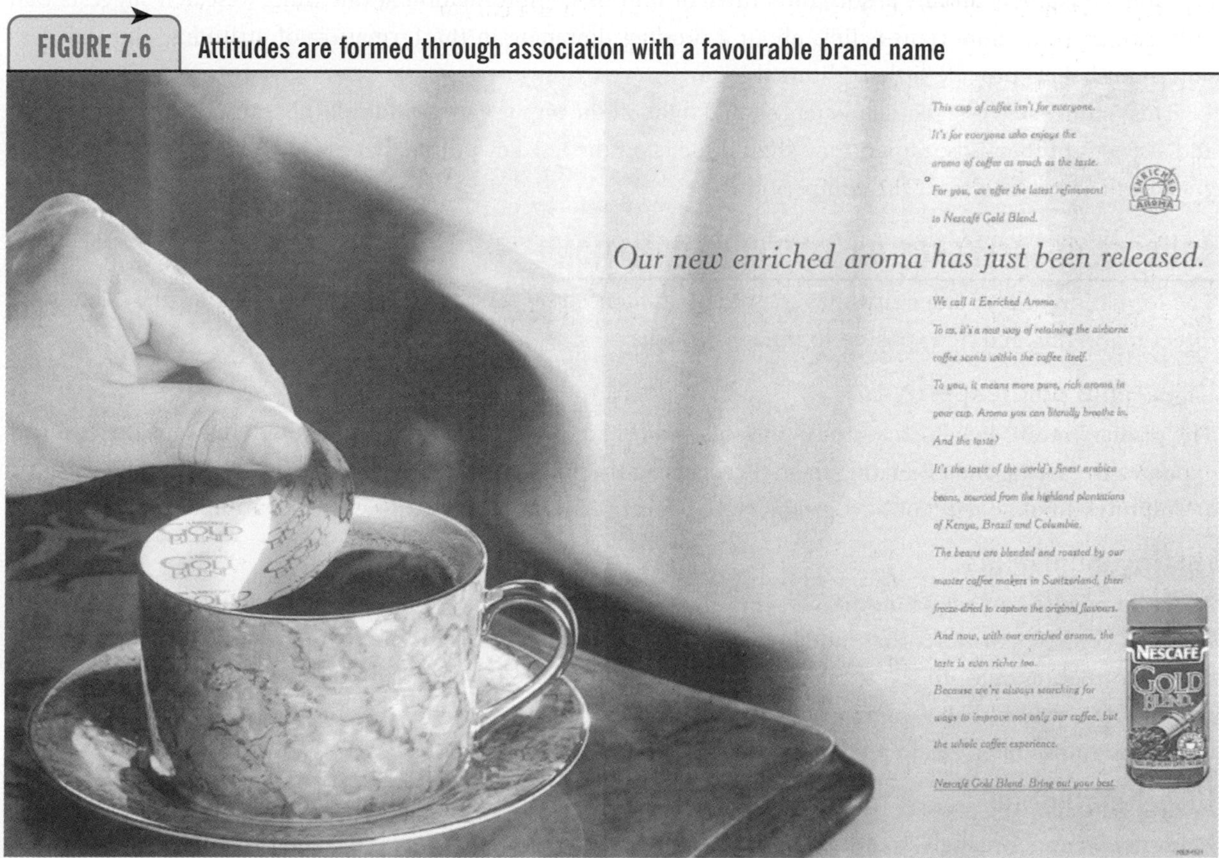

Source: **Nescafé Gold Blend is the registered trademark of Société des Produits Nestlé S.A. Vevey, Switzerland.**

recognition and goodwill (the positive attitude) the celebrity enjoys is transferred to the product so that potential consumers will quickly form positive attitudes towards the new product.

Instrumental conditioning

Sometimes attitudes follow the purchase and consumption of a product. For example, a consumer may purchase a brand-name product without having a prior attitude towards it, because it is the only product of its kind available (e.g. the last tube of toothpaste in a hotel pharmacy). Consumers also make trial purchases of new brands from product categories in which they have little personal involvement (see Chapter 4). If they find the purchased brand satisfactory, they are likely to develop a favourable attitude towards it.

Cognitive learning theory

In situations where consumers seek information about a product in order to solve a problem or satisfy a need, they are likely to form attitudes (either positive or negative) about products on the basis of an information search and their own cognitions (knowledge and beliefs). For instance, teenage Cathy likes pavlova and has thought about making a pavlova for a party, yet imagines that making a 'good' pavlova is tricky. When Cathy learns that Glad has a product that promises to make 'even the stickiest meringue non-stick', she is likely to form a positive attitude towards Glad Bake.

In general, the more information consumers have about a product or service, the more likely they are to form attitudes about it—either positive or negative. However, regardless of available information, consumers are not always ready or willing to process product-related information. Furthermore, consumers often use only a limited amount of the information available to them. As discussed later in the text in relation to communication, consumers usually absorb only three or four bits of information at one time. Research suggests that only two or three important beliefs about a product dominate in the formation of attitudes, and that less important beliefs provide little additional input.[23]

This finding suggests that marketers should fight off the impulse to include all the features of their products and services in their ads; rather, they should focus on the few key points that are at the heart of what distinguishes their product from the competition.

SOURCES OF INFLUENCE ON ATTITUDE FORMATION

The formation of consumer attitudes is strongly influenced by personal experience, by family and friends, by direct marketing and by exposure to the mass media.

Direct and past experience

The primary means by which attitudes towards goods and services are formed is through the consumer's direct experience of trying and evaluating them. Recognising the importance of direct experience, marketers frequently attempt to stimulate trials of new products by offering cents-off coupons or even free samples.[24]

Family and friends

As we come into contact with others, especially family, close friends and admired individuals (e.g. a respected teacher), we form attitudes that influence our lives. The family is an extremely important source of influence on the formation of attitudes, for it is the family that provides us with many of our basic values and a wide range of less central beliefs. For instance, young children who are rewarded for good behaviour with sweet foods and lollies often retain a taste for (and positive attitude towards) sweets as adults.

Direct marketing

Marketers are increasingly using highly-focused direct marketing programs to target small consumer niches with products and services that fit their interests and lifestyles. (**Niche marketing** is sometimes called *micromarketing*.) Marketers very carefully target customers on the basis of their demographic, psychographic or geodemographic profiles with highly personalised product offerings (e.g. golf clubs for left-handed people) and messages that show they understand their special needs and desires.

Direct marketing is also useful to appeal to those who desire to experience the lifestyle, atmosphere and unique facilities of the 1850s in the Australian historical replica town of Sovereign Hill, in Victoria.

Direct marketing efforts have an excellent chance of favourably influencing target consumers' attitudes, because the products and services offered, and the promotional messages conveyed, are very carefully designed to address the individual segment's needs and concerns, and are thus able to achieve a higher 'hit rate' than mass marketing.

Mass media exposure

In a country like Australia, where people have relatively easy access to newspapers and an almost infinite variety of general and special-interest magazines and television channels, consumers are constantly exposed to new ideas, products, opinions and advertisements. These mass media communications are an important source of information that influences the formation of consumer attitudes.

PERSONALITY FACTORS

Personality also plays a critical role in attitude formation. For example, individuals with a high need for cognition (i.e. those who crave information and enjoy thinking) are likely to form positive attitudes in response to ads that are rich in product-related information. On the other hand, consumers who are relatively low in the need for cognition are more likely to form positive attitudes in response to ads that feature an attractive model or well-known celebrity. (See Chapter 6 for relevant applications of the central-and-peripheral-routes-to-persuasion theory.) In a similar fashion, attitudes towards new products and new consumption situations are strongly influenced by the specific personality characteristics of consumers.

Attitude change

It is important to recognise that much that has been said about *attitude formation* is also basically true of *attitude change*. That is, attitude changes are learned; they are influenced by personal experience and other sources of information. Personality affects both the receptivity and the speed with which attitudes are likely to be altered.

STRATEGIES OF ATTITUDE CHANGE

Altering consumer attitudes is a key strategy consideration for most marketers. For marketers who are fortunate enough to be market leaders and enjoy a significant amount of customer goodwill and loyalty, the overriding goal is to fortify the existing positive attitudes of customers so that they will not succumb to competitors' special offers and other enticements designed to win them over. For instance, in many product categories (e.g. kitchen products, where Jif has dominated for years, or greetings cards, where Hallmark has been the leader), most competitors take aim at the market leaders when developing their marketing strategies. Their objective is to change the attitudes of the market leaders' customers and win them over. Among the attitude change strategies available to them are:

- changing the consumer's basic motivational function
- associating the product with an admired group or event
- relating two conflicting attitudes

- altering components of the multi-attribute model
- changing consumer beliefs about competitors' brands
- the elaboration likelihood model (ELM).

Changing the basic motivational function

An effective strategy for changing consumer attitudes towards a product or brand is to make new needs prominent. One method for changing basic motivations is known as the **functional approach.**[25] According to this approach, attitudes can be classified in terms of four functions: the utilitarian function; the ego-defensive function; the value-expressive function; and the knowledge function. Importantly, different consumers can hold different attitudes towards the same focal object for quite different reasons. Also an attitude can serve more than one of the four functions at the same time, however, generally one function will dominate or be dominant.

The utilitarian function

We hold certain brand attitudes partly because of a brand's utility. If a product has helped us in the past, even in a small way, our attitude towards it tends to be favourable. One way of changing attitudes in favour of a product is by showing people that it can serve a **utilitarian function** they may not have considered. For example, the advertisement for SunRice in Figure 7.7 stresses a utilitarian benefit.

The ego-defensive function

The **ego-defensive function** relates to the fact that most people want to protect their self-image from inner feelings of doubt. By acknowledging this need, ads for cosmetics, personal hygiene products, clothing and apparel increase both their relevance to the consumer and the likelihood of a favourable attitude by offering reassurance to the consumer's self-concept. Advertising that focuses on the fear a consumer may have about being ostracised socially by emphasising greater acceptance through the brand is effective in targeting the ego-defensive function of attitudes. Within such contexts consumers generally form positive attitudes towards brands associated with social acceptance, approval or image enhancement. The enhancement of the self-concept or ego is seen in the simple message about how the brand 'tells most about who you are' in Figure 7.8.

FIGURE 7.7 An example of an advertised brand appealing to a single utilitarian benefit

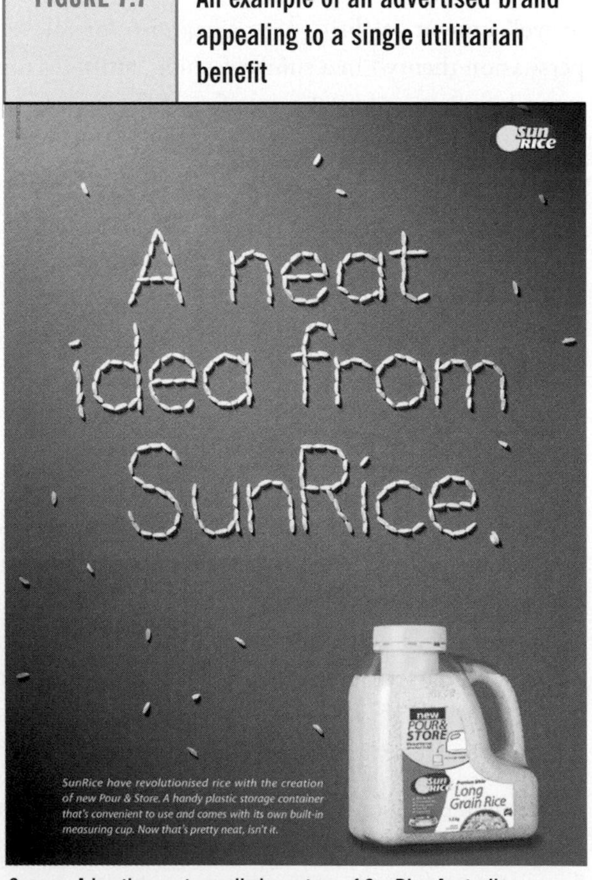

Source: Advertisement supplied courtesy of SunRice Australia.

The value-expressive function

The **value-expressive function** demonstrates how individuals' attitudes are related to their expression of general values, lifestyle and outlook. If a segment of consumers has a positive attitude towards being 'in fashion', then we could expect their attitudes towards high-fashion clothing to reflect this viewpoint. Thus, by knowing target consumers' attitudes, marketers can anticipate their values, lifestyle and outlook more skilfully, and reflect these characteristics in their ads. For

FIGURE 7.8 Example of advertised brand targeting ego-defensive function

IT'S NOT YOUR CAR.
IT'S NOT YOUR FRIENDS.
IT'S NOT YOUR JOB.

IT'S YOUR WATCH THAT
TELLS MOST ABOUT WHO YOU ARE.

ARCTURA
KINETIC
CHRONOGRAPH
SNL001P $1200.
KINETIC CHRONOGRAPH.
SAPPHIRE GLASS.
100M WATER RESISTANT.
SEIKO
seiko.com.au

Source: Courtesy of Seiko Australia Pty Ltd.

FIGURE 7.9 An example of an advertised brand appealing to the value-expressive function

brilliant
brunette.
Expose your glamorous side.
Your stunning, luminous,
BRUNETTE GODDESS side.
Introducing Brilliant Brunette®
the first shampoo, conditioner and styling line just for brunettes
Be a little more stare-worthy. Illuminate your full range of brunette - amber to maple, chestnut to espresso - without changing the color that makes you a stunning brunette. Show off your highlights. Get multi-dimensional shine. Brilliant Brunette. Expose your goddess side.
www.johnfrieda.com
JOHN FRIEDA.
london-paris-new york

Source: Courtesy of Kao Brands.

example, the John Frieda ad in Figure 7.9 appeals to the desire to express yourself with the tagline 'Expose your glamorous side'.

The knowledge function

The **knowledge function** recognises that individuals usually have a strong need to know and understand the people and things they come into contact with. The consumers' 'need to know', a cognitive need, is important to marketers concerned with product positioning. Indeed, most product and brand positionings are attempts to satisfy consumers' need to know, and to improve their attitudes towards the brand by clarifying its advantages over competitive brands. For instance, recent advertisements for Kellogg's Nutri-Grain boasted its higher level of proteins compared with other breakfast cereals. An ad for Ambre Solaire claims that photo-stable filtration allows for better protection from harmful UVA rays.

Combining several functions

Since different consumers may like or dislike the same product or service for different reasons, a functional framework for examining attitudes can be very useful. For instance, the ad for Hirudoid in Figure 7.10 (page 246) fulfils a variety of functions: the number of functions and the benefits appeal to the utilitarian function; the knowledge that you will be confident and not embarrassed satisfies the ego-defensive function; and the knowledge function is fulfilled by listing the benefits.

theory of reasoned action *(p. 230)*
theory of trying *(p. 232)*
tricomponent attitude model *(p. 224)*
utilitarian function *(p. 242)*
value-expressive function *(p. 242)*

Endnotes

1. Richard J. Lutz, 'The role of attitude theory in marketing', in Harold H. Kassarjian and Thomas S. Robertson (eds), *Perspectives in Consumer Behavior*, 4th edn (Englewood Cliffs, NJ: Prentice Hall, 1991), pp. 317–339.
2. Lesley Williams and Brian Imrie, 'Current issues in New Zealand marketing: Services marketing—the New Zealand experience', in Ken Grant and Ian Walker (eds), *Proceedings of the Seventh Bi-Annual World Marketing Congress*, 1995, Vol. VII-II, 8-108 to 8-115.
3. Joel B. Cohen and Charles S. Areni, 'Affect and consumer behavior', in Harold H. Kassarjian and Thomas S. Robertson (eds), op. cit., pp. 188–240; and Madeline Johnson and George M. Zinkhan, 'Emotional responses to a professional service encounter', *Journal of Service Marketing*, 5, Spring 1991, pp. 5–16.
4. Icek Ajzen and Martin Fishbein, *Understanding Attitudes and Predicting Social Behavior* (Englewood Cliffs, NJ: Prentice Hall, 1980); and Martin Fishbein and Icek Ajzen, *Belief, Attitude, Intentions, and Behavior* (Reading, MA: Addison-Wesley, 1975).
5. Martin Fishbein, 'An investigation of the relationships between beliefs about an object and the attitude toward the object', *Human Relations*, 16, 1963, pp. 233–240; and Martin Fishbein, 'A behavioral theory approach to the relations between beliefs about an object and the attitude toward the object', in Martin Fishbein (ed.), *Readings in Attitude Theory and Measurement* (New York: Wiley, 1967), pp. 389–400.
6. Ajzen and Fishbein, op. cit., pp. 62–63; also Robert E. Burnkrant, H. Rao Unnava and Thomas J. Page Jr, 'Effects of experience on attitude structure', in Rebecca H. Holman and Michael R. Solomon (eds), *Advances in Consumer Research*, 18 (Provo, UT: Association for Consumer Research, 1991), pp. 28–29.
7. Richard P. Bagozzi and Susan K. Kimmel, 'A comparison of leading theories for the prediction of goal-directed behaviours', *British Journal of Social Psychology*, 34(4), 1995, pp. 437–461.
8. Terence A. Shimp and Alican Kavas, 'The theory of reasoned action applied to coupon usage', *Journal of Consumer Research*, 11, December 1984, pp. 795–809; Blair H. Shepard, Jon Hartwick and Paul R. Warshaw, 'The theory of reasoned action: a meta-analysis of past research with recommendations for modifications and future research', *Journal of Consumer Research*, 15, September 1986, pp. 325–343; Sharon E. Beatly and Lynn R. Kahle, 'Alternative hierarchies of the attitude-behavior relationship: The impact of brand commitment and habit', *Journal of the Academy of Marketing Science*, 16, Summer 1988, pp. 1–10; and Richard P. Bagozzi, Hans Baumgartner and Youjae Yi, 'Coupon usage and the theory of reasoned action', in Rebecca H. Holman and Michael R. Solomon (eds), *Advances in Consumer Research*, 18 (Provo, UT: Association for Consumer Research, 1991), pp. 24–27.
9. Richard P. Bagozzi and Paul R. Warsaw, 'Trying to consume', *Journal of Consumer Research*, 17, September 1990, pp. 127–140.
10. Rajeev Batra and Michael L. Ray, 'Affective responses mediating acceptance of advertising', *Journal of Consumer Research*, 13, September 1986, pp. 236–239; Julie A. Edell and Marian Chapman Burke, 'The power of feelings in understanding advertising effects', *Journal of Consumer Research*, 14, December 1987, pp. 421–433; and Marian Chapman Burke and Julie A. Edell, 'The impact of feelings on ad-based affect and cognition', *Journal of Marketing Research*, 26, February 1989, pp. 69–83.
11. Thomas J. Madden, Chris T. Allen and Jacquelyn L. Twible, 'Attitude toward the ad: An assessment of diverse measurement indices under different processing "sets"', *Journal of Marketing Research*, 25, August 1988, pp. 242–252; and Scot Button and Donald R. Lictenstein, 'The effect of ad claims and ad context on attitude toward the advertisement', *Journal of Advertising*, 17, 1988, pp. 3–11.
12. Edell and Burke, op. cit., pp. 421–433.
13. Meryl P. Gardener, 'Mood states and consumer behavior: A critical review', *Journal of Consumer Research*, 12, December 1985, pp. 281–300.
14. David A. Aaker, Douglas M. Stayman and Michael R. Hagerty, 'Warmth in advertising: Measurement, impact

and sequence effects', *Journal of Consumer Research*, 12, March 1986, pp. 365–381.

15. Burke and Edell, op. cit., pp. 82–83.
16. Amitava Chattopadhyay and Prakash Nedungadi, 'Does attitude toward the ad endure? The moderating effects of attention and delay', *Journal of Consumer Research*, 19, June 1992, pp. 26–33.
17. Gabriel Bielhal, Debra Stephens and Eleonora Curlo, 'Attitude toward the ad and brand choice', *Journal of Advertising*, 21, September 1992, pp. 19–39.
18. Rajeev Batra and Douglas M. Stayman, 'The role of mood in advertising', *Journal of Consumer Research*, 17, September 1990, pp. 203–214; Michael J. Innes and Cheryl R. Ahrens, 'Positive moods, processing goals and the effect of information on evaluative judgment', in Joseph P. Forgas (ed.), *Emotion and Social Judgments* (New York: Pergamon Press, 1991), pp. 221–239.
19. Andrew A. Aylesworth and Scott B. MacKenzie. 'Context is the key: The effect of program-induced mood on thoughts about the ad', *Journal of Advertising*, 27(2), 1998, pp. 17–31.
20. Dena Saliagas Cox and William B. Locander, 'Product novelty: Does it moderate the relationship between ad attitudes and brand attitudes?', *Journal of Advertising*, 16, 1987, pp. 39–44.
21. Edell and Burke, op. cit., pp. 430–433.
22. Darrel D. Muehling, 'Comparative advertising: the influence of attitude-toward-the-ad on brand evaluation', *Journal of Advertising*, 16, 1987, pp. 43–49; and Darrel D. Muehling, 'The influence of attitudes-toward-advertising-in-general on attitudes-toward-an-ad', in Terence A. Shimp et al. (eds), *1986 AMA Educators' Proceedings* (Chicago: American Marketing Association, 1986), pp. 29–34.
23. Morris B. Holbrook, David A. Velez and Gerard J. Tabouret, 'Attitude structure and search: An integrative model of importance-directed information processing', in Kent B. Monroe (ed.), *Advances in Consumer Research*, 8 (Ann Arbor: Association for Consumer Research, 1981), pp. 35–41.
24. Richard P. Bagozzi, Hans Baumgartner and Yougae Yi, 'Coupon usage and the theory of reasoned action', in Rebecca H. Holman and Michael R. Solomon (eds), *Advances in Consumer Research*, 18 (Provo, UT: Association for Consumer Research, 1991), pp. 24–27.
25. Daniel Katz, 'The functional approach to the study of attitudes', *Public Opinion Quarterly*, 24, Summer 1960, pp. 163–191; Sharon Shavitt, 'Products, personality and situations in attitude functions: Implications for consumer behaviour', in Thomas K. Srull (ed.), *Advances in Consumer Research*, 16 (Provo, UT: Association for Consumer Research, 1989), pp. 300–305.
26. Carl I. Hovland, O.J. Harvey and Muzafer Sherif, 'Assimilation and contrast effects in reactions to communication and attitude change', *Journal of Abnormal and Social Psychology*, 55, July 1957, pp. 244–252.
27. Richard E. Petty et al., 'Theories of attitude change', in H. Kassarjian and T. Robertson (eds), *Handbook of Consumer Theory and Research* (Englewood Cliffs, NJ: Prentice Hall, 1991); and Richard E. Petty, John T. Cacioppo and David Schumann, 'Central and peripheral routes to advertising effectiveness: The moderating role of involvement', *Journal of Consumer Research*, 10, September 1983, pp. 135–146; also Curtis P. Haugtvedt and Alan J. Strathman, 'Situational product relevance and attitude persistence', in Marvin E. Goldberg, Gerald Gorn and Richard W. Pollay (eds), *Advances in Consumer Research*, 17 (Provo, UT: Association for Consumer Research, 1990), pp. 766–769; and Scott B. MacKenzie and Richard A. Spreng, 'How does motivation moderate the impact of central and peripheral processing on brand attitudes and intentions?', *Journal of Consumer Research*, 18, March 1992, pp. 519–529.
28. Edward E. Jones et al., *Attribution: Perceiving the Causes of Behavior* (Morristown, NJ: General Learning Press, 1972).
29. Chris T. Allen and William R. Dillon, 'Self-perception development and consumer choice criteria: Is there a linkage?', in Richard P. Bagozzi and Alice M. Tybout (eds), *Advances in Consumer Research*, 10 (Ann Arbor: Association for Consumer Research, 1983), pp. 45–50.
30. See, for example, Leslie Lazar Kanuk, *Mail Questionnaire Response Behavior as a Function of Motivational Treatment* (New York: CUNY, 1974).
31. Valerie S. Folkes, 'Consumer reactions to product failure: An attributional approach', *Journal of Consumer Research*, 10, March 1984, pp. 398–409; and 'Recent attribution research in consumer behavior: A review and new dimensions', *Journal of Consumer Research*, 14, March 1988, pp. 548–565.
32. Harold H. Kelley, 'Attribution theory in social psychology', in David Levine (ed.), *Nebraska Symposium on Motivation*, 15 (Lincoln: University of Nebraska Press, 1967), p. 197.

Consumers in their social and cultural settings

PART 3

Part 3 moves beyond the realm of the individual consumer to the social world of the society in which the consumer lives. In Chapter 8 we examine a broad range of social influences on the consumer, particularly the mass media and reference groups. Then in Chapter 9 we look at the family, both as a means of consumer socialisation and as a buying group with defined roles and needs which change throughout the family lifecycle. Finally this section sets consumer behaviour within a series of social contexts that include social class (Chapter 10), culture as a whole (Chapter 11), specific subcultures within society (Chapter 12) and finally cross-cultural and global influences (Chapter 13).

DECISION-MAKING MODEL

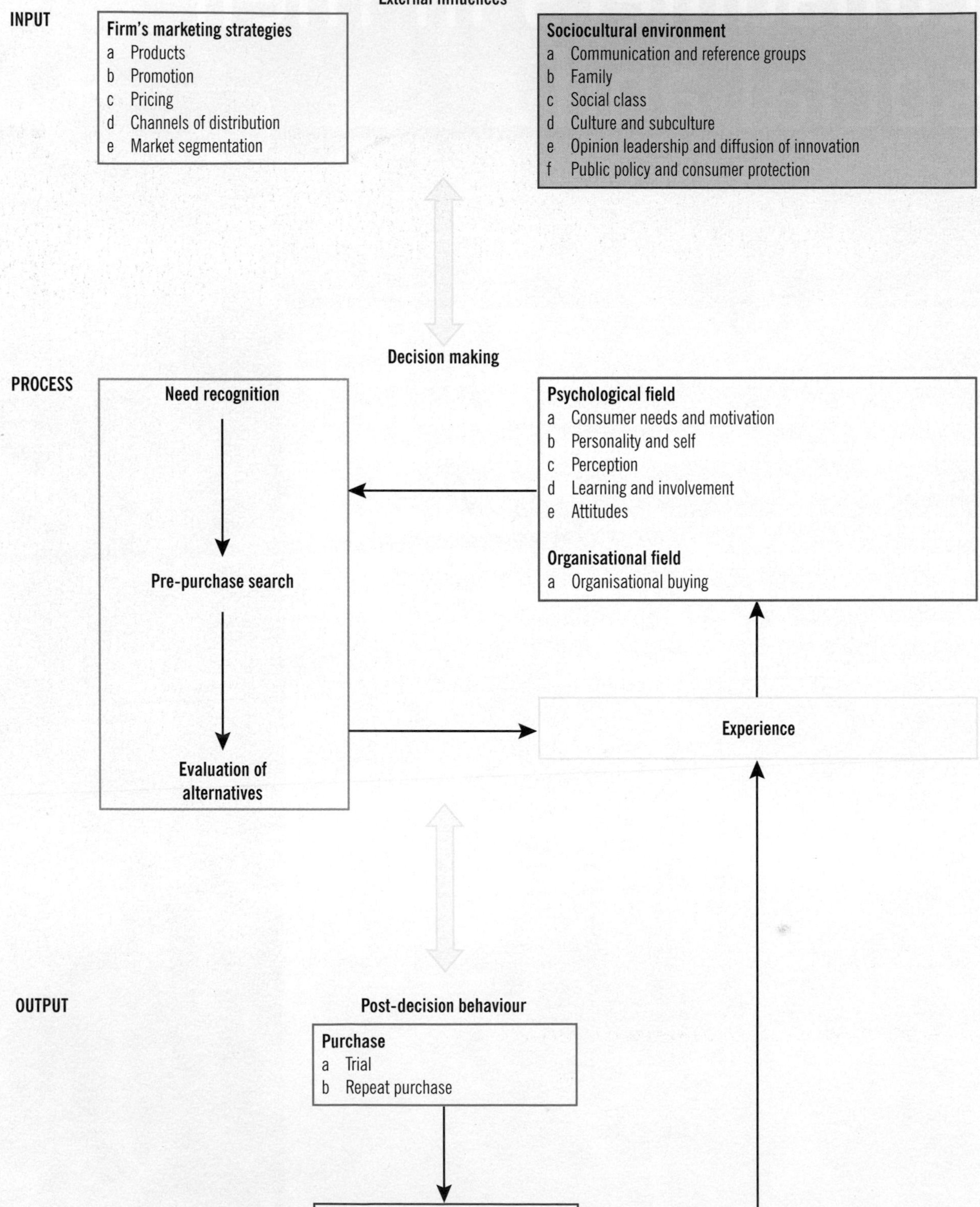

Social influences on buyer behaviour

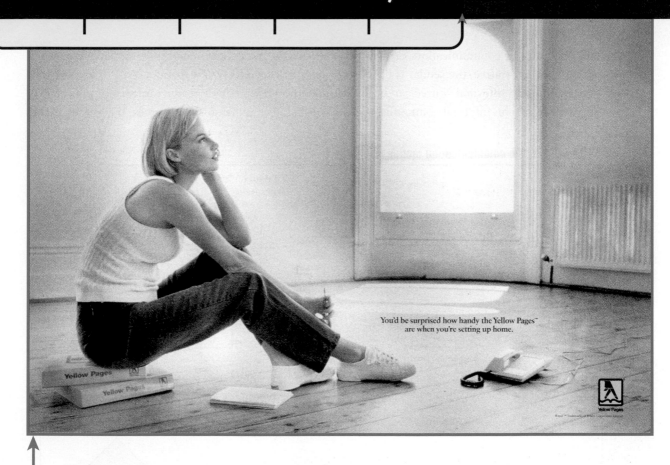

You'd be surprised how handy the Yellow Pages™ are when you're setting up home.

Yellow Pages

Source: © Telstra Corporation Limited 1999. Printed with permission.

The views of others have a profound effect on consumer behaviour. Many advertisers will attempt to wield this influence directly through mass media, particularly television, radio, the print media and the ubiquitous email spam, while others use targeted communication through direct mail or tailored websites. In this chapter we will look at mass communication from the perspective of the consumer who has to deal with these multiple messages. We will then turn more specifically to the issue of reference groups—those groups of people who influence buyers, both positively and negatively in the products they desire, seek, buy and use. The integrating theme for the chapter is *communication*.

Communication via the media

In its most basic form, communication is the transmission of a message from a sender to a receiver via a medium of some sort. An essential component of communication is **feedback**, which alerts the sender as to whether the intended message was in fact received. Figure 8.1 depicts this basic communication model.

THE SENDER

The sender initiates the communication. Using appropriate words, images and symbols the sender encodes the message. As a **formal source**, the sender is likely to represent either a for-profit (commercial) or a non-profit organisation; while an **informal source** can be a parent or a friend who gives product information or advice. Consumers often rely on informal communication sources because, unlike formal sources, the sender appar-

FIGURE 8.1 Basic communication model

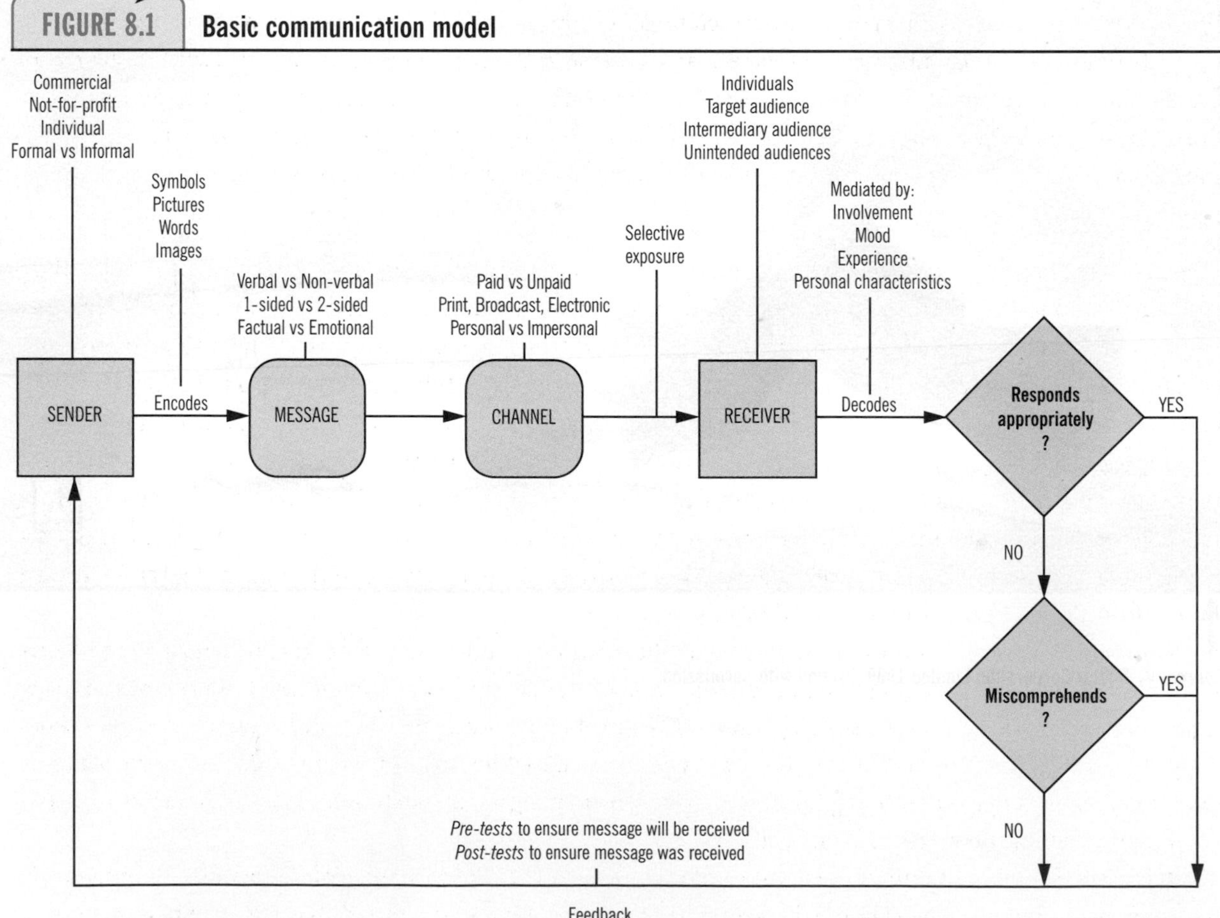

ently has nothing to gain from the receiver's subsequent actions. For that reason, informal **word-of-mouth** communication tends to be highly persuasive.

THE MESSAGE

The message can be verbal (spoken or written) or non-verbal (a photograph) or a combination of the two. A verbal message, whether spoken or written, usually contains more specific product information than does a non-verbal message. Sometimes, both are combined to provide more information to the receiver than either would alone. Non-verbal information takes the form of symbolic communication, such as a logo or a symbol[1] exclusively associated with their brand. The Coca-Cola Company, for example, has trademarked both the word 'Coke' in a specific font and the shape of the traditional Coke bottle—both are instantly recognisable to consumers as symbols of the company's best-selling soft drink.[2] The study of semiotics (see Chapter 11) is the study of the social meanings implied by such signs and symbols.

Communication strategy

In developing its message, the sponsor must establish the primary communication objectives. These might consist of creating awareness of a service, promoting sales of a product, encouraging (or discouraging) certain practices, attracting retail patronage, reducing post-purchase dissonance, creating goodwill, a favourable image, or any combination of these and other communication objectives. In addition, messages may be aimed at **reinforcing** beliefs, not changing them, e.g. FlyBuys ads may be aimed at keeping users loyal to the program. An essential component of a communication strategy is selecting the appropriate target audiences. This enables the marketer to create specific messages for each target group, and run them in specific media that are accessed by each target group. Companies that have many diverse audiences sometimes find it useful to develop a communication strategy that consists of an overall (i.e. umbrella) communications message to all their audiences, from which they spin off a series of related messages targeted directly at the specific interests of each individual segment. For example, Telstra has used Bert Newton to advertise a range of its services.

Persuasive message strategies

Persuasive messages should begin with an appeal to the needs and interests of the audience, and end with an appeal relevant to the marketers' own needs. Advertisements that do not conclude with an action closing tend to provoke much less response from the consumer than those that do. Advertisers need to recognise that consumers are increasingly knowledgeable about how advertising strategies are developed and the devices used to attract attention and persuade.[3] Senders must also know their target audiences' characteristics in terms of education, interests, needs and realms of experience. Senders must then try to phrase their messages so that their audiences decode the messages in the ways intended.[4] A strong fit between the receiver and the message on both the emotional and cognitive levels is known as **resonance**.[5] Using insights from semiotics, researchers have found that by manipulating the resonance of an ad, they could improve liking for the ad, brand attitudes and unaided recall of ad headlines.[6]

Non-verbal stimuli, such as photographs or illustrations, tend to reinforce verbal message arguments. A number of studies have manipulated the proportion of visual and verbal content used in print ads to investigate their relative impact on learning and persuasion, but the findings were inconclusive. At times, body copy alone was more effective than the body copy plus visuals, while in other experiments the reverse was true. One study showed that when verbal information was low in imagery, the inclusion of visual examples increased consumer recall of the verbal information.[7]

Researchers study not only the semantics of ad messages (i.e. the meanings of the words used and resulting inferences) but also the syntax (the sentence structure). One study found that ads using simple syntax produced greater levels of recall, regardless of the strength of the argument, than ads of greater complexity.[8] Researchers also focus on the rhetoric of advertising.[9] The major focus of rhetorical research is to discover the most effective way to express a message in a given situation. Researchers are interested in rhetorical forms, such as Hertz's 'The sooner you're out of our sight the better' (i.e. fast checkout) ad. The purpose of these studies is to discover the best way to phrase an advertising proposition to encourage processing that results in persuasion. Research findings suggest that rhetorical speech is most effective with unmotivated consumers, who would not otherwise process the ad.

Involvement theory (see Chapter 6) suggests that individuals are more likely to devote active cognitive effort to evaluating the pros and cons of a product in a high-involvement purchase situation, and more likely to focus on peripheral message cues in a low-involvement situation (the Elaboration Likelihood Model). Marketers should follow the **central route to persuasion** by presenting advertising with strong, well-documented, issue-relevant arguments that encourage cognitive processing. When involvement is low, marketers should follow the **peripheral route to persuasion** by emphasising non-content message elements such as background scenery, music or celebrity spokespeople. Such highly visual or symbolic cues provide the consumer with pleasant, indirect associations with the product, and provoke favourable inferences about its merits.[10] Figure 8.2 features an ad taking the peripheral route.

Despite the fact that many marketers have found that action closings tend to be more effective in encouraging consumer response, researchers have also found that, for high-involvement audiences, open-ended advertisements (that is, ads that do not draw explicit conclusions) can be highly effective in terms of creating positive brand attitudes and purchase intentions.[11]

FIGURE 8.2 **The peripheral route to persuasion**

Source: © 2004 Kimberly-Clark Worldwide, Inc. Reprinted with permission.

OVERCOMING BARRIERS TO COMMUNICATION

As we saw in Chapter 5, selective perception and advertising clutter can reduce the nication. The best way for a sender to overcome clutter (or noise) is simply to re times, much as a sailor does when sending an SOS message over and over again tc (The effects of repetition on learning were discussed in Chapter 6.) Repeated e message (redundancy of the advertising appeal) helps surmount psychological ba and thus facilitates message reception. Australian advertisers pioneered the practice of repe version of an ad at the end of a long commercial break in which it earlier appeared. Copywriters often use contrast (see Chapter 6) to achieve cut through. Two techniques, forcing (jolting the consumer's attention) and subverting (producing something unexpected or disconcerting) are often used.[12]

MESSAGE FRAMING

Should marketers stress the benefits to be gained by using a specific product (positive framing) or the benefits to be lost by not using it (negatively)? (See prospect theory as discussed in Chapter 5.) Research suggests that the appropriate message-framing decision depends on the product category. One study found that positively-framed messages are more persuasive in low-involvement situations where there is little emphasis on detailed cognitive processing, and negatively-framed messages are more persuasive in situations encouraging detailed information processing.[13] Research into consumers who had not used their credit cards in the previous three months found that negative framing (e.g. what they may lose by not using their card) had a stronger effect on later usage than positive framing.[14] This is consistent with the prospect theory view that losses are more keenly felt than gains. However, in high involvement decisions with the consumer doing much cognitive processing, negative framing appears less successful.[15]

ONE-SIDED VERSUS TWO-SIDED MESSAGES

Some marketers stress only positive factors about their products, and pretend that competition doesn't exist. However, when competition does exist, and when it is likely to be vocal, such advertisers tend to lose credibility with the consumer. Claim **credibility** can sometimes be enhanced by actually disclaiming superiority of some product features. Communication researchers have investigated ways to insulate existing customers from outside persuasion.[16] Their findings suggest that two-sided messages containing both positive and negative arguments about the brand serve to inoculate consumers against arguments that may be raised by competitors. In effect, this strategy provides consumers with **counterarguments** with which to dilute future attacks by competing brands. This is very important in political marketing, where one of the main aims of campaigns is to maintain current supporters.

If the audience is friendly (e.g. if it uses the advertiser's products), if it initially favours the communicator's position, or if it is not likely to hear an opposing argument, then a **one-sided (supportive) message** that stresses only favourable information is most effective. However, if the audience is critical or unfriendly (e.g. if it uses competitive products), if it is well-educated, or if it is likely to hear opposing claims, then a **two-sided (refutational) message** is likely to be more effective. Two-sided advertising messages are more credible than one-sided advertising messages because they acknowledge that the advertised brand has shortcomings. Such an approach tends to be effective in personal selling, PR campaigns designed to address negative publicity, when consumers are likely to see competitors' negative counter-claims or when consumer attitudes to a brand are already negative.[17]

FIGURE 8.3 **Fear appeal**

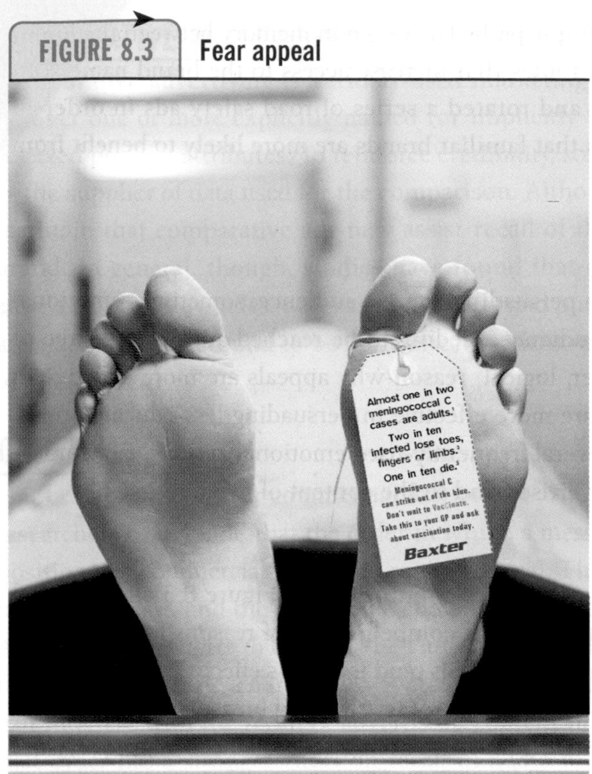

Source: Courtesy of Baxter Healthcare.

- humour is more effective with existing products than with new products
- humour is more appropriate for low-involvement products and 'feeling-oriented' products than for high-involvement products.

Consumer cynicism about advertising has led marketers, especially those targeting younger groups, to use humour as an attention gaining device. The infamous Toohey's Extra Dry commercial featuring a man's tongue detaching itself to go in search of a bottle of beer is an obvious example. Figure 8.4 for Orica glues uses a gentler form of humour to reflect the adhesive properties of the product. So long as humour does not detract from the message, it is likely to be an effective attention gaining device.

Agony advertising

All of us have, at one time or another, been repelled by so-called agony commercials, which depict in diagrammatic detail the internal or intestinal effects of heartburn, indigestion, clogged sinus cavities or hammer-induced headaches. Nevertheless, pharmaceutical companies continue to run such commercials

FIGURE 8.4 **Use of humour**

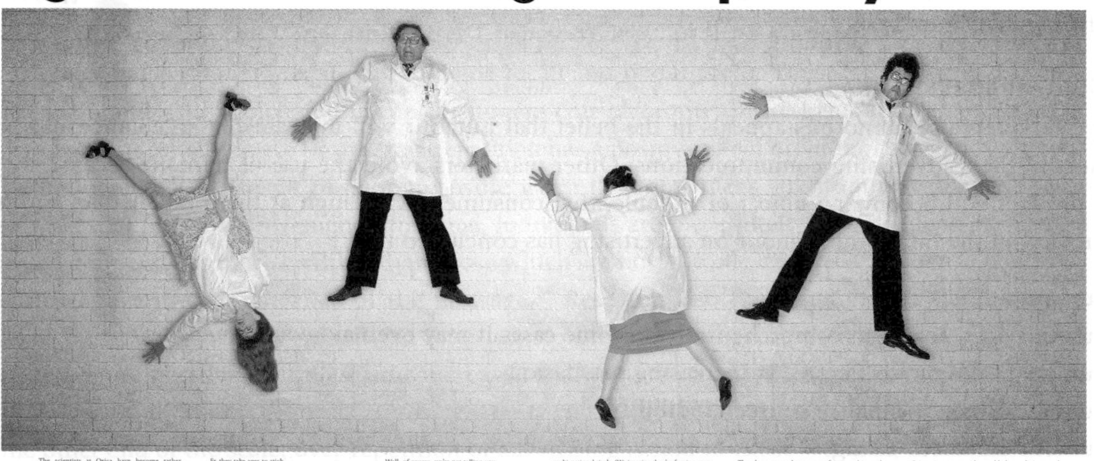

Source: Courtesy of Orica Limited.

with great success because they appeal to a certain segment of the population that suffers from ailments that are not visible, and which therefore elicit little sympathy from family and friends. Their complaints are legitimised by commercials with which they immediately identify. With the sponsor's credibility established ('They really understand the misery I'm going through'), the message itself tends to be highly persuasive in getting consumers to buy the advertised product.

Abrasive advertising

How effective can unpleasant or annoying ads be? Studies of the **sleeper effect** indicate that the effectiveness of an advertising message can increase over time, despite the initial presence of a negative cue. It suggests that the memory of an unpleasant commercial that saturates the media and antagonises listeners or viewers may dissipate in the end, leaving only the brand name and the persuasive message in the minds of consumers. Late-night television viewers will experience many ads of this type, with nauseating ads for clearance sales, lighting and rugs being prime examples. There is stronger evidence for entertaining advertising being effective in communicating positive brand images.[33]

Sex in advertising

In our highly permissive society, sex in advertising seems to permeate the print media and the airwaves. Sex in advertising ranges from the blatancy of nudes and obvious *double entendre* to devices so subtle it takes a trained observer to recognise them. (See, for example, the discussion of sexual embeds in Chapter 5.) Australian media have generally been more permissive than the usually conservative Americans, but are less overt than the Europeans. There are many instances where advertisers who have used sex as a thematic appeal have been very successful. In other instances, such advertising has proved to interfere with **message comprehension**, especially when there is a lot of information to process.[34] When visual sexual content is present, the same research shows consumers tend to be distracted from the cognitive ad content. So why do advertisers continue to use sex in their advertising? The answer is simple. There are few appeals in advertising that equal its attention-getting value.

There are strong indications that the type of interest that sex evokes often stops exactly where it started—with sex. If a sexually suggestive or explicit illustration is not relevant to the product advertised, it makes no selling impression on the reader. Researchers who investigated the impact of female nudity in advertisements have concluded that nudity may negatively impact the product message.[35] One thread seems to run through all the research findings about sex in advertising: the advertiser must be sure that the product, the ad, the target audience, and the use of sexual themes and elements all work together. When sex is relevant to the product, it can be an extremely potent copy theme, as the controversial ad for Lovable lingerie illustrates in Figure 8.5.

FIGURE 8.5 Appropriate use of sexuality in advertising

Source: Courtesy of Lovable.

THE CHANNEL (MEDIUM)

The medium or communications channel can be either personal (a conversation between people) or impersonal. Personal conversations may involve opinion leaders (see below), salespeople and their customers. Direct marketers, many of whom use sophisticated database marketing techniques, seek individual responses from advertisements placed in all the mass media: broadcast, print, Internet, as well as from **direct mail**. People who demonstrate an interest in a particular website are now routinely asked, as part of **permission marketing**, to consent to further emails about these topics.

Impersonal communication includes the **mass media**—print (newspapers, magazines, billboards, *Yellow Pages*), broadcast (radio, free-to-air television, pay television), cinema, outdoor advertising and electronic media (Internet, SMS, search engines like Google). Of national advertising, TV networks accounted for 30%, print media 59% and radio 7%, outdoor 3% and cinema 1%.[36] Despite the general use of the term 'mass media' to describe impersonal media, there is also a growing trend towards **media demassification** as publishers and broadcasters shift their focus from large, general interest audiences to smaller, more specialised audiences. The huge growth in special interest and women's magazine titles in Australia has been a clear indication of this.

Broadband Internet connections offer fast access to a growing group of consumers and most larger businesses. These modes permit the audiences of mass media to have a direct dialogue with most providers and thus have blurred the distinction between interpersonal and impersonal communication. The growth of spam (unsolicited email advertising) brought legislation in 2004 to restrict its use from sites located in Australia. Email viruses and worms have further limited the effectiveness of this medium.

Mass media strategy

Media strategy is an essential component of most communication plans. It calls for the placement of ads in the specific media that are read, viewed or heard by selected target markets. Remember, as noted in Chapter 3, accessibility of the audience is one of the criteria for successful market segmentation. To accomplish this, advertisers develop, through research, a consumer profile of their target customers that includes the specific media they read or watch. A cost-effective media choice is one that closely matches the advertiser's **consumer profile** to a medium's **audience profile**. Table 8.1 shows radio listening profiles collected by Nielsen Media Research. It would appear that popular FM and ABC radio stations appeal to very different audiences.

Before selecting specific media vehicles, advertisers must select general media categories that will carry their messages. Many advertisers use a multimedia campaign strategy, with one primary category carrying the major burden of the campaign (often television), and other categories providing supplemental support.

TABLE 8.1 Average share of audience (Monday–Sunday)

Radio station	All people 10+	Grocery buyers	18–24	55+
NOVA (Sydney)	11.8	8.5	34.4	0.6
ABC702	9.1	10.0	1.7	15.9
3AW (Melbourne)	14.2	17.2	1.0	27.9
ABC774 (Melbourne)	10.7	11.8	2.5	19.3
B105 (Brisbane)	18.4	16.6	30.2	3.3
ABC612 (Brisbane)	8.4	8.3	2.0	20.6
SAFM (Adelaide)	20.4	17.3	30.6	3.3
ABC891 (Adelaide)	9.9	11.5	0.9	20.8
94.5FM (Perth)	21.9	24.0	10.4	14.4
ABC720 (Perth)	11.1	11.9	2.2	24.6

Source: **Adapted from Nielsen Media Research, see <www.nielsenmedia.com.au> (February 2004). Based on Survey No. 1 covering 18 January–14 February 2004.**

Each media category has its own specific advantages. For example, print media and the Internet allow unlimited message length; broadcast messages have fixed durations and some media permit very timely messages.[37] Where possible, marketers place ads in specialised media where there is less **psychological noise**. For example, studies show that ads placed within the context of computer and video games and in movie theatres are recalled better than similar ads placed in more general media.[38] Choice of media will depend on the particular product message. For example, a retailer who wants to advertise a clearance sale should advertise in daily newspapers, since that is where consumers are accustomed to looking for sales announcements. A marketer who wants to promote a power lawn-mower with unique cutting features would be wise to use a medium like television, on which the mower can be demonstrated in action. Once marketers have identified the appropriate media category (e.g. magazines), they can then choose the specific medium in that category (e.g. *Women's Weekly*) that reaches their intended audiences. One medium often overlooked is the *Yellow Pages*, a prolific advertising medium run by Sensis (which is owned by Telstra). Case Study 8.1 shows how this medium has positioned itself. Finally, advertisers have to decide how often and how intensively they should schedule their ads.[39] The term **reach** refers to the number of different people or households that are exposed to the advertisement (either because they hear or watch the program or read the newspaper or magazine); **frequency** refers to how often they are exposed to it during a specified period of time. The term **effective reach** combines both concepts and has been defined as a minimum of three confirmed vehicle exposures to an individual member of a target group over an agreed-upon time period.[40]

THE RECEIVER

The receiver is likely to be a targeted prospect or a customer. There are also many intermediary, and even unintended, audiences for marketing communications. Examples of **intermediary audiences** are wholesalers, distributors and retailers, who are sent trade advertising designed to persuade them to order and stock merchandise, and relevant professionals (such as architects or physicians) who are sent professional advertising in the hope that they will specify or prescribe the marketer's products. **Unintended audiences** often include stakeholders that are important to the marketer, such as employees, shareholders, creditors, suppliers, bankers and the local community, in addition to the general public.[41] As some people are in multiple stakeholder roles, advertisers may need to keep their communication consistent.

Message comprehension is the amount of meaning accurately derived from the message and is a function of the message characteristics, the receiver's opportunity and ability to **encode** (or process) the message, and the receiver's motivation.[42] Our demographics (e.g. age, gender, marital status), sociocultural memberships (social class, race, religion), personality and lifestyle are all key determinants in how a message is interpreted. Marketers sometimes assume that audiences receive the message in the way they intended. Unfortunately, communication can fail. A US study showed that one-third of consumers did not understand the main message in a direct mail piece, despite it being written at year-eight reading level.[43]

Our level of involvement (see Chapter 6) plays a key role in how much attention is paid to the message, and how carefully it is decoded. People who have a low level of interest in home theatre systems, for example, may not pay much attention to an ad for specially-designed speakers, but may note how compactly they fit into a living-room setting. Mood or affect plays a significant role in how a message is decoded. A consumer's mood affects the way in which an advertisement is perceived, recalled and acted upon.[44] Research indicates that the consumer's mood states are often influenced by the context in which the advertising message appears (e.g. the adjacent TV program or newspaper story) and the content of the ad itself, which in turn may affect the consumer's evaluation and recall of the message.[45] High arousal may limit central (i.e. cognitive) processing, increasing reliance on peripheral cues.[46] Positive feelings induced by a commercial may enhance the likelihood that consumers will buy the advertised product (e.g. a plasma TV). Similarly, depressing commercials may induce negative moods that may in fact be congruent with the marketer's objectives: consumers may be persuaded that a negative outcome will occur if they don't buy the advertised product (e.g. accident insurance) or take the recommended action. For example, road safety ads may point out the lifelong guilt they would suffer if they drink and drive, then kill or maim a friend. The negative mood will encourage them to change their behaviour.

In addition to inducing positive or negative cognitive moods, marketers can also induce non-cognitive moods through the use of advertising stimuli such as background music and scenery. Singapore Airlines creates a mood of elegance and traditional service in press and TV ads that serves to enhance consumer attitudes towards the company's service.

Credibility

The perceived honesty and objectivity of the source of the communication has an enormous influence on how the communication is accepted by the receiver. If the source is well respected and highly thought of by the intended audience, the message is much more likely to be believed. Conversely, messages from a source considered unreliable or untrustworthy will be received with scepticism and may be rejected.

Credibility is built on a number of factors, the most important being the perceived intentions of the source. For example, if a garage offers a free brake check for your car, you may ask, 'What does he stand to gain if I do what is suggested? No doubt he wants to find faults and get me to pay to have them fixed.' As we shall see below, opinion leaders are thought to be credible because they perceived as having little to gain.

Formal sources such as non-profit organisations and neutral rating services (such as *Choice*[47] magazine) have greater credibility than commercial sources because of the likelihood that they are more objective in their product assessments. That is why publicity is so valuable to a supplier: citations of a product in an editorial context, rather than in a paid advertisement, give the reader much more confidence in the message. In Australia, the 'cash-for-comment' scandals saw radio announcers failing to disclose their commercial relationship with companies and other organisations. Once the vested interests were known, the announcers and the organisations lost credibility.

When the intentions of a source are clearly profit-making, then reputation, expertise and knowledge become important factors in message credibility. The credibility of commercial messages is often based on the composite evaluation of the reputations of the sender encapsulated in the brand of the product or store.

The reputation of the medium that carries the advertisement also affects the credibility of the message—for example, 'as advertised on television'. For example, ADMA, the association of the **direct marketing** industry, has promoted its 'Direct Marketing Code of Practice',[48] while the Australian Made campaign uses its exclusive kangaroo symbol.[49] Spokespeople can also add to credibility, as we shall see below.

FEEDBACK

Feedback is an essential component of both interpersonal and impersonal communications. Since marketing communications are usually designed to persuade a target audience to act in a desired way (to purchase a product, to vote for a specific candidate, to drive safely), the ultimate test of their success is the receiver's response. For this reason, it is essential for the sender to obtain feedback as promptly and accurately as possible. Only through feedback can the sender determine if and how well the message has been received.

An important advantage of **interpersonal communication** is the ability to obtain immediate feedback through verbal as well as non-verbal cues. Experienced communicators are very attentive to feedback and constantly modify their messages based on what they see or hear from the audience. Immediate feedback is the factor that makes personal selling so effective. It enables the salesperson to tailor the sales pitch to the expressed needs and observed reactions of each prospect. Similarly, it enables a political candidate to selectively stress specific aspects of his or her platform in response to questions posed by prospective voters in face-to-face meetings.

For mass communication, feedback is harder to obtain. While advertisers would like to measure the direct effect of advertising on sales and profits, this is often difficult to research.[50] Measures such as changes in sales of the advertised product,[51] inquiries to their call centre or hits on their website are used.

Market research is extensively used, in three main ways. The first is **pre-testing**. Consumer reaction is tested before ads are in their final form. The results can be used to reshape or even remake ads, as well as altering their scheduling.[52] However, there is some considerable debate about the effectiveness of pre-testing.[53] The second strategy is **advertising tracking** where responses to ads (typically awareness and message comprehension) are measured repeatedly to see how they change in response to advertising. The third is **post-campaign research.** Table 8.2 shows the results from 537 Australian advertising campaign studies (mainly on television) conducted by Newspoll Market Research. It is clear from the results that campaigns differ markedly in their effectiveness. Branding recall of advertsing is also a problem. Most people who had seen or heard the campaigns were unable to recall the brand being promoted. At times, respondents are just as likely to 'remember' the competitor's brand as the one being advertised. These results show just how difficult it is for advertisers to communicate effectively. Advertisers rely on media ratings to plan the scheduling and placement of their ads, such as television, radio and Internet ratings for electronic media and the readership research of the print media.[54]

Audience participation

The provision of feedback changes the communication process from one-way to two-way communication. This is important to senders, because it enables them to determine whether and how well communication has taken place. But feedback is also important to receivers, because it enables them to participate, to be involved, to experience in some way the message itself. Participation by the receiver reinforces the message. An experienced communicator will ask questions and opinions of an audience to draw them into the discussion. Many lecturers use the participative approach in classrooms rather than the more sterile lecture format because they recognise that student participation tends to facilitate internalisation of the information discussed.

Reference groups

One communication strategy used with telling effect by marketers is to employ reference groups—a collection of social role models—who affect consumer behaviour. To understand this approach, we will first look at the concept of a group and then its application to the reference group context.

WHAT IS A GROUP?

A **group** may be defined as two or more people who interact to accomplish either individual or mutual goals. The broad scope of this definition includes an intimate 'group' of two neighbours attending a Neighbourhood Watch meeting or a larger, more formal group, such as a local scuba diving club, whose members are mutually interested in scuba equipment, training, and diving trips. Included in this definition, too, are a kind of 'one-sided grouping' in which an individual consumer observes the appearance or actions of others, who unknowingly serve as consumption-related role models. Table 8.3 (page 275) shows various ways groups can be classified.

REFERENCE GROUPS

A **reference group** is any person or group that serves as a point of comparison (or reference) for an individual in forming either general or specific values, attitudes, or a specific guide for behaviour. From a marketing

At the same time, consumers did not always identify closely with the situations depicted. Television advertising for the *Yellow Pages* has taken a broader, mass market approach emphasising genuine Australians, often in humorous situations involving the *Yellow Pages* (the books propping up the wheel of the broken down ute at the top of the hill, the man using pages from the directories as packing material, and the reprise of the Gogomobile). Because the magazine advertising took place in the midst of these other campaigns, it was difficult to assess its separate, long-term influence. However, market research over the period revealed a growth in the number of women who would consider the *Yellow Pages* as the first place they would look to find a new supplier. The ads themselves have won a number of international and domestic advertising awards.

Case Study Questions

1. If you were remaking the *Yellow Pages* magazine ads to target the YO, SA and SB groups, what changes to the communication approach would you make?
2. Consumers often say they would prefer 'real people' rather than 'attractive models' in advertising? Why does most advertising not use such 'real people' in their campaigns?

Summary

Communication is defined as the transmission of a message from a sender to a receiver through some kind of channel or medium. There are five basic components of communication: the sender, the receiver, the medium, the message, and some form of feedback (the receiver's response). In the communication process, the sender encodes the message using words, pictures, symbols or spokespeople, and sends it through a selected channel of communication. Decoding, or interpreting, the message is based on the receiver's personal characteristics and experience; the receiver's response (or lack of response) is based on such factors as comprehension, psychological noise, selective exposure and selective attention.

There are two types of communication: interpersonal and impersonal (or mass) communication. Interpersonal communication occurs on a personal level between two or more people, and may be verbal or non-verbal. In mass communication, there is no direct contact between source and receiver. Interpersonal communication takes place in person, by telephone, or by email or mail; mass communication uses such impersonal media as television, radio, newspapers and magazines. In both types of communication, feedback is an essential component because it provides the sender with some idea of whether, and how well, the message has been received.

The credibility of the source, a vital element in message persuasiveness, is often based on the source's perceived intentions. Informal sources and neutral or editorial sources are generally considered highly objective and, therefore, very credible. The credibility of a commercial source is more problematic, and is usually based on a composite evaluation of its reputation, expertise and knowledge, and of the medium, the retail channel, and the company spokespeople it uses.

Media selection depends on the product, the audience and the advertising objectives of the campaign. In addition to consumers, a marketer's audiences include selling intermediaries and other publics that are relevant to the organisation's success.

The manner in which a message is presented influences its impact. For example, one-sided messages are more effective in some situations and with some audiences; two-sided messages are more effective with others. High-involvement products (i.e. those with great relevance to a consumer segment) are best advertised through the central route to persuasion, which encourages active cognitive effort. Low-involvement products are best promoted through peripheral cues such as background scenery, music or celebrity spokespeople.

Emotional appeals frequently used in advertising include fear appeals, humorous appeals, 'agony' appeals and sexual appeals. When sexual themes are relevant to the product, they can be very effective; when used solely as attention-getters, they rarely achieve brand recall. Audience participation is a very effective communication strategy because it encourages internalisation of the advertising message.

Almost all individuals regularly interact with other people who directly or indirectly influence their purchase decisions. Thus, the study of groups and their impact on the individual is of great importance to marketers concerned with influencing consumer behaviour. Groups may be classified according to regularity of contact (primary or secondary groups), by structure and hierarchy (formal or informal groups), by size or complexity (large or small groups), and by membership or aspiration (membership or symbolic groups).

There are several types of consumer-relevant groups that influence the consumption behaviour of individuals: the family, friendship groups, shopping groups, work groups, virtual groups/communities, brand communities and consumer action groups.

Consumer reference groups are groups that serve as a frame of reference for individuals in their purchase decisions. Any or all of the groups listed above can serve as reference groups. Reference groups that influence general values or behaviour are called normative reference groups; those that influence specific attitudes are called comparative reference groups. The concept of consumer reference groups has been broadened to include groups with which consumers have no direct face-to-face contact, such as celebrities, political figures and social classes.

Reference groups that are classified in terms of a person's membership and the positive or negative influences they exert include contactual groups, aspirational groups, disclaimant groups and avoidance groups. The credibility, attractiveness and power of the reference group affect the degree of influence it has. Reference group appeals are used very effectively by some advertisers in promoting their goods and services because they subtly induce the prospective consumer to identify with the pictured user of the product.

The types of reference groups most commonly used in marketing are celebrities, experts and the trade- or spokes-character. Celebrities are used to give testimonials or endorsements, as actors, or as company spokespersons. Experts may be recognised experts in the product category or actors playing the part of experts (e.g. a motor mechanic).

Reference group appeals are effective promotional strategies because they serve to increase brand awareness and reduce perceived risk among prospective consumers.

Discussion questions

1. Explain the differences between feedback from interpersonal communications and feedback from impersonal communications. How can the marketer obtain and use each kind of feedback?
2. List and discuss the effects of psychological barriers on the communication process. How can a marketer overcome the communication barrier known as 'noise'?
3. (a) What factors influence the perceived credibility of an informal communication source? List and discuss factors that determine the credibility of formal communication sources of product information.
   (b) What are the implications of the sleeper effect for the selection of spokespeople and the scheduling of advertising messages?
4. The Commonwealth Bank uses both magazines and the Internet itself to promote its on-line share brokerage business. How would you measure the advertising effectiveness of the two media for promoting the service? Which is likely to be the more effective?
5. For what kinds of audiences would you consider using comparative advertising? Why?
6. You are the marketing manager for a headache remedy tablet sold over the counter at pharmacies. Your advertising agency has just presented you with two different promotional strategies, one using a humorous approach and one taking an 'agony' approach. Which approach would you adopt? Why?
7. Suppose you were the PR manager of a large food firm which had to withdraw its main food product from the market while an outbreak of food poisoning allegedly caused by the product was being investigated. What crisis communication plan would have helped the companies handle the adverse publicity? Describe the components of such a plan.
8. You are the marketing vice president of a large soft-drink company. Your company's advertising agency is in the process of negotiating a contract to employ a female singing superstar to promote your product. Discuss the reference group factors that you would raise before the celebrity is hired.

Exercises

1. Bring two advertisements to class: one illustrating a one-sided message and one a two-sided message. Suggest why each marketer may have chosen that specific message strategy and evaluate its effectiveness.
2. Choose a television commercial that uses a humorous appeal. Interview other members of your family who saw the same commercial and measure:
   (a) their recall of the brand advertised
   (b) their recall of the information presented
   (c) their like or dislike of the commercial
   (d) their preference for the brand advertised.
   How would you explain your findings in view of the research evidence on humour in advertising presented in this chapter?
3. Find three print ads that use a fear, sex and audience participation appeal and present them in class. For each ad, discuss whether you think the appeal used is effective, and why.
4. Create two television advertisements for your university or TAFE college, conveying two different moods or affects. During which period of the year would you use each ad? Explain.
5. Watch one hour of TV on a single channel during prime time and record the broadcast. List all the commercials you can recall seeing. On the basis of memory alone, identify for each commercial:
   (a) the message framing approach used
   (b) whether the message was one-sided or two-sided
   (c) whether the commercial was shown closer to the beginning or end of the commercial break.
   Compare your list with the actual taped broadcast. Explain any discrepancies between your recollections and the actual broadcast by using the material discussed in this chapter.
6. Prepare a list of formal and informal groups to which you belong and give examples of purchases for which each served as a reference group. In which of the groups you listed is the pressure to conform the greatest? Why?

Key terms

advertising tracking *(p. 273)*
audience profile *(p. 270)*
celebrity credibility *(p. 281)*
celebrity endorser *(p. 280)*
central route to persuasion *(p. 264)*
comparative advertising *(p. 266)*
comparative reference groups *(p. 275)*
conspicuous product *(p. 277)*
consumer-action group *(p. 280)*
consumer conformity *(p. 278)*
consumer profile *(p. 270)*
counterarguments *(p. 265)*
credibility *(p. 265)*
direct mail *(p. 270)*
direct marketing *(p. 272)*
effective reach *(p. 271)*
encode *(p. 271)*
endorsement *(p. 280)*
feedback *(p. 262)*
formal source *(p. 262)*
frequency *(p. 271)*
group *(p. 273)*
indirect reference groups *(p. 275)*
informal groups *(p. 278)*
informal source *(p. 262)*
intermediary audiences *(p. 271)*
interpersonal communication *(p. 272)*
mass media *(p. 270)*
media demassification *(p. 270)*
media strategy *(p. 270)*
message comprehension *(p. 269)*
message framing *(p. 265)*
negative influence *(p. 275)*
normative reference groups *(p. 275)*
one-sided (supportive) message *(p. 265)*
ordered protection motivation (OPM) model *(p. 267)*
peripheral route to persuasion *(p. 264)*
permission marketing *(p. 270)*
post-campaign research *(p. 273)*
power groups *(p. 277)*
pre-testing *(p. 273)*
psychological noise *(p. 271)*
reach *(p. 271)*
reference group *(p. 273)*
reinforcing *(p. 263)*
resonance *(p. 263)*

shopping group (*p. 278*)
sleeper effect (*p. 269*)
source credibility (*p. 267*)
spokesperson (*p. 280*)
testimonial (*p. 280*)
two-sided (refutational) message (*p. 265*)
unintended audiences (*p. 271*)
word-of-mouth (*p. 263*)

Endnotes

1. Pamela W. Henderson and Joseph A. Cote, 'Guidelines for selecting or modifying logos', *Journal of Marketing*, April 1998, pp. 14–30.
2. Paul N. Bloom and Torger Reve, 'Transmitting signals to consumers for competitive advantage', *Business Horizons*, July/August 1990, pp. 58–66.
3. Stephanie O'Donahoe and Caroline Tynan, 'Beyond sophistication: Dimensions of advertising literacy', *International Journal of Advertising*, 17(4), 1998, pp. 467–482.
4. D. Vakratsas and T. Ambler, 'How advertising works: What do we really know?', *Journal of Marketing*, 63(1), 1999, pp. 26–43.
5. Tony Schwartz, *The Responsive Chord* (New York: Doubleday, 1974).
6. Edward F. McQuarrie and David Glen Mick, 'On resonance: A critical pluralistic inquiry into advertising rhetoric', *Journal of Consumer Research*, 19, September 1992, pp. 180–197.
7. H. Rao Unnava and Robert E. Burnkrant, 'An imagery-processing view of the role of pictures in print advertisements', *Journal of Marketing Research*, 28, May 1991, pp. 226–231.
8. Tina A. Lowrey, 'The relation between syntactic complexity and advertising persuasiveness', *Advances in Consumer Research*, 19, 1992, pp. 270–274.
9. Edward F. McQuarrie and David Glen Mick, 'Figures of rhetoric in advertising language', *Journal of Consumer Research*, 22, March 1996, pp. 424–438.
10. J. Craig Andrews and Terence A. Shimp, 'Effects of involvement, argument strength, and source characteristics on central and peripheral processing of advertising', *Psychology & Marketing*, 7(3), Fall 1990, pp. 195–214.
11. Alan G. Sawyer and Daniel J. Howard, 'Effects of omitting conclusions in advertisements to involved and uninvolved audiences', *Journal of Marketing Research*, 28, November 1991, pp. 467–474.
12. Arthur J. Kover, 'Copywriters' implicit theories of communication: An exploration', *Journal of Consumer Research*, 21, March 1995, pp. 596–611.
13. Durairaj Maheswaran and Joan Meyers-Levy, 'The influence of message framing and issue involvement', *Journal of Marketing Research*, 27, August 1990, pp. 361–370.
14. Yoav Ganzach and Nili Karsahi, 'Message framing and buyer behaviour: A field experiment', *Journal of Business Research*, 32, 1995, pp. 11–17.
15. Baba Shiv et al., 'Factors affecting the impact of negatively and positively framed ad messages', *Journal of Consumer Research*, 24, December 1997, pp. 285–294.
16. Michael A. Kamins and Henry Assael, 'Two-sided versus one-sided appeals: A cognitive perspective on argumentation, source derogation, and the effect of disconfirming trial on belief change', *Journal of Marketing Research*, 24, 1987, pp. 29–39.
17. Ayn E. Crowley and Wayne D. Hoyer, 'An integrative framework for understanding two-sided persuasion', *Journal of Consumer Research*, 20, March 1994, pp. 561–574.
18. Randall L. Rose, Paul W. Miniard, Michael J. Barone, Kenneth C. Manning and Brian D. Till, 'When persuasion goes undetected: The case of comparative advertising', *Journal of Marketing Research*, 30, August 1993, pp. 315–330; see also Cornelia Pechmann and S. Ratneshwar, 'The use of comparative advertising for brand positioning: Association versus differentiation', *Journal of Consumer Research*, 18, September 1991, pp. 145–160, and Cornelia Pechmann and David W. Stewart, 'The effects of comparative advertising on attention, memory and purchase intentions', *Journal of Consumer Research*, 20(1), 1991, pp. 299–302.
19. Paul W. Miniard, Michael J. Barone, Randall L. Rose and Kenneth C. Manning, 'A re-examination of the relative persuasiveness of comparative and non-comparative advertising', *Advances in Consumer Behaviour*, 21, 1994, pp. 299–302. See also Kenneth C. Manning, Paul W. Miniard, Michael J. Barone and Randall L. Rose, 'Understanding the mental representation created by comparative advertising', *Journal of Advertising*, Summer 2001, pp. 27–39.
20. Curtis P. Haugtvedt and Duane T. Wegener, 'Message order

effect in persuasion: An attitude strength perspective', *Journal of Consumer Research*, 21, June 1994, pp. 205–218.
21. Valerie Starr and Charles A. Lowe, 'The influence of program context and order of ad presentation on immediate and delayed responses to television advertisements', *Advances in Consumer Behaviour*, 21, 1995, pp. 184–190. For basic readings in this area, see Carl I. Hovland (ed.), *The Order of Presentation in Persuasion* (New Haven: Yale University Press, 1957). See also Australian research by David Bednall and Marie Hannaford, *Television and Children: Recall of Television Advertising and Programs by Children* (Melbourne: Australian Broadcasting Tribunal, 1980).
22. H. Rao Unnava, Robert E. Burnkrant and Sunil Erevelles, 'Effects of presentation order and communication modality on recall and attitude', *Journal of Consumer Research*, 21, December 1994, pp. 481–490.
23. Scott Sutherland, Mark Gabbott and Kerryn Jackson, 'A preliminary study investigating the mere exposure effect using divided and full attention conditions', *Australasian Marketing Journal*, 7(2), 1999, pp. 39–48.
24. Scott A. Hawkins and Stephen J. Hoch, 'Low-involvement learning: Memory without evaluation', *Journal of Consumer Research*, 19, September 1992, pp. 212–225.
25. Curtis P. Haugtvedt et al., 'Advertising repetition and variation strategies: Implications for understanding attitude strength', *Journal of Consumer Research*, 21, June 1994, pp. 176–189.
26. H. Rao Unnava and Robert E. Burnkrant, 'Effects of repeating varied ad executions on brand name memory', *Journal of Marketing Research*, 28, November 1991, pp. 406–416.
27. M. Cameron, N. Haworth, J. Oxley, S. Newstead and T. Le, *Evaluation of Transport Accident Commission Road Safety Advertising* (Melbourne: Monash University Accident Research Centre, 1993) and Tim R. Fry, *Advertising Wearout in the Transport Accident Commission Road Safety Campaigns* (Melbourne: Department of Econometrics, Monash University, 1994).
28. Anurag G. Hingorani, 'The effect of ad variation and brand familiarity on brand name and claim recall: A theoretical perspective', in Jack Cadeaux and Mark Uncles (eds), *Marketing in the Third Millennium: Proceedings of ANZMAC 99* (no pagination).
29. Robert A.C. Ruiter, Gerjo Kok, Bas Verplanken and Gerdien van Eersel, 'Strengthening the persuasive impact of fear appeals: The role of action framing', *The Journal of Social Psychology*, 14(3), 2003, pp. 397–400.
30. Denise D. Schoenbachler and Tommy E.Whittler, 'Adolescent processing of social and physical threat communications', *Journal of Advertising*, 35, 4, Winter 1996, pp. 37–54.
31. James B. Hunt, John F. Tanner Jr and David R. Eppright, 'Forty years of fear appeal research: Support for the ordered protection motivation model', *American Marketing Association*, 6, Winter 1995, pp. 147–153. See also John F. Tanner Jr, James B. Hunt and David R. Eppright, 'The protection motivation model: A normative model of fear appeals', *Journal of Marketing*, 55, July 1991, pp. 36–45. See also Nadine Henley and Rob Donovan, 'Unintended consequences of arousing fear in social marketing', in Jack Cadeaux and Mark Uncles (eds), *Marketing in the Third Millennium: Proceedings of ANZMAC 99* (no pagination). See also Nicky Shore and Brendan J. Gray, 'Teen reactions to anti-drink driving fear appeals', in Jack Cadeaux and Mark Uncles (eds), *Marketing in the Third Millennium: Proceedings of ANZMAC 99* (no pagination).
32. Marc G. Weinberger and Charles S. Gulas, 'The impact of humor in advertising: A review', *Journal of Advertising*, 21(4), December 1992, pp. 35–59.
33. Barbara Stern and Judith Lynne Zaichowsky, 'The impact of "entertaining" advertising on consumer responses', *Australian Marketing Researcher*, 14(1), 1991, pp. 68–80.
34. Jessica Severn, George E. Belch and Michael A. Belch, 'The effects of sexual and non-sexual advertising appeals and information level on cognitive processing and communication effectiveness', *Journal of Advertising*, 19(1), 1990, pp. 14–22.
35. Michael S. LaTour, Robert E. Pitts and David C. Snook-Luther, 'Female nudity, arousal and ad response: An experimental investigation', *Journal of Advertising*, 19(4), 1990, pp. 51–62.
36. Each year the Commercial Economic Advisory Service of Australia publishes figures on main media spending. These figures based on calendar year 1994. See <www.ceasa.com.au> (29 February 2004).
37. Joseph C. Philport and Jerry Arbittier, 'Advertising brand communications styles in established media and the Internet', *Journal of Advertising Research*, 37(2), March–April 1997, pp. 68–76.
38. For example, Michael T. Ewing, Erik Du Plessis and Charles Foster, 'Cinema advertising re-considered', *Journal of Advertising Research,* January/February 2001, pp. 78–85; Michelle R. Nelson, 'Recall of brand

placements in computer/video games', *Journal of Advertising Research*, March/April 2002, pp. 80–92.
39. Colin McDonald, 'From "frequency" to "continuity"—is it a new dawn?', *Journal of Advertising Research*, 37(4), July–August 1997, pp. 21–25.
40. George B. Murray and John R. Jenkins, 'The concept of "effective reach" in advertising', *Journal of Advertising Research*, May/June 1992, pp. 34–42.
41. Mary C. Gilly and Mary Wolfinbarger, 'Advertising's internal audience', *Journal of Marketing*, 62, January 1998, pp. 69–88 and Stewart Shapiro et al., 'The effects of incidental ad exposure on the formation of consideration sets', *Journal of Consumer Research*, 24, June 1997, pp. 94–104.
42. David Glen Mick, 'Levels of subjective comprehension in advertising processing and their relations to ad perceptions, attitudes and memory', *Journal of Consumer Research*, 18, 1992, pp. 411–424.
43. Jean Harrison-Walker, 'The import of illiteracy to marketing communication', *Journal of Consumer Marketing*, 12, 1, 1995, pp. 50–64.
44. William R. Swinyard, 'The effects of mood, involvement, and quality of store experience on shopping intentions', *Journal of Consumer Research*, 20, September 1993, pp. 271–280.
45. Mahima Mathur and Amitava Chattopadhyay, 'The impact of moods generated by television programs on responses to advertising', *Psychology & Marketing*, 8(1), 1991, pp. 59–77.
46. Michel Tuan Pham, 'Cue representation and selection effects of arousal on persuasion', *Journal of Consumer Research*, 22, March 1996, pp. 373–387.
47. <www.choice.com.au> (1 January 2004).
48. <www.adma.com.au/asp/index.asp?pgid=2001> (29 February 2004).
49. <www.australianmade.com.au> (26 January 2004).
50. For an extensive review of research in this area, see Leonard M. Lodish, Magid Abraham, Stuart Kalmenson, Jeanne Livelsberger, Beth Lubetkin, Bruce Richardson and Mary Ellen Stevens, 'How TV advertising works: A meta analysis of 389 real world split cable experiments', *Journal of Marketing Research*, 32(2), 1995, pp. 125–139.
51. John Roberts and Garry Haberecht, 'Improving the effectiveness of promotional expenditures using scanner data', *Australian Marketing Researcher*, 13(1), 1990, pp. 3–17.
52. See Max Sutherland, *Advertising and the Mind of the Consumer: What Works, What Doesn't and Why* (Sydney: Allen & Unwin, 1993).
53. John Rossiter and Rob Donovan, 'Why you shouldn't test ads in focus groups', *Australian Marketing Researcher* 7(2), 1983, pp. 43–48; Robert Sherr, 'The pre-testing of TV commercials: An empirical study', same issue, pp. 29–42.
54. See <www.oztam.com.au> (television), <www.nielsenmedia.com.au> (radio), <www.hitwise.com.au> (Internet ratings) and <www.roymorgan.com> (readership). Roy Morgan Research offers a *Single Source* service which produces usage information on all main media, plus the Internet for each individual.
55. Robert Madrigal, 'The influence of social alliances with sports teams on intentions to purchase corporate sponsors' products', *Journal of Advertising,* 29, Winter 2000, pp. 13–24.
56. Pamela Kicker and Cathy L. Hartman, 'Purchase pal use: Why buyers choose to shop with others', in *1993 AMA Winter Educators' Proceedings*, 4, eds Rajan Varadarajan and Bernard Jaworski (Chicago: American Marketing Association, 1993), pp. 378–384.
57. Eve M. Kahn and Julie Lasky, 'Out of the pantry and partying on', *The New York Times*, 8 November 2001, p. F9.
58. <www.whirlpool.net.au> (6 March 2004). A site where consumers can get information about broadband services and where consumers can air their grievances (and delights) about broadband service providers.
59. Cara Okleshen and Sanford Grossbart, 'Usenet groups, virtual community and consumer behaviour', in *Advances in Consumer Research*, 25, eds Joseph W. Alba and J. Wesley Hutchinson (Provo, UT: Association for Consumer Research, 1998), pp. 276–282.
60. Birud Sindhav, 'A sociological perspective on web-related consumer marketing', *Proceedings of the Summer Educators Conference* (Chicago: American Marketing Association, 1999), pp. 226–227. S. Elizabeth Bird, 'Chatting on Cynthia's porch: Creating community in an e-mail fan group', *Southern Communication Journal,* (65)1, Fall 1999, pp. 49–65.
61. John Harney, 'Cyber bazaars', *IntelligentKM*, 8 March 2001, pp. 58–62.
62. 'Startec acquires Chinese web community', *PR Newswire* (7 March 2000), p. 1.
63. Eileen Fischer, Julia Bristor and Brenda Gainer, 'Creating or escaping community? An exploratory study of Internet consumers' behaviours', *Advances in Consumer Research*, 23 (Provo, UT: Association for Consumer Research, 1996), pp. 178–182; Siok Kuan Tambyah, 'Life

on the Net: The reconstruction of self and community', *Advances in Consumer Research*, 23 (Provo, UT: Association for Consumer Research, 1996), pp. 172–177.

64. Albert M. Muniz Jr and Thomas C. O'Guinn, 'Brand community', *Journal of Consumer Research,* 27, March 2001, pp. 412–432.
65. See <www.harleydavidson.com> and <www.mgcc.com.au> (6 March 2004).
66. James H. McAlexander, John W. Schouten and Harold F. Koenig, 'Building brand community', *Journal of Marketing,* 66, January 2002, pp. 38–54.
67. B. Zafer Erdogan, Michael J. Baker and Stephen Tagg, 'Selecting celebrity endorsers: The practitioner's perspective', *Journal of Advertising Research,* May/June 2001, pp. 39–48.
68. David Nielsen, 'Tiger on verge of becoming No. 1 pitchman in sports', *Cincinnati Post*, 21 June 2000, p. 8B.
69. Roobina Ohanian, 'The impact of celebrity spokespersons: Perceived image on consumers' intention to purchase', *Journal of Advertising Research*, February–March 1991, pp. 46–54.
70. Carolyn Tripp, Thomas D. Jensen and Les Carlson, 'The effects of multiple product endorsements by celebrities on consumers' attitudes and intentions', *Journal of Consumer Research*, 20, March 1994, pp. 535–547; and David C. Bojanic, Patricia K. Voli and James B. Hunt, 'Can consumers match celebrity endorsers with products?', in *Developments in Marketing Science*, ed. Robert L. King (Richmond, VA: Academy of Marketing Science, 1991), pp. 303–307.
71. David H.B. Bednall and Anthony Collings, 'Effect of public disgrace on celebrity endorser value', *Australasian Journal of Marketing*, 8(2), 2000, pp. 47–57.
72. Richard Morin, 'When celebrity endorsers go bad', *The Washington Post,* 3 February 2002, p. B5.
73. Margaret F. Callcott and Wei-Na Lee, 'Establishing the spokes-character in academic inquiry: Historical overview and framework for definition', in *Advances in Consumer Research*, 22, eds Frank R. Kardes and Mita Sujan (Provo, UT: Association for Consumer Research, 1995), pp. 144–151.
74. Andrea Petersen, 'If product's invisible, can it be placed?', *Wall Street Journal,* 9 April 2001, p. B1.
75. Source MINDSET™. Devised in conjunction with Colin Benjamin of the Horizon Network.
76. Tony Schwartz, *The Responsive Chord* (New York: Doubleday, 1974).

CHAPTER 9

The family

GRANDIS
MITSUBISHI MOTORS
engineered to excite
FURNITURE
New Mitsubishi Grandis.
Soon as you see it you'll want to start a family.
At Mitsubishi we are pleased to announce the arrival of the new seven - seater Grandis. At its heart lies a 2.4 litre engine with revolutionary MIVEC technology. Fathered by Mitsubishi's rally cars, MIVEC delivers better fuel economy and more power;* an impressive 121kW. Add to that an automatic transmission with Sports Mode sequential control and it really moves. Grandis is also the first car in its class with front, side and curtain airbags as standard. It has a unique 'Hide and Seat' interior where the 6th and 7th seats fold underneath the floor and a host of storage compartments. So before you start up a family, start up a Grandis at your Mitsubishi dealer. Call us on 1300 13 12 11 or visit www.mitsubishi-motors.com.au
*than an equivalent, non-MIVEC equipped engine.

Source: Courtesy of Mitsubishi Motors Australia Ltd.

The family as a social unit has a major influence on the behaviour of its members, particularly consumption-related behaviours. The family is where our training as consumers begins, and continues to develop for sometime. As an entity, families are also the major consumption units within any society. Traditionally the family has been the focus of much marketing effort, and the household continues to be an important consuming unit for many products and services. Marketers are interested in the number and kinds of households that own and/or buy certain products. They are also interested in determining the demographic and media profiles of the household *decision maker* (the person involved in the actual selection of the product) in order to develop appropriate marketing strategies.

There are many examples of how the family influences the consumption behaviour of its members. A child learns how to eat lollies by observing an older brother or sister, and comes to understand the use and value of money by listening to and watching parents. Decisions about a new car, holidays or the merits of different educational institutions are consumer decisions usually made within the context of a family setting. The family commonly provides the opportunity for product exposure and trial, and imparts consumption values to its members. As a major consumption unit, the family is a prime target for the marketing of many products and services.

To determine how the family makes its purchase decisions and how the family affects the future purchase behaviour of its members, it is useful to understand the structure, processes and the roles played by family members, to fulfil their consumption needs. The chapter will examine the roles of husband, wife and the parent-children in the purchase decision-making process.

Foundations of the family

Although the term 'family' is a basic concept, used in everyday language, the structure, composition and functions of the family are not as easy to understand as one might assume. This is so because of the complex roles played by family members and the fact that such roles vary considerably from culture to culture. Even in Australia, considerable diversity in types of families exists. Figure 9.1 captures the diversity in Australian families, indicating the variety that exists in contemporary families. The **family** is a subset of the more general and encompassing classification, the household. Traditionally, a family has been defined as *two or more people related by blood, marriage or adoption who reside together in the same household.* In a more dynamic sense, the individuals who constitute a family might be described as members of the most basic social group, who live together and interact to satisfy their personal and mutual needs. From a consumer behaviour perspective, these needs include the consumption of products and services. Though families are sometimes referred to as **households**, not all households are families. For example, a household might include individuals who are not

FIGURE 9.1 Advertisement showing the diversity of Australian families

Source: **Courtesy of Mitsubishi Electric.**

related by blood, marriage or adoption, such as unmarried couples, family friends, room-mates or boarders. These are referred to as group households.

Over the last three decades, the structure of Australian families has changed considerably and Table 9.1 shows further predicted changes in the three household types. An important point for marketers is that we are seeing a decrease in the traditional family in Australia—they made up 72.5% of the population in 1996 but are predicted to fall to 67.55% in 2021. However, other non-traditional family structures are emerging and, in particular, lone-person households are predicted to increase as a percentage of overall households.[1] These changes have an important impact on the behaviour of consumers and the strategies of marketers, because the family is a major consumption unit within our society. In most Western societies, three types of families dominate: the married couple, the nuclear family, and the extended family.

Important demographic changes reflect the dynamic nature of the family. For example, marriage customs in Australia are changing, and the age at which people are getting married for the first time continues to rise, while the marriage rate for teenagers is now at an all-time low. Fewer people are opting for traditional marriage and the number of de facto unions continues to rise. The divorce rate has also risen, as has the proportion of remarriages and single-parent families.[2] There has, in Australia, been a decline in family households from 1991 when 72.7% of all households were families to 2001 where 70.31% of households were families. Interestingly, the proportion of lone-person households rose from 19.3% in 1991 to 25.21% in 2001. Household sizes are also projected to decline across many countries, as indicated in Table 9.2. These trends have important implications for marketers who target families, as they are an important consumer group.

TABLE 9.1 Projected household percentages by type

	1996 %	2001 %	2006 %	2011 %	2016 %	2021 %
Family households	72.50	70.31	69.08	68.33	68.00	67.55
Group households	4.36	4.49	4.49	4.43	4.29	4.09
Lone-person households	23.14	25.21	26.42	27.23	27.71	28.36
Total	100.00	100.00	100.00	100.00	100.00	100.00

Source: **Based on *Household and Family Projections Australia 1996 to 2021*, Australian Bureau of Statistics, 1999, Catalogue No. 3236.0 (Series B: Low rate of change).**

TABLE 9.2 Projected household growth (selected countries)

Country	Projected average annual household growth rate %	Average household size 1996 no.	Average household size 2011 no.
Australia	1.4	2.6	2.3
Canada	1.6	2.7	2.5
New Zealand	1.2	2.9	2.7
England	0.6	2.4	2.3
United States	1.1	2.6	2.5

Source: **Based on *Household and Family Projections Australia 1996 to 2021*, Australian Bureau of Statistics, 1999, Catalogue No. 3236.0.**

Over the last three decades, the family in Australia has undergone significant changes that will continue to affect household composition for many years. While there is no single cause behind the structural changes occurring in the Australian family, it is clear that changing social attitudes (to work, marriage, sex and other social issues) have played a critical role and are likely to continue impacting on the family in the years to come. This is partly due to increasing divorce rates, separation and out-of-wedlock births, and a general decline in the number of marriages. The number of **single-parent family** households (consisting of one parent and at least one child) has grown. Importantly for marketers, there has also been a widening of the concept of family to include same-sex couples. Non-family households have also grown in number, for both single-person households (those who live alone) and group households (households consisting of two or more people who are unrelated, e.g. university students sharing a house).

Such social trends have influenced changes to the law—for example, the Commonwealth *Sex Discrimination Act 1984* and *Child Care Act 1991*. Also important are the economic changes of the last two decades. The initial rise in interest rates in the 1980s, the recession and the decline in real earnings for individuals in the latter half of the 1980s, together with changing community attitudes, have given rise to increasing female labour force participation. The subsequent fall in interest rates has also impacted significantly on the buyer behaviour of families. The extent to which these changes will affect the form of Australian families in the next decade and the mechanisms by which this will occur are matters of ongoing interest to marketers, consumer researchers and policy makers.

In Australia, the majority of households are families with two or more people in them and are of four main types:

- couple only families
- two-parent families
- one-parent families
- other families.

The *couple only* family is generally representative of a newly-married couple who have no children yet, or older couples who have already raised their children. A two-parent family includes a husband, wife and one or more children and constitutes the **nuclear family** which is still the cornerstone of family life. The nuclear family, when living together with at least one grandparent in the household, is called an **extended family**. This three-generation family, which at one time was most representative of the family, has become comparatively less common in Australia than in developing countries in regions such as Asia and South America. In particular, the incidence of the extended family has suffered in Australia because of the geographic mobility that was commonplace among young people during the 1970s and 1980s and is still a major occurrence in Australian society. The one-parent family represents those families which are headed by a single parent (female or male) and have one or more children.

The family as a social institution is now viewed outside the traditional framework of marriage. From 1987 to the present we have seen a reduction of the marriage rate in Australia.[3] While the structural changes are not dramatic, they correspond with an ongoing social change where people choose to enter into de facto relationships or to live alone. However, the number of traditional families is still substantially greater than that of emerging non-traditional families and will continue to be so. A survey of US homemakers reported that, in 1990, more than 23 million (21.6%) of the 109 million homemakers were adult males.[4] This trend is expected to continue to rise and both in countries such as the US and Australia single homemakers are expected to play an increasingly important part in marketers' plans in the future. As indicated in Table 9.3 the forecasts show that, while there is projected growth in the lone-person and group household, the family is still predicted to dominate the social landscape in Australia.

TABLE 9.3 Classification of trends by family and household type

Family and household type	1996 %	2001 %	2006 %	2011 %	2016 %	2021 %
Couples/families with children	49.13	45.76	43.58	41.91	40.95	40.14
Couples/families without children	34.32	36.50	38.24	39.85	41.07	42.08
Single-parent families	14.68	15.94	16.39	16.47	16.27	16.13
Other families	1.87	1.81	1.79	1.76	1.71	1.65
Total families	100.00	100.00	100.00	100.00	100.00	100.00
Group households	4.36	4.49	4.49	4.43	4.29	4.09
Lone-person households	23.14	25.21	26.42	27.23	27.71	28.36

Source: **Based on *Household and Family Projections Australia 1996 to 2021*, Australian Bureau of Statistics, 1999, Catalogue No. 3236.0 (Series B: Low rate of change).**

Functions of the family

The family performs four basic functions—family-member socialisation, economic well-being, emotional support and provision of a family lifestyle, all of which are important to the study of consumer behaviour.

SOCIALISATION OF FAMILY MEMBERS

The **socialisation** of family members, ranging from young children to adults, is a central function of the family. In large part, this process consists of imparting to children (and other family members) the basic values and modes of behaviour consistent with the culture. Socialisation skills (manners, goals, values and other qualities) are imparted to a child directly through instruction, and indirectly through observation of the behaviour of parents and older siblings. These generally include moral and religious principles, interpersonal skills, dress and grooming standards, appropriate manners and speech, and the selection of suitable educational, occupational and career goals. To illustrate how this socialisation responsibility is expanding, parents are increasingly anxious to see their children possess adequate computer skills, almost before they can talk or walk—as early as 12 months after birth. Because parents are so interested in their young children learning to use a computer, hardware and software developers are rapidly creating products targeted at parents seeking to buy such items for their young children. Marketers often target parents looking for assistance in the task of socialising pre- and post-adolescent children. To this end marketers are sensitive to the fact that the socialisation of young children provides an opportunity to establish a foundation on which later experiences continue to build throughout life.

Consumer socialisation

Consumer socialisation is the process by which people acquire skills, knowledge, attitudes and preferences relevant to their own functioning and participation in the marketplace. Consumer socialisation has two distinct components: socialisation *directly* related to consumption, such as the acquisition of skills, knowledge and attitudes concerned with budgeting, pricing and brand attitudes; and socialisation *indirectly* related to consumption, such as the underlying motivations that spur a youth to purchase his first razor or a young girl to want her first bra. Both types of socialisation are significant. The indirect component of consumer socialisation specific to individual product categories is of more interest to marketers, who want to understand *why* people buy their products. The direct component of consumer socialisation is often of greatest interest to academic consumer behaviour researchers, who have broader goals of understanding all aspects of consumer behaviour.

Child consumer socialisation

Society teaches children marketplace behaviour via the family unit, where they learn about consuming and purchasing from parents and siblings. Importantly, while the mass media have a persuasive impact on what children see and hear about products and their consumption, it is still the family that is instrumental in teaching children the fundamental aspects of purchasing and consumption. Many children acquire their consumer behaviour norms through observation of their parents, who function as role models. While pre-adolescent children tend to rely on their parents and older siblings as the major source of cues for basic consumption learning, teenagers are likely to look to their friends and peers as models of consumer behaviour.[5] Marketers today are paying more attention to the influence of children in family decision-making. With a majority of mothers in the work force, large numbers of Australian children are becoming 'latchkey kids' (children with no parent at home after school). These children take on the responsibility for buying products such as food. As a result, children become the prime purchasers of a wide variety of products, even though parents are often still the ultimate decision makers.

Figure 9.2 presents a simple model of the socialisation process that focuses on the socialisation of young children, but can be extended to family members of all ages. Note that the arrows run both ways between the young person and other family members, and between the young person and his or her friends. These two-directional arrows signify that socialisation is really a two-way process, in which young people undergo socialisation themselves, but also influence those who are doing the socialising. It must be remembered that the child often influences the opinions and behaviour of parents. For example, a fashion-conscious teenager

FIGURE 9.2 **A simple model of the socialisation process**

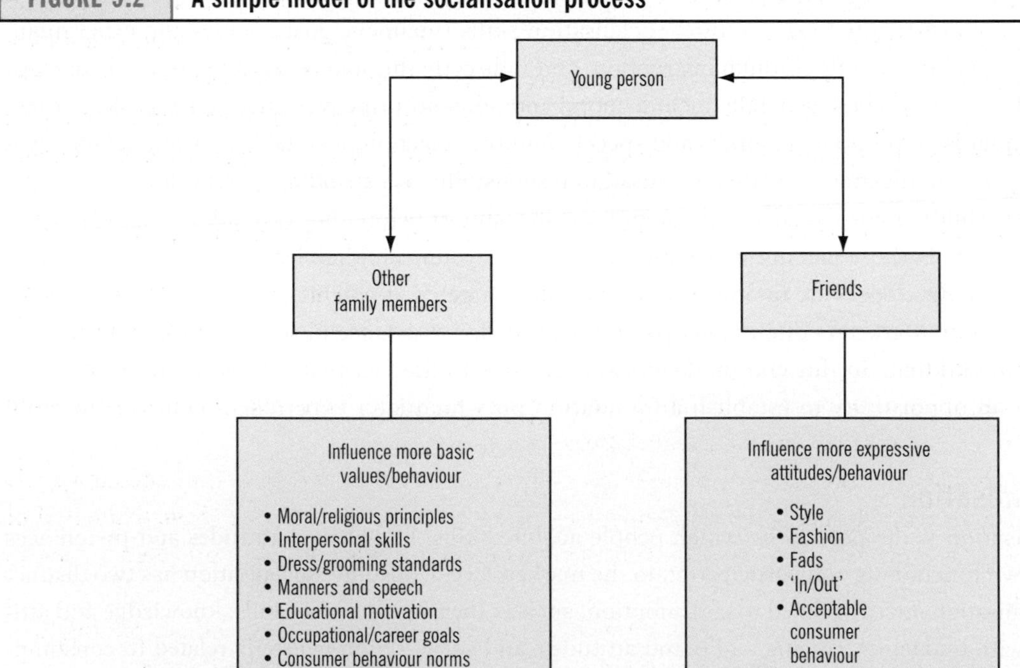

responding to peer pressure will endeavour to persuade her parents to buy a brand name product like Doc Marten boots.

However, children are still constantly exposed to parents' views on which products are of value, what advertising is good and what attitudes and behaviours to accept or reject. We also have to realise that children are often exposed to the same media influences and programming as their parents. For example, pre-teens will often share the same television experience as their parents, a fact that can be quite useful for marketers when targeting children. Several years of research indicates that children are increasingly knowledgeable about the purpose of advertising and the media in general. Programs such as *Neighbours*, *Home and Away* or any of a dozen television shows that are popular with Australian children—including American programs such as *Eight Simple Rules* and *Seventh Heaven*—include aspects of storylines where subtle product marketing exists. Children will look to the key characters as role models in terms of hairstyle, type of clothing worn, the food and beverages consumed and even the music playing in the background. For example, companies such as Kellogg's and Coca-Cola paid large sums of money to shows such as *Seinfeld* (when it was in production) to have their products displayed and used by the actors in the series. In terms of cultural change, many young Australians are now influenced by the fashions, trends and values of the youth culture in the United States. The concept of Australian 'street kids' is one expression of the transmission of an influential genre of street culture influenced by black culture, rap music, sport and war games from the United States. The traditional 'Aussie' icons of the country and rural outback have been dramatically superseded by life in the fast lane and toughing it out. Ultimately, the youth market is one that advertisers need continually to re-evaluate, given that children have greater access to information and choices than their parents.

The role of parents (and parental communication) in the consumer socialisation of children has been the focus of a number of studies. It has been found that children from families characterised by a more open conceptual style of communication had more consumer-related knowledge. They were better able to filter puffery in advertising and to manage budgets, and were more knowledgeable about products. Children from families characterised by more socially oriented communication tended to rely more on peer groups and mass media sources than their parents. Such findings seem to indicate that parents are the main source of consumer socialisation for children when they encourage communication and independence in children; while peer groups and television are stronger sources of socialisation when parents encourage obedience and deference in their children.[6]

Another study identified four important family types in the child consumer socialisation process.[7]

1. *Authoritarian parents*: seek a high level of control over their children and expect unquestioned obedience. They attempt to shield their children from outside influences and are more likely to engage in socially oriented communication.
2. *Neglecting parents*: are distant from their children and do not exert much control over them. Minimal effort is undertaken to encourage their children's capabilities.
3. *Democratic parents*: foster a balance between the rights of parents and their children. They encourage self-expression and autonomy. They are warm and supportive, but expect mature behaviour from their children and use discipline as a mechanism to punish. It is the democratic parents who are more likely to engage in conceptually oriented communication.
4. *Permissive parents*: seek to remove as many restraints from their children as possible, without putting them in danger. This parental style believes that children have adult rights but few responsibilities.

It appears that democratic and, to a lesser extent, permissive parents have the most active roles in children's socialisation as consumers. These parents tend to shop with their children and are more likely to seek their advice on consumption decisions compared with authoritarian and neglecting parents. Democratic parents are also more likely to view television with their children, express more concern about advertising to their children and attempt to control television viewing habits. Authoritarian parents place the most restrictions on children's consumer behaviour.

A further study also found four family types: (1) *tactical families*, where issues are open for discussion but where parents retain control; (2) *easygoing families*, where parents agree with their children most of the time; (3) *autocratic families*, where parents have authority and power; and (4) *malleable families*, where children get what they want if they are persistent.[8] The implication of such research is that, without proper analysis to determine the makeup of a marketplace, shopping centre managers and retailers are unable to match their marketing communications to the appropriate decision maker and decision-making processes within families. An important finding of this study is that the families who most involve children in consumer-related behaviours are also most concerned about advertising to children. Marketers should try to increase the integrity of advertising in the eyes of this type of family, by providing more information on the features and characteristics of the product/brand. Such features would include, for example, food products identifying nutrition value and toys with product-safety issues. This would alleviate some of the concerns of democratic parents by showing the positive aspects of advertising in aiding the consumer socialisation of children.

Shared shopping experiences (i.e. co-shopping—when a parent and child shop together) give children the opportunity to acquire in-store shopping skills. Possibly because of their busier lifestyles, working mothers are more likely to shop with their children than non-working mothers.[9] Shopping is also a way of spending time with one's children while at the same time accomplishing a necessary task. Through this socialisation process, children learn how to shop, how to evaluate the attributes of the store or product, and even how to select brands; and they will either learn that shopping is a chore or that it is fun depending largely on how their parents perceive shopping. As children mature they learn about money, and the different ways of paying, through shopping experiences with their parents. In addition, parents frequently use the promise or reward of material goods as a method of modifying or controlling a child's behaviour. A parent may reward their child if the child does something to please them, or withhold or remove the reward if the child disobeys.

Whether the agents of the socialisation process are family members, peers or the media, several consequences result from the process. Children can and often do simply adopt products or specific brands through encountering or seeing them in use by family members, friends or in the media. Children can also learn that certain products and brands are available at specific retail outlets, that certain products and brands have features that others do not and that some retailers are more expensive than others.

Adult consumer socialisation

The socialisation process is not confined to childhood; rather, it is an ongoing process. It is now accepted that socialisation begins in early childhood and continues throughout a person's entire life. For example, when a newly-married couple establishes a household, their adjustment to living and consuming together is part of this continuing process. Similarly, the adjustment (to the State's way of life) of a retired couple who decide to move to Queensland is also part of the ongoing socialisation process. As such, the model of the socialisation process depicted in Figure 9.2 is also relevant to understanding older consumers.

Such directionality across the generations is seen in the intergenerational influences of consumer behaviour. *Intergenerational* consumer behaviour influences means 'across or between generations' and refers to those aspects of purchasing and consumption that are passed from parents to children and vice versa. Research into intergenerational influences suggests that this effect is stronger for convenience goods, has a similar effect across males and females, and declines with ageing. Further, intergenerational effects on consumer behaviour are stronger for extended families than the more conventional nuclear families that exist in Australia.[10]

ECONOMIC WELL-BEING

Financial security is a basic function of the family. How the family divides its responsibilities for the provision of economic security and prosperity has changed considerably over the past three decades. The traditional roles of husband as the economic provider and wife as homemaker and child-rearer have changed dramatically. Most married women in Australia are employed outside the home and married men now share more of the household responsibilities.[11] These changes to the economic character and input of husband and wife in the family have altered the buying behaviour of many families—particularly in regard to which partner makes the financial contribution and performs the buying tasks, and the nature of the purchases made. The economic role of children has also changed considerably. Today many teenage children work, but they rarely assist the family financially. Instead, many teenagers are expected to pay for some of their clothes and their entertainment. Others are expected to contribute to the costs of their formal education and prepare themselves to be financially independent.

EMOTIONAL SUPPORT

An important function of the family is to provide emotional support (including love, affection and intimacy) to its members. In fulfilling this function, the family provides support and encouragement and assists its members to cope with personal and social problems.[12] A fairly recent development that has affected family dynamics is the recognition of a need to link family issues to working life. Australian companies are participating in programs to help provide for employees as caregivers. This has meant introducing flexible work hours, working from home, and casual, part-time and contract work to allow employees time to fulfil their other (emotional) responsibilities. Flexibility in working hours allows parents to attend school concerts, sports events and open days, enabling them to demonstrate love and support for their children. Many companies now target the emotional role of family members in their social interactions with each other. The loss of a loved one, for example, can be very distressing; to alleviate this aspect Australian InsuranceLine promotes its product with an appeal to the emotional comfort and support that their insurance brings to the family at a time of loss. The firm Kiddisafe also uses the emotional support of making parents feel at ease with aspects of their range of learn-to-swim products.

PROVISION OF FAMILY LIFESTYLE

Another important family function in terms of consumer behaviour is the establishment of a suitable lifestyle for the family. Upbringing, experience and the personal and jointly held goals of the spouses determine the importance placed on education or career, on reading and television viewing, on the frequency and quality of dining out, and on the selection of other entertainment and recreational activities. Family lifestyle commitments, including the allocation of time, greatly influence consumption patterns. For example, the increase in the number of married women working outside the home has reduced the time they have available for household duties, and created a market for convenience products, fast-food restaurants and domestic home help. Also, with both parents working, increased emphasis is placed on the notion of *quality time*, rather than the *quantity of time*, spent with children and other family members. Time pressure as an issue has the potential to impact marketplace behaviour. The notion of time and feeling pressured may influence our behaviour in the context of family activities and what products and services we buy. Importantly, the feeling of time pressure does differ across life stages as shown in Table 9.4.

Researchers have identified a shift in the nature of family 'togetherness'. Whereas a family being together once meant doing things together; today it means being in the same household with each person doing his or her own thing.[13] Realising the scarcity of quality time, some innovative retailers have positioned their

TABLE 9.4 Life stage and time pressure

Life stage	Always/often %	Sometimes %	Rarely/never %	Not stated %
Couples with dependent children	53.4	32.7	9.4	4.5
Couples with non-dependent children (15 and over)	36.7	36.1	23.5	3.9
Lone parents	41.3	31.2	22.6	4.9
Couples without children	25.2	33.4	36.5	4.9
Lone persons	17.2	33.2	45.8	3.8
Neither parent nor partner (in family household)	28.0	43.8	25.1	3.2

***Source:* *How Australians Use Their Time*, Australian Bureau of Statistics 1998, 4153.0.**

products and services as providers of such quality time. Pizza Hut targets families for an evening out and many shopping malls are now designed for the 'family shopping experience', making such an experience part of the lifestyle of families as consumer units. The family is an important market for many retailers and restaurants, who plan their strategies around appealing to the family and their lifestyle needs.[14]

➤ The family life cycle

The concept of the family life cycle is based on the notion of a progression of stages through which the majority of families pass. There will, of course, be exceptions and the exact timing of each stage will differ across individuals. Nevertheless, all people are born into, and almost all people grow up through, some form of family structure. The four functions discussed earlier are interrelated with the family life-cycle stages. A family's needs, spending patterns and lifestyle are affected by such factors as the number of people (adults and children) in the family unit, the ages and employment status of its members and their economic, social, emotional and lifestyle needs.

The **family life cycle (FLC)** has been utilised by consumer researchers and marketers as a way to classify family units into meaningful stages to examine their purchase and consumption behaviour. The FLC is a composite variable created by systematically combining such commonly used demographic variables as marital status, size of family, age of family members (usually oldest or youngest child) and employment status of the head of household. The ages of the parents and the relative amount of disposable income are usually inferred from the stage in the family life cycle. FLC analysis is a strategic tool that enables marketers to segment families into a series of stages spanning the life course of a family unit and thereby understand their purchasing and consumption behaviour.

Our treatment of the family life-cycle concept focuses first on the traditional family life-cycle perspective that has dominated most of the thinking about the FLC and, second, on alternative family life-cycle stages, including the increasingly important non-traditional family structure.

TRADITIONAL FAMILY LIFE CYCLE

The family life cycle is generally acknowledged to start with *singles*, moving on to *marriage* (and creation of the basic family unit), then to *family growth* (with the birth of children), to *family contraction* (as grown children leave the household) and ends with the *dissolution* of the basic unit (due to the death of one spouse). Although different researchers have expressed various preferences in terms of the number of FLC stages, the traditional FLC models that have been proposed over the years can be synthesised into five basic stages.

Stage I	Young singles	a young single adult living apart from parents
Stage II	Young marrieds	a young married couple
Stage III	Parenthood	a married couple with at least one child living at home
Stage IV	Post-parenthood	an older married couple with no children living at home
Stage V	Dissolution	one surviving spouse

Spending patterns will vary by type of household depending on the age of the household members, their marital status and whether there are children in the home. Importantly, for marketers, spending patterns and consumption will change as a household develops and the family changes its structure or composition during the family life-cycle stages.

STAGE I: YOUNG SINGLES

The young singles FLC stage consists of young single men and women who have established households apart from their parents. Most young singles are employed, although many are tertiary students who have left their parents' homes and often share housing with other young singles. Young single adults are apt to spend their incomes on rent, basic home furnishings, the purchase and maintenance of cars, travel and entertainment, and clothing and accessories. They frequently have sufficient disposable income to indulge themselves.

Marketers target young singles for a wide variety of products and services. In most large cities, one can find travel agents, housing developments, health clubs, sports clubs, and so forth, that find this FLC stage a lucrative target market for products and services. It is relatively easy to reach this segment, since many special-interest publications cater to them. For example, *Inside Sport*, *GQ*, *Men's Health* and *Penthouse* are directed to a young, sophisticated, single male audience, while *Cosmopolitan* and *Cleo* are directed to young single females.

Marriage marks the transition from the young singles stage to the young marrieds stage. Engaged and soon-to-be-married couples are the target for many products and services (the bridal industry is an incredible spending market).

STAGE II: YOUNG MARRIEDS

The young marrieds stage starts immediately after the marriage vows and generally continues until the arrival of the first child. Because many young husbands and wives both work, these couples have a high combined disposable income that often permits a pleasure-seeking lifestyle. Young marrieds have considerable start-up expenses in establishing a new home (major and minor appliances, bedroom and living room furniture, carpeting, curtains, dishes, and a host of utensils and accessory items). During this stage, the advice and experience of other married couples are likely to be important to young marrieds. Also an important source of new product information are so-called lifestyle magazines, such as *Better Homes and Gardens, House and Garden* and *Home Beautiful*, coupled with lifestyle TV programs such as *Better Homes and Gardens*, *Backyard Blitz* and *Ground Force*.

Many young marrieds are career-oriented and seeking to create a stable and secure environment in which to start a family. Within the young marrieds stage, some couples will be happy to function along traditional lines where the husband works and the wife maintains the home, while others will prefer to continue their careers despite their marriage.

STAGE III: PARENTHOOD

When a couple has its first child, the young married stage has moved to a close. The parenthood stage (sometimes referred to as the 'full-nest stage') usually extends over more than a 20-year period. Due to its long duration, it is useful to divide this stage into shorter phases—the preschool phase, the primary school phase, the high school phase and the tertiary phase. Throughout these parenthood phases, the interrelationships of family members and the structure of the family gradually change. Figure 9.3 shows an advertisement for Mitsubishi which illustrates the use of young marrieds' movement into parenthood (family) in an appeal to the target market for Mitsubishi Grandis. The financial resources of the family change significantly as one (or both) parent(s) progress in a career, and as child-rearing and educational responsibilities gradually increase and then decrease as children grow and become self-supporting or leave home.

New parents are often now older, better educated and more affluent, and they spend money accordingly. These parents become a target for companies that serve the baby market. They are also an important target for many investment and insurance companies with schemes such as school fees planning. Many magazines cater to the entertainment and information needs of parents and children. The *Australian Women's Weekly* each month presents a children's section, and specific publications such as *Disney Adventure Magazine* and *Winnie the Pooh and Friends* target the sibling market. As children leave home, the family moves into another stage—post-parenthood.

STAGE IV: POST-PARENTHOOD

The post-parent or so-called **empty-nest stage** signifies for many parents either a traumatic or liberating 'rebirth'. It is a time for doing all the things they could not do while the children were at home and had to spend substantial amounts on raising their children.

FIGURE 9.3 Advertisement for Mitsubishi emphasising family appeal

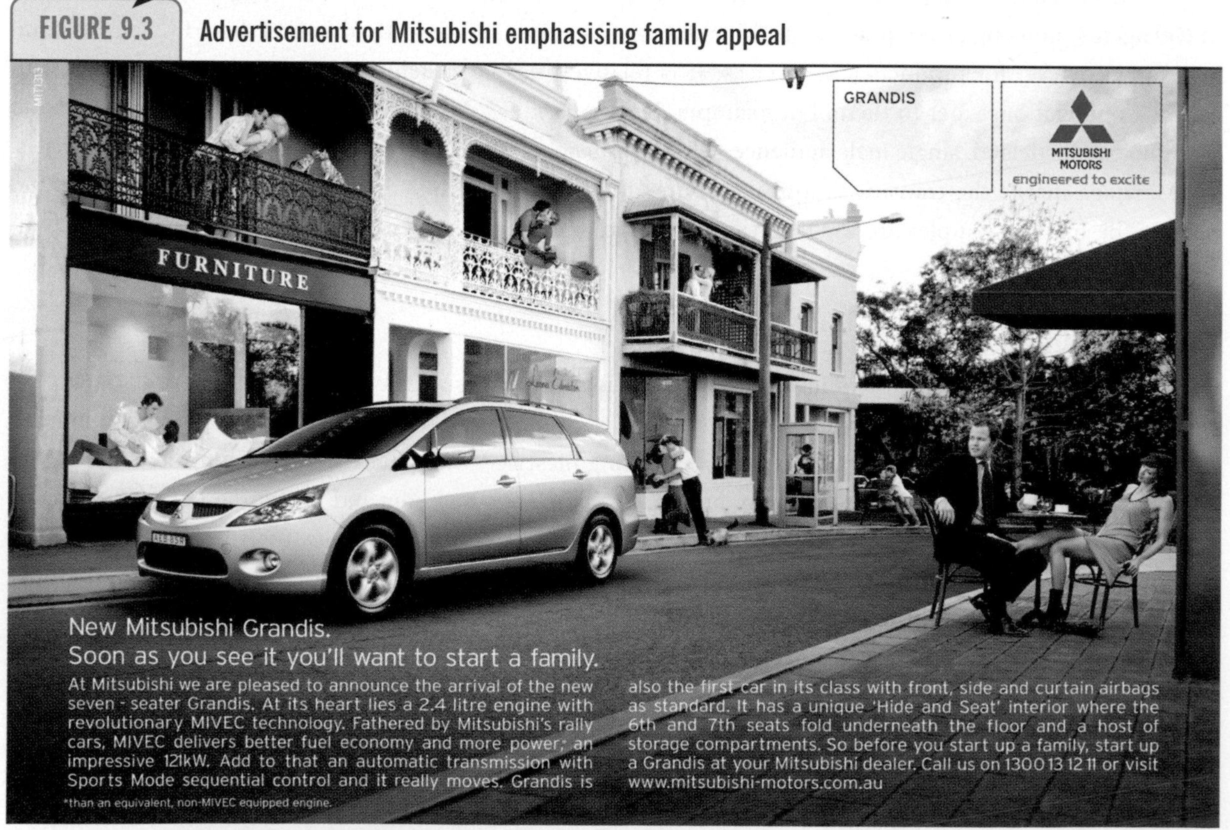
GRANDIS
MITSUBISHI MOTORS
engineered to excite
FURNITURE
New Mitsubishi Grandis.
Soon as you see it you'll want to start a family.
At Mitsubishi we are pleased to announce the arrival of the new seven - seater Grandis. At its heart lies a 2.4 litre engine with revolutionary MIVEC technology. Fathered by Mitsubishi's rally cars, MIVEC delivers better fuel economy and more power; an impressive 121kW. Add to that an automatic transmission with Sports Mode sequential control and it really moves. Grandis is also the first car in its class with front, side and curtain airbags as standard. It has a unique 'Hide and Seat' interior where the 6th and 7th seats fold underneath the floor and a host of storage compartments. So before you start up a family, start up a Grandis at your Mitsubishi dealer. Call us on 1300 13 12 11 or visit www.mitsubishi-motors.com.au
*than an equivalent, non-MIVEC equipped engine.

***Source:* Courtesy of Mitsubishi Motors Australia Ltd.**

It is during this stage that married couples tend to be most comfortable financially. With the option of early retirement, many empty-nesters retire while they are still in good health. Retirement provides the opportunity to pursue new interests, to travel and fulfil unsatisfied needs. The growth in retirement villages with a country club atmosphere or nurturing environment are a direct result of the needs expressed by this group. Today's empty-nesters have more leisure time, travel more frequently, take extended vacations and are often likely to purchase a second home in a warmer part of Australia. In traditional families, for the wife, it is a time to further her education, to enter or re-enter the job market, to seek new interests. For the husband, it is a time to indulge in new hobbies. For both, it is the time to travel, to entertain, perhaps to refurnish their home or to sell it in favour of downsizing to a smaller but more luxurious home or townhouse. They have a higher disposable income because of savings, investments and superannuation earnings, and fewer expenses (no mortgage or school fees). For all these reasons, families in the post-parenthood stage are an important market for luxury goods, such as new cars, expensive furniture and trips to faraway places. Older consumers tend to use television as an important source of information and entertainment. They favour programs that provide the opportunity to 'keep up with things', especially news and current affairs programs. In addition, there are magazines that cater to this market, such as *Family Circle*, *Woman's Day* and *Women's Weekly*. (Chapter 12 contains a more detailed discussion of the older consumer as a subcultural market segment.)

On the other hand, for older couples without adequate savings or income, retirement is a completely different picture, and very restrictive. Some empty-nesters receive a surprise in difficult economic times with the return of an adult child. For almost a decade, there has been a trend for young adults of 18–24 years to return home. There are many reasons behind a return to the 'nest'—completion of university, unemployment, underemployment, desire for more disposable income and a more comfortable lifestyle, separation or divorce. In many cases, the parents (especially mothers) welcome home the returning offspring.[15]

STAGE V: DISSOLUTION

With advancing age, the dissolution of the basic family unit occurs with the death of one spouse. The solitary survivor in the dissolved family experiences distinct changes in consumption behaviour. If the surviving spouse is in good health, is working or has adequate savings, and has a supportive family and friends, the adjustment is easier. The surviving spouse (usually the wife) often tends to follow a more economical lifestyle. Many surviving spouses seek each other out for companionship, while some enter into another marriage.

To complete the discussion of the traditional FLC stages, Table 9.5 presents various product types and the percentages of purchases and use in the family life stages used by Roy Morgan Research, which correspond quite closely to the FLC stages just examined. For example, Table 9.5 shows that young parents and mid-life households are the highest consumers of alcoholic beverages and older households are small consumers of muesli/health bars.

MODIFICATIONS TO THE FLC MODEL

The traditional FLC model outlined above was once typical of the vast majority of Australian families, which tended to progress uniformly through the stages discussed. Today, while the traditional FLC stages are still the most common type of family progression, some researchers have attempted to expand the FLC to give a better picture of the diversity of family and lifestyle arrangements.[16]

The underlying sociodemographic forces that drive the modified FLC model include divorce and later marriages, with and without the presence of children. While greater reality is provided by these subtle inclusions, this modified FLC model (see Figure 9.4) only recognises families that started in marriage—ignoring such single-parent households as unmarried mothers and families formed when one or more single people adopt a child.

family purchase decisions', in Frank R. Kardes and Mita Sujan (eds), *Advances in Consumer Research*, 22 (Provo, UT: Association for Consumer Research, 1995), pp. 723–728.

7. Leah Haran, 'Families together differently today', *Advertising Age*, 23 October 1995, pp. 1–12.
8. N. Brumback, 'Restaurant business', *Family Matters*, No. 47, 1997, pp. 57–58.
9. George P. Moschis, Roy L. Moore and Ruth B. Smith, 'The impact of family communication on adolescent consumer socialisation', in Thomas C. Kinnear (ed.), *Advances in Consumer Research*, 11 (Provo, UT: Association for Consumer Research, 1983), pp. 314–319. See also Les Carlson and Sanford Grossbart, 'Parental style and consumer socialisation of children', *Journal of Consumer Research*, 15, June 1988, pp. 77–94; Scott Ward, 'Consumer socialisation', *Journal of Consumer Research*, 1, September 1974, p. 9; and George P. Moschis and Roy L. Moore, 'Decision making among the young: A socialization perspective', *Journal of Consumer Research*, 6, September 1979, pp. 101–112.
10. George P. Moschis, 'The role of family communication in consumer socialization of children and adolescents', *Journal of Consumer Research*, 11, March 1985, pp. 898–913.
11. Les Carlson and Sanford Grossbart, 'Parental style and consumer socialization of children', *Journal of Consumer Research*, 15, June 1988, pp. 77–94.
12. Subha Narayanan, 'Category type determines who makes the decision', *Retail World*, 50(5), March 1997, p. 7.
13. Sanford Grossbart, Les Carlson and Ann Walsh, 'Consumer socialisation motives for shopping with children', *1988 AMA Educators' Proceedings* (Chicago: American Marketing Association, 1988), p. 78.
14. Larry G. Woodson, Terry L. Childers and Paul R. Winn, 'Intergenerational influences in the purchase of auto insurance', in W. Locander (ed.), *Marketing Look Outward: 1976 Business Proceedings* (Chicago: American Marketing Association, 1976), pp. 43–49; Terry Childers and Ashay Rao, 'The influence of familial and peer-based reference groups on consumer decisions', *Journal of Consumer Research*, 19, September 1992, pp. 198–211; Patriya Tansuhaj, Ellen Foxman and Jong Hee Park, 'Intergenerational differences in product importance perceptions: The role of societal change', *Journal of International Consumer Marketing*, 5(2), pp. 21–38.
15. Christy Fisher, 'It's all in the family: Empty nesters, kids moving back home', *Advertising Age*, 3(56), 27 April 1992; 'Grown children return to flexible mothers', *Wall Street Journal*, 3 March 1991, p. B1; and Alan L. Otten, 'Grown kids at home? Most parents don't mind', *Wall Street Journal*, 26 September 1990, p. B1.
16. Charles M. Schaninger and William D. Danko, 'A conceptual and empirical comparison of alternative household life cycle models', *Journal of Consumer Research*, 19, March 1993, pp. 580–594.
17. Rebecca Valenzuela, 'Costs of children in Australian households', *Family Matters*, No. 53, 1999, pp. 71–76.
18. AMF Campaign Launch, p. 4.
19. T. Colebatch, 'One-wage families are new poor: Study', *The Age*, 5 August 1993, p. 2.
20. Alan R. Andreason, 'Life status changes and changes in consumer preferences and satisfaction', *Journal of Consumer Research*, 11, December 1994, pp. 784–794.
21. Sunil Gupta, Michael Hagerty and John Myers, 'New directions in family decision-making research', in Richard Bagozzi and Alice Tybout (eds), *Advances in Consumer Research*, 10, 1983, pp. 445–450.
22. Janeen Baxter and Mark Western, 'Women's satisfaction with the domestic division of labour', *Family Matters*, No. 47, 1997, pp. 16–20.
23. Ken Dempsey, 'Women's perceptions of fairness and the persistence of an unequal division of housework', *Family Matters*, No. 48, 1997, pp. 15–19.
24. Kim P. Corfman, 'Perceptions of relative influence: Formation and measurement', *Journal of Marketing Research*, 28, May 1991, pp. 125–136. Also see Irene Raj Foster and Richard W. Olshavsky, 'An exploratory study of family decision making using a new taxonomy of family role structure', in Thomas K. Srull (ed.), *Advances in Consumer Research*, 16 (Provo, UT: Association for Consumer Research, 1989), pp. 665–670.
25. JoAnne Stilley Hooper, 'Family financial decision making: Implications for marketing strategy', *Journal of Services Marketing*, 9(1), 1995, pp. 24–32.
26. Amardeep Assar and George S. Bobinski, 'Financial decision making of baby boomer couples', in R. Holman and M. Solomon (eds), *Advances in Consumer Research*, 18 (Provo, UT: Association for Consumer Research, 1991), pp. 657–665.
27. James U. McNeal and Chyon-Hwa Yeh, 'Development of consumer behavior patterns among Chinese children', *Journal of Consumer Marketing*, 14, 1997, pp. 45–59.

28. Gopala Ganesh, 'Spousal influence in consumer decisions: A study of cultural assimilation', *Journal of Consumer Marketing*, 14, 1997, pp. 132–145.

29. See William J. Qualls, 'Toward understanding the dynamics of household decision conflict behavior', in Michael Houston (ed.), *Advances in Consumer Research*, 15 (Provo, UT: Association for Consumer Research, 1988), pp. 442–448; and William J. Qualls, 'Household decision behavior: The impact of husbands' and wives' sex role orientation', *Journal of Consumer Research*, 14, September 1987, pp.264–278. See also Erich Kirchler, 'Spouses' influence strategies in purchase decisions as dependent on conflict type and relationship characteristics', *Journal of Economic Psychology* 11, March 1990, pp. 101–178.

30. James Geary, 'Childhood's end?', *Time*, August 1999, pp. 50–52.

31. Elaine Sherman and Nejdet Delener, 'The impact of demographics on household personal computer purchasing decisions', *Journal of the Academy of Marketing Science*, 15, 1987, pp. 25–32.

32. Dick Lester, 'Cashed-up kids', *Dynamic Small Business*, December–January 1994, p. 13.

33. McCann Monitor Special Report, *Kids Who Spend What?* (Sydney: McCann Information Service, 1994).

34. James U. McNeal, 'The littlest shoppers', *American Demographics,* February 1992, pp. 48–53; and James U. McNeal, 'Planning priorities for marketing to children', *Journal of Business Strategy,* May/June 1991, pp. 12–15.

35. M. Carole Macklin, 'Preschoolers' understanding of the information function of television advertising', *Journal of Consumer Research*, 14, September 1987, pp. 229–239; Mary Ann Stutts and Garland G. Hunnicutt, 'Can young children understand disclaimers in television commercials?', *Journal of Advertising*, 16, 1987, pp. 41–46; and Mariea Grubbs Hoy, 'The toddler years: The missing sample in marketing research with children', in A. Parasuraman, William Bearden et al. (eds), *AMA Educators' Proceedings* (Chicago: American Marketing Association, 1990), pp. 112–117.

36. For relevant American research in this area, see Gerald J. Gorn and Renee Florsheim, 'The effects of commercials for adult products on children', *Journal of Consumer Research*, 11, March 1985, pp. 962–967.

37. Russell Belk, Robert Mayer and Amy Driscoll, 'Children's recognition of consumption symbolism in children's products', *Journal of Consumer Research*, 10, March 1984, pp. 386–397.

38. Angela Jackson, 'Kids use ads to escape: Survey', *Ad News*, 28 January 1994, p. 19.

39. Sally Rawlings, 'Teenage marketing: How to bridge the generation gap', *B&T*, 23 October 1992. See also 'Teenage essentials', *Choice*, June 1996, p. 45.

40. *Harrison Teenpower IV Report*, 1989.

41. Elizabeth S. Moore-Shay and Richard J. Lutz, 'Intergenerational influences on the formation of consumer attitudes and beliefs about the marketplace: Mothers and daughters', in Michael Houston (ed.), *Advances in Consumer Research*, 15, op. cit., pp. 461–467.

CHAPTER 10

Social class and consumer behaviour

NO. 6 ON THE LIST OF
SIGHTS WORTH THE INOCULATIONS

Number 8 is hand feeding fish in Antigua.
Number 7 is hiking through Morocco's Atlas mountain range.
But it's number 6 that will really send shivers down your spine –
with the help of American Express® Membership Rewards®.
Because every time you spend on the Card, you earn points you can exchange
for the flights you want, to countless destinations.
So start dreaming where you'll escape to.
For more ideas on what the Card can do for you, or to apply,
visit americanexpress.com.au/dreams
FOR WHATEVER DREAMS ARE ON YOUR LIST

Source: Courtesy of American Express.

Social class relates to the levels or hierarchy of groups within society. Some forms of class structure or social stratification has existed in all societies throughout human history. Australia has had a reputation for being a relatively **classless society**. However, inspection of the historical evidence shows this has never really been true[1] and few Australians believe it.[2] In addition, there appears to be a growing gap between rich and poor.[3] As an indication of the presence of social classes in Australia, people who are better educated or have more prestigious occupations generally have higher status than people with little education or in less prestigious occupations. For example, the occupations of lawyer or doctor are often more highly valued than those of truck driver or cleaner. Yet all four occupations are necessary for our society's well-being. Moreover, a wide range of differences in values, attitudes and behaviour has been shown to exist among members of different social classes.

This chapter examines issues related to social class and its role in consumer behaviour. The chapter examines the importance of social class for marketers, how it is measured, how members of specific social class groups behave and how social-class-linked attitudes and behaviour influence consumer behaviour.

What is social class?

Although social class can be thought of as a continuum, where individuals in society are placed into social positions, researchers prefer to divide the continuum into a small number of discrete social classes, or **strata**. Within this framework, the concept of social class is used to assign individuals or families to a social class category. Consistent with this practice, **social class** is defined as *the division of members of a society into a hierarchy of distinct status classes, so that members of each class have relatively the same status and members of all other classes have either more or less status.*

To appreciate more fully the complexity of social class, we now briefly consider several underlying concepts.

SOCIAL CLASS AND SOCIAL STATUS

Social class is often measured in terms of **social status**; that is, each social class is defined by the amount of status the members of that class have in comparison with members of other social classes. In social class research, *status* is frequently conceptualised as the relative rankings of members of each social class in terms of specific status factors. For example, relative *wealth* (amount of economic assets), *power* (the degree of personal choice or influence over others) and *prestige* (the degree of recognition received from others) are three popular factors frequently employed in the estimation of social class. When considering consumer behaviour and marketing research, social status is often defined in terms of one or more of the following demographic (socioeconomic) variables: *family income, occupational status* and *educational attainment*. These socioeconomic variables, as expressions of status, are used by marketing practitioners on a daily basis to measure social class and are used in appeals to various market segments.

Social class is hierarchical

Social class categories are usually ranked in a hierarchy ranging from low to high status. Thus, members of a specific social class perceive members of other social classes as having either more or less status than they do. To many people, social class categories suggest that others are either equal to them (about the same social class), superior to them (higher social class) or inferior to them (lower social class).

Within this context, social class membership serves as a reference (or a reference group) for the development of an individual consumer's attitudes and behaviours. In the context of reference groups, members of a specific social class may be expected to turn most often to other members of the same class for cues (or clues) regarding appropriate behaviour. In other cases, members of a particular social class (e.g. upper-lower class) may aspire to advance their social class standing by emulating the behaviour of members of the middle class. To accomplish this goal, they might read middle-class magazines, do middle-class things (such as visit museums and advance their education) and hang out at middle-class restaurants so that they can observe middle-class behaviour.[4] Thus, the middle class becomes a reference group for such upper-lower class individuals. (For a detailed discussion of reference groups see Chapter 8.) Products made for upper-class groups often 'trickle down' to other classes, in cheaper formats. For example, when Mercedes-Benz introduced fluted tail lights on their cars for practical reasons (to reduce the build-up of road grime), makers of cheaper cars emulated the look. When mobile car phones were first introduced into Australia, some people bought plastic replicas for their cars.

The hierarchical aspect of social class is important to marketers. Consumers may purchase certain products because they are favoured by members of their own or a higher social class (e.g. fine French champagne), and they may avoid other products because they perceive them to be lower-class or *down-market* products (such as a digital wristwatch as a dress watch). Therefore, the various social class strata provide a natural basis for market segmentation for many products and services. In many instances, consumer researchers have been able to relate product usage to social class membership.

Marketers can effectively tailor products or services, channels of distribution and promotional messages to the needs and interests of specific social strata (see Figure 10.1, page 332). In using class as a basis for segmentation, the marketer has to assume relative stability in this measure. For example, Australian evidence suggests that class is more stable among men than women.[5]

Researchers often measure social class in terms of social status; that is, they define each social class by the amount of status the members of that class have in comparison with members of other social classes. To better understand how status operates within the minds of consumers, researchers have explored the idea of social comparison theory. According to this social-psychological concept, individuals quite normally compare their own material possessions with those owned by others in order to determine their relative social standing. This is especially important in a marketing society where status is often associated with consumers' purchasing power (or how much can be purchased). Simply stated, individuals with more purchasing power or a greater ability to make purchases have more status. Those who have more restrictions on what they can or cannot buy have less status. Because visible or conspicuous possessions are easy to spot, they especially serve as markers or indicators of one's own status and the status of others. Not surprisingly, recent research confirmed that a key ingredient of status is a consumer's possessions compared with others' similar possessions (possibly one's home versus another person's home). In making such a comparison, an individual consumer might decide to compare himself with someone who is worse off (i.e. a downward comparison) in order to bolster his self-esteem; or alternatively a consumer might elect to compare upward with another consumer 'with more' or some idealised media image (e.g. a beautiful home in a magazine advertisement), which is likely to make the consumer feel somewhat inferior.

A related concept is status consumption—the process by which consumers endeavour to increase their social standing through purchase and consumption of possessions. As the market for status products (and brands) continues to grow, there is a growing need for marketers to identify and understand which consumers especially seek out such status-enhancing possessions, as well as the relationship between status consumption, social class and branding. Such understanding can be enhanced with the measurement of status consumption tendencies using measures such as those below which tap into the use of product to gain status and the belief that some products indicate status:

- Some products are symbols of success.
- Some products are symbols of prestige.
- Some products indicate wealth.
- Some products indicate achievement.
- I am interested in status.
- Status is important to me.
- Status enhances my image.

The acquisition of material goods for status purposes is one of the strongest measures of social success and achievement. Thus in reality status and consumption of specific brands are increasingly common practice in contemporary culture. Thus, increasingly the role of consumption is used to examine status.[6] Often communications about brand benefits and attributes are intertwined with notions of status and style as shown in Figure 10.2. Both advertisements for the brand identify the notion of status through copy expressing style and glamour.

SOCIAL CLASS CATEGORIES

Little agreement exists among sociologists on how many distinct class divisions are necessary to adequately describe the class structure of various countries. Most early studies divided the members of specific communities into five or six social class groups. However, other researchers have found nine, four, three, and even two class schemas suitable for their purposes. The choice of how many separate classes to use depends on the amount of detail the researcher believes is necessary to explain adequately the attitudes and behaviours of communities under study. The classification of society's members into a small number of social classes has also enabled researchers to identify the existence of shared values, attitudes and behavioural patterns among members within each social class, and differing values, attitudes and behaviours between social classes. Consumer researchers have been able to relate social class standing to consumer attitudes concerning specific products and to examine social class influences on the actual consumption of products. Market research companies, such as AGB McNair, use five class categories—A, B, C, D and E—based on income, education and head of household occupation.[7] Table 10.1 illustrates the number and diversity of social class level schemas. However, it must be remembered that much of the research comes from other countries and cannot be applied to Australian society without great care.

TABLE 10.1 Variations in the number and types of social class categories

TWO-CATEGORY SOCIAL CLASS SCHEMAS
- Blue collar, white collar
- Lower, upper
- Lower, middle

THREE-CATEGORY SOCIAL CLASS SCHEMAS
- Blue collar, grey collar, white collar
- Lower, middle, upper

FOUR-CATEGORY SOCIAL CLASS SCHEMA
- Lower, lower-middle, upper-middle, upper

FIVE-CATEGORY SOCIAL CLASS SCHEMAS
- Lower, working class, lower-middle, upper-middle, upper
- Lower, lower-middle, middle, upper-middle, upper

SIX-CATEGORY SOCIAL CLASS SCHEMA
- Lower-lower, upper-lower, lower-middle, upper-middle, lower-upper, upper-upper

SEVEN-CATEGORY SOCIAL CLASS SCHEMA
- Real lower-lower, a lower group of people but not the lowest, working class, middle class, upper-middle, lower-upper, upper-upper

NINE-CATEGORY SOCIAL CLASS SCHEMA
- Lower-lower, middle-lower, upper-lower, lower-middle, middle-middle, upper-middle, lower-upper, middle-upper, upper-upper

FIGURE 10.1 **Appeal using images and symbols of social status**

NO. 6 ON THE LIST OF
SIGHTS WORTH THE INOCULATIONS
Number 8 is hand feeding fish in Antigua.
Number 7 is hiking through Morocco's Atlas mountain range.
But it's number 6 that will really send shivers down your spine –
with the help of American Express Membership Rewards
Because every time you spend on the Card, you earn points you can exchange
for the flights you want, to countless destinations.
So start dreaming where you'll escape to.
For more ideas on what the Card can do for you, or to apply,
visit americanexpress.com.au/dreams
FOR WHATEVER DREAMS ARE ON YOUR LIST
3760
C L BROOKS
Subject to the terms and conditions of the Membership Rewards and Partner Programs. Membership Rewards and Partner Programs enrolment required.
An annual fee applies. American Express Australia Limited. ABN 92 108 952 085. ® Registered Trademark of American Express Company. AMECON0707

Source: Courtesy of American Express.

There are a number of reasons to approach the use of social class with caution. First, Australia is a far smaller market than, say, the United States or the United Kingdom, and it makes little sense to use an extensive set of class categories if some categories have few members.[8] Second, the distribution of wealth in Australia has been more even than in some other societies,[9] even though the gap between rich and poor is slowly widening (see Figure 10.3). The percentage of Australia's national income earned by each *decile* (the lowest decile contains the bottom 10% of family incomes, the highest decile contains the top 10%) varies significantly. Third, social mobility has been relatively high, with fewer barriers than exist in other cultures.[10] Fourth, there are ideological disagreements between sociologists of the relevance of the class concept.[11] Finally, a variety of methods has been used to measure social class in Australia, which causes some concerns regarding what is being measured and differing outcomes and social class groups that result from different measures.

FIGURE 10.2 **Advertisements communicating key aspects of status and style for the brand**

Experience the glamour
Capture the glamorous lifestyle of Beverly Hills in a bottle with the fresh, sensual and unforgettable fragrance of Giorgio Beverly Hills. One of the world's most classic fragrances for a woman who likes to be remembered.
Giorgio BEVERLY HILLS
GIORGIO BEVERLY HILLS

A GIORGIO BEVERLY HILLS PROMOTION
Bold, feminine and floral, the Giorgio Beverly Hills fragrance is one of the world's great fragrance classics.
Comprised of 450 precious ingredients, which include the natural perfume oils of jasmine, rose, gardenia, orange flowers, chamomile, sandalwood and patchouli, Giorgio Beverly Hills is a fragrance that's totally unforgettable.
Unlike any other perfume available, Giorgio Beverly Hills was designed as a signature fragrance to encapsulate the style and fashion of Giorgio Beverly Hills boutique on Rodeo Drive, Beverly Hills.
Provocative, dynamic, stylish and memorable, Giorgio Beverly Hills is one fragrance that every mother will love to receive this Mother's Day.

GIORGIO BEVERLY HILLS
Classic style
All mothers deserve the best on Mother's Day and the beautiful fragrance of Giorgio Beverly Hills is the perfect way to spoil her in style.

Source: Courtesy of Giorgio Beverly Hills Inc., the registered trademark and copyright owners of Giorgio Beverly Hills.

FIGURE 10.3 Changes in distribution of Australian equivalised disposable household income

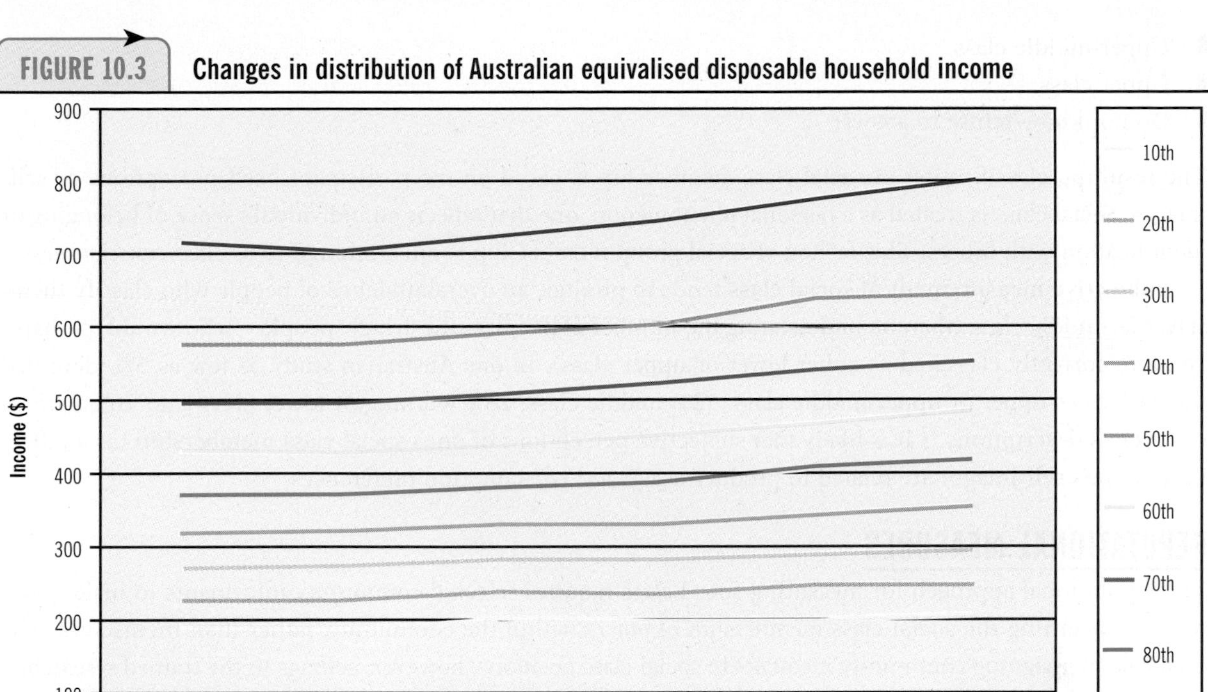

Source: Adapted from Australian Bureau of Statistics, *Household Income and Income Distribution*, 2003, Catalogue No. 6523.0.

The measurement of social class

Although social class is a valid and useful concept, its measurement can be somewhat problematic. There is still disagreement among researchers as to what constitutes the underlying dimensions of social class structure. To attempt to resolve this dilemma, researchers have employed a wide range of measurement techniques which they believe give a 'fair' approximation of social class. Systematic approaches for measuring social class fall into three broad categories: *subjective measures*, *reputational measures* and *objective measures*. Consumer researchers, however, are concerned with the measurement of social class in order to obtain a better understanding of markets and consumption behaviour, not of social structure. Potentially, these measures could be used by marketers to segment consumers according to class and develop marketing mix strategies focusing on class.

SUBJECTIVE MEASURES

In the subjective approach to measuring social class, individuals are asked to estimate their own social class positions. Typical of this approach is the following question:

Which one of the following categories best describes your own social class?

- Working class
- Lower-middle class

- Upper-middle class
- Upper class
- Do not know/refuse to answer

The resulting classification of social class membership is based on the participants' self-perceptions or self-images. Social class is treated as a personal phenomenon, one that reflects an individual's sense of belonging or identification with others. This feeling of social group membership is often referred to as *class consciousness*.

Subjective measurement of social class tends to produce an overabundance of people who classify themselves as middle class (thereby understating the number of people—the 'fringe' people—who would, perhaps, be more correctly classified as either lower or upper class). In one Australian study, as few as 5% identified themselves as upper or upper-middle class, 52% middle class, 28% working or lower class, and 16% various other class descriptions.[12] It is likely that subjective perceptions of one's social class membership (as a reflection of one's self-image) are related to product usage and consumption preferences.

REPUTATIONAL MEASURES

The reputational approach for measuring social class requires selected community informants to make judgments concerning the social class membership of *others* within the community, rather than themselves. The final task of assigning community members to social class positions, however, belongs to the trained researcher. Sociologists have employed the reputational approach to obtain a better understanding of the specific class structures of communities under study. In Australia, an extensive series of studies has looked at class on the basis of occupational status, which in turn is based on **reputational measures** of prestige.[13]

In regard to the more focused goal of understanding purchase and consumption behaviour, the reputational approach has proved to be somewhat impractical.

OBJECTIVE MEASURES

In contrast to the subjective and reputational methods, which require people to evaluate their own class standing or that of other community members, **objective measurement of social class** consists of selected demographic or socioeconomic variables concerning the individual(s) under study. These variables are measured through questionnaires which ask respondents to answer several factual questions about themselves, their family, or their place of residence. When selecting objective measures of social class, most researchers favour one or more of the following variables: *occupation*, *amount of income* and *education*. To these socioeconomic factors they sometimes add *geodemographic* market data in the form of postcodes and residence-neighbourhood information. These socioeconomic indicators are especially important as a means of locating concentrations of consumers with specific social class membership.

Socioeconomic measures of social class are of considerable value to marketers concerned with segmenting markets. Marketing managers who have developed **socioeconomic profiles** of their target markets can locate these markets (i.e. identify and measure them) by studying the socioeconomic data periodically issued by the Australian Bureau of Statistics and numerous commercial geodemographic data services, such as Pacific Micromarketing (a division of Pacific New Media), Apasco and Telstra's Spatial Decision Systems. In order to reach a desired target market, marketers match the *socioeconomic profiles* of their target audiences to the *audience profiles* of selected advertising media). Socioeconomic audience profiles are regularly developed and routinely made available to potential advertisers by most of the mass media. For example, Table 10.2 shows reader characteristics for two magazines in Australia. This data comes from readership research conducted by Roy Morgan Research and shows the readership profiles of *Woman's Day* and *Picture*, by gender, income, education, occupation and socioeconomic scale.

TABLE 10.2 Socioeconomic profile of readers of *Woman's Day* and *Picture*

	Read *Woman's Day* or *Picture*	*Woman's Day*	*Picture*
Gender			
Women	2 044 000	79.27%	16.97%
Men	692 000	20.73%	83.03%
Major demographics			
Main Grocery Buyer	1 845 000	69.21%	43.62%
Household income			
Less than $30 000	588 000	22.02%	15.80%
$30 000–$59 999	588 000	21.22%	24.84%
$60 000 & over	873 000	31.21%	39.23%
Socio-economic scale			
AB quintile	381 000	14.58%	5.33%
C quintile	515 000	19.09%	15.01%
D quintile	613 000	22.30%	23.19%
E quintile	620 000	21.91%	31.54%
FG quintile	607 000	22.12%	24.93%
Occupation of respondent (all workers)—summary			
Professional/manager	231 000	8.67%	5.66%
White collar workers	333 000	12.58%	6.47%
Skilled workers	133 000	3.62%	21.32%
Others (incl. semi/unskilled)	212 000	5.92%	30.55%
Full-time workers	912 000	30.91%	64.01%
TOTAL not employed	1 222 000	46.31%	22.62%
Education of reader			
Primary school	96 000	3.66%	1.32%
Secondary	1 831 000	65.50%	86.37%
Tertiary	809 000	30.85%	12.30%

Source: **Roy Morgan Single Source Australia: April 2003–March 2004.**

Objective measures of social class fall into two basic categories: single-variable indexes and composite-variable indexes.

Single-variable indexes

A **single-variable index** uses just one socioeconomic variable to evaluate social class membership. Some of the variables that are used for this purpose are discussed below.

Occupation Occupation is a widely accepted and probably the best documented measure of social class because it reflects **occupational status**. The importance of occupation as a social class indicator is seen by the frequency with which people ask others they meet for the first time, 'What do you do for a living?' The response to this question serves as a guide in 'sizing up' (i.e. evaluating and forming opinions of) others.[14]

Marketers frequently think in terms of specific occupations when defining a target market for their products (such as doctors and lawyers for stationery products) or broader occupational categories (targeting cars and holiday destinations to business executives and professionals). The likelihood that particular occupations will be receptive to certain products or services often provides the basis for a screener requirement for participation in focus groups or survey research, and for marketers to select occupational databases to target with direct marketing campaigns (e.g. a list of male lawyers practising in Melbourne; business executives for Qantas Club Business Lounges or American Express Gold Card).

Table 10.3 presents estimates of the relative prestige that people assign to many basic occupational titles.[15] Rankings were made on a 7-point scale where one was 'highest social status', four was 'middle social standing' and seven was 'lowest social standing'. The occupations listed towards the top of Table 10.3 tend to earn the greatest incomes and require the most formal education. As we move down the list of occupational rankings, the amount of income and required formal education tends to decrease. This suggests that there is a close association between occupational status, income and education.

Education The level of a person's formal education is another commonly accepted approximation of social class standing. Generally speaking, the more education people have, the more likely it is that they are well paid (i.e. have a higher income) and hold an admired or respected position (i.e. occupational status). When targeting specific products or services, marketers frequently speak in terms of occupational groups ('Accountants and lawyers are really good customers for our electronic organiser') or broader occupational categories ('We target our imported leather luggage to executives and professionals'). Data from the Australian Bureau of Statistics and from companies such as Roy Morgan Research supports the close relationship between educational attainment and amount of household income, as indicated in Table 10.4.

Income Individual or family income is another socioeconomic variable frequently used to approximate social class standing.[16] Researchers who favour income as a measure of social class use either the amount or source of income. Detailed information collected by the Australian Bureau of Statistics confirms that expenditure patterns vary considerably with household income. Table 10.5 shows the percentage of household income devoted to key areas by each of the five income **quintiles**.[17] Recent evidence suggests that income works best in accounting for leisure consumption when measured in terms of engaging in (either doing or not doing) a particular leisure activity (such as golf or snow skiing).[18]

Although income is a popular estimate of social class, not all consumer researchers agree that it is an appropriate index of social class. Some argue that a blue-collar plumber and a white-collar high school principal may both earn $50 000 a year, yet because of (or as a reflection of) social class differences, each will spend that income in a different way. How they decide to spend their income reflects different values, attitudes and **lifestyles**. Within this context, it is the difference in *values* that is an important discriminant of social class between people, not the *amount of income* they earn. Australian researchers Paul Henry and Margaret Craig-Lees have shown that 'professionals' value change, achievement and rationality. In contrast, the working class was more likely to favour stability and to take a more pessimistic view of life when change was involved.[19]

Supporting this viewpoint is American research into the marketplace behaviour of 'underprivileged' upper-class and 'overprivileged' middle-class families with the same basic annual income. Specifically, overprivileged middle-class consumers can be differentiated from underprivileged upper-class consumers by their likely ownership of such products as campervans, motorboats, four-wheel-drive vehicles and backyard swimming pools. In contrast, underprivileged upper-class consumers with the same income spend relatively greater amounts on private club memberships, special educational experiences for their children, and cultural objects and events.[20]

Although contemporary Australian society had its origins just over 200 years ago, it has been common to talk about 'old' versus 'new' money, or of groups such as the 'Adelaide Establishment'. We should be careful

TABLE 10.3 Occupational ratings by workforce sectors in Australia

Occupation	Rating	Occupation	Rating	Occupation	Rating
Judge	1.2	Draftsman	3.4	Bar manager	4.7
Cabinet minister	1.5	Systems analyst	3.4	Motor mechanic	4.7
Medical specialist	1.5	Social worker	3.5	Hairdresser	4.8
Barrister	1.7	Chiropractor	3.5	Sergeant, army, female	4.8
Church leader	1.7	Health inspector	3.5	Undertaker	4.8
Professor	1.8	Playwright	3.5	Fitter and turner	4.8
Military General	1.8	Speech therapist	3.5	Telephone technician	4.8
Managing director	1.8	Dietitian	3.5	Toolmaker	4.8
General, army	1.9	Secondary school teacher	3.5	Printer	4.9
International pilot	2.0	Media news reader	3.6	Sales representative	4.9
Department head (govt)	2.2	Kindergarten directress	3.6	Potter	5.0
Architect	2.2	Electrician, business	3.6	Typist	5.0
Dentist	2.3	Restaurateur	3.6	Bookie	5.0
Mayor	2.3	TV actor	3.6	Punchcard operator	5.1
Solicitor, male	2.3	Private secretary	3.7	Butcher, wages	5.2
Parliamentarian	2.4	Personnel officer	3.7	Bricklayer	5.2
Engineer, professional	2.4	Professional fisherman	3.7	Telephonist	5.2
Research scientist	2.4	Librarian	3.8	Milkman	5.2
Solicitor, female	2.5	Registered nurse, female	3.8	Plasterer	5.3
Veterinary surgeon	2.5	Assistant minister religion	3.8	Nightwatchman	5.4
University lecturer	2.5	Primary school teacher	3.8	Car salesman	5.4
Bank manager	2.5	Bank officer	3.9	Postman	5.5
Government medical officer	2.6	Owner small business	3.9	Taxi driver	5.5
School principal	2.6	Professional model	3.9	Nurse aide	5.5
Chartered accountant	2.6	Research officer	4.0	Sailor	5.6
Economist	2.6	Laboratory technician	4.0	Professional punter	5.6
Colonel	2.7	Air hostess	4.0	Clerk, junior	5.6
Owner large business	2.7	Chef	4.0	Shearer	5.6
Psychologist	2.7	Publican	4.0	Bus driver	5.6
Government legal officer	2.7	Registered nurse, male	4.0	Housekeeper	5.6
Geologist	2.7	Ambulanceman	4.0	Waiter	5.6
Orchestra conductor	2.8	Professional footballer	4.1	Waitress	5.7
Director, nursing	2.8	Acupuncturist	4.1	Sales assistant	5.7
Newspaper editor	2.8	Farm manager	4.1	Barman	5.8
Accountant	2.9	Professional golfer	4.2	Truck driver	5.8
Minister religion, own parish	2.9	Small landowner	4.2	Storeman	5.9
Producer, TV program	3.0	Advertising agent	4.2	Jackaroo	5.9
Lecturer, tech college	3.1	Foreman	4.2	Machinist	6.0
Surveyor	3.1	Trade union secretary	4.2	Barmaid	6.0
Large farm owner	3.1	Real estate agent	4.2	Domestic worker	6.0
Second division officer	3.2	Policeman	4.2	Debt collector	6.2
Physiotherapist	3.2	Photographer	4.3	Car assembly worker	6.2
Grazier	3.2	Carpenter	4.3	Farm labourer	6.3
Stockbroker	3.2	Contract cleaner	4.3	Service station attendant	6.3
Works manager	3.3	TV technician	4.4	Process worker	6.4
Superior, religious	3.3	Jockey	4.5	Builder's labourer	6.4
Master builder	3.3	Trainer, racehorses	4.5	Ticket collector	6.4
Journalist	3.4	Electrician, wages	4.5	Wharfie	6.5
Computer programmer	3.4	Stenographer	4.5	Seasonal labourer	6.6
Senior clerk	4.4	Insurance agent	4.6	Cleaner	6.6
Policewoman	4.4	Bank teller	4.6	Massage parlour operator	6.6
Disc jockey	4.4	Beauty consultant	4.6	Garbage collector	6.7
Airline steward	4.4	Housewife	4.6	Road sweeper	6.7
Fireman	4.4	Sergeant, army, male	4.7	Prostitute	6.9

Source: **Craig McGregor, *Class in Australia*, Penguin, 1997.**

TABLE 10.4 **Education attainment and income**

Education level	Personal income			
	< $29 999	$30 000–$49 999	$50 000–$69 999	$70 000 and over
Finished primary school	3.96%	0.79%	0.21%	0.39%
Intermediate/Form 4/Year 10	16.40%	12.64%	7.50%	6.11%
Finished/now doing matric/HSC/Year 12	9.48%	10.07%	6.23%	4.80%
Finished tech or commercial college	8.69%	12.69%	11.42%	7.90%
Tertiary diploma, not uni	6.87%	11.00%	12.23%	10.25%
University degree	9.72%	23.22%	41.45%	53.59%

Source: **Roy Morgan Single Source Australia: April 2003–March 2004.**

TABLE 10.5 **Percentage of household income on various expenditure items**

Item	Lowest quintile	Second quintile	Third quintile	Fourth quintile	Highest quintile
Total housing costs	15.6%	15.3%	14.7%	14.4%	12.8%
Food	19.8%	20.3%	18.9%	18.1%	17.2%
Clothing and footwear	4.5%	4.4%	5.3%	5.8%	6.5%
Medical and health	4.9%	4.3%	4.2%	4.5%	4.6%
Transport	13.3%	15.3%	15.6%	16.3%	15.8%
Recreation	12.6%	11.8%	12.6%	12.5%	14.7%
Average weekly expenditure	$303	$426	$573	$714	$994

Source: Household Expenditure Survey Australia: Detailed Expenditure Items**, Australian Bureau of Statistics, 1999, Catalogue No. 6535.0.**

about this—people cannot live a lifestyle beyond their means for any length of time, no matter what their values. A relevant concept here is **contestable income**, that is, the amount of income that is left over after the necessities of life (e.g. rent, rates, food, clothing, power bills, transport to work, repayments) have been bought.

Further indicating the importance of consumers' personal values, rather than amount of income, is the observation that affluence may be more a function of attitude or behaviour than income level.[21] These attitudinally affluent consumers represent a broad segment who do not have the income needed to be considered affluent in today's society, yet they desire to have the best. They buy less but buy better quality, assigning priorities and gradually working their way towards having everything they want.

Other variables *Quality of neighbourhood* and *dollar-value of residence* are rarely used as sole measures of social class. However, they are frequently used to support or verify social class membership assigned on the basis of occupational status or income. Some suburbs in Australian cities, such as Killara, Toorak, Vaucluse and Hamilton, are considered prestigious even though some of the housing is quite modest. More systematically, companies such as Pacific Micromarketing use geodemographic segmentation to measure geographical areas. Examples for Sydney and Melbourne are shown in Figures 10.4 and 10.5.

Finally, *possessions* have been used by sociologists as an index of social class. The best known and most elaborate rating scheme for evaluating possessions is **Chapin's Social Status Scale**, which focuses on the presence of certain items of furniture and accessories in the lounge room (type of floor or floor covering, curtains, fireplace, library table, telephone, bookcases) and the condition of the room (cleanliness, organisation, general atmosphere).[22] Conclusions are drawn about a family's social class on the basis of such observations. To illustrate how home decorations reflect social class standing, it has been identified that lower-class families are likely to place their television sets in the lounge room, while middle- and upper-class families usually place their television sets in the bedroom or family room.[23] The marketing implications of such insights suggest that advertisements for television sets targeted at lower-class consumers should show the set in the lounge room, while advertisements directed to middle- or upper-class consumers should show the sets in a bedroom or family room.

Composite-variable indexes

Composite-variable indexes, such as the A–G classification used by Roy Morgan Research and others, systematically combine a number of socioeconomic factors to form one overall measure of social class standing.[24] Such indexes are of interest to consumer researchers because they reflect the complexity of social class better than single-variable indexes.

For instance, research exploring consumers' perceptions of mail and phone shopping reveals that the higher the socioeconomic status (in terms of a composite of income, occupational status and education), the more positive are the consumers' rating of mail and phone order buying, relative to in-store shopping.[25] The research also found that downscale consumers (a composite of lower scores on three variables) were less positive towards magazine and catalogue shopping and more positive towards in-store shopping than more upscale socioeconomic groupings.[26] With such information, retailers like Kmart and Big-W that largely target merchandise to working-class (more downscale) consumers would have a real challenge using direct marketing catalogues and telephone selling approaches. In contrast, retailers concentrating on upscale consumers, such as David Jones and Myer, would be more successful in developing catalogue programs targeting specific segments of affluent consumers. Three of the more important composite indexes are the Index of Status Characteristics, the Socioeconomic Status Score and Coleman's Status Index.

Index of Status Characteristics A classic composite measure of social class is Warner's Index of Status Characteristics (ISC).[27] The ISC is a weighted measure of: occupation (40% of weighting); source of income (*not* amount of income—30%); house type (20%); and dwelling area (quality of neighbourhood—10%).

Socioeconomic Status Score This score, developed by the United States Bureau of the Census, is sometimes referred to as SES. It combines three basic socioeconomic variables: occupation, family income and educational attainment.

Coleman's Status Index Coleman's computerised status index (CSI) is a composite measure of status that has been used quite often by consumer researchers. The index has a number of variations, including scaling for employed women, and another where occupation is weighted double in determining the total score for status. Box 10.1 shows an example of the CSI.

Australian social class measures

There have been several approaches to social class among Australian sociologists and market researchers. The most thorough objective description of class has come from an Australian study[28] that was part of an international project. The classification is based on three classes of asset ownership—ownership of enterprises, ownership of organisational resources (managerial level) and skills ownership (level of professionalism). The

FIGURE 10.4 **MOSAIC types of Sydney (analysis level—18 households)**

Lindfield
North Ryde
Roseville
Chatswood
Seaforth
Artarmon
Lane Cove
Northbridge
Gladesville
Cammeray
Crows Nest
Hunters Hill
Cremorne
Neutral Bay
Mosman
North Sydney
Abbotsford
Drummoyne
Milsons Point
Balmain
Rozelle
SYDNEY
Potts Point
Haberfield
Pyrmont
Ashfield
Leichhardt
Annandale
Darlinghurst
Double Bay
Rose Bay
Edgecliff
Bellevue Hill
Summer Hill
Camperdown
Sydney University
Chippendale
Paddington
Petersham
Redfern
Dulwich Hill
Newtown
Marrickville
Bondi Junction
Erskineville
St Peters
Kingsford
Highways
Main Roads
Rivers
A01 Champagne and Chardonnay
A02 Asset Rich Commuters
A03 Educated Influentials
A04 Suburban Success Stories
B05 Miners and Military
B06 Pools and Barbies
B07 Elevated Lifestyles
B08 Creating a Future
B09 House and Land Package
B10 Blue Collar Plurality
C11 Ethnic Enterprise
C12 Villas and Mansions
C13 New Arrivals, New Hope
C14 Close-Knit and Debt-Free
C15 Time for Change
D16 Affluent Apartments
D17 Café Society
D18 Oriental Expresso
D19 Starting Out
D20 Student Union
E21 Cosmopolitan and Cultural
E22 Urban Renewal
E23 Non-Family Fringe
E24 Something Old, Something New
E25 Elderly Singles in Units
F26 Independent Elders
F27 Caravans and Cabins
F28 Anglo-Australian Alliance
F29 Retiring Retreats
F30 Seaside Seniors
F31 Twilight Zone
G32 True Blue Blues
G33 Country Town Challenge
G34 Safety Net
G35 Short Term Parking
H36 Country Comforts
H37 Families on the Fringe
H38 Rural Provisions
I39 Processors and Packers
I40 Roadside Properties
I41 Red Earth
Copyright (c) Pacific Micromarketing; Map Copyright 1996 - PSMA.
Drawn with centre (1989861,6105551) at scale 1:64835

Source: **Courtesy of Pacific Micromarketing.**

FIGURE 10.5 MOSAIC types of Melbourne (analysis level—18 households)

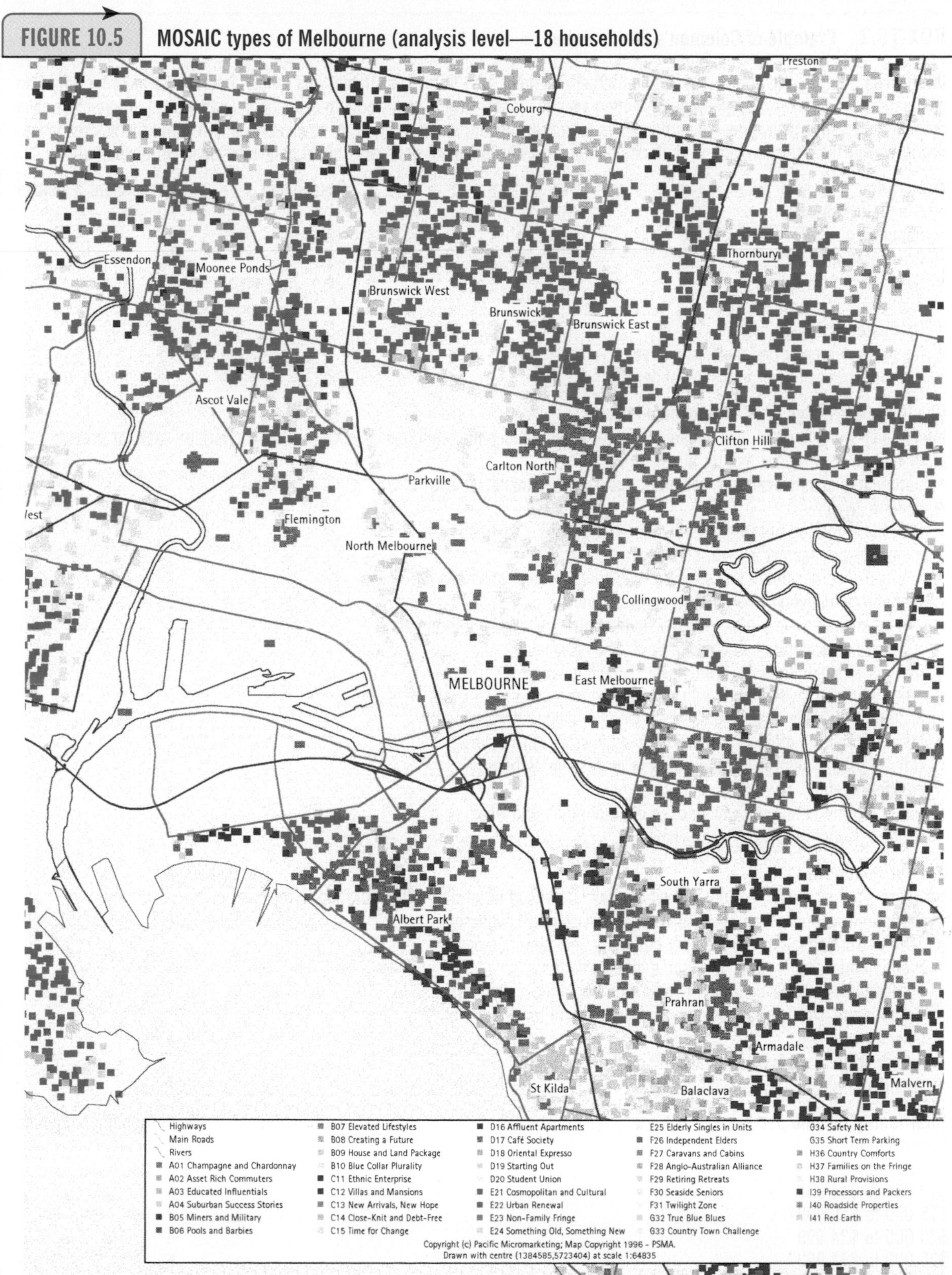

Source: Courtesy of Pacific Micromarketing.

BOX 10.1 Example of Coleman's Status Index

Interviewer circles code numbers which in his/her judgment best fit the respondent and family. Interviewer asks for detail on occupation, then makes rating. Interviewer often asks the respondent in own words to describe neighbourhood. Interviewer asks respondent to specify income—a card is given to the respondent showing the eight brackets—and records the R's response. If interviewer feels this is over- or understatement, a better-judgment estimate should be given, along with explanation.

Education	Respondent	Respondent's spouse
• Grammar school	–1	–1
• Some high school	–2	–2
• Graduated high school	–3	–3
• Some post-high school	–4	–4
• Two, three years of college	–5	–5
• Graduated four-year college	–6	–6
• Master's degree or professional degree	–7	–7
• PhD or six/seven year professional degree	–8	–8

Occupation prestige level of household head

Interviewer's judgment of how household head rates in occupational status. Respondent's description—ask for previous job if retired or, if widow, ask for husband's job:

• Chronically unemployed; day labourer, unskilled; on social security benefit.	–	0
• Steadily employed but in marginal semi-skilled jobs: custodians, minimum-pay factory worker, service worker, etc.	–	1
• Average-skill assembly-line workers, bus/truck drivers, police and firefighters, deliverymen, carpenters, bricklayers.	–	2
• Skilled craftsman (e.g. electrician), small contractors, factory foremen, low-pay sales clerks, office worker, postal employees.	–	3
• Owners of small firms (2–4 employees), technicians, salespeople, office workers, civil servant with average salary.	–	4
• Middle management, teachers, social workers, lesser professionals.	–	5
• Lesser corporate officials, owners of middle-sized businesses (10–20 employees), moderate-success professionals (dentists, engineers, etc.).	–	6
• Top corporate executives, successful in corporate world (leading doctors, lawyers, rich business owners).	–	7

Area of residence

Interviewer's impressions of the immediate neighbourhood in terms of its reputation in the eyes of the community.

• Slum area: people on social security benefits, common labourers.	–	1
• Strictly working class: not slummy but some very poor housing.	–	2
• Predominantly blue-collar with some office workers.	–	3
• Predominantly white-collar with some well paid blue-collar workers.	–	4
• Better white-collar area; not many executives, but hardly any blue-collar either.	–	5
• Excellent area: professional and well paid managers.	–	6
• Wealthy or society-type neighbourhood.	–	7

Total family income per year	Respondent	Respondent's spouse
Under $5000	–	1
$5000 to $9 999	–	2
$10 000 to $14 999	–	3
$15 000 to $19 999	–	4
$20 000 to $24 999	–	5
$25 000 to $34 999	–	6
$35 000 to $49 999	–	7
$50 000 and over	–	8

Total score ______________________________

Estimated status

Married ______ Divorced/Separated ______ Widowed ______ Single ______ (Code)

Source: Adapted from Richard P. Coleman, 'The continuing significance of social class to marketing', *Journal of Consumer Research*, 10, December 1983, pp. 265–280.

classification can trace its origins back to Marxist theory. The various assets can be combined into a large number of possible combinations, but the authors have reduced these to seven (Table 10.6 shows the details). Their study then used survey data to estimate the incidence of these in Australian society. Since the study was conducted, the recession of the early 1990s and the reorganisation of many businesses has seen a marked reduction in the number of middle managers. In addition, unemployment has drastically lifted the number of the **proletariat** and the number of small business people (the petty bourgeoisie).

The Baxter study also highlighted the relationship between class and other key social segmentation methods, including occupation, gender and age. The Australian Standard Classification of Occupations (ASCO) was developed by the Australian Bureau of Statistics.[29] Table 10.7 shows occupation classified by these class categories. Clearly, there is a relationship, with labourers, operators, sales and clerical workers more likely to be classified as members of the proletariat.

Table 10.8 shows class analysed by gender and age. Males were more often represented among the managerial and ownership classes, women more among the proletariat. Older people were less likely to belong to the proletariat. Presumably this reflects increases in ownership, skills and organisational assets over time. Given its origins in theoretical sociology, it is hardly surprising that marketers have not used this classification directly. However, categories such as small business are recognised as key groups by marketers, while publications directed at professional and executive groups are common.

With an improved understanding of society and its social bases, derived through social class measures, marketers are in a position to examine differences in lifestyle profiles of social classes.

TABLE 10.6 Australian social class classification

Class	Percentage
Employers (owners of enterprises with two or more employees)	4.2
Petty bourgeoisie (owners with one or zero employees)	9.2
Managers	26.1
Supervisors (of one or more employees)	9.0
Expert non-managers	1.9
Skilled workers (semi-credentialled)	9.8
Proletariat (those with no ownership, organisational or skills assets)	39.8

***Source:* J. Baxter et al., *The Australian and New Zealand Journal of Sociology*, 25(1), 1989, pp. 100–120.**

TABLE 10.7 Class by ASCO occupation group

Class	Occupation							
	Manager-administrator	Professional	Para-professional	Trades	Clerks	Sales/ Personal services	Operators	Labourers
	%	%	%	%	%	%	%	%
Employer	17.2	2.5	1.9	3.2	4.0	0.9	1.1	1.9
Petty bourgeoisie	19.8	6.5	3.9	20.8	2.1	5.4	10.8	4.7
Managers	52.6	43.2	34.7	17.5	24.1	21.8	14.7	7.4
Supervisors	6.8	8.2	16.7	9.7	10.3	9.6	8.0	5.2
Expert non-managers	1.8	12.3	3.4	0.0	0.0	0.0	0.0	0.0
Skilled workers	1.8	27.3	39.3	23.3	0.5	0.0	0.0	0.0
Proletariat	0.0	0.0	0.0	25.4	58.9	62.4	65.4	80.7

Source: J. Baxter et al., *The Australian and New Zealand Journal of Sociology*, 25(1), 1989, pp. 100–120.

TABLE 10.8 Class by gender and age group

Class	Gender		Age group		
	Males	Females	18–30 years	31–45 years	45+ years
	%	%	%	%	%
Employer	4.7	3.5	2.5	5.2	5.0
Petty bourgeoisie	11.3	6.4	4.7	10.5	13.8
Managers	29.5	21.8	23.3	28.3	26.4
Supervisors	8.0	10.2	7.7	9.3	10.5
Expert non-managers	1.8	2.5	1.9	2.4	1.0
Skilled workers	10.9	8.5	12.5	8.8	6.9
Proletariat	33.8	47.5	47.4	35.5	36.5

Source: J. Baxter et al., *The Australian and New Zealand Journal of Sociology*, 25(1), 1989, pp. 100–120.

Lifestyle profiles of the social classes

Consumer research has found evidence that within each of the social classes there is a constellation of specific lifestyle factors (shared beliefs, attitudes, activities and behaviours) that tend to distinguish the members of each class from the members of all other social classes.[30] To capture the lifestyle composition of the various social class groupings, Table 10.9 presents a consolidated portrait, pieced together from various sources, of the members of the following six social classes: upper-upper class; lower-upper class; upper-middle class; lower-middle class; upper-lower class; lower-lower class. Each profile is only a generalised picture of the class. People in any class may possess values, attitudes and behavioural patterns that are a hybrid of two or more classes.

TABLE 10.9 **Social class profiles**

The upper-upper class—country club establishment
- Small number of well-established families
- Belong to best country clubs and sponsor major charity events
- Serve as trustees for local colleges and hospitals
- Prominent physicians and lawyers
- May be heads of major financial institutions, owners of major long-established firms
- Accustomed to wealth, so do not spend money conspicuously

The lower-upper class—new wealth
- Not quite accepted by the upper crust of society
- Represent 'new money'
- Successful business executives
- Conspicuous users of their new wealth

The upper-middle class—achieving professionals
- Have neither family status nor unusual wealth
- Career-oriented
- Young successful professionals, corporate managers and business owners
- Most are college graduates, many with advanced degrees
- Active in professional, community and social activities
- Have a keen interest in obtaining the 'better things in life'
- Their homes serve as symbols of their achievements
- Consumption is often conspicuous
- Very child-oriented

The lower-middle class—faithful followers
- Primary non-managerial white-collar workers and highly paid blue-collar workers
- Want to achieve 'respectability' and be accepted as good citizens
- Want their children to be well-behaved
- Tend to be churchgoers and are often involved in church-sponsored activities
- Prefer a neat and clean appearance and tend to avoid faddish or highly styled clothing
- Constitute a major market for do-it-yourself products

The upper-lower class—security-minded majority
- The largest social class segment
- Solidly blue collar
- Strive for security (sometimes gained from union membership)
- View work as a means to 'buy' enjoyment
- Want children to behave properly
- High wage earners in this group may spend impulsively
- Interested in items that enhance their leisure time (e.g. TV sets, hunting equipment)
- Husbands typically have a strong 'macho' self-image
- Males are sports fans, heavy smokers, beer drinkers

The lower-lower class—rock bottom
- Poorly educated, unskilled labourers
- Often out of work
- Children are often poorly treated
- Tend to live a day-to-day existence

The most consistent Australian attempt to use such a classification comes from the values segments developed by Roy Morgan Research, in conjunction with Colin Benjamin of The Horizons Network. Using the family life cycle (see Chapter 9), income and questions on values (such as the importance of family life), a 10-category classification was devised. The 10 groups are called:

- Basic needs
- Fairer deal
- Traditional family life
- Conventional family life
- Look at me
- Something better
- Real conservatism
- Young optimism
- Visible achievement
- Socially aware

A full description of each values category is given in Chapter 11.

China in pursuit of a middle-class lifestyle

In recent years, established marketers from all over the world have singled out China as a highly desirable growth market for their brands. These marketers have been anxious to satisfy China's rapidly expanding urban middle class's appetite for consumer goods. Specifically, the wealthiest 20% of urban Chinese households (about 80 million people) constitutes a highly attractive market. These relatively affluent urban Chinese consumers are primarily composed of the two following segments: (1) 'little rich'—those 15% with annual household income of about $3200, and (2) 'yuppies'—those 5% with annual household income of about $9500.[31] Although household incomes between $3200 and $9500, on first glance, do not seem like much, this conclusion can be a real error. With small families and housing and other costs subsidised by the government, an urban Chinese family is able to have a relatively good lifestyle on a relatively small income. The 'secret' is that a fairly large amount of a family's income is discretionary income (i.e. income that can be spent on a wide range of non-necessities). Table 10.10 reveals more about the lifestyles of these two urban Chinese middle-class consumer groups, and Table 10.11 presents a comparison of their consumption patterns for selected products. Interestingly, the two middle-class segments tend to differ more in terms of their consumption patterns than in terms of their attitudes, lifestyles and media behaviour.

Social class mobility

Social class membership in Australia is not as concrete as it is in some other countries and cultures. Although individuals can move either up *or* down in social class standing from the class position held by their parents, Australians think primarily in terms of **upward mobility** because of the availability of widely affordable education and opportunities for self-development and self-advancement. Australia has many examples of people, such as A.C. Packer (grandfather of Kerry), Kerry Stokes and Gerry Harvey, who achieved wealth and status despite humble origins. Today, many young men and women with ambition to get ahead dream of going to university and eventually starting their own successful businesses.

Because upward mobility has always been attainable in our society, the higher social classes often become reference groups for ambitious men and women of lower social status. The junior manager tries to dress like

TABLE 10.10 Two urban socioeconomic segments in China: Psychographic, lifestyle activities and media behaviour

Segments/dimensions	Little rich	Yuppies
Consumer attitudes		
Work hard and get rich	43%	32%
Satisfaction with life	73%	80%
Live one's own life	37%	48%
Live a pure and honest life	10%	5%
Willing to pay for brands	43%	68%
Prefer foreign goods	28%	48%
Lifestyle activities		
Reading	8%	80%
Going to movies	48%	51%
Going to parks	45%	60%
Domestic travel	53%	68%
Karaoke bar	48%	50%
Media use (minutes)		
Television time	143	146
Radio time	41	42
Newspaper time	52	60
Magazine time	67	61

Note: Based on media used the previous day and the amount of time each medium was used.

Source: Geng Cui and Qiming Liu, 'Executive insights: Emerging market segments in a transitional economy: A study of urban consumers in china,' *Journal of International Marketing*, 9, no. 1, 2001, p. 91. Reprinted with permission from the American Marketing Association.

TABLE 10.11 Two urban socioeconomic segments in China: Selective consumption patterns

Segments/products	Little rich	Yuppies
Color TV	94%	100%
Microwave oven	12%	22%
Air conditioner	19%	47%
Compact disc player	32%	55%
Mobile telephone	12%	33%
Computer	5%	14%
Private car	5%	12%
Tea	92%	92%
Ice cream	34%	37%
Soft drinks	47%	60%
Beer	50%	72%
Credit card	11%	40%
Life insurance	42%	41%

Note: Based on media used the previous day and the amount of time each medium was used.

Source: Geng Cui and Qiming Liu, 'Executive insights: Emerging market segments in a transitional economy: A study of urban consumers in china,' *Journal of International Marketing*, 9, no. 1, 2001, p. 94. Reprinted with permission from the American Marketing Association.

his boss; the middle manager aspires to belong to the CEOs' golf club; the graduate of a suburban high school wants to send his son to a grammar school. Recognising that individuals often aspire to membership in higher social classes, marketers frequently incorporate the symbols of higher-class membership, both as products and props, in advertisements targeted to lower social class audiences. Ads often display marketers' products within an upper-class setting—for example, a board game is displayed on a table in front of a fireplace with a beautiful mantel; a domestic wine is shown being consumed by fashionably (European) dressed models; a new model car is seen parked outside a famous exclusive restaurant.

Sometimes a more direct appeal to consumers' sense of owning products that are normally restricted to members of other social classes can be an effective message. For example, if a direct marketer of consumer electronics were to promote a top-of-the-line notebook computer (such as a high-end model of an IBM ThinkPad), usually purchased by senior business executives, with 'Now it's your turn to have what Fortune 500 executives have enjoyed' (it's been marked down about 50% of original price), this would be a marketing message that encourages 'ordinary consumers' to own a 'dream machine'. Ads often depict an affluent-looking suburban family, thus creating a comfortable, middle-class image for their products. Another characteristic of social class mobility is the way that products and services traditionally within the realm of one social class may filter down to lower social classes. For example, cosmetic surgery was once affordable only by movie stars and other wealthy consumers. Today, consumers of all economic strata undergo cosmetic surgery.[32]

SIGNS OF DOWNWARD MOBILITY

Although Australia is frequently associated with upward mobility, because it has been the rule for much of its history, there are now signs of **downward mobility**. Social commentators have suggested that some young adults (such as members of the X-generation, described in Chapter 12) are not only likely to find it difficult to 'do better' than their parents (better jobs, own homes, more disposable income, more savings) but may not even do as well as their parents. As long as community wealth increased, as it did for much of the post-World War II period, it was simple to think that all classes were upwardly mobile. Now, after a period of increasingly frequent recessions, social disparity is gradually growing. In the last 15 years, executive salaries have grown at twice the rate of award wages. Some Australian CEOs were in 1995 reportedly earning more than $1.5 million in annual salary, and in 2004 some are earning between $1.145 million and $4.15 million.[33] In effect, this means that a smaller, elite group is growing in wealth and status, but that it is harder for large numbers of people to aspire to the top ranks.

➤ Geodemographic clustering

In recent years, traditional social class measures have been enhanced by the linkage of geographic and socio-economic consumer data to create more powerful geodemographic clusters. The underlying rationale for **geodemographic clustering** is that 'birds of a feather flock together'.

There are several competing clustering services in Australia, such as Pacific Micromarketing, Apasco and Spatial Decision Systems. Comparable services exist elsewhere, especially in the United States, where $PRIZM_{NE}$ is one of the most popular (demographic and lifestyle) clustering services. $PRIZM_{NE}$ assigns all the US households (postcode + 4 areas), census tract, block group, postcode, media market, county, state and nation providing the ability to shift between traditional demographic segmentation and household level segmentation. All households are assigned to one of 66 PRIZM clusters, which can be further collapsed into 14 groups based on urbancity and affluence. Box 10.2 shows an example of $PRIZM_{NE}$ social groups. Marketers in the United States can superimpose these geodemographic clusters onto a host of product and service usage data, media-exposure data and lifestyles data (such as VALS) to create a refined picture of their target markets. Segments are placed in one of the four urbancity categories, which are determined by the population density of an area and its neighbouring areas. A density score of between 1 (low) and 99 (high) is then assigned to each of the areas. Once this occurs all segments are sorted into groupings based on affluence. To illustrate the usefulness of such information, Box 10.3 presents the profiles of the S3 Middleburbs group. The five segments that comprise Middleburbs share a middle-class, suburban perspective, but there the similarity ends. Two groups are filled with very young residents, two are filled with seniors and one is middle-aged. In addition, S3 includes a mix of both homeowners and renters as well as high school graduates and college alums. With good jobs and money in their jeans, the members of Middleburbs tend to have plenty of discretionary income to visit nightclubs and casual-dining restaurants, shop at midscale department stores, buy dance and easy listening CDs by the dozen and travel across the US and Canada.

Pacific Micromarketing, Apasco and Spatial each identify a host of socioeconomic and demographic factors (education, income, occupation, family life cycle, ethnicity, housing, urbanisation) drawn from Australian

BOX 10.2 Sample of $PRIZM_{NE}$ social groups

Urbancity category

- Urban areas (U) have population density scores between 85 and 99. They include both the downtowns of major cities and surrounding neighbourhoods. These areas often extend beyond the city limits and into surrounding jurisdictions.
- Second cities (C) are less densely populated than urban areas, with population density scores between 40 and 85. They are surrounded by areas of moderate or low population density, so that population density usually decreases on all sides of a second city. They can be independent cities or satellite cities in major metro areas.
- Suburbs (S) have population density scores between 40 and 90, and are clearly dependent on urban areas or second cities. Population density rises as you approach the city, and decreases as you move away from it.
- Town and rural areas (T) have population density scores under 40. This category includes exurbs, towns, farming communities, and a wide range of other rural areas.

Source: © 2003, Claritas, Inc. $PRIZM_{NE}$ and Claritas are registered trademarks of Claritas, Inc. The 66 PRIZM cluster nicknames. Used with permission.

BOX 10.3 Profiles of $PRIZM_{NE}$ S3 group

21 Gray Power

The steady rise of older, healthier Americans over the past decade has produced one important by-product: middle-class, home-owning suburbanites who are ageing in place rather than moving to retirement communities. Gray Power reflects this trend, a segment of older, midscale singles and couples who live in quiet comfort.

22 Young Influentials

Once known as the home of the nation's yuppies, Young Influentials reflects the fading glow of acquisitive yuppiedom. Today, the segment is a common address for young, middle-class singles and couples who are more preoccupied with balancing work and leisure pursuits. Having recently left college dorms, they now live in apartment complexes surrounded by ball fields, health clubs and casual-dining restaurants.

30 Suburban Sprawl

Suburban Sprawl is an unusual American lifestyle: a collection of midscale, middle-aged singles and couples living in the heart of suburbia. Typically members of the Baby Boom generation, they hold decent jobs, own older homes and condos, and pursue conservative versions of the American Dream. Among their favourite activities are jogging on treadmills, playing trivia games and renting videos.

36 Blue-Chip Blues

Blue-Chip Blues in known as a comfortable lifestyle for young, sprawling families with well-paying blue-collar jobs. Ethnically diverse—with a significant presence of Hispanics and African-American— the segment's ageing neighbourhoods feature compact, modestly priced homes surrounded by commercial centres that cater to child-filled households.

39 Domestic Duos

Domestic Duos represents a middle-class mix of mainly over-55 singles and married couples living in older suburban homes. With their high-school educations and fixed incomes, segment residents maintain an easy-going lifestyle. Residents like to socialise by going bowling, seeing a play, meeting at the local fraternal order or going out to eat.

Source: © 2003, Claritas, Inc. $PRIZM_{NE}$ and Claritas are registered trademarks of Claritas, Inc. The 66 PRIZM cluster nicknames. Used with permission.

Bureau of Statistics data and electoral rolls. This material is combined with survey and panel data on actual consumer behaviour (e.g. product purchase and usage, mail order buying, media exposure habits) to locate concentrations of consumers with similar characteristics.

Pacific Micromarketing, for example, assigns every Australian household to one of nine groups (A to I) and 41 types (1 to 41), based on available census data, car vehicle registrations, housing commencements, income tax statistics and unemployment statistics. Box 10.4 shows a description of the groups and types.

BOX 10.4 Pacific Micromarketing: MOSAIC Classification

Group A White Collar Affluents (7.2%)

- Mature families found in affluent and leafy suburbs
- Enjoy playing tennis, golf, swimming
- Professional occupations
- Read newspapers and business magazines
- High users of mobile phones and the Internet

Group B Pioneering Young Families (18.5%)

- Often have two or more young children with both parents working
- High home mortgage repayments
- Busy lifestyles with shopping usually completed after hours
- Value for money is generally more of a consideration than fashion in decision-making process

Group C Emerging Ethnic Enclaves (12.0%)

- High proportion of individuals from non-English-speaking backgrounds
- Wide range of incomes and unemployment rates reflect contrasting experiences since migration
- Tend to be extremely brand loyal

Group D Independent Young Achievers (8.9%)

- A mix of students and stylish young professionals living in inner suburban apartments earning mid to high incomes
- Success is important to this educated group
- Cultured, appreciate art and fine food

Group E Suburban Singles and Sharers (13.1%)

- Represents low to middle income households found in the mid to outer suburbs
- Fashionable, culturally aware individuals who regularly attend art galleries and appreciate the finer things in life, albeit on a challenging budget
- Suburban Singles and Sharers, some of whom are elderly, use public transport to commute although they often have cars

Group F Retired Simplicity (17.2%)

- Can be found in coastal and country towns where a seasonal influx of tourists can be expected
- Elderly couples play golf and lawn bowls—doubling as exercise and an opportunity to meet with friends
- They are proud of their country and prefer to buy Australian wherever possible

Group G Disadvantaged and Dependent (4.3%)

- A mix of young and old living alone
- Can often be found in neighbourhoods that offer cheap services and accommodation
- Typically have a low disposable income and are struggling financially

Group H Self-sufficient Provincials (13.3%)

- Can be found in low-cost housing in outer areas
- Predominantly older families live in these areas, although there has been a recent influx of young families making the most of low-cost housing
- Generally not fashion-conscious, instead spending their money on practical items

Group I Aussie Farmers (5.5%)

- Can be found in country farming areas and service towns
- School-aged children with middle-aged parents and grandparents
- Prefer Aussie tucker to multicultural food—not renowned for their adventurous cooking

Source: Courtesy of Pacific Micromarketing.

The groups are based on a statistical technique that groups small areas on the basis of similar profiles. It is sometimes surprising to see which geodemographic features go together, but the classifications reflect the diversity actually found in the different areas of Australia. Figure 10.4 illustrates how these groups are distributed around Sydney (the 32 categories are further grouped into seven). Figure 10.5 shows a comparable map for Melbourne grouped into seven main types.

The affluent consumer

Affluent households constitute an especially attractive target segment because their members have incomes that provide them with a disproportionately larger share of all discretionary income—allowing the purchase of luxury cruises, foreign sports cars, fashion clothing and fine jewellery, expensive alcohol and increased leisure activities. As Figure 10.6 shows, many alcoholic drinks are targeted at the **affluent consumer** via appeals that include a brand name that suggests affluence and copy that praises the 'uniquely smooth taste' and the aromas of the drink.

Table 10.12 (page 353) shows the relationship between household income and possessions in the home. Clearly, there is a strong relationship for the most expensive items. Eventually, appliances that were initially owned by the affluent spread throughout society. The micrwave oven is an example of this, and the DVD player is another. The relevant measure is what economists call *contestable income*—that is, income (or savings) that can be diverted to another product choice. For example, a family might cut down on gambling so that they can afford a subscription to pay television. In contrast, money spent on transport to work is not contestable in this sense.

While there will always be an opportunity to sell expensive houses, cars, travel and goods to the affluent in Australia, the market is limited. Unlike the United States, it makes little sense to segment this market further, unless a highly specialised product or service (such as an exclusive golf club) is being promoted. Such products need to have very high markups for distributors to make a profit from selling or producing them.

THE MEDIA EXPOSURE OF THE AFFLUENT CONSUMER

As might be expected, the media habits of the affluent differ from those of the general population. For example, among main household income earners who earn more than $60 000 annually, 9.9% read *The Weekend Australian* magazine, compared with 3.0% of those earning less than $20 000 annually. Comparable figures for the *Good Weekend* magazine are 21.4% and 5.8% and, for *Business Review Weekly*, 4.2% and 0.6%. Similarly, 3.8% of those earning over $60 000 read the *Bulletin*, compared with less than 1.0% of those earning less than $20 000.[34]

FIGURE 10.6 **Appeal to segment of affluent consumers**

Source: **Courtesy of Bacardi Lion. Bombay Sapphire and Sapphire are registered trademarks.**

Social classes also differ by their selective exposure to various types of mass media. In the selection of specific television programs and program types, higher social class members tend to prefer current events and drama, while lower-class individuals prefer soap operas, quiz shows and situation comedies. Higher-class consumers tend to have greater exposure to magazines and newspapers and watch less TV than do their lower-class counterparts. Lower-class consumers are likely to have greater exposure to publications that dramatise romance and the lifestyles of movie and television celebrities. For example, magazines like *New Idea*, *Women's Weekly* and *Woman's Day* appeal heavily to blue-collar or working-class women (middle Australia), who enjoy reading about the problems, fame and fortune of others.

SEGMENTING THE AFFLUENT MARKET

In most countries the affluent market is not one single market. Contrary to popular stereotypes, the wealth in countries like America and Australia is not found only behind 'the tall cloistered walls of suburban country clubs'. Wealth is spread in niches, including (but not limited to) Asian and European immigrants.

Because not all affluent consumers share the same lifestyle (i.e. activities, interests and opinions), various marketers have tried to isolate meaningful segments of the affluent market. To assist those interested in reaching subsegments of the affluent market, a US firm, Mediamark Research, Inc. (MRI), has developed for the US market the following affluent market-segmentation schema (or the Upper Deck—defined as the top 10% of households in terms of income).[35]

1. *Well-feathered nests:* Households that have at least one high-income earner and children present (37% of the Upper Deck).
2. *No strings attached:* Households that have at least one high-income earner and no children (32% of the Upper Deck).
3. *Nanny's in charge:* Households that have two or more earners, none earning high incomes, and children present (11% of the Upper Deck).
4. *Two careers:* Households that have two or more earners, neither earning high incomes, and no children present (14% of the Upper Deck).
5. *The good life:* Households that have a high degree of affluence with no person employed or with the head of the household not employed (6% of the Upper Deck).

Armed with these affluent lifestyle segments, MRI provides subscribing companies with profiles of users of a variety of goods and services frequently targeted to the affluent consumer (e.g. domestic and foreign travel, leisure clothing, lawn-care services and various types of recreational activities). For example, in the United States, in terms of recreation, the well–feathered nester may be found on the tennis court, the good lifer may be playing golf, while the two-career couple may be off sailing.[36]

TABLE 10.12 Relationship between household income and possessions

	Under $15 000 %	$15 000–$19 999 %	$20 000–$24 999 %	$25 000–$29 999 %	$30 000–$34 999 %	$35 000–$39 999 %	$40 000–$49 999 %	$50 000–$59 999 %	$60 000–$69 999 %	$70 000+ %
APPLIANCES/ITEMS OWNED										
Microwave	74.67	80.18	78.22	82.66	82.23	84.14	85.92	84.18	89.03	88.95
Air conditioner	40.59	43.84	47.45	45.65	43.82	45.86	47.49	50.96	53.80	55.82
Swimming pool	4.37	4.42	5.62	5.92	7.05	10.25	9.67	11.25	14.75	20.36
Dishwasher	18.05	16.94	22.96	23.82	25.27	27.54	32.29	36.06	43.49	60.39
Personal computer	45.67	44.75	54.64	63.37	69.33	70.99	75.59	81.58	83.10	92.35
Camera $150+	32.88	35.46	40.41	45.60	46.66	48.73	54.85	61.81	65.65	74.55
Stove, oven or hotplate	79.13	82.57	84.85	84.50	83.62	86.06	87.19	86.30	89.68	90.65
Personal CD/cassette/radio (e.g. Walkman)	32.39	32.03	36.17	41.47	40.75	42.20	45.18	45.02	50.15	57.35
Portable combined CD/cassette/radio	36.88	38.68	37.85	39.62	36.52	46.23	41.32	43.32	46.41	48.65
DVD player	24.30	26.62	29.38	32.26	41.37	38.97	48.92	49.53	55.36	64.05
Clothes dryer	36.57	40.92	42.77	47.81	49.96	55.98	54.77	56.54	61.80	68.75

Source: Roy Morgan Single Source Australia: April 2003–March 2004.

With few local marketers vying for their business, the rural affluent represent an untapped (and somewhat difficult to pinpoint) subsegment of the affluent market. The rural affluent fall into four categories:[37]

1. *Suburban transplants:* Those who move to the country but still commute to high-paying urban jobs.
2. *Equity-rich suburban expatriates:* Urbanites who sell their homes for a huge profit, buy a far less expensive home in a small town and live off the difference.
3. *City folks with country homes:* Wealthy snowbirds and vacationers who spend winters or summers in scenic rural areas, especially mountainous or coastal areas.
4. *Wealthy landowners:* Wealthy farmers and others who make a comfortable living off the land.

The non-affluent consumer

Although many advertisers would prefer to show their products as part of an affluent lifestyle, blue-collar and other non-professional people represent a large group of consumers that marketers cannot ignore. After all, everyone needs 'the necessities of life'—a roof over our heads, clothes, security, basic health services and something to eat. In Australia, necessities would normally also include items such as refrigerators, electricity and furniture, although many live below the poverty line[38] and exist without such items.

The arrival of the 'techno-class'

The degree of literacy, familiarity and competency with technology, especially computers and the Internet, appears to be a new basis for a kind of 'class standing', status or prestige. Those who are unfamiliar with computers and lack computer skills are being referred to as 'technologically underclassed'.[39] Educators, business leaders and government officials have warned that the inability to use technology adequately has a negative impact on lifestyle and quality of life.

Fuelling this perception, the business press regularly runs cover stories featuring technological superstars like Bill Gates. The copy describes their accomplishments and enviable lifestyles that include $30 million residences and other luxuries, and serves to motivate readers to duplicate their accomplishments. Even factory workers in highly successful start-up technology firms in some countries have become millionaires on their employee profit-sharing and stock options.

These stories of entrepreneurial and technological accomplishment, coupled with a general sense of not wanting to be left out of the 'sweep of computer technology', have propelled parents to seek computer training for their children, even infant children. Parents realise that an understanding of computer usage is a necessary tool of 'competitive achievement' and success. Even older professionals (55 and older), who were initially reluctant to 'learn computers', are now seeking personal computer training—they no longer want to be left out, nor do they want to be embarrassed by having to admit that they 'don't know computers'.

Consumers throughout the world have come to believe that it is critical to acquire a functional understanding of computers to ensure they do not become obsolete or hinder themselves socially or professionally. In this sense, there is a 'technological class structure' that centres around the extent of one's computer skills. It appears that those without necessary computer skills will increasingly find themselves 'underclassed' and 'disadvantaged'.

Selected consumer behaviour applications of class

Social class profiles provide a broad picture of the values, attitudes and behaviour that distinguish the members of various social classes. This section focuses on specific consumer research that relates social class to the development of marketing strategy.

CLOTHING, FASHION AND SHOPPING

A Greek philosopher once said: 'Know, first, who you are; and then adorn yourself accordingly.'[40] This piece of wisdom is relevant to clothing marketers today, since most people dress to fit their self-images, which include their perceptions of their own social class membership.

Members of specific social classes differ in terms of what they consider fashionable or in good taste. For instance, lower-middle-class consumers have a strong preference for t-shirts, caps and other clothing that offers an external point of identification, such as the name of an admired person or group (e.g. Ricky Ponting, David Beckham), a respected company or brand name (Hot Tuna) or a valued trademark (Nike). These consumers are prime targets for licensed goods. In contrast, upper-class consumers are likely to buy clothing that is free from such 'supporting' associations. Upper-class consumers may seek clothing with a more subtle look, such as the kind of sportswear found overseas, rather than high-status jeans.

In Shanghai, the public wearing of pyjamas is a sign of status and possibly a signal of an economically developing society (historically, its citizens could not afford the luxury of wearing pyjamas).[41] In a similar manner, people in Asia can be observed wearing outer clothing with the well-known designer labels still on the garment's sleeves. Again, this is a sign of status, of being able to afford expensive luxury clothing.

Social class may also be important in determining where a consumer shops. It would appear that retailing is dividing into mass market stores, such as Kmart, Big-W and Woolworths, and specialty stores, like Robins Kitchen, Colorado, Myer and David Jones. Among the specialty stores many target the affluent,[42] and an inspection of the newer shopping malls will demonstrate this pattern. People tend to avoid stores that have an image of appealing to a social class very different from their own. In the past, some mass merchandisers who tried to appeal to a higher class of consumers found themselves alienating their traditional customers. This implies that retailers should pay attention to the social class of their customer base and the social class of their store appeal to ensure that they send the appropriate message through advertisements.

HOME DECORATION

To the extent that a family's home is its castle, the decor of the home should provide clues to the family's social class position. Of all the rooms in the home, the living room seems to express most clearly how a family wants to be seen by those it entertains. Therefore, living-room furnishings are likely to be particularly sensitive to class influences. As noted earlier, Chapin's Social Status Scale uses the presence and condition of living-room furnishings to measure a family's social class standing. The appropriateness of using living-room furnishings as a barometer of social class standing is based on the premise that the living-room is the 'face' a family shows to its guests.

The Australian magazines *Home Beautiful* and *Vogue Living* reflect social class differences by emphasising high-status and luxury home settings. For example, the style or status appeal is conveyed in Figure 10.7 through the copy 'beautiful, durable flooring for all walks of life'.

THE PURSUIT OF LEISURE

Social class membership is also closely related to the choice of recreational and leisure time activities (such as tennis and golf). Upper-class consumers are likely to attend the theatre and concerts, to play bridge and to use a PC for Internet browsing. Lower-class consumers tend to be avid television watchers and fishing enthusiasts and enjoy attending sports such as drag racing and football. The lower-class consumer also spends more time on commercial types of activities (visiting clubs and hotels) and craft activities (model building, painting, woodworking projects), rather than cerebral activities (reading, visiting museums).[43] Unemployed Australians spend an average of 342 minutes a day on recreation and leisure, while full-time workers spend around 277.[44] In 1988–89, high-status professionals were estimated to spend an average of $34 a week on cultural activities (e.g. cinema, theatre, CDs) compared with $19 a week spent by labourers.[45] It appears that, whether we are describing middle-class or working-class consumers, there is a growing trend towards more spending on 'experiences' that bring the family together (family holidays or activities) and less on 'things'.[46]

FIGURE 10.7 **An advertisement for home decoration 'flooring' emphasising style and class**

Amtico
Beautiful, Durable Flooring for all Walks of Life

Source: Courtesy of Amtico.

SAVING, SPENDING AND CREDIT

Saving, spending and credit-card use all seem to be related to social class standing. Upper-class consumers are more future-oriented and confident of their financial acumen; they are more willing to invest in insurance, stocks and shares, and real estate. In comparison, lower-class consumers are generally more concerned with immediate gratification; when they do save, they are primarily interested in safety and security. Therefore, it is not surprising that members of the lower social classes tend to use their bank credit cards for instalment purchases, while members of the middle and upper social classes pay their credit card bills in full each month. In other words, lower-class purchasers tend to use their credit cards to 'buy now and pay later' for things they might not otherwise be able to afford, while upper-class purchasers use their credit cards as a convenient substitute for cash.

This is evidenced by the relative importance that affluent consumers place on bank services compared with non-affluent consumers. Affluent consumers seem to be more adventurous financially than their non-affluent counterparts, being more likely to seek financial advice and to take out large mortgages. The non-affluent consumer typically wants more traditional products and services, such as passbook savings accounts.[47]

SOCIAL CLASS AND COMMUNICATION

Social class groupings differ in their media habits and in how they transmit and receive communications. Knowledge of these differences is invaluable to marketers who segment their markets on the basis of social class.

When describing their world, lower-class consumers tend to portray it in personal and concrete terms, while middle-class consumers are able to describe their experiences from a number of perspectives. A simple example illustrates that members of different social classes tend to see the world differently. The following responses to a question asking where the respondent usually bought petrol were received:

- Upper-middle-class answer: At Mobil or Shell.
- Lower-middle-class answer: At the station on Napper Road.
- Lower-class answer: At Ed's.

Such variations in response indicate that middle-class consumers have a broader or more general view of the world, while lower-class consumers tend to have a narrower or more personal view, seeing the world through their own immediate experiences.

Regional differences in terminology, choice of words and phrases, and patterns of usage also tend to increase as we move down the social class ladder. Therefore, in creating messages targeted to the lower classes, marketers should try to word advertisements to reflect the particular regional preferences that exist throughout Australia.

CASE STUDY 10.1

Milk—Are You Getting Enough?

Dr Gillian Sullivan Mort, Graduate School of Management, University of Queensland
Dr Jay Weerawardena, Graduate School of Management, University of Queensland
Nick Parkington, University of Melbourne

Some beverages are the 'Real Thing', some are for the 'New Generation'. Sometimes we are told they have B vitamins, others simply make our break or get us cruising in the fast lane. The beverage market is a crowded one and the soft beverage market even more so. The difficulty for dairy producers has been to try to compete and increase consumption in this crowded beverage marketplace, especially against the innovative, high-spending firms with the well-packaged, well-known brands in the carbonated beverage segment.

Milk production

While farm numbers have decreased over the last 20 years, milk output has steadily increased since 1985, due to improved cow yields and, in more recent years, increasing cow numbers (Figure 10.8).

Australian milk production is highly seasonal (Figure 10.9). This reflects both the pasture-based nature of the industry and the importance of long shelf life manufactured products—particularly in the south-east of Australia, the dominant dairy region. Milk production peaks in October, tapering off in the colder months of May and June. Milk output in some other States, such as New South Wales and Queensland, is less seasonal due to a greater focus on drinking milk and fresh products in the product mix (Figure 10.10).

Australian milk production peaked in 2001/02 at 11 271 million litres, whilst the industry experienced a decrease of 8.4% in 2002/03 to record a production output of 10 326 million litres for that year (Table 10.13).

The number of dairy cows continued to increase to 2000/01, reflected in the record production of milk, however the estimated number of cattle in 2002/03 is 3.7% lower than that of 2001/02 (Table 10.14, page 361).

FIGURE 10.8 Australian milk production 1985–2003

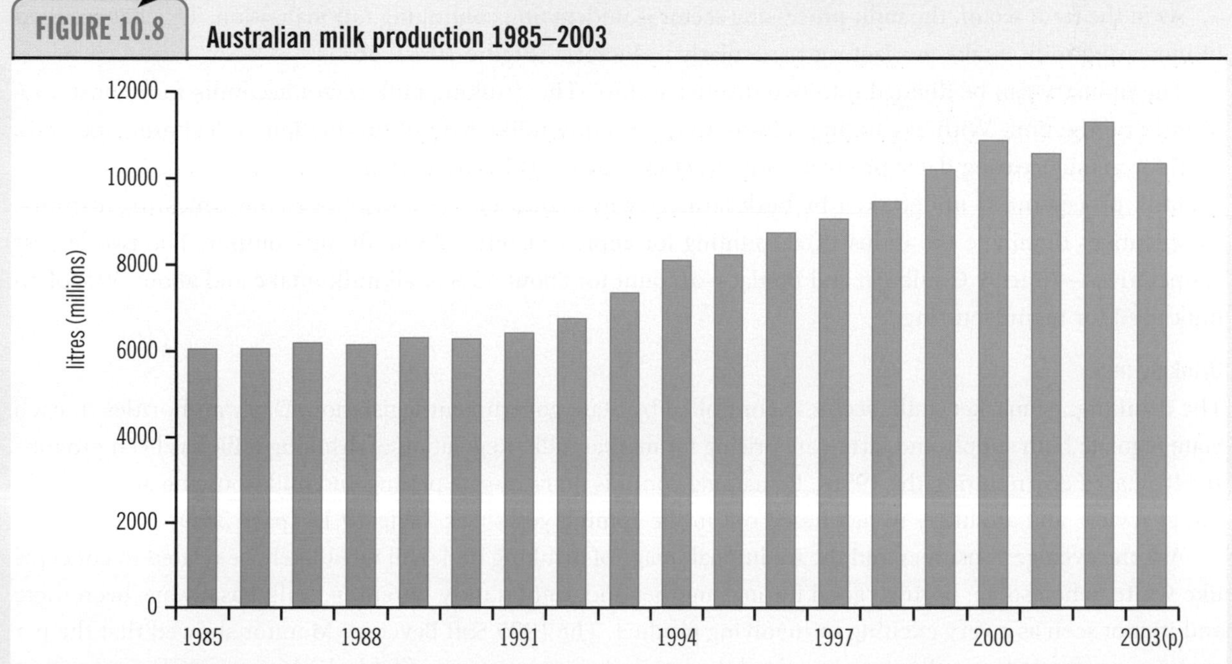

Source: Dairy Australia Limited.

FIGURE 10.9 Seasonality of milk production in Australia

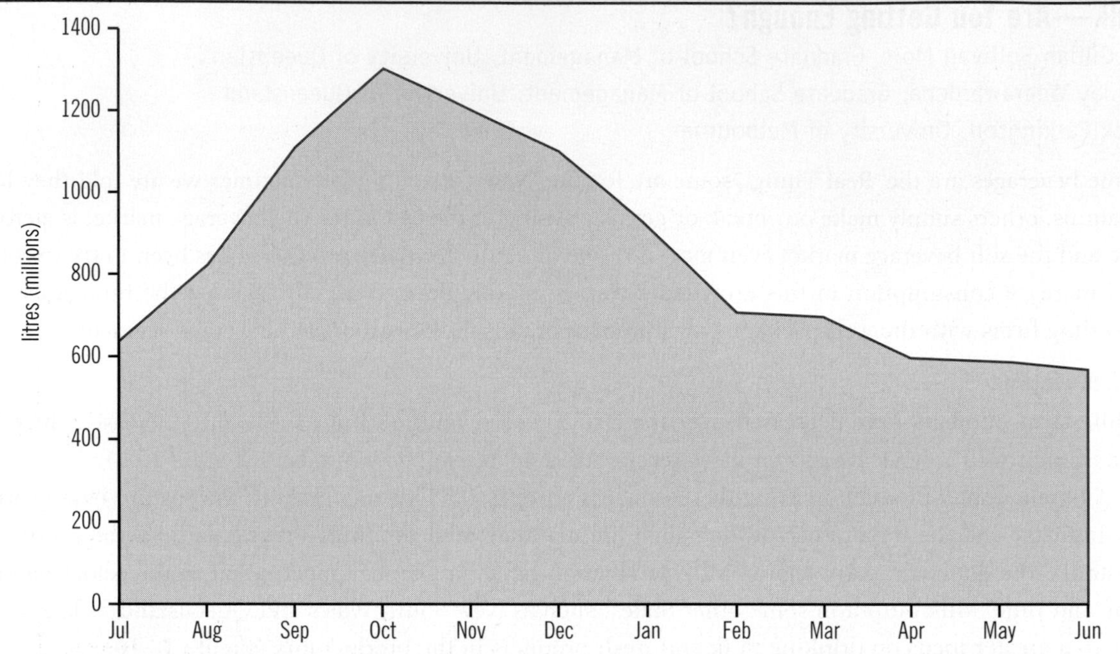

Source: **Dairy Australia Limited.**

Milk production is concentrated in the south-east corner of Australia, with Victoria accounting for over 60% of total output (Figure 10.11, page 360).

As in the farm sector, the milk-processing sector is undergoing continuing rationalisation. This has resulted in increasing milk intake per factory, particularly in Victoria (Figure 10.12, 361).

The industry can be divided into two distinct sectors. The drinking milk sector accounts for almost 19% of milk production. With expanding milk output, drinking milk share of production is declining and milk used for manufacturing dairy products is increasing (Figure 10.13, page 362).

Milk processing is undertaken by both farmer-owned cooperatives and public companies in Australia. Cooperatives dominate the industry, accounting for approximately 75% of all milk output. The two largest cooperatives—Murray Goulburn and Bonlac—account for about 45% of all milk intake and about 50% of all milk used for manufacturing.

Drinking milk

The drinking, or market, milk sector is controlled by State government legislation. Dairy authorities in each State regulate both supply and farm-gate pricing for market milk. Regulation of drinking milk has been progressively phased down during the 1990s. Remaining controls on farm-gate pricing and milk sourcing are currently under review, and are likely to be phased out in the coming years. See Table 10.15 (page 362).

Ask the average consumer and the traditional image of drinking milk will most likely be related to concepts like white, wholesome, boring, 'good for me', mother and, importantly, fattening. Milk has always been there and it's not seen as a very exciting or involving product. The 1995 Soft Beverage Monitor showed that the per capita consumption of milk as a plain drink had room for improvement (Table 10.16, page 363).

FIGURE 10.10 Seasonality of milk production by State (Average 1997/98–2001/02 compared with 2002/03)

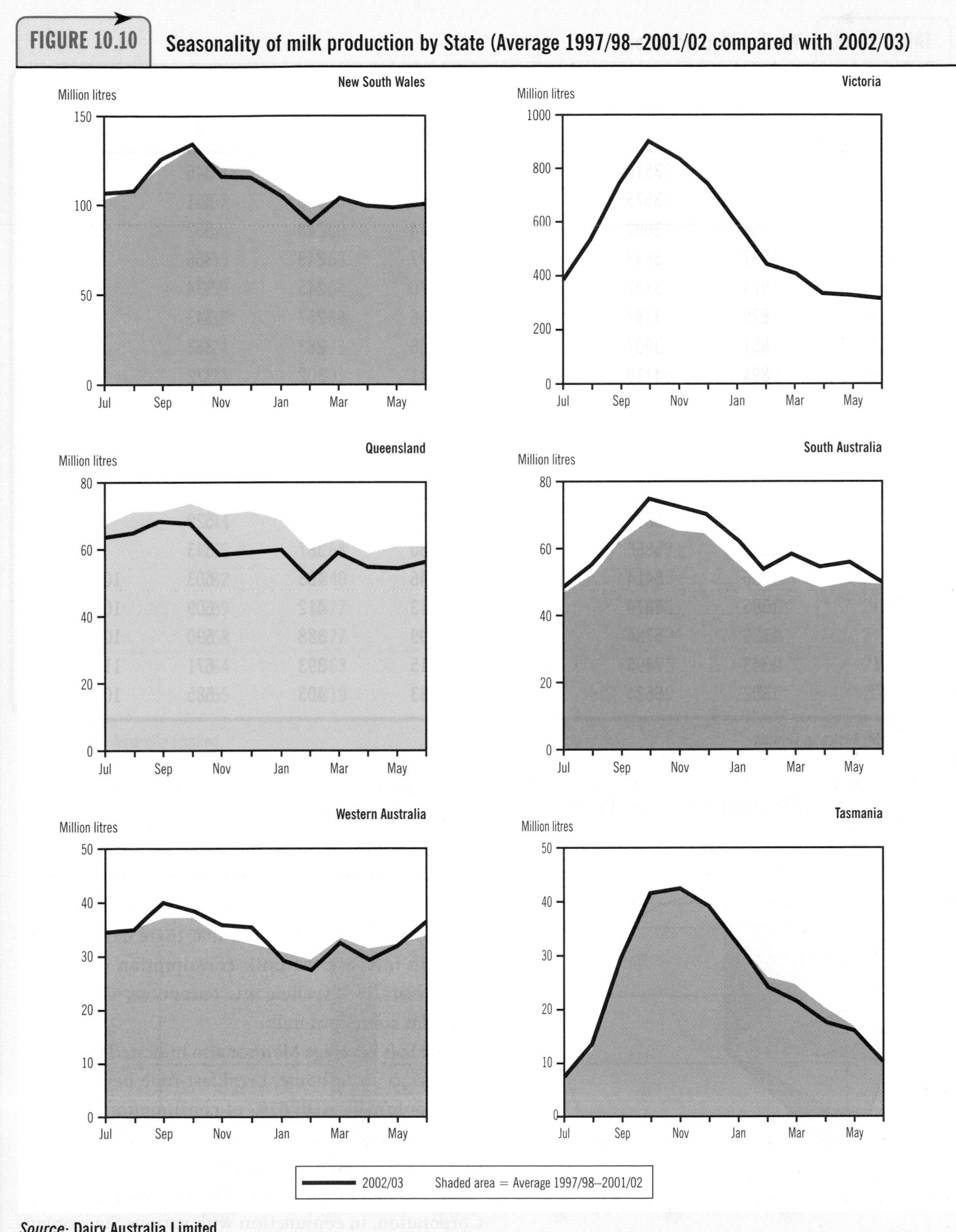

Source: Dairy Australia Limited.

measures rely on an individual's self-perception, reputational measures rely on an individual's perceptions of others, and objective measures use specific socioeconomic measures, either alone (as a single-variable index) or in combination with others (as a composite-variable index). Composite-variable indexes combine a number of socioeconomic factors to form one overall measure of social class standing.

Class structures range from two-class to nine-class systems. A common way of describing class is to use the upper, middle and working class classification, while others (such as market research companies) classify people into quintiles based on income, education and occupation. From sociological theory, Australian researchers have used the classification into employers, petty bourgeoisie, managers, supervisors, expert non-managers, skilled workers and proletariat to describe class groups. Another frequently used system classifies six classes: upper-upper, lower-upper, upper-middle, lower-middle, upper-lower and lower-lower. Profiles of class groups indicate that the socioeconomic differences between classes are reflected in differences in attitudes, leisure activities, shopping, personal finances and media consumption habits. That is why segmentation by social class is of special interest to marketers. Given that the top fifth of families earn just under half the nation's income, it is hardly surprising that marketers target the affluent.

In recent years some marketers have turned to geodemographic clustering as an alternative to a strict social class typology. Geodemographic clustering is a technique that combines geographic and socioeconomic factors to locate concentrations of consumers with particular characteristics. Particular attention is currently being directed to affluent consumers, who represent the fastest-growing segment in our population; however, some marketers are finding it extremely profitable to cater to the needs of non-affluent consumers.

Research has revealed social class differences in clothing habits, home decoration, leisure activities and saving, spending and credit habits. Thus, astute marketers tailor specific product and promotional strategies for each social class target segment.

Discussion questions

1. Marketing researchers have generally used the objective method to measure social class, rather than the subjective or reputational methods. Why has the objective method been preferred by researchers?
2. Under what circumstances would you expect income to be a better predictor of consumer behaviour than a composite measure of social class (based on income, education and occupation)? When would you expect the composite social class measure to be superior?
3. Describe the correlation between social status (or prestige) and income. Which is a more useful segmentation variable? Discuss.
4. Which status-related variable—occupation, education or income—is the most appropriate segmentation base for: (a) expensive holidays; (b) opera subscriptions; (c) people magazine subscriptions; (d) fat-free foods; (e) personal computers; (f) pocket-sized mobile phones; (g) health clubs?
5. Consider the Rolex watch, which has a retail price range starting at about $2000 for a stainless steel model to thousands of dollars for a solid gold model. How might the Rolex company make use of geodemographic clustering in its marketing efforts?
6. How would you use the research evidence on affluent households presented in this chapter to segment the market for: (a) home exercise equipment; (b) holidays; (c) banking services?
7. How can a marketer use knowledge of consumer behaviour to develop financial services for affluent consumers? For 'downscale' consumers?
8. You are the owner of two furniture stores, one catering to upper-middle-class consumers and the other to lower-class consumers. How do social class differences influence each store's: (a) product lines and styles; (b) advertising media selection; (c) the copy and communications style used in the ads; (d) payment policies?

Exercises

1. Copy the list of occupations in Table 10.3 and ask students majoring in areas other than marketing to rank the relative prestige of these occupations. Are any differences in rankings related to the students' majors? Explain.
2. Find three print ads from popular magazines. Using the social class characteristics listed in Table 10.1, identify the social class targeted by each ad and evaluate the effectiveness of the advertising appeals used.
3. Select two households featured in two different TV series or sitcoms. Classify each household into one of the social classes discussed in the text and analyse its lifestyle and consumption behaviour.
4. Analyse the social class of the main characters in two television comedy or drama series made in Australia, in terms of lifestyle, affluence and values.

Key terms

affluent consumer *(p. 351)*
Chapin's Social Status Scale *(p. 339)*
classless society *(p. 329)*
composite-variable indexes *(p. 339)*
contestable income *(p. 338)*
downward mobility *(p. 348)*
geodemographic clustering *(p. 348)*
lifestyle *(p. 336)*
objective measurement of social class *(p. 334)*
occupational status *(p. 335)*
proletariat *(p. 343)*
quintiles *(p. 336)*
reputational measures *(p. 334)*
single-variable indexes *(p. 335)*
social class *(p. 329)*
social status *(p. 329)*
socioeconomic profiles *(p. 334)*
strata *(p. 329)*
subjective measurement of social class *(p. 334)*
upward mobility *(p. 346)*

Endnotes

1. R.W. Connell and T.H. Irving, *Class Structure in Australian History* (Melbourne: Longman Cheshire, 1980).
2. Around 61% of Australians disagree that Australia is a classless society. See *True Who? An Analysis of What Today's Australian is Really Like* (Sydney: The Campaign Palace, 1988).
3. Data from the Australian Bureau of Statistics showed that, over the period 1981–82 to 1989–90, the top 20% of family units increased their share of the national income from 43% to 46.7%. See *Social Indicators: Australia, 1992*, p. 244. For household data, see *Household Expenditure Survey Australia: 1993–94: Detailed Expenditure Items* (Canberra: Australian Bureau of Statistics, 1996), Catalogue No. 6535.0.
4. Douglas B. Holt, 'Does cultural capital structure American consumption?', *Journal of Consumer Research*, 25, June 1998, p. 19.
5. Mark Western, 'International class mobility among women and men', *Australian and New Zealand Journal of Sociology*, 30(3), 1994, pp. 303–321.
6. Aron O'Cass and Hmily Frost, 'Status brands: Examining the effects of non-product related brand associations on status and conspicuous consumption', *Journal of Product & Brand Management*, 11(2), 2002, pp. 67–88; Aron O'Cass and Hmily McEwan, 'Exploring consumer status and conspicuous consumption', *Journal of Consumer Behaviour* (in press).
7. *AGB Consumer Market Profiles*, 1992. Each person is scored on income, education and occupation of head of household scales. The scales are given equal weight and added. The resulting scores are divided into five equal groups, to give the different classes.
8. In the American edition of this book, Schiffman and Kanuk describe social class categories that include up to nine groups, such as 'lower-upper' and 'middle-middle'. See Leon G. Schiffman and Leslie Lazar Kanuk, *Consumer Behavior*, 5th edn (New Jersey: Prentice Hall, 1994), p. 380.
9. Connell and Irving, op. cit.
10. F.L. Jones and P. Davis, 'Closure and fluidity in the class structure', *Australian and New Zealand Journal of Sociology*, 24(2), 1988, pp. 226–247.
11. G. Dow and G. Lafferty, 'From class analysis to class politics: A critique of sociological interpretations of class', *Australian and New Zealand Journal of Sociology*, 26(1), 1990, pp. 3–35.
12. B. Graetz, 'Social structure and class consciousness: Facts, fictions and fantasies', *Australian and New Zealand Journal of Sociology*, 22(1), 1986, pp. 46–64. The results were based on a national survey conducted in 1973. See also Chris Chamberlain, *Class Consciousness in Australia* (Sydney: George Allen & Unwin, 1983).
13. F.L. Jones, 'Stratification approaches to class measurement', *Australian and New Zealand Journal of Sociology*, 24(2), 1988, pp. 279–284; and F.L. Jones, 'Occupational prestige in Australia: A new scale', *Australian and New Zealand Journal of Sociology*, 25(2), pp. 187–199.
14. Paul Leinberger, 'The monitor: Clued up on the intelligent consumer', *Australian Professional Marketing*, February 1993, pp. 38–39.
15. Craig McGregor, *Class in Australia*, Penguin, 1997. Although other research shows reasonable agreement about social status across the community, care should be taken in generalising the results.
16. Bob Connell, 'The money measure: Social inequality of wealth and income', in Jan O'Leary and Rachel Sharp (eds), *Inequality in Australia: Slicing the Cake* (Port Melbourne: William Heinemann, 1991).
17. *1988–89 Household Expenditure Survey Australia: Detailed Expenditure Items* (Canberra: Australian Bureau of Statistics, 1990), Catalogue No. 6535.0.
18. Eugene Sivadas, George Mathew and David J. Curry, 'A preliminary examination of the continued significance of social class to marketing: A geodemographic replication', *Journal of Consumer Marketing*, 14(6), 1997, p. 469.

19. Paul Henry and Margaret Craig-Lees, 'The differing "world views" of social classes in Australia', in K. Grant and I. Walker (eds), *Proceedings of the Seventh Bi-Annual World Marketing Congress* (Melbourne: Academy of Marketing Science, 1995) Vol. VII-1, 2-84 to 2-91.
20. Richard P. Coleman, 'The continuing significance of social class to marketing', *Journal of Consumer Research,* 10, 1983, p. 274.
21. Dennis Rodkin, 'Wealthy attitude wins over healthy wallet: Consumers prove affluence is a state of mind', *Advertising Age*, 9 July 1990, pp. S4, S6.
22. F. Stuart Chapin, *Contemporary American Institutions* (New York: Harper, 1935), pp. 373–397.
23. Joan Kron, *Home-Psych* (New York: Potter, 1983), pp. 90–102.
24. For examples of research using this classification, see Tim Gill and Jim Harnwell, 'The AB market: Cash in on cashed up—selectively', *B&T*, 13 May 1994, pp. 15–16; Greg Graham, 'New slant on age-old AB quandary', ibid., pp. 20–21.
25. Robert B. Settle, Pamela L. Alreck and Denny E. McCorkle, 'Consumer perceptions of mail/phone order shopping media', *Journal of Direct Marketing*, 8, Summer 1994, pp. 30–45.
26. Ibid.
27. W. Lloyd Warner, Marchia Meeker and Kenneth Eells, *Social Class in America: Manual of Procedure for the Measurement of Social Status* (New York: Harper & Brothers, 1960).
28. J.H. Baxter, P.R. Boreham, S.R. Clegg, J.M. Emmison, G.M. Gibson, G.N. Marks, J.S. Western and M.C. Western, 'The Australian class structure: Some preliminary results from the Australian Class Project', *Australian and New Zealand Journal of Sociology*, 25(1), 1989, pp. 100–120; J. Baxter, M. Emerson and J. Western, *Class Analysis and Contemporary Analysis* (Melbourne: Macmillan, 1991).
29. Australian Bureau of Statistics, *Australian Standard Classification of Occupations* (Canberra: Australian Bureau of Statistics, 1986).
30. One of the early Australian attempts is contained in *The Age Lifestyle Study* (Melbourne: *The Age*, 1982).
31. Geng Cui and Quiming Liu, 'Executive insights: Emerging market segments in a transitional economy: A study of urban consumers in China', *Journal of International Marketing*, 9(1), 2001, pp. 84–106.
32. 'The perfect face', *Adweek's Marketing Week*, 5 August 1991, p. 16.
33. 'Why the top few earn big dollars', *Sunday Age*, 26 March 1995; *Career Journal.com* <http://salaryexpert.com>, June 2004; 'Top salaries defy industry fall', *Australian Financial Review*, 9 September 2003.
34. Roy Morgan Single Source Australia: April 2003–March 2004. For US data, see Ronald Alsop, 'Wealth of affluent magazines vie for advertisers' attention', *Wall Street Journal*, 9 January 1986, p. 23.
35. The Upper Deck (Mediamark Research, Inc., 1998).
36. For further insights into the affluence of dual-income households, see Diane Crispell, 'The very rich are sort of different', *American Demographics*, March 1994, pp. 11–13.
37. Sharon O'Malley, 'Country gold', *American Demographics*, July 1992, pp. 26–34.
38. See Connell, op. cit.
39. Steve Rosenbush, 'Techno leaders warn of great divide', *USA Today*, 17 June 1998, p. B1.
40. Epictetus (2nd century), 'Discourses', in *The Enchiridon*, 2nd edn, trans. by Thomas Higginson (Indianapolis: Bobbs-Merrill, 1955).
41. Seth Faison, 'A city of sleepwalkers? No, they just like PJ's', *New York Times*, 6 August 1997, p. A4.
42. For US research in this area, see John P. Dickson and Douglas L. MacLachan, 'Social distance and shopping behavior', *Journal of the Academy of Marketing Science*, 18, 1990, pp. 153–161.
43. The evidence on which this is based is largely American. See Schiffman and Kanuk, op. cit., p. 403.
44. Australian Bureau of Statistics, *How Australians Use Their Time*, Catalogue No. 4153.0, 1997.
45. Australian Bureau of Statistics, *Cultural Trends in Australia: No.1: A Statistical Overview* (Canberra: ABS, 1994).
46. Christina Duff, 'Indulging in inconspicuous consumption', *Wall Street Journal*, 14 April 1997, pp. B1, B2; and Christina Duff, 'Two family budgets: Different means, similar ends', *Wall Street Journal*, 14 April 1997, pp. B1, B2.
47. Edward G. Thomas, S.R. Rao and Rajshekar G. Javalgi, 'Affluent and non-affluent consumers' needs: Attitudes and information-seeking behavior in the financial services marketplace', *Journal of Services Marketing*, 4, 1990, pp. 41–54.
48. The evidence on which this is based is largely American. See Schiffman and Kanuk, op. cit., p. 403.
49. Australian Bureau of Statistics, *Cultural Trends in Australia: No. 1: A Statistical Overview* (Canberra: ABS, 1994).
50. Christina Duff, 'Indulging in inconspicuous consumption', *Wall Street Journal*, 14 April 1997, pp. B1, B2; and Christina Duff, 'Two family budgets: Different means, similar ends', *Wall Street Journal*, 14 April 1997, pp. B1, B2. Mosiac profiles supplied by Pacific Micromarketing, 1999. Used with permission.

CHAPTER 11

The influence of culture on consumer behaviour

NEW! NIGHT RESCUE

WAKE UP TO YOUNGER LOOKING SKIN

LAB SERIES FOR MEN

NIGHT RESCUE
SKIN REVITALIZING THERAPY
Réparateur Intense Nuit
1.7 FL. OZ./50 ml ℮
aramis

WITH NIGHT RESCUE SKIN REVITALIZING THERAPY SEE*:

Up to 33% improved hydration
Helps repair and revitalize the skin's appearance

Up to 30% fewer visible lines and wrinkles
Protects skin leaving it smoother and younger looking

Up to 29% increased firmness
Improves tone and texture

*After 8 weeks of daily use

Powerful breakthrough formula helps repair, protect and revitalize the skin's appearance while you sleep—targeting men's key anti-aging concerns. Provides advanced moisturisation and anti-oxidant protection as it reduces the appearance of lines and wrinkles. Awaken to younger looking skin!

LAB SERIES FOR MEN
aramis

Source: Courtesy of Estée Lauder.

The study of culture is a challenging undertaking because its primary focus is on the broadest component of social behaviour—an entire society. In contrast to the psychologist, who is principally concerned with the study of individual behaviour, or the sociologist, who is concerned with the study of groups, the anthropologist is primarily interested in identifying the very fabric of society itself.

This chapter explores the basic concepts of culture, with particular emphasis on the role that culture plays in influencing consumer behaviour in Australian society. We first consider the specific dimensions of culture that make it a powerful force in regulating human behaviour. After reviewing several measurement approaches that researchers employ in their efforts to understand the impact of culture on consumption behaviour, we show how a variety of multicultural values influence consumer behaviour. This chapter is concerned with the more general aspects of *culture*; the following two chapters focus on *subcultures* and on *cross-culture* and show how marketers can use such knowledge to shape and modify their marketing strategies.

What is culture?

Given the broad and pervasive nature of culture, its study generally requires a broad examination of the character of the total society, including such factors as language, knowledge, laws, religions, food customs, music, rituals, art, technology, work patterns, products and other artifacts that give the society its distinctive flavour. In a sense, culture is a society's personality. For this reason, it is not easy to define its boundaries.

Since our objective is to understand the influence of culture on consumer behaviour, we define **culture** as the *sum total of learned beliefs, values and customs that serve to direct the consumer behaviour of members of a particular society*. The belief and value components of our definition refer to the accumulated feelings and priorities that individuals have about behaviours, possessions and goals. More precisely, **beliefs** consist of the very large number of mental or verbal statements (i.e. 'I believe . . .') that reflect our particular knowledge and assessment of something (another person, a store, a product, a brand). **Values** are also beliefs. However, values differ from other beliefs in that they meet the following criteria:

1. They are relatively few in number.
2. They serve as a guide for culturally appropriate behaviour.
3. They are enduring or difficult to change.
4. They are not tied to specific objects or situations.
5. They are widely accepted by the members of a society.

Therefore, in a broad sense, both values and beliefs are *mental images* that affect a wide range of specific attitudes, which in turn influence the way a person is likely to respond in a specific situation. For example, the criteria we use to evaluate alternative brands in a product category (e.g. a Holden Commodore versus a Mazda 6) and our eventual decision regarding these brands are influenced both by our general *values* (e.g. perceptions as to quality, country of origin, production skills, status, design and aesthetics) and by specific *beliefs* (e.g. *particular* perceptions about the quality, production skills, status, design and aesthetics of the Holden and the Mazda). Institutions such as our homes, schools and the media[1] transmit our basic and evolving culture to each generation.

In contrast to beliefs and values, **customs** are *overt modes of behaviour that constitute culturally approved or acceptable ways of behaving in specific situations*. Customs consist of everyday behaviour as well as accepted rituals around times like Christmas. For example, a consumer's everyday behaviour, such as having a cappucino with lunch or giving Christmas presents, are customs. Thus, while beliefs and values are *guides* for behaviour, customs are *usual and acceptable ways of behaving*.

Using this broad approach, it is easy to see how an understanding of the beliefs, values and customs of a society helps marketers to predict consumer acceptance of their products.

THE INVISIBLE HAND OF CULTURE

The impact of culture is so natural and so automatic that its influence on behaviour is usually taken for granted. For example, when consumer researchers ask people why they do certain things, they frequently answer 'Because it's the right thing to do'. This seemingly superficial response partially reflects the ingrained influence of culture on our behaviour. Often, it is only when we are exposed to people with different cultural values or customs (e.g. when visiting a different country, or as an overseas student in Australia) that we become aware of how culture has moulded our own behaviour. Thus, a true appreciation of the influence culture has on our daily life requires some knowledge of at least one other society with different cultural characteristics. For example, a mundane item like toilet paper is not used in some cultures. Even in Australia, 4% of households in a panel survey reported buying no toilet paper over the course of a year.[2]

CULTURE SATISFIES NEEDS

Culture exists to satisfy the needs of the people within a society. It offers *order*, *direction* and *guidance* in all phases of human problem solving by providing 'tried and true' methods of satisfying physiological, personal and social needs. For example, culture provides standards and 'rules' about when to eat, where to eat, what is appropriate to eat for breakfast, lunch, dinner and snacks, and what to serve to guests at a dinner party, picnic or wedding. Soft drink companies would prefer that consumers received their morning 'jolt' of caffeine from one of their products, rather than from coffee. Because most Australians do not consider soft drink to be a suitable breakfast beverage, the real challenge for soft drink companies is to overcome culture, not competition. One approach for a company like Coca-Cola has been to market fruit juices and other acceptable breakfast drinks.

Cultural beliefs, values and customs continue to be followed as long as they yield satisfaction. However, when a specific standard no longer satisfies the members of a society, it is modified or replaced, so that the resulting standard is more in line with current needs and desires. Thus, culture gradually but continually evolves to meet the needs of society. While home cooking was once considered largely women's work, the rapid growth in the number of working women has led advertisers to emphasise meals that are quick to prepare and can be cooked by either men or women. Many workplaces with strict dress codes have been replaced by more casual styles. Look at the dress codes followed by your lecturers or instructors—have they followed this trend?

In a cultural context, a firm's products and services can be viewed as offering appropriate or acceptable solutions for individual or societal needs. If a product is no longer acceptable because a value or custom that is related to its use does not adequately satisfy human needs, then the firm producing it must be ready to revise its product offering. Marketers must also be alert to newly embraced customs and values. For example, as Australians have become more conscious of health and fitness, there has been an increase in the number of walkers, joggers and cyclists on the nation's streets. Astute shoe manufacturers who responded by offering an increased variety of appropriate footwear have been able to improve their market positions. In contrast, marketers who were not perceptive enough to note the opportunities created by changing values and lifestyles lost market share and, in some cases, were squeezed out of the market.

CULTURE IS LEARNED

Unlike innate biological characteristics (e.g. sex, skin, hair colour, intelligence), culture is *learned*. At an early age we begin to acquire from our social environment a set of beliefs, values and customs that constitute our culture. Play and the use of toys in particular is one of the ways children learn cultural values and practices. Later in life, lessons learned in play are taken into adult life.

How culture is learned

Anthropologists have identified three distinct forms of cultural learning:

1. **formal learning**, in which adults and older siblings teach a young family member 'how to behave'
2. **informal learning**, in which a child learns primarily by imitating or modelling the behaviour of selected others (family, friends, sporting heroes)
3. **technical learning**, in which teachers instruct the child in an educational environment as to *what* should be done, *how* it should be done, and *why* it should be done.

Although a firm's advertising can influence all three types of cultural learning, it is likely that many product advertisements enhance informal cultural learning by providing the audience with a model of behaviour to imitate (see Figure 11.1). This is especially true for visible or conspicuous products (such as clothing, MP3 players or mobile phones) or language where peer influence is likely to play an important role.[3]

The repetition of advertising messages both creates and reinforces cultural beliefs and values. For example, many advertisers continually stress the same selected benefits as integral features of their products or brands. Ads for mobile phones often stress features such as free air time, unlimited talk time and ability to send pictures. It is difficult to say whether product owners, after several years of cumulative exposure to such potent advertising appeals, *inherently* desire these benefits from their mobile phones or have been *taught* by marketers to desire them. In a sense, although specific product advertising may reinforce the benefits that consumers want from the product (as determined by consumer behaviour research), such advertising also 'teaches' future generations of consumers to expect the same benefits from the product category.

FIGURE 11.1 Informal learning of culture

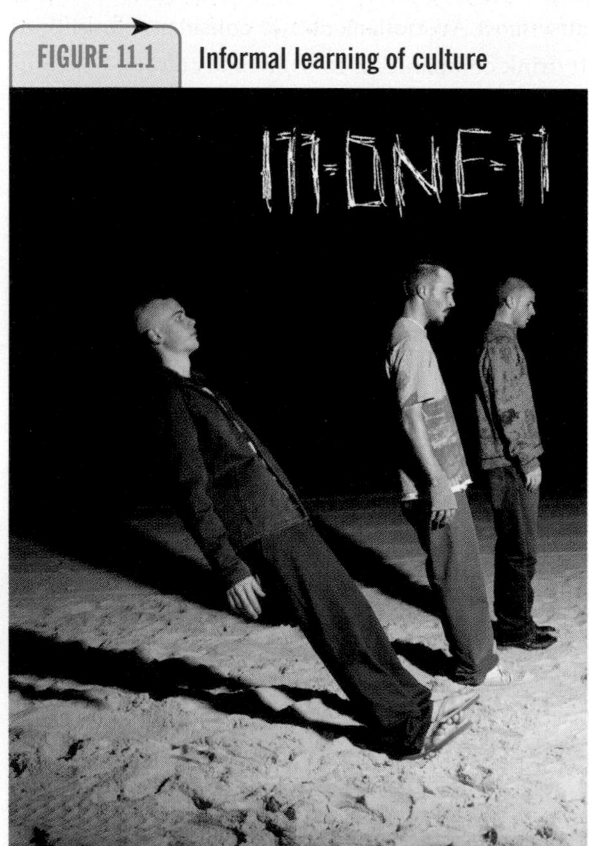

Source: M-one-11, Winter 2004. Photographer: Harold David. Creative: Daniela Marich. Reproduced by permission.

Figure 11.2 shows that cultural meaning moves from the culturally constituted world to consumer goods, and from there to the individual consumer by means of various consumption-related vehicles. For example, the ever-popular T-shirt can furnish cultural meaning for wearers (see Table 11.1). Many of the symbols on T-shirts ('Hard Rock Cafe' or 'Manchester United') are common across the world. Specifically, T-shirts can function as *trophies* (e.g. proof of participation, travel) or as self-proclaimed labels of *belonging to a cultural category* (e.g. Brisbane Lions, Barmy Army). T-shirts can also be used as a means of *self-expression*, which may provide wearers with the additional benefit of serving as a 'topic' initiating social dialogue with others.[4]

Enculturation and acculturation

In discussing the acquisition of culture, anthropologists often distinguish between the learning of one's own, or *native*, culture and the learning of some other culture. The learning of one's own culture is known as **enculturation**. The learning of a new or foreign culture is known as **acculturation**. In Chapter 15 we see that acculturation is an important concept for marketers who plan to sell their products in foreign or multinational markets. In such cases, marketers must study the specific culture(s) of their potential target market in order to determine whether their products will be acceptable to its members and, if so, how they can best communicate the characteristics of their products to persuade the target market to buy.

FIGURE 11.2 The movement of cultural meaning

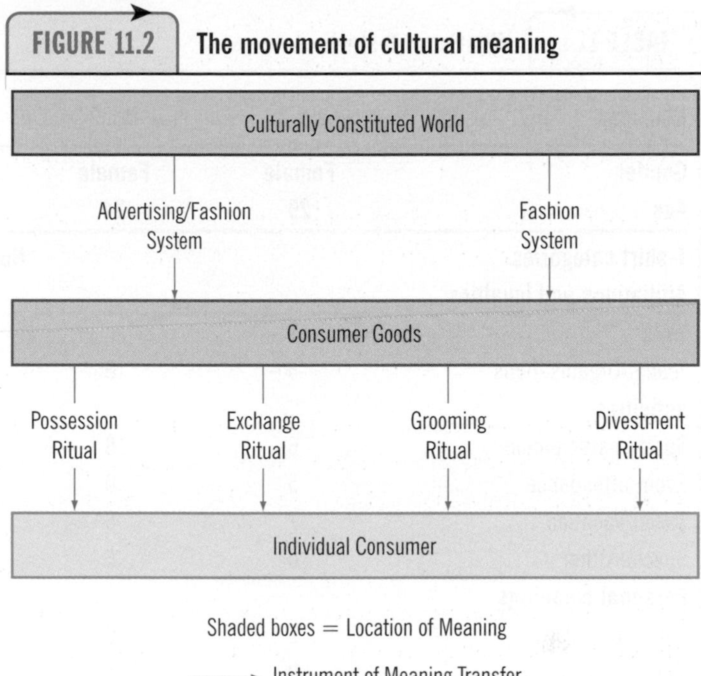

Source: **Grant McCracken, 'Culture and consumption: A theatrical account of the structure and movement of the cultural meaning of consumer goods', *Journal of Consumer Research*, 13, June 1986, p. 72. Reprinted by permission of The University of Chicago Press.**

Language and symbols

To acquire a common culture, the members of a society must be able to communicate with each other through a common language. Without a common language, shared meaning could not exist and true communication would not take place (see Chapter 8).

To communicate effectively with their audiences, marketers must use appropriate *symbols* to convey desired product images or characteristics. These symbols can be *verbal* or *non-verbal*. Verbal symbols may include a television or radio announcement[5] (e.g. 'Where do you want to go today?' Microsoft's slogan) or an advertisement in a magazine. Non-verbal communication includes the use of such symbols as figures (e.g. 'Louie the Fly'—for Mortein (see Figure 11.3)), colours (the red of Nestlé's KitKat), shapes (Cadbury's glass-and-a-half symbol) and even textures to lend additional meaning to print or broadcast advertisements, to trademarks, and to packaging or product designs.

Basically, it is the symbolic nature of human language that sets it apart from all other animal communication. A **symbol** is anything that stands for something else. Any word is a symbol. The word 'razor' calls forth a specific image related to an individual's own knowledge and experience. The word 'cyclone' not only invokes the notion of wind and rain but also has the power to stir us emotionally, arousing feelings of danger and the need for protection and safety. Similarly, the word 'jaguar' has symbolic meaning; to some it suggests a fine luxury car; to others it implies wealth and status; to still others it suggests an animal to be seen at the zoo. The philosophy of *semiotics* (signs and their cultural meaning) has been adopted by marketers to help them understand the appropriate cultural symbols to use. Box 11.1 shows six key semiotic concepts that can be used to gain an insight into products and communications.[6]

The capacity to learn symbolically is primarily a human phenomenon; most other animals learn by direct experience. Clearly, the ability of humans to understand symbolically how a product, service or idea can satisfy their needs makes it easier for marketers to 'sell' the features and benefits of their offerings.[7] Through a shared language and culture, individuals already know what the image means; thus, an association can be made without actively thinking about it. Figure 11.3 shows examples of symbols found in Australian advertising.

TABLE 11.1 **What's on T-shirts**

Consumer*	No. 1	No. 2	No. 3	No. 4	No. 5
Gender	**Female**	**Female**	**Female**	**Male**	**Male**
Age	**29**	**34**	**39**	**26**	**45**
T-shirt categories			**Number of T-shirts**		
Affiliations and loyalties					
Work	1	0	1	1	3
Teams/Organisations	6	0	2	5	4
Activities					
Sports participation	6	18	4	6	0
Event attendance	5	0	2	5	3
Travel/Vacation	7	6	7	2	8
Special/Other	0	6	0	0	0
Personal meanings					
Self-expression	1	0	1	2	7
Gifts	0	5	5	0	0
Impersonal					
Company/Product	4	0	0	1	4
Fashion	0	2	0	0	0
Totals	30	37	22	22	29

Note: *The first consumer was the author of the article—T. Bettina Cornwell.

Source: **Adapted from T. Bettina Cornwell, 'T-shirts as wearable diary: An examination of artifact consumption and garnering related to life events', in M. E. Goldberg, G. Gorne & R. W. Pollay (eds), *Advances in Consumer Research*, 17 (Provo, UT: Association for Consumer Research, 1990), p. 377. Reprinted by permission.**

FIGURE 11.3 **Symbols in Australian marketing**

Louie the Fly

Rosella Foods

Early Kooka Stoves

Collage of icons

Source: **<www.mortein.com.au/louie_friends.html>; Mimmo Cozzolino and Fysh Rutherford, *Symbols of Australia*, <www.symbolsofaustralia.com.au>.**

A symbol may have several, even contradictory, meanings so it is important that the advertiser ascertain exactly what the symbols are communicating to an intended audience. For example, the advertiser who uses a trademark depicting an old craftsman to symbolise careful workmanship may instead be communicating an

BOX 11.1 | Key semiotic concepts

Concept	Explanation	Examples
Synchronic vs diachronic	One particular moment in time vs evolving trend.	At one time smoking was seen as fashionable and sophisticated, progressively it has been socially vilified.
Langue vs parole	Rules of communication vs a specific implementation of them.	Agreed use of a colour like blue or red to convey emotion (langue) vs a specific ad for Coca-Cola using red.
Signifier vs signified	The communication object vs all the content attached to the signifier.	A brand name such as Rolls-Royce and all the meaning attached to it (wealth, status, refinement).
Denotation vs connotation	Literal meaning vs the cultural meaning attached to a concept.	The marked price of a product is often used by consumers to connote quality.
Syntagmatic vs paradigmatic relations	A linear combination of symbols, such as words in a sentence vs all the possible symbols that could be used in one place in the sequence.	For example, advertisements may adopt a linear format of using an attention getting device, showing a product, branding a product and finishing with a tag line (syntagmatic). All possible tag lines would be in a paradigmatic relationship with one another.
Metonymy vs metaphor	Literal language or imagery vs non-literal imagery or hidden meanings.	The use of the concepts of 'family' or 'economic rationalism' in political marketing.

Source: Adapted from Malcolm Evans, 'Semiotics: Culture and communications—common sense of the 21st century.' Paper presented to the Annual Conference of the Market Research Society of Australia, Adelaide, October 1999. Reproduced with the kind permission of the Australian Market and Social Research Society.

image of outmoded methods and lack of style. The marketer who uses slang in an advertisement to attract a teenage audience must do so with great care. Slang that is offensive or outdated will symbolically date the marketer's firm and product.

Price and channels of distribution are also significant symbols of the marketer and the marketer's product. For example, price often implies quality to potential buyers (see Chapter 5). For certain products (e.g. clothing), the type of store in which the product is sold is also an important symbol of quality. In fact, all the elements of the marketing mix—the product, its promotion, its price, its packaging and the stores at which it is available—are symbols that communicate a range of quality to potential buyers.

Ritual

In addition to language and symbols, culture includes various ritualised experiences and behaviours that, until recently, have been neglected by consumer researchers. A **ritual** is a type of symbolic activity consisting of a series of steps (*multiple behaviours*) occurring in a fixed sequence and repeated over time.[8]

In practice, rituals extend over the human life cycle from birth to death, including a host of intermediate events (e.g. eighteenth birthdays, graduation, marriage). These rituals can be very public, elaborate, religious or civil ceremonies, or they can be as mundane as an individual's grooming behaviour.[9] Ritualised behaviour is typically rather formal, and is often scripted behaviour (e.g. a religious service requiring a prayer book, or the code of proper conduct in a court of law). It is also likely to occur repeatedly over time (e.g. singing the national anthem before the football grand final). Most important from the standpoint of marketers, rituals tend to be replete with ritual *artifacts* (products) that are associated with or somehow enhance performance of the ritual. For instance, a tree, stocking and a turkey are linked to the ritual of Christmas celebration; other rituals (such as a graduation, a wedding or the Saturday afternoon football match) have their own specific artifacts associated with them (see Table 11.2).

In addition to a ritual, which is the way that something is traditionally done, there is also **ritualistic behaviour**, which can be defined as *any behaviour that a person has made into a ritual*. For example, a family may have a tradition of where and how they celebrate Christmas, down to the foods that are prepared, the people who are invited and the gifts that are given.

TABLE 11.2 **Selected rituals and associated artifacts**

Ritual	Typical artifacts
Graduation	Gown and cloak, procession, formal photographs, afternoon tea
Valentine's Day	Card, flowers, newspaper notice
Retirement	Company party, watch, plaque
Wedding	White gown, reception
Funeral	Hearse, flowers, wake
Football	Beer, meat pies
Birth of child	Baby spoon, celebratory drinks
Going to the gym	Towel, leotard, water bottle
Christmas	Presents for friends and families, office parties

CULTURE IS SHARED

To be considered a cultural characteristic, a particular belief, value or practice must be shared by a significant portion of the society. Accordingly, culture is frequently viewed as *group customs* that link together the members of a society. Of course, common language is the critical cultural component that makes it possible for people to share values, experience and customs.

Various social institutions within a society transmit the elements of culture and make the sharing of culture a reality. Chief among such institutions is the *family*, which serves as the primary agent for enculturation, the passing along of basic cultural beliefs, values and customs to society's newest members. A vital part of the enculturation role of the family is the consumer socialisation of the young (see Chapter 9). This includes the teaching of such basic consumer-related values and skills as the meaning of money, the relationship between price and quality, the establishment of product tastes, preferences and habits, and appropriate methods of response to advertising.

In addition to the family, two other institutions traditionally share much of the responsibility for the transfer of selected aspects of culture—the educational institution and the religious body. Educational institutions are specifically charged with imparting basic learning skills, history, patriotism, citizenship and the technical training needed to prepare people for significant roles within society. Religious institutions provide a moral leadership for society even in a relatively secular society like Australia. Although the young receive much of their consumer training in the family setting, the educational and religious systems reinforce such training through the teaching of economic and ethical concepts.

A fourth social institution that plays a major role in the transfer of culture throughout society is the mass media. Given the extensive exposure of the Australian population to both print, Internet and broadcast media, and the easily ingested, entertaining format in which the contents of such media are usually presented, it is not surprising that the mass media are an important vehicle for imparting, reinforcing and occasionally changing a wide range of cultural values. Australians have a clear example of this with SBS television. One of its major benefits may be termed *cultural maintenance*, that is, helping Australians of a non-English-speaking background (NESB) to celebrate their cultural origins.[10]

We are exposed daily to advertising, an important component of the media. It not only underwrites, or makes economically feasible, the editorial or programming content of the media, but also transmits much about our culture. Without advertising, it would be almost impossible to disseminate information about products, ideas and causes. Consumers receive important cultural information from advertising. For example, it has been hypothesised that one of the roles of advertising in sophisticated magazines like *Vanity Fair* is to instruct readers how to dress, how to decorate their homes, and what foods and wines to serve to guests—in other words, what types of behaviour are most appropriate to their particular social class.[11]

Thus, while the scope of advertising is often considered to be limited to influencing the demand for specific products or services, in a cultural context advertising has the expanded mission of reinforcing established cultural values and aiding in the dissemination of new tastes, habits and customs. In planning their advertising, marketers should recognise that advertising is an important agent for social change in our society.

CULTURE IS DYNAMIC

To fulfil its need-gratifying role, culture must continually evolve if it is to function in the best interests of a society. For this reason, the marketer must carefully monitor the sociocultural environment in order to market an existing product more effectively, or to develop promising new products. This is not an easy task, since many factors are likely to produce cultural changes within a given society (new technology, population shifts, resource shortages, wars, changing values, customs borrowed from other cultures). For example, a major cultural change in our society is the expanding role choices of Australian women. Today, most women work outside the home, frequently in careers that were once considered exclusively male. Also, women are increasingly active in social and athletic activities outside the home. Advertising is now reflecting that reality.

All this adds up to a blurring of traditional male-female sex roles. These changes mean that marketers have had to reconsider *who* are the purchasers and the users of their products (males only, females only, or both), *when* they do their shopping, *how* and *where* they can be reached by the media, and what new product and service needs are emerging. For example, with the spread of AIDS, condom manufacturers, who had traditionally marketed their product exclusively to men, now also target condoms to women; indeed, some brands are specifically named, packaged and advertised to female purchasers.

Marketers who monitor cultural changes often find new opportunities to increase corporate profitability. The recent cultural changes in the role of women have justified such changes in marketing focus. Marketers of life insurance, leisure wear, toy electric trains and small cigars are among those who have attempted to take advantage of the dramatically shifting sense of what is feminine. Banks now market products to single women. This sex-role shift has also had an impact on traditional male roles. Today, cosmetic firms such as Aramis are successfully marketing skin care and other cosmetic products to men. From time to time, magazines publish a list of 'what's hot and what's not' which details fashion trends.

The measurement of culture

A wide range of measurement techniques is employed in the study of culture. The major approaches are reviewed here.

CONTENT ANALYSIS

Conclusions about a society, or specific aspects of a society, can sometimes be drawn from an examination of the content of its messages. **Content analysis**, as the name implies, focuses on the content of verbal, written and pictorial communications (e.g. the copy and art composition of an advertisement). It provides a relatively objective means of determining whether social and cultural changes have occurred in a specific society.[12] For instance, consumer researchers can use content analysis to examine how migrants, families, women and the elderly have been depicted in the mass media.[13] Content analysis could also be used to explore trends in the style and layout of various types of advertising.

Content analysis is useful to both marketers and public policy makers interested in comparing the advertising claims of competitors within a specific industry, and for evaluating the nature of advertising claims targeted to specific audiences (e.g. women, the elderly, children). A content analysis of 263 ads appearing in eight issues of the US *Seventeen* magazine, four Japanese issues and four American issues, found that teenage girls are portrayed differently. The research concluded that these 'differences correspond to each country's central concepts of self and society.' While American teen girls are often associated with images of 'independence and determination,' Japanese teen girls are most often portrayed with a 'happy, playful, childlike girlish image.'[14] In another content analysis study—this one comparing American and Chinese television commercials targeted to children—the research revealed that 82% of the Chinese ads aimed at children were for food products; whereas 56% of the ads directed at American children were for toys.[15]

Consumer fieldwork

In examining a specific society, anthropologists frequently immerse themselves in the environment under study. As trained researchers, they are likely to select a small group of people from a particular society and carefully observe their behaviour. Based on their observations, they then draw conclusions about the values, beliefs and customs of the society under investigation. For example, if researchers were interested in how people select a DVD to rent, they might position trained observers in movie rental stores and note how specific types of movies are selected (new release movies, 'blockbusters' versus classics, action versus horror films, cartoons versus R-rated content). The researchers might also be interested in the degree of search that accompanies the choice; that is, how often consumers take a DVD off the shelf, read the description and put it back again before selecting the DVD they finally rent. Such information would be of interest to a company such as Blockbuster and also to providers of movie services such as *video-on-demand* (available on pay television).

The distinct characteristics of **field observation** are (1) it takes place within a natural environment, (2) it is sometimes performed without the subjects' awareness, and (3) it focuses on observation of behaviour. Since the emphasis is on a natural environment and observable behaviour, field observation concerned with consumer behaviour often focuses on in-store shopping behaviour and less frequently on in-home preparation and consumption.[16]

In some cases, instead of just observing behaviour, researchers become *participant-observers* (i.e. they become active members of the environment they are studying). In commercial market research, this is normally known as **shadow shopping**. For example, a researcher interested in examining how women select new clothes might take a sales position in a women's clothing store in order to observe directly, and even interact with, customers in the transaction process.

Both field observation and participant-observer research require highly skilled researchers who can separate their own emotions from what they actually observe in their professional roles. Both techniques provide valuable insights that might not easily be obtained through survey research that simply asks consumers questions about their behaviour. Care should be taken with such research; it would be unethical to disadvantage individuals (e.g. service staff in a store) who are unwittingly taking part.

In addition to fieldwork methods, in-depth interviews and focus groups (using techniques such as storytelling to elicit social metaphors, critical incident research and semiotic approaches) are also quite often employed by marketers to get a 'first look' at an emerging social or cultural change. In the relatively informal atmosphere of group discussions or depth interviews, consumers are apt to reveal attitudes or behaviour that could signal a shift in values that in turn might affect the long-run market acceptance of a product or service. For example, car insurance companies might investigate all the hassles, lost time, delays and inconvenience faced by customers in getting their cars fixed after an accident. By reducing the tasks required to be done by customers, companies have found that they can identify ways to add value.

An approach that has grown in popularity is the use of **means-end chains** to understand the ultimate values that drive behaviour. Using the interview technique of *laddering*, researchers ask consumers to give an account of their behaviour. For each answer given, the researchers ask for further elaboration until the ultimate reasons (terminal values or motives) are uncovered.[17] The approach is often useful because it links motives to the means of satisfying them. Once values are identified they can be used in survey research to quantify market opportunities. Like all qualitative research techniques, its value depends greatly on the questioning and interpretive skills of the researcher. Morris Holbrook has proposed a typology of experienced consumer value to synthesise previous research. The classification is shown in Table 11.3.

VALUE MEASUREMENT SURVEY INSTRUMENTS

Anthropologists have traditionally observed the behaviour of members of a specific society and *inferred* from such behaviour the dominant or underlying values of the society. In recent years, however, there has been a gradual shift to measuring values directly by means of survey (questionnaire) research.[18] Researchers use data collection instruments called **values instruments** to ask people how they feel about such basic personal and social concepts as freedom, comfort, national security and peace.

Several value instruments have been used in consumer behaviour studies. The **Rokeach Value Survey**, a self-administered value inventory, is divided into two complementary parts. The first part consists of 18 *terminal value* items, which are designed to measure the relative importance of **end-states of existence** (i.e. fundamental personal goals). The second part consists of 18 *instrumental value* items, which measure basic *approaches* an individual might take to reach end-state values. Thus, the first half of the measurement instrument deals with *ends*, while the second half considers *means*.[19]

TABLE 11.3 Typology of experienced consumer value

		Extrinsic	Intrinsic
Self-oriented	Active	EFFICIENCY (O/I, convenience)	PLAY (fun)
	Reactive	EXCELLENCE (quality)	AESTHETICS (beauty)
Other-oriented	Active	STATUS (success, impression management)	ETHICS (virtue, justice, morality)
	Reactive	ESTEEM (reputation, materialism, possessions)	SPIRITUALITY (faith, ecstasy, sacredness, magic)

Source: **Morris B. Holbrook, 'Introduction to consumer value', in Morris B. Holbrook (ed.), *Consumer Value: A Framework for Analysis and Research* (London: Routledge, 1999).**

Studies in a number of countries have shown a relationship between these values and consumer behaviour. One US study found that a subset of 24 of the 36 value items in the Rokeach Value Survey were particularly relevant to product consumption.[20] In a Brazilian study, Rokeach value measures were used to segment consumers into six groups. Two of these segments were correlated with consumer behaviour. One of these, concerned with a less materialistic and non-hedonist orientation, was related to behaviour such as gardening, reading and going out with the family. The other, mostly concerned with self-centred values, was found to be related to a preference for provocative clothes in the latest fashion, an active lifestyle and a desire to try new products.[21]

The Kahle's **List of Values (LOV)** instrument has been designed specifically to study consumers' personal values. It asks consumers to choose their two most important values from a nine-value list (such as 'warm relationships with others', 'a sense of belonging', 'a sense of accomplishment') based on the terminal values of the Rokeach Value Survey.[22] The Schwartz Value Survey, also having its origin in the Rokeach value measures, attempts to describe a universal list of values.[23] It is discussed in more detail below. Psychographic measures, like VALS (see Chapter 2) implicitly incorporate values into their inventories of Activities, Interests and Opinions (AIOs). In Australia, commercial measures of values have been used, particularly the Roy Morgan Research Values Segments.

AUSTRALIAN VALUES SEGMENTS

This approach to segmentation was devised by Colin Benjamin of the Horizons Network, in conjunction with Roy Morgan Research. The ten segments are based on responses to seven questions concerning values about matters such as family life, religion and leading an exciting life. These were combined with five demographic variables (including family life cycle and income) and factor analysed, assigning individuals to one of nine groups. One of the groups, Family Life, was further subdivided into two groups, Traditional Family Life, representing the responses of people who were likely to be *empty nesters*, and Conventional Family Life, representing younger families focused on the quality of life for their children. Box 11.2 describes the ten segments that were produced.

BOX 11.2 Australian Values Segments

Basic Needs© (3%)

This pattern of thinking or MINDSET™ is usually associated with older people who are retired, pensioners or people on social security payments who have an active community focus to their lives, and with people on sickness benefits or workers compensation who have to reduce their expectations in line with reduced income.

Fairer Deal© (5%)

This pattern of thinking is generally found among unskilled and semi-skilled workers who left school to start learning from friends who share blue-denim values. This MINDSET™ is more likely to experience unemployment, family pressures and the feeling of getting a raw deal out of life.

Traditional Family Life© (20%)

This pattern of thinking personifies middle-aging Australian home owners with relatively stable incomes that meet the needs of the smaller household. Energies revolve around the ideal of becoming grandparents or getting children to come home for visits or at least to keep in touch. Health and spirituality dominate a sense of meaning and purpose in life, and being well-respected in the community is very important.

Conventional Family Life© (9%)

This pattern of thinking is most closely associated with suburban families devoting all their time and efforts to building a 'home' to give their children the opportunities they deserve, striving to improve their home, enjoying family life and having enough time to keep in touch with their parents and friends.

Look-at-Me© (12%)

This pattern of thinking is associated with active, unsophisticated, somewhat self-centred and peer-driven behaviour that sees success as a kind of game and not to be measured by family standards. This is the pattern of the 'decibel generation' that lives in McDonald's, drinks Pepsi, burns up money (their own and their parents'), spends hours watching commercial TV and can't wait to be somewhere else.

Something Better© (7%)

This pattern of thinking is associated with people who are very competitive, seeking to clinch a bigger, better deal that will develop a little bit more to help pay off an excessive mortgage on the new family home. This MINDSET™ has extensive debts and a strong preference for more power, improved status and security.

Real Conservatism© (4%)

This pattern of thinking is associated with people who are mature and mid-career, holding conservative social, moral and ethical values, and seeking a disciplined, ordered society that is safe and predictable. There is a strong tendency towards authoritarian, blue-chip, business-oriented preferences that offer security and the feeling of being very much in control. This is a common pattern in rural settings.

Young Optimism© (8%)

This pattern of thinking is associated with young professionals, technocrats and students whose thoughts are focused on achieving a good career, overseas travel and generally improving their prospects in life, having a sense of fulfilment and a chance to enjoy an outgoing lifestyle. It is generally more prevalent in inner-city and urban lifestyle settings.

Visible Achievement© (18%)

This pattern of thinking is associated with the proof of having made it up the seemingly never-ending social ladder. Personal recognition, higher incomes, job satisfaction and other tangible rewards of success such as travel, recreation and high-quality homes, vehicles and holiday locations provide the very best of visible good living.

Socially Aware© (14%)

This pattern of thinking is usually associated with the highest socioeconomic group in the community. This MINDSET™ is the specialty of public servants, pressure groups, business analysts and politicians of all political colours. These 'insatiable information vacuum cleaners' are addicted to finding out or trying anything that's new or different and persuading others to accept their opinions, priorities and lifestyle preferences.

Source: Roy Morgan Single Source Australia: April 2003–March 2004. Based on a sample of 55 687 Australians aged 14 and over. Developed in conjunction with Colin Benjamin of The Horizons Network.

These values segments have been used to analyse a broad range of marketing data collected by Roy Morgan Research for products ranging from motor vehicles to magazines and fast-moving consumer goods.[24] In Table 11.4, a list of magazines is shown and analysed in terms of the readership by the ten values segments. In looking at the results, it can be seen that some magazines, (e.g. *Women's Weekly*) have high readership among all values segments and that some values segments (e.g. Basic Needs) read magazines less often than the other segments. Bearing this in mind, it is evident that some segments are disproportionately likely to

TABLE 11.4 Readership of magazines by values segment

	Basic Needs %	Fairer Deal %	Traditional Family %	Conventional Family %	Look-at-Me %	Something Better %	Real Conservatism %	Young Optimism %	Visible Achievement %	Socially Aware %
Australian PC User	0.8	3.0	1.3	2.4	2.6	2.1	1.4	3.7	2.8	3.4
Australian Reader's Digest	8.4	5.2	9.5	5.9	3.3	4.6	7.4	4.3	6.5	4.9
BRW	0.2	0.7	0.7	0.6	0.5	0.7	0.6	2.2	2.7	4.3
Cleo	0.9	8.9	0.6	3.1	13.5	5.3	1.4	13.4	2.4	2.7
Cosmopolitan	1.1	9.0	0.9	4.0	15.8	6.3	1.3	15.8	2.9	3.1
Dolly	0.4	8.1	0.2	2.1	13.7	2.5	0.9	2.8	1.1	0.8
Family Circle	4.5	2.7	3.7	3.6	1.5	3.1	3.1	1.5	3.5	2.1
Good Weekend (NSW/Vic)	4.5	3.0	8.6	4.2	5.1	5.7	7.5	14.1	14.3	28.8
Home Beautiful	2.0	1.6	1.9	2.7	1.0	2.0	2.3	1.8	3.3	3.8
House & Garden	2.9	1.9	3.8	4.4	2.0	3.3	4.2	2.0	5.8	5.8
Inside Sport	0.1	0.9	0.2	1.2	3.2	1.9	0.4	2.9	1.2	1.5
New Idea	15.6	14.3	13.9	13.9	12.6	12.6	13.3	11.3	11.3	9.2
Ralph	0.1	4.4	0.3	2.3	9.0	4.8	0.9	8.6	2.1	2.5
Rolling Stone	0.1	2.3	0.1	0.9	5.2	2.3	0.4	6.2	0.8	2.3
That's Life	11.5	16.4	8.2	11.3	8.3	11.7	8.0	4.5	5.1	2.3
Time	0.9	1.9	1.7	1.5	2.0	1.8	1.5	4.4	3.1	5.3
TV Week	6.3	12.8	5.6	8.8	14.1	8.1	7.3	9.2	5.4	3.2
Vogue Australia	1.3	2.5	1.1	1.9	2.9	1.7	1.2	3.7	1.9	3.1
Woman's Day	17.5	17.2	17.0	19.2	16.3	17.5	18.0	14.2	15.0	11.0
Women's Weekly	19.3	14.0	19.9	19.0	11.4	14.6	17.5	11.8	18.6	14.3

Source: **Roy Morgan Single Source Australia: April 2003–March 2004. Based on national average readership among a sample of 55 687 Australians aged 14 and over. Developed in conjunction with Colin Benjamin of The Horizons Network.**

read some magazines. For example, the Basic Needs segment had a high proportion who read *TV Week* while *Good Weekend* had its highest readership among the Socially Aware segment. Members of this latter segment are less likely to be readers of popular women's magazines, such as *New Idea*.

Such analyses are of use to two groups of marketers. Among magazine publishers, the results help them understand who their readers are and the extent to which they are correctly positioned. For example, certain magazines may wish to target groups with high levels of disposable income. To attract such readers, they may have to change the content of the magazine to reflect the values held by the segment. Among advertisers, there will be interest in knowing the values segments for which the magazine has special appeal. They may also wish to vary the themes in their advertising, depending on the magazine in which they are promoting their services and products.

Recently, the values segments have been aligned with a hybrid segmentation tool known as the ColourGrid™ (see Figure 11.4). At a household level, it combines household composition and geodemographic data to produce a 16-segment view of Australia. By modelling the relationship between the grid segments on one hand and media and values data on the other, the system aims to answer the question, 'Who should I target, where should I target them, with what message, delivered in what medium?'

By modelling the relationship between the segments and values data, they can be said to represent several key cultural dimensions[25] as Figure 11.5 (page 390) shows:

1. Individualism/collectivism—'I' versus 'we'
2. Power distance—'Them' versus 'us'

FIGURE 11.4 **ColourGrid™ Segments Map**

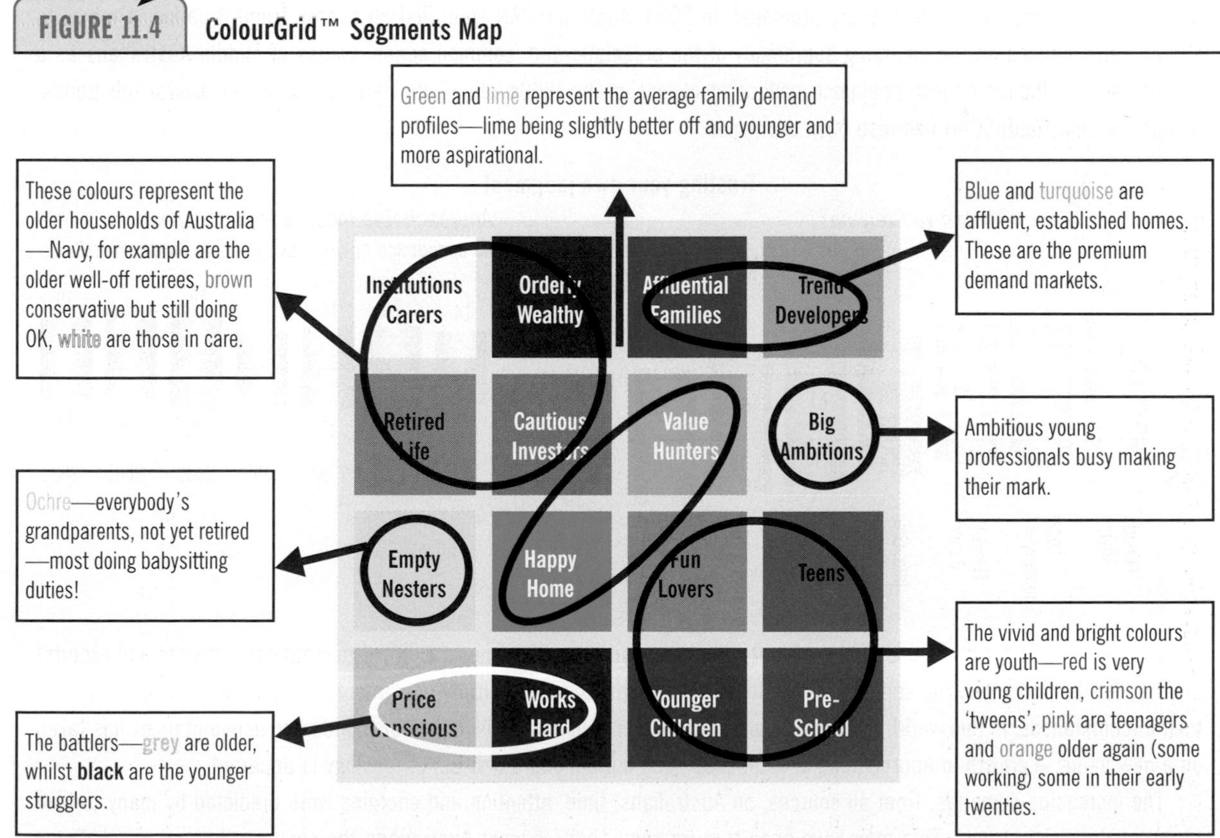

Green and lime represent the average family demand profiles—lime being slightly better off and younger and more aspirational.
These colours represent the older households of Australia —Navy, for example are the older well-off retirees, brown conservative but still doing OK, white are those in care.
Blue and turquoise are affluent, established homes. These are the premium demand markets.
Institutions Carers
Orderly Wealthy
Affluential Families
Trend Developers
Retired Life
Cautious Investors
Value Hunters
Big Ambitions
Ambitious young professionals busy making their mark.
Ochre—everybody's grandparents, not yet retired —most doing babysitting duties!
Empty Nesters
Happy Home
Fun Lovers
Teens
The vivid and bright colours are youth—red is very young children, crimson the 'tweens', pink are teenagers and orange older again (some working) some in their early twenties.
Price Conscious
Works Hard
Younger Children
Pre-School
The battlers—grey are older, whilst black are the younger strugglers.

Source: © Intellectual Property Holdings Pty Ltd—Colin Benjamin.

3. Uncertainty avoidance/acceptance
4. Past present or future orientation.

The nearly eight million households in Australia are arranged into privacy pods™ of about 200 households each. Each pod can then be profiled in terms of the 16 typologies. This enables geographic targeting by a range of marketers including retailers, political parties, financial organisations and product companies such as Bang & Olufsen to select which markets to target.

SOCIAL TRENDS RESEARCH

The spotting of social trends is also of interest to marketers. Several commercial services in the US and elsewhere track emerging values and social trends for businesses and government agencies. These include AustraliaSCAN™[26] (see Box 11.3), which is based on the US DYG SCAN®.[27] It aims to discover and track a range of social trends of interest to marketers. By carefully interpreting social trends and determining which demographic segments are most affected by a particular group of trends, marketers may gain advance warnings of likely shifts in demand for various product and service categories.

BOX 11.3 AustraliaSCAN™ Social Trends Monitor

AustraliaSCAN™ is based on an wide-ranging annual survey of 2000 consumers, plus qualitative research. As well as values measurement, it records a wealth of other data on Australians and their lives, their aspirations, their fears, their beliefs and their relationships with government, business, markets and brands. Companies use the data to develop their product offerings and the manner in which they are promoted. In 2003, AustraliaSCAN identified an overall trend it called 'a return to Middle Earth,' based on the emerging supremacy of the pragmatic and 'common sense' values of Middle Australians as a reaction against the more theoretical post-modern 'ideologies' of the 1990s 'elites'. Its view was based on several sub-trends. A youth version, YouthSCAN has also been developed.

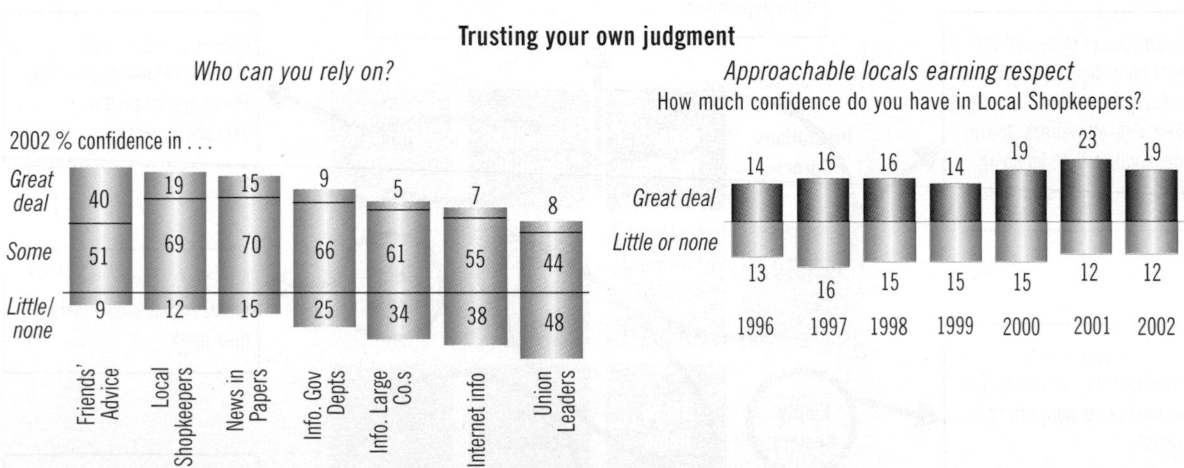

Growing scepticism has eroded the credibility of all the institutions (business, church, government, activists and experts) and has left behind a growing self-confidence in people's ability to form their own judgments as to what is right for them in their circumstances. In this world, direct personal experience and the recommendation of friends and acquaintances has taken on a new value. A growth in appreciation of local shops and outlets and a distrust of ideology is apparent.

The increasing demands, from all sources, on Australians' time, attention and energies were predicted by many to lead to an 'epidemic of stress'. This may have been true for some, but for most Australians the converse has occurred. Today

Filter and focus

The epidemic of stress

AustraliaSCAN Stress Index

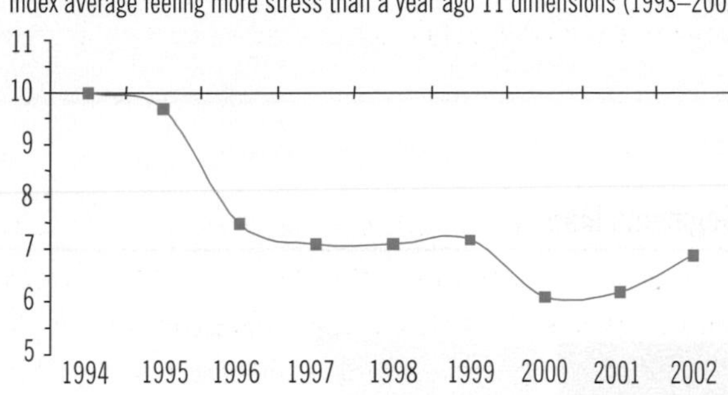

Focusing on what's really important

In the past year, have you spent more time, less time or the same amount of time . . .

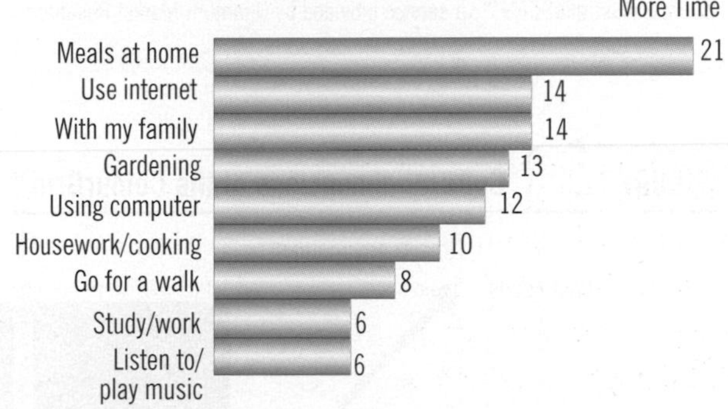

Australians are more 'relaxed and comfortable' than they have been for a decade. Armed with a new self-confidence in their own judgment, Australians have focused on those aspects of their lives that are most important to them (as opposed to what others tell them should be important) and filtered out the extraneous, irrelevant, unproductive, or merely fashionable. What Australians judge to be 'most important' can be gauged by looking at how they perceive their leisure time changing. The winners are clearly activities focused on home and family. Home theatre, a better selection of meals and home improvement television reflects this trend.

Practicality over ideology

Business: Not necessarily to be trusted on its own

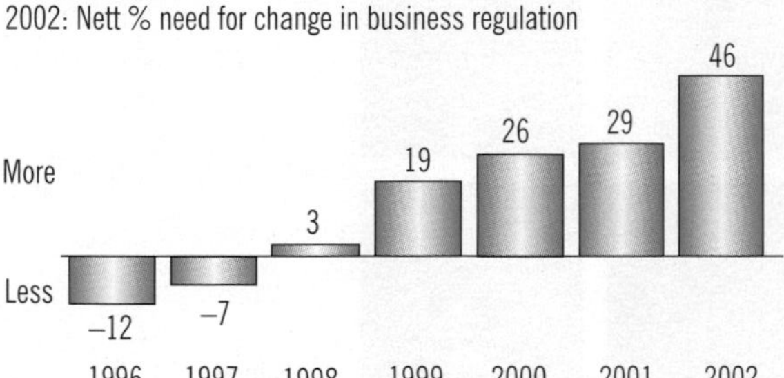

Base: Those perceiving need for a change.

Happy to help: But only if it works

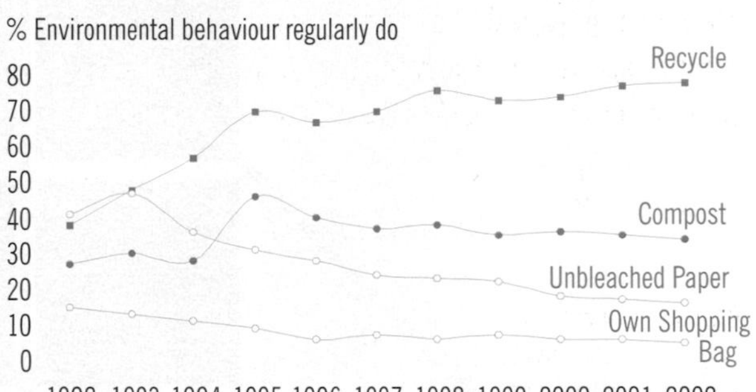

Idealism about nature, the environment or dealings with other cultures has been replaced with a more pragmatic approach.

Growth of authentic brands

'Big Brands' Wane

Top 2 Best Brands

% 10–17 Year Olds: Spontaneous

50
40
30
20
10
0

Nike

Adidas

1995 1997 1999 2001

Source: YouthSCAN.

'Authentic Brands' Bloom

Top 3 Best Brands

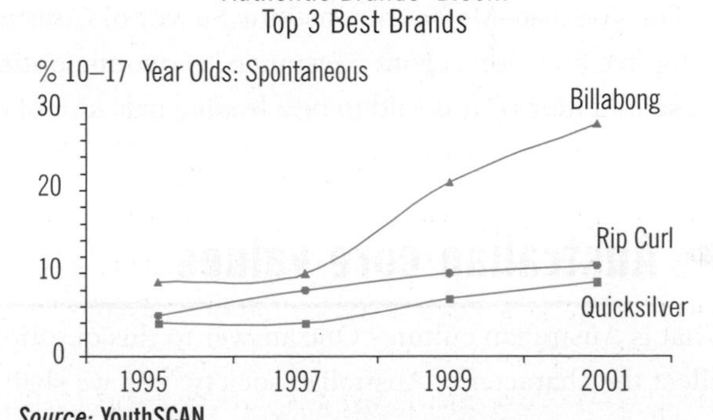

Source: YouthSCAN.

Figures taken from Youth Scan, a related monitor among 1000 young people aged 10–17. In simplistic terms this can be represented as the inversion of the classic 'top-down' model where the dominant factor was main media advertising. Today's new brands are more likely to be grown by a 'bottom-up' approach where the power of local delivery and word-of-mouth recommendation is the focus.

Source: AustraliaSCAN™: a service provided by Quantum Market Research.

FIGURE 11.5 **Cultural dimensions of the ColourGrid™ Segments Map**

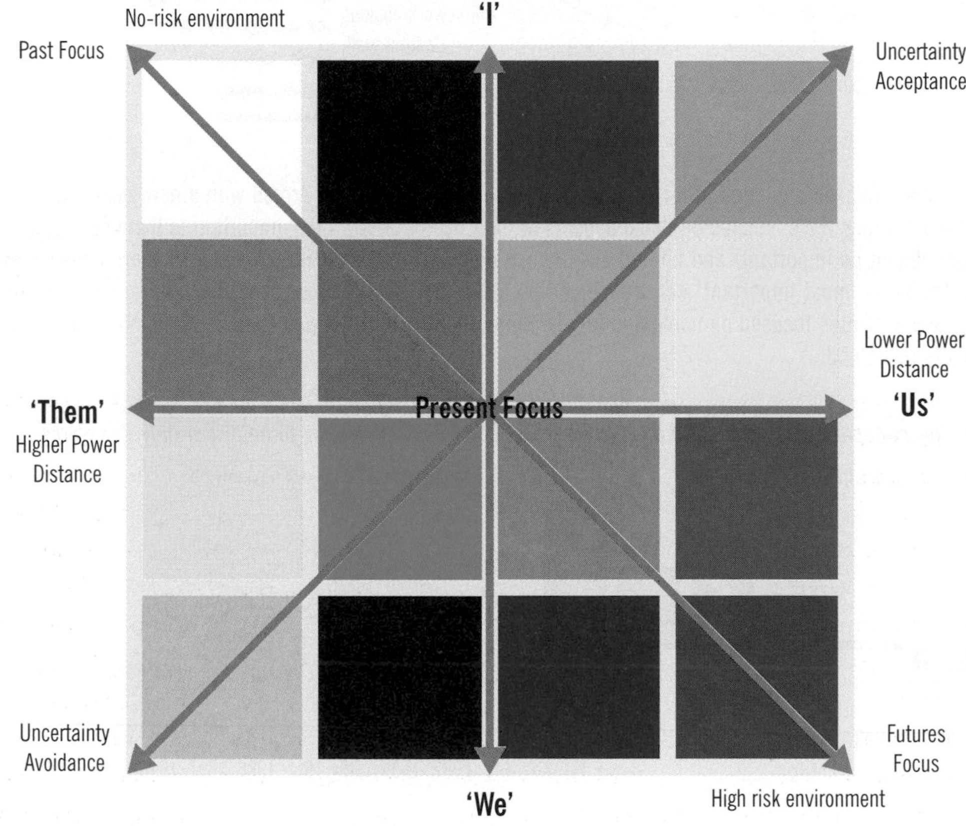

Source: **© Intellectual Property Holdings Pty Ltd—Colin Benjamin.**

The Westpac–Melbourne Institute Survey of Consumer Sentiment[28] has been collected monthly since 1975. Using five questions about consumers' economic optimism (e.g. whether today is the right time to buy major household items). It is said to be a *leading indicator* of consumer economic activity. Figure 11.6 shows changes in the monthly Index between 1990 and 2003. The figures have been deseasonalised.

Australian core values

What is Australian culture? One answer to this question is that there is a set of **core values** that both affect and reflect the character of Australian society.[29] As we shall see, the evidence is far from consistent. First, Australia is a diverse country, consisting of a variety of **subcultures** (religious, ethnic, regional, racial and economic

FIGURE 11.6 **Survey of Consumer Sentiment**

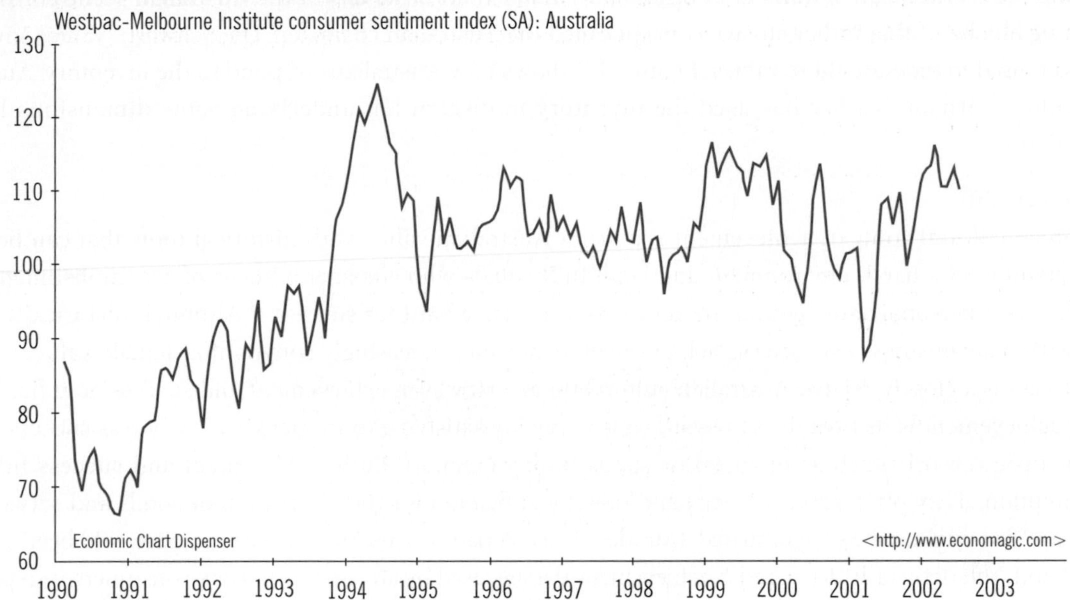

Source: **Melbourne Institute of Applied Economic and Social Research at the University of Melbourne.**

groups), each of which interprets and responds to society's basic beliefs and values in its own specific way (see Chapter 12). Second, Australia is a dynamic society that has undergone almost constant change in response to migration, the economy and technology. This element of rapid change makes it especially difficult to monitor changes in cultural values. Finally, the existence of contradictory values in society is obvious. As an example, Australians traditionally embrace freedom of choice and individualism, while simultaneously valuing the collective ideal of mateship. In the context of consumer behaviour, Australians like to have a wide choice of products (such as cars and electronics) from around the world, yet 'Buy Australian' and 'Australian made—Australian owned' campaigns encourage people to consider locally produced and owned merchandise.[30]

Australian researchers have argued that key personal values (such as personal competence) and social values (such as having enjoyable spare-time activities and a good family life) contribute to the satisfaction and happiness that people get out of life.[31] For people in service industries and other white-collar professions, the expression of personal competence at work has resulted in longer and longer hours, compromising those very social values.

With all this diversity, it would be easy for marketers to overreact and ignore values. But when you ask sojourners in Australia (such as consumer marketing students from the Asia-Pacific region) about this, their answers are clear. There does seem to be a set of common, *core* values that apply to most Australians, most of the time. The key issue for marketers is to understand when and with whom they are relevant.

Essentially, a core value must fulfil three criteria:

1. *The value must be pervasive.* A significant portion of the Australian people must accept the value and use it as a guide for their attitudes and actions.
2. *The value must be relatively enduring.* The specific value must have influenced the actions of the Australian people over an extended period of time (as distinguished from a short-run trend).
3. If the value is to be useful to marketers, it must be *consumer-related.* The specific value must provide insights that help us understand the consumption actions of the Australian people.

TEN CORE AUSTRALIAN VALUES

Meeting these criteria are a number of basic values that expert observers of the Australian scene consider the 'building blocks' of that rather elusive concept called the Australian character. The Schwartz Values Inventory has been used to measure these values. Figure 11.7 shows how Australians respond to the inventory. Australian researcher Norman Feather has used the inventory to discern ten underlying value dimensions held by Australians.[32]

Achievement

In a broad cultural context, achievement is a major Australian value, with historical roots that can be traced to the taming of a harsh environment and land. Individuals who consider a 'sense of accomplishment' to be an important personal value tend to be achievers who strive hard for success.[33] Although historically associated with male business executives, 'achievement' is now an increasingly sought after female value.

Success is a closely-related Australian cultural theme. However, achievement and success do differ. Specifically, achievement is its own direct reward (it is implicitly satisfying to the achiever); whereas success implies an extrinsic reward (such as financial or status improvements). Both achievement and success influence consumption. They often serve as social and moral justification for the acquisition of goods and services. For example, 'You ought to be congratulated' (Meadow Lea), 'A hard-earned thirst deserves an ice cold beer' (Victoria Bitter) and 'You deserve it' are popular achievement themes used by advertisers to coax consumers into purchasing their products. And, regardless of gender, achievement-oriented people often enjoy conspicuous consumption because it allows them to display symbols of their achievement. When it comes to personal development and preparation for future careers, the themes of achievement and success are especially appropriate.

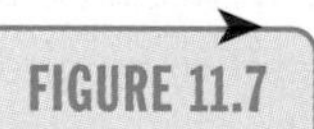

Australian values based on the Schwartz Values Inventory

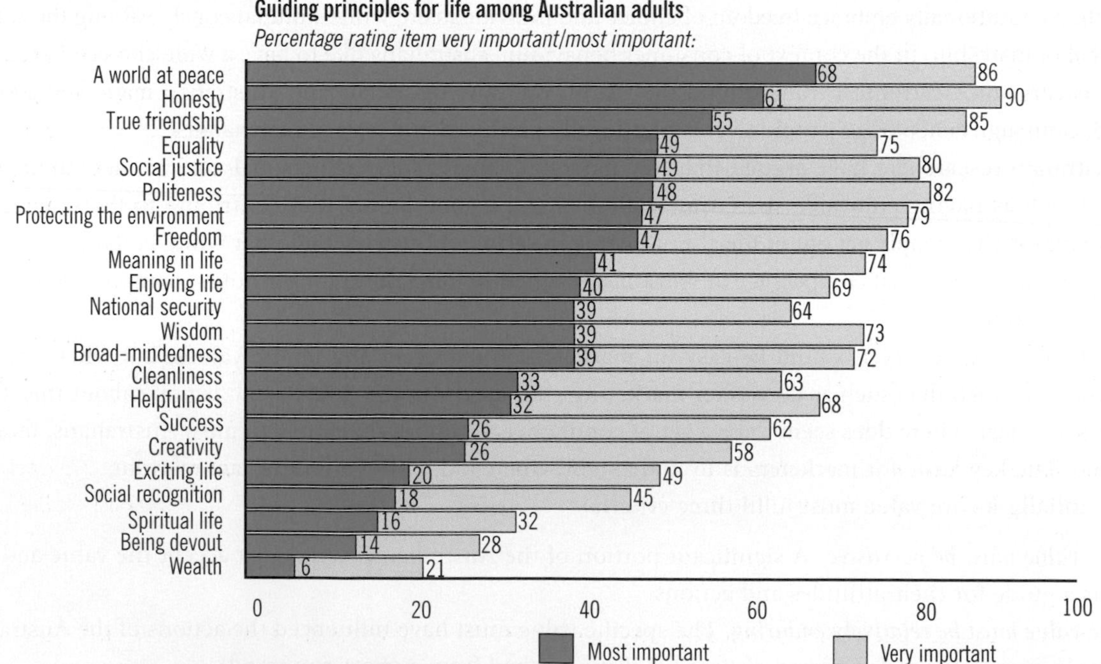

Source: **P. Hughes, S. Bond, J. Bellamy & A. Black, *Exploring What Australians Value* (Adelaide: Openbook Publishers, 2003), p. 11. (A joint publication between Edith Cowan University, Christian Research Association & NCLS Research.)**

Power

This value relates to having social power, wealth, public image and authority. Often the social power is reflected in high-quality overseas products brought to Australia. For example, prestige car advertising for Lexus reflects the social (and economic) power embodied in this value. Hotel and resort advertising often portrays this value in business magazines. As shown in Chapter 10, there are increasing discrepancies in wealth in Australia. Despite this, Australians are often suspicious of the public display of social power. The classic Stella Artois 'About as sophisticated as a beer can get' advertising (which depicts just the opposite) reflects this tension. In the Australian context, it is all right for advertisers to show individuals that they can enjoy having social power, so long as they do not imply that people will flaunt it. Australians are said to dislike 'tall poppies'.

Hedonism

Hedonists look to indulge themselves, for the sheer pleasure of doing so. Peters 'Heaven on a Stick' advertising, Diet Coke's 'Just for the taste of it' and Magnum ice-cream 'The most fun you can have at home' advertising reflect this value.

Stimulation

This reflects a desire for change and excitement. Pepsi Max advertising and the Toyota Corolla 'Looks like it wants to Mooove!' slogan provide clear examples of this, while the ubiquitous 'new' reflects a common need for change in much advertising. Advertising for hair shampoo consistently shows this approach. Brands are forever being launched, improved, relaunched or given new ingredients.

Self-direction

Self-directed people value freedom, creativity, curiosity and the choice to be whatever they want to be. All those many jeans commercials with the free spirits riding their bikes (or planes) off into the West reflect this value.

Universalism

This reflects wisdom, a world of beauty, social justice, equality and unity with nature. The Pyrenees Victoria advertisement in Figure 11.8 shows this value in an Australian context. Other examples include the Nescafé Gold commercials set in Africa, 'Dolphin-free' commercials for tuna and World Vision appeals. While there are cultural variations about what constitutes beauty, current Australian society regards youthfulness as an important indicator. This is a common theme in much advertising, traditionally aimed at women but also aimed at men these days. See Figure 11.9 for an example.

Benevolence

Benevolent people value honesty, loyalty, helpfulness, forgiveness and responsibility. Perhaps this value is best embodied in the Christian Television Association announcements or in advertising for the Salvation Army.

Tradition

This shows itself in a respect for tradition, devotion and being moderate. The value is expressed in the Mercantile Mutual 'cricket' campaign, the 'Aussie kids are Weet-Bix kids' campaign and ads for Vegemite showing children of an earlier era.

Conformity

Conformists value self-discipline, obedience, politeness and the honouring of parents and elders. In traditional European, African and Asian societies, the elderly are revered for having the wisdom of experience that comes with age. In Australia, this is far less obvious with perhaps only former sports heroes such as Steve Waugh or ex-prime ministers such as Malcolm Fraser enjoying this public status.

FIGURE 11.8 Ad featuring core values

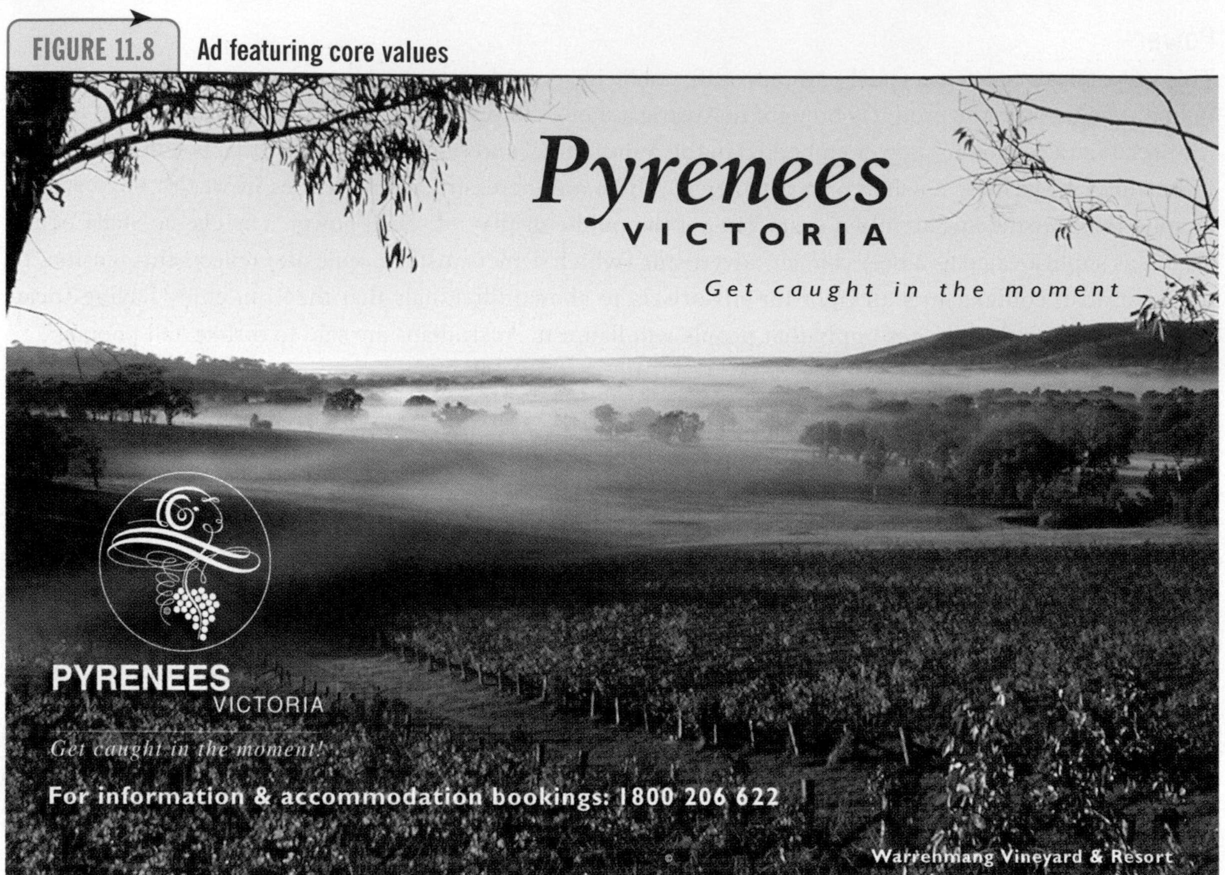

Source: Coursey of Pyrenees Victoria.

Conformity to one's peer group, however, is strong. One of this book's authors was travelling in Greece and was confronted by a lad dressed in exactly the same way as his teenage son: hairstyle, joggers, jeans and T-shirt all carried the same universal look. Particularly among teenagers, universal deviation from the adult world is cool!

Security

This reflects family security, national security, social order and cleanliness. Advertising that picked up this theme included the campaigns for 'Be alert, not alarmed' anti-terrorism and the Domestos 'hospital strength' disinfectant. Polticians are masters at playing on perceived threats to national security, such as asylum seekers or terrorists.

Overall, these values could provide a useful means for segmenting consumers, with respect to what they are likely to notice and buy. They may underpin how Australians see their national identity. Phillips has described two approaches to this issue: *inclusive Australian identity* refers to an overall approach to the concept of being Australian, with Australians showing higher levels of pride than most other peoples, endorsing patriotism as a value and supporting Australian institutions such as the legal system; an *exclusive* approach attempts to define traditional ways of life or to define out-groups not considered to be a genuine part of Australian society or even a threat to it.[34]

CORE VALUES FOR SERVICES

FIGURE 11.9 **Staying youthful**

Source: Courtesy of Estée Lauder.

Another approach to core values is to understand what consumers are seeking from the services that they use. Because services essentially involve an interaction between buyer and supplier in order to deliver, service providers especially recognise core instrumental values they must satisfy on the way to meeting consumer terminal needs. We may describe them as *consistency*, *timeliness*, *effectiveness*, *efficiency*, *ease* and *responsiveness*.

Consistency

This involves the concepts of *predictability* and *reliability*. There is nothing more upsetting to a user of a service than inconsistency or variability. Consumers can make adjustment for a service that is poor, if it is reliable. For example, if a train service is always at least two minutes late, then the consumer can adjust to this. But if the train sometimes arrives two minutes early, sometimes on time and sometimes late, the consumer has a dilemma. She has to arrive at the railway station two minutes early, just in case. She expects the worst, but judges the service against the best. In this case, she knows the train service can arrive on time and condemns it when it does not do so.

Timeliness

Consumers want services at the time they need them, not at the convenience of service providers. They also dislike waiting in queues or similar delays. Telstra advertised its Big Pond service as having a fast connection time, while McDonald's has at times promised consumers a guaranteed time between placing an order and receiving it.

Effectiveness

Consumers want the service or product to do the job. While it is pleasant that an appliance repair service has friendly people who take an interest in the customer, the service is perceived as being no good if they cannot fix the faulty appliance.

Efficiency

When it comes to efficiency, Australians admire anything that saves them time and money. In terms of practicality, they are generally receptive to any new product that makes tasks easier and can help solve problems. Insurance companies now advertise their fast and efficient service for settling claims. The frequency with which Australians look at their watches, and the importance attached to having an accurate timepiece, tend to support the Australian value of punctuality (certainly in comparison with other countries in the Asia-Pacific region).

Ease

Services are essentially co-productions between the supplier and the buyer. For example, to get service from a bank teller, a consumer typically has to fill in forms and wait in a queue. The more service providers require

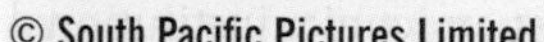

© South Pacific Pictures Limited.

© South Pacific Pictures Limited.

having to deal with a patient committing suicide. *Shortland Street* has drawn acclaim for addressing such social concerns. How the characters deal with the fictional dramas teach the audience how to deal with such issues in real life. In this way, *Shortland Street* holds a remarkably responsible position in New Zealand society. This responsibility is taken in hand, and often at the end of an episode, contact details for relevant organisations (e.g. Alcoholics Anonymous) are provided. South Pacific Pictures also works with health-related campaigns such as Daffodil Day (for cancer awareness), smoke-free campaigns and the Hillary Commission (for exercise). Posters promoting such campaigns pervade the set of *Shortland Street*.

So should the makers of *Shortland Street* be conscious of the impact they have on their audience's behaviour? Is it possible that a half-hour television program can influence how the public deals with different societal issues? Just because the characters on *Shortland Street* wear large earrings, or refer to a handsome male as a 'hunk', does that mean the viewers of *Shortland Street* will dress and speak in the same way? The answer is unclear, but the impact of *Shortland Street* can perhaps best be seen in the response of the viewers to different storylines and characters. As explained by Rachel Lorimer, publicist for *Shortland Street*, 'we recognise the power we hold. We are well aware that viewers can imitate behaviour from the characters on this program, modelling what they say and even how they dress.' There have been cases, for example, where viewers have called the studio enquiring after a particular outfit worn by a character. 'They'll ring up and say, "we saw Waverly wearing that amazing screen printed top. Where can I get it from"?' (Because of such demand, South Pacific Pictures often works with local designers in the selection of the cast's wardrobe.)

While South Pacific Pictures is aware of its influence on New Zealand culture via this weekday television drama, measuring audience reactions to *Shortland Street* is left in the hands of the broadcaster TVNZ. TVNZ conducts ongoing research, primarily via focus groups, with viewers to determine how they are responding to particular characters and storylines. While such market research can help refine the program elements, this research does not explore broader societal influences. But is it even possible to research the impact of *Shortland Street* on New Zealand culture? How could one determine the direct influence of this program, as separate from other ways that culture is learned?

The passion of *Shortland Street* fans is evident in the numerous conversations that pervade the staff tea rooms of organisations throughout New Zealand. Over the morning coffee, fans discuss the previous evening's episode, and speculate on what will happen next. Those who unfortunately missed the program are filled in on the developments, step by step, in remarkable detail. It is as if we know these people personally. They are a part of our life, and whether or not we realise it, they influence us, as much as our family and friends.

Note: Many thanks to Rachel Lorimer, Publicist—*Shortland Street*, South Pacific Pictures, for her valuable assistance in putting this case study together.

Case Study Questions

1. Discuss how the viewing of *Shortland Street* might be considered ritualistic behaviour.
2. How might *Shortland Street* affect a fan's behaviour?
3. The case study poses the question: 'should the makers of *Shortland Street* be conscious of the impact they have on their audiences' behaviour?' Take a stance either for or against this issue, and debate your response.
4. The case study suggests culture is learned, in an informal manner, through media programs such as *Shortland Street*. In what other ways might a consumer informally learn about their culture?
5. The chapter suggests that measurement techniques can be employed in the study of culture. What measurement methods could be applied to *Shortland Street* in order to measure the impact of this television program?

Summary

The study of culture is the study of all aspects of a society—its language, knowledge, laws, customs—that give that society its distinctive character and personality. In the context of consumer behaviour, culture is defined as the sum total of learned beliefs, values and customs that serve to regulate the consumer behaviour of members of a particular society. Beliefs and values are guides for consumer behaviour; customs are usual and accepted ways of behaving.

The impact of culture on society is so natural and so ingrained that its influence on behaviour is rarely noted. Yet culture offers order, direction and guidance to members of society in all phases of human problem solving. Culture is dynamic, and gradually and continually evolves to meet the needs of society. In Australia, the influx of migrants from many cultures has stressed multiculturalism—the pluralist expression of multiple values within a narrower legal and social framework. Culture is learned as part of social experience. Children acquire from their environment a set of beliefs, values and customs that constitute culture (i.e. they are 'encultured'). These are acquired through formal learning, informal learning and technical learning. Advertising enhances formal learning by reinforcing desired modes of behaviour and expectations; it enhances informal learning by providing models for behaviour.

Culture is communicated to members of the society through a common language and through commonly shared symbols. Because the human mind has the ability to absorb and process symbolic communication, marketers can successfully promote both tangible and intangible products and product concepts to consumers through the mass media.

All the elements in the marketing mix serve to communicate symbolically with the audience. Products project images of their own; so does promotion; price and retail outlets symbolically convey images concerning the quality of the product.

The elements of culture are transmitted by three pervasive social institutions: the family, the church and the school. A fourth social institution that plays a major role in the transmission of culture is the mass media—both through editorial content and through advertising.

A wide range of measurement techniques are employed to study culture. These include projective techniques, attitude measurement methods, field observation, participant observation, content analysis and value measurement survey techniques.

Several core values of the Australian people appear to be relevant to the study of consumer behaviour. These include achievement, power, hedonism, stimulation, self-direction, universalism, benevolence, tradition, conformity and security.

A number of commercial techniques are available to the marketer for measuring values and using them as a means of targeting or segmenting markets.

Discussion questions

1. Distinguish between beliefs, values and customs. Illustrate how the clothing a person wears at different times or for different occasions is influenced by customs.
2. Give a consumer behaviour example from your own experience of each of the following types of cultural learning:
   (a) formal learning
   (b) informal learning
   (c) technical learning.
3. How would you decide whether it was worth measuring social values in order to develop an advertising campaign?
4. Describe how a marketer can use some of the social trends examined by AustraliaSCAN™ or the ColourGrid™ segmentation tool.
5. Suppose the Australian Horticultural Corporation was planning a promotional campaign to encourage the eating of apples in situations where many consumers normally eat a snack food. Using the Schwartz Values, identify relevant cultural, consumption-specific and product-specific values for apples as an alternative to snack foods. What are the implications of these values for an advertising campaign designed to increase the consumption of apples?
6. As the media planner for a large advertising agency, you have been asked by top management to identify recent cultural changes that affect your selection of media in which to place clients' advertising. List five cultural changes you believe have bearing on the selection of television shows as vehicles for advertising different types of products.
7. For each of the products and activities listed below: (a) identify the values most relevant to their purchase and use, (b) determine whether these values encourage or discourage use or ownership, and (c) determine whether these core values are shifting and, if so, in what direction. The products and activities are:
   (a) donating money to charities
   (b) diet soft drinks
   (c) DVD players
   (d) subscribing to pay television
   (e) foreign travel
   (f) opening a new bank account
   (g) a new nightclub
   (h) coffee
   (i) Australian-made items
   (j) illegal drugs like ecstasy or GHB.

Exercises

1. Identify a singer or pop group you like and discuss the symbolic function of the clothes that person (or group) wears.
2 Think of the various routines in your everyday life (e.g. grooming, eating). Examine one ritual and describe it. In your view, is this ritual shared by others? If so, to what extent? What are the implications of your routinised or ritualistic behaviours for marketers?
3. Summarise an episode of a recent television series made in Australia and compare it with another made in America. What social values are endorsed or condemned in each? How can you explain any differences you find?
4. Look at two commercials for each of the products, services and charities categories. Summarise the values in each.
5. Analyse perfume or cosmetic advertising directed at men and at women. Compare the values presented in each type.

Key terms

acculturation *(p. 377)*
beliefs *(p. 374)*
content analysis *(p. 382)*
core values *(p. 390)*
culture *(p. 374)*
customs *(p. 374)*
enculturation *(p. 377)*
end-states of existence *(p. 383)*
field observation *(p. 382)*
formal/informal/technical learning of culture *(p. 376)*
List of Values (LOV) *(p. 384)*
means-end chains *(p. 383)*

ritual (*p. 379*)
ritualistic behaviour (*p. 380*)
Rokeach Value Survey (*p. 383*)
shadow shopping (*p. 382*)
subcultures (*p. 390*)
symbol (*p. 377*)
values (*p. 374*)
values instruments (*p. 383*)

Endnotes

1. Thomas C. O'Guinn and L.J. Shrum, 'The role of television in the construction of consumer reality', *Journal of Consumer Research*, 23, March 1997, pp. 278–295.
2. Based on Roy Morgan Research Consumer Panel, 1993.
3. Gwen Rae Bachmann, Deborah Roedder John and Akshay Rao, 'Children's susceptibility to peer group purchase influence: An exploratory investigation', in Leigh McAlister and Michael L. Rothschild (eds), *Advances in Consumer Research*, 20 (Provo, UT: Association for Consumer Research, 1993), pp. 463–469.
4. T. Bettina Cornwell, 'T-shirts as wearable diary: An examination of artifact consumption and garnering related to life events', in Marvin E. Goldberg, Gerald Gorn and Richard W. Pollay (eds), *Advances in Consumer Research*, 17 (Provo, UT: Association for Consumer Research, 1990), pp. 375–379.
5. See <www.adslogans.com> (March 2004).
6. Malcolm Evans, 'Semiotics: Culture and communications—common sense of the 21st century', Paper presented to the Annual Conference of the Market Research Society of Australia, Adelaide, October 1999.
7. Stuart Cunningham, 'The unworthy discourse? Advertising and national culture', in *Framing Culture: Criticism and Policy in Australia* (Sydney: Allen & Unwin, 1992).
8. Dennis W. Rook, 'The ritual dimension of consumer behavior', *Journal of Consumer Research*, 12, 1985, pp. 251–264.
9. Dennis W. Rook, 'Ritual behavior and consumer symbolism', in Thomas C. Kinnear (ed.), *Advances in Consumer Research*, 11 (Ann Arbor, MI: Association for Consumer Research, 1984), pp. 279–284.
10. David Bednall, *Media and Immigrant Settlement* (Canberra: Australian Government Publishing Service, 1992).
11. Russell W. Belk and Richard W. Pollay, 'Images of ourselves: The good life in twentieth century advertising', *Journal of Consumer Research*, 11, 1985, p. 888.
12. Shay Sayre, 'Content analysis as a tool for consumer research', *Journal of Consumer Marketing*, 9, Winter 1992, pp. 15–25.
13. Donald E. Stewart, *The Television Family: A Content Analysis of the Portrayal of Family Life on Prime Time Television* (Melbourne: Institute of Family Studies, 1983); Peter Beilby (ed.), 'Commercial break', in *Australian TV: The First 25 Years* (Melbourne: Thomas Nelson, 1981); and Tomiko Kodama, 'Rhetoric of the image of women in a Japanese television advertisement: A semiotic analysis', *Australian Journal of Communication*, 18(2), 1991, pp. 42–65.
14. Michael L. Maynard and Charles R. Taylor, 'Girlish images across cultures: Analyzing Japanese versus US *Seventeen* magazine ads', *Journal of Advertising*, 28, No. 1, Spring 1999, pp. 39–45.
15. Mindy F. Ji and James U. McNeal, 'How Chinese children's commercials differ from those of the United States: A content analysis,' *Journal of Advertising*, Vol. 30, No. 3, Fall 2001, pp. 79–92.
16 Lawrence Osborne, 'Consuming rituals of the suburban tribe', *The New York Times Magazine*, 13 January 2002, pp. 28–31, Margaret Littman, 'Science shopping', *Crain's Chicago Business*, 11 January 1999, p. 3, and Marvin Matises, 'Top of mind: Send ethnographers into new-SKU jungle', *Brandweek*, 25 September 2000, pp. 32–33.
17. Jonathon Gutman, 'Means-end chains as goal hierarchies', *Psychology & Marketing*, 14(6), September 1997, pp. 545–560.
18. Steven M. Burgess, 'Personal values and consumer research: An historical perspective', in Jagdish M. Sheth (ed.), *Research in Marketing: Volume 11, 1992* (Greenwich, Connecticut: JAI Press, 1992). For a ten-nation study of values (including Australia, Japan and the United States), see Branmir Sverko, 'The structure and hierarchy of values viewed cross-nationally', in Donald E. Super et al. (eds), *Life Roles, Values and Careers: International Findings of the Work Importance Study* (San Francisco: Jossey-Bass Inc., 1995).
19. N.T. Feather, 'Human values and the work situation: Two studies', *Australian Psychologist*, 14(2), 1979, pp. 131–141.
20. J. Michael Munson and Edward F. McQuarrie, 'Shortening the Rokeach Value Survey for use in consumer

research', *Academy for Consumer Research*, 15, 1988, pp. 381–386.

21. Wagner A. Kamakura and Jose Afonso Mazzon, 'Value segmentation: A model for the measurement of values and value systems', *Journal of Consumer Research*, 18, September 1991, pp. 208–218.
22. Lynn R. Kahle and Larry Chiagouris (eds), *Values, Lifestyles and Psychographics* (New Jersey: Lawrence Erlbaum, 1997); Sharon E. Beatty et al., 'Alternative measurement approaches to consumer values: The List of Values and the Rokeach Value Survey', *Psychology & Marketing*, 2, 1985, pp. 181–200; and Lynn R. Kahle et al., 'Empirical relationships between cognitive style and LOV: Implications for values and value systems', in Frank J. Kardes and Mita Sujan (eds), *Advances in Consumer Research*, 22 (Provo, UT: Association for Consumer Research, 1995), pp. 141–146; Jeffrey F. Durgee, Gina C. O'Connor and Robert W. Veryzer, 'Observations: Translating values into product wants', *Journal of Advertising Research*, 36(6), Nov/Dec 1996, pp. 90–100; and Boris W. Becker, 'Values in advertising research: A methodological caveat', *Journal of Advertising Research*, 38(4), 1998, pp. 57–60.
23. Norman T. Feather, 'Values and national identification: Australian evidence', *Australian Journal of Psychology*, 46(1), 1994, pp. 35–40.
24. David Bednall, Ian Walker and Peter Grant, 'Impact of values and demographic data in accounting for patterns of brand and store loyalty in an Australian consumer panel', in *Proceedings of the Seventh Bi-Annual World Marketing Congress* (Melbourne: Academy of Marketing Sciences, 1995).
25. Geert H. Hofstede, *Culture's Consequences: Comparing Values, Behaviors, Institutions and Organizations Across Nations*, 2nd edn (Thousand Oaks, CA: Sage, 2001).
26. See <http://www.qmr.com.au/austscan.htm> (March 2004).
27. DYG SCAN® <www.dyg.com/dygscan.htm> (accessed September 2004).
28. The Survey of Consumer Sentiment is collected by Westpac and the Melbourne Institute of Applied Economic and Social Research at the University of Melbourne. See <http://www.ecom.unimelb.edu.au/iaesrwww/indicators/ consumer.html> (March 2004).
29. Jerzy Jaroslaw Smolicz, *What is an Australian? Identity, Core Values and Resilience of Culture* (Adelaide: Multicultural Education Coordinating Committee, 1989).
30. <http://www.ausbuy.com.au/> and <http://www.australianmade.com.au> (March 2004).
31. Bruce Headey, 'The life satisfactions and priorities of Australians', in Jonathon Kelley and Clive Bean (eds), *Australian Attitudes: Social and Political Analyses from the National Social Science Survey* (Sydney: Allen & Unwin, 1988).
32. N.T. Feather, 'Values and national identification: Australian evidence', op. cit. The values are based on the Schwartz Value Survey, which in turn draws on the terminal and instrumental values described by Rokeach.
33. David C. McClelland, *The Achieving Society* (New York: Free Press, 1961), pp. 150–151.
34. T. Phillips, 'Popular views about Australian identity: Research and analysis', *Journal of Sociology*, 34(3), 1998, pp. 281–302. See also, 'Peace and honesty top list of what Australians most value, finds study' <http://www.ncls.org.au> (March 2004).
35. George M. Zinkhan and Penelope J. Prenshaw, 'Good life images and brand associations: Evidence from Asia, America, and Europe', in Chris T. Allen and Deborah Roedder (eds), *Advances in Consumer Research*, 21 (Provo, UT: Association for Consumer Research, 1994) pp. 496–500.

CHAPTER 12

Subcultural aspects of consumer behaviour

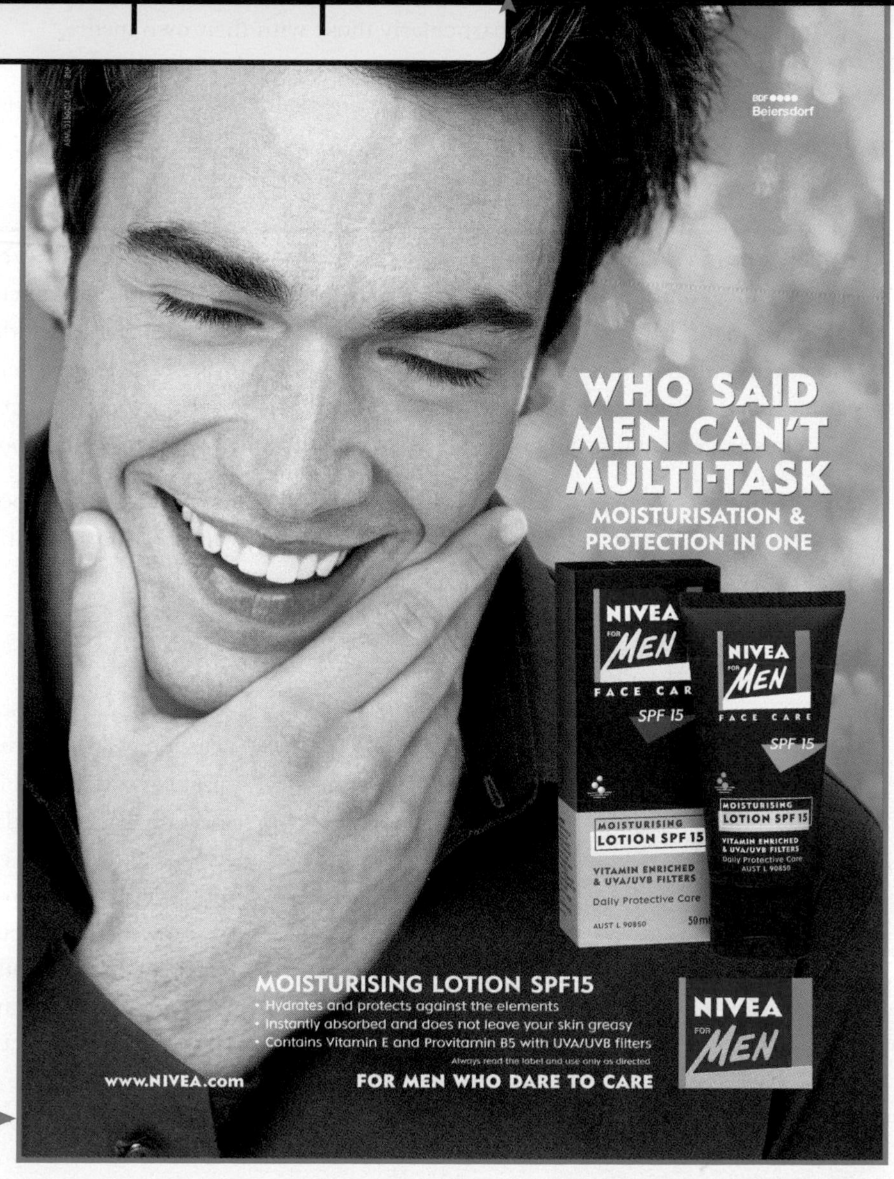

Source: Courtesy of Foote Cone & Belding.

Culture has a potent influence on all consumer behaviour. Individuals are brought up to follow the beliefs, values and customs of their society and to avoid behaviour that is frowned upon or considered taboo. In addition to cultural segmentation, marketers have begun to segment the larger society into smaller subgroups (subcultures) that identify themselves as members of these groups and who share similar customs and ways of behaving. These subcultures provide important marketing opportunities for astute marketing strategists.

Our discussion of subcultures, therefore, has a narrower focus than the discussion of culture. Instead of examining the dominant beliefs, values and customs that exist within an entire society, this chapter explores the marketing opportunities created by the existence of certain beliefs, values and customs specific to subcultural groups within society. These subcultural divisions are based on a variety of sociocultural and demographic variables, such as ethnicity, religion, race, age, gender, sexual preference and working status. In the Australian and New Zealand context, it must be understood that the *small size* of many subcultural markets may make fine-grained marketing segmentation impractical. However, unless marketers consider subcultural segments, they could:

- miss viable niche markets, particularly those with their own media;
- alienate significant numbers of customers in the subcultures;
- miss opportunities to use subcultural channels for distribution and marketing.

What is a subculture?

A subculture can be thought of as a distinct cultural group that exists as an identifiable segment within a larger, more complex multicultural society.[1] The members of a specific subculture possess beliefs, values and customs that set them apart from other members of the same society. In addition, they adhere to most of the dominant cultural beliefs, values and behavioural patterns of the larger society. We define **subculture**, then, as *a distinct cultural group that exists as an identifiable segment within a larger, more complex society.*

Thus the cultural profile of a society or nation can be viewed as a composite of four distinct elements:

1. the unique beliefs, values, and customs subscribed to by members of specific subcultures;
2. the central or core cultural themes that are shared by most of the population, regardless of specific subcultural memberships;
3. language used; and
4. self-identification.

FIGURE 12.1 Relationship between culture and subcultures

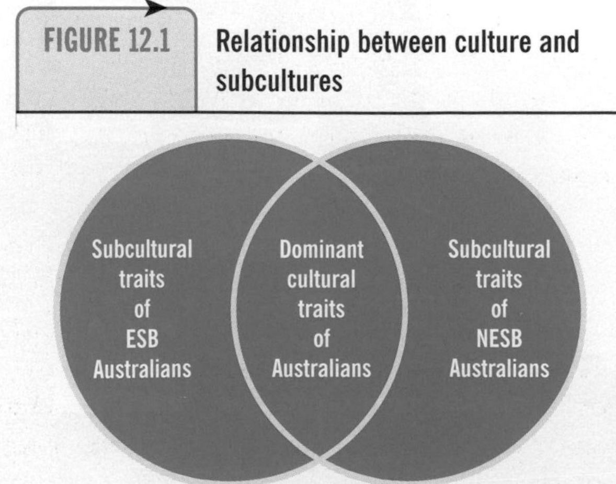

Figure 12.1 presents a model of the relationship between two subcultural groups—people with English-speaking background (ESB) and those with non-English-speaking backgrounds (NESB)—and the larger culture. As the figure depicts, each subculture has its own unique traits, yet both groups share the dominant traits of the overall Australian culture.[2] In this way, Australia is considered to be a **culturally diverse society**.

Let us look at it another way. Each Australian is in large part a product of the 'Australian way of life'. However, at the same time, each Australian is a member of various subcultures. For example, an 18-year-old girl may simultaneously be of Vietnamese origin, from a

Chinese family, a Buddhist, a teenager and a Queenslander. We would expect that membership in each different subculture would provide its own set of specific beliefs, values, attitudes and customs. Table 12.1 lists typical subcultural categories and corresponding examples of specific subcultural groups. This list is by no means exhaustive: university graduates, feminists, conservationists, bikers, single parents—in fact, any group that shares common beliefs and customs and who self-identify as a distinct group may be classified as a subculture.

Subcultural analysis enables the marketing manager to focus on natural, though not necessarily large, market segments. In carrying out such analyses, however, the marketer must determine whether the beliefs, values and customs shared by members of a specific subgroup make them desirable candidates for special marketing attention. Subcultures are therefore relevant units of analysis for marketing.

The following sections examine a number of important subcultural categories: ethnicity, religion, geographic location, race, age and sex. (Occupational and social class subgroups are discussed in detail in Chapter 10.)

TABLE 12.1 Subcultural categories

Subcultural category	Examples
First-language background	English (ESB), non-English (NESB)
Birthplace	Vietnam, Greece, New Zealand, Somalia, Australia
Background	Chinese, Vietnamese, Australian, British, American
Region	Capital cities, regional Australia, outback, Northern Australia
Gender	Male, female
Age	Generation Y, Generation X, baby boomers, teenagers
Sexual preference	Gay, straight
Religion	Catholic, Buddhist, Muslim, Atheist
Occupation	White collar, blue collar, professional

Ethnic subcultures

While most Australian citizens, especially those born in Australia, see themselves as Australians, they frequently retain a sense of identification and pride in the language and customs of their ancestors. When it comes to consumer behaviour, this ancestral pride is manifested most strongly in the viewing of ethnic-specific programs on SBS television,[3] the consumption of ethnic foods, in travel or telephone calls to relatives in the 'homeland' and in the purchase of cultural artefacts (ethnic clothing, art, music, NESB language newspapers). Interest in such goods and services has expanded rapidly as younger Australians attempt to understand their origins better and associate themselves more closely with their ethnic roots, and as the pleasures of this multicultural diversity extend to a wider group. Until recently, Australian marketers knew comparatively little about **ethnic subcultures**, especially those based on NESB groups.

NESB CULTURES IN AUSTRALIA

There are over 200 **community languages** in common use in Australia, including nearly 50 Aboriginal languages. This reflects the heritage of Aboriginal languages in Australia and the long periods of mass migration to Australia, particularly in the sixty years following World War II. Around 28% of Australians were born overseas[4] and net migration continues at around 135 000 people each year.[5] Table 12.2 shows the main community languages used in Australia, based on the language spoken at home.[6]

TABLE 12.2 **Languages spoken at home**

Language	Speakers x 000s	Language	Speakers x 000s
English only	15 014.0	Spanish	93.6
Italian	353.6	Tagalog (Filipino)	78.9
Greek	263.7	Macedonian	72.0
Cantonese	225.3	Croatian	69.9
Arabic	209.4	Polish	59.1
Vietnamese	174.2	Turkish	50.7
Mandarin	139.3	Serbian	49.2

Source: **Derived from ABS *Basic Community Profiles*, 2001 Census, Table B08.**

Understanding NESB consumer behaviour

Much of the research in this area has come from the American market, particularly when dealing with the differences between Anglo and Hispanic markets.[7] In Australia, there are significant markets for people of an NESB. In 2001, the Census asked people for the first time to describe their ancestry, going back to three generations ago. Some people named more than one ancestry. Table 12.3 shows the main ancestries claimed, analysed by the birthplace of their parents. The table shows just how diverse Australian society is. In the older immigrant communities (people from the United Kingdom, Italy, Greece, Germany and Holland), parents and grandparents are far more likely to be Australian-born. The opposite is the case of more recent arrivals, including those from Vietnam and China.

TABLE 12.3 **Ancestry by birthplace of parents**

Ancestry claimed	Both parents born in Australia x 000s	One or both parents born outside Australia x 000s	Birthplace of parents unspecified x 000s	Total claimed ancestry x 000s
Australian	5452.8	1095.1	191.8	6739.6
English	3773.3	2421.7	163.8	6358.9
Irish	1367.0	510.9	41.7	1919.7
Italian	196.6	580.0	23.7	800.3
German	428.3	298.2	15.7	742.2
Chinese	29.1	510.8	16.7	556.6
Scottish	242.1	287.8	10.1	540.0
Greek	60.3	302.2	13.1	375.7
Lebanese	10.3	143.4	8.5	162.2
Indian	3.3	148.7	4.6	156.6
Vietnamese	0.7	147.3	8.7	156.6
Polish	18.6	129.3	3.1	150.9

Source: **Derived from ABS *Basic Community Profiles*, 2001 Census, Tables B05A and B05B.**

The extent of marketing activities to ethnic groups can be gauged by the great strength of the ethnic press in Australia.[8] Over 100 publications in over 35 languages other than English are published regularly.[9] An Australian study by one of the authors of this book showed that up to 96% of adults of particular language backgrounds were reading one or more ethnic newspapers in their own language.[10] Some Australians would be surprised to learn that Australia has daily newspapers in Chinese and Greek and an ethnic newspaper (*Le Courier*) dating back to 1892.[11]

Table 12.4 gives an indication of this richness and activity by listing newspapers from several languages and cultures and their websites where available. For communities where mass migration occurred mostly one or two generations ago, parts of the publication are likely to be in English. In looking at the advertising contained in such newspapers, several products and services predominate:

- Travel, telecommunications and freight services—e.g. Shamrock Travel (*Irish Echo*) and Denny's Travel (*Greek Herald*), Polonez carrier service (*Express Wieczorny*);
- Food—e.g. Harrigan's Irish Pub (*Irish Echo*), the Dutch Company's imported foods (*Dutch Courier*);
- Festivals relevant to communities—e.g. St Patrick's Day (*Irish Echo*), Queen's Day (*Dutch Courier*);
- Immigration advocates and lawyers—e.g. United Lawyers Barristers and Solicitors (*Chinese Melbourne Daily*);
- Financial services—e.g. Provident Capital (*Greek Herald*); and see Figure 12.2 (page 410); and
- Culturally appropriate services, such as funeral directors, or services where someone speaks the language.

TABLE 12.4 **Some ethnic newspapers in Australia**

Newspaper	Website	Newspaper	Website
Arabic		**Hungarian**	
El Telegraph		*Magyar Elet*	<www.nlc.net.au/~erika>
Middle East Herald	<www.ualm.org.au/meh_ci.asp>	**Indian**	
Chinese		*Indian Link*	<www.indianlink.com.au>
Australian Chinese Daily	<www.ausdaily.net.au>	*Indian Downunder*	<www.indiandownunder.com.au>
Sing Tao	<www.singtao.com>	**Irish**	
Czech		*Irish Echo*	<www.irishecho.com.au>
Noviny	<www.coleoptera.org/noviny>	**Italian**	
Croatian		Il Globo	
Nova Hrvatska	<http://homepages.ihug.com.au/~franjo>	**Japanese**	
		Nichigo Press	<www.nichigo.com.au>
Spremnost Croatian Weekly	<www.magna.com.au/~sprem>	**Jewish**	
Dutch		*Australian Jewish News*	<www.ajn.com.au>
Dutch Weekly	<www.dal.com.au/DW>	**Serbian**	
Egyptian		*Glas (Serbian)*	<www.glasslovenije.com.au>
El Massry Newspaper	<www.elmassry.com>	**Sri Lankan**	
Greek		*Serendib News (Sri Lankan)*	<www.serendibnews.com>
Neos Kosmos	<www.neoskosmos.com.au>	**Thai**	
Greek Herald		*Thai Oz News*	<www.thaioz.com.au/newspaper>
Nea Patrida		**Vietnamese**	
		Viet Luan	<www.vietluan.com.au>

Surprisingly, there is little government advertising in these papers. Although the numbers in each community are often not enough to allow a fine-grained segmentation, we should not assume that each ethnic group is homogeneous. For example, Spanish-speaking people in Australia may have come from South America (Argentina or Chile), not necessarily from Spain. Few of Australia's Hispanics are from Puerto Rico or Mexico (unlike the United States).

In addition to the ethnic press, advertisers have access to ethnic-specific audiences on SBS television,[12] while government advertisers can use national SBS radio services. Channel 31 offers TV programs in many languages. NESB pay television services were the first on air,[13] starting with Chinese, Greek and Italian language channels. They also carry advertising. Commercial radio stations such as 2CR (Chinese) and Radio Hellas (Greek) also offer advertising opportunities.

Australian marketers have been given more insight into marketing among and by these communities[14] by the Ethnic Business Awards.[15] One pioneer in the field was the unforgettable 'memories' telephone campaign, directed to persuading immigrant communities to ring family members in their homelands. Western Union has recently targeted ethnic groups and travellers to Australia wanting to transfer money to and from other countries (see Case Study 12.1). In 2004, Qantas celebrated the Year of the Monkey by combining the company's kangaroo symbol with a red monkey in its advertising to the Chinese community.[16] As immigrant groups become more established, elements of their culture disperse into the general community. Restaurants are the clearest example of this; holidays and international tourism are others.

Academic research in Australia has investigated ethnic group differences in consumer behaviour. In a qualitative study, Constance Hill and Celia Romm showed differences between ESB families and Sino-Vietnamese families in terms of gift giving[17]. For most ESB families, gift buying was a high-involvement activity aimed at giving recipients high-status gifts designed to deliver gratification in the short term. Their timing reflected birthdays, Christmas and Mother's and Father's Day. In contrast, the Sino-Vietnamese gave gifts as a low-priority activity. They were more directed to longer-term issues (like saving for education) and were more likely to involve financial risk. The timing was less tied to Western events like birthdays, though Chinese New Year was a common time of gift giving. These outcomes reflect both ethnic differences (e.g. Chinese New Year rather than Christmas) and cohort differences (being newer arrivals, the Sino-Vietnamese were more likely to value education as a way of ensuring their children's future in Australia). In studying ethnic markets, both factors need to be considered.

Planning an ethnic-specific campaign involves several issues beyond ordinary advertising:

- You cannot assume a community is homogeneous simply because they all speak the same language. In particular, NESB people born in Australia are likely to have somewhat different views, values and degree of affluence than their parents' generation.[18] **Self-identification** and *degree* of identification are important (see Table 12.5).
- You cannot assume that all people are literate in their own first language.
- While there is a relative scarcity of programs in the NESB audiences' first languages, do not assume that any advertising placed in these programs, no matter how poor, will be attended to.
- Most ethnic communities watch and use a lot of ESB media.[19] Campaigns should be consistent across media.
- Advertising prepared in English and translated into other languages should be back-translated to check accuracy and cultural appropriateness. Brand names can be especially problematic if simply taken into another language (see Chapter 13 for some cross-cultural examples). In addition, apparently minor details, such as colour, can have great cultural significance and this aspect should also be checked with several people from that culture.[20] Symbols, such as lucky numbers for Chinese-speakers, can have great significance for the audience.

TABLE 12.5 **Ways in which 'Italian' has been defined**

Indicator	Comments
Surname	Not definitive, since a non-Italian person may have an Italian surname and vice versa.
Country of origin	While most Italian-Australians have come from Italy, some have come from other parts of Europe, Africa or even South America. Of course, the children (and now grandchildren) of Italian postwar immigrants are Australian-born.
Country of family ancestry	Some Italians may have come from Egypt or Libya, rather than Italy.
Italian spoken at home	English is often spoken at home.
Self-identification	How the person regards themselves, the type of passport they own and the sports team (Italy or Australia) they support more strongly.
Degree of identification	Strength of beliefs and behaviours (use of language, values, food and other habits).

ASIAN-AUSTRALIAN CONSUMERS

It is possible to examine the large number of ethnic groups separately, though typically there is little public information about marketing to specific groups. Although Asian-Australians (primarily Chinese and Vietnamese) currently number less than one million, they are the fastest-growing Australian minority. Because they are largely family-oriented, highly industrious and strongly driven to achieve a middle-class lifestyle, Asian-Australians are an attractive niche market. As we have seen, there is a booming newspaper market for Chinese and Vietnamese readers. US research[21] confirms that ethnic-specific advertising was more effective than general advertising for the same product. An ad for stereo speakers using an Asian model evoked a far more positive result than the same ad using a Caucasian model.

Characteristics

Asian-Australians largely lead urban lives and are presently concentrated in Sydney, Melbourne and Brisbane. Although they tend to speak many different languages and dialects, the majority also speak English reasonably well. The overwhelming majority of Asian-Australians value a close-knit family life, the attainment of formal education, and personal achievement. Like most newly-arrived groups, Asian-Australians have shown themselves to be hard-working, very family-oriented, and strive for excellence in educational pursuits (both for themselves and their children). The evidence suggests that this relatively new community in Australia, like many immigrant groups before them, is strongly motivated towards self-sufficiency. If they do not own their own business, they or their children are often found in professional, technical or managerial occupations.

Asian-Australian consumer behaviour

Currently there is limited information about Asian-Australians as consumers. It is important to remember that Asian-Australians are really drawn from diverse cultural backgrounds. Those with limited acculturation to mainstream Australia or with a well-developed social network within their own culture are more likely to rely on their subculture.[22] US research showed that Vietnamese-Americans were more likely to follow the traditional model, wherein the man makes the decision for large purchases; however, Chinese-American husbands and wives are more likely to share in the decision-making process.[23] Vietnamese-Americans also frowned on credit, because in their culture owing money is negatively viewed. In contrast, Korean-Americans and Chinese-Americans, many of whom have been in the US for years, readily use credit.[24] The use of Asian models in advertising is effective in reaching this market segment.

FIGURE 12.2 **Subcultural financial services marketing**

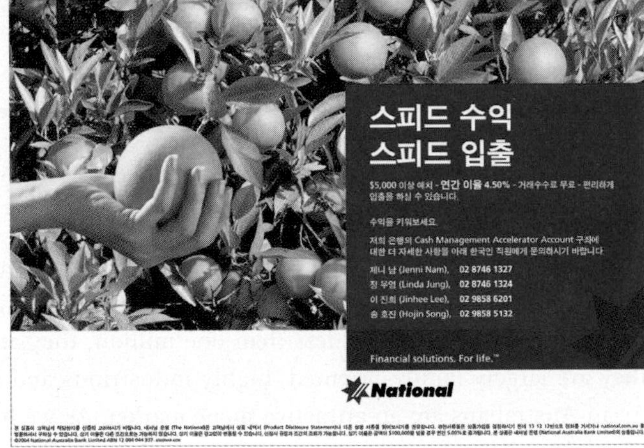

Source: **Courtesy of National Australia Bank Limited.**

SOJOURNERS

In considering ethnic-specific marketing, we should look beyond the ethnic groups currently settled in Australia. For example, there are large numbers of sojourners in Australia (people visiting for study or holiday). In 2003, these included 303 000 international students, with China, Hong Kong, Korea, Indonesia, Malaysia, Japan, Thailand, India, the USA and Singapore being the main countries of origin.[25] Companies like Western Union, national home country airlines[26] and phonecard companies offering cheap rates to specific overseas countries have specifically targeted these groups.

ABORIGINAL AND TORRES STRAIT ISLANDER CONSUMER BEHAVIOUR

Australia's Aboriginal and Torres Strait Islander population is of moderate size (around 460 000 people) but because of economic disadvantage they have been of limited interest to generalist marketers. Some 30% of Australia's indigenous population live in major cities, compared with 67% of other Australians. Approximately 12% speak an indigenous language at home, the remainder mainly use English. Whilst education levels are increasing, indigenous people are less likely to attend a university (but more likely to attend TAFE) than their non-indigenous counterparts. Unemployment is much higher in these groups, while household income is only 62% of that of non-indigenous Australians. Use of consumer items like cars, computers and the Internet are also lower.[27] There are various indigenous media[28], including Imparja which offers a commercial television service by satellite to most areas of Australia. Under its licence conditions, it is often not available in areas where there are other commercial television stations. Imparja also operates radio services.[29] Imparja carries mainstream national advertising, along with community services announcements. A particular series of these, featuring the well-respected indigenous leader Michael Long, focuses on consumer advice, e.g. buying a car or some other consumer product. One very sensitive issue is to ensure that no commercial (or other program content) features people who have died. Thus, if an actor in a commercial subsequently dies, Imparja can no longer carry that ad unless the actor's image is removed.

There has been little direct research into indigenous consumer behaviour. One exception was research led by US consumer researcher Russell Belk who studied the influence of first-world consumer culture on remote communities in northern Western Australia. The research showed heavy use of consumer products such as television, video games, cars and refrigerators, amongst some community poverty and ill-health. While the indigenous culture was affected, and even threatened by the imported consumer culture, Belk and his colleagues also found occasions where it was used to strengthen traditional cultural practices and values.[30]

➤ Religious subcultures

Most of the world's major religions (and many of the minor ones) are represented in Australia. Table 12.6 lists the main religious denominations in Australia, based on the 2001 census. The largest single religious group is Catholic Christians, though collectively they are outnumbered by other Christian denominations. Non-Christian adherents are also present in considerable numbers. Perhaps surprising is the small number of Jewish adherents. It is understood that some Jewish people do not identify themselves as Jewish by religion or do not report their religion on the Census.

The members of all these religious groups are at times likely to make purchase decisions that are influenced by their religious identity. For many Australians in the postwar period, Sunday was a day devoid of shopping, professional sport and entertainment. Catholics used to eat fish on Fridays. However, as Australian life has become increasingly secularised (i.e. as religion plays less of a central role in determining basic customs, beliefs and values), adherence to traditional religious rules has diminished. Nevertheless, consumer behaviour is directly affected by religion in terms of products that are *symbolically* and *ritualistically* associated with the celebration of various religious holidays. For example, Christmas has become the major gift-purchasing season of the year, while Easter festivals mean no more than a long holiday break to many Australians. Some religious groups have their own media, such as the *Australian Jewish News*. Religious requirements or practices sometimes take on an expanded meaning beyond their original purpose. For instance, dietary laws for an observant Jewish family represent an obligation, so there are a range of Kosher foods and products that at times find a wider market. Similarly, Australia is a large producer of Halal food prepared for export as well as the local market. Figure 12.3 shows certification symbols used on Halal and Kosher food produced in Australia. These religious rules mostly describe what animals can be eaten, how they should be slaughtered and how food should be prepared. Pig meat, for example, is prohibited in both religions.[31]

TABLE 12.6 **Religious affiliation of people living in Australia**

Religious adherence	%	Religious adherence	%
Catholic	26.4	Buddhism	1.9
Anglican	20.5	Islam	1.5
Uniting Church	6.6	Hinduism	0.5
Orthodox	2.8	Judaism	0.4
Other Christian	10.5	None	15.3

Source: **Derived from ABS *Basic Community Profiles*, 2001 Census, Table B10. Excludes other religions, inadequately described and overseas visitors.**

FIGURE 12.3 Certification symbols for Halal and Kosher food sold in Australia

Very little consumer research has been devoted to examining how religious affiliation and commitment influences consumer preferences and loyalties. One stream of research that examined leisure activities of individuals with different religious backgrounds found a number of interesting distinctions: in the United States, Protestant and Catholic consumers were found to have a stronger orientation towards solitary leisure pursuits, whereas Jewish consumers preferred activities that provided companionship and/or sensory stimulation. Related research indicated that many New York Jewish consumers were innovators and often served as generalised opinion leaders[32] These US studies are not easily transferable to the Australian market when we consider the comparatively small number of Jewish people and other minority subgroups in Australia.

Research into the family (see Chapter 10) indicated that husband and wife decision making was also related to religious orientation. In US research involving one of the authors of this book, examining differences in pro-religious and non-religious Catholic and Jewish households, it was found that husbands in Catholic and pro-religious families had the most influence in making specific purchase decisions; while in both Jewish and non-religious families, husbands and wives shared equally in making most decisions.[33]

Geographic and regional subcultures

Australia is a large country, one that enjoys a wide range of climatic and geographic conditions. Given the country's size and physical diversity, it is only natural that the Australian people have a sense of regional identification and use this identification as a way of describing others (e.g. those people from 'down south', a term used by Northern Territorians to describe people south of Alice Springs). In fact the majority of Australians live in large urban centres, with most of the country remaining largely unoccupied.

Despite this, differences between areas depend mainly on climate and remoteness of location. For example, the use of solar water heaters is common in northern Australia, yet rare in the southerly parts of the country. Australians show a great love for sport, but culturally there are differences between the Queensland/NSW/ACT mania for rugby and the fervour for AFL football in the other States. Given Australia's vast distances between population centres, communication systems have always been of great importance.[34] Television, phones, airlines and an efficient postal system have made most products and services widely available, limiting cultural differences. Minor variations do exist; for example, the luncheon meat 'Strasbourg' in one state is called 'Devon' in the next, but generally Australia shows few regional variations. Despite improving communications technology, people in regional areas have witnessed a flight of services, jobs and opportunities to the cities, stranding an angry group of consumers. Such city–country differences may become entrenched in Australian society, given the widening gap in household income. We may become more like the US in this respect.[35]

Racial subcultures

Within the United States, some attention has been given by marketers to racial differences, with a focus on African-Americans, Asian-Americans and Hispanic-Americans. Australian marketers are far more likely to focus on ethnic groups than on race, for several reasons. The time of arrival of NESB immigrant groups and their socioeconomic background are more critical to their economic status than anything to do with race. Recently-arrived groups tend to be younger and less affluent than earlier arrivals and work in lower-status jobs. They are more typically at the earlier stage of the family life cycle, struggling to establish a home for themselves and a future for their children. Recent Asian immigrants fit this pattern, while the older established communities of settlers, such as the Dutch, Italians and Greeks, are typically older and more affluent. In addition, many Australians appear uncomfortable using race as a legitimate means of segmenting society, let alone markets.

American research on racial sub-segments is of interest to Australian marketers because it shows how sub-segments need to be well understood before they can be targeted. Race may provide a means of segmentation in some overseas markets that Australian marketers are attempting to enter. Table 12.7 shows how there can be large differences (and many similarities) in purchasing patterns between sub-groups based on different cultural practices.

TABLE 12.7 Purchase patterns of Anglo-White, African-American, and Hispanic-American households

Product/Activity	Anglo-White	African–American	Hispanic–American
Dental floss	102	86	98
Mouthwash	97	124	105
Hand and body cream	98	117	100
Vitamin/mineral supplements	103	77	86
Energy drinks	96	124	132
Car rental—business use	94	131	78
Camera film	104	66	89
Greeting card	103	83	85
Instant breakfast	97	112	105
Barbeque and seasoning sauces	100	103	89
Ready-to-drink iced cappuccino	95	113	121
Cat treat	110	42	84
Charcoal	93	148	109
Attend movies/last 6 months	101	90	106
Went camping/past 12 months	110	31	89
Own a full-size van	112	19	130
Own a camera	106	60	83

Source: **Mediamark Research, Inc. Doublebase 2001 Report. All rights reserved. Reprinted by permission. Based on an index of 100 which represented average purchase across all groups.**

Age subcultures

All major age subgroupings of the population might be thought of as separate subcultures. Each stage of the family life cycle (active seekers, young achievers, parenthood, post-parenthood and dissolution) could be considered a separate subculture, since important shifts occur in the demand for specific types of products and services. Figure 12.4 shows the age distribution, for males and females for 1983 and 2003.

It is clear that Australia has an ageing population, with smaller numbers of the younger age groups. In addition, there is a large group of people nearing or at retiring age (the baby boomers, see below). These demographic trends are the result of Australians living longer—life expectancy has increased by a remarkable 6.2 years for males (whose median age at death is 76.2 years) and by 5.0 years for females (whose median age

FIGURE 12.4 Age distribution 1983 and 2003

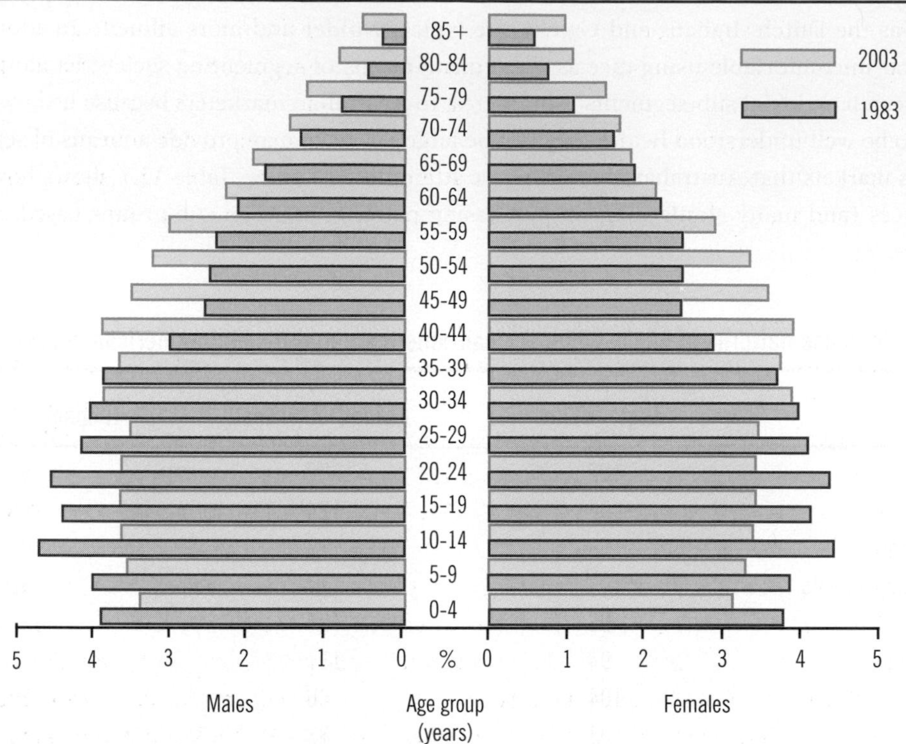

Source: ABS, *Population by Age and Sex, Australian States and Territories*. Catalogue No. 3201.0. ABS, 2003.

at death has risen to 82.2 years) between 1982 and 2003. People who survive into adulthood are now expected to live into their late 80s. Fertility has stabilised at around 1.75 babies per woman, and in general these children are being born to older mothers.[36]

Age **cohorts** (a cohort is a group of individuals born over a relatively short and continuous period of time) have been used to describe groups of individuals who were born in a particular era. In this section we will limit our examination of age subcultures to four groups: Generation Y, Generation X, baby boomers and the elderly. These segments have been singled out because their distinctive lifestyles qualify them for consideration as subcultural groups. There is some debate among academics about how valid this cohort approach is,[37] but it has certainly proved useful to practitioners. One age cohort, the baby boomers, corresponded to a period of a drastically increased birthrate and a period of strong economic prosperity in the years after World War II. The labels given to subsequent generations, Generation X and Generation Y reflect the fact that these later generations were less easy to characterise. Similarly, different writers have used slightly different dates for these last two groups.

GENERATION Y MARKET

This age cohort includes the approximately 3.9 million Australians born between the years 1980 and 1994. They are mostly the children of baby boomers and are thus also known as 'echo boomers' and the 'millennium generation'. They can be divided into three subsegments: Gen Y adults, Gen Y teens and Gen Y kids, or 'tweens'. According to US research, members of **Generation Y** are often described as pragmatic, savvy, socially and environmentally aware, and open to new experiences.[38] The teen segment of Generation Y have grown up with the Internet and in a media-saturated environment and tend to be aware of 'marketing hype'. For example, they would tend to immediately understand that when a shopping centre locates popular teen stores at opposite ends of the mall they are being encouraged 'to walk the mall.'[39] This age cohort has shifted some of its TV viewing time to the Internet and, when compared with their parents, they are less likely to read newspapers and often do not trust the stores that their parents shop in.[40] Some US retailers have found it profitable to develop websites specifically targeted to the interests of the Gen Y consumer, such as Rave Girl <www.goravegirl.com>. This generation is characterised by mobile telephone use and informal posses of friends who keep in regular contact. It also has its own media such as *Girlfriend* <www.girlfriend.com.au> and *Dolly* magazines <http://dolly.ninemsn.com.au/dolly/Default.asp>.

GENERATION X MARKET

Generation X, also referred to as *Xers*, consists of people born from 1965–79, numbering approximately four million Australians. They are one of the most educated generations, but are less likely to own a home and slower to start a family than earlier generations. They were not good savers and many still live with their parents. They tend to spend disproportionately more on recreation.[41] As we saw in Chapter 8, they are heavy users of commercial FM radio, but infrequent users of ABC AM talk shows. Australian research suggests that value for money is a powerful influence on purchase.[42]

According to US research, this generation do not like labels, are cynical and do not want to be singled out and marketed to. They matured during an era of rising divorce rates and 'latchkey children'.[43] Also, unlike their parents, who are frequently baby boomers, they are in no rush to marry or start a family. For Generation X consumers, job satisfaction is typically more important than salary. It has been said, for example, that 'baby boomers live to work, Gen Xers work to live!' Xers reject the values of older co-workers who may neglect their families while striving to secure higher salaries and career advancement, and many have observed their parents getting laid off after many years of loyalty to an employer. Xers, therefore, are not particularly interested in long-term employment with a single company but instead prefer to work for a company that can offer some work/life flexibility and can bring some fun aspects into the environment. Xers understand the necessity of money but do not view salary as a sufficient reason for staying with a company—the quality of the work itself and the relationships built on the job are much more important.[44] For Generation X, it is more important to enjoy life and to have a lifestyle that provides freedom and flexibility. Yet, inevitably all groups age and many Gen Xers are in their 30s and fighting the early signs of ageing. Figure 12.5 shows an ad targeting this group.

Members of Generation X often pride themselves on their sophistication. Although they are not necessarily materialistic, they do purchase good brand names but not necessarily designer labels. They want to be recognised by marketers as a group in their own right and not as mini–baby boomers. Therefore, advertisements targeted to this audience must focus on their

FIGURE 12.5 **Targeting Generation X**

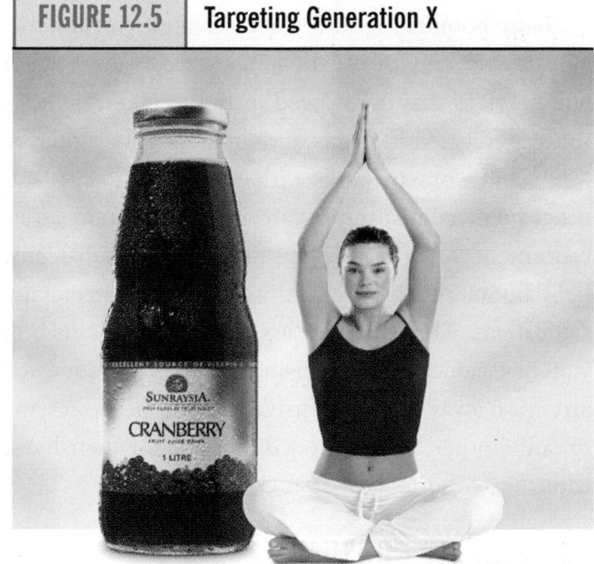

Source: **Courtesy of The Sunraysia Natural Beverage Company.**

style in music, fashions, and language. One key for marketers appears to be sincerity. Xers are not against advertising are only opposed to insincerity. Baby boomer media does not work with Generation X members. For example, in the US, 65% of 50–64-year-olds, and 55% of 30–49-year-olds read a newspaper regularly, only 39% of adults under 30 (the younger Xers) regularly read a newspaper.[45] Xers are the MTV generation and in the US, heavy viewers of the Fox network which claims that 38% of its viewers are in this age group. (The Fox network news and other programs provide multiple channels on Foxtel in Australia.)

THE BABY BOOMER MARKET

In recent years, marketers have found **baby boomers** to be a particularly desirable target audience because:

1. they are the single largest distinctive age category alive today;
2. they frequently make important consumer purchase decisions;
3. they have reached or are reaching retirement age and, together with inherited wealth from their parents, are at the peak of affluence.

Who are the baby boomers?

When we speak of baby boomers, we are referring to the age segment of the population that was born between 1946 and 1964. Thus, baby boomers are in the broad age category that extends from the early 40s to the late 50s. They constitute a large proportion of the adult population, currently estimated at 5.1 million people. Given their age and affluence, baby boomers form a desirable market segment. Although each year more baby boomers turn 50 years of age, they do not necessarily like the idea. In the US, increases in health club memberships and a boom in the sales of vitamin and health supplements are evidence that these consumers are trying hard to look and feel 'young'—they do not want to age gracefully, but will fight and kick and pay whatever is necessary to look young. For example, 35–50-year-olds are the largest market for plastic surgery in the US, and the majority of cosmetic dentistry patients are 40–49 years of age.[46]

Baby boomers tend to be motivated consumers. They enjoy buying for themselves, for their homes or apartments, and for others—they are consumption oriented. As baby boomers age, the nature of the products and services they most need or desire changes. For example, because of the ageing of this market segment, sales of 'relaxed fit' jeans and 'lineless' bifocal glasses are up substantially, as are the sales of walking shoes. Men's and women's pants with elastic waistbands are also enjoying strong sales. Recently, bank marketers and other financial institutions are also paying more attention to assisting boomers who are starting to think about retirement. A previously upwardly mobile sub-segment, yuppies, is by far the most sought-after subgroup of baby boomers. They generally are well-off financially, well educated, and in enviable professional or managerial careers. They often are associated with status brand names, such as BMWs or Volvo station wagons, Rolex watches, cable TV, and Cuisinart food processors. Today, as many yuppies are maturing, they are shifting their attention away from expensive status-type possessions to travel, physical fitness, planning for second careers, or some other form of new directions for their lives. Table 12.8 contrasts the differing views taken by these three age cohorts, based on US research.

THE ELDERLY CONSUMER

Australia's population is ageing. The number of **elderly consumers** is growing faster than the overall population. In 1871, only 2% of the population were aged 65 or over. By 2003, this had grown to 10.7% representing over 2.5 million Australians.[47] By the year 2051, this figure is projected to rise to 8.9 million.[48] This expected growth in the elderly population can be explained by a sustained low birth-rate, the ageing of the baby boomers, and improved medical diagnoses and treatment.

TABLE 12.8 **Comparison of selected age cohorts across marketing-related issues**

Themes	Generation Y	Generation X	Boomers
Purchasing behaviour	Savvy, pragmatic	Materialistic	Narcissistic
Coming-of-age technology	Computer in every home	Microwave in every home	TV in every home
Price–quality attitude	Value oriented: weighing price–quality relationships	Price oriented: concerned about the cost of individual items	Conspicuous consumption: buying for indulgence
Attitude toward brands	Brand embracing	Against branding	Brand loyal
Behaviour toward ads	Rebel against hype	Rebel against hype	Respond to image-building hype

Source: Stephanie M. Noble and Charles H. Noble, 'Getting to know Y: The consumption behaviors of a new cohort', AMA Winter Educators' Conference 11 (Chicago: American Marketing Association, 2000), Marketing Theory, Conference Proceedings, p. 294. Reprinted with permission of the American Marketing Association.

Who are the elderly?

In Australia, 'old age' is assumed to begin with our 65th birthday (i.e. when we qualify for the age pension and the age at which retirement used to be mandatory). However, many people who are 70 years old still tend to view themselves as 'middle-aged'. Research consistently suggests that our *perceptions* of our age are more important in determining behaviour than our *chronological age* (i.e. the number of years lived). In fact, we may have a number of different **cognitive (or perceived) ages** at the same time.

Elderly consumers perceive themselves to be younger than their chronological age on four perceived age dimensions:

1. *feel age* (how old they feel);
2. *look age* (how old they look);
3. *do age* (how involved they are in activities favoured by members of their specific age group);
4. *interest age* (how similar their interests are to those of members of a specific age group).[49]

The results support other research that indicates that elderly consumers are more likely to consider themselves younger (i.e. have a younger cognitive age) than their *chronological age*. Figure 12.6, based on US research, shows the relationship between actual *chronological age*, *cognitive age* and **ideal age** (the age a person might wish to be). Younger adults (20–24) are likely to want to be, or feel, older than their chronological age. For the 25–29 group, the three age measures are in balance. After the chronological age of 30, cognitive and ideal age drop further and further below chronological age. Such results are readily extended to Australian society, with its emphasis on youth and youth-related products. However, we cannot assume that these results will apply to other societies in the Asia-Pacific region, where the elderly are more often revered for their wisdom and given high status in society.

One consumer gerontologist has suggested that the elderly are more diverse in interests, opinions, and actions than other segments of the adult population.[50] Although this view runs counter to the popular myth that the elderly are uniform in terms of attitudes and lifestyles, both gerontologists and market researchers have repeatedly demonstrated that age is not necessarily a major factor in determining how older consumers respond to marketing activities. With an increased appreciation that the elderly constitute a diverse age segment, more attention is now being given to identifying ways to segment the elderly into meaningful groupings.[51] One relatively simple segmentation scheme partitions the elderly into three chronological age categories: the young-old (65 to 74 years of age), the old (those 75 to 84); and the old-old (those 85 years of age and older).

The elderly can also be segmented in terms of motivations and quality-of-life orientation. Table 12.9 (page 419) presents a side-by-side comparison of **new-age elderly** consumers and the more traditional older

FIGURE 12.6 A comparison of different measures of age across chronological age levels

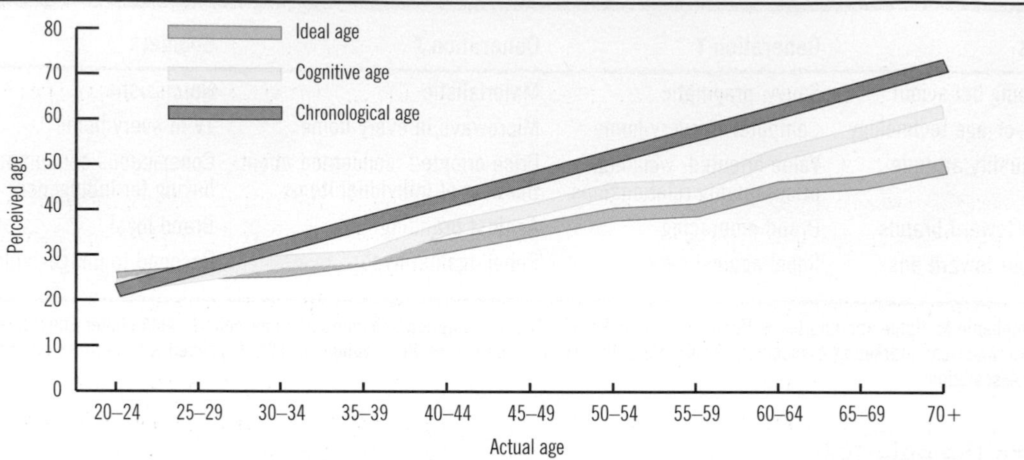

***Source:* L.R. Lepisto, 'The effect of cognitive age and sex on consumer well-being'. Conference on the Elderly Consumer, University of Florida, March 1989.**

consumers. The increased presence of the new-age elderly suggests that marketers need to respond to the value orientations of older consumers whose lifestyles remain relatively ageless. Clearly, the new-age elderly are individuals who feel, think, and do according to a cognitive age that is younger than their chronological age. An examination of several recent studies on ageing suggests an 'erosion of chronological age as a central indicator of the experience of ageing'.[52]

Cyberseniors

Although some people might think of older Australians as luddites who are generally resistant to change, this stereotype is far from the truth. According to US research, few older consumers are fearful of new technology, and there are more Internet users over the age of 50 than under the age of 20. Research studies have found that those over-55 are more likely than the average adult to use the Internet to purchase books, stocks, and computer equipment—92% of surfing seniors have shopped online and 78% have purchased online.[53]

What's the attraction for seniors to go online? Certainly, the Internet is a great way to communicate with friends and family members living in other states, including grandchildren at university. But the Web is also a place to find information (e.g. stock prices, health and medication-related information), entertainment, and a sense of community. There also appears to be a relationship between the amount of time an older adult spends on the Internet and his or her level of out-of-home mobility (using the Internet may serve as a substitute for going out of the house). Having a computer and modem 'empowers' older consumers—it allows them to regain some of the control that was lost due to the physical and/or social deterioration in their lives. For example, a consumer can pay bills, shop, and e-mail friends without leaving their home.

Marketing to the older consumer

Older consumers do want to be marketed to, but only for the 'right' kinds of products and services and using the 'right' advertising presentation. For example, older models tend to be underrepresented in advertisements or are often shown as being infirm or feeble. Part of the problem, according to some writers on the subject, is that the advertising professionals who create the ads are often in their twenties and thirties and have little understanding or empathy for older consumers. Seniors often want to be identified not for what they did in the past, but by what they would like to accomplish in the future. Retirement or moving to a sunbelt community is viewed as the opening of a new chapter in life, and not a quiet withdrawal. Figure 12.7 gives a good

TABLE 12.9 **Comparison of new-age and traditional elderly**

New-age elderly	Traditional/stereotypical elderly
Perceive themselves to be different in outlook from other people their age	Perceive all older people to be about the same in outlook
Age is seen as a state of mind	See age as more of a physical state
See themselves as younger than their chronological age	See themselves at or near their chronological age
Feel younger, think younger, and 'do' younger	Tend to feel, think, and do things that they feel match their chronological age
Have a genuinely youthful outlook	Feel that one should act one's age
Feel there is a considerable adventure to living	
Feel more in control of their own lives	Normal sense of being in control of their own lives
Have greater self-confidence when it comes to making consumer decisions	Normal range of self-confidence when it comes to making consumer decisions
Less concerned that they will make a mistake when buying something	Some concern that they will make a mistake when buying something
Especially knowledgeable and alert consumers	Low-to-average consumer capabilities
Selectively innovative	Not innovative
Seek new experiences and personal challenges	Seek stability and a secure routine
Less interested in accumulating possessions	Normal range of interest in accumulating possessions
Higher measured life satisfaction	Lower measured life satisfaction
Less likely to want to live their lives over differently	Have some regrets as to how they lived their lives
Perceive themselves to be healthier	Perceive themselves to be of normal health for their age
Feel financially more secure	Somewhat concerned about financial security

Source: **Reprinted from 'The value orientation of new-age elderly: The coming of an ageless market', by Leon G. Schiffman and Elaine Sherman, *Journal of Business Research*, 22, April 1991, pp. 187–194. Copyright 1991, with permission from Elsevier.**

FIGURE 12.7 **Advertising targeted at the over-50s**

Source: **Courtesy of OFM Investment Group.**

illustration of this. In the same vein, the increase in the number of older adults taking vacation cruises and joining health clubs signifies a strong commitment to remaining 'functionally young'.[54]

Sex as a subculture

Since **sex roles** are largely culturally determined, it is quite fitting to examine gender as a subcultural category.

SEX ROLES AND CONSUMER BEHAVIOUR

All known societies assign certain traits and roles to males and others to females. In Western society, for instance, aggressiveness, competitiveness, independence and self-confidence were long considered to be traditional masculine traits; neatness, tactfulness, gentleness and talkativeness were considered to be traditional feminine traits.[55] In terms of role differences, women have historically been cast as homemakers with responsibility for child care, and men as the providers or breadwinners. While such traits and roles are no longer as strongly associated with members of a specific sex, they are nevertheless still prevalent. Many advertisers still appeal to such sex-linked roles, and consumer tastes are frequently influenced by sex role factors. Meadow Lea has spent a product life cycle of time on female cooks in the family, with its 'You ought to be congratulated' theme.

Consumer products and sex roles

Within every society, it is quite common to find products that are either exclusively or strongly associated with members of one sex. In Australia, for example, shaving equipment, pants, ties and work clothing were historically male products; bracelets, wedding rings, hair spray, hair dryers and perfumes were generally considered to be feminine products. For most of these products, the sex link has either diminished or disappeared; for others, the prohibition still lingers. For this reason, marketers should consider not only the sex of their target market, but also the *perceived gender identity* of the product category, in the development of advertising campaigns. Table 12.10 suggests very different usage segments between male and female Internet users.

TABLE 12.10 Male and female Internet user segments

	Key usage situation	Favourite Internet materials
Female segments		
Social Sally	Making friends	Chat and personal Web page
New-age crusader	Fight for causes	Books and government information
Cautious mom	Nurture children	Cooking and medical facts
Playful pretender	Role play	Chat and games
Master producer	Job productivity	White Pages and government information
Male segments		
Bits and bytes	Computers and hobbies	Investments, discovery, software
Practical Pete	Personal productivity	Investments, company listings
Viking gamer	Competing and winning	Games, chat, software
Sensitive Sam	Help family and friends	Investments, government information
World citizen	Connecting with world	Discovery, software, investments

Source: Scott M. Smith and David B. Whitlark, 'Men and women online: What makes them click?' *Marketing Research*, 13, 2, Summer 2001, p. 23.

WOMEN IN PAID EMPLOYMENT

Marketers and consumer researchers have been increasingly interested in the working woman, especially the married working woman. They recognise that working wives are a large and growing market segment whose needs differ from those of women who do not work outside the home. It is the size of the working woman market that makes it so attractive. Figure 12.8 shows the proportion of employed women and men in the 15 and over age group between 1978 and 2004. A striking trend is the increase in part-time work, for both genders. Overall, 53% of women in this age range had jobs in 2004. With many more women in work and the increasing age of marriage and childbearing, many women establish their own households. Young women, with young children, are an important segment in the female workforce, though with increasing *casualisation* of the workforce (more temporary, part-time, casual work) family incomes may be less assured.

Because there are now so many female business travellers, hotels have begun to realise that it pays to provide the services women want, such as healthy foods, gyms, spas and wellness centres. Female business travellers are also concerned about hotel security and frequently use room service because they do not want to go to the hotel bar or restaurant. The Paris Hilton, for example, discreetly hands key cards to female patrons, offers valet parking, and allows women to receive guests in an executive lounge located on the hotel's business floor. And bathrooms feature roses, shampoos, and bath gels.[56]

Segmenting the working woman market

To provide a richer framework for segmentation, marketers have developed categories that differentiate the motivations of women in paid work and those whose work (typically at home or in a helping role) is unpaid. For instance, some studies have divided the female population into four segments: stay-at-home housewives; plan-to-work housewives; just-a-job working women; and career-oriented working women.[57] The distinction between 'just-a-job' and 'career-oriented' working women is particularly meaningful. 'Just-a-job' working women are often motivated to work primarily by a sense that the family requires the additional income, whereas 'career-oriented' working women, who tend to be in managerial or professional positions, are driven more by a need to achieve and succeed in their chosen careers. Today, though, with more and more female graduates in the workforce, the percentage of career-oriented working women is on the rise.

Shopping patterns of women who work in paid employment

Women in paid work spend less time shopping than do other women. They accomplish this 'time economy' not by shopping less often, but by minimising the total time spent shopping. Not surprisingly, these women are also more likely to shop during evening hours and on weekends, as well as to buy through direct-mail catalogues. For everyday items, they will tend to swap stores at their convenience. For key items, brand and store loyalty are likely to be strong. Because they are short of time, but earning an income, they are less likely to be price conscious.

Businesses that advertise to women should also be aware of US research which shows that magazines are now delivering a larger women's audience than television shows.[58] Advertising campaigns, such as those for beef shortcuts and Chicken Tonight, emphasise the nutritional value and speed of preparation of their products. Women reporting role overload are more likely to serve convenience foods and to own time-saving kitchen and household products. However, they are more likely to be worried about the healthiness of their diet.[59] Figure 12.9 shows an ad targeting modern women.

AND WHAT ABOUT MEN?

In the late 90s it appeared that many Australian men had become uncertain about their roles, with many saying they were unprepared for nurturing or family relationships. One Australian whitegoods manufacturer advertised a refrigerator by showing a man storing his laundry detergent in it, looking very stupid when his mistake was discovered. While women may feel that this type of ad redressed the balance for demeaning commercials featuring women, advertisers should recognise that males are also involved in purchase decisions for such products. While incompetence humour is permissible in settings outside the family, it will alienate men if set within the family.[60] Men relate to ads that show them in positive roles (e.g. Gillette's 'Father and Son' commercials) or in

FIGURE 12.8 **Employment trends 1978–2004 males and females**

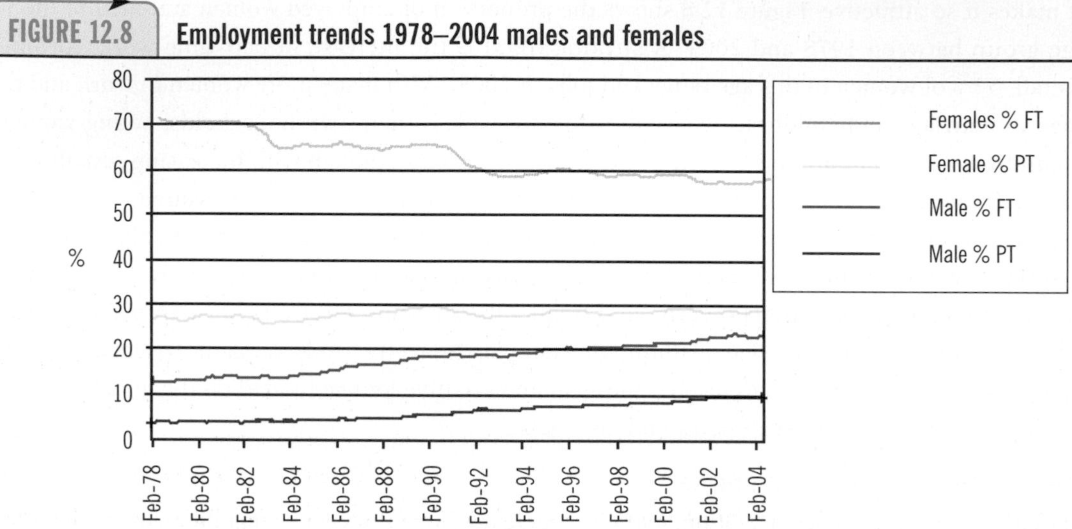

Source: ABS. *Labour Force, Australia*. Catalogue 6202.0. ABS Canberra. Based on all persons aged 15 and over.

FIGURE 12.9 **A Diet Pepsi ad targeting modern women**

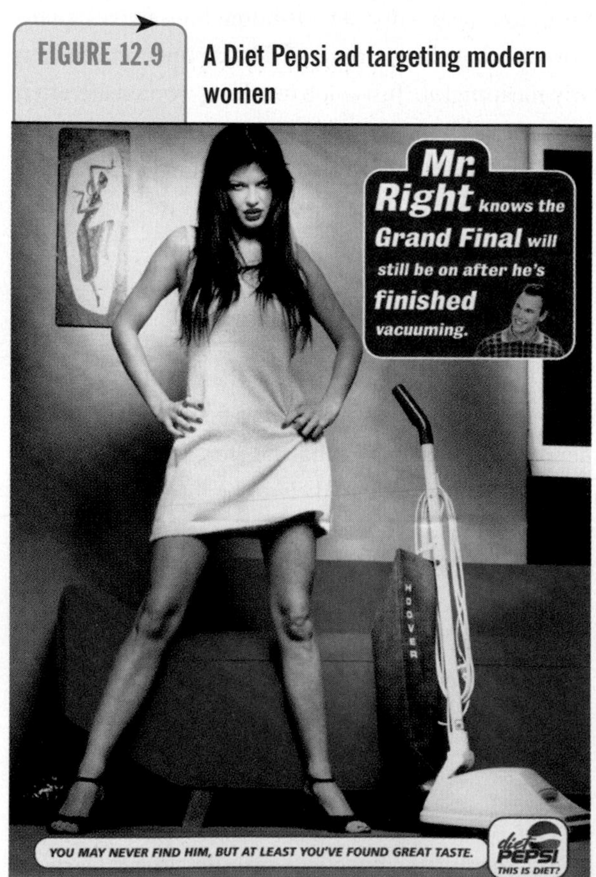

Source: Courtesy of PepsiCo Australia Holdings.

FIGURE 12.10 **Advertising targeting metrosexual men**

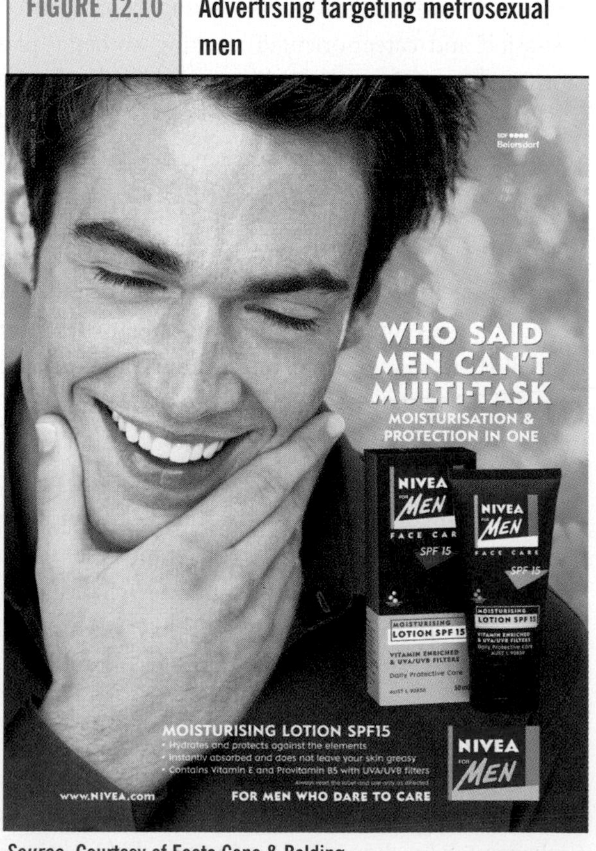

Source: Courtesy of Foote Cone & Belding.

control (e.g. King Gee, Solo). Younger males may be showing signs of getting it together—being positive about their sexuality, more knowledgeable about their inner-selves while at the same time applauding and promoting equality of the sexes. This has been encompassed by the term 'metrosexual', heterosexual males with an interest in appearance, clothes, pampering of the body and style. Sports stars like Ian Thorpe and David Beckham were said to be examples. Whether this is a passing fad of the early years of the millennium or a long-term trend cannot yet be discerned.[61] Figure 12.10 (page 422) shows an ad directed at this group.

Like other sub-groups, men have their own media, though traditional pin-up magazines like *Playboy* and *Penthouse* appeared to be in decline, while magazines like *Ralph, Men's Health* and *Inside Sport* had sizeable readerships.[62] Of course, a magazine such as *New Idea* may have more male readers than magazines specifically aimed at men.

THE GAY MARKET

In a pluralist society such as Australia, **gay subcultures** take their place as part of its rich social diversity. One sign of acceptance is the community's interest in, and enjoyment of, the gay and lesbian Mardi Gras held in Sydney.[63] Similarly, programs featuring gay men have entered the mainstream media, e.g. *Queer Eye for the Straight Guy*. In other cultures in the Asia-Pacific region, gay behaviour is restricted and even outlawed.

While it is difficult to estimate the size of this market in Australia, the gay market has its own media such as *DNA*, *Refresh* and *Bent* magazines, a newspaper the *Sydney Star Observer* <www.ssonet.com.au> and TV programs like *Queer as Folk*. The *Pink Directory* contains a detailed listing of services and products for gay and lesbian consumers <www.thepinkdirectory. com. au>. Like many other subgroups, these subcultural media attract a vast range of minority and mainstream advertisers. Brands that may appeal to gay men include Calvin Klein, Downunderpants, Coast Clothing and Avis car rental. Australian research suggests that the gay and lesbian market comprises a largely affluent group[64] so it is little wonder that advertisers target it. Figure 12.11 shows an ad targeting the gay market. Consumer behaviour theorist Steve Kates has shown how gay communities may form powerful relationships (both positive and negative) with particular brands.[65] He has also shown how advertisers may end up 'heterosexualising' advertisements aimed at the gay community, inadvertently undermining their message.[66]

FIGURE 12.11 Gay market advertising

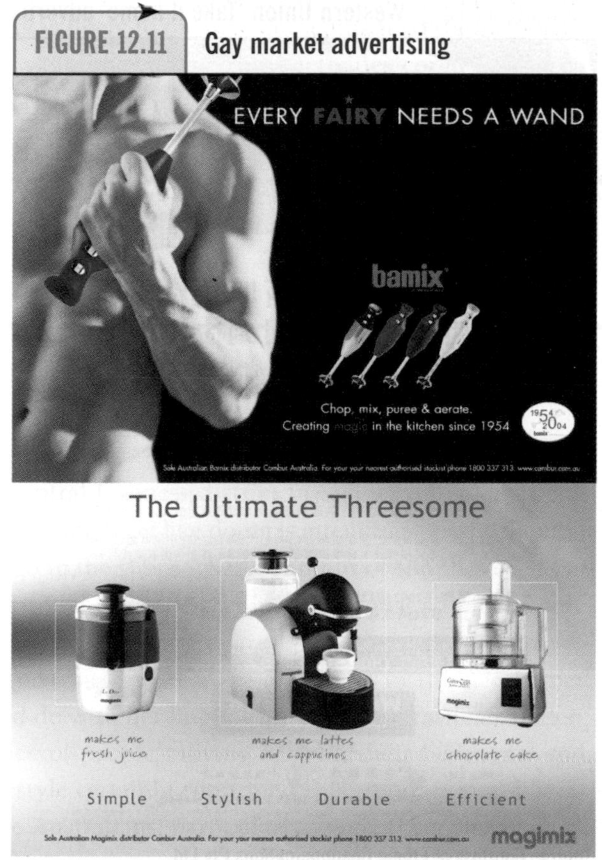

Source: Courtesy of Cambur Australia & Power Advertising 2004.

Subcultural interaction

It should be remembered that all consumers are simultaneously members of more than one subcultural segment (e.g. a consumer may be a young, Vietnamese, Catholic, working wife living in the Western suburbs of Sydney). For this reason, marketers should strive to understand how multiple subcultural memberships *interact* to influence target consumers' relevant consumption behaviour. Promotional strategy should not be limited to a single subcultural membership.

Between the Sheets

Sex facts from the suburbs...

- 640 000 Australians are on adult video mailing lists. It is the second largest direct mail list in the country behind the Coles-Myer FlyBuys scheme. Interestingly, a third of all mail order customers are from Queensland, Australia's most conservative state. It is estimated that 70% of customers are buying for a partner, amounting to 1.1 million Australians or 8% of the adult voting population.
- There are approximately 250 adult shops operating around Australia with a turnover of about $100 million. The shops employ about 2300 people.
- In Australia's adult shops and through mail order catalogues, 1 million vibrators are sold each year, with an estimated 8 million vibrators already in Australian homes.
- There are close to 800 legal brothels, escort agencies and sexual massage services in Australia, with another 350 operating illegally. Each year there are over 12 million visits to sex workers.
- There are five sexual contact magazines published in Australia, which advertise an average of 2000 new messages each issue. Approximately half these messages are from suburban couples seeking a partner to share sexual activity, while a quarter are from heterosexual singles and the remaining quarter from the gay community.
- Each month there are 1.4 million phone calls made to adult phone lines. This is all about to change with amendments made to the *Telecommunications Act* stipulating the requirement of a PIN to access adult phone lines.
- Australia's most popular magazines have a strong emphasis on frank discussions on sexuality, from *Cosmopolitan* to *Cleo*. In recent years there has been a boom in the men's magazine market with the establishment of such titles as *Ralph*, *FHM* and *GQ*.
- There are magazines that deal exclusively with sexuality—*Australian Penthouse* and *Hustler*. There are also the weekly publications of *The Picture*, *People* and *Scoop*—with a combined weekly circulation of 250 000.
- Each year 55 million condoms are imported into Australia. On a per capita basis we use condoms at the same rate as adults in Europe and the United States.

Source: <www.eros.com.au>.

References

Laughter & Light—Inside Australia's Sex Industry, 1997, The Eros Foundation Inc.

Adult Industry Review, Vol. 2, No. 3–4, 1999, The Eros Foundation Inc.

D.K. Davidson, *Selling Sin: The Marketing of Socially Unacceptable Products*, Westport, CT: Quorum Books, 1996.

D. Malina and R. Schmidt, 'It's business doing pleasure with you: Sh! A women's sex shop case', *Marketing Intelligence & Planning*, 15/7, 1997, pp. 352–360.

R. Ostrow, 'Sexual healing', *The Weekend Australian*, 14–15 August 1999.

Case Study Questions

1. What are the most significant sociocultural factors that have prompted Tamrah to set up Sugar & Spice?
2. Tamrah has clearly segmented her market on gender. Discuss whether this subcultural segmentation can be further segmented.
3. Is Tamrah's belief that Australian society is becoming more sexually liberated and experimental justified?
4. What recommendation/s would you give Tamrah in relation to (a) product assortment and (b) distribution?
5. What can Tamrah do to change negative attitudes and misconceptions about her business?

Summary

A subculture is a distinct cultural group that exists as an identifiable segment within a larger, more complex society. Its members possess beliefs, values, and customs that set them apart from other members of the same society; at the same time, they hold to the dominant beliefs of the overall society. Subcultural analysis enables marketers to segment their markets to meet the specific needs, motivations, perceptions and attitudes shared by members of a specific subcultural group.

Major subcultural categories in Australia include ethnicity, religion, and indigenous background, urban versus rural location, age and sex. Each of these can be broken down into smaller segments which can be reached through special copy appeals and selective media choices. In some cases (e.g. the elderly consumer), product characteristics can be tailored to the specialised needs of the market segment.

Since all consumers are simultaneously members of several subcultural groups, marketers must determine for their product category how specific subcultural memberships interact to influence consumers' purchase decisions. Like any form of segmentation, the marketer must make sure that subcultures are readily identified and easy to reach. In addition, the benefits must outweigh the costs in the relatively small Australian market.

Discussion questions

1. Discuss the importance of subcultures in segmenting the market for food products. Identify a particular product and show how it should be marketed differently to various ethnic groups.
2. Consider the role of nudity in advertising. Discuss how it could be made appealing or off-putting to working mothers, career women, young singles and stay-at-home housewives.
3. What allowance should be made for the ability of the elderly to process complex information in making product purchase decisions?
4. Foxtel is marketing pay television services in Australia. What approach should it take to households where the main decision makers are:
   (a) baby boomers
   (b) Generation X?
5. In view of the anticipated growth of the 50-plus market, should Oil of Ulan consider a new strategy for its face cream? Would it be wiser to develop a new brand, or can it successfully market the same product to the under- and over-50s?
6. Marketers are beginning to realise that people of the same age often exhibit very different lifestyles. Discuss whether developers of retirement housing can use lifestyles to segment their markets more effectively.
7. What type of subcultural segmentation would best assist the marketer with the following products and services?
   (a) a digital videophone;
   (b) a DVD player;
   (c) jeans;
   (d) snap-chill meals;
   (e) a new alcoholic lemonade;
   (f) a tourist package to Vietnam or Pakistan;
   (g) a personal phone number.

Exercises

1. Using *one* of the subculture categories in Table 12.1, identify a group that can be regarded as a subculture within your university or TAFE.
   (a) Describe the norms, values and behaviours of the subculture's members.
   (b) Interview five members of that subculture about their attitudes to the use of mobile phones.
   (c) What are the implications for the marketing of credit and debit cards to this group?
2. Interview one elderly person, one baby boomer and one Generation Xer about their knowledge and likely purchase of a digital television set. Are the differences between these people based on age?
3. Many of your perceptions regarding price versus value are likely to be different from those of your parents or grandparents. Researchers attribute such differences to *cohort effects*, which are based on the premise that consumption patterns are determined early in life.

Therefore, individuals who have experienced different economic, political and cultural environments during their youth are likely to be different types of consumers as adults. Describe instances in which your parents or grandparents disagreed with or criticised purchases you had made. Describe the cohort effects that explain each party's position during these disagreements.

4. Advertisers are often accused of portraying older consumers in a stereotypical fashion. Find one print ad that depicts older consumers in a stereotypical way and another ad that you feel constitutes a more effective way to communicate with older consumers. Do they depict the concept of perceived age? How could these ads be improved?

Key terms

age subcultures *(p. 413)*
baby boomers *(p. 416)*
cognitive (or perceived) age *(p. 417)*
cohort *(p. 414)*
community languages *(p. 405)*
culturally diverse society *(p. 404)*
elderly consumers *(p. 416)*
ethnic subcultures *(p. 405)*
gay subcultures *(p. 423)*
Generation X *(p. 415)*
Generation Y *(p. 414)*
ideal age *(p. 417)*
new-age elderly *(p. 417)*
racial subcultures *(p. 412)*
regional subcultures *(p. 412)*
religious subcultures *(p. 411)*
self-identification *(p. 408)*
sex roles *(p. 420)*
subcultural interaction *(p. 423)*
subculture *(p. 404)*

Endnotes

1. See David Goodman, D.J. O'Hearn and Chris Wallace-Crabbe (eds), *Multicultural Australia: The Challenges of Change* (Newham, Victoria: Scribe Publications, 1991).
2. For a detailed discussion of this issue, see Adam Jamrozik, Cathy Boland and Robert Urquhart, *Social Change and Cultural Transformation in Australia* (Melbourne: Cambridge University Press, 1995). Politically the term 'multiculturalism' seems to have lost currency in Australia, even though this term best describes subcultural diversity. See also <www.multiculturalaustralia.com.au> (March 2004).
3. David Bednall, *Media and Immigrant Settlement* (Canberra: Australian Government Publishing Service, 1992).
4. See <www.fecca.org.au/census/fCensusIndex.html> (March 2004). Based on ABS 2001 Census data.
5. ABS, *Migration, Australia.* Catalogue No. 3412.0 (Canberra: ABS, May 2003).
6. See <www.fecca.org.au/census/fCensusIndex.html>, op. cit.
7. Denise T. Ogden. James R. Ogden and Hope Jensen Schau, 'Exploring the impact of culture and acculturation on consumer purchase decisions: Toward a microcultural perspective', *Academy of Marketing Science Review*, No. 3, 2004, pp. 1–22. See also John Robinson, Bart Landry and Ronica Rooks, 'Time and the melting pot', *American Demographics*, June 1998, pp. 18–24; Eric Schmitt, 'New census shows Hispanics are even with Blacks in US', *New York Times*, 8 March 2001, pp. A1, A21; Brad Edmondson, 'Hispanic Americans in 2001', *American Demographics*, January 1997, p. 17; Soyeon Shim and Kenneth C. Gehrt, 'Native American and Hispanic adolescent consumers: Examination of shopping orientation, socialization factors and social structure variables', in 1995 AMA *Educators' Proceedings*, eds Barbara B. Stern and George M. Zinkan (Chicago: American Marketing Association, 1995), pp. 297–298; Sandra Yin, 'Hola, you've got mail!' *American Demographics*, 23(12), December 2001, pp. 13–16; Catharine P. Taylor, 'Barbie Latina says "Hola" to Net', *Advertising Age*, 1 October 2001, p. 54; and Rohit Deshpandè, Wayne D. Hoyer and Naveen Donthu, 'The intensity of ethnic affiliation: A study of the sociology of hispanic consumption', *Journal of Consumer Research*, 13, September 1986, pp. 214–220; and Cynthia Webster, 'The role of Hispanic ethnic identification on reference group influence', in *Advances in Consumer Research*, 21, eds Chris T. Allen and Deborah Roedder John (Provo, UT: Association for Consumer Research, 1994), pp. 458–463.

8. A.W. Ata and C. Ryan (eds), *The Ethnic Press in Australia* (Melbourne: Academic Press and Footprint Publications, 1989); see also Mike Zafiropoulos, 'The ethnic media in Australia', *BIPR Bulletin 12*, 1994, pp. 28–29.
9. According to the Community Relations Commission of NSW. See <www.crc.nsw.gov.au/ethnicmedia/index.htm> (March 2004).
10. See Bednall, op. cit., p. 27.
11. Geoff Strong, '*Hãy tim doc sô dăc biêt này*: That's "Read all about it" in Vietnamese. But what are our ethnic media really saying?' *The Sunday Age*, 13 June 1993, Agenda 3.
12. David Robinson, 'Using the media to reach multicultural communities', Paper presented on behalf of SBS television (Melbourne: 1994). See also <www.sbs.com.au> and <www.immi.gov.au/research/topics.htm> (Federal Department of Immigration and Multicultural Affairs).
13. 'Pay TV planner sees money in ethnic market', *Multicultural Marketing News*, March–April 1993, p. 8.
14. Paul Leeds, 'How to prepare an effective media plan to reach NESB communities' (Melbourne: Leeds Media & Communication Services, 1994).
15. Ethnic communities have produced many business entrepreneurs. See C.L. Kermond, K.E. Luscombe, K.W. Strahan and A.J.Williams, *Immigrant Women Entrepreneurs in Australia* (Wollongong: Centre for Multicultural Studies, University of Wollongong, 1991); Office of Multicultural Affairs, *Asian Entrepreneurs in Australia: Ethnic Small Business in the Chinese and Indian Communities of Brisbane and Sydney* (Canberra: Australian Government Publishing Service, 1991); Stephen Castles, 'From migrant worker to ethnic entrepreneur', in Goodman, O'Hearn and Wallace-Crabbe, op. cit.
16. See <www.etcom.com.au> (March 2004). See also Michael Kiely, 'Big money in ethnic marketing', *Marketing*, June 1994, pp. 10–14.
17. Constance Hill and Celia T. Romm, 'Gift-giving family styles: A cross-cultural study with consumer socialisation implications', in Ken Grant and Ian Walker (eds), *Proceedings of the Seventh Bi-annual World Marketing Congress* (Melbourne: Academy of Marketing Science, 1995), Vol. VII-III, 14-68 to 14-86. Sino-Vietnamese are people from Vietnam, but of Chinese ethnicity.
18. Des Storer, 'Introduction', in Des Storer (ed.), *Ethnic Family Values in Australia* (Sydney: Prentice Hall of Australia, 1985). See also Stephen Castles, Caroline Alcorso, Gaetano Rando and Ellie Vasra (eds), *Australia's Italians: Culture and Community in a Changing Society* (Sydney: Allen & Unwin, 1992).
19. See Bednall, op. cit.; and 'Do ads reflect our cultural diversity?', *Ad News*, 2 July 1993, p. 42.
20. Alvin M. Chan, 'Multicultural marketing in Australia', in Grant and Walker (eds), op. cit., Vol. VII-I, 2-71 to 2-76.
21. Judy Cohen, 'White consumer response to Asian models in advertising', *Journal of Consumer Advertising*, Spring 1992, pp. 17–27.
22. Melissa J. Chaw and M. Yunis Ali, Impact of acculturation, ethnic identity and ethnic ties on the consumption behaviour of ethnic Chinese consumers in Australia. Proceedings, ANZMAC 2002, Melbourne, 161–169 [CD-ROM].
23. John Steere, 'How Asian-Americans make purchase decisions', *Marketing News*, 13 March 1995, p. 9.
24. Simpson, 'The future cardholder', *Credit Card Management*, 14, 13, March 2002, pp. 36–42.
25. <http://aei.dest.gov.au/general/stats/StudentVisaData/RecentAnnualData/RecentData.htm> (April 2004)
26. Tekle Shanka, 'Students' preference for "National Carrier" on their overseas holidays'. Proceedings, ANZMAC 2000, Gold Coast, 1123–1129. [CD-ROM].
27. ABS, *Population Characteristics, Aboriginal and Torres Strait Islander Australians*. Catalogue No. 4713.0 (Canberra: ABS, 2003).
28. <www.cbonline.org.au/index.cfm?pageId=36,94,22,0> (April 2004).
29. <www.imparja.com.au> (April 2004).
30. Russell W. Belk, Ron Groves and Per Østergaard, 'Aboriginal consumer culture', in Russell W. Belk, Janeen Costa and John Schouten (eds) *Research in Consumer Behaviour*, Volume 9 (Stamford, CT: Jai Press, 2000).
31. <www.icca.org.au/HalalInfo/HalalHaram.htm> and <www.ka.org.au>.
32. Elizabeth C. Hirschman, 'Ethnic variation in leisure activities and motives', in Bruce J. Walker et al. (eds), *An Assessment of Marketing Thought and Practice* (Chicago: American Marketing Association, 1982), pp. 93–98; and Elizabeth C. Hirschman, 'American Jewish ethnicity: Its relationship to some selected aspects of consumer behavior', *Journal of Marketing*, 45, 1981, pp. 102–110. See also Kevin Michael Grace, 'Is this Kosher?' *Report Newsmagazine*, 27, 1, 8 May 2000, p. 37; Laura Bird, 'Major brands look for the Kosher label', *Adweek's Marketing Week*, 1 April 1991, pp. 18–19; and Judith Waldrop, 'Everything's Kosher', *American Demographics*, March 1991, p. 4.
33. Nejdet Delener and Leon G. Schiffman, 'Family decision making: The impact of religious factors', in Gary Frazier

et al. (eds), *1988 AMA Educators' Proceedings* (Chicago: American Marketing Association, 1988), pp. 80–83.

34. Ann Moyal, *Clear Across Australia: A History of Telecommunications* (Melbourne: Nelson, 1984).
35. Lynn R. Kahle, 'The nine nations of North America and the value basis of geographic segmentation', *Journal of Marketing*, 50, 1986, pp. 37–47.
36. ABS, *Births Australia*, Catalogue No. 3301.0 (2003); ABS, *Deaths Australia*, Catalogue No. 3302.0 (2003).
37. Stephanie M. Noble and Charles D. Schewe, 'Cohort segmentation: An elaboration of its validity', *Journal of Business Research*, 56(12), 2003, pp. 979–987.
38. Stephanie M. Noble and Charles H. Noble, 'Getting to know Y: The consumption behaviors of a new cohort', in *2000 AMA Winter Educators' Conference*, 11, eds John P. Workman and William D. Perreault (Chicago: American Marketing Association, 2000), pp. 293–303; and Pamela Paul, 'Getting inside Gen Y', *American Demographics*, 23(9), September 2001, pp. 42–49; Joyce M. Wolburg and James Pokrywczynski, 'A psychographic analysis of Generation Y college students', *Journal of Advertising Research*, 41(5), September/October 2001, pp. 33–52.
39. Lauren Keating, 'The in crowds', *Shopping Center World*, 29(5), May 2000, pp. 160–165.
40. Chantal Todè, 'Evolution of tweens' tastes keeps retailers on their toes', *Advertising Age*, 12, February 2001, p. S6
41. *Income and Wealth of Generation X*. AMP: Natsem Income and Wealth Report, Issue 6, November 2003.
42. John Hall, Binta Abubakar and Peter Oppenheim, 'Factors influencing the airline choice of Generation X', ANZMAC Conference, Auckland [CD-ROM]. See also Don Porritt, 'Generation X—the moving target', *Australian Professional Marketing*, May 1994, pp. 37–38.
43. Keating, op. cit.
44. E. Loomis, 'Generation X,' *Rough Notes*, 143(9), September 2000, pp. 52–54.
45. Paula M. Poindexter and Dominic L. Lasorsa, 'Generation X: Is its meaning understood?' *Newspaper Research Journal*, 20(4), Fall 1999, pp. 28–36.
46. 'Boomer facts,' *American Demographics*, January 1996, p. 14. Also see Diane Crispell, 'U.S. population forecasts decline for 2000, but rise slightly for 2050', *Wall Street Journal*, 25 March 1996, p. B3; and Cindy Hearn and Doug Hammond, 'Cosmetic dentistry: The "boom" is upon us!' *Dental Economics*, 91(9), September 2001, pp. 118–122.
47. ABS, *Population by Age and Sex, Australian States and Territories*, Catalogue No. 3201.0 (ABS, 2003).
48. Projections rest on assumptions about birth-rate, mortality and net migration. See ABS, *Population Projections Australia*, Catalogue No. 3222.0 (ABS, 2003), Table A9.
49. Benny Barak and Leon G. Schiffman, 'Cognitive age: A nonchronological age variable', in *Advances in Consumer Research*, 8, ed. Kent B. Monroe (Ann Arbor, MI: Association for Consumer Research, 1981), pp. 602–606; Elaine Sherman, Leon G. Schiffman, and William R. Dillon, 'Age/gender segments and quality of life differences', in *1988 Winter Educators' Conference*, ed. Stanley Shapiro and A. H. Walle (Chicago: American Marketing Association, 1988), pp. 319–320; Stuart Van Auken and Thomas E. Barry, 'An assessment of the trait validity of cognitive age', *Journal of Consumer Psychology*, 1995, pp. 107–132; Robert E. Wilkes, 'A structural modeling approach to the measurement and meaning of cognitive age', *Journal of Consumer Research*, September 1992, pp. 292–301; and Chad Rubel, 'Mature market often misunderstood', *Marketing News*, 28 August 1995, pp. 28–29.
50. A quote from Professor Elaine Sherman, in David B. Wolfe, 'The ageless market', *American Demographics*, July 1987, pp. 26–28 and 55–56. See also Elaine Sherman, Leon G. Schiffman and William R. Dillon, 'Age/gender segments and quality of life differences', in Stanley Shapiro and A. H. Walle (eds), *1988 Winter Educators' Conference* (Chicago: American Marketing Association, 1988), pp. 319–320.
51. Carol M. Morgan and Doran J. Levy, 'Understanding mature consumers', *Marketing Review*, January 1996, pp. 12–13, 25; and Elaine Sherman and Leon G. Schiffman, 'Quality-of-life (QOL) assessment of older consumers: A retrospective review', *Journal of Business and Psychology*, Fall 1991, pp. 107–119.
52. Don E. Bradley and Charles F. Longino, Jr., 'How older people think about images of aging in advertising and the media', *Generations*, 25(3), Fall 2001, pp. 17–21.
53. Isabelle Szmigin and Marylyn Carrigan, 'Leisure and tourism services and the older innovator', *The Service Industries Journal* (London), 21(3), July 2001, pp. 113–129; and Polyak, 'The center of attention', p. 32.
54. Isabelle Szmigin and Marylyn Carrigan, 'Learning to love the older consumer', *Journal of Consumer Behaviour* (London), 1, 1 June 2001, pp. 22–34; Bill Radford, 'Age-old trend/health-conscious seniors displacing

younger fitness-club patrons', *The Gazette*, 12 November 2001, LIFE1; and Bradley and Longino, 'How older people think . . .', pp. 17–21.

55. Inge K. Broverman, Susan Raymond Vogel, Donald M. Broverman, Frank E. Clarkson and Paul S. Rosenkrantz, 'Sex role stereotypes: A current appraisal', *Journal of Social Issues*, 28, 1972, p. 63.
56. Anjuman Ali, 'Women travellers: Marooned no more', *Wall Street Journal Europe*, 6–7 July 2001, p. 29.
57. Thomas Barry, Mary Gilly, and Lindley Doran, 'Advertising to women with different career orientations', *Journal of Advertising Research*, 25, April–May 1985, pp. 26–35.
58. Alison Stein Wellner, 'The female persuasion', *American Demographics*, 24(2), February 2002, pp. 24–29.
59. *Trends in Australia: Consumer Attitudes and the Supermarket* (Washington: Food Market Institute, 1992).
60. Peter Stickels, 'The 90s man: Keep me in control and don't let my family think I'm stupid', *Ad News*, 24 September 1993, pp. 12–14. See also Heather Payne and Monica Klimek, 'RIO (Research International Observer): Men of today and tomorrow', paper presented to the MRSA National Conference, Melbourne, October 1998.
61. 'The rise of the metrosexual', *Sydney Morning Herald*, 11 March 2003. See also Steve Drew, 'The style evolution of the modern man', *Sunday Life*, 7 March 2003, pp. 15–17.
62. <www.roymorgan.com/news/press-releases/2004/296> (April 2004). See also Tony Schirato and Susan Yell, 'The "new" men's magazines and the performance of masculinity', *Media International Australia Incorporating Culture and Policy*, No. 92, 1999, pp. 81–90.
63. Steven M. Kates, 'Producing and consuming gendered representations: An interpretation of the Sydney gay and lesbian Mardi Gras', *Consumption, Markets and Culture*, 6(1), 2003, pp. 5–22.
64. Angela Jackson, 'Gay market valuable: Survey', *Ad News*, 22 October 1993, p. 4.
65. Steven M. Kates, 'The protean quality of subcultural consumption: An ethnographic account of gay consumers', *Journal of Consumer Research*, 29 (December), 2002, pp. 383–399.
66. Steven M. Kates, 'Making the ad perfectly queer: Marketing "Normality" to the gay men's community?' *Journal of Advertising*, 28(1), 1999, pp. 25–37.

CHAPTER 13

Cross-cultural consumer behaviour: An international perspective

Source: Courtesy of Telstra.

In our examination of psychological, social, and cultural factors, we have consistently pointed out how various segments of the Australian consuming public differ. If so much diversity exists among segments of a single society, then even more diversity is likely to exist among the members of two or more societies. To succeed, international marketers must understand the nature and extent of differences between the consumers of different societies—cross-cultural differences—so that they can develop effective targeted marketing strategies to use in each foreign market of interest.

Foreign markets, including those in the Asia-Pacific region, are of great significance to Australia. The domestic market of 20 million people is small, and trade agreements within Europe and elsewhere block our access to some markets. Table 13.1 shows Australia's trade with its major market partners.

In this chapter, we broaden the scope of our analysis and consider the marketing implications of cultural differences and similarities that exist between the people of two or more nations. We also compare the views that pit a global marketing perspective—one that stresses the similarities of consumers worldwide—against a localised marketing strategy that stresses the diversity of consumers in different nations and their specific cultural orientations. Our own view is that marketers must be aware of and sensitive to cross-cultural similarities and differences that can provide expanded sales and profit opportunities. Multinational marketers must be ready to tailor their marketing mixes to the specific customs of each nation that they want to target.

TABLE 13.1 Imports and exports by region ($A m) 2002–2003

Region	Imports		Exports	
	Services	Merchandise	Services	Merchandise
China (excl Hong Kong)	923	13 788	976	8 800
Hong Kong	1 664	1 233	1 308	3 214
Indonesia	523	4 600	972	2 909
Japan	2 100	16 337	3 377	21 727
Korea	409	4 752	837	9 115
Malaysia	692	4 261	885	2 146
New Zealand	1 809	5 018	2 339	8 126
Singapore	2 450	4 370	2 089	4 659
South Africa	291	1 060	236	1 315
Taiwan	173	3 378	352	4 311
Thailand	812	3 471	479	2 480
United Kingdom	3 686	5 770	3 672	7 235
United States	6 067	22 493	5187	10 365
APEC	18 952	92 245	19 733	83 021
ASEAN	5 047	20 748	4763	13 855
European Union	7 405	31 397	6187	15 863
OECD	19 362	84 776	18 612	68 361
TOTAL	32 909	133 128	32 471	115 480

Source: **ABS, *International Trade in Goods and Services, Australia 2003*, Catalogue No. 5368.0. Covers 2002–2003.**

The imperative to be multinational

Today, almost all major corporations are actively marketing their products beyond their original homeland borders. In fact, the issue is generally not whether to market a brand in other countries but rather how to do it (as the same product with the same 'global' advertising campaign, or 'tailored' products and localised ads for each country). Because of this emphasis on operating multinationally, the vocabulary of marketing now includes terms such as glocal, which refers to companies that are both 'global' and 'local'; that is, they include in their marketing efforts a blend of standardised and local elements in order to secure the benefits of each strategy.[1]

This challenge has been given special meaning by the efforts of the **European Union (EU)** to form a single market. Although the movement of goods and services among community members has been eased, it is unclear whether this diverse market will really be transformed into a single market of homogeneous 'Euro-consumers' with the same (or very similar) wants and needs. It is likely that the Euro, the common EU currency, will help shape Europe into a huge, powerful, unified market, but one with barriers to entry to those outside this massive economic zone. Furthermore, the rapid acceptance of market economies by many Eastern European countries also presents a major opportunity and challenge to marketers. Global firms such as Coca-Cola and Gillette have been investing extensive sums in product development and marketing to satisfy the needs of Eastern European consumer markets.[2]

The **North American Free Trade Agreement (NAFTA)**, which currently consists of the United States, Canada, and Mexico, provides market access to more than 400 million consumers. The USA–Australia Free Trade Agreement was passed by parliament and the US Congress in 2004. It should offer opportunities for futher trade with the US, while moving the balance of imports away from the Asia-Pacific. Recent US trade agreements with Singapore and Thailand may also affect the balance of trade in the region. The Association of Southeast Asian Nations (ASEAN), consisting of Indonesia, Singapore, Thailand, the Philippines, Malaysia, Brunei Darussalam and Vietnam, is another important economic alliance that offers marketers new global markets. The members of this group have formed the **ASEAN** Free Trade Area (AFTA) to promote regional trade. APEC (the forum for Asia Pacific Economic Cooperation) includes most countries around the Asia-Pacific rim, including the US, Australia, China, Vietnam, Japan and Chile. It is a discussion forum, rather than a trade bloc. Finally, Australia and New Zealand have a Closer Economic Relationship (CER) which allows free trade between the two countries.

Many firms are developing strategies to take advantage of these and other emerging economic opportunities. A substantial number of firms now jockey for market share in foreign markets. Starbucks has opened a store within the Forbidden City in Beijing, China, and MTV Networks has formed a partnership with @Japan-Media to establish a new 24-hour Japanese language music TV channel.[3] Firms which orginated in Australia like News International, BHP Billiton, Telstra and Foster's Brewing have made many attempts to enter world markets, with a mixture of success and failure.

With the buildup of 'multinational fever' and the general attractiveness of multinational markets, products or services originating in one country are increasingly being sought out by consumers in other parts of the world. An Australian-built car may contain components from the US and the Asia-Pacific region. Firms are selling their products worldwide for a variety of reasons. First, many firms have learned that overseas markets represent the single most important opportunity for their future growth when their home markets reach maturity. This realisation is propelling them to expand their horizons and seek consumers in other markets. Moreover, consumers all over the world are increasingly eager to try 'foreign' products that are popular in different and far-off places.

Attempts are often made to estimate which are the most valuable **world brands**. Table 13.2 shows one such list. As expected, US brands predominate, partly based on their own huge domestic market. For example, it has been claimed that if California alone were a nation it would be in the top ten economies by size in the world, certainly larger than Australia.[4]

TABLE 13.2 Top world brands

Rank	Brand	2001 brand value ($US billion)
1	Coca-Cola	69.6
2	Microsoft	64.1
3	IBM	51.2
4	GE	41.3
5	Intel	30.9
6	Nokia	30.0
7	Disney	29.3
8	McDonald's	26.4
9	Marlboro	24.2
10	Mercedes	21.0

***Note*: Only includes brands that sell at least 20% outside of their home country or region.**

***Source:* Based on <http://www.finfacts.com/brands.htm> (July 2004). See also *Business Week*, 4 August 2003, p. 72.**

ACQUIRING EXPOSURE TO OTHER CULTURES

As more and more consumers come in contact with the material goods and lifestyles of people living in other parts of the world, they have the opportunity to adopt these different products and practices. How consumers in one culture secure exposure to the goods of people living in other cultures is an important part of consumer behaviour. It impacts the well-being of consumers worldwide and of marketers trying to gain acceptance for their products in countries that are often quite different from their home country.

A portion of consumers' exposure to different cultures tends to come about through consumers' own initiatives—their travel, their living and working in foreign countries, or even their immigration to a different country. Additionally, consumers obtain a 'taste' of different cultures from contact with foreign movies, theatre, art and artifacts and, most certainly, from exposure to unfamiliar and different products. This second major category of cultural exposure is often fostered by marketers seeking to expand their markets by bringing new products, services, practices, ideas, and experiences to potential consumers residing in a different country and possessing a different cultural view. Within this context, international marketing provides a form of 'culture transfer'.[5] Japanese popular culture, particularly Anime, has spread widely to the West. Australia's own *Gaijin* ('foreigner' in Japanese) magazine was introduced in 2003 and is an example of how culture spreads both ways.[6]

COUNTRY-OF-ORIGIN EFFECTS

When consumers are making purchase decisions, they may take into consideration the countries of origin of their choices. Researchers have shown that consumers use their knowledge of where products are made in the evaluation of their purchase options.[7] Such a country-of-origin effect seems to come about because consumers are often aware that a particular firm or brand name is associated with a particular country.[8] It's hard to think of BMW or Mercedes except in the context of their being German; a Mini or a Jaguar is linked with Britishness (despite the fact that both brands are now under overseas ownership); and Ferrari is a brand that is Italian before it's anything else at all.

In general, many consumers associate France with wine, fashion clothing, and perfume and other beauty products; Italy with pasta, designer clothing, furniture, shoes, and sports cars; Japan with cameras and consumer electronics; and Germany with cars, tools, and machinery. Given that many of the components in such products come from many countries, some writers have suggested that what counts is the country of origin of the brand.[9] Although in the late 1980s there were US consumers who preferred a Japanese-made Honda to the same model made in the US, today the general attitude is 'as long as it's a Honda, it doesn't matter where it's made'.

Moreover, consumers tend to have an attitude or even a preference when it comes to a particular product being made in a particular country. This attitude might be positive, negative, or neutral, depending on perceptions or experience. For instance, a consumer in one country might positively value a particular product made in another country (e.g. affluent Australian consumers may feel that an Italian Prada handbag or a Swiss Rolex watch are worthwhile investments. In contrast, another consumer might be negatively influenced when he learns that a DVD player he is considering is made in a country he does not associate with fine electronics). Such country-of-origin effects influence how consumers rate quality and which brands they will ultimately select.[10] Recent research suggests, though, that when consumer motivation is high and when a specific model of a product is being evaluated (as opposed to a range of products manufactured in a particular country), then consumers are less likely to base judgments on country-of-origin information.[11]

In addition to perceptions of a product's attributes based on its country of manufacture, research evidence exists that suggests that some consumers may refrain from purchasing products from particular countries due to animosity. A study of this issue found that high-animosity consumers in the People's Republic of China owned fewer Japanese products than low-animosity consumers (during World War II, Japan occupied parts of China). Although some Chinese consumers might consider Sony to be a high-end, high-quality brand (or perceptions of the product itself might be very positive), they might nevertheless refuse to bring a product manufactured in Japan into the home. Similarly, some Jewish consumers might avoid purchasing German-made products due to the Holocaust, and some New Zealand and Australian consumers considered boycotting French products due to France's nuclear tests in the South Pacific.[12] A multicountry study asked both US and Thai students, 'Are you willing to buy a Sony product if it is "made in China" at the same price as one "made in Japan?"' Although 81% of the Thai students answered, 'no', 81% of US students answered 'yes'.[13]

➤ Cross-cultural consumer analysis

To determine whether and how to enter a foreign market, marketers need to conduct some form of **cross-cultural consumer analysis**. Within the scope of this discussion, cross-cultural consumer analysis is defined as, *the effort to determine to what extent the consumers of two or more nations are similar or different*. Such analyses can provide marketers with an understanding of the psychological, social, and cultural characteristics of the foreign consumers they wish to target, so that they can design effective marketing strategies for the specific national markets involved.

SIMILARITIES AND DIFFERENCES AMONG PEOPLE

A major objective of cross-cultural consumer analysis is to determine how consumers in two or more societies are similar and how they are different. Such an understanding of the similarities and differences that exist between nations is critical to the multinational marketer who must devise appropriate strategies to reach consumers in specific foreign markets. The greater the similarity between nations, the more feasible it is to use relatively similar marketing strategies in each nation. On the other hand, if the cultural beliefs, values, and customs of specific target countries are found to differ widely, then a highly individualised marketing strategy is indicated for each country. To illustrate this, the IKEA furniture company's generic global website uses English and the firm also offers 14 localised websites and 30 minisites that only provide contact information. Whereas the IKEA Italian website shows a group of people frolicking on their IKEA furniture (nudity is acceptable and commonplace in Italian advertising), the Saudi Arabian website uses extremely conservative photographs.[14] Another study examined brand choice and personal values among young British and Spanish girls (11–12-year-olds) and found that the Spanish girls were seeking fun and individual satisfaction from snack food brands (individual pleasure seekers), whereas their British counterparts were seeking friendship, sociability, and a sense of well-being (reassurance seekers).[15]

A firm's success in marketing a product or service in a number of foreign countries is likely to be influenced by how similar the beliefs, values, and customs are that govern the use of the product in the various countries. For example, the worldwide TV commercials of major international airlines (including American Airlines, Qantas, Air France, Lufthansa, Swissair, United Airlines, and British Airways) tend to depict the luxury and pampering offered to their business-class and first-class international travellers. The reason for their general cross-cultural appeal is that these commercials speak to the same types of individuals worldwide—upscale international business travellers—who share much in common. Figure 13.1 shows an example. In contrast, knowing that 'typical' Western advertising would not work in China, Nike hired Chinese-speaking art directors and copywriters to develop specific commercials that would appeal to the Chinese consumer within the boundaries of the Chinese culture. The resulting advertising campaign appealed to national pride in China.[16] Table 13.3 contrasts the values depicted in Chinese and US advertisments on their home television services.

FIGURE 13.1 **International traveller's advertising**

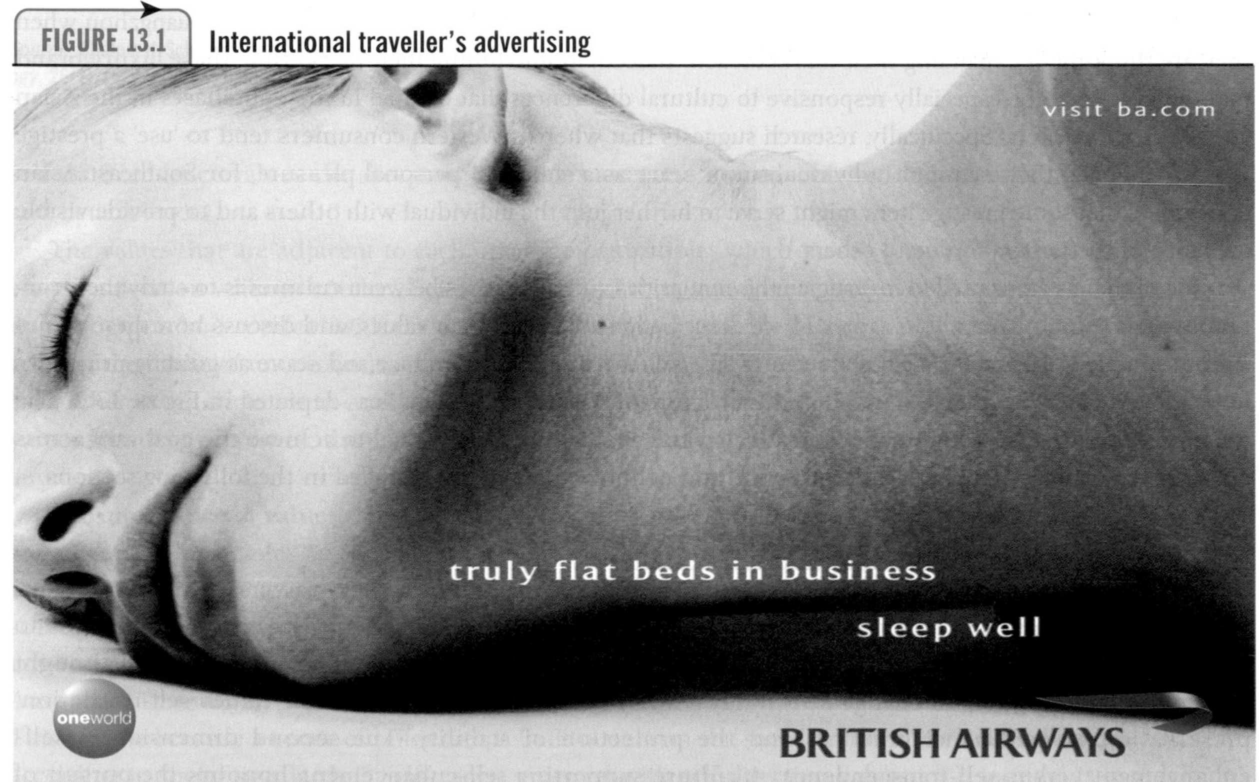

Source: Courtesy of British Airways.

9. Mercedes-Benz, a German car manufacturer, is using cross-cultural psychographic segmentation to develop marketing campaigns for a new two-seater sports car directed at consumers in different countries. How should the company market the car in the United States? How should it market the car in Japan?
10. What advice would you give to an Australian retailer who wants to sell women's clothing in the US?
11. Select two of the marketing mistakes discussed in the text. Discuss how these mistakes could have been avoided if the companies involved had adequately researched some of the issues listed in Table 13.5.

Exercises

1. Write some questions for a consumer research survey into areas such as credit cards, soup, toilet paper, perfume or mobile phones. Ask a student who is bilingual to translate the questions into his or her own language. Ask another person to translate them back into English. Compare the two versions and determine why there are differences. What differences in cultural sensitivity does this exercise reveal?
2. What difficulties do credit card companies, beer producers and McDonald's have in introducing their products into countries in the Asia-Pacific region? How would India and China differ from Malaysia and Indonesia?
3. How big is the cross-cultural market for educational services provided by Australia to companies and individuals in the Asia-Pacific region? How would you go about increasing Australia's share of this market?
4. If you are a student studying in another country, please identify some of the differences in values, behaviour, and consumption patterns you noted between people in your home country and the country in which you are now studying? If you are studying in your own country, find a student from another country and see what they say.
5. Compare the your views of how consumers behave in your culture with the views of someone who has visited that culture. Are there agreements? What accounts for different experiences or perceptions?
6. Select one of the following countries: Indonesia, Germany, Singapore, Israel, Japan, the US or China. Assume that a significant number of people in the country you chose would like to visit Australia and have the financial means to do so. Now, imagine you are a consultant for the Australian government and that you have been charged with developing a promotional strategy to attract tourists from the country you chose. Focusing on accommodation, food and travel services explain what approaches you would use.

Key terms

acculturation *(p. 444)*
ASEAN *(p. 436)*
back translation *(p. 446)*
cross-cultural consumer analysis *(p. 438)*
cross-cultural consumer research *(p. 445)*
cross-cultural psychographic segmentation *(p. 451)*
European Union (EU) *(p. 436)*
global advertising strategy *(p. 447)*
multinational strategies *(p. 449)*
North American Free Trade Agreement (NAFTA) *(p. 436)*
product standardisation *(p. 450)*
world brand *(p. 437)*

Endnotes

1. Thomas L. Friedman, 'Big Mac II', *New York Times*, 11 December 1996, p. A27.
2. Betsy McKay and Steven Gutterman, 'For ads, Russian revolution lives', *Advertising Age*, 7 March 1994, p. 40.
3. Larry Roellig, 'Designing global brands: Critical lessons', *Design Management Journal*, 12(4), Fall 2001, pp. 40–45; and 'MTV: Music television and H&Q Asia-Pacific's @Japan Media Group to launch new 24-Hour channel in Japan', *PR Newswire*, 29 August 2000, p. 1.
4. See <www.e-edge.org/special/GDP.htm> (March 2004).
5. Michael Silk and David L. Andrews, 'Beyond a boundary? Sport, transnational advertising, and the

reimagining of national culture', *Journal of Sport and Social Issues*, 25(2), May 2001, pp. 180–201.

6. <www.gaijinmag.com/magazine.asp> (March 2004).
7. Sharyne Merritt and Vernon Staubb, 'A cross-cultural exploration of country-of-origin preference', in *1995 AMA Winter Educators' Proceedings*, (eds) David W. Stewart and Naufel J. Vilcassim (Chicago: American Marketing Association, 1995), p. 380; Jill Gabrielle Klein, Richard Ettenson and Marlene D. Morris, 'The animosity model of foreign product purchase: An empirical test in the People's Republic of China', *Journal of Marketing*, 62, January 1998, pp. 89–100; and Gillian Sullivan Mort, Hume Winzar and C. Min Han, 'Country image effects in international services: A conceptual model and cross-national empirical test', in *2001 AMA Educators' Proceedings*, 12, (eds) Greg W. Marshall and Stephen J. Grove (Chicago: American Marketing Association, 2001), pp. 43–44.
8. Simon Anholt, 'The nation as brand', *Across the Board*, 37(10), December 2000, pp. 22–27.
9. Ian Phau and Gerard Prendergast, 'Conceptualizing the country of origin of brand', *Journal of Marketing Communications*, 6, 2000, pp. 159–170.
10. Israel D. Nebenzahl, Eugene D. Jaffe, and Shlomo I. Lampert, 'Towards a theory of country image effect on product evaluation', *Management International Review*, 37, 1997, pp. 27–49.
11. Zeynep Gurhan-Canli and Durairaj Maheswaran, 'Determinants of country-of-origin evaluations', *Journal of Consumer Research*, 27, June 2000, pp. 96–108.
12. Jill Gabrielle Klein, Richard Ettenson and Marlene Morris, 'The animosity model of foreign product purchase: An empirical test in the People's Republic of China, *Journal of Marketing*, 62(1), 1998, pp. 89–100; Rick Yan, 'To reach China's consumers, adapt to Guo Qing', *Harvard Business Review*, September–October 1994, pp. 66–67.
13. Lyn S. Amine and Sang-Heun Shin, 'A comparion of consumer nationality as a determinant of COO preferences', *Multinational Business Review*, 10(1), Spring 2002, pp. 45–53; and Paul Chao, 'The moderating effects of country of assembly, country of parts, and country of design on hybrid product evaluations', *Journal of Advertising*, 30(4), Winter 2001, pp. 67–81.
14. Olin Lagon, 'Culturally correct site design', *Web Techniques*, 5(9), September 2000, pp. 49–51.
15. Anne Dibley and Susan Baker, 'Uncovering the links between brand choice and personal values among young British and Spanish girls', *Journal of Consumer Behaviour* (London), 1(1), June 2001, pp. 77–93.
16. Robert G. Tian and Charles Emery, 'Cross-cultural issues in Internet marketing', *Journal of American Academy of Business*, 1(2), March 2002, pp. 217–224.
17. Nancy Y. Wong and Aaron C. Ahuvia, 'Personal taste and family face: Luxury consumption in Confucian and Western societies', *Psychology & Marketing*, 15(5), August 1998, pp. 423–441. Also see Sarah Ellison, 'Sex-themed ads often don't travel well', *Wall Street Journal*, 31 March 2000, p. 87.
18. Clyde Kluckholn, 'Values and value-orientations in the theory of action: An exploration in the definition and classification', in T. Parsons and E. Shils (eds), *Toward a General Theory of Action* (Cambridge, MA: Harvard University Press, 1951); Milton J. Rokeach, *The Nature of Human Values* (New York: The Free Press, 1973).
19. Shalom H. Schwartz and Lilach Sagiv, 'Identifying culture-specifics in the content and structure of values', *Journal of Cross-Cultural Psychology*, 26, January 1995, pp. 92–116.
20. Robert Levine, 'The pace of life in 31 countries', *American Demographics*, November 1997, pp. 20–29.
21. Robert Levine, 'Re-learning to tell time', *American Demographics*, January 1998, pp. 20–25.
22. Chip Walker, 'The global middle class', *American Demographics*, September 1995, pp. 40–46; Paula Kephart, 'How big is the Mexican market?' *American Demographics*, October 1995, pp. 17–18; and Rahul Jacob, 'The big rise', *Fortune*, 30 May 1994, pp. 74–90.
23. Rainer Hengst, 'Plotting your global strategy', *Direct Marketing*, August 2000, p. 55.
24. Mookyu Lee and Francis M. Ulgado, 'Consumer evaluations of fast-food services: A cross-national comparison', *Journal of Services Marketing*, 11(1), 1997, pp. 39–52.
25. Hengst, 'Plotting your global strategy', pp. 52–57.
26. Rick Yan, 'To reach China's consumers, Adapt to Guo Qing', *Harvard Business Review*, September–October 1994, pp. 66–67.
27. Kathy Chen, 'Chinese babies are coveted consumers', *Wall Street Journal*, 15 May 1998, p. B1; and Fara Warner, 'Western markets send researchers to China to plumb consumers' minds', *Wall Street Journal*, 28 March 1997, p. B5.
28. Mindy F. Ji and James U. McNeal, 'How Chinese childen's commercials differ from those of the United

States: A content analysis', *Journal of Advertising*, 30(3), Fall 2001, pp. 78–92.

29. Tara Parker-Pope, 'Non-alcoholic beer hits the spot in Mideast', *Wall Street Journal*, 6 December 1995, p. B1.
30. Warner, 'Western markets send researchers', p. B5.
31. Paul Howard Berent, 'International research is different', in Edward M. Mazze (ed.), *1975 Combined Proceedings* (Chicago: American Marketing Association, 1975), p. 294.
32. Gaurav Bhalla and Lynn Y. S. Lin, 'Cross-cultural marketing research: A discussion of equivalence issues and measurement strategies', *Psychology and Marketing* 4, 1987, pp. 275–285.
33 Elizabeth Cowley, 'East-West consumer confidence and accuracy in memory for product information', *Journal of Business Research*, 55, 2002, pp. 915–921.
34. Vanessa O'Connell, 'Exxon "centralizes" new global campaign', *Wall Street Journal*, 11 July 2001, p. B6.
35. Robert L. Wehling, 'Even at P&G, only 3 brands make truly global grade so far', *Advertising Age International*, January 1998, p. 8.
36. Friedman, 'Big Mac II', *New York Times*, 11 December 1996, p. A27; and Drew Martin and Paul Herbig, 'Marketing implications of Japan's social-cultural underpinnings', *Journal of Brand Management*, 9, 3, January 2002, pp. 171–179.
37. Pamela Buxton, 'Helping brands take on the world', *Marketing* (London), 13 May 1999, p. 32.
38. Martin S. Roth, 'The effects of culture and socio-economics on the performance of global brand image strategies', *Journal of Marketing Research*, 32, 1995, pp. 163–175.
39. Roellig, 'Designing global brands', *Design Management Journal*, 12(4), Fall 2001, p. 43.
40. Betsy McKay, 'Drinks for developing countries', *Wall Street Journal*, 27 November 2001, pp. B1, B6.
41. Sharon Shavitt, Michelle R. Nelson and Rose Mei Len Yuan, 'Exploring cross-cultural differences in cognitive responding to ads', in *Advances in Consumer Research*, 24, (eds) Merrie Brucks and Deborah J. MacInnis (Provo, UT: Association for Consumer Research, 1997), pp. 245–250.
42. Michael A. Callow, Dawn B. Lerman and Mayo de Juan Vigaray, 'Motivational appeals in advertising: A comparative content analysis of United States and Spanish advertising', in *Proceedings of the Sixth Symposium on Cross-Cultural Consumer and Business Studies*, (ed.) Scott M. Smith (Honolulu, HI: Association of Consumer Research and the Society for Consumer Psychology, 1997), pp. 392–396.
43. Dean Foster, 'Playing with China dollars', *Brandweek*, 10 November 1997, pp. 20–23.
44. Kip D. Cassino, 'A world of advertising', *American Demographics*, November 1997, p. 60.
45. Jiafei Yin, 'International advertising strategies in China: A worldwide survey of foreign advertisers', *Journal of Advertising Research*, 39(6), November/December 1999, pp. 25–35.
46. Robert Frank, 'Potato chips to go global—or so Pepsi bets', *Wall Street Journal*, 30 November 1995, p. B1.
47. Teresa Domzal and Lynette Unger, 'Emerging positioning strategies in global marketing', *Journal of Consumer Marketing*, 4, Fall 1987, pp. 27–29.
48. Zafar U. Ahmed, James P. Johnson, Xia Yang, Cheng Keng Fatt, Han Sack Teng and Lim Chee Boon, 'Does country of origin matter for low-involvement products?' *International Marketing Review*, 21(1), 2004, pp. 102–120.
49. Sangeeta Ramarapu, John E. Timmerman and Narender Ramarapu, 'Choosing between globalization and localization as a strategic thrust for your international marketing effort', *Journal of Marketing Theory and Practice*, 7(2), 1999, pp. 97–105.
50. David Kirkpatrick, 'Europe's technology gap is getting scary', *Fortune*, 17 March 1997, pp. 26–27.
51. <www.clickz.com/stats/big_picture/demographics/article.php/5901_408521> (March 2004).
52. Ben Vickers, 'In Internet age, Europe looks to define its many cultures against U.S. online', *Wall Street Journal*, 2 April 2001, p. B9F.
53. Jack Russell, 'Working women give Japan culture shock', *Advertising Age*, 16 January 1995, p. 24.
54. Sidney J. Levy, 'Myth and meaning in marketing', *1974 Combined Proceedings*, (ed.) Ronald C. Curhan (Chicago: American Marketing Association, 1975), pp. 555–556.
55. Stuart Elliott, 'Research finds consumers worldwide belong to six basic groups that cross national lines', *New York Times*, 25 June 1998, p. D8.
56. Pamela Paul, 'Global generation gap', *American Demographics*, 24(3), March 2002, pp. 18–19.
57. Norihiko Shirouzu, 'Snapple in Japan: Splash dried up', *Wall Street Journal*, 15 April 1996, pp. B1, B6.
58. John Tagliabue, 'Spoon-to-spoon combat overseas', *New York Times*, 7 January 1995, p. 17.
59. Ernest Beck and Rekha Balu, 'Europe is deaf to Snap!

Crackle! Pop!', *Wall Street Journal*, 22 June 1998, pp. B1, B2.

60. Yumiko Ono, 'Some kids won't eat the middle of an Oreo', *Wall Street Journal*, 20 November 1991, p. B1.
61. Julia Flynn and Lori Bongiorno, 'IKEA's new game plan', *Business Week*, 6 October 1997, pp. 99–102.
62. Colin Jevons, 'Misplaced marketing', *Journal of Consumer Marketing*, 17(1), 2000, pp. 7–8.
63. Linda J. Coleman, Ernest F. Cooke and Chandra M. Kochunny, 'What is meant by global marketing?' in *Developments in Marketing Science*, (eds) J. M. Hawes and G. B. Gilsan (Akron, OH: Academy of Marketing Science, 1987), 10, p. 178.
64. Toddi Gutner, 'Never give a Mandarin a clock, and other rules', *Business Week*, 9 December 1996, p. 192.
65. Deborah Klosky, 'Spanish viewership cries "Foul" on lurid TV', *Advertising Age*, 17 April 1995, pp. 1–20.
66. Seth Stevenson, 'I'd like to buy the world a shelf-stable children's lactic drink', *New York Times Magazine*, 10 March 2002, pp. 38–43.
67. David E. Sanger, 'An epidemic adverted: Foot-in-mouth disease', *New York Times*, 11 December 1994, p. 22.
68 Heath McDonald, Penny Darbyshire and Colin Jevons, 'Shop often, buy little: The Vietnamese reaction to supermarket retailing', *Journal of Global Marketing*, 13(4), 2000, pp. 53–71.
69. Gustavo Mendex-Kuhn, 'MEXICO: What Bell?', *Brandweek*, 5 May 1997, p. 26.
70. Lisa A. Petrison, Masaru Ariga and Paul Wang, 'Strategies for penetrating the Japanese market', *Journal of Direct Marketing*, 8, Winter 1994, pp. 44–58.

The decision-making process

PART 4

Part 4 explores various aspects of consumer decision making. This section offers the reader a simple model of consumer decision making that ties together the psychological, social and cultural concepts examined throughout the book. This is followed by an examination of opinion leadership and its role in the diffusion of innovations. Part 4 concludes with a chapter on organisational buyer behaviour.

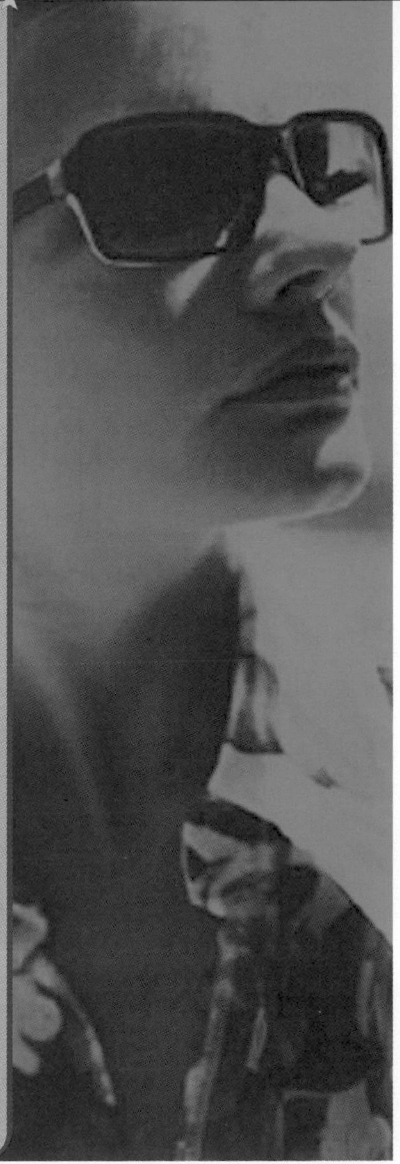

DECISION-MAKING MODEL

External influences

INPUT

Firm's marketing strategies

a Products
b Promotion
c Pricing
d Channels of distribution
e Market segmentation

Sociocultural environment

a Communication and reference groups
b Family
c Social class
d Culture and subculture
e Opinion leadership and diffusion of innovation
f Public policy and consumer protection

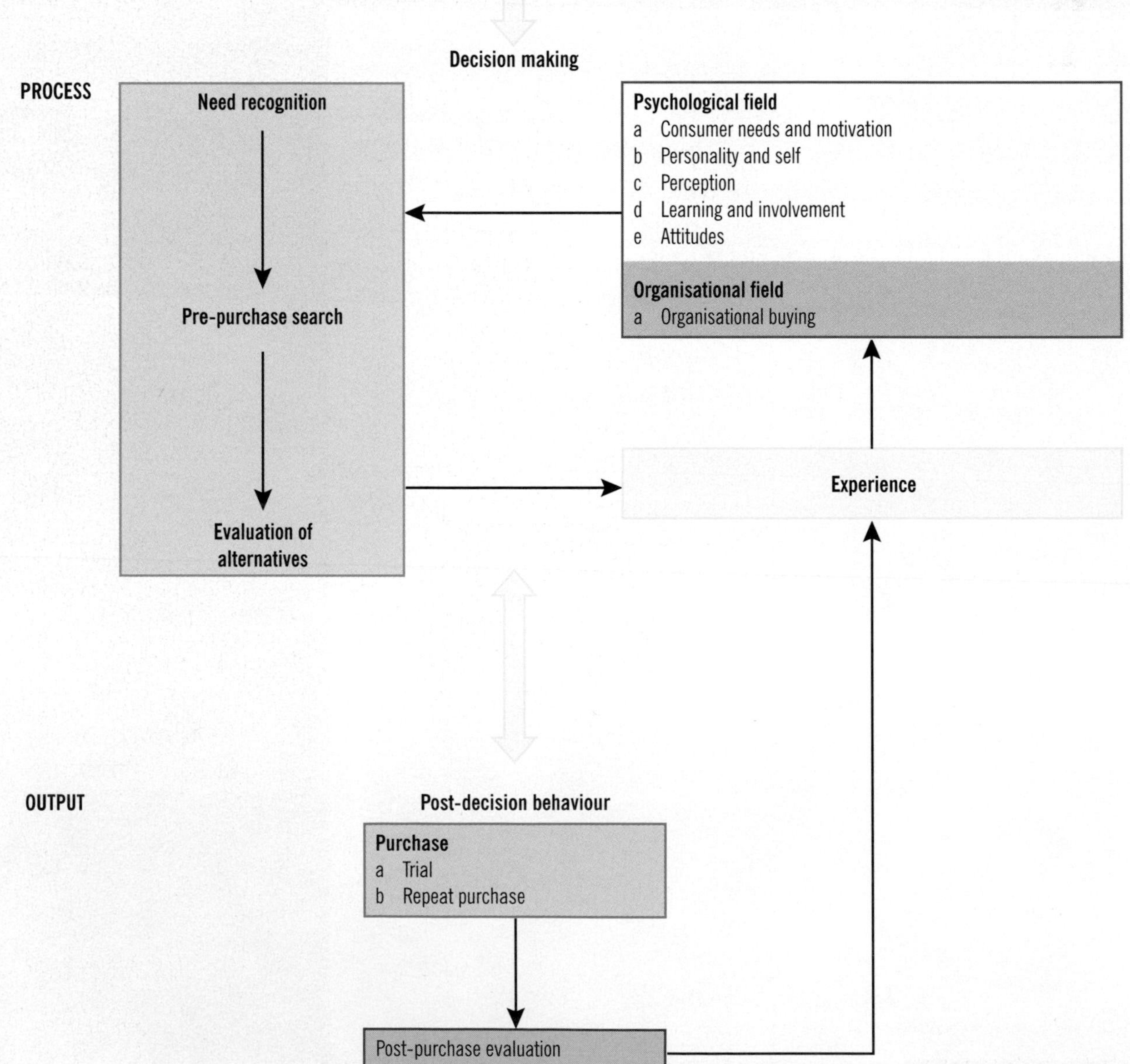

CHAPTER 14

Decision making

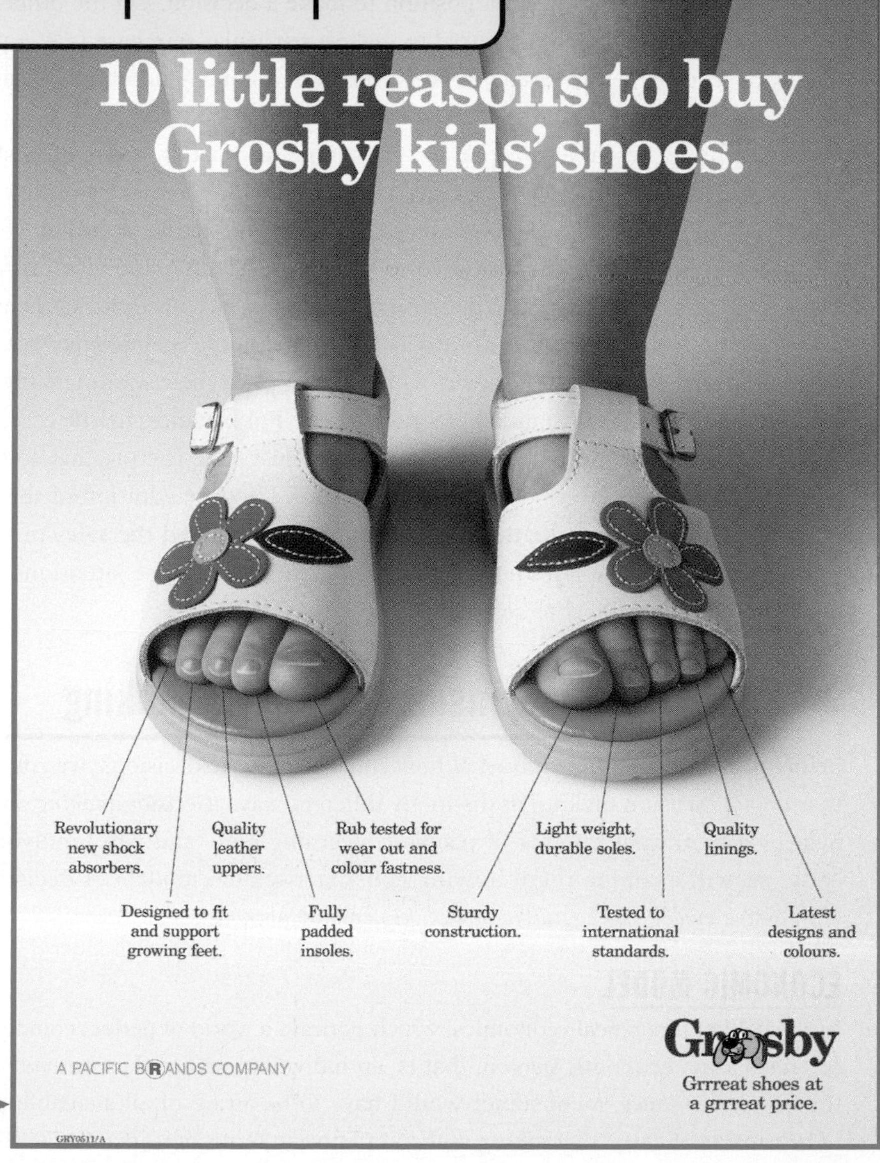

10 little reasons to buy Grosby kids' shoes.
Revolutionary new shock absorbers.
Quality leather uppers.
Rub tested for wear out and colour fastness.
Light weight, durable soles.
Quality linings.
Designed to fit and support growing feet.
Fully padded insoles.
Sturdy construction.
Tested to international standards.
Latest designs and colours.
A PACIFIC BRANDS COMPANY
Grosby
Grrreat shoes at a grrreat price.

Source: Courtesy of Grosby.

This chapter draws many of the psychological, social and cultural concepts developed throughout the book into a simple framework for understanding how consumers make decisions. Unlike Chapter 15, which will examine the dynamics of new product adoption, this chapter takes a broader perspective and examines consumer decision making in the context of all types of consumption choices, ranging from the consumption of new products to the use of old and established products.

What is a decision?

Every day, each of us makes numerous decisions concerning every aspect of our daily lives. However, we generally make these decisions without stopping to think about *how* we make them and what is involved in the decision-making process itself. In the most general terms, a decision is the *selection of an action from two or more alternative choices*. In other words, for us to make a decision, a choice of alternatives must be available. If we have a choice between making a purchase and not making a purchase, or a choice between brand X and brand Y, then we are in a position to make a decision. On the other hand, if we have no alternatives from which to choose and are *forced* to make a particular purchase (e.g. a prescribed medication), then this single 'no-choice' action does not constitute a decision. A no-choice decision is commonly referred to as 'Hobson's choice'.

In actuality, a no-choice purchase or consumption situation is rare in Australian society. However, it is very common through habit or circumstance for consumers *not* to make an active choice. We do not choose which brand of bank to use each time we make a banking transaction, although we may choose a different communication link (e.g. ATM). Similarly, we do not choose which brand of laundry detergent to use if someone else is the main grocery buyer. Thus, decision making must be considered in the context in which it occurs. Generally however, if there is almost always a choice, then there is almost always an opportunity for consumers to make decisions. Providing consumers with a choice when there was originally none can be a very good business strategy, one that can substantially increase sales.[1] For instance, in one case, a direct-mail electrical appliance catalogue displayed two coffeemakers instead of just one. The original coffeemaker was priced at $149 and a 'new' only slightly larger model was priced at $229. The addition of the second comparison coffeemaker stimulated consumer evaluation that significantly increased the sales of the original coffeemaker. For the remainder of this chapter, and Chapter 16, we focus on those situations where consumers actually make decisions about products or services.

Four views of consumer decision making

Before presenting a simple model of how consumers make decisions, we consider several models of consumers that depict decision making in distinctly different ways. *Decision-making models* refer to general perspectives held by a significant number of people concerning how (and why) individuals behave as they do.[2] Specifically, we will examine the following consumer-related models of decision making: (1) *economic model*; (2) *passive model*; (3) *cognitive model*; (4) *emotional model*.

ECONOMIC MODEL

In the field of theoretical economics, which portrays a world of perfect competition, the consumer is often characterised as an economic person; that is, an individual who makes *rational* decisions. To behave rationally in the economic sense, a consumer would have to be aware of all available product alternatives, would have to be capable of correctly ranking each alternative in terms of its benefits and disadvantages, and would have to be able to identify the one best alternative. This model has been criticised by consumer researchers because consumers rarely have enough information, sufficiently accurate information, or an adequate degree of involvement or motivation to make perfect decisions.

According to a leading social scientist, the economic model is unrealistic for the following reasons: (a) people are limited by their existing skills, habits and reflexes; (b) people are limited by their existing values and goals; and (c) people are limited by the extent of their knowledge.[3] Consumers operate in an imperfect world, in which they do not maximise their decisions in terms of economic considerations such as price–quantity relationships, marginal utility or indifference curves. Indeed, the consumer is generally unwilling to engage in extensive decision-making activities and will settle instead for a 'satisfactory' decision, one that is 'good enough'.[4] For this reason, the economic model is often rejected as too idealistic and simplistic. There may often be another set of motives that could account for a consumer's behaviour. As an example, recent research has found that consumers' primary motivation for price haggling, which was long thought to be the desire to obtain a better price (i.e. better dollar value for the purchase), may instead be related to the need for achievement, affiliation, and dominance.[5]

PASSIVE MODEL

Quite opposite to the economic view is the passive model, which depicts the consumer as submissive to the self-serving interests and promotional efforts of marketers. Consumers are perceived as impulsive and irrational purchasers, ready to yield to the arms and aims of marketers. At least to some degree, the passive model of the consumer was subscribed to by the hard-driving supersalesmen of old, who were trained to regard the consumer as an object to be manipulated.

The principal limitation of the passive model is that it fails to recognise that the consumer can play an equal, if not dominant, role in many buying situations. It does this by seeking information about product alternatives and selecting the product that appears to offer the greatest satisfaction and at other times by impulsively selecting a product that satisfies the mood or emotion of the moment. All that we have studied about motivation (see Chapter 3), selective perception (Chapter 5), attitudes (Chapter 7), and opinion leadership (Chapter 8) serves to support the proposition that consumers are rarely objects of manipulation. However, there are situations (discussed in Chapter 6) where consumers can be conditioned by the rewards of the marketer, or when they are in a low-involvement state and can be somewhat passive in their learning.

COGNITIVE MODEL

The third model portrays the consumer as a thinking *problem solver*. Within this framework, consumers are frequently pictured as either receptive to, or actively seeking, products and services that fulfil their needs and enrich their lives. The cognitive model focuses on the *processes* by which consumers seek and evaluate information about selected brands and retail outlets.

In this model, consumers are viewed as *information-processing systems*. Information processing leads to the formation of preferences and ultimately to purchase intentions. Consumers may also use a *preference formation strategy* that is 'other-based', in which they allow another person—a trusted friend, an interior decorator, an expert retail salesperson—to establish preferences for them.[6]

From a cognitive perspective, consumers are rational given the limitations of their ability to process and remember information, and their varying interests and priorities. This concept of *bounded rationality*[7] suggests that consumers cannot be rational in the economic sense, but they strive to make the best decisions possible given these limitations. The consumer is unlikely even to attempt to obtain all available information about every choice. Instead, the consumer's information-seeking efforts are likely to cease when what is perceived as *sufficient information* about some of the alternatives is obtained—enough information to enable an 'adequate' decision to be made. As this information-processing viewpoint suggests, consumers often develop short-cut decision rules (called **heuristics**) to ease the decision-making process. They might also use decision rules to cope with exposure to too much information, a condition known as **information overload**.

The cognitive, or problem-solving, model describes a consumer who falls somewhere between the extremes of the economic and passive model. This consumer does not (or cannot) have total knowledge about available product alternatives. Therefore, this individual cannot make perfect decisions, but nonetheless actively seeks information and attempts to make satisfactory decisions.

Consistent with the problem-solving model is the notion that a great deal of consumer behavior is goal directed. For example, a consumer might purchase a computer in order to manage finances or look for a laundry detergent that will be gentle on fabrics. Goal setting is especially important when it comes to the adoption of new products because the greater the degree of 'newness,' the more difficult it would be for the consumer to evaluate the product and relate it to his or her need (because of a lack of experience with the product).[8] Figure 14.1 diagrams goal setting and goal pursuit in consumer behaviour.

The cognitive model allows for the consumer to be actively involved in the decision-making process, but does not predict economically rational decisions. Our discussions of specific aspects of consumer decision making throughout the book have frequently depicted a consumer who is consistent with the cognitive model.

EMOTIONAL MODEL

Marketers frequently prefer to think of consumers in terms of either economic or passive models. In reality however, each of us is likely to associate deep feelings or emotions—joy, fear, love, hope, sexuality, fantasy, even

FIGURE 14.1 **Goal setting and goal pursuit in consumer behaviour**

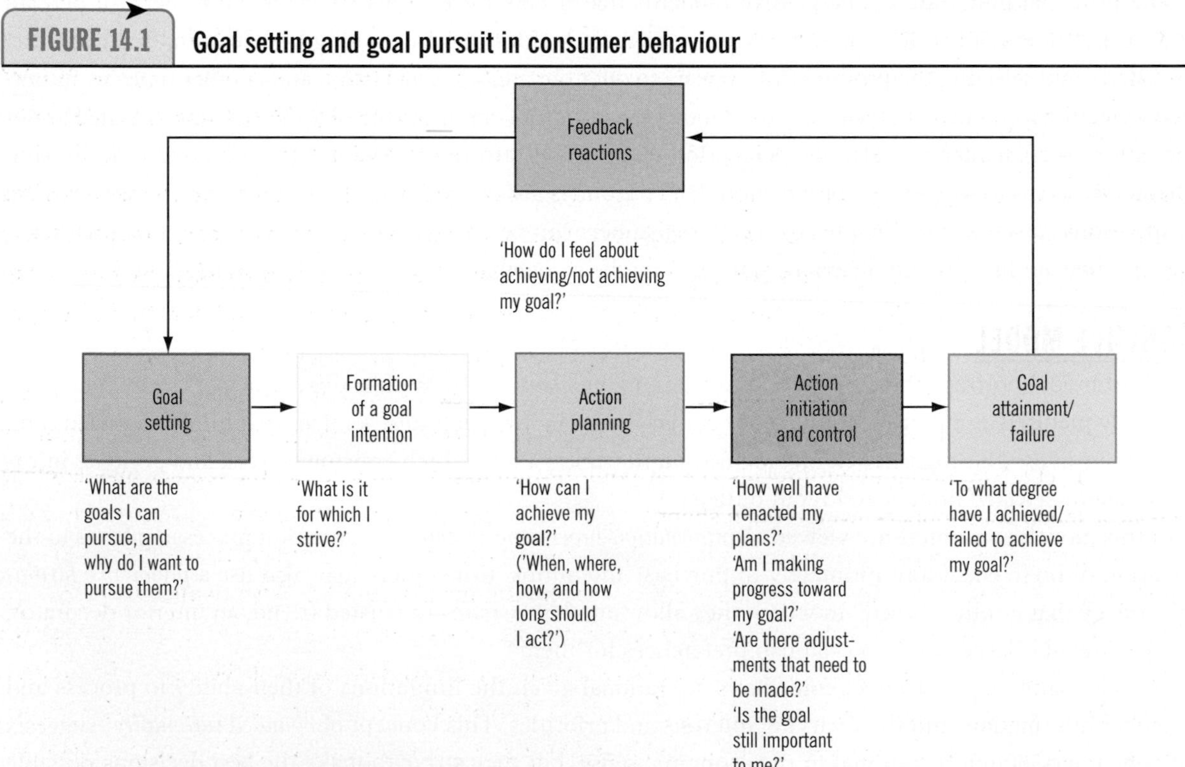

Source: Richard P. Bagozzi and Utpal Dholaki, 'Goal setting and goal striving in consumer behaviour', _Journal of Marketing_, 63, 1991, p. 21. Reprinted with permission from the _Journal of Marketing_, published by the American Marketing Association.

a little 'magic'—when it comes to certain purchases or possessions. These feelings or emotions are likely to be highly involving. For instance, a writer who misplaces a favourite pen might go to great lengths to look for it, despite the fact that he has six others at hand.

Possessions may also serve to preserve a sense of the past and act as familiar transitional objects when one is confronted with an uncertain future. For example, members of the armed services invariably carry photographs as memorabilia of 'the girl (or guy) back home', their families, and their lives in earlier times. These objects serve as hopeful reminders that normal activities will resume some day.[9] If we were to reflect on the nature of our recent purchases, we might be surprised to realise just how impulsive some of them were. Rather than carefully searching, deliberating and evaluating alternatives before buying, we are just as likely to have made many of these purchases on impulse or because we were emotionally driven.

When a consumer makes what is basically an emotional purchase decision, less emphasis is placed on the search for pre-purchase information. Rather than carefully searching, deliberating and evaluating alternatives before buying, we are just as likely to have made many of these purchases on impulse or a whim or because we were 'emotionally driven'. Emphasis is placed on current mood and feelings—'Go for it!' This is not to say that the decisions made by an emotional decision maker are irrational. As Chapter 3 points out, buying products that allow emotional satisfaction is a perfectly rational consumer decision. Some emotional decisions are expressions that 'you deserve it' or 'treat yourself'. For instance, many consumers buy designer-label clothing, not because they look any better in it, but because status labels make them feel better. This is a rational decision. Of course, if a man with a wife and three children purchases a two-seater BMW Z3 <www.bmw.com> for himself, the neighbours might wonder about his level of rationality (although some might think it was deviously high). No such question would arise if the same man selected a box of Lindt Lindor chocolate <www.lindt.com>, instead of a Cadbury Milk Tray <www.cadbury.com.au>, although in both instances, each might be an impulsive, emotional purchase decision. Furthermore, in the case of a good number of products, the choice of one brand over another has little to do with rationality. Advertisers are recognising with renewed interest the importance of emotional or *feeling-oriented* advertising.[10]

Like emotion, consumers' *moods* are also important to decision making. Mood can be defined as a 'feeling state' or 'state of mind'.[11] Unlike an emotion, which is a *response* to a particular environment, a mood is more typically an unfocused, *pre-existing* state already present when a consumer experiences an advertisement, retail environment, brand or product.[12] Compared to emotions, moods are generally lower in intensity and longer lasting. They are not as directly coupled with action tendencies and explicit actions as emotions.[13]

Mood appears to be important to consumer decision making because it influences when consumers shop, where they shop, and whether they shop alone or with others. It is also likely to influence how the consumer responds to actual shopping environments (i.e. at point-of-purchase).[14] In a sense, the retailer may attempt to create a 'mood' for shoppers, even though shoppers enter the store with a pre-existing mood. Recent research suggests that a store's image or atmosphere can affect shoppers' moods and, in turn, shoppers' moods can influence how long they stay in the store, as well as other behaviour that retailers wish to encourage.[15]

In general, individuals in a positive mood recall more information about a product than those in a negative mood. As the results of one study suggested, however, inducing a positive mood at the point-of-purchase decision (e.g. through background music, point-of-purchase displays) is unlikely to have a meaningful impact on specific brand choice unless a previously stored brand evaluation already exists.[16] Additionally, consumers in a positive mood typically employ a mood maintenance strategy. This is designed to avoid investing cognitive effort in any task unless it promises to maintain or enhance the positive mood.[17]

A model of consumer decision making

This section presents a simple model of consumer decision making that reflects the *cognitive*, or *problem-solving*, consumer, and to some degree the *emotional* consumer. The model is designed to tie together many of the ideas on consumer decision making and consumption behaviour discussed throughout the book. It does not presume to provide an exhaustive picture of the complexities of consumer decision making. Rather, it is designed to synthesise and coordinate relevant concepts into a significant whole. The model, presented in Figure 14.2, has three major components: input, process and output. It is important to remember that not all consumer decision situations receive (or require) the same degree of information search (see Chapter 6). If all decisions required extensive effort, consumer decision making would be an exhausting process that left

FIGURE 14.2 A simple model of consumer decision making

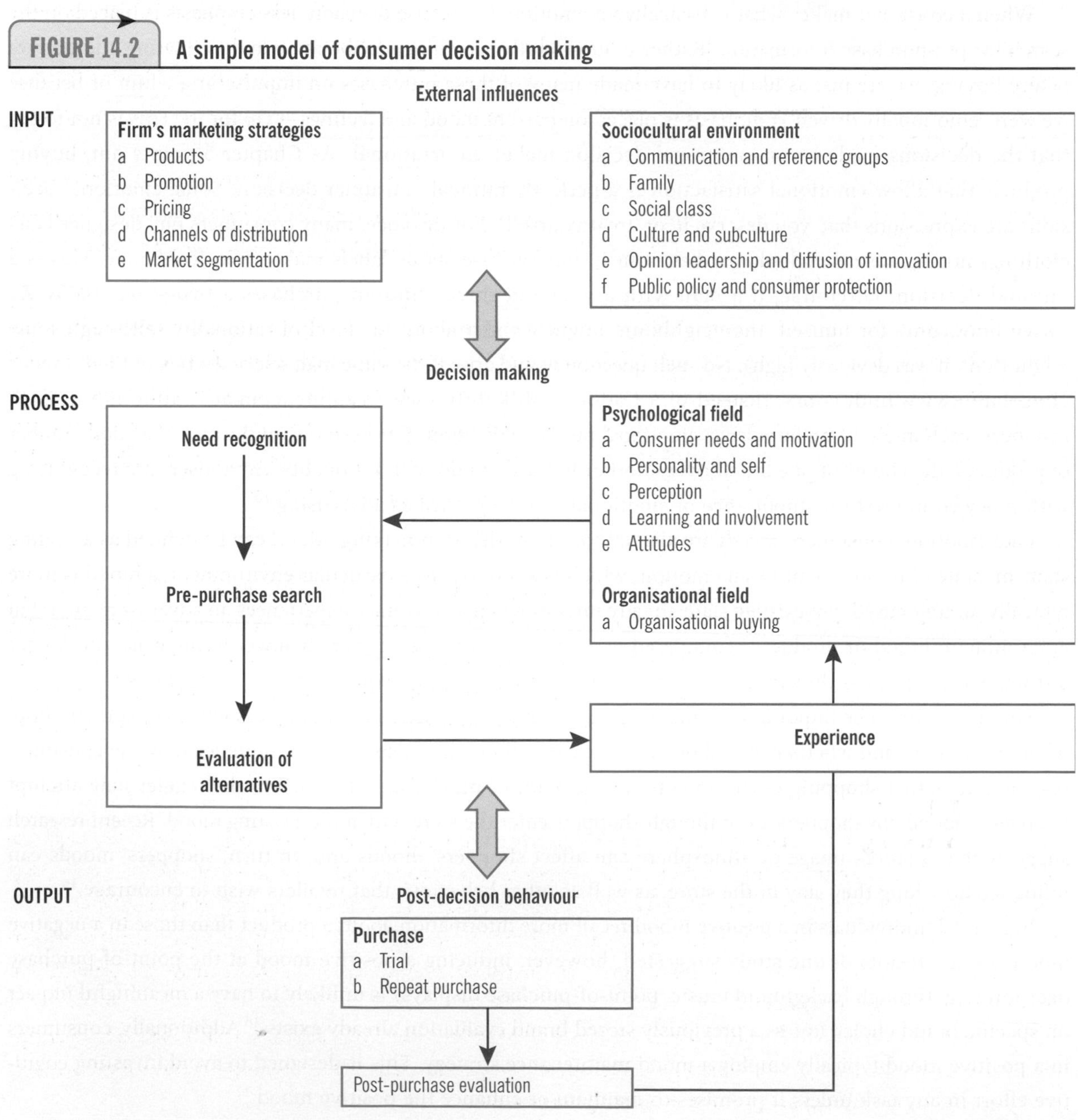

little time for anything else. On the other hand, if all purchases were routine, they would tend to be monotonous and would provide little pleasure or novelty. On a continuum of effort ranging from very high to very low, we can distinguish three specific levels of consumer decision making: **extensive problem solving, limited problem solving** and **routinised response behaviour**.[18]

- *Extensive problem solving* When consumers have not established criteria for evaluating a product category or specific brands in that category, or have not narrowed the number of brands to be considered to a small, manageable subset (the evoked set), their decision-making efforts can be classified as extensive problem solving. At this level, the consumer needs a great deal of information to establish a set of criteria on which to judge specific brands and a correspondingly large amount of information concerning each of the brands to be considered.
- *Limited problem solving* At this level of problem solving, consumers have already established the basic criteria for evaluating the product category and the various brands in the category. However, they have not fully established preferences concerning a select group of brands. Their search for additional information is more like 'fine-tuning'; they must gather additional brand information to discriminate among the various brands.
- *Routinised response behaviour* At this level, consumers have some experience with the product category and a well-established set of criteria with which to evaluate the brands in their evoked sets. In some situations, they may search for a small amount of additional information; in others, they simply purchase out of habit or review what they already know.

Just how extensive the problem-solving task is depends on how well established consumers' criteria for selection are, how much information they have about each brand being considered, and how narrow the set of brands (the evoked set) is from which the choice will be made. Clearly, extensive problem solving implies that consumers must seek more information to make a choice, while routinised response behaviour implies little need for additional information. The model as specified in Figure 14.2 is an extensive problem-solving model, but it can be adapted to represent limited and routine problem-solving situations as well.

INPUT

The *input* component of our consumer decision-making model draws on external influences that serve as sources of information about a particular product and influence a consumer's product-related values, attitudes and behaviour. The most important input factors are the *marketing inputs*, which include the activities of organisations that attempt to communicate the benefits of their products and services to potential consumers, and the non-marketing *sociocultural inputs* which, when internalised, influence the consumer's purchase decisions.

Marketing inputs

The firm's **marketing activities** are a direct attempt to reach, inform and persuade consumers to buy and use its products. These inputs to the consumer's decision-making process take the form of specific marketing strategies that consist of the product itself (including its package, size and guarantees); mass media advertising, direct marketing, personal selling and other promotional efforts; pricing policy; the selection of distribution channels to move the product from the manufacturer to the consumer; market segmentation and the implementation strategies.

Ultimately, the impact of a firm's marketing efforts is governed to a large degree by the consumer's perception of these efforts. Thus, marketers do well to remain diligently alert to consumer perceptions, rather than to rely on the intended impact of their marketing messages.

Sociocultural inputs

The second type of input, the **sociocultural environment**, also exerts a major influence on the consumer. Sociocultural inputs (examined in Part 3) consist of a wide range of non-commercial influences. For example, the comments of a friend, an editorial in the newspaper, usage by a family member, an article in *Choice* or the views of experienced consumers participating in a special interest discussion group on the Internet are all specific and direct non-commercial sources of information. The influences of social class, culture and subculture, though less tangible, are important input factors that are internalised and affect how consumers evaluate and ultimately adopt (or reject) products and services.

The unwritten codes of conduct communicated by culture subtly indicate which consumption behaviour is considered 'right' or 'wrong' at a particular point in time. For example, until the 1970s, most men would not have considered using a hair dryer or hairspray to keep their hair in place. Similarly, skin care products and makeup would not have been considered for purchase by men. However, the advent of the 'metrosexual' in the new millennium has seen this consumption behaviour change.[19] Now all of these products are often used by men. (See also Chapter 12.)

Unlike the firm's marketing efforts, sociocultural inputs do not necessarily *support* the purchase or consumption of a specific product, but may influence consumers to *avoid* a product. For example, animal rights activists (such as former French actor Brigitte Bardot) have attempted to educate consumers about the cruelty inflicted on animals when obtaining the raw materials necessary for fur coats. In some areas of the world and in some circles, these messages have discouraged women from buying and wearing furs.

The cumulative impact of each firm's marketing efforts, the influence of family, friends and neighbours, and society's existing code of behaviour are all inputs that are likely to affect what consumers purchase and how they use what they buy. Because these influences may be directed *to* the individual or actively sought *by* the individual, a two-headed arrow is used to link the *input* and *process* segments of the model (see Figure 14.2).

PROCESS

The *process* component of the model is concerned with how consumers make decisions. To understand this process, we must consider the influence of the psychological concepts examined in Part 2. The **psychological field** represents the internal influences (consumer needs and motivation, perception, learning and involvement, personality and self as well as attitudes) that affect consumers' decision-making processes (what they need or want, their awareness of various product choices, their information-gathering activities and their **evaluation of alternatives**). Included in the psychological field are two key concepts that are functions of consumer perceptions—*perceived risk* and the *evoked set*. We discuss these later in the chapter.

The act of making decisions

As pictured in the *process* component of the simple decision model in Figure 14.2, the act of making a consumer decision consists of three stages:

1. need recognition
2. pre-purchase search
3. evaluation of alternatives.

Need recognition The recognition of a need is likely to occur when a consumer is faced with a 'problem'. This takes place when the tension caused by the difference between *actual state* and *desired state* is above a threshold level set by the consumer. The actual state is consumers' perception of their present situation. The desired state is consumers' perception of the situation they would like to be in. There is usually a difference, however minor, between our current situation and our desired situation. The difference between these two states creates tension; if the tension rises above an acceptable threshold, the consumer will recognise the need for change (Figure 14.3). This process is not unlike the tension discussed in Chapter 3. For example, John, a university student in Sydney, relies on public transport because he does not have access to a car, motorbike or push bike. John has been in this situation for some time now. Today, after he had waited half an hour for a bus to arrive, only to be told he could not get on because the bus was too full, he decided to begin shopping immediately for a used car. John perceives his actual state as undesirable because he must depend on public transport. John's desired state is one of independence, which he believes he will achieve by owning his own car. It is important to note that John's actual state is his perception of the situation. Michael, another university student, is currently also reliant on public transport. Michael, however, perceives his situation to be one of worry-free, responsibility-free transport. Michael's perception is different because he has just had his car towed to the wreckers after months of costly repair bills and parking charges. The actual state depends on a comparison with past situations. It can also depend on comparisons with relevant reference groups.

Take another example: consider the case of Adrian, a busy marketing executive for the Australian branch of a major multinational food company, and husband of Michelle. Most of Adrian's family lives in Victoria. The imminent birth of their first child, which will be his family's first grandchild, is of great importance. However, as Adrian's family lives in another state, there is limited opportunity to share the 'magic moments' of the new grandchild. Of course, Adrian and Michelle also want a way of recording important events for their own future enjoyment. This leads them to consider a way of recording the antics of the new child. They briefly consider various ways of doing this (audio cassettes, photographs, a diary, video cassettes, web cam). Taking into account convenience, ease of use, practicality and value for money, Adrian and Michelle *recognise a possible need* for a video camera.

Among consumers, there seem to be two different problem-recognition situations. Some consumers face *actual state* decisions, where they perceive a problem with a product that fails to perform satisfactorily (e.g. a watch that no longer keeps accurate time). In contrast, other consumers face *desired state* decisions, where the desire for something new may trigger the decision process.[20] (Adrian, in his consideration of a video camera, appears to be basing his decision on his *desired state*.)

Need or problem recognition can also be viewed as either *simple* or *complex*. Simple problem recognition refers to needs that occur frequently and that can be dealt with almost automatically, such as becoming hungry and buying a chocolate bar from a nearby vending machine. Complex problem recognition, however, is

FIGURE 14.3 **Need recognition: actual versus desired state model**

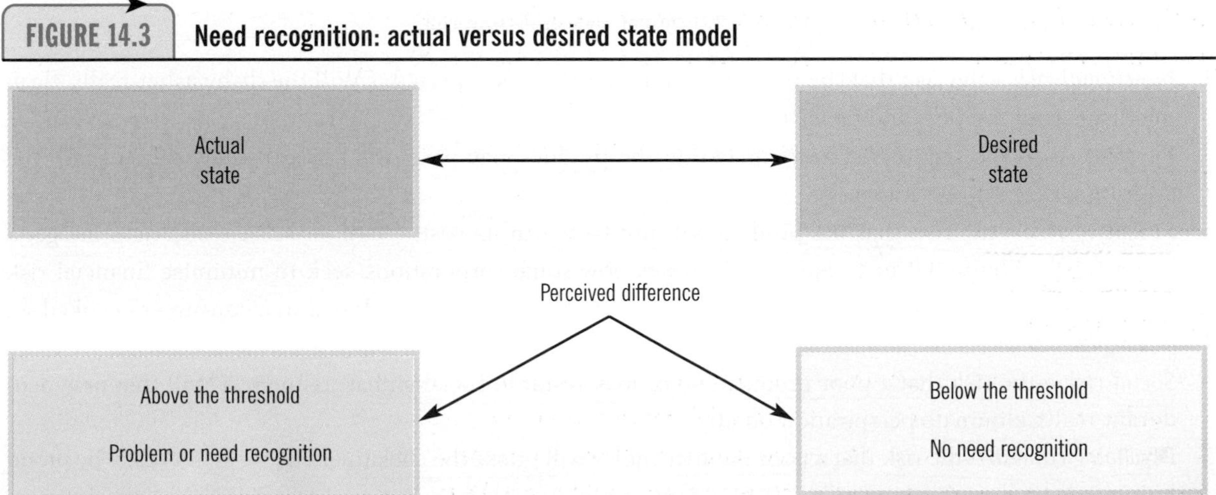

characterised as a state in which a problem develops over time, as the *actual state* and the *desired state* gradually move apart.[21] In the case of Adrian and Michelle, the closer the birth became, the more pressing the need. We should also note that, in this stage of the decision-making process, a family decision model is the most appropriate.

Pre-purchase search **Pre-purchase search** begins when a consumer perceives a need that might be satisfied by the purchase and consumption of a product. A consumer who senses a need for information on which to base a choice is in this stage. The recollection of past experiences (drawn from long-term memory storage) might provide the consumer with adequate information to make the present choice. Past experience is considered an *internal* source of information. If the consumer cannot retrieve enough information from memory or is unsure of the credibility of the information in memory, he or she may have to engage in a search of the outside environment for useful information on which to base a choice.

The amount of *external* search depends on the previous knowledge and experience of the consumer, the perceived risk involved in the decision, and other factors related to the information itself. The relationship between the amount of external search and the product category knowledge held by the consumer before the search is the source of some debate. In one study it was demonstrated that the amount of external search is greater for consumers with little product category knowledge.[22] Other studies have shown that high-knowledge consumers are more likely to engage in extended information search.[23] Low-knowledge consumers may find the task of collecting information too difficult if the product category is complex and the choice problem is perceived to be too difficult. Many consumer decisions are based on a combination of past experience (internal sources) and marketing and non-commercial information (external sources).

The degree of perceived risk can also influence this stage of the decision process. In high-risk situations, consumers are likely to engage in complex information search and evaluation; in low-risk situations they are likely to use very simple search and evaluation tactics.[24] **Perceived risk** is defined as *the uncertainty that consumers face when they cannot foresee all the consequences of their purchase decisions.* This definition highlights two relevant dimensions of perceived risk: uncertainty and consequences. (Perceived risk was discussed also in Chapter 5). It should be stressed that consumers are influenced only by the risk they *perceive*, whether or not such risk actually exists. Risk that is not perceived (no matter how real or how dangerous) does not influence consumer behaviour. Furthermore, the amount of money involved in the purchase is not directly related to the amount of risk perceived. Selecting the right brand of sports shoe may present as great a social risk to a particular consumer as selecting a new television set.

The major types of risks that consumers perceive when making product decisions include functional risk, physical risk, financial risk, social risk, psychological risk and time risk.

1. *Functional risk*—the risk that the product will not perform as expected. ('Will the dishwasher really clean my dishes and my pots and pans?')
2. *Physical risk*—the risk to self and others that the product may pose. ('Is this car really safe, or will the steering wheel nut work loose?')
3. *Financial risk*—the risk that the product will not be worth its cost. ('Will an MBA really help me get a better job?'). Figure 3.9 in Chapter 3 illustrates how some corporations seek to minimise financial risk to the consumer in their advertisements. In doing so, they hope to be included in a consumer's evoked set of brands.
4. *Social risk*—the risk that a poor product choice may result in social embarrassment. ('Will that new deodorant really eliminate perspiration odour?')
5. *Psychological risk*—the risk that a poor product choice will bruise the consumer's ego. ('Will I really be proud to invite friends to this house?')

6. *Time risk*—the risk that the time spent in product search may be wasted if the product does not perform as expected. ('Will I have to go through the shopping effort all over again?')

As the level of perceived risk increases, so too will the perceived payoff for the search.[25] Adrian visited several retailers—Myer, Dick Smith Electronics, JB Hi-Fi, airport duty free—as well as several discount stores. There he saw many video cameras, but concentrated on familiar brands such as Sony, JVC and Sharp.

The act of shopping is an important form of external information. According to a recent consumer study, there is a big difference between men and women in terms of their response to shopping. Unlike men, most women claim to like the experience of shopping. Although the majority of women found shopping to be relaxing and enjoyable, the majority of men did not have the same response.[26] In addition to gender differences, research reveals that price considerations can also play a role in determining the extent of the search process. For instance, consumers may engage in smart shopping, which indicates a willingness to invest a considerable amount of time and effort to seek and use promotion-related information in order to obtain a price savings. For such consumers, this search constitutes doing their 'homework' prior to making a purchase.[27]

An examination of the external search effort associated with the purchase of different product categories (TVs, VCRs, or personal computers) found that, as the amount of total search effort increased, consumer attitudes toward shopping became more positive, and more time was made available for shopping. Not surprisingly, the external search effort was greatest for consumers who had the least amount of product category knowledge.[28] It follows that the less consumers know about a product category and the more important the purchase is to them, the more time they will make available and the more extensive their pre-purchase search activity is likely to be. Conversely, research studies have indicated that consumers high in subjective knowledge (a self-assessment of how much they know about the product category) rely more on their own evaluations than on dealer recommendations.[29]

Other important factors that influence the amount of external search a consumer engages in are: (1) the perceived impact the information will have on the quality of the decision; (2) the time available; and (3) the ease of access to the information. If consumers believe that there are great differences in the brands available, and that the information available will help them to understand the differences between the brands, they will be more motivated to search for the information. On the other hand, if the information is difficult for them to understand, or if the brands are perceived to be very similar, consumers may not see the advantage in collecting information. The time available can be constrained either by the need to purchase the product immediately, or by other demands on consumers' time. In either case, as the time available decreases, so too will the amount of search. Finally, if the information is easy to access then more information will be sought.[30]

It is also important to point out that the Internet has had a great impact on pre-purchase search. Rather than visiting a store to find out about a product or calling the manufacturer and asking for a brochure, manufacturers' websites can provide consumers with much of the information they need about the products and services they are considering. For example, many automobile websites provide product specifications, sticker prices and dealer cost information, reviews, and even comparisons with competing vehicles. Jaguar's website <www.jaguar.com>, for example, lets you 'build' your own Jaguar, and see how it would look in different colours. Some websites will even list a particular auto dealer's new and used car inventory. Then there are websites such as <www.reflect.com> that allow women to customise any number of cosmetic and beauty care products. Similarly, <www.customatix.com> allows its customers to design shoes.[31]

At the most fundamental level, search alternatives can be classified as either personal or impersonal. Personal search alternatives include more than a consumer's past experience with the product or service. They also include asking for information and advice from friends, relatives, coworkers and sales representatives. Table 14.1 presents some of the sources of information that a consumer might use as part of her/his pre-purchase search.

TABLE 14.1 Alternative pre-purchase information sources for an ultralight laptop

Personal	Impersonal
Friends	Newspaper articles
Neighbours	Magazine articles
Relatives	*Choice*
Coworkers	Direct-mail brochures
Computer salespeople	Information from product advertisements
	Internal websites

Any or all of these sources might be used as part of a consumer's search process.

Consumers collect information from a number of different sources. Information sources can be categorised on two dimensions: direct/mediated and marketing/non-marketing. *Direct sources* are available for two-way communication, while *mediated sources* involve communicating via television, radio or print media. The *marketing/non-marketing dimension* captures the motivation of the source. For non-marketing sources, the motivation to inform or advise exists without any direct benefit from the final choice. Marketing sources may also inform or advise, but they will benefit from one choice more than another. Their information, therefore, may be biased. See Box 14.1 for examples of the types of information sources.

Direct, non-marketing information sources are assumed to provide 'unbiased' information tailored to the decision maker's needs. Direct marketing sources, such as a sales clerk, may be perceived as providing information that will benefit the clerk more than the consumer. The advantage of collecting information from direct marketing sources is that they are considered to be knowledgeable about the product. Dependence on the source varies with consumers' confidence in their knowledge in a product category. Consumers with little confidence in their knowledge of the product category are more likely to use a non-marketing source. Consumers with more confidence in their knowledge of the product category will use direct marketing sources.[32]

Mediated sources can be categorised as marketing information or non-marketing information. Mediated marketing information, such as brochures and advertisements, is created by one of the groups marketing the product. Mediated non-marketing information, such as the reviews published in *Choice*, is considered to be unbiased. An unbiased source is perceived as more credible than advertising and will be more persuasive when the consumer is first exposed to the information. Over time, however, a consumer's memory for the source fades before the content of the memory. The result is that the discounting in the persuasive impact of the 'biased' source and the increase in persuasive impact of the 'unbiased' source also fade. Hence, the difference in the persuasive impact of the two sources is reduced with time.[33] For example, as you collect information about CD players, you gather facts and impressions from brochures and advertisements in magazines, and from an article in *Choice*. After a few weeks of collecting information, you may catch yourself saying, 'I can't remember where I read this but … .'

Evaluation of alternatives Making a selection from a sample of all possible brands (or models) is a human characteristic that helps to simplify the decision-making process. When evaluating potential alternatives, consumers tend to use two types of information:

1. a 'list' of brands (and stores) from which they plan to make their selection (the evoked set)
2. the criteria they will use to evaluate each brand.

The **evoked set** refers to the set of brands a consumer considers in making a purchase choice in a particular product category. (The evoked set is also called the *consideration set*.) A consumer's evoked set is distinguished from his or her **inept set**, which consists of brands the consumer excludes from purchase consideration, and

BOX 14.1 Factors that are likely to increase pre-purchase search

Product factors

Long interpurchase time (a long-lasting or infrequently used product)
Frequent changes in product styling
Frequent price changes
Volume purchasing (large number of units)
High price
Many alternative brands
Much variation in features

Situational factors

Experience:

- First-time purchase
- No past experience because the product is new
- Unsatisfactory past experience within the product category

Social acceptability:

- The purchase is for a gift
- The product is socially visible

Value-related considerations:

- Purchase is discretionary rather than necessary
- All alternatives have both desirable and undesirable consequences
- Family members disagree on product requirements or evaluation of alternatives
- Product usage deviates from important reference group
- The purchase involves ecological considerations
- Many sources of conflicting information

Personal factors

Demographic characteristics of consumer:

- Well-educated
- High income
- White-collar occupation
- Under 35 years of age

Personality:

- Low dogmatic (open-minded)
- Low-risk perceiver (broad categoriser)
- Other personal factors, such as high product involvement and enjoyment of shopping and search

from the **inert set**, which consists of brands the consumer is indifferent towards because they are perceived as not having any particular advantages. Regardless of the total number of brands in a product category, a consumer's evoked set tends to be quite small—on average, only three to five brands.[34] However, research indicates that a consumer's consideration set increases in size as experience with a product category grows.[35]

Among those brands with which the consumer is familiar, there are *acceptable* brands, *unacceptable* brands, *indifferent* brands and *overlooked* (or forgotten) brands. The evoked set consists of the small number of brands the consumer is familiar with, remembers and finds acceptable for further evaluation. Figure 14.4 presents a simple depiction of the evoked set as a subset of all available brands in a product category. As the figure indicates, it is essential that a product be part of a consumer's evoked set if it is to be considered at all. The five terminal positions in the model do *not* end in a purchase for the following reasons: (1) brands may be *unknown* because of the consumer's selective exposure to advertising media and selective perception of advertising stimuli; (2) brands may be *unacceptable* because of poor or inappropriate positioning in either advertising or product characteristics; (3) brands may be perceived as not having any special benefits and are regarded *indifferently* by the consumer; (4) brands may be *overlooked* because they have not been clearly positioned or sharply targeted at the consumer market segment under study; and (5) brands may not be selected because they are perceived by consumers as *unable to satisfy* perceived needs as fully as the brand that is chosen.

In each of these instances, the implication for marketers is that promotional techniques should be designed to impart a more favourable, perhaps more relevant, product image to the target consumer. This may also require a change in product features or attributes (more or better features). An alternative strategy is to invite consumers in a particular target segment to consider a specific offering and possibly put it in their evoked set. It should also be pointed out that at times a consumer may feel as if he or she is being offered too many choices. For example, the brand proliferation on supermarket shelves may result in our trying a new brand, liking it, and then never being able to find it again.[36]

The criteria consumers use to evaluate the brands that constitute their evoked sets are usually expressed in terms of important product attributes. Examples of product attributes that consumers have used as criteria in evaluating nine product categories are listed in Box 14.2.

Table 14.2 presents a comparison of consumers by different age groups in terms of their ratings of attributes that 'strongly influence' their car purchase decisions. While all consumers, regardless of age, value cars that are reliable and durable, there are some age differences. For instance, while the youngest car buyers (those 16 to 29 years of age) are more concerned with owning cars that offer the latest technology, the oldest car buyers (those 50 years of age and older) appear to be the least price-conscious, to rely more on trusted brand names, and to value 'easy-to-use' factors. Because baby boomers are moving into this older-age cohort, car

FIGURE 14.4 The evoked set as a subset of all brands in a product class

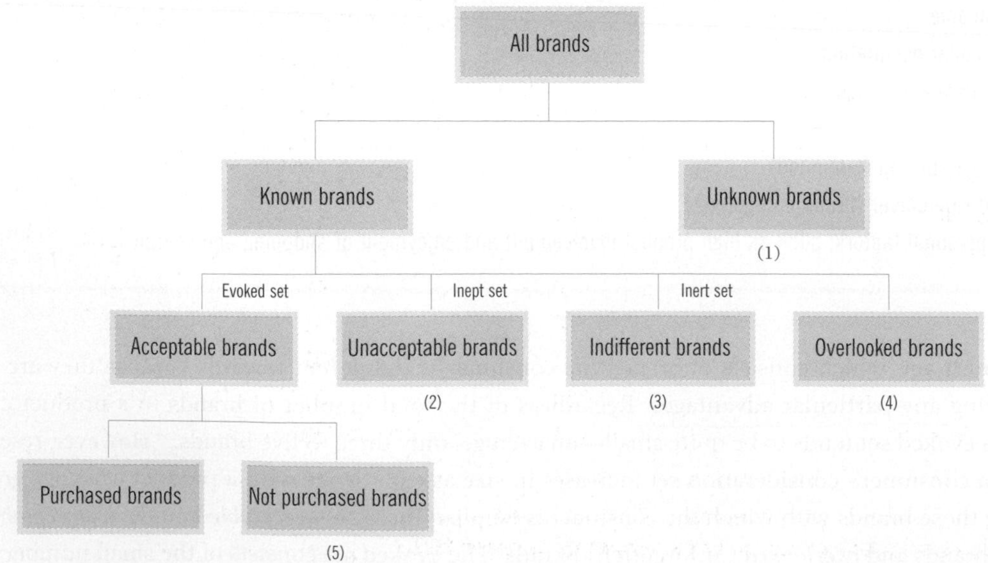

BOX 14.2 Possible product attributes used as purchase criteria for nine product categories

Personal computers
- Processing speed
- Price
- Type of display
- DVD/CD-RW drive
- Runs Windows XP
- Laptop or desktop

Video cameras
- Autofocusing and zoom ratio
- Digital recording
- Ease of use
- LCD colour screen and viewfinder
- Size and weight
- Scan type and pixels

Watches
- Wrist band
- Alarms
- Price
- Water-resistant
- Quartz movement
- Size of face

Paper towels
- Strength
- Design
- Price
- Colour
- Package size
- Absorbency

Colour TVs
- Picture quality
- Length of warranty
- Pay TV ready
- Price
- Videotext
- Size of screen

Frozen dinner
- Taste
- Type of main course
- Type of side dishes
- Serving size
- Preparation requirements
- Kilojoule count

Shaving cream
- Fragrance
- Consistency
- Price
- Size
- Smoothness of shave

Fountain pen
- Balance
- Price
- Shape
- Smoothness
- Size

Air conditioners
- Cooling capacity
- Energy efficiency rating
- Quietness
- Warranty
- Price

TABLE 14.2 The influence of selected automobile attributes on purchase decisions, by age

	Per cent rating as 'Strongly Influence'		
	Age category		
	16–29	30–49	50+
Reliable, works as it should	68	85	73
Long-lasting, durable	63	78	72
Easy to fix, maintain	39	49	53
Low price	40	42	30
Easy to use	38	40	46
Easy to purchase	33	31	25
Known, trusted brand name	26	32	43
Latest technology, styles	20	13	14
Many options, features	18	11	13

Source: **'Drawing a bead on car buyers for the nineties',** ***Brandweek*****, September 1992.**

FIGURE 14.5 Ad suggesting criteria for decision making

10 little reasons to buy Grosby kids' shoes.
Revolutionary new shock absorbers.
Quality leather uppers.
Rub tested for wear out and colour fastness.
Light weight, durable soles.
Quality linings.
Designed to fit and support growing feet.
Fully padded insoles.
Sturdy construction.
Tested to international standards.
Latest designs and colours.
A PACIFIC BRANDS COMPANY
Grosby
Grrreat shoes at a grrreat price.

Source: Courtesy of Grosby.

manufacturers would be wise to give more thought to the human engineering of their cars to make them easier to use.[37]

When a company knows that consumers will be evaluating alternatives, it sometimes advertises in a way that recommends the criteria that consumers should use in assessing product or service options. Figure 14.5 illustrates the effective use of criteria to assist the consumer with their decision making. Such information is designed to educate and assist potential consumers in their decision-making processes. Furthermore, research reveals, if evaluations are made online, information acquired later (the recency effect) is given more weight than information that had been acquired earlier. This, however, decreases with the amount of knowledge that consumers already possess.[38] In another study, the mere possession of a rebate coupon (whether it is used or not) for a product purchase enhances consumers' preference for that object.[39] In fact, techniques such as free samples, test drives, coupons and comprehensive warranties are all used by the marketer to minimise the risk perceived by the consumer.[40] There is also evidence to show that when making a 'remote' purchase (i.e. the consumer is shopping from home or office rather than in the actual store), the leniency of the retailer's return policy can influence the decision process because it reduces consumer risk.[41]

Let's return for a moment to Adrian, the marketing executive who is contemplating buying a video camera. After visiting several stores, Adrian's evoked set might consist of eight brands—Sony, JVC, Sharp, Philips, Canon, Hitachi, Samsung and Panasonic.

As part of his search process, Adrian has also acquired information about other relevant issues (or attributes) that could influence his final choice. On the basis of his recently acquired information, Adrian has tentatively decided that the video camera he wants should have the following features: simple to use, compact, long battery life, ability to record the baby in low light, light to carry, able to sustain wear and tear outside, be technologically up to date, and looking 'good or acceptable'.

At this point in the evaluation process, we need to consider consumer decision rules. **Consumer decision rules**, often referred to as *heuristics*, *decision strategies* or *information-processing strategies*, are procedures used by consumers to facilitate brand (or other consumption-related) choices. These rules reduce the burden of making complex decisions by providing guidelines or routines that make the process less taxing.

Consumer decision rules Consumer decision rules have been broadly classified into two major categories: compensatory and non-compensatory. In following a **compensatory decision rule**, a consumer evaluates brand options in terms of each relevant attribute and computes a weighted or summated score for each brand. The computed score reflects the brand's relative merit as a potential purchase choice. The assumption is that the consumer will select the brand that scores highest among the alternatives evaluated. Table 14.3 shows

TABLE 14.3 Hypothetical ratings for three models of video camera

Feature	Model X	Model Y	Model Z
Ease of use	10	7	5
Low-light capability	8	9	4
Zoom magnification	9	9	4
Weight	9	2	7
Size	8	2	4
Battery life	4	4	5
Latest technology	9	10	8
Compatible with VCR	2	10	8
Digital effects	5	10	10
Picture quality	7	8	10
Sound quality	5	9	7
Price	8	3	6
Total	**84**	**83**	**78**

hypothetical ratings for three video cameras where the consumer used a 10-point scale. Model X scored the highest, though the consumer had to trade-off ease of use and price against picture quality and compatibility with the home VCR.

An even more sophisticated consumer could assign weights to each feature. For example, price might have a weight of 60, while sound quality might have a weight of 12. In which case, the sum of the weighted ratings would be used. Some consumers will actually sit down and work out their choice as systematically as Table 14.3 suggests. Others will approximate this process, weighing up features before coming to a decision. Often advertisers will assist this process by describing a list of features included in their product (e.g. word-processing packages).

A unique feature of a compensatory decision rule is that it allows a positive evaluation of a brand on one attribute to balance out a negative evaluation on some other attribute. For example, a positive assessment of a particular brand of car in terms of performance may offset an unacceptable assessment of its high petrol consumption.

In contrast, **non-compensatory decision rules** do not allow consumers to balance positive evaluations of a brand on one attribute against a negative evaluation on some other attribute. For instance, in the case of a car, a negative (unacceptable) rating on the vehicle's fuel economy would not be offset by a positive evaluation of performance. Instead, this particular car model would be disqualified from further consideration. In Adrian's case, the choice of video camera was a non-compensatory one. Mazda is encouraging a non-compensatory approach in their advertisement that shows the consumer that Eunos has attributes that Audi and BMW do not. See Figure 14.6 (page 486).

Four non-compensatory rules are considered briefly here: the conjunctive rule, the disjunctive rule, the lexicographic rule and the elimination-by-aspects rule.

When using a **conjunctive decision rule**, the consumer establishes a separate, minimally acceptable level as a cut-off point for each attribute. If any particular brand falls below the cut-off point on any one attribute, the brand is eliminated from further consideration. This is the approach that Adrian took to video cameras (and retailers). In the end, he was left with three brands (Sony, JVC and Panasonic) and three stores (JB Hi-Fi, Myer and airport duty free). Because the conjunctive rule can result in several acceptable alternatives, it becomes necessary in such cases for the consumer to apply an additional decision rule to arrive at a final selection—for example, to accept the first satisfactory brand. The conjunctive rule is particularly useful in quickly reducing the number of alternatives to be considered. The consumer can then apply another, more refined decision rule to arrive at a final choice.

The **disjunctive rule** allows for trade-offs between attributes of the choice alternatives. For example, Adrian might say that the video camera he would be willing to purchase should have the highest quality picture in low light or, if it has only good quality picture in low light, it must also have the sharpest image. Although there are also trade-offs in the compensatory model, the nature of the trade-offs differs between the compensatory and the disjunctive rules. The disjunctive model considers only the sheer presence or absence of the attribute, not the amount of the attribute the brand possesses. The trade-off in the disjunctive model tends to be between two attributes relating to the same benefit, in this case picture quality. In the compensatory model, the attributes included in the trade-off need not serve the same purpose. A trade-off in the compensatory model could be between picture quality and warranty or service features.

In following a **lexicographic decision rule**, the consumer first ranks the attributes in terms of perceived relevance or importance. The consumer then compares the various brand alternatives in terms of the single attribute that is considered most important. If one brand scores sufficiently high on this top-ranked attribute (regardless of the score on any of the other attributes), it is selected and the process ends. If there are two or more surviving brand alternatives, the process is repeated with the second highest-ranked attribute (and so on) until reaching the point when one of the brands is selected because it exceeds the others on a particular attribute.

With the lexicographic rule, the highest-ranked attribute (the one applied first) may reveal something about the individual's basic consumer (or shopping) orientation. For instance, a 'buy the best' rule might indicate that the consumer is *quality-oriented*; a 'buy the most prestigious brand' rule might indicate that the consumer is *status-oriented*; a 'buy the least expensive' rule might reveal that the consumer is *price-oriented*; a 'buying the most expensive brand or model' strategy might reveal that the consumer is trying to reduce the risk of making an inappropriate decision, or is *risk-averse*.

The **elimination-by-aspects rule** is similar to the lexicographic rule in the first stage. Consumers rate the attributes in order of importance and set minimum cut-off values. The most important attribute is considered first and any brand that does not have the minimum acceptable amount of the attribute is eliminated. Then, the second most important attribute is considered and any brand that does not have the minimum acceptable amount of the attribute is eliminated. This process continues through the attributes until there is only one brand remaining.

A variety of decision rules appear quite commonplace. According to a consumer survey, 9 out of 10 shoppers who go to the store for frequently purchased items possess a specific shopping strategy for saving money. The consumer segment and the specific shopping rules that these segments employ are:[42]

1. Practical loyalists—those who look for ways to save on the brands and products they would buy anyway.
2. Bottom-line price shoppers—those who buy the lowest-priced item with little or no regard for brand.
3. Opportunistic switchers—those who use coupons or sales to decide among brands and products that fall within their evoked set.
4. Deal hunters—those who look for the best bargain and are not brand loyal.

We have considered only the most basic of an almost infinite number of consumer decision rules. Most of the decision rules described here can be combined to form hybrid rules; for example, conjunctive-compensatory, conjunctive-disjunctive or disjunctive-conjunctive. Consumer researchers have described hybrid rules as two-stage.[43] In the first stage, the *alternative elimination stage*, the consumer uses a less effortful non-compensatory rule in order to reduce the set of brands to be considered more carefully. In the second stage, the *alternative selection stage*, the smaller set is considered in more detail. With a smaller set of brands for consideration, the consumer can afford to use a more compensatory rule.

It is likely that, for many purchase decisions, consumers maintain overall evaluations of the brands in evoked sets in long-term memory. This would make assessment by individual attributes unnecessary. Instead, the consumer would simply select the brand with the highest perceived overall rating. This type of synthesised decision rule is known as the **affect referral rule** and may represent the simplest of all rules.

Table 14.4 summarises the essence of many of the decision rules considered in this chapter, in terms of the kind of mental statements that Adrian, our marketing executive, might make in selecting a video camera.

In many choice situations, consumers face incomplete information on which to base decisions and must use alternative strategies to cope with the missing elements. Missing information may result from advertisements or packaging that mention only certain attributes, the consumer's own imperfect memory of attributes for non-present alternatives, or because some attributes are experiential and can only be evaluated after product use.[44] There are at least four alternative strategies that consumers can adopt for coping with missing information:[45]

1. Consumers may delay the decision until missing information is obtained. This strategy is likely to be employed for high-risk decisions.
2. Consumers may ignore missing information and decide to continue with the current decision rule (e.g. compensatory or non-compensatory), using the available attribute information.
3. Consumers may change the customarily used decision strategy to one which better accommodates missing information.
4. Consumers may infer ('construct') the missing information.

Recent research has demonstrated that consumers tend to deal with missing information by purchasing the option that is deemed to be superior on the common attribute (i.e. basing the decision on the information that is available for all of the options or brands being considered). For marketers, therefore, the decision as to what information to provide or not to provide can help determine the product's success or failure in the marketplace.[46]

In discussing consumer decision rules, we have assumed that a choice is made from among the brands evaluated. Of course, a consumer may also conclude that none of the alternatives offers sufficient benefits to

TABLE 14.4 Hypothetical use of popular decision rules in making a video camera purchase decision

Decision rule	Mental statement
Compensatory rule	'I selected the video camera that came out best when I balanced the good features against the bad features.'
Conjunctive rule	'I picked the video camera that had no bad features.'
Disjunctive rule	'The video camera that I selected had either the highest quality picture in low light or the sharpest image.'
Lexicographic rule	'The most important thing about a video camera is ease of use in all conditions. I selected the camera that was easiest to use.'
Affect referral rule	'Sony has the best appliances, so naturally I selected one of their video cameras.'

FIGURE 14.6 An ad promoting non-compensatory decision rules

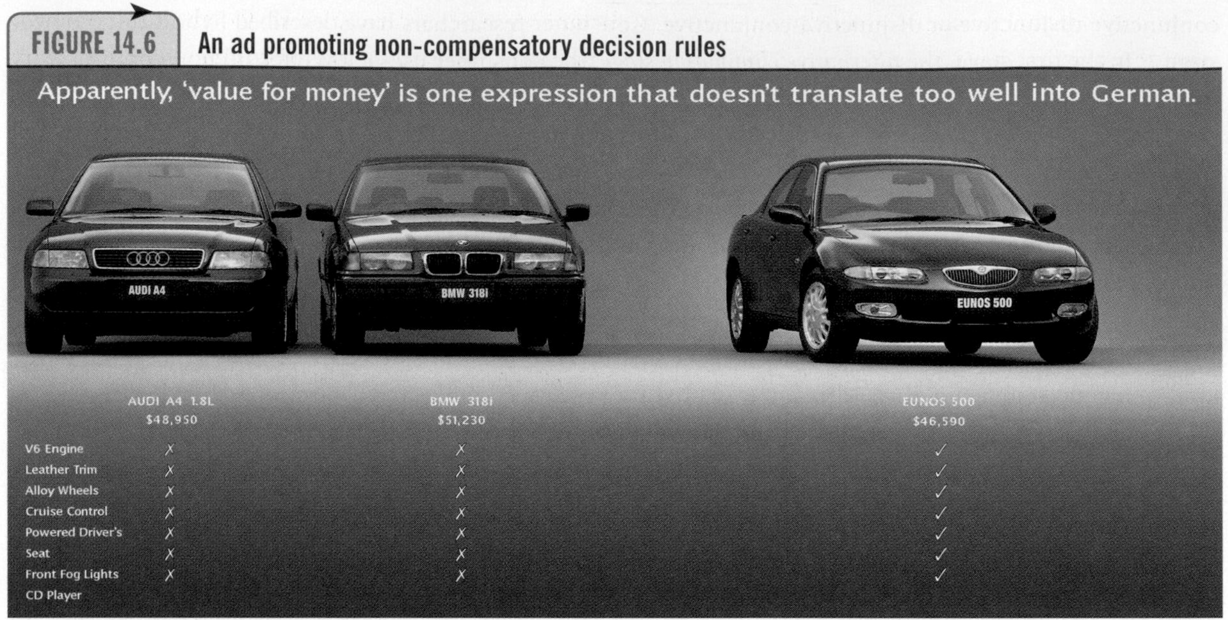

Source: Courtesy of Mazda.

warrant purchase. If this were to occur with a necessity such as a refrigerator, the consumer would probably either lower his or her expectations and settle for the best of the available alternatives, or seek information about additional brands, hoping to find one that met predetermined criteria more closely. On the other hand, if the purchase is more discretionary (e.g. a second or third pair of jeans), the consumer would probably postpone the purchase. In this case, information gained from the search up to that point would be transferred to long-term storage (in the psychological field) and retrieved and reintroduced as input when and if the consumer regains interest in making such a purchase.

It should be noted that, in applying decision rules, consumers may at times attempt to compare dissimilar (non-comparable) alternatives. For example, a consumer may be undecided about whether to buy a new car or rent a holiday house, because he can only afford one expenditure. Another example: a consumer may try to decide between buying a portable compact disc player or a 34-cm remote-control colour TV. When there is great dissimilarity in the alternative ways of allocating available funds, consumers abstract the products to a level where comparisons are possible.[47] In the examples cited above, a consumer might weigh the alternatives (new car versus holiday rental; compact disc player versus colour TV) in terms of which alternative would offer the most pleasure or which, if either, is more of a 'necessity'.

We should also note the effect of situation on choice. The consumer may go to a store seeking a specific model of a video camera, only to see some other model at a special price and buy that. For fast-moving consumer goods in supermarkets, shoppers walking past the gondola bins at the start of the aisles are prone to this type of decision-making behaviour. It is likely that the consumer uses a hybrid, or two-stage, decision in this instance. The consumer might use a non-compensatory rule to narrow down the alternatives, and a compensatory rule in the store, where all the information is available. Conversely, the consumer might use a compensatory rule to narrow down the alternatives, and a non-compensatory rule at the store, such as 'choosing the cheapest' of the alternatives remaining in the consideration set.

Going online to secure assistance in decision making For the past several years researchers have been examining how using the Internet has impacted the way consumers make decisions. Research demonstrates that as a result of having limited information-processing capacity, consumers must develop a choice strategy based on both individual factors (e.g. knowledge, personality traits, demographics) and contextual factors (characteristics of the decision tasks). The three major contextual factors that have been researched are task complexity (number of alternatives and amount of information available for each alternative), information organisation (presentation, format, and content), and time constraint (more or less time to decide).[48] Table 14.5 compares these contextual factors for both the electronic and traditional environments.

Lifestyles as a consumer decision strategy An individual's or family's decisions to be committed to a particular lifestyle (e.g. devoted followers of a particular religion) impacts on a wide range of specific everyday consumer behaviour. For instance, the Trends Research Institute has identified 'voluntary simplicity' as one of the top 10 lifestyle trends.[49] Researchers there estimate that 15% of all 'boomers' seek a simpler lifestyle with reduced emphasis on ownership and possessions. (See also Chapter 12.) Voluntary simplifiers are making do with less clothing and fewer credit cards (with no outstanding balances) and moving to smaller, yet still adequate,

TABLE 14.5 Comparison of electronic and traditional information environment

		Electronic environment	Traditional environment
Assumption		**Consumers use both 'heads' and computers to make decisions. The total capacity is extended.**	**Consumers use 'heads' to make decisions. Their cognitive capacity is fixed.**
Contextual factors	Task complexity	More alternatives and more information for each alternative are available. Information is more accessible.	Information is scattered and information search is costly.
	Information organisation	Information presentation format is flexible. It can be reorganised and controlled by consumers. Product utilities can be calculated by computers without consumers' direct examination of the attributes.	Information presentation format and organisation are fixed. They can only be 'edited' by consumers manually (e.g. using pencil and paper).
	Time constraint	Time is saved by using computers to execute the decision rules; extra time is needed to learn how to use the application.	Complex choice strategies require more time to formulate and execute.

Source: Lan Xia, 'Consumer choice strategies and choice confidence in the electronic environment', *American Marketing Association Conference Proceedings*, American Marketing Association, 10, 1999, p. 272. Reprinted with permission of the American Marketing Association.

homes or apartments in less populated communities. Most importantly, it is not that these consumers can no longer afford their affluence or 'lifestyle of abundance'; rather, they are seeking new, 'reduced', less extravagant lifestyles. As part of this new lifestyle commitment, some individuals are seeking less stressful and lower-salary careers or jobs. In a telephone survey, for example, 33% of those contacted claimed that they would be willing to take a 20% pay cut in return for working fewer hours.[50] Time pressure may also play a role in the consumer's decision process, as research has positively associated this factor with both sale proneness (i.e. respond positively to cents-off coupons or special offers) and display proneness (e.g. respond positively to in-store displays offering a special price).[51]

A series of decisions Although we have discussed the purchase decision as if it were a single decision, in reality, a purchase can involve a number of decisions. For example, when purchasing an automobile, consumers are involved in multiple decisions. These include choosing the make or country of origin of the car (foreign versus domestic), the dealer, the financing, and particular options. A study found that consumers who replace their cars after only a few years were more concerned with the car's styling and image or status and were less concerned with cost. In contrast, those who replace their cars after many years undertook a greater amount of information and dealer search and were greatly influenced by friends.[52]

Since deciding how to pay for a purchase is one of the decisions facing consumers, it is of interest to point out that the use of debit cards has been gaining popularity in the United States as a payment option. Whereas in 1999, according to one study, 22% of purchases were made with credit cards and 21% with debit cards, by 2001 credit cards accounted for only 21% of purchases and debit card usage had risen to 26%. Online point-of-sale debit card transactions were also expected to rise. In contrast, the average American writes 21 cheques monthly, about half of them at the time of purchase.[53] The evidence in Australia suggests that consumers have in fact increased their credit card usage and avoided the use of cheques.[54] In fact, at the end of 2003, credit card balances in Australia totalled $24.1 billion.[55]

Decision rules are important in marketing strategy. An understanding of which decision rules consumers apply in selecting a particular product or service is useful to marketers concerned with formulating a promotional program. A marketer familiar with the prevailing decision rule can prepare a promotional message in a format that would facilitate consumer information processing. The promotional message might even suggest how potential consumers should make a decision. For instance, a direct-mail piece for a desktop computer might tell potential consumers 'what to look for in a new PC'. This mail piece might specifically ask consumers to consider the attributes of hard disk size, amount of memory, processor speed, monitor size and maximum resolution, video card memory, and CD burner speed.

Consumption vision researchers have recently proposed 'consumption vision' as a non-orthodox, but potentially accurate, portrayal of decision making for those situations in which the consumer has little experience and the problems are not well structured, as well as those in which there is a considerable amount of emotion. Under such circumstances, the consumer may turn to a consumption vision, a mental picture or visual image of specific usage outcomes and/or consumption consequences.[56] Such visions (e.g. a new college graduate envisioning working for a large corporation versus working for his dad's small manufacturing firm, or a consumer visualising lying on a beach in Hawaii) allow consumers to imagine or vicariously participate in the consumption of the product or service prior to making an actual decision. After 'trying out' a number of different alternatives in one's mind, so to speak, the consumer then makes his or her decision.[57] In a recent study, consumers were more likely to construct consumption visions when they saw an advertisement presenting the product's attributes in concrete and detailed language or visually with pictures.[58] There is also research evidence to indicate that a consumer's preferences may change depending on the degree to which anticipated satisfaction is evoked. When anticipating satisfaction, the consumer forms mental images—consumption visions—of one or more of the options, and the final decision is very likely going to be based on this imagery. To illustrate, a real estate agent selling an expensive home might encourage clients to ask themselves (i.e. 'envision') how satisfied they would likely be to live in such a home.[59]

OUTPUT

The *output* portion of the consumer decision-making model concerns two closely associated kinds of post-decision activity: **purchase behaviour** and **post-purchase evaluation**. The objective of both activities is to increase the consumer's satisfaction with his or her purchase.

Purchase behaviour

At the end of the *process* portion of the model, the consumer should have identified a 'best' brand or alternative. The identification of the 'best' alternative may change if new information is encountered in the retail environment. Point-of-purchase material may infuse new information into the evaluation. When the consumer arrives at the retail outlet, there may be new information that alters the evaluation of one or more of the brands. It is unlikely that the consumer will alter one of the inputs to the decision and re-evaluate all the brands in the consideration set. Instead, the consumer will alter the overall evaluation in a more positive or negative direction.

Consumers make three types of purchases: trial purchases, repeat purchases, and long-term commitment purchases. When a consumer purchases a product (or brand) for the first time and buys a smaller quantity than usual, this purchase would be considered a trial. Thus, a trial is the exploratory phase of purchase behaviour in which consumers attempt to evaluate a product through direct use. For instance, when consumers purchase a new brand of laundry detergent about which they may be uncertain, they are likely to purchase smaller trial quantities than if it were a familiar brand. Consumers can also be encouraged to try a new product through such promotional tactics as competitions, free samples, coupons, and/or sale prices. This ideal is reflected in Figure 14.7.

When a new brand in an established product category (toothpaste, chewing gum, or cola) is found by trial to be more satisfactory or better than other brands, consumers are likely to repeat the purchase. Repeat purchase behaviour is closely related to the concept of brand loyalty, which most firms try to encourage because it contributes to greater stability in the marketplace (see Chapter 5). Unlike trial, in which the consumer uses the product on a small scale and without any commitment, a repeat purchase usually signifies that the product meets with the consumer's approval and that he or she is willing to use it again and in larger quantities.

Trial, of course, is not always feasible. For example, with most durable goods (refrigerators, washing machines, or electric ranges), a consumer usually moves directly from evaluation to a long-term commitment (through purchase) without the opportunity for an actual trial. While purchasers of the new Volkswagen Beetle were awaiting delivery of their just purchased cars, they were kept 'warm' by being sent a mailing that included a psychographic tool called 'Total Visual Imagery' that was personalised to the point that it showed them the precise model and colour they had ordered.[60]

The Internet has greatly changed how people search for information and ultimately make a purchase. As usage grows, some authorities are forecasting that early in the twenty-first century some consumers will be purchasing food and other basic household needs via in-home television computer systems. Choices will be made by the shopper after viewing brands and prices on the screen. So the purchasing process itself may change dramatically in the coming decades.[61]

To this point, the discussion has focused on planned purchases. There are many purchases that are not planned, or may be delayed depending on the atmosphere of the retail environment. Several variables might affect the atmosphere in a retail setting: music, lighting, colours, store layout, crowding, etc. For instance,

FIGURE 14.7 Encouraging product trial to reduce purchase risk

Try it for two weeks and see if you glow from the inside out.
Body Smart WheatBran Flakes
new & improved taste
Kellogg's
Body Smart
WheatBran Flakes
High in fibre for digestive health
inner health glows on the outside
A diet high in fibre helps keep you healthy on the inside, so you'll glow with vitality on the outside. That's why we've created new Kellogg's Body Smart. High in fibre and great in taste, it's an easy, everyday way to help maintain your inner health. In fact, we challenge you to try it for just two weeks and see if you feel the difference.

Source: Courtesy of Kellogg (Aust) Pty Ltd.

when the tempo of the music is slow, shoppers stay longer and spend more money. When the tempo of the music was manipulated in a grocery store, consumers spent 38% more when the music was slow compared with a condition where the tempo of the music was fast.[62] Playing classical music has been demonstrated to encourage the choice of more expensive wines in a wine cellar.[63] The classical music was supposed to cue more upmarket purchasing.

A model of the relationship between retail atmosphere and behaviour suggests that the atmosphere alters the mood state of the consumer, which results in a change in behaviour[64] (see Figure 14.8). Like emotion, consumers' *moods* are also important to decision making. Unlike an emotion, which is a *response* to a particular environment, a mood is more typically an unfocused, *pre-existing* state already present when a consumer experiences an advertisement, retail environment, brand or product.[65] A study carried out in a discount department store in Australia supported this model. More specifically, pleasure experienced in the store environment resulted in consumers spending more time and more money than they had intended. Consumers experiencing displeasure in the store environment resulted in their spending less time, but not necessarily less money, unless the mood was intense.[66] Most of these studies suggest that aspects of the retail environment can result in an increase in purchasing, although there may be aspects of the retail environment that encourage consumers to delay purchasing. Every setting has its optimal number of occupants. A store with no one in it may seem unpopular; whereas a store full of other shoppers may not be appealing due to the reduction in service. A restaurant that is empty may be perceived as low in quality or value; a full restaurant may seem like the place to be and be considered appealing. For some consumers, crowding can cause stress and result in the omission of purchases and less exploratory behaviour,[67] as well as more comparison shopping and greater price sensitivity.[68]

Consider Adrian, who was in and out of many retail outlets at the end of his evaluation process. The purchase, however, was made quickly. Early on a fine, warm Saturday morning, Adrian went into one of

FIGURE 14.8 Retail environment, mood and behaviour

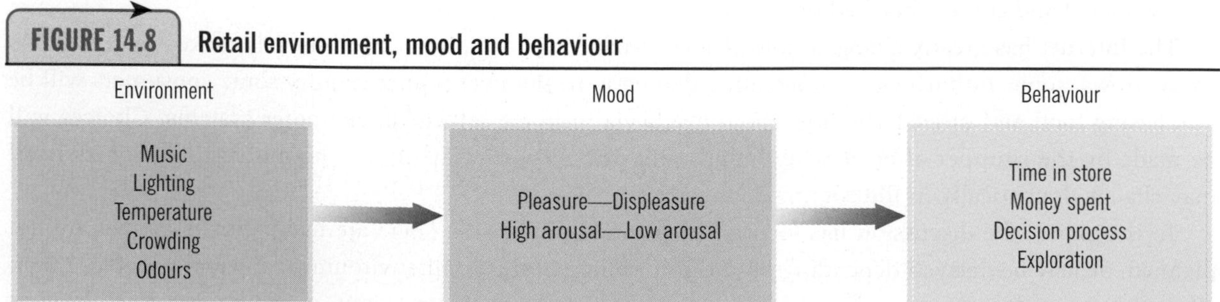

the stores near his home. He was in a good mood, the clerk was friendly, the store was bright and clean. He made his decision—he decided to buy the Sony Digital 8 HandyCam DCRTRV250. He also picked up two new cassettes and an extra carry case without searching for information about these items at other outlets.

Post-purchase evaluation

An important component of post-purchase evaluation is the reduction of any uncertainty or doubt that the consumer might have had about the selection. As part of their post-purchase analyses, consumers try to reassure themselves that their choice was a wise one; that is, they attempt to reduce **post-purchase cognitive dissonance.** As Chapter 7 indicated, they do this by adopting one of the following strategies: they may rationalise the decision as being wise; they may seek advertisements that support their choice and avoid those of competitive brands; they may attempt to persuade friends or neighbours to buy the same brand (thus confirming their own choice); or they may turn to other satisfied owners for reassurance.

As consumers use a product, particularly during a trial purchase, they evaluate its performance in light of their own expectations. In the simplest model, consumers are satisfied if their expectations are met or exceeded. Consider a situation where you have been going to lectures in one of your courses for the entire term and the lecturer has been boring every week. It's week eleven, you are expecting to go to the lecture and be very bored. If you go to the lecture and the lecturer is dull, are you satisfied? After all, the experience was equivalent to your expectations.

There are three types of expectations:

1. Equitable performance expectation—what the product or service performance ought to be
2. Ideal performance expectation—the best possible product or service performance
3. Expected performance—the expected level of product or service performance.

If the actual performance matches or exceeds equitable performance expectations, the consumer will be satisfied. If the actual performance matches or exceeds the ideal performance expectation, the consumer will be extremely satisfied. If the actual performance matches the expected performance expectations, the consumer will not be surprised, but may not necessarily be satisfied. Marketers are increasingly incorporating the notion of expectations into their advertisements as illustrated in Figure 14.9.

FIGURE 14.9 Highlighting the importance of expectations

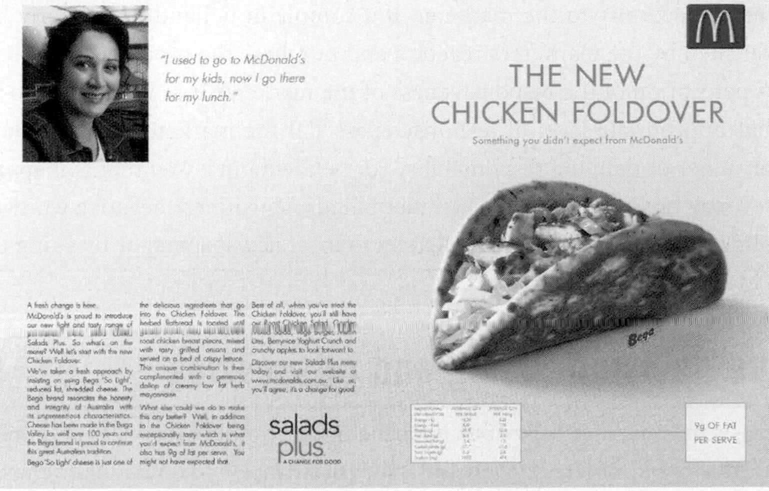

***Source:* Courtesy of McDonald's Australia.**

The degree of post-purchase analysis that consumers undertake depends on the importance of the product decision and the experience acquired in using the product. If the product lives up to expectations, they will probably buy it again. If the product's performance is disappointing or does not meet expectations, however, they will search for more suitable alternatives. Thus, the consumer's post-purchase evaluation 'feeds back' as *experience* to the consumer's psychological field and serves to influence future related decisions. Although it would be logical to assume that customer satisfaction is related to customer retention (i.e. if a consumer is satisfied with his Hugo Boss suit he will buy other Hugo Boss products), a recent study found no direct relationship between satisfaction and retention. The findings show that customer retention may be more a matter of the brand's reputation—especially for products consumers find difficult to evaluate.[69]

What was Adrian's post-purchase evaluation of the Sony video camera? He found that it performed even better than he had imagined it would. Initially he had some reservations in charging the batteries and getting it going but he found it was very easy and, after a few practice attempts, he was able to bypass the manual and use the camera in a variety of situations.

Adrian also learned by experience that he could easily hook up the camera to his VCR, TV set and computer. He experimented with the various settings and was pleased to see that the camera would still record an acceptable picture in a room lit by three large candles. The sports and close-up modes were also easy to use, though sometimes Adrian forgot these settings were being used when filming.

In summary, Adrian was enthusiastic about his Sony video camera and was eagerly awaiting the birth of his child. One of his friends at work was thinking about a video camera for an overseas trip and was impressed by what Adrian said about the camera.

How do consumers behave when they are not satisfied with their purchase? Consumers have three choices when dissatisfied with the performance of a product or service. One option is never to purchase the brand again. In this case, the marketer will not be aware of the consumer's dissatisfaction. Another option is to complain to the marketer. Complaining is more likely if:

1. the product or service is perceived by the consumer to be important;
2. the gap between equitable expectations and performance is large;
3. the consumer cannot attribute blame to their use of the product, and can attribute blame to the marketer; or
4. the consumer believes that the marketer will act on the basis of their complaint.

Complaining offers an opportunity to the marketer. If a complaint is handled properly by the marketer, the consumer may feel satisfied by the marketer's reaction and purchase the product or service again. This occurs when the consumer's perception of the responsiveness of the marketer is at least equal to what that consumer believes is the 'normal' appropriate level of responsiveness.[70] If the marketer does not handle the complaint well, ignoring the consumer or denying responsibility (or behaving in a way that is inappropriate in the mind of the consumer), they may not only lose the consumer but also encourage negative word-of-mouth.[71] The last option is to take public or legal action by writing letters to local newspapers, or by suing the company—obviously, an option the marketer would like to avoid.

Beyond the decision: Using and possessing

Historically, the emphasis in consumer behaviour has been on the product (service) and brand choice decisions. As shown throughout this book, however, there are many more facets to consumer behaviour. The *experience* of using products and services, as well as the sense of pleasure derived from *possessing* or *consuming* things and experiences (e.g. a VCR or a vacation), contribute to consumer satisfaction. These consumption outcomes, in turn, affect consumers' future decision processes.

Thus, given the importance of possessions and experiences, a broader perspective of consumer behaviour might view choice as the *beginning* of a **consumption process**, not merely the *end* of consumer decision-making efforts.[72] In this context, choice is an *input* into a process of establishing a *consumption set* (an assortment or portfolio of products and/or their attributes) and a *consuming style* (how the individual fulfils his or her consumption requirements). The *process* stage of a simple model of consumption from the consumer's perspective might include the *using*, *possessing*, *collecting* and *disposing* of things and experiences. The *output* stage of this process would include changes in a wide range of feelings, moods, attitudes and behaviour, as well as reinforcement (positive or negative) of a particular lifestyle, enhancement of a sense of self and the level of consumer satisfaction and quality of life.[73] Figure 14.10 presents a simple model of consumption that reflects the ideas discussed here and throughout the text.

Possessions (e.g. photographs, souvenirs, trophies and everyday objects) assist consumers in their efforts to create and maintain a sense of *past,* which is essential to having a sense of self.[74] Furthermore, 'objects of the past' are often acquired and retained intentionally (some become antiques or even heirlooms) to 'memorialise' pleasant or momentous times in one's past. It has been suggested that nostalgia permits people to maintain their identity after some major change in their life. This nostalgia can be based on family and friends; on objects such as toys, books, jewellery, and cars; or on special events, such as graduations, weddings, and holidays.[75] Older consumers are often faced with the issue of how they should dispose of such special possessions. Indeed, in the past several years, a number of researchers have examined this subject area. Often the older person wants to pass a family legacy on to a child, ensure a good home for a cherished collection, and/or influence the lives of others. The aim is not to 'sell' the items, because they could do that themselves.[76]

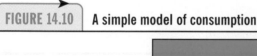

FIGURE 14.10 A simple model of consumption

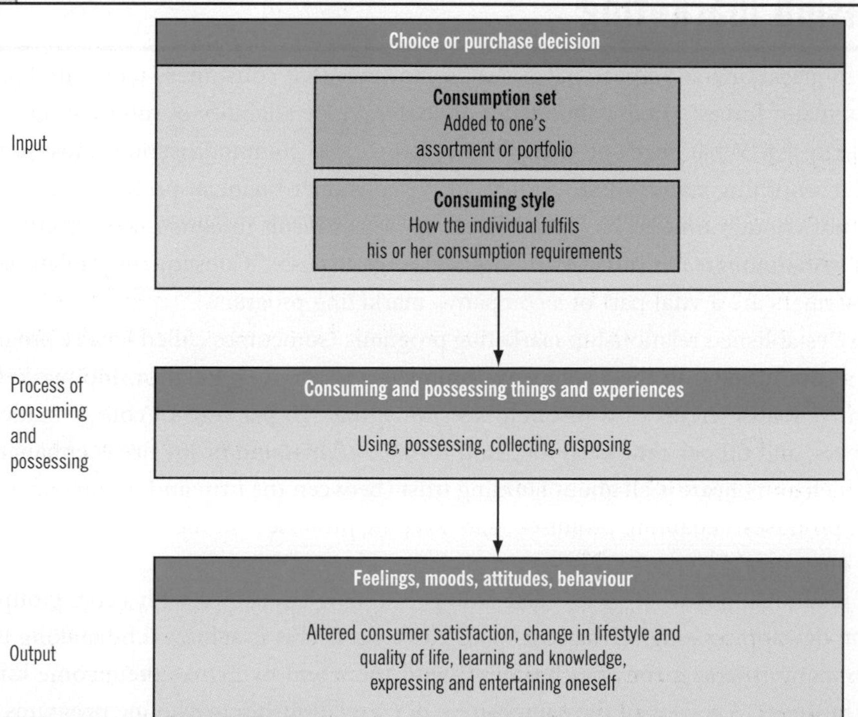

TABLE 14.6 Reported circumstances and motivations for self-gift behaviour

Circumstances	Motivations
• Personal accomplishment	• To reward oneself
• Feeling down	• To be nice to oneself
• Holiday	• To cheer oneself up
• Feeling stressed	• To fulfil a need
• Have some extra money	• To celebrate
• Need	• To relieve stress
• Had not bought for self in a while	• To maintain a good feeling
• Attainment of a desired goal	• To provide an incentive towards a goal
• Others	• Others

Source: David Glen Mick and Mitchelle DeMoss, 'To me from me: A descriptive phenomenology of self-gifts', in Marvin E. Goldberg, Gerald Gorn and Richard W. Pollay (eds), *Advances in Consumer Research*, 17 (Provo, UT: Association for Consumer Research, 1990), pp. 677–682.

Similarly, products chosen for gift-giving also represent more than ordinary 'everyday' purchase decisions because of their symbolic meanings. Gift-giving is an interpersonal act of symbolic communication, with explicit and implicit meanings ranging from congratulations, love or regret to obligation or dominance. Moreover, some personal acquisitions, because of their context or meaning, serve as **self-gifts**. Table 14.6 illustrates specific circumstances and motivations that might lead a consumer to engage in self-gift behaviour. Consumers may treat themselves to self-gifts that are products (e.g. clothing, compact discs, jewellery), services (e.g. hair styling, restaurant meals, spa membership) or experiences (e.g. socialising with friends).[77]

Relationship marketing

Why is relationship marketing so important? Research indicates that consumers today are less loyal than in the past, due to six major forces: (1) the abundance of choice, (2) availability of information, (3) entitlement (consumers repeatedly ask 'What have you done for me lately?'), (4) commoditisation (most products/services appear to be similar—nothing stands out), (5) insecurity (consumer financial problems reduce loyalty), and (6) time scarcity (not enough time to be loyal). These six forces result in consumer defections, complaints, cynicism, reduced affiliation, greater price sensitivity, and litigiousness.[78] Consequently, relationship programs that can retain customers are a vital part of a company's marketing program.

Many firms have established relationship marketing programs (sometimes called loyalty programs) to foster usage loyalty and a commitment to their company's products and services. Relationship marketing is exceedingly logical when we realise credit card research has shown that '75 per cent of college students keep their first card for 15 years, and 60 per cent keep that card for life.'[79] This kind of loyalty is enhanced by relationship marketing, which at its heart is all about building trust (between the firm and its customers) and keeping promises ('making promises', 'enabling promises', and 'keeping promises' on the part of the firm and, possibly, on the part of the customer).[80]

It is the aim of relationship marketing to create strong, lasting relationships with a core group of customers. The emphasis is on developing long-term bonds with customers. This is achieved by making them feel good about how the company interacts (or does business) with them and by giving them some kind of personal connection to the business. A review of the composition of 66 relationship marketing programs revealed three elements shared by more than 50% of the programs. They are (1) fostering ongoing communication with customers (73% of the programs); (2) furnishing loyalty by building in extras like upgrades and other perks (68% of the programs); and (3) stimulating a sense of belonging by providing a 'club membership' format (50% of the programs).[81] A real relationship marketing program is more than the use of database marketing tactics to better target customers. The consumer must feel that he or she has received something for being a participant in the relationship.[82] In a positive vein, businesses have been finding that the Internet is an inexpensive, efficient, and more productive way to extend customer services.[83] This has resulted in the new phrase 'permission marketing' to enter our vocabularies. It is the 'art of asking consumers if they would like to receive a targeted email ad, promotion, or message before it appears in their in-box'. The opposite tack, sending a consumer spam and offering the option to 'Click here to opt out', annoys consumers and is not permission marketing.[84]

An analogy can be drawn between two individuals who build an interpersonal relationship and the type of relationship marketers attempt to build between the company (or its products) and the consumer. Like personal relationships between individuals who are willing to do favours for each other, relationship marketers offer loyal customers special services, discounts, increased communications, and attention beyond the core product or service, without expecting an immediate payback. However, they are hoping that, over time, they will reap the advantages of sustained and increasing transactions with a core group of loyal customers. Jaguar, for example, two years prior to opening its South Coast Jaguar dealership in the midst of the biggest luxury car market in the United States (California), started underwriting fund-raising events for local charities and targeting about 500 leading philanthropists and business executives who live in the area. According to the head of the South Coast project for Jaguar, the marketing opportunity was seen as follows:[85]

> *It's not about bricks and mortar, or even about cars. It's about the overall experience. These are people who can afford to buy all the luxury goods they want. What we have set out to do is to create a retail experience that they cannot buy—one that shows them how important they are. Everything else will flow from that.*

Although direct marketing, sales promotion, and general advertising may be used as part of a relationship marketing strategy, relationship marketing stresses long-term commitment to the individual customer. Advances in technology (such as UPC scanning equipment, and relational databases) have provided techniques that make tracking customers simpler, thus influencing the trend toward relationship marketing. Wal-Mart's database is second in size only to the database of the US government.[86] Furthermore, a recent study suggests that relationship marketing programs are more likely to succeed if the product or service is one that buyers consider to be high involvement due to its association with financial, social, or physical risk.[87]

Relationship marketing programs have been used in a wide variety of product and service categories. Many companies call their relationship programs a club, and some even charge a fee to join. Membership in a club may serve as a means to convey to customers the notions of permanence and exclusivity inherent in a committed relationship. Those firms that charge a fee (such as the American Express Platinum card) increase customers' investment in the relationship that may, in turn, lead to greater commitment to the relationship and increased usage loyalty.

Airlines and major hotel chains, in particular, use relationship marketing techniques by awarding points to frequent customers that can be used to obtain additional goods or services from the company. This kind of point system may act as an exit barrier because starting a new relationship would mean giving up the potential future value of the points and starting from ground zero with a new service provider. Moreover, companies have recently been broadening the scope of such relationship programs. For example, Table 14.7 lists the many products and services offered to participants in the Qantas Frequent Flyer Program.

TABLE 14.7 Broad-based relationship program

Airlines	Hotels continued
American Airlines	Holiday Inns
Cathay Pacific Airlines	Inter-Continental Hotels
British Airways	Sheraton Hotels & Resorts
Aer Lingus	Marriott Hotels, Resorts, and Suites
Lan Chile	Mercure
Iberia	Radisson
Alitalia	**Car Rental**
US Airways	Avis
Hotels	Hertz
All Seasons	**Other**
Best Western	Citibank
Crowne Plaza Hotels & Resorts	HomeScreen DVD rental services
Four Seasons	Travelex
Hilton International Hotels	Woolworths Ezy Rewards

Ultimately, it is to a firm's advantage to develop long-term relationships with existing customers because it is easier and less expensive to make an additional sale to an existing customer than to make a new sale to a new consumer.[88] This is why, for example, Lands' End tells consumers that if they are not 100% satisfied with their purchase, they can return it at any time, for any reason.[89] However, the effort involved in developing and maintaining a customer relationship must be weighed against the expected long-term benefits. Marketers must determine the lifetime value of a customer to ensure that the costs of obtaining, servicing, and communicating with the customer do not exceed the potential profits.[90] Recent research also suggests that a consumer's participation in a relationship marketing program is not only based on past and present experiences but also incorporates expected future usage and expected future satisfaction levels with the program.[91] Figure 14.11 portrays some of the characteristics of the relationship between the firm and the customer within the spirit of relationship marketing.

FIGURE 14.11 A portrayal of the characteristics of relationship marketing

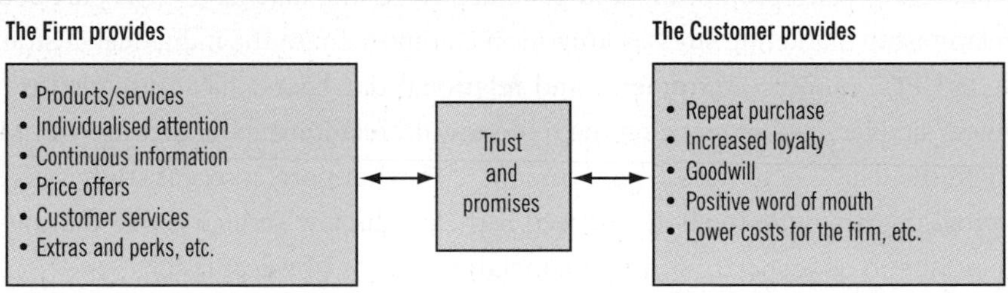

Source: In part, this portrayal was inspired by: Mary Long, Leon Schiffman, and Elaine Sherman, 'Understanding the relationships in consumer marketing relationship programs: A content analysis', in *Proceedings of the World Marketing Congress* VII-II, eds K. Grant and I. Walker (Melbourne, Australia: Academy of Marketing Science, 1995), 10/27–10/26.

CASE STUDY 14.1

Auctions

Dr Clare D'Souza, La Trobe University

Auctions are a thriving business. Christie's and Sotheby's both started selling by auction in London in the 18th century. Edward Hiscock of the National Auction Association in Overland Park, Kansas, reports that there are 11 000 full-time auctioneers in the United States and 29 000 more selling their wares on a part-time basis. Marketing through auctions is not a new phenomenon—the Ancient Romans did it all the time. In recent years, the advantages of buying and selling in a public forum are becoming apparent to a wider audience.[92] The lure of a bargain or something unique, antique or different makes auctions attractive.

There are four main types of auction design:[93]

1. *English:* Most popular of the four; also known as the ascending-bid auction. It starts with a low first bid or specified reservation price—a price below which the item will not be sold—and the auctioneer solicits increasingly higher bids.
2. *Dutch auction:* Known as the descending-bid auction. The auction here is initiated with a high price which then drops until someone decides to bid.
3. *First or discriminatory price auction:* Also known as the First Price Sealed Bid (FPSB). Bidders submit bids in sealed envelopes and the highest bid wins, paying the bid price for the good. When multiple units are auctioned at the same time, the procedure is called a discriminatory auction.
4. *Second uniform price auction:* This is also known as a Sealed Bid (SPSB) or Vickrey auction as it was first suggested by Vickrey. It is an unpopular form of auction; it involves bidders submitting sealed bids with the highest bidder winning *but only paying a price equal to the second highest bid.*

Auctions and consumer behaviour

Auctions provide solutions to an industry where demand and, particularly, supply are open to significant fluctuations. Despite intense criticisms and abuses of the system, the demand from affluent and acquisitive societies keeps auctions alive. Buying at auctions is different from buying at retail or wholesale. It is pure supply and demand, with buyers determining the selling price based on a limited supply of goods. You bid at an auction. There is no product worth a specific 'retail value'. Experienced buyers have their own bidding tactics. Auctions are known for inducing a craze ('winner's curse') that drives people to keep bidding to win, eventually, wanting to beat the other customer who outbid you.[94]

Consumers experience an 'emotional risk' when purchasing at auctions. In the consumer decision-making process, it is the intensity of the need for the product and willingness to pay that determines the price. It is the perception of the value of the product obtained at that particular time. 'Going, going, gone . . .' is the phrase for a lost opportunity for both buyer and seller. It gives buyers that urgent craving—you either buy it now or you miss getting the value. The emotional process that consumers go through during an auction is intense, especially at English (open cry) auctions where the atmosphere is vibrant with many bidders. Auctioneers prefer a large crowd as many bids make the auction exciting and interesting. They get people involved. The consumer who reaches the highest bid can suffer high levels of stress in a competitive environment. The auctioneer conducts the bids at a fast pace, giving little time for consumers to decide. And every competitor's desire to win increases the price of the product. At a live auction, everything happens very fast. Consumers normally make up their minds at the auction preview, with a reference price for the product, but they can go over their limit.

Post-purchase dissonance is experienced when pressure under competitive bidding increases the consumer's risk of suffering from the 'winner's curse'. The type of bidding used often gives bidders the opportunity to communicate within the competitive structure of an English auction. Aggressive bidding intimidates consumers and discourages competition. Open-exit bidding does not allow for jump bidding.[95] Here the auctioneer raises the price incrementally. The auction process in English and Dutch auctions creates a complex behavioural situation where consumers have to purchase in a vibrant atmosphere against their desire to win or obtain the product.

In practice, auctions account for both cheap and expensive items. For example, the most anyone has ever paid for a manuscript is $30.8 million, which was a Leonardo da Vinci manuscript purchased in 1994 by Microsoft's Bill Gates.[96] No item fetches the same amount time after time. In the case of Albert Einstein's handwritten manuscript on the theory of relativity, which failed to sell at Sotheby's auction house, time may not be absolute, though money definitely is. The problem was not that no one wanted the 72-page manuscript. In fact, bidders were willing to pay more than twice the amount paid for it in 1987. It's just that the owner wanted even more than that. Sotheby's had reportedly hoped to sell the manuscript, written in German in 1912, at somewhere between $4 million and $6 million. The manuscript sold to an American private collector in 1987 for $1.2 million because of its scientific importance.

Crown Auctions

Crown Auctions is a registered business in Australia, owned by a private family company. The business started in July 1994 and held its first auction in August 1994. The intention was to provide income-producing opportunities for the owners allied to a lifestyle environment that was flexible, subject to a minimum of external formalities and restrictions, and with minimum exposure to financial risk. The business idea was to provide a service to two markets—namely, sellers and buyers, with a commission fee being payable by each party to the provider, Crown Auctions. Thus, Crown Auctions holds the dual responsibility of that most important marketing job—trying to convince sellers as well as buyers. It is here that auction houses have to create an image to gain the attention of the sellers, thereby giving them the competitive edge.

Crown Auctions has completed in excess of 100 public auctions of antiques, collectibles and general merchandise over a 10-year period. These were held at different venues, with more than 50 onsite auctions in the vendor's house and the balance in public halls and rooms. Profitability has increased, and reputation and expertise have been established. The business has embraced the Internet and now has an email list of more than 1600 prospective buyers. The original mailing list has been discontinued because of the success of the Website. Crown Auctions is operated by the two principal shareholders with casual assistance. Crown seeks every opportunity to draw sellers. Some auction houses have found it easy to draw sellers, especially in the case of bankruptcy and debtors. Under these circumstances, auction houses in the UK put goods worth tens of thousands of pounds under the hammer every day of the week, and very often auction prices fetch a mere fraction of the real value. These sales have become a nourishing business in the case of bankrupt stocks and liquidated goods and equipment.[97]

Present situation

- *External macro environment.* Very little in the existing environment is adverse or detrimental to the operation of the business in its present form or in future preferred directions. In tight economic circumstances there will always be sellers, while buyers within the various target segments are always present. The relative weakness of the Australian dollar, particularly against Sterling/US dollar, is expected to contribute to a shortage of imported antiques from the United Kingdom and the United States in the short run. This should eventually help to push up domestic prices. There is very little effect on the industry from other macro environmental factors such as political, legal, social or green considerations. Technology creates opportunities to access sellers and buyers in different ways—for example, 'virtual' auctions are being conducted via the Internet.

In recent times, the advent of cheaper furniture alternatives and the ease with which consumers can receive favourable credit terms has had a significant effect on consumers' behaviour. This is because many consumers have committed to large fixed mortgage repayments as a result of the boom in house prices and the need to borrow significantly greater amounts. Thus the available funds to spend on furnishings etc. have been reduced. Therefore these potential buyers have opted to have furniture of a lesser quality for an interim period, until financial pressures ease. They will very likely replace this inferior furniture with antiques in the future, but the pressure is adverse on prices in the antique sector.

- *Industry environment.* The auction industry is very crowded. Many segments are not attractive to Crown Auctions for a variety of reasons and need not be considered at this time. The industry segment in which Crown operates deals with antique furniture, collectibles, period furniture, restorable and reproduction furniture. These are the preferred items. General merchandise needs to be considered because there are many times when supply of preferred items is contingent on acceptance of these general goods. The expectation by the public that auction houses are expert in all things offered for sale presents a particular problem. No one person can be an expert at everything. Commission rates charged to vendors are variable and are often used as a tool to obtain business at the expense of other auction houses. Crown Auctions does not favour cutting rates, and will do so only in special circumstances, such as the realisation of major collections.

Competition

Competition in the segment includes the following:

1. *International auction houses and their affiliates:* Sotheby's, Christie's and Phillips are all world auction houses. Their main focus is on the upper level of the market, with preferred goods categories bringing extremely high prices. This group is not seen as a threat to Crown as their clientele are generally much more wealthy and do not operate in Crown's environment.
2. *Established trade auction houses in Melbourne:* Ainger's, Long's, Leonard Joel, E&R and Eastern Suburbs are all basically trade auction houses. Their sellers and buyers are predominantly trade-associated. This group poses a threat because there is no restriction on the general public bidding at their auctions.
3. *Established auction houses in country centres:* They offer a variety of goods, and generally have a loyal and regular support base. Kittelty's in Ballarat, Woodlands in Ocean Grove, Valentine's in Bendigo and Kerley's in Geelong are all formidable competition.
4. *General auctioneers, real estate agents, stock and station agents:* They sometimes hold clearing sales and realisations that conflict with Crown. They provide competition because their terms of sale are generally less stringent (no buyer premium) with mostly unreserved prices.
5. *Other smaller auction houses:* Those that operate in direct competition with Crown Auctions include Bragg's, Roycrofts, Paters and Manton's. In the last 18 months more smaller competitors have entered the market. The effect is not expected to be detrimental. In fact, Crown has established a working relationship with some of these firms and is now participating in an ad hoc cross-selling arrangement. This is not a formal agreement to attempt to influence either the buyer or seller markets, but rather a way to put each firm before those markets. Really, it is seen as a method to increase the size of the pie, not the slice. These businesses conduct auctions on Sundays, which is the day preferred by Crown. They have a similar range of goods on offer and they target the same buying groups. Lastly, auctions on the Internet provide a variety of products for consumers.

Consumer segments

1. *Private buyers:* This segment of the market perceives the value obtained by buying at auctions. Frank Ward, owner of Crown Auctions, has identified that there is no defined consumer within the set market. Their motivations to purchase include:

- the need to buy a specific item;
- the need to be seen as wealthy enough to buy in company with peers;
- the opportunity to buy something unusual—the exotic or erotic;
- an inability to say 'no';
- to bid for winning;
- the perception of receiving value, even if the item is not really wanted—a bargain;
- the 'emotion' of an auction, buying for the fun of it.

Buyers in this category will pay more for goods than any others except serious collectors (for certain items only).

2. *Serious collectors:* This group has one common attribute: they are passionate about collecting in their chosen field. If they can acquire something they do not have in their collection, their usual reaction is to buy at almost any price. However, they will not buy in quantity and they will not buy often. Their focus is on their collection only.
3. *Regular auction-goers:* This group of potential buyers attends auctions almost as a way of life. They get satisfaction from attending, without necessarily buying.
4. *Trade buyers:* Motivation is to make money. They do this by buying and then selling on at a profit. This group of buyers is really needed. They push prices up to trade level and motivate private buyers to pay more. They can, in effect, set the market price for goods. Occasionally, they will pay excessive prices for items that may complement their own stock, thus helping them to create a sale.
5. *Furniture restorers, amateur and professional:* As the title implies, this group buys furniture that needs and is capable of restoration. They always try to buy as cheaply as possible. After restoration, the goods are resold at a higher price.
6. *Commission buyers:* These are professional buyers who buy on behalf of principals and who charge fees to those principals. It is good to have them attend inspections, as they are generally specialists and know a lot about the needs of a number of potential buyers. They act as referral agents to their principals.

Crown Auctions' intention is to target private buyers, trade buyers and restorers during the next 12 months. They seek to expand the business and will actively pursue several options.

Note: The author gratefully acknowledges Mr Frank Ward, the owner of Crown Auctions, PO Box 538, Rosanna, Victoria, Australia, for all the information, support and encouragement he has provided.

Case Study Questions

1. Consumers have both innate and acquired needs. How are consumers motivated to buy at an auction?
2. Price is an indicator of product quality, perception and value. At auctions, bidders bid at much higher prices for some products. Discuss.
3. What suggestions could you provide to help Crown Auctions increase their profits in the next three years?
4. Auctions are the way capitalism was supposed to be—with buyers determining the selling price (also known as the '*winner's curse*'). Comment on this statement.

Summary

The consumer's decision to purchase or reject a product is the moment of final truth for the marketer. It signifies whether the marketing strategy has been wise, insightful and effective, or whether it was poorly planned and missed the mark. Thus, marketers are particularly interested in the consumer's decision-making process. For a consumer to make a decision, more than one alternative must be available. (The decision not to buy is also an alternative.)

Theories of consumer decision making vary, depending on the researcher's assumptions about the nature of human kind. The various consumer decision-making models (economic, passive, cognitive and emotional) depict consumers and their decision-making processes in distinctly different ways.

A simple consumer decision-making model ties together the psychological, social and cultural concepts examined in Parts II and III into an easily understood framework. This decision model has three sets of variables: input variables, process variables and output variables.

Input variables that affect the decision-making process include commercial marketing efforts as well as non-commercial influences from the consumer's sociocultural environment. The decision process variables are influenced by the consumer's psychological field, including the evoked set (i.e. the brands in a particular product category considered in making a purchase choice), level of perceived risk and risk-reduction strategies. Taken as a whole, the psychological field influences the consumer's recognition of a need, the pre-purchase search for information and the evaluation of alternatives.

The output phase of the model includes the actual purchase (either trial or repeat purchase) and post-purchase evaluation. Both pre-purchase and post-purchase evaluations feed back in the form of experience into the consumer's psychological field, and serve to influence future decision processing.

Consumer behaviour is not just about making the decision or the act of purchasing; it also includes a full range of experiences associated with using or consuming the product or service. It includes the sense of pleasure and satisfaction derived from possessing or collecting things. The outputs of consumption are changes in feelings, moods or attitudes; reinforcement of lifestyles; an enhanced sense of self; satisfaction of a consumer-related need; belonging to a group; and entertaining oneself.

Discussion questions

1. Compare and contrast the economic, passive, cognitive and emotional models of consumer decision making.
2. What kinds of marketing and sociocultural inputs would influence the purchase of:
   (a) a TV with a built-in VCR;
   (b) a concentrated liquid laundry detergent;
   (c) fat-reduced ice-cream; and
   (d) pay television?
   Explain your answers.
3. Define extensive problem solving, limited problem solving, and routinised response behaviour. What are the differences between the three decision-making approaches? What type of decision process would you expect most consumers to follow in their first purchase of a new product or brand in each of the following areas?
   (a) chewing gum
   (b) sugar
   (c) men's aftershave lotion
   (d) carpeting
   (e) paper towels
   (f) mobile telephone
   (g) new bank account
   (h) luxury car.
   Explain your answers.
4. (a) Identify three different products that you believe require reasonably intensive pre-purchase search by a consumer. Then, using Box 14.1 as a guide, identify the specific characteristics of these products that make intensive pre-purchase search likely.
   (b) For each of the products you have listed, identify the perceived risks that a consumer is likely to experience prior to purchase. Discuss how the marketers of these products can reduce these perceived risks.
5. Let's assume that this coming winter you are planning to spend a month touring Europe and are therefore in need of a good video camera.
   (a) Develop a list of product attributes that you will use as the purchase criteria in evaluating various video cameras—such as format and picture resolution.

(b) Distinguish the differences that would occur in your decision process if you were to employ compensatory versus non-compensatory decision rules.

6 How can a marketer of very light, very powerful laptop computers use its knowledge of customers' expectations in designing a marketing strategy?

7. How do consumers reduce post-purchase dissonance? How can marketers provide positive reinforcement to consumers after the purchase in order to reduce their dissonance?

8. The Gillette Company, which produces the highly successful Sensor shaving blade, has recently introduced a clear gel antiperspirant and deodorant for men. Identify the perceived risks associated with the purchase of this new product and outline a strategy designed to reduce these perceived risks during the product's introduction.

9. Albert Einstein once wrote that 'the whole of science is nothing more than a refinement of everyday thinking'. Do you think this statement applies to the development of the consumer decision-making model presented in Figure 14.2?

Exercises

1. Find two print advertisements: one that illustrates the cognitive model of consumer decision making and one that illustrates the emotional model. Explain your choices. In your view, why did the marketers choose the approaches depicted in the advertisements?
2. Describe the need recognition process that took place before you purchased your last can of soft drink. How did it differ from the process that preceded the purchase of a new pair of joggers? What role, if any, did advertising play in your need recognition?
3. List the places that you considered when choosing which TAFE or university to attend, and the criteria you used to evaluate them. Describe how you acquired information on the different places about the different attributes that were important to you and how you made your decision. Be sure to specify whether you used compensatory or non-compensatory decision rules.
4. Select *one* of the following product categories:
   - compact disc players
   - fast-food restaurants
   - shampoo

   (a) Write down the brands that constitute your evoked set.

   (b) Identify brands that are not part of your evoked set.

   (c) Discuss how the brands included in your evoked set differ from those that are not included, in terms of important attributes.
5. Select a newspaper or magazine advertisement that attempts:

   (a) to provide the consumer with a decision strategy to follow in making a purchase decision; or

   (b) to reduce the perceived risk(s) associated with a purchase.

Key terms

affect referral rule *(p. 485)*
compensatory decision rule *(p. 482)*
conjunctive decision rule *(p. 483)*
consumer decision rules *(p. 482)*
consumption process *(p. 493)*
disjunctive rule *(p. 484)*
elimination-by-aspects rule *(p. 484)*
evaluation of alternatives *(p. 474)*
evoked set *(p. 478)*
extensive problem solving *(p. 473)*
heuristics *(p. 470)*
inept set *(p. 478)*
inert set *(p. 479)*
information overload *(p. 470)*
lexicographic decision rule *(p. 484)*
limited problem solving *(p. 473)*
marketing activities *(p. 473)*
need recognition *(p. 474)*
non-compensatory decision rules *(p. 483)*
perceived risk *(p. 476)*
post-purchase cognitive dissonance *(p. 491)*
post-purchase evaluation *(p. 489)*
pre-purchase search *(p. 476)*
psychological field *(p. 474)*
purchase behaviour *(p. 489)*
routinised response behaviour *(p. 473)*
self-gifts *(p. 494)*
sociocultural environment *(p. 474)*

Endnotes

1. Itamar Simonson, 'Shoppers' easily influenced choices', *New York Times*, 6 November 1994, p. 11.
2. There are several approaches to such an issue. See Jagdish N. Sheth, Bruce I. Newman and Barbara L. Gross, 'Why we buy what we buy: A theory of consumption values', *Journal of Business Research*, 22, 1991, pp. 159–170.
3. Herbert A. Simon, *Administrative Behavior*, 2nd edn (New York: Free Press, 1965), p. 40.
4. James G. March and Herbert A. Simon, *Organizations* (New York: John Wiley, 1958), pp. 140–141.
5. Michael A. Jones, Philip J. Trocchia and David L. Mothersbaugh, 'Non-economic motivations for price haggling: An exploratory study', in *Advances in Consumer Research,* 24, eds Merrie Brucks and Deborah J. MacInnis (Provo, UT: Association for Consumer Research, 1997), pp. 388–391.
6. Richard W. Olskavsky, 'Towards a more comprehensive theory of choice', in Elizabeth C. Hirschman and Morris B. Holbrook (eds), *Advances in Consumer Research*, 12 (Provo, UT: Association for Consumer Research, 1985), pp. 465–470.
7. Herbert A. Simon, 'A behavioral model of rational choice', *Quarterly Journal of Economics*, 69, 1955, pp. 99–118.
8. Richard P. Bagozzi and Utpal Dholakia, 'Goal setting and goal striving in consumer behavior', *Journal of Marketing*, 63, 1999, pp. 19–32.
9. Russell W. Belk, 'The role of possessions in constructing and maintaining a sense of past', in Marvin E. Goldberg, Gerald Gorn and Richard W. Pollay (eds), *Advances in Consumer Research*, 17 (Provo, UT: Association for Consumer Research, 1990), pp. 669–676.
10. For an example of research that focuses on emotional advertising, see Marian Friestad and Esther Thorson, 'Emotion-eliciting advertising: Effects on long-term memory and judgment', in Richard J. Lutz (ed.), *Advances in Consumer Research*, 13 (Provo, UT: Association for Consumer Research, 1986), pp. 111–115; and Rajeev Batra and Douglas M. Stayman, 'The role of mood in advertising effectiveness', *Journal of Consumer Research*, 17, 1990, pp. 203–214.
11. Meryl Paula Gardner, 'Mood states and consumer behavior: A critical review', *Journal of Consumer Research*, 12, 1985, pp. 281–300; and Robert A. Peterson and Matthew Sauber, 'A mood scale for survey research', in Patrick E. Murphy et al. (eds), *1983 AMA Educators' Proceedings* (Chicago: American Marketing Association, 1983), pp. 409–414.
12. Barry J. Babin, William R. Darden and Mitch Griffin, 'Some comments on the role of emotions in consumer behavior', in Robert P. Leone, V. Kumor et al. (eds), *1992 AMA Educators' Proceedings* (Chicago: American Marketing Association, 1992), pp. 130–139; and Patricia A. Knowles, Stephen J. Grove and W. Jeffrey Burroughs, 'An experimental examination of mood effects on retrieval and evaluation of advertisement and brand information', *Journal of the Academy of Marketing Science*, 12, 1993, pp. 135–142.
13. Richard P. Bagozzi, Mahesh Gopinath and Prashanth U. Nyer, 'The role of emotions in marketing', *Academy of Marketing Science Journal*, 27(2), Spring 1999, pp. 184–206; and Gardner, 'Mood states and consumer behavior'.
14. Gardner, op. cit.
15. Ruth Belk Smith and Elaine Sherman, 'Effects of store image and mood on consumer behavior: A theoretical and empirical analysis', in Leigh McAlister and Michael L. Rothschild (eds), *Advances in Consumer Research*, 20 (Provo, UT: Association for Consumer Research, 1993), p. 631.
16. Knowles, Grove and Burroughs, op. cit.
17. Bagozzi et al., 'The role of emotions in marketing'.
18. John A. Howard and Jagdish N. Sheth, *The Theory of Buyer Behavior* (New York: Wiley, 1969), pp. 46–47. See also John Howard, *Consumer Behavior in Marketing Strategy* (Englewood Cliffs, NJ: Prentice Hall, 1989).
19. Neil Shoebridge, 'The metrosexual myth', *Business Review Weekly*, 18–24 September 2003, p. 63.
20. Gordon C. Bruner II, 'The effect of problem-recognition style on information seeking', *Journal of the Academy of Marketing Science*, 15(1), 1987, pp. 33–41.
21. Gordon C. Bruner II and Richard J. Pomazal, 'Problem recognition: The crucial first stage of the consumer decision process', *Journal of Consumer Marketing*, 5, 1969, pp. 53–63.
22. Sharon E. Beatty and Scott M. Smith, 'External search effort: An investigation across several product categories', *Journal of Consumer Research*, 14, 1987, pp. 83–95.
23. James R. Bettman and C. Won Park, 'Effects of prior knowledge and experience on consumer decision

processes: A protocol analysis', *Journal of Consumer Research*, 7, 1980, pp. 234–248.

24. Rohit Deshpande and Wayne D. Hoyer, 'Consumer decision making: Strategies, cognitive effort and perceived risk', in Patrick E. Murphy et al. (eds), *1983 AMA Educators' Proceedings*, op. cit., pp. 88–91. See also Wayne D. Hoyer, 'An examination of consumer decision making for a common repeat purchase product', *Journal of Consumer Research*, 11, 1984, pp. 822–829; and Keith B. Murray, 'A test of services marketing theory: Consumer information acquisition activities', *Journal of Marketing*, 55(1), 1991, pp. 10–25.
25. N. Srinivasan and Brian T. Ratchford, 'An empirical test of a model of external search for automobiles', *Journal of Consumer Research*, 18, September 1991, pp. 233–242.
26. Matthew Klein, 'He shops, she shops', *American Demographics*, March 1998, pp. 34–35.
27. Haim Mano and Michael T. Elliott, 'Smart shopping: The origins and consequences of price savings', *Advances in Consumer Research*, eds Brucks and MacInnis, pp. 504–510.
28. James R. Bettman and C. Won Park, 'Effects of prior knowledge and experience on consumer decision processes: A protocol analysis', pp. 234–248.
29. Rohit Deshpande and Wayne D. Hoyer, 'Consumer decision making: Strategies, cognitive effort and perceived risk', in Patrick E. Murphy et al. (eds), *1983 AMA Educators' Proceedings*, op. cit., pp. 89–91. See also Wayne D. Hoyer, pp. 822–829; and Keith B. Murray, 'A test of services marketing theory: Consumer information acquisition activities', pp. 10–25.
30. James R. Bettman, *An Information Processing Theory of Consumer Choice* (Reading, MA: Addison-Wesley Publishing Company, 1979); and M.J. Culnan, 'Environmental scanning: The effects of task complexity and source accessibility on information gathering behaviour', *Decision Sciences*, 14, 1983, pp. 314–326.
31. Krizner, 'Individuality extends into manufacturing', *Frontline Solutions*, 2(3), March 2001, pp. 1, 18.
32. Dale F. Duhan, Scott D. Johnson, James B. Wilcox, Gilbert D. Harrell, 'Influences on consumer use of word-of-mouth recommendation sources', *Journal of the Academy of Marketing Science*, 25(4), 1997, pp. 283–295.
33. Darlene B. Hannah and Brian Sternthal, 'Detecting and explaining the sleeper effect', *Journal of Consumer Research*, 11, September 1984, pp. 632–642.
34. Ayn E. Crowley and John H. Williams, 'An information theoretic approach to understanding the consideration set/awareness set proportion', in Rebecca H. Holman and Michael R. Solomon (eds), *Advances in Consumer Research*, 18 (Provo, UT: Association for Consumer Research, 1991), pp. 780–787; John R. Hauser and Wernerfelt Birger, 'An evaluation cost model of consideration sets', *Journal of Consumer Research*, 19, 1990, pp. 393–408; and Prakash Nedungadi, 'Recall and consumer consideration sets: Influencing choice without altering brand evaluations', *Journal of Consumer Research*, 17, 1990, pp. 263–276.
35. Michael D. Johnson and Donald R. Lehmann, 'Consumer experience and consideration sets for brands and product categories', *Advances in Consumer Research*, eds Brucks and MacInnis, pp. 295–300.
36. Thomas T. Semon, 'Too much choice not ideal, but not enough choice likely worse', *Marketing News*, 5 November 2001, p. 9.
37. 'Drawing a bead on car buyers for the nineties', *Brandweek*, 14 September 1992, pp. 17, 20.
38. Gita Venkataramani Johar, Kamel Jedidi, and Jacob Jacoby, 'A varying-parameter averaging model on on-line brand evaluations', *Journal of Consumer Research*, 24, September 1997, pp. 232–247.
39. Sankar Sen and Eric J. Johnson, 'Mere-possession effects without possession in consumer choice', *Journal of Consumer Research*, 24, June 1997, pp. 105–117.
40. Pinson, C.R. and Roberto, E.L., 'Consumer behaviour and the marketing activities of firms', *Handbook of Economic Psychology*, eds W.F van Raaij, G.M van Veldhoven and K-E Warneryd (Dordrecht: Kluwer, 1988), pp. 294–331.
41. Stacy L. Wood, 'Remote purchase environments: The influence of return policy leniency on two-stage decision processes', *Journal of Marketing Research*, 38(2), May 2001, pp. 157–169.
42. Laurie Peterson, 'The strategic shopper', *Adweek's Marketing Week*, 30 March 1992, pp. 18–20.
43. Bettman and Park, op. cit.
44. Sandra J. Burke, 'The effects of missing information on decision strategy selection', Marvin E. Goldberg, Gerald Gorn and Richard W. Pollay (eds), *Advances in Consumer Research*, 17 (Provo, UT: Association for Consumer Research, 1990), pp. 250–256.
45. Sarah Fisher Gardial and David W. Schumann, 'In search of the elusive consumer inference', Goldberg et al. (eds), op. cit., pp. 283–287. See also Burke, ibid.
46. Ran Kivetz and Itamar Simonson, 'The effects of incomplete information on consumer choice', *Journal of*

Marketing Research, 37(4), November 2000, pp. 427–448.

47. Michael D. Johnson, 'Consumer choice strategy for comparing non-comparable alternatives', *Journal of Consumer Research*, 11, 1984, pp. 741–750.
48. Lan Xia, 'Consumer choice strategies and choice confidence in the electronic environment', *1999 AMA Educators Proceedings*, 10, eds Stephen P. Brown and D. Sudharshan (Chicago: American Marketing Association, 1999), pp. 270–277.
49. Carey Goldberg, 'Choosing the joys of a simplified life', *New York Times*, 21 September 1995, pp. C1, C9.
50. Ibid.
51. Nancy Spears, 'The time pressured consumer and deal proneness: Theoretical framework and empirical evidence', *2000 AMA Winter Educators' Conference*, 11, eds John P. Workman and William D. Perreault (Chicago: American Marketing Association, 2000), pp. 35–40.
52. Barry L. Bayus, 'The consumer durable replacement buyer', *Journal of Marketing*, 55, January 1991, pp. 42–51.
53. Calmetta Coleman, 'Debit cards look to give credit cards a run for consumers' money', *Wall Street Journal*, 3 December 2001, pp. B1, B4; 'Understanding debit cards', <www.aarp.org/confacts/money/debitcards/html>; and 'Debit cards', <www.mcvisa.com/debi.html>.
54. Garnaut, J., 'The cheque's no longer in the mail, we're using credit instead', *Sydney Morning Herald*, 22 July 2003, p. 3.
55. 'Credit card debt hits record high', <www.theage.com.au/articles/2004/04/01/1080544618371.html>.
56. Diane M. Phillips, Jerry C. Olson, and Hans Baumgartner, 'Consumption visions in consumer decision making', *Advances in Consumer Research*, 22, eds Frank R. Kardes and Mita Sujan (Provo, UT: Association for Consumer Research, 1995), p. 280.
57. Ibid., pp. 280–284.
58. Diane M. Phillips, 'Anticipating the future: The role of consumption visions in consumer behavior', *Advances in Consumer Research*, 23, eds Kim P. Corfman and John G. Lynch, Jr (Provo, UT: Association for Consumer Research, 1996), pp. 70–75.
59. Baba Shiv and Joel Huber, 'The impact of anticipating satisfaction on consumer choice', *Journal of Consumer Research*, 27(2), September 2000, pp. 202–216.
60. Emily Booth, 'Getting inside a shopper's mind', *Marketing* (U.K.), 3 June 1999, p. 33.
61. Robert A. Peterson, Sridhar Balasubramanian and Bart J. Bronnenberg, 'Exploring the implications of the Internet for consumer marketing', *Journal of the Academy of Marketing Sciences*, 25, 1997, pp. 329–346.
62. R.E. Milliman, 'Using background music to affect the behaviour of supermarket shoppers', *Journal of Marketing*, 46, 1982, pp. 86–91.
63. Charles S. Areni and David Kim, 'The influence of background music on shopping behavior: Classical versus top-forty music in a wine store', in Leigh McAllister and Michael L. Rothschild (eds), *Advances in Consumer Research*, 20 (Provo, UT: Association for Consumer Research, 1993), pp. 336–340.
64. A. Mehrabian and James A. Russell, *An Approach to Environmental Psychology* (Cambridge MA: MIT Press, 1974).
65. Babin, op. cit.
66. Robert J. Donovan, John R. Rossiter, Gilian Marcoolyn and Andrew Nesdale, 'Store atmosphere and purchasing behaviour', *Journal of Retailing*, 70(3), 1994, pp. 283–294.
67. S. Milgram, 'The experience of living in cities', *Science*, 167, 1970, pp. 1464–1468.
68. Linda K. Anglin, J. Kathleen Stuenkel and Lawrence R. Lepisto, 'The effect of stress on price sensitivity and comparison shopping', in Chris T. Allen and Deborah Roedder John (eds), *Advances in Consumer Research*, 21 (Provo, UT: Association for Consumer Research, 1994), pp. 126–131.
69. Kare Sandvik, Kjell Gronhaug, and Frank Lindberg, 'Routes to customer retention: The importance of customer satisfaction, performance quality, brand reputation and customer knowledge', in *AMA Winter Conference*, eds Debbie Thorne LeClair and Michael Hartline (Chicago: American Marketing Association, 1997), pp. 211–217.
70. Jagdip Singh and Robert E. Widing II, 'What occurs once consumers complain? A theoretical model for understanding satisfaction/dissatisfaction outcomes of complaint responses', *European Journal of Marketing*, 25(5), 1991, pp. 30–47
71. Ibid.
72. Kathleen M. Rassuli and Gilbert D. Harrell, 'A new perspective on choice', in Goldberg et al. (eds), op. cit., pp. 737–744.
73. Ibid.
74. Russell W. Belk, 'The role of possessions in constructing and maintaining a sense of past', in Goldberg et al. (eds), op. cit., pp. 669–676.

75. Stacey Menzel Baker and Patricia F. Kennedy, 'Death by nostalgia: A diagnosis of context-specific cases', *Advances in Consumer Research*, 21, eds Chris T. Allen and Deborah Roedder John (Provo, UT: Association for Consumer Research, 1994), pp. 169–174.
76. Linda L. Price, Eric J. Arnould and Carolyn Folkman Curasi, 'Older consumers' disposition of special possessions', *Journal of Consumer Research*, 27(2), September 2001, pp. 179–201.
77. David Glen Mick and Mitchelle DeMoss, 'To me from me: A descriptive phenomenology of self-gifts', in Goldberg et al. (eds), op. cit., pp. 677–682.
78. Steve Schriver, 'Consumer loyalty: Going, going…', *American Demographics*, September 1997, pp. 201–223.
79. Robert Bryce, 'Here's a course in personal finance 101, the hard way', *New York Times*, 30 April 1995, p. F11.
80. Susan M. Lloyd, 'Toward understanding relationship marketing from the consumer's perspective: What relationships are and why consumers choose to enter them', in *2000 AMA Educators' Proceedings*, 11, eds Gregory T. Gundlach and Patrick E. Murphy (Chicago: American Marketing Association, 2000), pp. 12–20; Leonard L. Berry, 'Relationship marketing of services—Growing interest, emerging perspectives', *Journal of the Academy of Marketing Science*, 23 (Fall 1995), pp. 236–245; and Mary Jo Bitner, 'Building service relationships: It's all about promises', *Journal of the Academy of Marketing Science*, 23 (Fall 1995), pp. 246–251.
81. Mary Long, Leon Schiffman and Elaine Sherman, 'Understanding the relationships in consumer marketing relationship programs: A content analysis', *Proceedings of the World Marketing Congress* VII-II, eds K. Grant and I. Walker (Melbourne, Australia: Academy of Marketing Science, 1995), 10/27–10/32.
82. Patricia A. Norberg, 'Relationship issues in business-to-consumer markets', *2001 AMA Educators' Proceedings*, 12, eds Greg W. Marshall and Stephen J. Grove (Chicago: American Marketing Association, 2001), pp. 381–390.
83. Marc E. Duncan, 'The Internet and relationship marketing: A framework for application', *2000 AMA Winter Educators' Conference*, 11, eds John P. Workman and William D. Perreault (Chicago: American Marketing Association, 2000), pp. 72–82.
84. Lauren Barack, 'Pretty, pretty, please', *Business*, 2.0, April 2000, pp. 176–180.
85. John O'Dell, 'Advertising & marketing; Jaguar is talking relationships; luxury car maker is wooing south O.C.'s elite before new dealership is built', *The Los Angeles Times*, 10 June 1999, p. 1.
86. Emily Nelson, 'Why Wal-Mart sings, "Yes, we have bananas"', *Wall Street Journal*, 6 October 1998, pp. B1, B4.
87. Mary Ellen Gordon and Kim McKeage, 'Relationship marketing effectiveness: Differences between women in New Zealand and the United States', in *1997 AMA Educators' Proceedings*, eds William M. Pride and G. Tomas M. Hult (Chicago: American Marketing Association, 1997), pp. 117–122.
88. Jagdish N. Sheth and Atul Parvatiyar, 'Relationship marketing in consumer marketing: Antecedents and consequences', *Journal of the Academy of Marketing Science*, 23, Fall 1995, pp. 255–271.
89. Barbara B. Stern, 'Advertising intimacy: Relationship marketing and the services consumer', *Journal of Advertising*, 26, Winter 1997, pp. 7–19.
90. Robert F. Dwyer, 'Customer lifetime valuation to support marketing decision making', *Journal of Direct Marketing*, 3, 1989, pp. 8–15; Jonathan R. Copulsky and Michael J. Wolf, 'Relationship marketing: Positioning for the future', *The Journal of Business Strategy*, July–August 1990, pp. 16–20; and Philip Kotler, 'Marketing's new paradigm: What's really happening out there', *Planning Review*, September–October 1992, pp. 50–52.
91. Katherine N. Lemon, Tiffany Barnett White, and Russell S. Winer, 'Dynamic customer relationship management: Incorporating future considerations into the service retention decision', *Journal of Marketing*, 66(1), January 2002, pp. 1–14.
92. A. Phaneuf, 'Going once, going twice', *Sales and Marketing Management*, 147(10), October 1995, pp. 136–137.
93. R. Feldman and R. Mehra, 'Auctions: A sampling of techniques', *Finance and Development*, 30(3), 1993, pp. 32–35.
94. J. Mardesich, 'Onsale takes auction gavel electronic', *Computer Reseller News* (691): 2, 32, 8 July 1996.
95. P. Migrom and R. Weber, 'A theory of auctions and competitive bidding', *Econometrica*, 50, pp. 1089–1122.
96. Associated Press and Reuters (1996) contributed to this report—*Einstein's manuscript goes unsold,* 17 March 1996—Cable News Network Inc. (author unknown).
97. P. Robson, 'Buying at auction: Under the hammer', *Purchasing and Supply Management*, July/August 1993, pp. 32–33.

CHAPTER 15

Consumer influence and diffusion of innovations

I wouldn't put just anything in my body.

That's why I always think twice about what I do.

Some decisions are hard to make.

But in the end, you've got to do what's right for you.

Panadol

It's my choice

ALWAYS READ THE LABEL. Use only as directed. For the temporary relief of pain and fever. Incorrect use could be harmful. Consult your health care professional if symptoms persist. Panadol is a Registered Trade Mark of the GlaxoSmithKline group of companies. ASMI/8747/1-07/03 GSK0867/YOG

Source: **Courtesy of GlaxoSmithKline Australia Pty Ltd.**

This chapter deals with two related issues—the informal influence that others have on consumers' behaviour and the dynamic processes that impact consumers' acceptance of new products and services. In the first part of this chapter, we examine the nature and dynamics of the influence that friends, neighbours, and acquaintances have on our consumer-related decisions. We will also consider the personality and motivations of those who influence (opinion leaders) and those who are influenced (opinion receivers). In the second part, we explore factors that encourage and discourage acceptance (or rejection) of new products and services. For consumers, new products and services may represent increased opportunities to satisfy individual and social needs. For the marketer, they provide an important mechanism for keeping the firm competitive and profitable.

What is opinion leadership?

Opinion leadership (or word-of-mouth communications) is the process by which one person (the opinion leader) informally influences the actions or attitudes of others. The key characteristic of the influence is that it is interpersonal and informal and takes place between two or more people, none of whom represents a commercial selling source that would gain directly from the sale of something. Word-of-mouth implies personal communication, through direct contact, or through a medium such as the telephone, email or a chat group. This communication process is likely, at times, to also be reinforced by non-verbal observations of the appearance and behaviour of others. In Chapter 8, we studied the influence reference groups have on consumers. The critical difference is that opinion leadership involves contact with people as individuals, not as the representative of a larger social group.

One of the parties in a word-of-mouth encounter usually offers advice or information about a product or service, such as which of several brands is best or how a particular product may be used. This person, the **opinion leader**, may become an opinion receiver when another product or service is brought up as part of the overall discussion. Individuals who actively seek information and advice about products sometimes are called **opinion seekers**. For purposes of simplicity, the terms **opinion receiver** and **opinion recipient** will be used interchangeably in the following discussion to identify both those who actively seek product information from others and those who receive unsolicited information. Simple examples of opinion leadership at work include the following:

1. during a tea break, someone talks about the movie he saw last night and recommends it;
2. a person shows photographs of his recent Kakadu holiday to a friend, and the friend suggests that using a polarising filter might produce better pictures of outdoor scenery;
3. a family decides that they would like a swimming pool for their backyard and ask neighbours who have pools which pool construction company they should call.

Most studies of opinion leadership are concerned with the measurement of behavioural impact that opinion leaders have on the consumption habits of others. Available research, for example, suggests that 'influentials' or opinion leaders are almost four times more likely than others to be asked about political and government issues, as well as how to handle teens; three times more likely to be asked about computers or investments; and twice as likely to be asked about health issues and restaurants.[1] Research also suggests that when an information seeker feels that he or she knows little about a particular product or service, a 'strong-tie source' will be sought (such as a friend or family member), but when the consumer has some prior knowledge of the subject area, a 'weak-tie source' is acceptable (acquaintances or strangers).[2]

With the proliferation of mobile phone usage and email (and the invention of combination devices like PDAs and Web-capable mobile phones), many people find themselves, by choice, to be 'always' available to friends, family, and business associates. Along with the explosion of Web-capable mobile phones is the creation of the 'thumb generation,' known in Japan as *oya yubi sedai*. Young people in Japan learn to send text messages from the mobile phones by using their thumbs to type in text, and some Japanese TV stations have even held thumbing speed contests. This is a natural extension of the thumb usage learned from using handheld computer games.[3] Picture and video phones have extended the contactibility of people, leading to informal groups of opinion leaders influencing each other about such everyday matters as where to eat and what movies to see.

VIRAL MARKETING

Viral marketing 'describes any strategy that encourages individuals to pass on a marketing message to others, creating the potential for exponential growth in the message's exposure and influence'.[4] Viral marketing is the marriage of word-of-mouth and electronic communication such as email, SMS or blog sites on the Web.[5] This type of marketing is named 'viral' because it allows a message to spread like a virus. Famous examples spreading around the world in this way were ads for John West Salmon and the Ford 'Evil Ka' ad in the UK. In the Australian market, the outrageous Toohey's Extra Dry 'tongue' ad and the controversial Lovable campaign (see Chapter 8) attempted to exploit this technique. Both released versions of their ads for downloading from the Net. One of the original users of this technique was Microsoft's Hotmail. By giving away free email addresses and services, and by attaching a tag to the bottom of every message that read 'Get your private, free email at http://www.hotmail.com', every time a Hotmail user sent an email, there was a good chance that the receiver of the email would consider signing up for a free Hotmail account. With estimated 100 million instant messenger (IM) users in 2004, companies are looking at ways to combine it with mobile phone and work-related uses to enhance the contactability of personal contacts.[6]

Dynamics of the opinion leadership process

The opinion leadership process is a very dynamic and powerful consumer force. As informal communication sources, opinion leaders are remarkably effective at influencing consumers in their product-related decisions. Some of the reasons for the effectiveness of opinion leaders are discussed below.

CREDIBILITY

Opinion leaders are highly credible sources of information because they are usually perceived as being objective concerning the product or service information or advice they dispense. Their intentions are perceived as being in the best interests of the opinion recipients, because they receive no compensation for the advice and apparently have no axe to grind. Because opinion leaders often base their product comments on firsthand experience, their advice reduces the perceived risk for opinion receivers and alleviates anxiety inherent in buying new products. In the US, it is estimated that the average person is exposed to anywhere from 200 to 1000 sales communications a day, but he or she is thousands of times more likely to act on the basis of a friend's or colleague's recommendation. Whereas the advertiser has a vested interest in the message being advertised, the opinion leader offers advice that does not have a commercial motive.[7]

POSITIVE AND NEGATIVE PRODUCT INFORMATION

Information provided by marketers is typically favourable to the product and/or brand. Thus, the very fact that opinion leaders provide both favourable and unfavourable information adds to their credibility. Consumers are especially likely to note such information and to avoid products or brands that receive negative evaluations. Over the years, a number of motion pictures have failed due to negative 'buzz' about the film, and one study

TABLE 15.1 **The factors leading to negative word-of-mouth behaviour**

Type of factor	Specific issues
Individual	Personality factors: Self-confidence Sociability Social responsibility
Attitudinal	Negative attitude to complaining Negative attitude to business in general Negative perceived reputation of firm
Involvement	Product involvement Purchase decision involvement
Situational	Proximity of others

Source: **Based on Geok Theng Lau and Sophia Ng, 'Individual and situational factors influencing negative word-of-mouth behaviour', *Revue Canadienne des Sciences de l'Administration* (Montreal), 18, September 2001, p. 168.**

found that negative word-of-mouth about a food product retarded sales more than twice as much as positive word-of-mouth promoted sales.[8] Consumers, it turns out, are generally three to ten times more likely to share a negative experience than a positive one.[9] Table 15.1 shows several factors which can contribute to negative word-of-mouth.

INFORMATION AND ADVICE

Opinion leaders are the source of both information and advice. They may simply talk about their experience with a product, relate what they know about a product, or, more aggressively, advise others to buy or to avoid a specific product. The kinds of product or service information that opinion leaders are likely to transmit during a conversation include the following:

1. Which of several brands is best: 'In my opinion, when you consider cost, Sanyo offers the best value in TV.'
2. How to best use a specific product: 'I find that my photos look best when I use genuine Kodak processing.'
3. Where to shop: 'When David Jones has a sale, the values are terrific.'
4. Who provides the best service: 'Over the last five years, I've had my car serviced at Ultratune, and I've never had a problem.'

Many of the messages being sent and received these days deal with movies, restaurants, shopping, computer games, and other areas of interest to young adults—word-of-mouth communication in the form of telephone or email.

OPINION LEADERSHIP IS CATEGORY SPECIFIC

Opinion leadership tends to be category specific; that is, opinion leaders often 'specialise' in certain product categories about which they offer information and advice. When other product categories are discussed, however, they are just as likely to reverse their roles and become opinion receivers. A person who is considered particularly knowledgeable about boats may be an opinion leader in terms of this subject, yet when it comes to purchasing a home theatre system, the same person may seek advice from someone else—perhaps even from someone who has formerly sought his advice on boats.

OPINION LEADERSHIP IS A TWO-WAY STREET

As the preceding example suggests, consumers who are opinion leaders in one product-related situation may become opinion receivers in another situation, even sometimes regarding the same product. A new home-owner thinking about buying a lawnmower may seek advice from other people in order to reduce his indecision about which brand to buy. Once the lawnmower has been bought, however, he may experience post-purchase dissonance and have a compelling need to talk favourably about the purchase to other people to confirm the correctness of his own choice. In the first instance, he is an opinion receiver (seeker); in the second, he assumes the role of opinion leader. An opinion leader may also be influenced by an opinion receiver as the result of a product-related conversation. For example, a person may tell a friend about the lawnmower, and, in response to comments from the opinion receiver, come to realise that the lawnmower has a small grass catcher that needs emptying all the time and is hard to start.

THE MOTIVATION BEHIND OPINION LEADERSHIP

What motivates a person to talk about a product or service? Motivation theory suggests that people may provide information or advice to others to satisfy some basic need of their own. However, opinion leaders may be unaware of their own underlying motives. As suggested earlier, opinion leaders may simply be trying to reduce their own post-purchase dissonance by confirming their own buying decisions. For instance, if Noah subscribes to an ADSL broadband service and then is uncertain that he made the right choice, he may try to reassure himself by 'talking up' the service's advantages to others. In this way, he relieves his own psychological discomfort. Furthermore, when he can influence a friend or neighbour to also get ADSL, he confirms his own good judgment in being first to select the service. Thus, the opinion leader's true motivation may really be self-confirmation or self-involvement. Furthermore, the information or advice that an opinion leader dispenses may provide all types of tangential personal benefits: It may confer attention, imply some type of status, grant superiority, demonstrate awareness and expertise, and give the feeling of possessing inside information and the satisfaction of converting less adventurous souls.

In addition to self-involvement, the opinion leader may also be motivated by product involvement, social involvement, and message involvement. Opinion leaders who are motivated by product involvement may find themselves so pleased or so disappointed with a product that they simply must tell others about it. Those who are motivated by social involvement need to share product-related experiences. In this type of situation, opinion leaders use their product-related conversations as expressions of friendship, neighbourliness, and love.[10]

The pervasiveness of advertising in our society encourages message involvement. Individuals who are bombarded with advertising messages and slogans tend to discuss them and the products they are designed to sell. Such word-of-mouth conversation is typified by the popular use in everyday conversation of slogans such as Microsoft's 'Where do you want to go today?' or Nike's 'Just do it!'[11]

THE NEEDS OF OPINION RECEIVERS

Opinion receivers satisfy a variety of needs by engaging in product-related conversations. First, they obtain new-product or new-usage information. Second, they reduce their perceived risk by receiving firsthand knowledge from a user about a specific product or brand. Third, they reduce the search time entailed in the identification of a needed product or service. Moreover, opinion receivers can be certain of receiving the approval of the opinion leader if they follow that person's product endorsement or advice and purchase the product. For all of these reasons, people often look to friends, neighbours, and other acquaintances for product information. Indeed, research examining the importance of four specific information sources on a hypothetical $100 purchase of consumer services revealed that advice from others was more important than the combined impact of sales representatives, advertising and promotion, and other sources.[12]

TABLE 15.2 **A comparison of the motivations of opinion leaders and opinion receivers**

Opinion leaders	Opinion receivers
Self-improvement motivations	
• Reduce post-purchase uncertainty or dissonance • Gain attention or status • Assert superiority and expertise • Feel like an adventurer • Experience the power of converting others	• Reduce risk in making a purchase commitment • Reduce search time (e.g. avoid the necessity of shopping around)
Product-involvement motivations	
• Express satisfaction or dissatisfaction with a product or service	• Learn what products are new in the marketplace • Learn how to use or consume a product
Social-involvement motivations	
• Express neighbourliness and friendship by discussing products or services that may be useful to others	• Buy products that have the approval of others, thereby ensuring acceptance
Message-involvement motivations	
• Express one's reaction to a stimulating advertisement by telling others about it	• Share social dialogue, have opportunity to pass message to others by becoming opinion leader

Table 15.2 compares the motivations of opinion receivers with those of opinion leaders.

SHOPPING BUDDIES

US researchers have also examined the influence of what they term 'purchase pals' as information sources who actually accompany consumers on shopping trips. Although purchase pals in one study were used only 9% of the time for grocery items, they were used 25% of the time for electronic equipment purchases (e.g. computers, VCRs, TV sets).[13] Interestingly, male purchase pals were more likely to be used as sources of product category expertise, product information, and retail store and price information. Female purchase pals are more often used for moral support and to increase confidence in the buyer's decisions. Similarly, research evidence suggests that when a weak tie exists between the purchase pal and the shopper (e.g. neighbour, classmate, or work colleague), the purchase pal's main contribution tends to be functional—the source's specific product experiences and general marketplace knowledge are being relied on. In contrast, when strong ties exist (such as mother, son, husband, or wife), what is relied on is the purchase pal's familiarity and understanding of the buyer's individual characteristics and needs (or tastes and preferences).[14]

SURROGATE BUYERS VERSUS OPINION LEADERS

Although the traditional model of new product adoption shows opinion leaders influencing the purchase of many new products and services, there are instances in which surrogate buyers replace opinion leaders in this role. For example, working women are increasingly turning to wardrobe consultants for help in purchasing business attire, most new drugs start out requiring a doctor's prescription, and many service providers make decisions for their clients (e.g. your service station decides which brand of disc brake pads to install on your car). Consequently, in an increasing number of decision situations, it is a surrogate buyer who primarily influences the purchase.[15] Table 15.3 presents the key differences between opinion leaders and surrogate buyers.

TABLE 15.3 **Key differences between opinion leaders and surrogate buyers**

Opinion leaders	Surrogate buyer
Informal relationship with end users	Formal relationship; occupation-related status
Information exchange occurs in the context of a casual interaction	Information exchange in the form of formal instructions/ advice
Homophilous (to a certain extent) to end users	Heterophilus to end users (that in fact is the source of power)
Does not get paid for advice	Usually hired, therefore gets paid
Usually socially more active than end users	Not necessarily socially more active than end users
Accountability limited regarding the outcome of advice	High level of accountability
As accountability limited, rigor in search and screening of alternatives low	Search and screening of alternatives more rigorous
Likely to have (although not always) used the product personally	May not have used the product for personal consumption
More than one can be consulted before making a final decision	Second opinion taken on rare occasions
Same person can be an opinion leader for a variety of related product categories	Usually specialises for a specific product/service category

Source: **Praveen Aggarwal and Taihoon Cha, 'Surrogate buyers and the new product adoption process: A conceptualization and managerial framework',** ***Journal of Consumer Marketing*****, 14(5), 1997, p. 394. Reprinted by permission.**

MEASUREMENT OF OPINION LEADERSHIP

In measuring opinion leadership, the researcher has a choice of four basic measurement techniques: In the **self-designating method**, respondents are asked to evaluate the extent to which they have provided others with information about a product category or specific brand or have otherwise influenced the purchase decisions of others. Figure 15.1 shows two types of self-designating question formats that can be used to determine a consumer's opinion leadership activity. The first consists of a single question, whereas the second consists of a series of questions. The use of multiple questions enables the researcher to determine a respondent's opinion

FIGURE 15.1 **Self-designating method approaches**

Single-question approach

1. In the past six months, have you been asked your advice or opinion about cosmetic products?*
   Yes______________ No______________

Multiple-question approach

(Measured on a 5-point bipolar Agree/Disagree scale)

1. Friends and neighbours frequently ask my advice about *cosmetic products*.
2. I sometimes influence the types of *cosmetic products* friends buy.
3. My friends come to me more often than I go to them about *cosmetic products*.
4. I feel that I am generally regarded by my friends as a good source of advice about *cosmetic products*.
5. I can think of at least three people I have spoken to in the past six months about *cosmetic products*.

*Researchers insert their own relevant product/service category.

leadership more reliably because the statements are interrelated.[16] The self-designating technique is used more often than other methods for measuring opinion leadership because consumer researchers find it easy to include in market research questionnaires. However, because this method relies on the respondent's self-evaluation, it may be open to bias should respondents perceive 'opinion leadership' (even though the term is not used) to be a desirable characteristic and, thus, overestimate their own roles as opinion leaders.

The **sociometric method** measures the person-to-person informal communication of consumers concerning products or product categories. In this method, respondents are asked to identify (a) the specific individuals (if any) to whom they provided advice or information about the product or brand under study and (b) the specific individuals (if any) who provided them with advice or information about the product or brand under study. In the first instance, if respondents identify one or more individuals to whom they have provided some form of product information, they are tentatively classified as opinion leaders. In the second instance, respondents are asked to identify the individuals (if any) who provided them with information about a product under investigation. Individuals designated by the primary respondent are tentatively classified as opinion leaders. In both cases, the researcher attempts to validate the determination by asking the individuals named whether they did, in fact, either provide or receive the relevant product information. Such methods are useful when there is a relatively stable social group, such as a firm or a family.

Opinion leadership can also be measured through the use of a **key informant**, a person who is keenly aware of or knowledgeable about the nature of social communications among members of a specific group. The key informant is asked to identify those individuals in the group who are most likely to be opinion leaders. The key informant does not have to be a member of the group under study. For example, a lecturer may serve as the key informant for a university class, identifying those students who are most likely to be opinion leaders with regard to a particular issue. This research method is relatively inexpensive because it requires that only one individual or at most several individuals be intensively interviewed, whereas the self-designating and sociometric methods require that a consumer sample or entire community be interviewed. However, the key informant method is generally not used by marketers because of the difficulties inherent in identifying an individual who can objectively identify opinion leaders in a relevant consumer group.

The key informant method would seem to be of greatest potential use in the study of industrial or institutional opinion leadership. For example, a firm's salespeople might serve as key informants in the identification of specific customers who are most likely to influence the purchase decisions of other potential customers. Similarly, the purchasing agent of a specific firm might serve as a key informant by providing a supplier's salesperson with the names of those persons in the firm who are most likely to influence the purchase decision. In the study of consumers, possible key informants include knowledgeable community members, such as the president of the women's club, the head of the local school council, or a prominent local business person.

Finally, the **objective method** of determining opinion leadership is much like a 'controlled experiment'—it involves placing new products or new-product information with selected individuals and then tracing the resulting 'web' of interpersonal communication concerning the relevant product(s). In a practical sense, a new restaurant in a business district might apply this approach to speed up the creation of a core customer base by sending out invitations to young, influential business executives to dine with their friends at a reduced introductory price any time during the first month of the restaurant's operations. If the restaurant's food and drink are judged to be superior, the restaurant is likely to enjoy the benefits of enhanced positive word-of-mouth generated by the systematic encouragement of the young clientele to try it out and who talk it up to their friends after experiencing the new restaurant.

Table 15.4 presents an overview of each of the four methods of measuring opinion leadership, together with advantages and limitations.

TABLE 15.4 Comparison of methods for measuring opinion leadership

Opinion leadership measurement method	Description of method	Sample questions asked	Advantages	Limitations
Self-designating method	Respondents are asked a series of questions to determine the degree to which they perceive themselves to be opinion leaders.	'Do you influence other people in their selection of products?'	Measures the individual's own perceptions of his or her opinion leadership.	Depends on the objectivity with which respondents can identify and report their personal influence.
Sociometric method	Members of a social system are asked to identify to whom they give advice and to whom they go for advice and information about a product category.	'Whom do you ask?' 'Who asks you for information about that product category?'	Sociometric questions have the greatest degree of validity and are easy to administer.	Very costly, and analysis is often very complex. Requires a large number of respondents. Not suitable for sample design where only a portion of the social system is interviewed.
Key informant method	Carefully selected key informants in a social system are asked to designate opinion leaders.	'Who are the most influential people in the group?'	Relatively inexpensive and less time-consuming than the sociometric method.	Informants who are not thoroughly familiar with the social system are likely to provide invalid information.
Objective method	Artificially places individuals in a position to act as opinion leaders and measures results of their efforts.	'Have you tried the product?'	Measures individual's ability to influence others under controlled circumstances.	Requires the establishment of an experimental design and the tracking of the resulting impact on the participants.

Source: **Adapted with permission of The Free Press, a Division of Simon & Schuster Adult Publishing Group, from *Diffusion of Innovations*, 4th edition, by Everett M. Rogers.**

A PROFILE OF THE OPINION LEADER

Just who are opinion leaders? Can they be recognised by any distinctive characteristics? Can they be reached through specific media? Marketers have long sought answers to these questions, for if they are able to identify the relevant opinion leaders for their products, they can design marketing messages that encourage them to communicate with and influence the consumption behaviour of others. For this reason, consumer researchers have attempted to develop a realistic profile of the opinion leader. This has not been easy to do. As was pointed out earlier, opinion leadership tends to be category specific; that is, an individual who is an opinion leader in one product category may be an opinion receiver in another product category. Thus, the generalised profile of opinion leaders is likely to be influenced by the context of specific product categories.

Although it is difficult to construct a generalised profile of the opinion leader without considering a particular category of interest (or a specific product or service category), Table 15.5 does present a summary of the

TABLE 15.5 Profile of opinion leaders

Generalised attributes across product categories	Category-specific attributes
Innovativeness	Interest
Willingness to talk	Knowledge
Self-confidence	Special-interest media exposure
Gregariousness	Same age
Cognitive differentiation	Same social status
	Social exposure outside group

generalised characteristics that appear to hold true, regardless of product category. The evidence indicates that opinion leaders across all product categories generally exhibit a variety of defining characteristics. First, they reveal a keen sense of knowledge and interest in the particular product or service area, and they are likely to be **consumer innovators**. They also demonstrate a greater willingness to talk about the product, service, or topic; they are more self-confident; and they are more outgoing and gregarious (more sociable). Furthermore, within the context of a specific subject area, opinion leaders receive more information via non-personal sources and are considered by members of their groups to have expertise in their area of influence. Indeed, a recent study found expertise of the source (the opinion leader) to be strongly associated with likely influence on the information seeker's decision-making process.[17] They also usually belong to the same socioeconomic and age groups as their opinion receivers.

When it comes to their mass-media exposure or habits, opinion leaders are likely to read special-interest publications devoted to the specific topic or product category in which they specialise. For example, scuba divers opinion leaders read publications such as *Rodale's Scuba Diving* magazine.[18] These special-interest magazines serve not only to inform scuba diving oriented consumers about new equipment and diving locations that may be of personal interest, but also provide them with the specialised knowledge that enables them to make recommendations to friends and relatives. Thus, the opinion leader tends to have greater exposure to media specifically relevant to his or her area of interest than the non-leader.

FREQUENCY AND OVERLAP OF OPINION LEADERSHIP

Opinion leadership is not a rare phenomenon. Often more than one-third of the people studied in a consumer research project are classified as opinion leaders with respect to some self-selected product category. The frequency of consumer opinion leadership suggests that people are sufficiently interested in at least one product or product category to talk about it and give advice concerning it to others. This leads to the interesting question: Do opinion leaders in one product category tend to be opinion leaders in other product categories? The answer comes from an area of research aptly referred to as opinion leadership overlap. Accordingly, opinion leadership tends to overlap across certain combinations of interest areas. Overlap is likely to be highest among product categories that involve similar interests (such as plasma TVs and DVD players, high-fashion clothing and cosmetics, household cleansers and detergents, expensive wristwatches and writing instruments, discount airlines and backpackers). Thus, opinion leaders in one product area often are opinion leaders in related areas in which they are also interested.

However, research does suggest the existence of a special category of opinion leader, the **market maven**.[19] These consumers possess a wide range of information about many different types of products, retail outlets, and other dimensions of markets. They both initiate discussions with other consumers and respond to requests for market information. Market mavens like to shop, and they also like to share their shopping expertise with others. However, although they appear to fit the profile of opinion leaders in that they have high levels of brand awareness and tend to try more brands, unlike opinion leaders their influence extends beyond the realm of high-involvement products. For example, market mavens may help diffuse information on such low-involvement products as razor blades and laundry detergent.[20] A US study also found that market mavens are value conscious and appear to know the best deals. In the US, this more often led them to redeem discount coupons which are common there.[21]

Market mavens are also distinguishable from other opinion leaders because their influence stems not so much from product experience but from a more general knowledge or market expertise that leads them to an early awareness of a wide array of new products and services. Part of this early awareness may come from the fact that market mavens have a more favourable attitude than non-mavens toward direct mail as a source of information.

THE SITUATIONAL ENVIRONMENT OF OPINION LEADERSHIP

Product-related discussions between two people do not take place in a vacuum. Two people are not likely to meet and spontaneously break into a discussion in which product-related information is sought or offered. Rather, product discussions generally occur within relevant situational contexts, such as when a specific product or a similar product is used or served or as an outgrowth of a more general discussion that touches on the product category. For example, while drinking tea, one person might tell the other person about a preferred brand of tea.

Moreover, opinion leaders and opinion receivers often are friends, neighbours, or work associates, as existing friendships provide numerous opportunities for conversation concerning product-related topics. Close physical proximity is likely to increase the occurrences of product-related conversations. The workplace, for example, is a common place where leisure activities are discussed. In a similar fashion, the rapid growth in the use of the Internet is also creating a type of close 'electronic proximity' or 'communities'—where people of like minds, attitudes, concerns, backgrounds and experiences are coming together in chat sessions to explore their common interests. A recent study identified personal involvement and continuing relationship as two important factors when examining people's reactions to a website and noted that 'information becomes a relationship on the WWW'.[22] Similarly consumer grudge sites allow people to vent their feelings (often negative) about a particular company. Sites like eBay get individual ratings of sellers (and buyers); while 'best buy' sites seek the opinions of buyers of the service they obtained. Online chat sites like TalkCity allow people to chat on a specified range of topics.[23]

THE INTERPERSONAL FLOW OF COMMUNICATION

A classic study of voting behaviour concluded that ideas often flow from radio and print media to opinion leaders and from them to the general public.[24] This so-called **two-step flow of communication theory** portrays opinion leaders as direct receivers of information from impersonal mass-media sources, who in turn transmit (and interpret) this information to the masses. This theory views the opinion leader as an intermediary between the impersonal mass media and the majority of society. Figure 15.2 presents a model of the two-step flow of communication theory. Information is depicted as flowing in a single direction (or one way) from the mass media to opinion leaders (Step 1) and then from the opinion leaders (who interpret, legitimise, and transmit the information) to friends, neighbours, and acquaintances, who constitute the 'masses' (Step 2).

A more comprehensive model of the interpersonal flow of communication depicts the transmission of information from the media as a multi-step flow. The revised model takes into account the fact that information

FIGURE 15.2 **Two-step flow of communication theory**

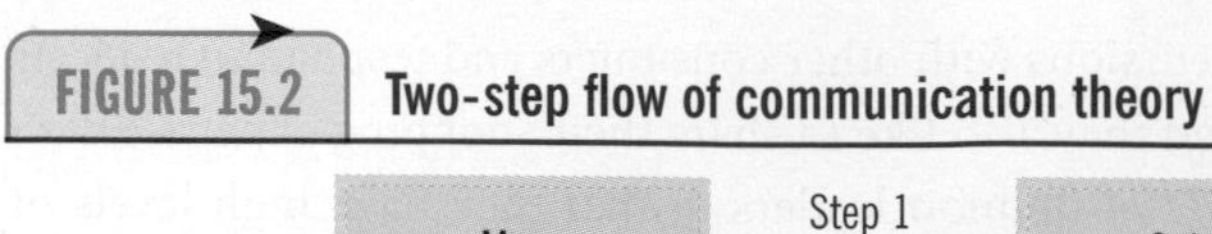

and influence often are two-way processes in which opinion leaders both influence and are influenced by opinion receivers. Figure 15.3 presents a model of the **multi-step flow of communication theory**. Steps 1a and 1b depict the flow of information from the mass media simultaneously to opinion leaders, opinion receivers/seekers, and information receivers (who neither influence nor are influenced by others). Step 2 shows the transmission of information and influence from opinion leaders to opinion receivers/seekers. Step 3 reflects the transfer of information and influence from opinion receivers to opinion leaders.

OPINION LEADERSHIP AND THE FIRM'S MARKETING STRATEGY

Marketers have long been aware of the power that opinion leadership exerts on consumers' preferences and actual purchase behaviour. For this reason many marketers either seek to stimulate opinion leadership or to simulate it (through the use of ads featuring testimonials or actors giving their 'personal' opinions).

Programs designed to stimulate opinion leadership

New-product designers take advantage of the effectiveness of word-of-mouth communication by deliberately designing products to have word-of-mouth potential. Examples of products and services that have had such word-of-mouth appeal include the Polaroid camera, the Sony Walkman, the Swatch watch, and Microsoft Windows. These revolutionary products have attained market share because consumers 'sell' them to each other by word-of-mouth means. Movies also appear to be one form of entertainment in which word-of-mouth operates with some degree of regularity and a large degree of impact. It is very common to be involved directly or overhear people discussing which movies they liked and which movies they advise others to skip. While critics can act as opinion leaders, consumer word-of-mouth can eventually overcome their views.[25]

A new product should give customers something to talk about ('buzz potential'). Box 15.1 describes the code of conduct of a US company BzzAgent[26] that recruits volunteers to try new products and then give others their honest opinion. As the code shows, this only works when people can give their honest opinion, good or bad. In this way the company aims directly to stimulate opinion leadership. In a promotional campaign

FIGURE 15.3 **Multi-step flow of communication theory**

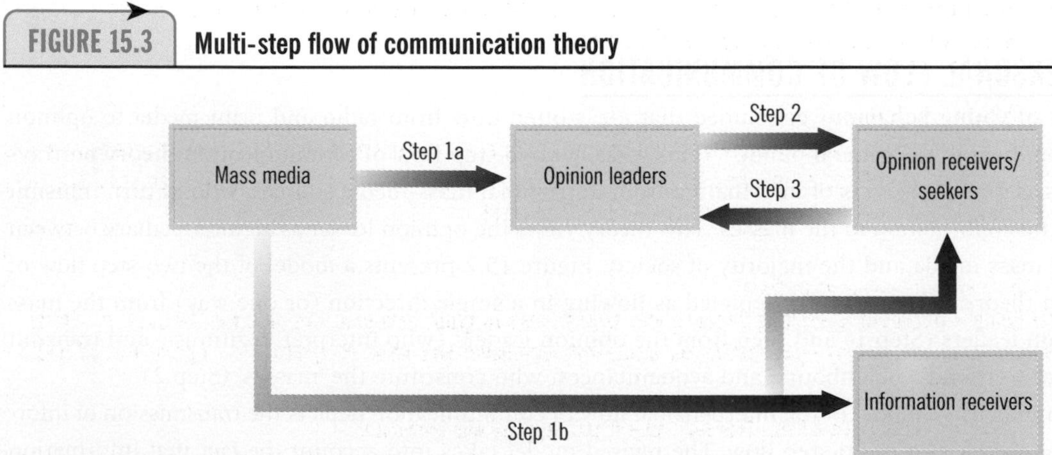

BOX 15.1 BzzAgent code of conduct for stimulating word-of-mouth

A BzzAgent is:

A natural communicator

Be yourself and share your opinions—All Bzz is good Bzz!

The first priority is to deliver authentic Bzz, or information and opinions, to other people. Of course, this should happen naturally in a cool, unforced way. You know how you can stop listening when you think someone is trying to sell you something? Well, other people do too. Stay natural!

Honest

Bzz is only effective when it's completely honest!

Bzz only works because it is honest—even if that means discussing the bad with the good. People are smart, and they will pick up on fake or dishonest Bzz. Your honest opinion is what matters!

Mindful

Everything you do communicates something to the people around you!

A **BzzAgent** watches other people and adapts to them. Keep in mind that you're constantly sending messages to the people around you, from what you say to the products you use. Bzz is an every day part of interacting with different people!

Influential

Knowledge is power . . . and so is Bzz!

BzzAgents are confident, smart, outgoing, and powerful! As a **BzzAgent**, you're part of a movement of people influencing other people through word-of-mouth. You are about the next wave of marketing, which is about marketing to consumers as opposed to at them.

Discreet

Be conscious of who you tell about BzzAgent!

To tell or not to tell? Should **BzzAgents** reveal their identities? That's a question for you to decide—carefully—when you're sharing the Bzz with someone. Some people might think it's cool. Other people might not understand. The choice is yours. Decide what's best for each conversation.

Not a salesperson

Don't exaggerate or 'sell' . . . just share your honest opinions!

During BzzActivities, you don't need to 'close the sale' or over-dramatize what you're saying. Billboards, TV commercials, and other advertisements already do that! Bzzing is about sharing honest opinions with people and raising awareness, never pressuring people.

A Listener

Pay attention to how people are responding to the Bzz!

Bzzing is a two-way street. Sure, you have information about exciting new products to share, but the people you're Bzzing also have opinions and experiences that they may want to share with you as well. Listening will help you to become a better, more informed **BzzAgent**. The more information you're able to gather, the better!

In Touch

Stay in contact with the Central Hive!

Stay alert for new BzzCampaigns and sign up quickly for the ones that interest you. Submit a detailed BzzReport whenever you get the chance to share the Bzz with someone. And let the staff at BzzAgent know about your experiences—good and bad—so we can keep BzzCampaigns fresh and exciting. You're our eyes and ears!

Bzzing for Fun

Bzz only works when you're having a good time!

Bees love to Bzz! Being a **BzzAgent** is exciting because you have access to great new products, and fun because you get to spread the Bzz in your own unique way—whenever you want, with whomever you want. No gimmicks, no pressure. Sit back and relax. Let the Bzz begin!

Source: BzzAgent Code of Conduct, © 2004, Dave Balter, President BzzAgent, LLC. Reprinted with permission.

for Hennessy Cognac, actors were paid to visit New York Manhattan bars and nightclubs and order cognac martinis, made with Hennessy. Although they were instructed to act as if they were ordering a new fad drink, in reality they were attempting to create a new fad drink.[27]

Small marketers with limited resources are unable to spend millions of dollars promoting their products. So in today's world, they try to create a buzz about their product. As an example, although iced coffee has been slow to catch on in the United States (in contrast, Coca-Cola's Georgia iced coffee is a very successful brand in Japan), the US market is expanding because many young adults were raised drinking cold drinks in the morning, allowing marketers to use this to build their brands.[28] Thus the objective of a promotional strategy of stimulation is to run advertisements which are so interesting that consumers will talk about them or to run a direct campaign based on generating word-of-mouth that will encourage opinion receivers to talk to others about the product.

SIMULATING OPINION LEADERSHIP

A firm's advertisements can also be designed to simulate product discussions by portraying people in the act of informal communication. This promotional tactic suggests that it is appropriate to discuss a particular subject or product. For example, simulated informal communications encounters between two or more women are often portrayed in TV advertising for personal care products to persuade women to discuss their use or contemplated use. Because these simulations often function as convenient substitutes, they reduce the need for consumers to actually seek product advice from others.

Figure 15.4 shows an ad which simulates the advice one consumer might give directly to another about Panadol.

FIGURE 15.4 **Ad simulating consumer opinion-giving**

I wouldn't put
just anything in my body.
That's why I always think
twice about what I do.
Some decisions are hard to make.
But in the end,
you've got to do what's
right for you.
Panadol
It's my choice
ALWAYS READ THE LABEL. Use only as directed. For the temporary relief of pain and fever. Incorrect use could be harmful. Consult your health care professional if symptoms persist. Panadol is a Registered Trade Mark of the GlaxoSmithKline group of companies. ASMI/8747/1-07/03 GSK0867/YOG

Source: **Courtesy of GlaxoSmithKline Australia Pty Ltd.**

WORD-OF-MOUTH MAY BE UNCONTROLLABLE

Although most marketing managers believe that word-of-mouth communication is extremely effective, one problem that they sometimes overlook is the fact that informal communication is difficult to control. Negative comments, frequently in the form of rumours that are untrue, can sweep through the marketplace to the detriment of a product. Indeed, a US study found that 90% or more of unhappy customers will not do business again with the company that is the source of their dissatisfaction. To make matters even worse, each dissatisfied customer will share his or her grievance with at least nine other people, and 13% of unhappy customers will tell more than 20 people about the negative experience.[29]

Some common rumour themes that have plagued marketers in recent years and unfavourably influenced sales include the following:

- The product was produced under unsanitary conditions.
- The product contained an unwholesome or culturally unacceptable ingredient.

- The product functioned as an undesirable depressant or stimulant.
- The product included a cancer-causing element or agent.
- The firm was owned or influenced by an unfriendly or misguided foreign country, governmental agency, or religious cult.

Cosmetics are especially prone to these type of rumours.[30]

Some marketers use toll-free telephone numbers in an attempt to head off negative word-of-mouth, displaying an 1800 number prominently on their products' labels. Customer relations managers want dissatisfied customers to call their companies' 1800 numbers and receive 'satisfaction' instead of telling their complaints to friends and relatives.

CREATION OF OPINION LEADERS

Marketing strategists agree that promotional efforts would be significantly improved if they could segment their markets into opinion leaders and opinion receivers.[31] They could then direct their promotional messages directly to the people most likely to 'carry the word' to the masses. However, because of the difficulties inherent in identifying appropriate opinion leaders, some researchers have suggested that it might be more fruitful to 'create' product-specific opinion leaders. In one classic US study, a group of socially influential high school students (including class presidents and sports captains) were asked to become members of a panel that would rate newly-released musical recordings. As part of their responsibilities, panel participants were encouraged to discuss their record choices with friends. Preliminary examination suggested that these influentials would not qualify as opinion leaders for musical recordings because of their relatively meagre ownership of the product category.[32] However, some of the records the group evaluated made the Top 10 charts in the cities in which the members of the group lived; these same recordings did not make the Top 10 charts in any other city. This study suggests that product-specific opinion leaders can be created by taking socially involved or influential people and deliberately increasing their enthusiasm for a product category.

A more recent US study explored the notion of increasing enthusiasm for a product category. Over a 12-week period, half the participants were assigned to look at corporate websites (i.e. marketer-generated information sources), and half were asked to look at online discussions (e.g. chat rooms, forums). Consumers who got their information from online discussions reported greater interest in the product category. It is felt that chat rooms and other forums provide consumers with personal experiences and may offer greater credibility, trustworthiness, relevance, and empathy than marketer-generated Internet websites.[33]

Diffusion of innovations

The second part of this chapter examines a major issue in marketing and consumer behaviour—the acceptance of new products and services. The framework for exploring consumer acceptance of new products is drawn from the area of research known as the **diffusion of innovations**. This consists of two closely related processes: the **diffusion process** and the **adoption process**. In the broadest sense, diffusion is a macro process concerned with the spread of a new product (an innovation) from its source to the consuming public. In contrast, adoption is a micro process that focuses on the stages through which an individual consumer passes when deciding to accept or reject a new product. In addition to an examination of these two interrelated processes, we present a profile of consumer innovators, those who are the first to purchase a new product. The ability of marketers to identify and reach this important group of consumers plays a major role in the success or failure of new-product introductions.

It is also of interest to note that diffusion models for particular types of goods and services may change over time. For example, until the 1960s, it was assumed that new fashions diffused in a top-down or trickle-down manner—new styles are first adopted by the upper-class elites and gradually diffuse to the middle and lower classes. However, since the 1960s, the bottom-up model has served as the better explanation of fashion diffusion—new styles develop in lower-status groups and are later adopted by higher-status groups. These innovative fashions typically emanate from urban communities that also serve as the seedbeds for other innovations, such as art and popular music.[34]

The diffusion process

The diffusion process is concerned with how innovations spread, that is, how they are assimilated within a market. More precisely, diffusion is the process by which the acceptance of an innovation (a new product, new service, new idea, or new practice) is spread by communication (mass media, salespeople, or informal conversations) to members of a social system (a target market) over a period of time. This definition includes the four basic elements of the diffusion process:

1. the innovation
2. the channels of communication
3. the social system
4. time.

THE INNOVATION

No universally accepted definition of the terms 'product innovation' or 'new product' exists. Instead, various approaches have been taken to define a new product or a new service; these can be classified as firm-oriented, product-oriented, market-oriented, and consumer-oriented definitions of **innovations**.

Firm-oriented definitions

A firm-oriented approach treats the newness of a product from the perspective of the company producing or marketing it. When the product is 'new' to the company, it is considered new. This definition ignores whether or not the product is actually new to the marketplace (i.e. to competitors or consumers). Consistent with this view, copies or modifications of a competitor's product would qualify as new. Although this definition has considerable merit when the objective is to examine the impact that a 'new' product has on the firm, it is not very useful when the goal is to understand consumer acceptance of a new product.

Product-oriented definitions

In contrast to firm-oriented definitions, a product-oriented approach focuses on the features inherent in the product itself and on the effects these features are likely to have on consumers' established usage patterns. One product-oriented framework considers the extent to which a new product is likely to disrupt established behaviour patterns. It defines the following three types of product innovations:[35]

1. A **continuous innovation** has the least disruptive influence on established patterns. It involves the introduction of a modified product rather than a totally new product. Examples include the redesigned Toyota Camry and the latest version of Microsoft PowerPoint. Figure 15.5 (page 524) is an ad for Gillette showing continuous innovation in the company's product range.
2. A **dynamically continuous innovation** is somewhat more disruptive than a continuous innovation but still does not alter established behaviour patterns. It may involve the creation of a new product or the modification of an existing product. Examples include digital camcorders, DVD players, antilock braking systems, erasable-ink pens, and disposable nappies.

3. A **discontinuous innovation** requires consumers to adopt new behaviour patterns. Examples include aeroplanes, radios, TVs, automobiles, home computers, videocassette recorders, medical self-test kits, and the Internet.

Figure 15.6 (page 525) shows how the telephone, a discontinuous innovation of major magnitude, has produced a variety of both dynamically continuous and continuous innovations and has even stimulated the development of other discontinuous innovations.

Market-oriented definitions

A market-oriented approach judges the newness of a product in terms of how much exposure consumers have to the new product. Two market-oriented definitions of product innovation have been used extensively in consumer studies:

1. A product is considered new if it has been purchased by a relatively small (fixed) percentage of the potential market.
2. A product is considered new if it has been on the market for a relatively short (specified) period of time.

Both of these market-oriented definitions are basically subjective because they leave the researcher with the task of establishing the degree of sales penetration within the market that qualifies the product as an 'innovation' (such as the initial 5% of the potential market to use the new product) or how long the product can be on the market and still be considered 'new' (i.e. the first three months that the product is available).

Consumer-oriented definitions

Although each of the three approaches described have been useful to consumer researchers in their study of the diffusion of innovations, some researchers have favoured a consumer-oriented approach in defining an innovation.[36] In this context, a 'new' product is any product that a potential consumer judges to be new. In other words, newness is based on the consumer's perception of the product rather than on physical features or market realities. Although the consumer-oriented approach has been endorsed by some advertising and marketing practitioners, it has received little systematic research attention.

Additionally, it should be pointed out that although this portion of the chapter deals primarily with what might be described as 'purchase' innovativeness (or time of adoption), a second type of innovativeness, 'use innovativeness', has been the subject of some thought and research. A consumer is being use innovative when he or she uses a previously adopted product in a novel or unusual way. In one study that dealt with the adoption of VCRs and computers, early adopters showed significantly higher use innovativeness than those who adopted somewhat later along the cycle of acceptance of the innovation.[37]

Product characteristics that influence diffusion

All products that are new do not have equal potential for consumer acceptance. Some products seem to catch on almost overnight (such as cordless telephones), whereas others take a very long time to gain acceptance or never seem to achieve widespread consumer acceptance (such as trash compactors).

The uncertainties of product marketing would be reduced if marketers could anticipate how consumers will react to their products. For example, if a marketer knew that a product contained inherent features that were likely to inhibit its acceptance, the marketer could develop a promotional strategy that would compensate for these features or decide not to market the product at all. In the US auto market, SUVs and pick-up trucks are big sellers. Pickup trucks are now being designed for the female driver, and manufacturers are careful to design door handles that do not break fingernails. Ford even offers adjustable accelerator and brake pedals.[38]

FIGURE 15.5 Continuous innovation

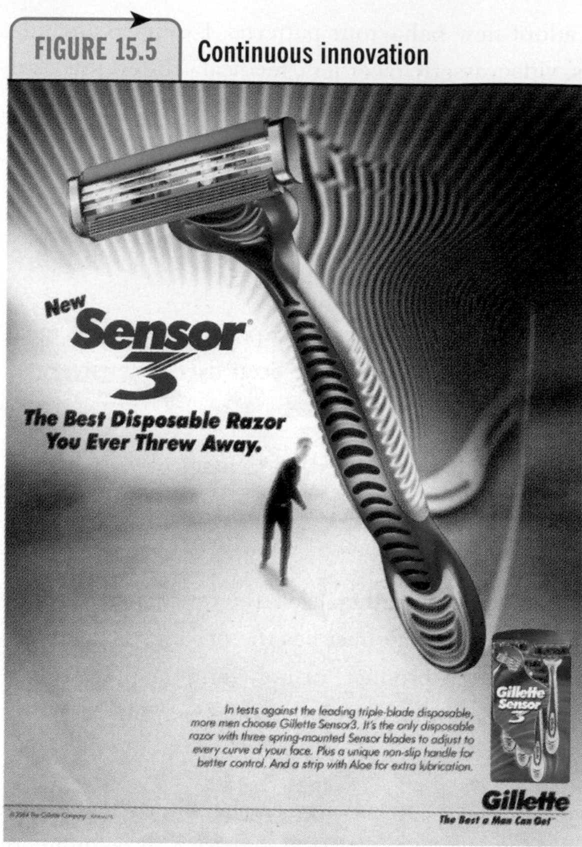

Source: Courtesy of Gillette Australia Pty Ltd.

Although there are no precise formulas by which marketers can evaluate a new product's likely acceptance, diffusion researchers have identified five product characteristics that seem to influence consumer acceptance of new products:[39]

1. relative advantage
2. compatibility
3. complexity
4. trialability
5. observability.

Based on available research, it has been estimated that these five product characteristics account for much of the dynamic nature of the rate or speed of adoption.[40] **Relative advantage** is the degree to which potential customers perceive a new product as superior to existing substitutes. For example, although pagers allowed business offices or families to contact staff, a mobile phone enables users to be in nearly instant communication with the world and allows users to both receive and place calls. The fax machine is another example of an innovation that offers users a significant relative advantage over systems it replaced, such as couriers and telex machines. Now faxes are being superseded by email with the ability to attach files or scan documents.

Compatibility is the degree to which potential consumers feel a new product is consistent with their present needs, values, and practices is a measure of its compatibility. For instance, an advantage of 3M's Scotch™ Pop-up Tape Strips is that they are easier to use than roll-tape for certain tasks (such as wrapping gifts), yet they represent no new learning for the user. Similarly, in the realm of shaving products, it is not too difficult to imagine that a few years ago when Gillette introduced the MACH3 razor, some men made the transition from inexpensive disposable razors and other men shifted from competitive non-disposable razors (including Gillette's own Sensor razors, see Figure 15.5). This new product is fully compatible with the established wet-shaving rituals of many men. However, it is difficult to imagine male shavers shifting to a new depilatory cream designed to remove facial hair. Although potentially simpler to use, a cream would be basically incompatible with most men's current values regarding daily shaving practices.

A study of purchasers of CD players and other technology-based products (such as computers, VCRs, and telephone answering machines) found that the key factors inhibiting product adoption were incompatibility with existing values and poor product quality.[41] And although it is possible, in theory, to make a mobile phone the size of a button (e.g. personal handy phones the size of a hairclip are popular in Japan), according to phone manufacturer Ericsson, American consumers do not like the feeling of talking into empty space.[42]

Complexity is the degree to which a new product is difficult to understand or use that affects the product's acceptance. Clearly, the easier it is to understand and use a product, the more likely it is to be accepted. For example, the acceptance of such convenience foods as frozen potato chips, instant puddings, and microwave dinners is generally due to their ease of preparation and use. Interestingly, home theatre equipment such as

FIGURE 15.6 The telephone has led to related innovations

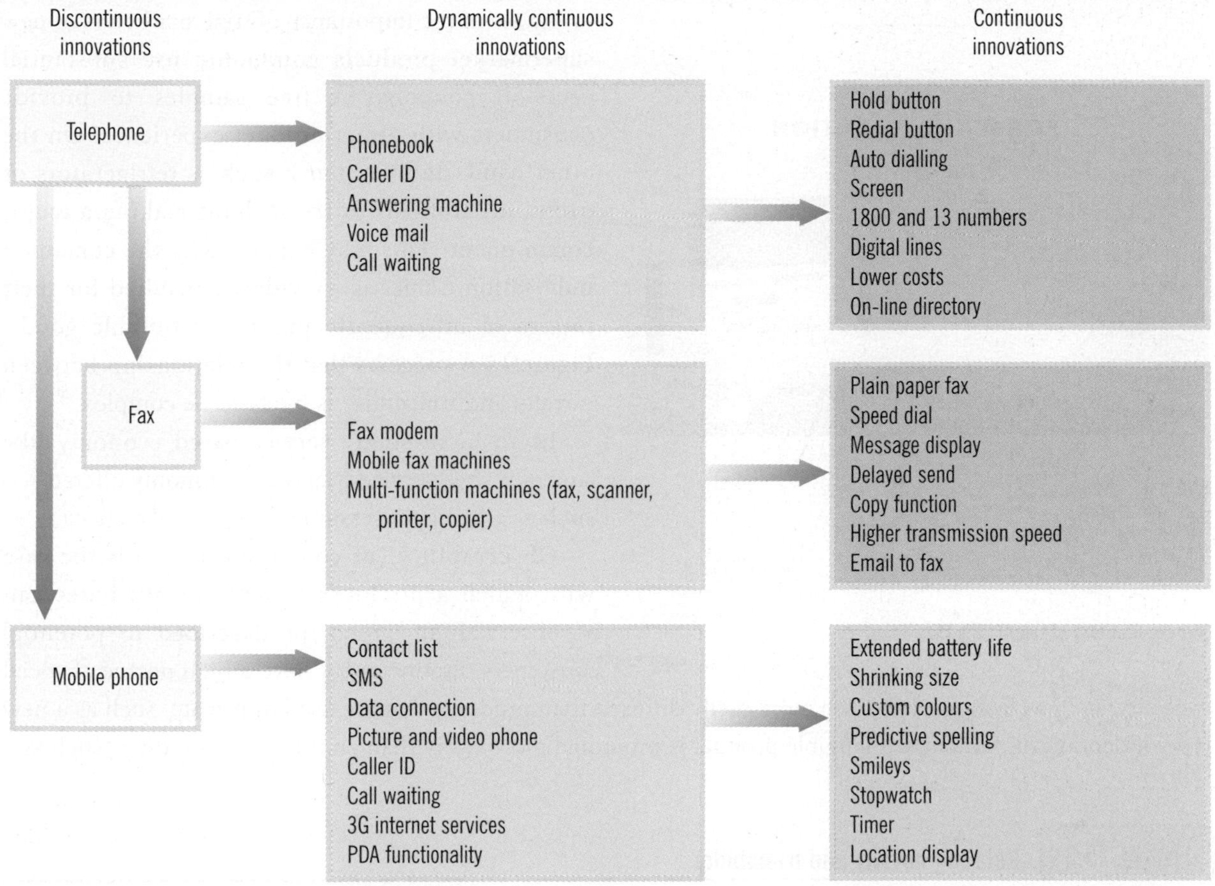

Discontinuous innovations	Dynamically continuous innovations	Continuous innovations
Telephone	Phonebook Caller ID Answering machine Voice mail Call waiting	Hold button Redial button Auto dialling Screen 1800 and 13 numbers Digital lines Lower costs On-line directory
Fax	Fax modem Mobile fax machines Multi-function machines (fax, scanner, printer, copier)	Plain paper fax Speed dial Message display Delayed send Copy function Higher transmission speed Email to fax
Mobile phone	Contact list SMS Data connection Picture and video phone Caller ID Call waiting 3G internet services PDA functionality	Extended battery life Shrinking size Custom colours Predictive spelling Smileys Stopwatch Timer Location display

amplifier/tuners and digital personal video recorders (PVRs) have more functions and buttons than consumers know how to use. The recognition of the need to overcome complexity has led to the need to introduce 'one touch' functions and on-screen help to guide the consumer through this maze.

The issue of complexity is especially important when attempting to gain market acceptance for high-tech consumer products. Four predominant types of 'technological fear' act as barriers to new product acceptance:

- fear of technical complexity
- fear of rapid obsolescence
- fear of social rejection
- fear of physical harm.

Of the four, technological complexity was the most widespread concern of consumer innovators.[43] Figure 15.7 presents an advertisement for a Jamo home theatre system emphasising simplicity of set-up and use.

Trialability refers to the degree to which a new product is capable of being tried on a limited basis. The greater the opportunity to try a new product, the easier it is for consumers to evaluate it and ultimately adopt it. In general, frequently purchased household products tend to have qualities that make trial relatively easy, such as the ability to purchase a small or 'trial' size. Because a computer program cannot be packaged in a smaller size, many computer software companies offer free working models of their latest software to encourage computer users to try the program and subsequently buy the program.

Aware of the importance of trial, marketers of new supermarket products commonly use substantial cents-off coupons or free samples to provide consumers with direct product experience. On the other hand, durable items, such as refrigerators or ovens, are difficult to try without making a major commitment. This may explain why the consumer publication *Choice* is so widely consulted for their ratings of infrequently purchased durable goods. Figure 15.8 suggests that the relationship between novelty and trialability is likely to be complex.[44]

In an increasingly service-based economy like Australia, free service trials are commonly offered[45]—such as a free gym session or a free brake check.

Observability (or communicability) is the ease with which a product's benefits or attributes can be observed, imagined, or described to potential consumers. Products that have a high degree of social visibility, such as fashion items, are more easily diffused than products that are used in private, such as a new type of deodorant. Similarly, a tangible product is promoted more easily than an intangible product (such as a

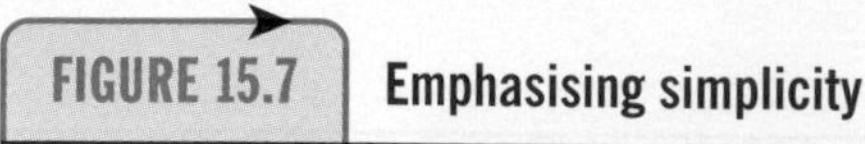

FIGURE 15.7 Emphasising simplicity

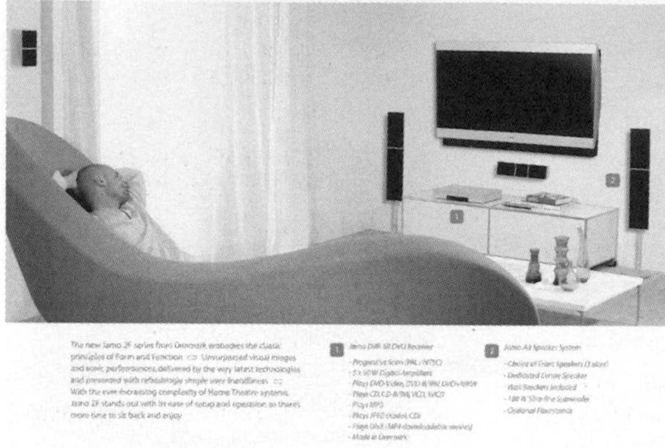

Source: Courtesy of QualiFi Pty Ltd.

FIGURE 15.8 Relating novelty and trialability

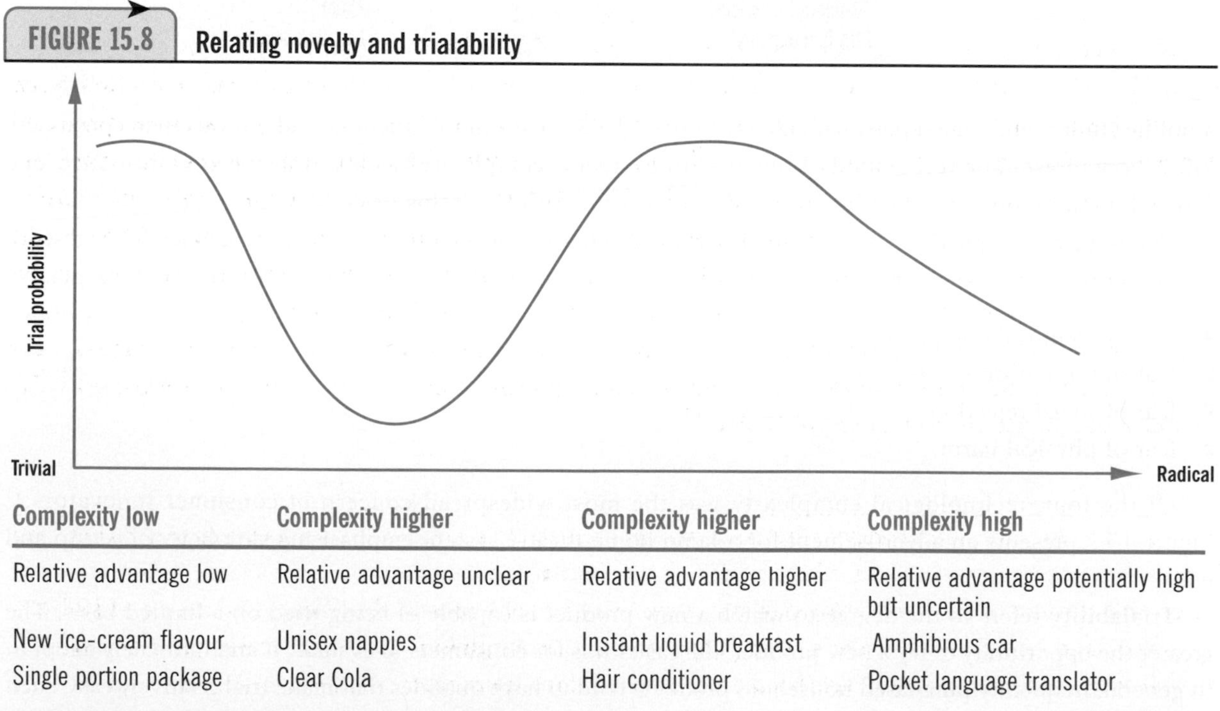

Complexity low	Complexity higher	Complexity higher	Complexity high
Relative advantage low	Relative advantage unclear	Relative advantage higher	Relative advantage potentially high but uncertain
New ice-cream flavour	Unisex nappies	Instant liquid breakfast	Amphibious car
Single portion package	Clear Cola	Hair conditioner	Pocket language translator

Source: Based on Jan-Benedict E.M. Steenkamp and Katrijn Gielens, 'Consumer and market drivers of the trial probability of new consumer packaged goods', *Journal of Consumer Research*, 30, December 2003, p. 381.

TABLE 15.6 **Product characteristics that influence diffusion**

Characteristics	Definition	Examples
Relative advantage	The degree to which potential customers perceive a new product as superior to existing substitutes	Air travel over train travel, cordless phones over corded telephones
Compatibility	The degree to which potential consumers feel a new product is consistent with their present needs, values, and practices	Gillette MACH3 over disposable razors, voicemail over machines using tape to make recordings
Complexity	The degree to which a new product is difficult to understand or use	Products low in complexity include frozen TV dinners, electric shavers, instant puddings
Trialability	The degree to which a new product is capable of being tried on a limited basis	Trial size jars and bottles of new products, free trials of software, free samples, cents-off coupons
Observability	The degree to which a product's benefits or attributes can be observed, imagined, or described to potential customers	Clothing, such as a new Tommy Hilfiger jacket, a car, wristwatches, eyeglasses

service). It is also important to recognise that a particular innovation may diffuse differently throughout different cultures. For example, SMS text messaging was slow to be adopted in the US market even though it became enormously popular elsewhere. Table 15.6 summarises the product characteristics that influence diffusion.

Resistance to innovation

What makes some new products almost instant successes, while others struggle to achieve consumer acceptance? To help answer such a question, marketers look at the product characteristics of an innovation. Such characteristics offer clues that help determine the extent of consumer resistance, which increases when perceived relative advantage, perceived compatibility, trialability, and communicability are low, and perceived complexity is high. The term 'innovation overload' is used to describe the situation in which the increase in information and options available to the consumer is so great that it seriously impairs decision-making. As a result, the consumer finds it difficult to make comparisons among the available choices. In a world where consumers often find themselves with too little time and too much stress, increased complexity of products wastes time and may delay the acceptance of the product.[46] Consider the fate of Sony's MiniDisc. Although a huge success in Japan, the product flopped in the United States and despite an attempt to revive it, was overcome by CD recorders and digital players like Apple's iPod.[47]

THE CHANNELS OF COMMUNICATION

How quickly an innovation spreads through a market depends to a great extent on communications between the marketer and consumers, as well as communication among consumers (word-of-mouth communication). Of central concern is the uncovering of the relative influence of impersonal sources (advertising and editorial matter) and interpersonal sources (salespeople and informal opinion leaders). In recent years, a variety of new channels of communication have been developed to inform consumers of innovative products and services. Consider the growth of interactive marketing messages, in which the consumer becomes an important part of the communication rather than just a 'passive' message recipient. For example, for the past several years, an increasing number of companies such as AOL have used CD-ROMs to promote their products. Many websites now ask the user if he or she would like to be informed about new products, discount offers, and so on, relevant to the focus of the site. If the answer is 'yes,' the consumer provides the website with an email address and will then receive periodic information from this source. This phenomenon is known as **permission marketing**.[48]

US examples of new media include Nike's Presto line of sneakers. Although the company spends about $US1 billion annually to promote its products, it was word-of-mouth that caused sales of the Presto to soar. Instead of ads in major publications and prime-time television, Nike used MTV and Comedy Central, offered a page of stickers in *YM* magazine, and rented a studio in Manhattan to display a wall containing 200 Presto sneakers. The firm also encouraged teens to log onto the Nike website to select Presto graphics, pair the graphics with music, and then email the mini–music videos to their friends (i.e. an example of viral marketing).[49]

The social system

The diffusion of a new product usually takes place in a social setting frequently referred to as a social system. In the context of consumer behaviour, the terms market segment and target market may be more relevant than the term social system used in diffusion research. A social system is a physical, social, or cultural environment to which people belong and within which they function. For example, for a new hybrid seed corn, the social system might consist of all farmers in a number of local communities. For a new drug, the social system might consist of all physicians within a specific medical specialty (e.g. all neurologists). For a new special diet product, the social system might include all residents of a geriatric community. As these examples indicate, the social system serves as the boundary within which the diffusion of a new product is examined.

The orientation of a social system, with its own special values or norms, is likely to influence the acceptance or rejection of new products. When a social system is modern in orientation, the acceptance of innovations is likely to be high. In contrast, when a social system is traditional in orientation, innovations that are perceived as radical or as infringements on established customs are likely to be avoided. According to one authority, the following characteristics typify a modern social system:[50]

- a positive attitude toward change
- an advanced technology and skilled labor force
- a general respect for education and science
- an emphasis on rational and ordered social relationships rather than on emotional ones
- an outreach perspective, in which members of the system frequently interact with outsiders, thus facilitating the entrance of new ideas into the social system
- a system in which members can readily see themselves in quite different roles

The orientations of a social system (either modern or traditional) may be national in scope and may influence members of an entire society or may exist at the local level and influence only those who live in a specific community. The key point to remember is that a social system's orientation is the climate in which marketers must operate to gain acceptance for their new products. For example, in recent years, there has been a decline in the demand for beef. The growing interest in health and fitness throughout has created a climate in which beef is considered too high in fat and in caloric content. At the same time, the consumption of chicken and fish has increased because these foods satisfy the prevailing nutritional values of a great number of consumers.

TIME

Time is the backbone of the diffusion process. It pervades the study of diffusion in three distinct but interrelated ways:

1. the amount of purchase time
2. the identification of adopter categories
3. the rate of adoption.

Purchase time

Purchase time refers to the amount of time that elapses between consumers' initial awareness of a new product or service and the point at which they purchase or reject it. Table 15.7 illustrates the scope of purchase time by tracking a hypothetical purchase of a new notebook computer. Table 15.7 illustrates not only the length and complexity of consumer decision making but also how different information sources become important at successive steps in the process.

Purchase time is an important concept because the average time a consumer takes to adopt a new product is a predictor of the overall length of time it will take for the new product to achieve widespread adoption. For example, when the individual purchase time is short, a marketer can expect that the overall rate of diffusion will be faster than when the individual purchase time is long. Some products are so attractive to consumers that supply cannot keep up with demand. For example, in the US the Miller Brewing Company had to introduce its plastic bottles to the national audience three months later than originally planned because demand for the bottles in sports arenas proved to be so strong.[51]

Adopter categories

The concept of **adopter categories** involves a classification scheme that indicates where a consumer stands in relation to other consumers in terms of time (or when the consumer adopts a new product). Five adopter categories are frequently cited in the diffusion literature: innovators, early adopters, early majority, late majority, and laggards. Table 15.8 (page 531) describes each of these adopter categories and estimates their relative proportions within the total population that eventually adopts the new product. It should also be mentioned that the person first to buy an innovation is often an individual who serves as a bridge to other networks, an opinion broker between groups, rather than within groups.[52]

As Figure 15.9 indicates, the adopter categories are generally depicted as taking on the characteristics of a normal distribution (a bell-shaped curve) that describes the total population that ultimately adopts a product. Some argue that the bell curve is an erroneous depiction because it may lead to the inaccurate conclusion that

FIGURE 15.9 **Sequence and proportion of adopter categories among the population that eventually adopts**

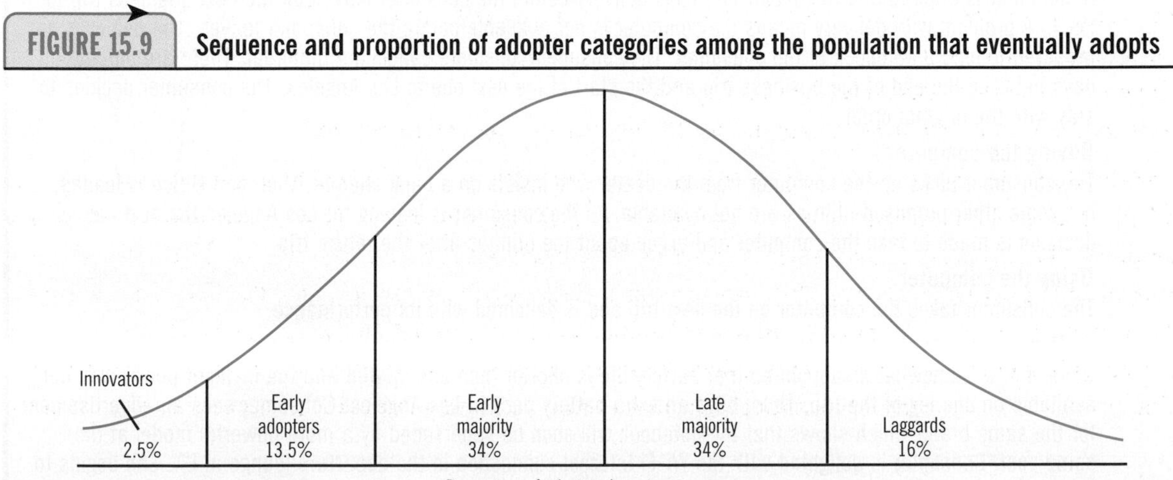

Source: Adapted with permission of The Free Press, a Division of Simon & Schuster Adult Publishing Group, from *Diffusion of Innovations*, 4th edition, by Everett M. Rogers. Copyright © 1995 by Everett M. Rogers. Copyright © 1962, 1971, 1983 by The Free Press. All rights reserved.

TABLE 15.7 **Timeline for selecting a new notebook computer**

Week	Activity
0	**Precipitating situations/factors** Consumer observes another passenger in the business class section of a flight from Sydney to London working for a long period on a small notebook computer connected to a power source in the seat. After asking about the computer, the consumer observes a small size, a colour screen running Windows, a convenient trackball and an in-flight Internet connection. The consumer realises that more productive use can be made of long travel times.
1–4	**Decision process begins** Consumer senses a need to learn more about the features and availability of notebook computers. Begins a process of getting and reading the latest computer magazines (*Australian Personal Computer*, *Your Computer*), computer sections of the local newspaper and manufacturer websites. Finds an issue of the American magazine, *PC Magazine*, which reviews 70 notebook computers, many of which are sold in Australia. Takes special interest in new Apple iMac, Toshiba and Fujitsu notebooks.
5–8	**The notebook computer is out of mind** Back at the home office, the consumer is overwhelmed by work and puts the idea of a notebook computer on the 'back burner'.
9	**Interest is retriggered** A series of long business trips is coming up and a notebook would be especially useful, particularly loaded with Microsoft Office. An apparently special deal in the computer section of *The Australian* further revives interest. **Consumer acquires a mentor (opinion leader)** The office 'techie' is asked and agrees to serve as a mentor (opinion leader) with regard to notebook options.
10	**Features and brand options are reviewed** With the advice of the mentor, various alternatives are narrowed down to two notebooks—the iMac and the Toshiba.
11	**Dealers are visited** Consumer visits four dealers. Takes an interest in one of the main brands. Although prices are similar, one dealer offers a special price on an older demonstration model, while another dealer mentions a new, more powerful model released in Japan and available in Australia 'soon'. The first business trip to Perth is only a week away. **Period of self-study** Consumer is faced with a choice of model, computing power, type of colour screen, hard disk capacity, displays, battery life, weight, dealer support, multimedia options and bundled software. Price is also a factor!
12	**Ordering the notebook** A computer is ordered and the dealer promises delivery before the consumer leaves on the next business trip to Perth. A problem with delivery means the computer is not available before the consumer leaves. The dealer is not prepared to lend a notebook to the consumer. The consumer considers cancelling the order. There are only two days between the end of the business trip and the start of the next one to Los Angeles. The consumer decides to stay with the original order.
13	**Buying the computer** The consumer picks up the computer from the dealer who insists on a bank cheque. Microsoft Office is loaded; but some other promised utilities are not available. As the consumer is leaving for Los Angeles the next day, a decision is made to take the computer and argue about the utilities after the return trip. **Using the computer** The consumer takes the computer on the next trip and is delighted with its performance.
14–20	**Post-purchase evaluation** Consumer is somewhat disappointed that battery life is shorter than anticipated and the in-flight power was not available on one leg of the trip. Thus, buys an extra battery pack in Los Angeles. Consumer sees an advertisement for the same brand which shows that the notebook will soon be superseded by a more powerful model at the same cost. Consumer is delighted with the Wi-Fi Internet connection in the departure lounge in LA. She begins to wonder how work could have been managed without the computer. Considers buying a financial analysis software package to take on the next trip.

TABLE 15.8 Adopter categories

Adopter category	Description	Relative percentage within the population that eventually adopts %
Innovators	*Venturesome*—very eager to try new ideas; acceptable if risk is daring; more cosmopolitan social relationships; communicate with other innovators	2.5
Early adopters	*Respectable*—more integrated into the local social systems; the people to check with before adopting a new idea; category contains greatest number of opinion leaders; are role models	13.5
Early majority	*Deliberate*—adopt new ideas just prior to the average time; seldom hold leadership positions; deliberate for some time before adopting	34.0
Late majority	*Sceptical*—adopt new ideas just after the average time; adopting may be both an economic necessity and a reaction to peer pressures; innovations approached cautiously	34.0
Laggards	*Traditional*—the last people to adopt an innovation; most 'localite' in outlook; oriented to the past; suspicious of the new	16.0
		100.0

Source: **Adapted with permission of The Free Press, a Division of Simon & Schuster Adult Publishing Group, from *Diffusion of Innovations*, 4th edition, by Everett M. Rogers. Copyright © 1995 by Everett M. Rogers. Copyright © 1962, 1971, 1983 by The Free Press. All rights reserved.**

100% of the members of the social system under study (the target market) eventually will accept the product innovation. This assumption is not in keeping with marketers' experiences, because very few, if any, products fit the precise needs of all potential consumers. For example, all purchasers of pre-recorded movies on videotape could theoretically be expected to use (or try) DVDs. In practice not all people will do so. For this reason, it is appropriate to add an additional category, that of non-adopters.

Researchers have used actual adoption data and tried to see which mathematical models best fit these data. Australian research has suggested[53] that adoption is part of the product life cycle which includes the phases of *innovative first purchases*, *imitative purchases*, *repeat purchases* and, finally, *substitution by alternatives*. The authors suggest that these stages actually overlap and their analyses show a reasonable fit to the data. Some consumer researchers have used other classification schemes, most of which consist of two or three categories that compare innovators or early triers with later triers or non-triers. As we will see, this focus on the innovator or early trier has produced several important generalisations that have practical significance for marketers planning the introduction of new products.

The overall pattern of adoption and eventual abandonment of products produces a **product life cycle**. The vinyl record would be a classic example of this product life cycle. Sweeping old 78 rpm records from the market, the vinyl record has now been virtually replaced by the CD. DVDs, MP3 players or some later technology will eventually replace the CD. Not all products have a lifecycle. Although it has introduced new varieties over the years, Coca-Cola continues with its basic cola product and is likely to do so while it continues in business.

Rate of adoption

The rate of adoption is concerned with how long it takes a new product or service to be adopted by members of a social system, that is, how quickly it takes a new product to be accepted by those who will ultimately adopt it. The general view is that the rate of adoption for new products is getting faster or shorter. Fashion adoption is a form of diffusion, one in which the rate of adoption is important. Cyclical fashion trends or 'fads' are extremely 'fast,' whereas 'fashion classics' may have extremely slow or 'long' cycles.

In general, the diffusion of products worldwide is becoming a more rapid phenomenon. Table 15.9 shows the growth in numbers of mobile phones in selected countries around the world between 1997 and 2002.

In most economies, the compound annual growth has been very high—explosive, in some cases. The actual adoption rate will depend on the existing communications infrastructure, age distribution and wealth. In Taiwan and Luxembourg, the ITU reported an average of 1.1 mobile phones per person!

The objective in marketing new products is usually to gain wide acceptance of the product as quickly as possible. Marketers desire a rapid rate of product adoption to penetrate the market and quickly establish market leadership (obtain the largest share of the market) before competition takes hold. A penetration policy is usually accompanied by a relatively low introductory price designed to discourage competition from entering the market. Rapid product adoption also demonstrates to marketing intermediaries (wholesalers and retailers) that the product is worthy of their full and continued support.

Under certain circumstances, marketers might prefer to avoid a rapid rate of adoption for a new product. For example, marketers who wish to use a pricing strategy that will enable them to recoup their development costs quickly might follow a skimming policy: They first make the product available at a very high price to consumers who are willing to pay top dollar and then gradually lower the price in a stepwise fashion to attract additional market segments at each price reduction plateau. When hi-fi stereo VCRs were first introduced in the 1980s, they retailed for over $A1200. By 2004, the price was less than $A200 with some manufacturers withdrawing from the market to focus on DVD players.

In addition to how long it takes from introduction to the point of adoption (or when the purchase actually occurs), it is useful to track the extent of adoption (the diffusion rate). For instance, a particular corporation

TABLE 15.9 Mobile phone growth

Country	1997 000s	2002 000s	Yearly % growth rate	Per 100 inhabitants
Australia	4578.0	12579.0	22.4	64.0
New Zealand	566.2	2449.0	34.0	62.2
Malaysia	2000.0	9241.4	35.8	37.7
Singapore	848.6	3312.6	31.3	79.6
China (Excl. Hong Kong)	13233.0	206620.0	73.3	16.1
Hong Kong	2229.9	6395.7	23.5	94.3
India	881.8	12687.6	70.5	1.2
Indonesia	916.2	11700.0	66.4	5.5
Japan	38253.9	81118.4	16.2	63.7
United States	55312.3	140766.8	20.5	48.8
Finland	2162.6	4516.8	15.9	86.7
United Kingdom	8841.0	49677.0	41.2	84.1
South Africa	1836.0	13814.0	49.7	30.4
Tanzania	20.2	670.0	101.4	2.0

***Source:* Adapted from International Telecommunications Union (ITU), *World Telecommunications Indicators*, December 2003. Reproduced with the kind permission of ITU.**

might not upgrade its employees' computer systems to the latest Windows environment until after many other companies in the area have already begun to do so. However, once it decides to upgrade, it might install the new version of Windows in a relatively short period of time on all of its employees' PCs. Thus, although the company was relatively 'late' with respect to time of adoption, its extent of adoption was very high.

The adoption process

The second major process in the diffusion of innovations is adoption. The focus of this process is the stages through which an individual consumer passes while arriving at a decision to try or not to try or to continue using or to discontinue using a new product. (The adoption process should not be confused with adopter categories.)

STAGES IN THE ADOPTION PROCESS

It is often assumed that the consumer moves through five stages in arriving at a decision to purchase or reject a new product:

1. awareness
2. interest
3. evaluation
4. trial
5. adoption (or rejection)

The assumption underlying the adoption process is that consumers engage in extensive information search, whereas consumer involvement theory suggests that for some products, a limited information search is more likely (for low-involvement products). The five **stages in the adoption process** are described in Table 15.10.

Although the traditional adoption process model is insightful in its simplicity, it does not adequately reflect the full complexity of the consumer adoption process. For one, it does not adequately acknowledge that there is quite often a need or problem-recognition stage that consumers face before acquiring an awareness of potential options or solutions (a need recognition preceding the awareness stage). Moreover, the adoption process does not adequately provide for the possibility of evaluation and rejection of a new product or service after each

TABLE 15.10 Stages in the adoption process

Awareness	During the first stage of the adoption process, consumers are exposed to the product innovation. This exposure is somewhat neutral, for they are not yet sufficiently interested to search for additional product information.
Interest	When consumers develop an interest in the product or product category, they search for information about how the innovation can benefit them.
Evaluation	Based on their information, consumers draw conclusions about the innovation or determine whether further information is necessary. The evaluation stage represents a kind of 'mental trial' of the product innovation. If the evaluation is satisfactory, the consumer will actually try the product innovation; if the mental trial is unsatisfactory, the product will be rejected.
Trial	At this stage, consumers use the product on a limited basis. Their experience with the product provides them with the critical information that they need to adopt or reject.
Adoption (rejection)	Based on their trials and/or favourable evaluation, consumers decide to use the product on a full rather than limited basis, or they decide to reject it.

FIGURE 15.10 **An enhanced view of the adoption process**

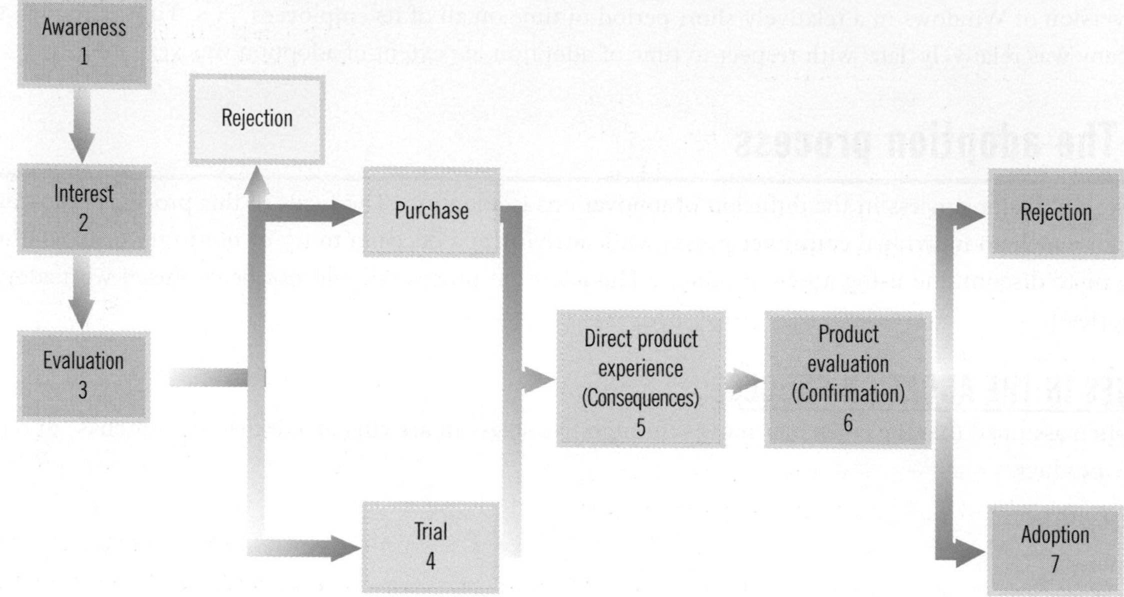

Source: **Adapted from John Antil, 'New product or service adoption: When does it happen?',** ***Journal of Consumer Marketing*****, 5, Spring 1988, p. 9.**

stage, especially after trial (i.e. a consumer may reject the product after trial or never use the product on a continuous basis). Finally, it does not explicitly include post-adoption or post-purchase evaluation, which can lead to a strengthened commitment or to a decision to discontinue use. Figure 15.10 presents an enhanced representation of the adoption process model, one that includes the additional dimensions or actions described here.

The adoption of some products and services may have minimal consequences, whereas the adoption of other innovations may lead to major behavioural and lifestyle changes. Examples of innovations with such major impact on society include the automobile, the telephone, the electric refrigerator, the television, the airplane, and the personal computer.

THE ADOPTION PROCESS AND INFORMATION SOURCES

The adoption process provides a framework for determining which types of information sources consumers find most important at specific decision stages. For example, early subscribers to a computer-linked data service, such as On-Australia (later BigPond), might first become aware of the service via mass-media sources (magazines and radio publicity). Then these early subscribers' final pre-trial information might be an outcome of informal discussions with personal sources. The key point is that impersonal mass-media sources tend to be most valuable for creating initial product awareness; as the purchase decision progresses, however, the relative importance of these sources declines while the relative importance of interpersonal sources (friends, salespeople, and others) increases. Figure 15.11 depicts this relationship.

➤ A profile of the consumer innovator

Who is the consumer innovator? What characteristics set the innovator apart from later adopters and from those who never purchase? How can the marketer reach and influence the innovator? These are key questions for the marketing practitioner about to introduce a new product or service.

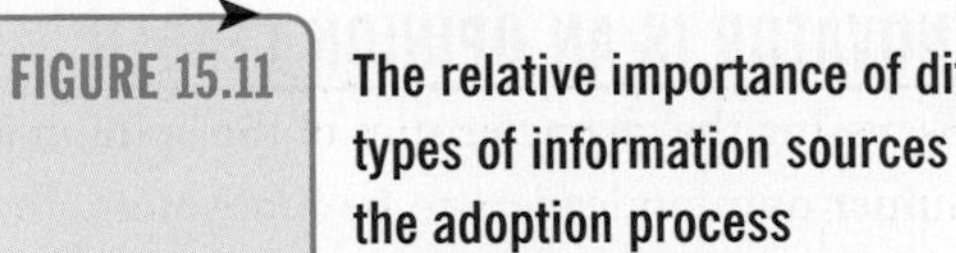
FIGURE 15.11 The relative importance of different types of information sources in the adoption process

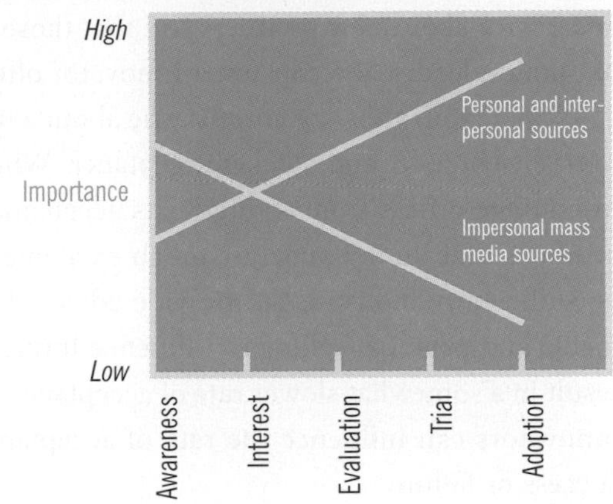

DEFINING THE CONSUMER INNOVATOR

Consumer innovators can be defined as the relatively small group of consumers who are the earliest purchasers of a new product. The problem with this definition, however, concerns the concept of earliest, which is, after all, a relative term. Sociologists have treated this issue by sometimes defining innovators as the first 2.5% of the social system to adopt an innovation. In many marketing diffusion studies, however, the definition of the consumer innovator has been derived from the status of the new product under investigation. For example, if researchers define a new product as an innovation for the first three months of its availability, then they define the consumers who purchase it during this period as 'innovators'. Other researchers have defined innovators in terms of their innovativeness, that is, their purchase of some minimum number of new products from a selected group of new products. For instance, in the adoption of new fashion items, innovators can be defined as those consumers who purchase more than one fashion product from a group of 10 new fashion products. Non-innovators would be defined as those who purchase none or only one of the new fashion products. In other instances, researchers have defined innovators as those falling within an arbitrary proportion of the total market (e.g. the first 10% of the population in a specified geographic area to buy the new product).

INTEREST IN THE PRODUCT CATEGORY

Not surprisingly, consumer innovators are much more interested than either later adopters or non-adopters in the product categories that they are among the first to purchase. If what is known from diffusion theory holds true in the future, the earliest purchasers of small hydrogen fuel cells cars are likely to have substantially greater interest in cars (they will enjoy looking at car magazines and will be interested in the performance and functioning of cars) than those who purchased conventional small cars during the same period or those who purchased fuel cell cars during a later period. Recent research examining early adopters of products containing a non-fat synthetic cooking oil (i.e. olestra) were found to have a high interest in such a product because of health and diet concerns.[54]

Consumer innovators are more likely than non-innovators to seek information concerning their specific interests from a variety of informal and mass-media sources. They are more likely to give greater deliberation to the purchase of new products or services in their areas of interest than non-innovators. Although innovators have generally been portrayed as heavy product category users, this may be true only for relatively continuous innovations. A recent study found that for discontinuous innovations, it is often novices that purchase the product, whereas experts in the subject area are often laggards with respect to product adoption. For example, serious amateur photographers with a great deal of camera knowledge and little computer literacy were found to be least likely to buy a digital camera, whereas individuals with high computer literacy and low photographic knowledge were most likely to purchase this product.[55] Therefore, it might be more important for the digital camera manufacturer to advertise in a computer rather than a photography magazine.

THE INNOVATOR IS AN OPINION LEADER

When discussing the characteristics of the opinion leader earlier in this chapter, we indicated a strong tendency for consumer opinion leaders to be innovators. In the present context, an impressive amount of research on the diffusion of innovations has found that consumer innovators provide other consumers with information and advice about new products and that those who receive such advice frequently follow it. Thus, in the role of opinion leader, the consumer innovator often influences the acceptance or rejection of new products.

When innovators are enthusiastic about a new product and encourage others to try it, the product is likely to receive broader and quicker acceptance. When consumer innovators are dissatisfied with a new product and discourage others from trying it, its acceptance will be severely limited, and it may die a quick death. For products that do not generate much excitement (either positive or negative), consumer innovators may not be sufficiently motivated to provide advice. In such cases, the marketer must rely almost entirely on mass media and personal selling to influence future purchasers; the absence of informal influence is also likely to result in a somewhat slower rate of acceptance (or rejection) of the new product. Because motivated consumer innovators can influence the rate of acceptance or rejection of a new product, they influence its eventual success or failure.

PERSONALITY TRAITS

In Chapter 4, we examined the personality traits that distinguish the consumer innovator from the non-innovator. In this section, we will briefly highlight what researchers have learned about the personality of the consumer innovator. First, consumer innovators generally are less dogmatic than non-innovators. They tend to approach new or unfamiliar products with considerable openness and little anxiety. In contrast, non-innovators seem to find new products threatening to the point where they prefer to delay purchase until the product's success has been clearly established.

Consistent with their open-mindedness, it appears that innovative behaviour is an expression of an individual's need for uniqueness.[56] Those new products, both branded and unbranded, that represent a greater change in a person's consumption habits were viewed as superior when it came to satisfying the need for uniqueness. Therefore, to gain more rapid acceptance of a new product, marketers might consider appealing to a consumer's need for uniqueness.

Still further, consumer innovators also differ from non-innovators in terms of social character. Consumer innovators are inner-directed; that is, they rely on their own values or standards when making a decision about a new product. In contrast, non-innovators are other-directed, relying on others for guidance on how to respond to a new product rather than trusting their own personal values or standards. Thus, the initial purchasers of a new line of automobiles might be inner-directed, whereas the later purchasers of the same automobile might be other-directed. This suggests that as acceptance of a product progresses from early to later adopters, a gradual shift occurs in the personality type of adopters from inner-directedness to other-directedness.

There also appears to be a link between optimum stimulation level and consumer innovativeness. Specifically, individuals who seek a lifestyle rich with novel, complex, and unusual experiences (high optimum stimulation levels) are more willing to risk trying new products, to be innovative, to seek purchase-related information, and to accept new retail facilities. Researchers have isolated a link between variety-seeking and purchase behaviour that provides insights into consumer innovators. Variety-seeking consumers tend to be brand switchers and purchasers of innovative products and services. They also possess the following innovator-related personality traits: They are open-minded (or low in dogmatism), extroverts, with liberal rather than conservative values, low in authoritarianism, able to deal with complex or ambiguous stimuli, and creative.[57]

To sum up, consumer innovators seem to be more receptive to the unfamiliar and the unique; they are more willing to rely on their own values or standards than on the judgment of others. They also are willing to run the risk of a poor product choice to increase their exposure to new products that will be satisfying. For the marketer, the personality traits that distinguish innovators from non-innovators suggest the need for separate promotional campaigns for innovators and for later adopters.

PERCEIVED RISK AND VENTURESOMENESS

Perceived risk is another measure of a consumer's likelihood to try new brands or products. Perceived risk is the degree of uncertainty or fear about the consequences of a purchase that a consumer feels when considering the purchase of a new product. For example, consumers experience uncertainty when they are concerned that a new product will not work properly or as well as other alternatives. Research on perceived risk and the trial of new products overwhelmingly indicates that consumer innovators are low-risk perceivers; that is, they experience little fear of trying new products or services. Consumers who perceive little or no risk in the purchase of a new product are much more likely to make innovative purchases than consumers who perceive a great deal of risk. In other words, high-risk perception limits innovativeness.

Venturesomeness is a broad-based measure of a consumer's willingness to accept the risk of purchasing new products. Measures of venturesomeness have been used to evaluate a person's general values or attitudes toward trying new products. A typical measurement scale might include such items as:

- I prefer to (try a toothpaste when it first comes out) (wait and learn how good it is before trying it).
- When I am shopping and see a brand of paper towels I know about but have never used, I am (very anxious or willing to try it), (hesitant about trying it), (very unwilling to try it).
- I like to be among the first people to buy and use new products that are on the market (measured on a five-point 'agreement' scale).

Research that has examined venturesomeness has generally found that consumers who indicate a willingness to try new products tend to be consumer innovators (as measured by their actual purchase of new products). On the other hand, consumers who express a reluctance to try new products are, in fact, less likely to purchase new products. Therefore, venturesomeness seems to be an effective barometer of actual innovative behaviour.

PURCHASE AND CONSUMPTION CHARACTERISTICS

Consumer innovators possess purchase and usage traits that set them apart from non-innovators. For example, consumer innovators are less brand loyal; that is, they are more apt to switch brands. This is not surprising, for brand loyalty would seriously impede a consumer's willingness to try new products. Consumer innovators are more likely to be deal prone (to take advantage of special promotional offers such as free samples and cents-off coupons). They are also likely to be heavy users of the product category in which they innovate. Specifically, they purchase larger quantities and consume more of the product than non-innovators. Finally, for products like DVDs, computers, microwave ovens, mobile phones, and food processors, usage variety is likely to be a relevant dimension of new-product diffusion. An understanding of how consumers might be 'usage innovators'—that is, finding or 'inventing' new uses for an innovation—might create entirely new market opportunities for marketers' products. SMS in mobile phones provides an example of a use which proved to be unexpectedly popular. It has created new, informed social networks.[58]

A positive relationship exists between innovative behaviour and heavy usage. Consumer innovators are not only an important market segment from the standpoint of being the first to use a new product, but they also represent a substantial market in terms of product volume. However, their propensity to switch brands or to use products in different or unique ways and their positive response to promotional deals also suggest that innovators will continue to use a specific brand only as long as they do not perceive that a new and potentially better alternative is available.

MEDIA HABITS

Comparisons of the media habits of innovators and non-innovators across such widely diverse areas of consumption as fashion clothing and new automotive services suggest that innovators have somewhat greater total exposure to magazines than non-innovators, particularly to special-interest magazines devoted to the product category in which they innovate. For example, fashion innovators are more likely to read magazines such as *GQ* and *Vogue* than non-innovators; financial services innovators have greater exposure to such special-interest investor magazines.

Consumer innovators are also less likely to watch television than non-innovators. This view is consistently supported by research that over the past decade or so has compared the magazine and TV exposure levels of consumer innovators. The evidence indicates that consumer innovators have higher-than-average magazine exposure and lower-than-average TV exposure. It will be interesting, though, to observe over the next few years what the impact the convergence of the Internet and television will be. Studies concerning the relationship between innovative behaviour and exposure to other mass media, such as radio and newspapers, have been too few, and the results have been too varied to draw any useful conclusions.

SOCIAL CHARACTERISTICS

Consumer innovators are more socially accepted and socially involved than non-innovators. For example, innovators are more socially integrated into the community, better accepted by others, and more socially involved; that is, they belong to more social groups and organisations than non-innovators. This greater social acceptance and involvement of consumer innovators may help explain why they function as effective opinion leaders.

DEMOGRAPHIC CHARACTERISTICS

It is reasonable to assume that the age of the consumer innovator is related to the specific product category in which he or she innovates; however, research suggests that consumer innovators tend to be younger than either late adopters or non-innovators. This is no doubt because many of the products selected for research attention (such as fashion, convenience grocery products, or new automobiles) are particularly attractive to younger consumers.

Consumer innovators have more formal education, have higher personal or family incomes, and are more likely to have higher occupational status (to be professionals or hold managerial positions) than late adopters or non-innovators. In other words, innovators tend to be more upscale than other consumer segments and can, therefore, better afford to make a mistake should the innovative new product or service being purchased prove to be unacceptable. Table 15.11 summarises the major differences between consumer innovators and late adopters or non-innovators. The table includes the major distinctions examined in our current presentation of the consumer innovator profile.

ARE THERE GENERALISED CONSUMER INNOVATORS?

Do consumer innovators in one product category tend to be consumer innovators in other product categories? The answer to this strategically important question is a guarded 'no'. The overlap of innovativeness across product categories, like opinion leadership, seems to be limited to product categories that are closely related to the same

TABLE 15.11 Comparative profiles of the consumer innovator and the non-innovator or late adopter

Characteristic	Innovator	Non-innovator (or Late adopter)
Product interest	More	Less
Opinion leadership	More	Less
Personality		
Dogmatism	Open-minded	Closed-minded
Need for uniqueness	Higher	Lower
Social character	Inner-directed	Other-directed
Optimum stimulation level	Higher	Lower
Variety seeking	Higher	Lower
Perceived risk	Less	More
Venturesomeness	More	Less
Purchase and consumption traits		
Brand loyalty	Less	More
Deal proneness	More	Less
Usage	More	Less
Media habits		
Total magazine exposure	More	Less
Special-interest magazines	More	Less
Television	Less	More
Internet	More	Less
Social characteristics		
Social integration	More	Less
Social striving (e.g. social, physical, and occupational mobility)	More	Less
Group memberships	More	Less
Demographic characteristics		
Age	Younger	Older
Income	Higher	Lower
Education	More	Less
Occupational status	Higher	Lower

basic interest area. Consumers who are innovators of one new food product or one new appliance are more likely to be innovators of other new products in the same general product category. In other words, although no single or generalised consumer-innovativeness trait seems to operate across broadly different product categories, evidence suggests that consumers who innovate within a specific product category will innovate again within the same product category. For example, up to the point of 'innovator burnout' (i.e. 'what I have is good enough'), a person who was an innovator in buying an original IBM PC for his or her home office in the early 1980s was most likely again an innovator in buying a PC with an Intel 80286 microprocessor, an Intel 80386 microprocessor, an Intel 80486 microprocessor, and an Intel Pentium microprocessor and is likely to again be an innovator when it comes to the next generation of microprocessors for personal computers.

For the marketer, such a pattern suggests that it is generally a good marketing strategy to target a new product to consumers who were the first to try other products in the same basic product category. In the realm of high-tech innovations, there is evidence suggesting that there is a generalised 'high-tech' innovator—known as a 'change leader'.[59] Such individuals tend to embrace and popularise many of the innovations that are ultimately accepted by the mainstream population, such as computers, mobile phones, and PDAs. They tend to have a wide range of personal and professional contacts representing different occupational and social groups; most often these contacts tend to be 'weak ties' or acquaintances.

Change leaders also appear to fall into one of two distinct groups: a younger group that can be characterised as being stimulation seeking, sociable, and having high levels of fashion awareness or a middle-aged group that is highly self-confident and has very high information-seeking needs.

Similar to change leaders, 'technophiles' are individuals who purchase technologically advanced products soon after their market debut. Such individuals tend to be technically curious people. Also, another group responding to technology are adults who are categorised as 'techthusiasts'—people who are most likely to purchase or subscribe to emerging products and services that are technologically oriented. These consumers are typically younger, better educated, and more affluent.[60]

CASE STUDY 15.1

The Horseless Carriage: From the Oruktor Amphibolos to the Flying Car

Margo Poole, University of Newcastle

Could you image hopping into your 'Oruktor Amphibolos' to go and pick up a few groceries at the supermarket? Well, as history goes, if it had been up to Oliver Evans, who patented a steam-powered, self-propelled vehicle in 1789, that chugged along on land and then dropped into the water and paddled around, we would all be driving about in an 'Oruktor'. However, as fate would have it, we have ended up with what is now commonly called a 'car', coming from the Celtic term 'carrus' (meaning a cart) or 'automobile', coming from the Greek term 'auto' (meaning self) and the Latin term 'mobils' (meaning moving).[61,62] Nevertheless, whatever name that was settled upon, there is little doubt that this innovation in personal transport has enormously impacted our daily lives.

Not only has the automobile influenced our mode of personal transport, it has also had a profound impact on our surrounding environment and, perhaps, how we may even meet our maker. Think about billboards, flashing neon signs, drive-in take-aways like McDonald's and giant signage icons like the Big Banana in New South Wales and the Big Pineapple in Queensland. The drive-in motel, that became so popular in the 1960s, is also a part of this sea change in society. This mode of transportation, unfortunately, has also been considered highly dangerous. But, more on that as we progress through the automobile's past, present and future development.

The first self-propelled personal vehicles were built in the late 1700s, powered by a steam engine. However, with a top speed of 2.3 mph and being highly cumbersome and noisy, they had an uphill battle competing with the already tried and true mode of transportation of the day, the horse-drawn cart.[63] Legislation brought in by the British government also put a stop to any further development of what was often referred to as the 'steam-carriage'. The legislation demanded that the vehicle be led by a gentleman, on foot, waving a red flag and blowing a loud horn. This legislation was not repealed until the late 1800s.[64] There was then some dabbling in internal combustion engines powered by gunpowder. For obvious reasons, this avenue was abandoned.

However, around 1886, two German inventors, Gottleib Daimler and Karl Benz, independently developed a revolutionary internal combustion engine that was powered by petrol.[65]

A little later in the US, in the late 1800s, Frank and Charles Duryea began manufacturing more than one automobile at a time. Then Charles King introduced the revolutionary four-cylinder engine. It travelled at a top speed of five mph. A young boy, W. Bronson Taylor, growing up during this era, recalls his first encounter with an automobile. He had heard that a lawyer in a town 18 miles away had purchased an automobile called an 'Olds'. People questioned the sanity of anyone crazy enough to do such a thing. Such transportation was prohibitively expensive with the average car costing around $US2500 while the average annual wage was a mere $US500. The automobile was considered to be a highly indulgent, expensive luxury that was dangerous and limited in any real practical value.[66] They had no roof, no windscreen and broke down continually. With great embarrassment, the driver would often have to walk to the closest farmer's house and ask if they could harness their horse to the front to get back home. Returning back along the street where the driver had so proudly showed off his new mode of transportation just an hour earlier was, of course, a humiliation.[67] Thus, the young Taylor, all of 12 years, immediately decided that he would never actually see this new acquisition because it would never be capable of travelling the distance of 18 miles to his town. However, soon after, his mate came running up in the street, he had seen the lawyer, and his car, in front of old Mrs Anderson's house. There stood the 'Olds', with a great deal of steam coming from under the seat where the engine lay with the lawyer standing nearby, looking very perplexed. Young Taylor suggested to him that maybe it needed some water. The lawyer sternly replied that it was a petrol engine and didn't use water. An investigation into the basic workings of the engine by young Taylor found that, indeed, water was a very important component of the working of the engine. With some tap water from old Mrs Anderson's, the 'Olds' was back on its way home.[68]

Then, an enthusiastic engineer by the name of Henry Ford brought about another advance in the history of the automobile. Henry began building a prototype that he called the 'Quadricicle'. Unfortunately, in his enthusiasm, he realised, a little too late, that it was too big to go through the shed door. So, to test drive his prototype, he had to use an axe to chop out a hole large enough to make for a safe exit. The 'Quadricicle' had a top speed of 20 mph. Henry then went for a job at the Winton Motor Carriage Company. Fortunately, in many ways, Alexander Winton was not impressed by Henry and decided not to hire him.[69] Subsequently, Henry Ford, through the development of the conveyor belt, then went on to make automobiles affordable for many more people. However, what still seemed to be an almost insurmountable problem was the roads. They were all dirt and built for horse-drawn carriages. In summer, the automobile would generate a remarkable amount of choking dust while in winter, when it rained, it would simply get bogged. Indeed, it was said at the time that 'the idea of roads which were passable all the time seemed more remote that a trip to the moon'.[70] How things have changed, man has travelled to the moon and, on the whole, we have passable roads; if only we could overcome the driver's nightmare, the traffic jam. Also, from the very beginning the automobile has been dangerous to both people and animals. Horses used to bolt when they saw one coming and people were, and still are, continually being injured or killed. It was even a dangerous procedure to crank start the early car. If it backfired at this time, the driver could end up with a broken arm.[71] Although there has been great advances, like the seat belt, anti-locking brakes and interior air bags, we continue to see carnage on the roads. There are also ongoing concerns about environmental damage through polluting emissions. So, with so many problems remaining, what does the future of personal transportation hold?

It appears that we have two options, the 'flying car' and the 'personal jetpack'. Both see the end to the traffic jam. Imagine just pressing a button and 'lifting off' into a third dimension, the sky. Have you ever seen the old TV cartoon of the 1960s where George Jetson takes off and flies to work? The 'flying car' is bringing this to reality and everything will be completely controlled by computers using computerised global positioning systems (GPS) over the Internet. The 'flying car' will take off and land vertically and can have a top speed of around 350 kph in the air and 105 kph on the road. So, at the flick of a switch your car lifts off, wings come out on each side and you're off, with a range of around 900 km. The cost? Initially about $US1 million, but this should reduce to around $US60 000 once mass produced.[72]

The alternative is the 'personal jetpack'. The 'solo track exo-skeletor flying vehicle' (XFV) also lifts off vertically. The fundamental difference from the 'flying car' is that you strap it to your back, step onto two little foot-stands, hold on to the levers and off you go. Of course, it only works in the air and not on the roads. But, you could 'lift off' from your back yard and 'land' where there are no roads at all. Average speed in the air is around 100 kph and it can climb as high as 3048 metres. Therefore, you could be sharing airspace with other light aircraft. The XFV is compact, weighing in at 130 kg, it can hover in a stationary position and has a handy parachute for any emergency. The left-hand lever controls speed while the right-hand one looks after the tilt. You can also lean sideways as well as back and forth, like being on a motor bike, for greater control.[73]

So, the manner in which humans attempt to transport themselves and their goods has evolved enormously over a very short time and, it would appear that we still have a remarkable future ahead.

Case Study Questions

1. Consider the characteristics that influence consumer acceptance of new products (the diffusion process) and apply them to the automobile.
2. Now consider the same characteristics to debate whether the 'flying car' or the 'personal jetpack' will become the future of personal transportation.
3. Consider the product characteristics in Table 15.6 (page 527) that influence diffusion. Apply them to the automobile.
4. There are five stages to the adoption process. Can these be identified with the adoption process of the automobile? Will this also be the case for the 'flying car'?
5. Does the case study illustrate the profile of the consumer innovator? Discuss and debate the similarities and/or differences?
6. Research automobile accessories like the headlamp, flashing turn signals and the bumper that have been adopted by consumers over the years. Choose three such innovations, research how they evolved and discuss them in relationship to the diffusion of innovations.

Summary

Opinion leadership is the process by which one person (the opinion leader) informally influences the actions or attitudes of others, who may be opinion seekers or merely opinion recipients. Opinion receivers perceive the opinion leader as a highly credible, objective source of product information who can help reduce their search time and perceived risk. Opinion leaders, in turn, are motivated to give information or advice to others, in part because doing so enhances their own status and self-image and because such advice tends to reduce any post-purchase dissonance that they may have. Other motives include product involvement, 'other' involvement, and message involvement.

Market researchers identify opinion leaders by such methods as self-designation, key informants, the sociometric method, and the objective method. Studies of opinion leadership indicate that this phenomenon tends to be product specific; that is, individuals 'specialise' in a product or product category in which they are highly interested. An opinion leader for one product category may be an opinion receiver for another.

Generally, opinion leaders are gregarious, self-confident, innovative people who like to talk. Additionally, they may feel differentiated from others and choose to act differently (or public individuation). They acquire information about their areas of interest through avid readership of special-interest magazines and by means of new-product trials. Their interests often overlap adjacent product areas; thus, their opinion leadership may extend into related areas. The market maven is an intense case of such a person. These consumers possess a wide range of information about many different types of products, retail outlets, and other dimensions of markets. They both initiate discussions with other consumers and respond to requests for market information over a wide range of products and services. Market mavens are also distinguishable from other opinion leaders, because their influence stems not so much from product experience but from a more general knowledge or market expertise that leads them to an early awareness of a wide array of new products and services.

The opinion leadership process usually takes place among friends, neighbours, and work associates who have frequent physical proximity and, thus, have ample opportunity to hold informal product-related conversations. These conversations usually occur naturally in the context of the product-category usage.

The two-step flow of communication theory highlights the role of interpersonal influence in the transmission of information from the mass media to the population at large. This theory provides the foundation for a revised multi-step flow of communication model, which takes into account the fact that information and influence often are two-way processes and that opinion leaders both influence and are influenced by opinion receivers.

Marketers recognise the strategic value of segmenting their audiences into opinion leaders and opinion receivers for their product categories. When marketers can direct their promotional efforts to the more influential segments of their markets, these individuals will transmit this information to those who seek product advice. Marketers try to both simulate and stimulate opinion leadership. They have also found that they can create opinion leaders for their products by taking socially involved or influential people and deliberately increasing their enthusiasm for a product category.

The diffusion process and the adoption process are two closely related concepts concerned with the acceptance of new products by consumers. The diffusion process is a macro process that focuses on the spread of an innovation (a new product, service, or idea) from its source to the consuming public. The adoption process is a micro process that examines the stages through which an individual consumer passes when making a decision to accept or reject a new product.

The definition of the term innovation can be firm-oriented (new to the firm), product-oriented (a continuous innovation, a dynamically continuous innovation, or a discontinuous innovation), market-oriented (how long the product has been on the market or an arbitrary percentage of the potential target market that has purchased it), or consumer-oriented (new to the consumer). Market-oriented definitions of innovation are most useful to consumer researchers in the study of the diffusion and adoption of new products.

Five product characteristics influence the consumer's acceptance of a new product: relative advantage, compatibility, complexity, trialability, and observability (or communicability).

Diffusion researchers are concerned with two aspects of communication—the channels through which word of a new product is spread to the consuming public and the types of messages that influence the adoption or rejection of new products. Diffusion is always examined in the context of a specific social system, such as a target market, a community, a region, or even a nation.

Time is an integral consideration in the diffusion process. Researchers are concerned with the amount of purchase time required for an individual consumer to adopt or reject a new product, with the rate of adoption, and with the identification of sequential adopters. The five adopter categories are innovators, early adopters, early majority, late majority, and laggards.

Marketing strategists try to control the rate of adoption through their new-product pricing policies. Marketers who wish to penetrate the market to achieve market leadership try to acquire wide adoption as quickly as possible by using low prices. Those who wish to recoup their developmental costs quickly use a skimming pricing policy but lengthen the adoption process.

The traditional adoption process model describes five stages through which an individual consumer passes to arrive at the decision to adopt or reject a new product: awareness, interest, evaluation, trial, and adoption. To make it more realistic, an enhanced model is suggested as one that considers the possibility of a pre-existing need or problem, the likelihood that some form of evaluation might occur through the entire process, and that even after adoption there will be post-adoption or purchase evaluation that might either strengthen the commitment or alternatively lead to discontinuation.

New-product marketers are vitally concerned with identifying the consumer innovator so that they may direct their promotional campaigns to the people who are most likely to try new products, adopt them, and influence others. Consumer research has identified a number of consumer-related characteristics, including product interest, opinion leadership, personality factors, purchase and consumption traits, media habits, social characteristics, and demographic variables that distinguish consumer innovators from later adopters. These serve as useful variables in the segmentation of markets for new-product introductions.

Discussion questions

1. a. Why is an opinion leader a more credible source of product information than an advertisement for the same product?
   b. Are there any circumstances in which information from advertisements is likely to be more influential than word of mouth?
2. Why would a consumer who has just purchased an expensive fax machine for home use attempt to influence the purchase behaviour of others?
3. A company that owns and operates gymnasiums across the country is opening one in your suburb. The company has retained you as its marketing research consultant and has asked you to identify opinion leaders for its service. Which of the following identification methods would you recommend: the self-designating method, the sociometric method, the key informant method, or the objective method? Explain your selection. In your answer, be sure to discuss the advantages and disadvantages of the four techniques as they relate to the marketing situation just described.
4. Do you have any 'market mavens' among your friends? Describe their personality traits and behaviours. Describe a situation in which a market maven has given you advice regarding a product or service and discuss what you believe was his or her motivation for doing so.
5. Describe how a manufacturer might use knowledge of the following product characteristics to speed up the acceptance of pocket-sized mobile telephones:
   a. Relative advantage
   b. Compatibility
   c. Complexity
   d. Trialability
   e. Observability
6. Fujitsu has introduced a compact laptop computer that weighs about one kilo, has wireless connectivity, but no disk drive. It has a powerful processor into which a full-size desktop screen and keyboard can be easily plugged. How can the company use the diffusion-of-innovations framework to develop promotional, pricing, and distribution strategies targeted to the following adopter categories?
   a. Innovators
   b. Early adopters
   c. Early majority
   d. Late majority
   e. Laggards
7. Is the curve that describes the sequence and proportion of adopter categories among the population (Figure 15.9) similar in shape to the product lifecycle curve? Explain your answer. How would you use both curves to develop a marketing strategy?
8. Sony is introducing an ultra high-definition 106 cm plasma TV bundled with a HDTV set-top box, a DVD recorder and a home theatre system that uses wireless technology to get the sound to the speakers. The system allows the viewer to watch two sources of video (e.g. DVD and the cricket) at the same time.
   a. What recommendations would you make to Sony regarding the initial target market for the new TV bundle?
   b. How would you identify the innovators for this product?
   c. Select three characteristics of consumer innovators (as summarised in Table 15.11). Explain how Sony might use each of these characteristics to influence the adoption process and speed up the diffusion of the new product.
   d. Should Sony follow a penetration or a skimming policy in introducing the product? Why?

Exercises

1. Describe two situations in which you served as an opinion leader and two situations in which you sought consumption-related advice or information from an opinion leader. Indicate your relationship to the persons with whom you interacted. Are the circumstances during which you engaged in word-of-mouth communications consistent with those in the text's material? Explain.

2. a. Find ads that simulate and ads that stimulate opinion leadership and present them in class.
   b. Can you think of negative rumours that you have heard recently about a company or a product? If so, present them in class.
3. Identify a product, service, or style that recently was adopted by you or some of your friends. Identify what type of innovation it is and describe its diffusion process up to this point in time. What are the characteristics of people who adopted it first? What types of people did not adopt it? What features of the product, service, or style are likely to determine its eventual success or failure?
4. With the advancement of digital technology, some companies plan to introduce interactive TV systems that will allow viewers to select films from video libraries and view them on demand. Among people you know, identify two who are likely to be the innovators for such a new service and construct consumer profiles using the characteristics of consumer innovators discussed in the text.

Key terms

adopter categories *(p. 529)*
adoption process *(p. 521)*
compatibility *(p. 524)*
complexity *(p. 524)*
consumer innovators *(p. 516)*
continuous innovation *(p. 522)*
diffusion of innovations *(p. 521)*
diffusion process *(p. 521)*
discontinuous innovation *(p. 523)*
dynamically continuous innovation *(p. 522)*
innovation *(p. 522)*
key informant *(p. 514)*
market maven *(p. 516)*
multi-step flow of communication theory *(p. 518)*
objective method *(p. 514)*
observability *(p. 526)*
opinion leader *(p. 508)*
opinion leadership *(p. 508)*
opinion receiver/recipient *(p. 508)*
opinion seekers *(p. 508)*
permission marketing *(p. 528)*
product life cycle *(p. 531)*
relative advantage *(p. 524)*
self-designating method *(p. 513)*
sociometric method *(p. 514)*
stages in the adoption process *(p. 533)*
trialability *(p. 525)*
two-step flow of communication theory *(p. 517)*
viral marketing *(p. 509)*

Endnotes

1. Chip Walker, 'Word of mouth', *American Demographics*, 17(7), July 1995, p. 42.
2. Dale F. Duhan, Scott D. Johnson, James B. Wilcox, and Gilbert D. Harrell, 'Influences on consumer use of word-of-mouth recommendation sources', *Journal of the Academy of Marketing Science*, 25(4), 1997, pp. 283–295.
3. James Brooke, 'Youth let their thumbs do the talking in Japan', *New York Times*, 30 April 2002, p. A14.
4. Ralph F. Wilson, 'The six simple principles of viral marketing', *Web Marketing Today*, 70, 1 February 2000, see <www.wilsonweb.com/wmt5/viral-principles.htm>; and <searchcrm.techtarget.com/sDefinition/0,sid11_gci213514,00.html>. Beth Snyder Bulik, 'Upping the cool quotient', *Business 2.0*, 22 August 2000, pp. 94–96; and John Gaffney, 'The cool kids are doing it. Should you?', *Business 2.0*, November 2001, pp. 140–141.
5. For example see <www.ragingcow.com/DrinkThis.asp>, website/blog produced by Dr Pepper (11 March 2004) and Jack Neff, 'P&G goes viral with test of innovation locations', *Advertising Age*, 4 September 2000, p. 4.
6. Ira Brodsky, 'IM expands its enterprise reach', *Network World*, 21(4), p. 49. See also Marc Weingarten, 'The medium is the instant message', *Business 2.0*, February 2002, pp. 98–99.
7. George Silverman, 'The power of word of mouth', *Direct Marketing*, 64(5), September 2001, pp. 47–52.
8. Geok Theng Lau and Sophia Ng, 'Individual and situational factors influencing negative word-of-mouth behaviour', *Revue Canadienne des Sciences de l'Administration* (Montreal), 18(3), September 2001, pp. 163–178.
9. See Silverman, op. cit.
10. S. Ramesh Kumar, 'The might of the word', *Businessline*, 2 September 1999, pp. 1–2.
11. See <www.adslogans.com/hof/index.html> (12 March 2004).
12. Pamala L. Alreck and Robert B. Settle, 'The importance

of word-of-mouth communications to service buyers', in *1995 AMA Winter Educators' Proceedings*, eds David W. Stewart and Naufel J. Vilcassim (Chicago: American Marketing Association, 1995), pp. 188–193.

13. Cathy L. Hartman and Pamela L. Kiecker, 'Marketplace influencers at the point of purchase: The role of purchase pals in consumer decision making', in *1991 AMA Educators' Proceedings*, eds Mary C. Gilly and F. Robert Dwyer et al. (Chicago: American Marketing Association, 1991), pp. 461–467.
14. Pamela Kiecker and Cathy L. Hartman, 'Predicting buyers' selection of interpersonal sources: The role of strong ties and weak ties', *Advances in Consumer Research*, 21, eds Chris T. Allen and Deborah Roedder John (Provo, UT: Association for Consumer Research, 1994), pp. 464–469.
15. Praveen Aggarwal and Taihoon Cha, 'Surrogate buyers and the new product adoption process: A conceptualization and managerial framework', *Journal of Consumer Marketing*, 14(5), 1997, pp. 391–400; and Stanley C. Hollander and Kathleen M. Rassuli, 'Shopping with other people's money: The marketing management implications of surrogate-mediated consumer decision making', *Journal of Marketing*, 63(2), April 1999, pp. 102–118.
16. Leisa Reinecke Flynn, Ronald E. Goldsmith, and Jacqueline K. Eastman, 'The King and Summers opinion leadership scale: Revision and refinement', *Journal of Business Research*, 31, 1994, pp. 55–64.
17. Mary C. Gilly, John L. Graham, Mary Finley Wolfinbarger, and Laura J. Yale, 'A Dyadic Study of Interpersonal Information Search', *Journal of the Academy of Marketing Science*, 26(2), 1998, pp. 83–100.
18. <www.scubadiving.com> (13 March 2004).
19. Lawrence F. Feick and Linda L. Price, 'The market maven: A diffuser of marketplace Information', *Journal of Marketing*, 51, January 1987, p. 85.
20. Michael T. Elliott and Anne E. Warfield, 'Do market mavens categorize brands differently?', *Advances in Consumer Research*, 20, eds Leigh McAlister and Michael L. Rothschild (Provo, UT: Association for Consumer Research, 1993), pp. 202–208; and Frank Alpert, 'Consumer market beliefs and their managerial implications: An empirical examination', *Journal of Consumer Marketing*, 10(2), 1993, pp. 56–70.
21. Brian T. Engelland, Christopher D. Hopkins, and Dee Anne Larson, 'Market mavenship as an influencer of service quality evaluation', *Journal of Marketing Theory and Practice*, 9(4), Fall 2001, pp. 15–26.
22. John Eighmey and Lola McCord, 'Adding value in the information age: Uses and gratifications of sites on the World Wide Web', *Journal of Business Research*, 41, 1998, pp. 187–194.
23. Roy Furchgott, 'Surfing for satisfaction: Consumer complaints go on-line', *New York Times*, 8 June 1997, p. 8. See also <www.notgoodenough.org>, <forums.baddealings.com>, <www.sucks.com> and <www.talkcity.com>.
24. Paul F. Lazarsfeld, Bernard Berelson, and Hazel Gaudet, *The People's Choice*, 2nd edn (New York: Columbia University Press, 1948), p. 151.
25. Suman Basuroy, Subimai Chatterjee and S. Abraham Ravid, 'How critical are critical reviews? The box office effects of film critics, star power, and budgets', *Journal of Marketing*, 67, October 2003, pp. 103–117.
26. <www.bzzagent.com> (12 March 2004). The site is discussed in Melanie Wells, 'Cross-pollinators', *Forbes*, 173(2), 2 February 2004, p. 86.
27. 'In the news: Ploys', *New York Times Magazine*, 13 February 1994, p. 19.
28. Kate MacArthur, 'Iced coffee market gains grounds', *Advertising Age*, 4 September 2000, p. 22.
29. Walker, op.cit.
30. 'Dangerous personal care products?', *Choice*, March 2004, pp. 24–29.
31. See, for example, Thomas W. Valente and Rebecca L. Davis, 'Accelerating the diffusion of innovations using opinion leaders', *Annals of the American Academy of Political and Social Science*, 566, November 1999, pp. 55–67.
32. Joseph R. Mancuso, 'Why not create opinion leaders for new product introduction?', *Journal of Marketing*, 33, July 1969, pp. 20–25.
33. Barbara Bickart and Robert M. Schindler, 'Internet forums as influential sources of consumer information', *Journal of Interactive Marketing*, 15(3), Summer 2001, pp. 31–39.
34. Diane Crane, 'Diffusion models and fashion: A reassessment', *Annals of the American Academy of Political and Social Sciences*, 566, November 1999, pp. 13–24.
35. Thomas S. Robertson, 'The process of innovation and the diffusion of innovation', *Journal of Marketing*, 31, January 1967, pp. 14–19.
36. Everett M. Rogers, *Diffusion of Innovations*, 4th edn (New York: Free Press, 1995); and Hubert Gatignon and Thomas S. Robertson, 'Innovative decision processes', *Handbook of Consumer Behavior*, eds Thomas S. Robert-

son and Harold H. Kassarjian (Upper Saddle River, NJ: Prentice Hall, 1991), pp. 316–348.

37. S. Ram and Hyung-Shik Jung, 'Innovativeness in product usage: A comparison of early adopters and early majority', *Psychology and Marketing*, 11, January–February 1994, pp. 57–67; A. R. Petrosky, 'Gender and use innovation: An inquiry into the socialization of innovative behavior', *1995 AMA Educators' Proceedings*, eds Barbara B. Stern and George M. Zinkan (Chicago: American Marketing Association, 1995), pp. 299–307; Kyungae Park and Carl L. Dyer, 'Consumer use innovative behavior: An approach toward its causes', *Advances in Consumer Research*, 22, eds Frank R. Kardes and Mita Sujan (Provo, UT: Association for Consumer Research, 1995), pp. 566–572.
38. Earle Eldridge, 'Pickups get women's touch', *USA Today*, 13 June 2001, pp. 1B, 2B.
39. Rogers, op. cit. pp. 15–16.
40. Hsiang Chen and Kevin Crowston, 'Comparative diffusion of the telephone and the World Wide Web: An analysis of rates of adoption', Suave Lobodzinski and Ivan Tomek (eds), *Proceedings of WebNet '97—World Conference of the WWW, Internet and Intranet*, Toronto, Canada, pp. 110–115.
41. Tina M. Lowrey, 'The use of diffusion theory in marketing: A qualitative approach to innovative consumer behavior', *Advances in Consumer Research*, 18, eds Rebecca H. Holman and Michael R. Solomon (Provo, UT: Association for Consumer Research, 1991), pp. 644–650.
42. Quentin Hardy, 'Will miniature phones ring up bigger sales?', *Wall Street Journal*, 4 December 1996, pp. B1, B4.
43. Susan H. Higgins and William L. Shanklin, 'Seeding mass market acceptance for high technology consumer products', *Journal of Consumer Marketing*, 9, Winter 1992, pp. 5–14.
44. Jan-Benedict E.M. Steenkamp and Katrijn Gielens, 'Consumer and market drivers of the trial probability of new consumer packaged goods', *Journal of Consumer Research*, 30, December 2003, pp. 368–384. The authors also drew on an earlier study for their conceptualisation. See Jacob Goldenberg, Donald R. Lehman and David Mazursky, 'The idea itself and the circumstances of its emergence as predictors of new product success', *Management Science*, 47(1), 2001, pp. 69–84.
45. Krongjit Laochumnanvanit and David Bednall, 'Consumers' evaluation of free service trial offers', Working paper, Monash University, 2004.
46. Paul A. Herbig and Hugh Kramer, 'The effect of information overload on the innovation choice process', *Journal of Consumer Marketing*, 11(2), 1994, pp. 45–54.
47. Walter S. Mossberg, 'Sony again attempts to sell its mini-CD, focusing on recording', *Wall Street Journal*, 28 May 1998, p. B1.
48. Steve Hemsley, 'Beg your pardon', *Precision Marketing*, 17(6), 2003, pp. 25–27.
49. Erin White, 'Word of mouth makes Nike slip-on sneakers take off', *Wall Street Journal*, 7 June 2001, p. B1.
50. Everett M. Rogers and F. Floyd Shoemaker, *Communication of Innovations*, 2nd edn (New York: Free Press, 1971), pp. 32–33; see also Elizabeth C. Hirschman, 'Consumer modernity, cognitive complexity, creativity and innovativeness', *Marketing in the 80's: Changes and Challenges*, ed. Richard P. Bagozzi et al. (Chicago: American Marketing Association, 1980), pp. 135–139.
51. Hilary Chura, 'Miller breaks ad effort for unbreakable bottles', *Advertising Age*, 4 September 2000, p. 8; and Micheline Maynard, 'When hot cars go cold', *New York Times*, 31 August 2001, p. F1.
52. Thomas W. Valente and Rebecca L. Davis, 'Accelerating the diffusion of innovations using opinion leaders', *Annals of the American Academy of Political and Social Sciences*, 566, November 1999, pp. 55–67; and Ronald S. Burt, 'The social capital of opinion leaders', *Annals of the American Academy of Political and Social Sciences*, 566, November 1999, pp. 37–54.
53. Paul R. Steffens and D.N.P. Murthy, 'A mathematical model for new product diffusion: The influence of innovators and imitators', *Mathematical Computer Modelling*, 16(4), 1992, pp. 11–26. See also Jacob Goldenberg, Barak Libai, and Eitan Muller, 'Riding the saddle: How cross-market communications can create a major slump in sales', *Journal of Marketing*, 66, April 2002, pp. 1–16.
54. Dianne Neumark-Sztainer et al., 'Early adopters of olestra-containing foods: Who are they?', *Journal of the American Dietetic Association*, 100(2), February 2000, pp. 198–204.
55. C. Page Moreau, Donald R. Lehmann, and Arthur B. Markman, 'Entrenched knowledge structures and consumer response to new products', *Journal of Marketing Research*, 38(1), February 2001, pp. 14–29.
56. David J. Burns and Robert F. Krampf, 'A semiotic perspective on innovative behavior', *Developments in*

Marketing Science, ed. Robert L. King (Richmond, VA: Academy of Marketing Science, 1991), pp. 32–35.

57. Wayne D. Hoyer and Nancy M. Ridgway, 'Variety seeking as an explanation for exploratory purchase behavior: A theoretical model', *Advances in Consumer Research*, 11, ed. Thomas C. Kinnear (Provo, UT: Association for Consumer Research, 1984), pp. 114–119.
58. <www.dis.unimelb.edu.au/staff/elizabethh/Novell2.htm> (10 March 2004). Describes informal social groups of up to 25 teenagers who communicate via SMS.
59. Bruce MacEvoy, 'Change leaders and the new media', *American Demographics*, January 1994, pp. 42–48.
60. Susan Mitchell, 'Technophiles and technophobes', *American Demographics*, February 1994, pp. 36–42.
61. Automotive 101, *Automotive History* <www.autoshop-online.com>, 2004.
62. Automobile, *Science Daily* <www.sciencedaily.com>, 2004.
63. Invention of the Automobile, *Idea Finder* <www.ideafinder.com/history/invetnions/story054.htm>, 2004.
64. Automobile, *Science Daily* <www.sciencedaily.com>, 2004.
65. W.W. Bottorff, T*he First Car—A History of the Automobile* <www.ausbcomp.com/~bbott/cars/carhist.htm>, 2004.
66. Horatio's Drive, *The Public Broadcasting Service* <www.pbs.org/horatio/educators/act05.html>.
67. Automotive 101, *Automotive History* <www.autoshop-online.com>, 2004.
68. W.B. Taylor, *Automobile History—As I remember the Automobile* (Article originally published: *Hobbies*, September 1942) <www.oldandsold.com/articles/article200.shtml>, 2004.
69. Celebrating the American Automobile, *Auto museum* <www.automuseum.com>, 2004.
70. W.B. Taylor, *Automobile History—As I remember the Automobile* (Article originally published: *Hobbies*, September 1942) <www.oldandsold.com/articles/article200.shtml>, 2004.
71. Starting a 1913 Ford Model T Ford Automobile, Phase Metrics <www.aureliasystems.com/samples/msword/indexa2.htm>, 1999.
72. How Flying Cars Will Work, *Howstuffworks* <www.howstuffworks.com>, 2004.
73. How Personal Jetpacks Will Work, *Howstuffworks* <www.howstuffworks.com>, 2004.

CHAPTER 16

Organisational buying

Home Search Favorites History

Our security software also protects your butt.

If it's your responsibility to ensure your company is protected from workers misusing the Internet and email, then it makes sense for you to have the best protection available today. SurfControl offers solutions for all your Internet filtering needs - web, email, AND peer-to-peer file sharing with an integrated suite of products from a single, reliable source. No one can offer you this kind of total solution. We can help you block inappropriate content, secure confidential data, optimise network bandwidth and add a layer of protection against viruses. Of course, you can always take your chances and risk your butt instead.

Download your free trial SurfControl software now for a free 30-day evaluation at **www.surfcontrol.com** or call 1800 73 2244.

The World's #1 Web and Email Filtering Company.

SurfControl®

Source: Courtesy of SurfControl.

Many items are also likely to reappear on the shelves year after year. Teddy bears and dolls are always available, along with toy trucks and cars. Although Mattel's Barbie dolls are brought out in new models each year, major retailers are likely to carry several lines of this enduring product at all times. Thomas the Tank Engine has been around since the 1950s, while long-running shows like *Sesame Street* and *Play School* ensure that a range of toys are staple items. Boys' and girls' markets are generally quite distinct. Retail store buyers know from experience what ranges of products and price points work best in their stores, although this may vary from area to area depending on the geodemographics of each store's catchment area.

Viewing supplier ranges was not actually found to be the next step in the cycle, but was a continuous preoccupation with buyers. One area where the buyers needed to be alert was around 'knock-offs'. These are toys that emulate most of the features of the branded faddish products but which can be sold at lower price points, thus generating higher profit margins. The smaller chains in Australia may also have limitations imposed on them by suppliers who are used to delivering products to US and European markets by the container load. The smaller quantities required by Australian retailers are often provided last, almost as remaindered stock. *Analysis and comparison of ranges* is a continuing task for retail buyers, though the smaller chains tend to pay greater heed to larger retailers like Kmart, rather than the other way round.

Order placement usually comes at defined times in the business year. Buying tends to be conducted in anticipation of two half-year sales periods (e.g. August–January and February–July) and within the planning period the retailer will be 'open-to-buy' products up to agreed budget levels. Because of the concentration of suppliers in the market, strong network relationships usually exist between buyers and suppliers. Occasionally, a buyer will need more stock urgently and in this case network contacts are useful.

Evaluation of merchandise purchased occurs from the moment the product goes on sale. In some stores, daily sales figures are available if required; in some buying groups there was a greater reliance on informal feedback, not actual sales data. One buyer described the life cycle of faddish toy products (such as action figures) as follows:

- in the first sale period, demand outstrips supply,
- in the next period the two are in balance,
- followed by oversupply,
- stock clearances and
- items deleted from store shelves.

In addition to actual sales, buyers evaluate the overall performance of the supplier in terms of sales support, reliability, range, quality and pricing.

Reorder and replacement can be difficult for faddish toy items in unexpectedly high demand. (Occasionally, toy items are so popular that parents have been known to resort to desperate measures to get a wanted item for their children. Voltron and Cabbage Patch dolls were examples.) Buyers make extensive use of their network of contacts in the toy companies in an attempt to get hold of high-demand stock. Retailers' buyers conduct a *re-evaluation of merchandise purchased* constantly. However, of greater concern is the overall service and relationship performance of the toy suppliers.

In general, Lyon's approach described the major parts of the retail toy-buying cycle, but did not take into account the constant searching for new, differentiated and high-turnover items. Although much of the buying could be described as a modified rebuy, new-task buying was extremely common. For the experienced buyers, a new-task buy was not daunting but a routine based on their well-tested theories of what appeals to boys and girls and what price points will work.

Case Study Questions

1. In what other areas of organisational buying is new-task buying as routinised as in the toy industry?
2. Given the small number of buyers and the dominance of large toy suppliers, how would a niche toy manufacturer in Australia go about arranging retail distribution?
3. How are online toy stores likely to affect the sales of traditional outlets?

Summary

Organisations buy more products than consumers, yet their role as buyers has been relatively neglected by researchers in marketing. The origins of demand in organisations can be largely accounted for by firmagraphics; that is, by understanding the industry, company size, transaction size, customer location and the structure of a firm we can largely predict what purchases they will need to make. In addition, business objectives represented by values such as entrepreneurship or environmental orientation affect buying policies. Stakeholder theory also identifies many players in and outside the firm that influence its buying decisions.

Most businesses in Western economies are small businesses and Australia is no exception, with only 33% of employees working in organisations with 100 or more employees. The downsizing of large corporations and the outsourcing of many of their activities has meant that there has been a growth in small office home office (SOHO) businesses. As these are typically controlled and run by an individual or family group, marketing approaches more akin to consumers may be appropriate. However, the limited marketing studies and theories in this area have typically referred to larger organisations and ignored the buying role of smaller businesses. Firms buy for their own immediate needs, as inputs into value-creating activities and as resellers (this especially applies to retailers). Some of these purchases have a regular cycle (like accounting services), others are ad hoc (such as a new computer for an additional staff member).

Like families, organisations have a variety of buying roles or stakeholders in the buying process. They include users, information gatekeepers, influencers, specifiers, financial controllers, deciders and actual buyers. In smaller businesses these roles tend to coalesce. In large firms, these roles are spread across the organisation and known collectively as the buying centre. The BUYGRID approach to organisational buying combines a decision-making process with types of buying. Decision-making is seen to follow the steps of need anticipation (or recognition); decisions on the amount, type and timing or purchase; search for suitable suppliers; evaluation of suppliers; evaluation of proposals from these suppliers; selection of supplier; placing an appropriate order; then evaluating the purchase. In the model, these steps vary considerably depending on whether the purchase is a straight rebuy, a modified rebuy or a new task.

While individuals with their preferences and prejudices have an influence on what is bought, the basic firmagraphics and values of the organisation are likely to be of greater significance. Within larger firms, with many stakeholders, there are likely to be more formalised buying and approval processes. Formalised buying often starts with a brief or an RFT, leading to a proposal, further negotiations and the signing of contracts.

In this era, businesses are changing and reforming themselves with great rapidity under the influence of communications technology and the globalising economy. As a result, selling organisations are likely to see their buyers reorganising, using flatter management structures and downsizing, making it difficult to maintain relationships with buyers. Globalisation is likely to put sellers in contact with buyers from other cultures who expect to negotiate differently. On the other hand, increased outsourcing and use of Compulsory Competitive Tenders (CCTs) has increased opportunities for business-to-business suppliers.

Newer business models emphasise that the buyer–supplier relationship is typically not a simple one, but involves the firm interacting on a number of levels (activity, resource and personal linkages) between several areas of each firm. A network approach is increasingly used to characterise these complex relationships. Organisational theorists have identified four emerging marketing network structures—internal networks, vertical synergistic networks, intermarket opportunity networks and networks designed to optimise customer opportunity. Each network model has its own requirements for buyer–seller relationships. Indeed, these relationships are fundamentally what determines the structure in the vertical and customer opportunity networks. Many of these networks are now global.

Embeddedness describes the degree to which the boundaries between business units or organisations become diffused—meaning that it is difficult to say which resources, activities or actors belong to which organisation specifically. For example, a selling company may station its staff within the buying organisation, if the volume of business is great enough, or the two firms may cooperate in devising a customer information system. The role of the buyer in this complex of relationships in a rapidly changing environment is a difficult one to maintain, especially when buying may not be the only role performed by the buyer in flatter, team-based structures apparent in larger organisations.

Discussion questions

1. Do all new business purchase decisions have an element of rebuying or new buying about them?
2. What categories of small business are similar to consumer markets when it comes to promoting and selling products to them?
3. Suppose you are supplier of office equipment to a fast changing organisation like Telstra? How do you establish activity, resource and actor relationships that will thrive as the buyer organisation changes?
4. Is it more efficient for a company like Nike to be a vertical network integrator rather than owning the network? Under what conditions would the opposite be true? How would this affect the buying process in Nike?
5. What are the costs and benefits to large organisations in abolishing separate buying departments and instead dispersing this responsibility across the organisation?
6. Compare an SME and a large business buying a computer network. What internal stakeholders are likely to be involved and what types of external suppliers?

Exercises

1. Find examples of advertising that target businesses. On the basis of firmagraphics, predict which business segments are most likely to buy these products.
2. Describe the supply chain for a new car, going all the way from the primary inputs to end-user. Identify all the buyer–seller dyads involved.
3. Do the same task for a packaged holiday (such as the Milford Track Guided Walk in New Zealand).
4. Find examples of the four marketing network types described by Achrol and Kotler.
5. Complete the BUYGRID for a large firm acquiring office supplies, a new payroll system and an Internet site which for the first time sells products online.

Key terms

activity relationship *(p. 563)*
actor relationship *(p. 563)*
briefs *(p. 558)*
BUYGRID *(p. 555)*
buying centre *(p. 554)*
Compulsory Competitive Tendering (CCT) *(p. 558)*
disintermediation *(p. 554)*
dyads *(p. 563)*
embeddedness *(p. 564)*
firmagraphics *(p. 551)*
keiretsu (p. 563)
modified rebuy *(p. 555)*
network *(p. 564)*
network integrator *(p. 562)*
new buy (task) *(p. 555)*
outsourcing *(p. 560)*
power imbalance *(p. 562)*
Request for Tender (RFT) *(p. 558)*
self-organising *(p. 564)*
straight rebuy *(p. 555)*
supply chain *(p. 552)*
virtual organisation *(p. 563)*

Endnotes

1. Derived from ABS (2003), *Australian National Accounts: National Income, Expenditure and Product*, Catalogue 5206.0.
2. Based on ABS (2002), *Small Business in Australia, 2001*, Catalogue 1321.0.
3. Geoff Alford, 'A new macro-level segmentation model for business-to-business marketing', Esomar Seminar on Business to Business Marketing, 9–11 November 1994 (London: Esomar).
4. Shawn L. Berman, Andrew C. Wicks, Suresh Kotha and Thomas M Jones, 'Does stakeholder orientation matter? The relationship between stakeholder management models and firm financial performance', *Academy of Management Journal*, 42(5), October 1999, pp. 488–506.
5. Frederick E. Webster and Yoram Wind, 'A general model for understanding organizational buying behavior', *Journal of Marketing*, 36, April 1972, p. 12.
6. Minette E. Drumwright, 'Socially responsible organizational buying: Environmental concern as a noneconomic buying criterion', *Journal of Marketing*, 58, July 1994, pp. 1–19.
7. Philip L. Dawes and Don Y. Lee, 'Communication intensity in large-scale organizational high technology purchasing decisions', *Journal of Business-to-Business Marketing*, 3(3), 1996, pp. 3–38.
8. Arch M. Woodside, T. Lukko and R. Vuori, 'Organizational buying of capital equipment involving persons across several authority levels', *The Journal of Business & Industrial Marketing*, 14(1), 1999, pp. 30–48.
9. Based on a classic formulation by P.J. Robinson, C.W. Faris and Y. Wind, *Industrial Buying Behavior and Creative Marketing* (Boston: Allyn and Bacon, 1967). Reproduced in Scott Ward and Frederick E. Webster, 'Organizational buyer behavior', in Thomas S. Robertson and Harold H. Kassarjian (eds), *Handbook of Consumer Behavior* (New Jersey: Prentice Hall, 1991).
10. R. Bruce Money, Mary C. Gilly and John L. Graham, 'Explorations of national culture and word-of-mouth referral behavior in the purchase of industrial services in the United States and Japan', *Journal of Marketing*, 62(4), October 1998, pp. 76–87.
11. Tony L. Henthorne, Michael S. LaTour and Alvin J. Williams, 'How organizational buyers reduce risk', *Industrial Marketing Management*, 22(1), 1993, pp. 41–48.
12. Leslie P. Willcocks and Wendy L. Currie, 'Information technology in public services: Towards the contractual organization?', *British Journal of Management*, 8 (Special issue), June 1997, pp. S107–120; 'Dealing with today's intermediaries: How to leverage the emerging network of value-added resellers, systems-integrators, facilities-managers, and outsourcing-providers', Chapter 4, in Bozidar G. Yovovich, *New Marketing Imperatives* (Englewood Cliffs: Prentice Hall, 1995); and Mary C. Lacity, Leslie P. Willcocks and David F. Feeny, 'IT outsourcing: Maximise flexibility and control', *Harvard Business Review*, 73(1), May–June 1995, pp. 84–93.
13. Joan Magretta, 'Fast, global, and entrepreneurial: Supply chain management, Hong Kong style', *Harvard Business Review*, 76(5), Sept–Oct 1998, pp. 103–114. See also Philip Evans and Thomas S. Wurster, 'Getting real about virtual commerce', *Harvard Business Review*, 77(6), Nov–Dec 1999, pp. 84–94.
14. Francis Buttle. *Customer relationship management: concepts and tools*. (Oxford: Elsevier Butterworth-Heinemann, 2004).
15. Ravi S. Achrol and Phillip Kotler, 'Marketing in the network economy', *Journal of Marketing*, 63, 1999, pp. 146–163. See also David W. Cravens and Nigel F. Piercy, 'Relationship marketing and collaborative networks in service organizations', *International Journal of Service Industry Management*, 5(5), 1994, pp. 39–53.
16. Jeffrey H. Dyer, 'How Chrysler created an American *keiretsu*', *Harvard Business Review*, 74(4), July–August 1996, pp. 42–56.
17. James C. Anderson, Håkan Håkansson and Jan Johanson, 'Dyadic business relationships within a business network context', *Journal of Marketing*, 58(1), October 1994, pp. 1–15.
18. Evert Gummesson, 'Service productivity, quality and relationship marketing', Paper presented to the 12th Quality Management Conference, Australian Quality Council, Sydney 1997. See also Evert Gummesson, 'Total relationship marketing: Experimenting with a synthesis of research frontiers', *Australasian Marketing Journal*, 7(1), 1999, pp. 72–85.
19. Martin Christopher, *Marketing Logistics* (London: Butterworth-Heinemann, 1997).
20. Cravens and Piercy, op. cit.
21. Kent Grayson and Tim Ambler, 'The darkside of long-term relationship in marketing services', *Journal of Marketing*, 36, February 1999, pp. 132–141.
22. Anderson et al., op. cit.

23. Keith G. Provan, 'Embeddedness, interdependence and opportunism in organizational supplier–buyer networks', *Journal of Management*, 19(4), 1993, pp. 841–856. See also M. Tina Dacin, Marc J. Ventresca and Brent D. Beal, 'The embeddedness of organizations: Dialogue and directions', *Journal of Management*, 25(3), 1999, pp. 317–356.
24. Kathleen M. Eisenhardt and D. Charles Galunic, 'Coevolving: At last, a way to make synergies work', *Harvard Business Review*, 78(1), 2000, pp. 91–101.
25. Philip Anderson, 'Complexity theory and organization science', *Organization Science*, 10(2), May/June 1999, pp. 216–232.
26. Neil Shoebridge, 'Toy soldiers find that war is hell', *BRW*, 20 July 1998, p. 42.
27. 'Survey: E-commerce: Something old, something new', *Economist*, 26 February 2000, pp. 15–27. See also <www.etoys.com>.
28. Kenneth Chan and David Bednall, 'The retail buyer's adoption process for new toys', paper delivered to ANZMEC, Melbourne, 1998.
29. B. Lyon, 'The merchandise decision-making process in apparel retailing', unpublished paper, Marketing Department, Caulfield Institute of Technology, 1979.

Consumer behaviour and society

PART 5

Part 5 focuses on the role of consumer behaviour in society. It examines public policy and its relationship with marketing and consumer behaviour.

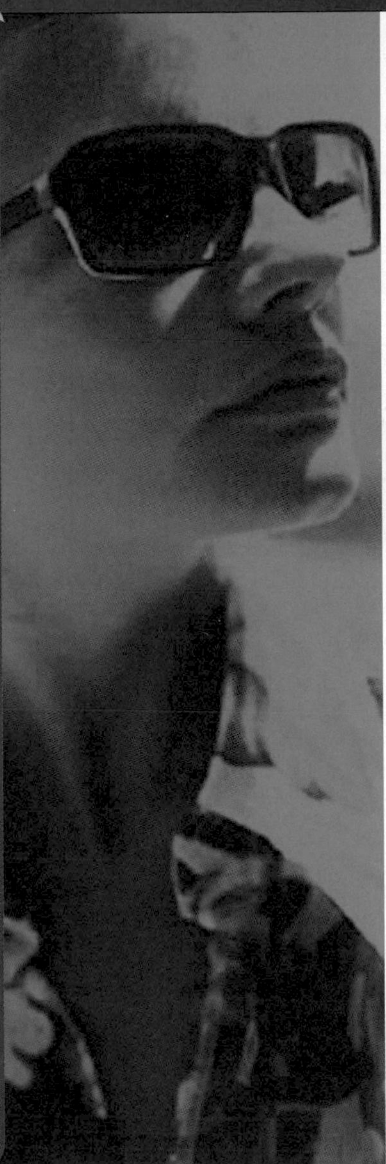

DECISION-MAKING MODEL

External influences

INPUT

Firm's marketing strategies
- a Products
- b Promotion
- c Pricing
- d Channels of distribution
- e Market segmentation

Sociocultural environment
- a Communication and reference groups
- b Family
- c Social class
- d Culture and subculture
- e Opinion leadership and diffusion of innovation
- f Public policy and consumer protection

Decision making

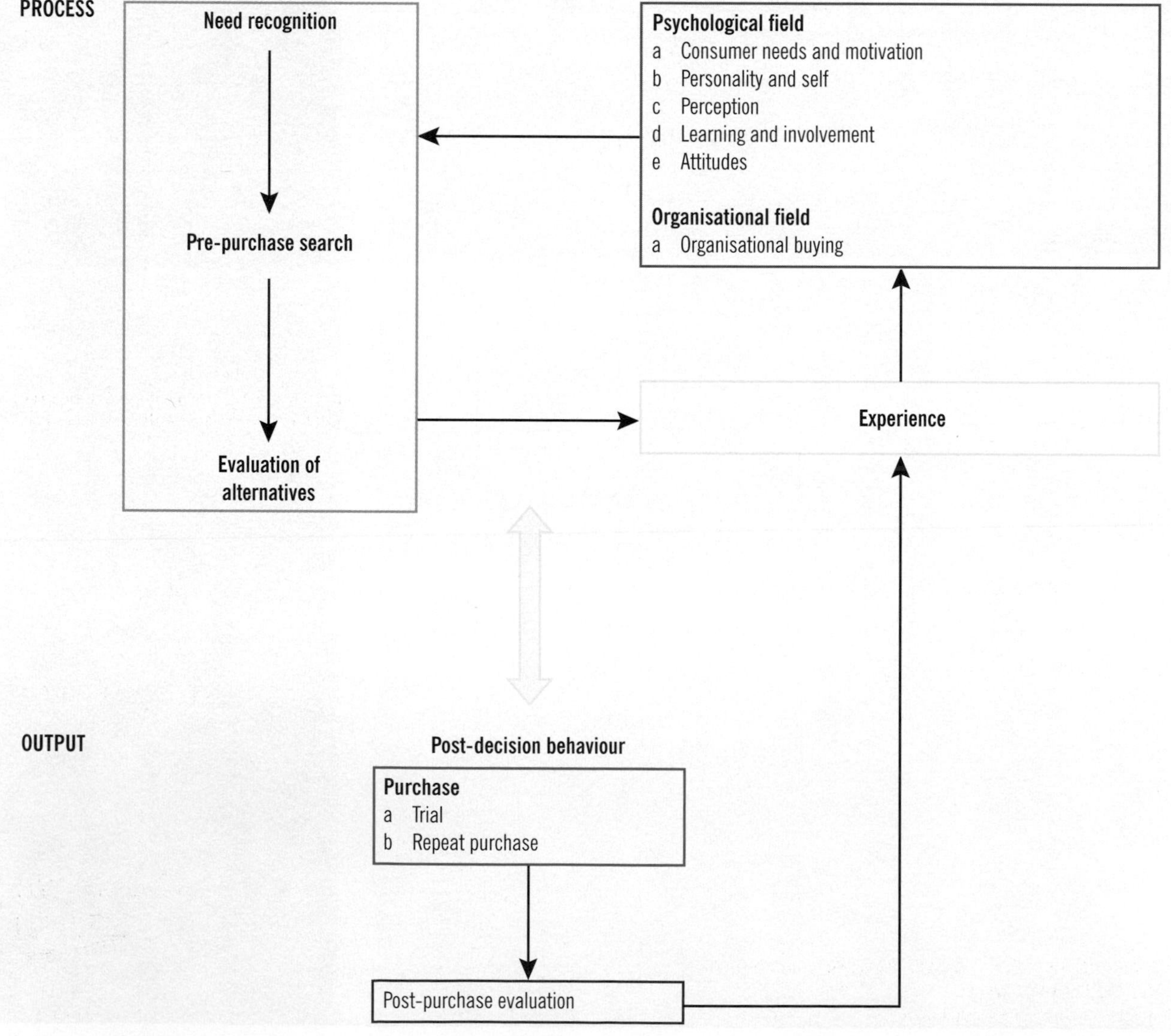

CHAPTER 17

Public policy and consumer protection

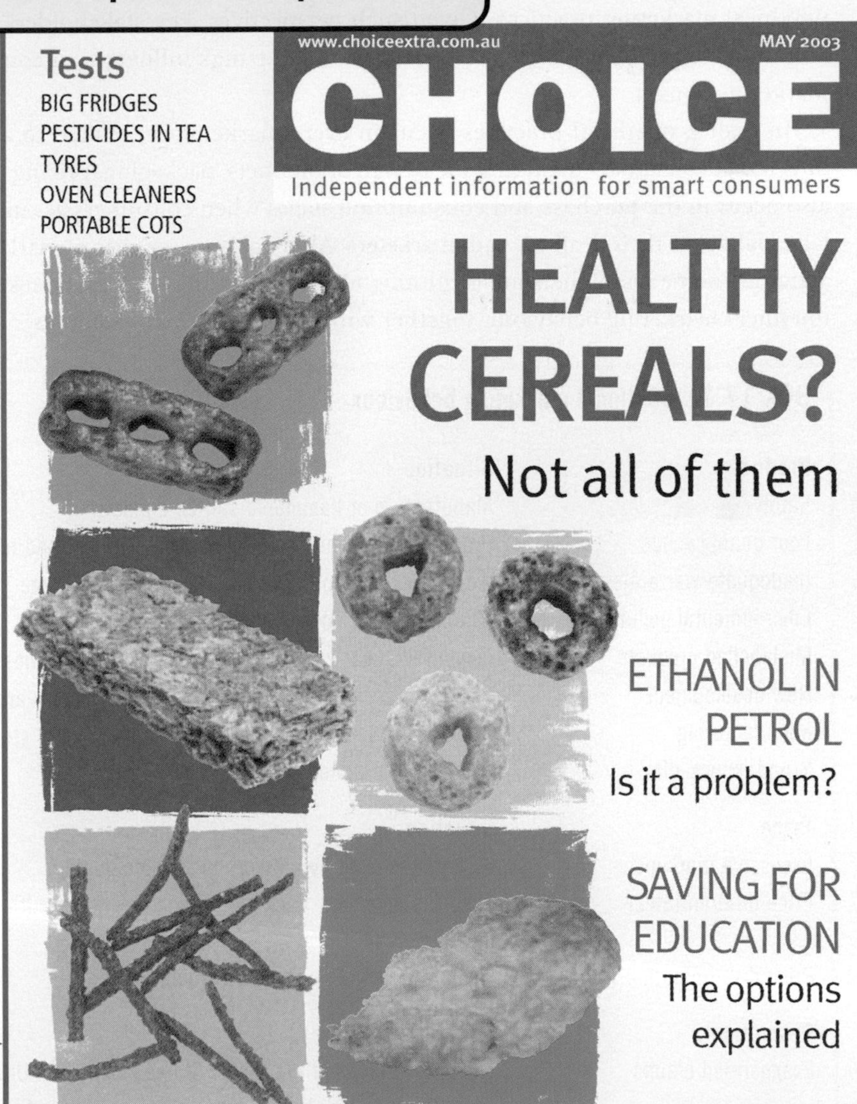

www.choiceextra.com.au
MAY 2003
CHOICE
Independent information for smart consumers
Tests
BIG FRIDGES
PESTICIDES IN TEA
TYRES
OVEN CLEANERS
PORTABLE COTS
HEALTHY CEREALS?
Not all of them
ETHANOL IN PETROL
Is it a problem?
SAVING FOR EDUCATION
The options explained

Source: Reprinted from the May 2003 edition of CHOICE with the permission of the Australian Consumers' Association.

The development of public policy and its inforcement through appropriate laws directed at protecting consumers has become an important issue for marketers, politicians, public policy advocates and consumers. Government regulation, industry self-regulation and consumer advocacy are the major forces shaping public policy. This chapter initially examines the role of ethics in consumer research and marketing as an important basis for acceptable marketing practices by firms. We then examine issues related to public policy and marketing and the application of consumer behaviour research to the development of public policy.

Ethics in marketing

The primary purpose for studying consumer behaviour is to understand why and how consumers make their purchase decisions. These insights enable marketers to design more effective marketing strategies. Yet some critics are concerned that an in-depth understanding of consumer behaviour makes it possible for unethical marketers to exploit human vulnerabilities in the marketplace. In short, they are concerned that knowledgeable insights into consumer behaviour give marketers an unfair advantage that enables them to engage in unethical marketing practices. Given such perspectives, key stakeholders have exerted pressure to develop and improve public policies as they relate to marketing's influence on consumers and consumer recourse to marketing abuses.

In reality, unethical practices occur in every marketplace, related to all elements of the marketing mix directed at consumers including the design of products, packaging, pricing, advertising and distribution. They also occur in the purchase and consumption stages when consumers act unethically (e.g. shoplifting, making false claims) in their dealings with marketers. Although most studies of marketing ethics focus on the marketer's activities, some researchers are beginning to study consumer ethics. Boxes 17.1 and 17.2 list various types of unethical marketing behaviour, together with some consumer examples.

BOX 17.1 Unethical marketing behaviour

Product	Situation
Safety	Manufacture of flammable stuffed animals
Poor quality goods	Products that cannot withstand ordinary wear and tear
Inadequate warranties	Warranties with insufficient time or parts coverage
Environmental pollution	Manufacture of non-biodegradable plastic products
Mislabelled products	Flavoured sugar water sold as apple juice for babies
New development	Bribery or corruption of officials to secure agency approval of generic pharmaceuticals
Manufacturing	Unauthorised substitutions in generic drugs after governmental approval
Brand 'knock-offs'	Counterfeit branded goods sold as originals
Price	**Situation**
Excessive markups	High prices used by retailers to connote quality
Price differentiation	Yield-management pricing of airline tickets, resulting in day-to-day differential pricing of adjacent seats[a]
Price discrimination	Favoured pricing to preferred groups
Promotion	**Situation**
Exaggerated claims	Wilkinson Blades in the United States claimed its Ultra Glide Razor offered 'the smoothest, most comfortable shave known to man', an assertion challenged by Gillette[b]

Tasteless advertising	Sexual innuendo and gender disparagement (e.g. Miller Brewing Company targeted college males with ads on 'how to scam babes')[c]
Deceptive advertising	Ads for economy accommodation depicting first-class facilities
Persuasive role	Celebrity spokespersons in beer and liquor ads targeted at youth models for inappropriate products
Telemarketing	Offers of fabulous prizes in return for credit card purchases of touted goods[d]
Distribution	**Situation**
Fraudulent sales	Phoney markdowns based on inflated retail list prices
Bait-and-switch tactics	Luring consumers with ads for low-priced merchandise for the purpose of switching them to higher-priced models
Direct marketing	Deceptive, misleading product size and performance claims[e]
Packaging	**Situation**
Deceptive quantities	Some marketers use 'packaging-to-price' tactics that mask a decrease in product quantity while maintaining the same price and traditional package size[f]

Adapted from

a Frank A. Weil '$540 on Saturday, $1560 on Monday', *New York Times*, 26 March 1989.
b 'Close shaves battling blades', *Time*, 5 June 1989, p. 57.
c 'Miller beer drops ad after protest', *New York Times*, 12 March 1989.
d Janice Castro, 'Reach out and rob someone', *Time*, 3 April 1989, pp. 38–39.
e 'Self-regulation will suppress direct marketing', 'Dark Side', *Marketing News*, 24 April 1989, p. B4.
f John B. Hinge, 'Critics call cuts in package size deceptive move', *Wall Street Journal*, 5 February 1991, p. B1

BOX 17.2 Unethical consumer practices

Shoplifting
Switching price tags
Returning clothing that has been worn
Abusing products and returning them as damaged goods
Redeeming coupons without the requisite purchase
Redeeming coupons that have expired
Returning clothing bought at full price and demanding a refund for the sales price differential
Returning products bought at sale and demanding the full-price refund
Stealing belts from store clothing
Cutting buttons off store merchandise
Returning partially-used products for full store credit
Abusing warranty or unconditional guarantee privileges
Damaging merchandise in a store and then demanding a sales discount
Copying copyrighted materials (e.g. books, videotapes, computer software) without permission

There is no universally accepted definition for the term 'ethics' but ethical philosophies can be grouped into two different theoretical perspectives: teleological theories and deontological theories. Teleological theory deals with the moral worth of behaviour as determined by its consequences. According to teleology, to be ethical, a decision should be based on what is best for everyone involved. Utilitarianism, a teleological theory, can be summarised by the notion of 'the greatest good for the greatest number'. According to this theory, it would be perfectly ethical for a pharmaceutical company to conceal potentially harmful side effects of a new diet drug that may affect just a few people, as long as a large number of people are likely to benefit once the product is perfected. To utilitarians, ethics are evaluated on the basis of a kind of cost-benefit analysis: if the benefits to society (or to a specific segment of society) exceed the costs—that is, if more people would benefit than would be harmed—a behaviour is considered ethical. However, a cost-benefit analysis should explore not only the financial but also the human consequences of a business decision, in both the short term and the long term. It is especially important that responsible decision makers anticipate all negative consequences that may occur and take action to avert such outcomes.

Deontological theory deals with the methods and intentions involved in a particular behaviour. Deontological theories focus on the results of a particular action, and tend to place greater weight on personal and social values than on economic values. Kant's categorical imperative is a deontological theory that suggests that individuals should be willing to have their actions become universal laws that would apply equally to themselves as to all others.[1] The reverse of the 'golden rule', which most of us learned in primary school, aptly expresses the notion of ethical behaviour in marketing: Do not do unto others what you would not have others do unto you (or your loved ones). Clearly, this is a deontological theory, not a utilitarian theory, since it depends on the results of your action. Of the two dominant traditions, most moral philosophers today favour deontology.[2]

Ethics is clearly a process of give and take and for the marketing process to work to the benefit of all society, marketers and consumers alike must understand and practise ethical behaviour.

THE SOCIAL RESPONSIBILITY OF MARKETERS

The corporate environment and corporate philosophy are crucial determinants of ethical behaviour among an organisation's employees. Many companies have developed codes of ethics that set the tone for decision making throughout the organisation. The Shell Group, for example, includes in its 'Statement of General Business Principles' a statement dealing with customers: 'To win and maintain customers by developing and providing products and services which offer value in terms of price, quality, safety and environmental impact, and which are supported by the requisite technological, environmental and commercial expertise.' Shell also includes general principles related to society, stating that 'to conduct business as responsible, corporate members of society, to observe the laws of the countries in which they operate, to express support for fundamental human rights in line with the legitimate role of business'. Other companies have also incorporated specific social goals into their mission statements, and programs in support of these goals have become an integral part of their strategic planning.

There are a number of reasons why a company would include social goals in its corporate philosophy. A very basic reason is that these goals reflect its founder's (or chairman's or board's) personal philosophy of social responsibility. Ethical practices by employees are very much a product of the corporate environment.[3] Employee surveys suggest that superiors often coerce those who engage in unethical practices into doing so.[4] Conversely, a highly ethical environment—one that espouses a strong moral code—encourages ethical practices among its employees.[5] Some companies recognise that socially responsible activities improve their image among consumers, stockholders, the financial community and other relevant interest groups. Ethical and socially responsible practices are simply good business: they result in a favourable image and, ultimately, in increased sales and decreased business costs.

Many industry associations have also developed codes of ethics because they recognise that **self-regulation** is in every member's best interests, in that it deters government from imposing its own regulations on the industry. Many professional associations also provide codes of conduct for their members. For example, the Australian Marketing Institute covers key issues in its code of professional conduct, including:

- 'Members shall conduct their professional activities with respect for the public interest.'
- 'Members shall at all times act with integrity in dealing with clients or employers past and present, with their fellow members and with the general public.' (see <www.ami.org.au>)

Many companies have incorporated specific goals into their mission statements and include programs in support of these goals as integral components of their plans. They believe that ethics and social responsibility are important components of organisational effectiveness. They have found that ethical and socially responsible practices are simply good business, resulting in a favourable image and increased sales. The converse is also true, where perceptions of a company's lack of social responsibility negatively affects consumer purchase decisions.

THE CONSUMER MOVEMENT

In the United States the consumers' bill of rights (subsequently expanded to include the rights to recourse and redress and to a physical environment that enhances the quality of life) set the stage for a consumer movement that started around 1964. Widespread consumer discontent with shoddy merchandise, inadequate warranties, arrogant marketers and widespread abuses in the marketplace triggered this bill of rights. The consumer movement is a mechanism that tries to correct the imbalance that had developed historically between buyers and sellers.

In Australia, parliaments have enacted various pieces of legislation designed to protect consumers (see Box 17.3). Consumer-oriented legislation, as with any other governmental policy, is constantly being reviewed and updated to cope with the changing nature of the commercial and social environment and various Federal, State and local government Acts cover consumers in Australia.

Ultimately, consumers express their approval or disapproval of a company's policies and practices by their actions in the marketplace (i.e. buy or not buy). In an effort to systematise approval and disapproval of a company's policies, some consumer groups have urged their members and other consumers to take action against specific marketers in the form of consumer boycotts. A boycott can be defined as the concerted (but non-mandatory) refusal by a group of consumers to do business with one or more companies for the purpose of expressing disapproval of certain policies, and attempting to coerce the target companies to modify those policies.[6] Under appropriate circumstances, consumer boycotts can be very effective. For example, a consumer boycott by animal rights advocates has resulted in the gradual elimination by cosmetic companies of product testing on animals.[7] In Australia, various interest groups exist that express concerns over various products and services. An example of a more consistent boycott stance has evolved through Australian consumers' response towards the purchase of French products such as perfumes and wines during French nuclear testing in the South Pacific. For a boycott to be successful, the consumer group must accurately assess the commitment of the target company to the disputed activity, and its own ability to generate sufficient economic pressure and significant negative publicity.

Consumers acting alone can also influence marketers to change certain policies. For example, in 1989, in the United States, companies such as Toyota withdrew TV advertisements because of widespread consumer

BOX 17.3 Consumer-oriented legislation

Statute	Purpose
Packages Act 1967 (SA)	Provides for the regulation of the packaging and labelling of consumer goods. Requires manufacturers to state what the package contains, who made it, and how much it contains. Permits industries' voluntary adoption of uniform packaging standards.
Smoking and Tobacco Products Advertisements (Prohibition) Act 1989 (Cth)	Bans the advertising of all tobacco products in print. Maximum upper limits of tar, nicotine and carbon monoxide required on domestic and imported cigarettes.
National Food Authority Act 1991 (Cth)	Requires that nutritional information be printed on food packaging, and uniform food standards be adhered to nationally.
Consumer Credit Act 1994 (Qld)	A new model or credit code to protect consumers through truth in lending by all credit providers. There must be ongoing disclosure of the progress of the account including any variation to interest rates and charges.
Sale of Goods Act 1895 (WA)	Stipulates that goods must be of merchantable quality, must fit the purpose intended and match the description.
Privacy Amendment Act 1990 (Cth)	Restricts the use and nature of all credit reporting, apart from some exceptions to the rule.
The Environment Protection (Impact of Proposals) Act 1974 (Cth)	The first Commonwealth law addressing matters related to environmental issues and covering all aspects of surroundings and individuals and groups.
Trades Standards Act 1979 (SA)	Protects consumers against unreasonable risk of injury, informs consumers about the safe use of products and ensures goods are fit for the purposes for which they are intended.

complaints about sexual themes and explicit language. In 1994 Toyota ran ads in Australia for the Paseo that also created some debate and negative consumer perceptions when they targeted gay consumers. Unlike organised consumer movements in the 1970s and early 1980s, which were led by religious and educational groups (primarily to protest against violence on TV), these protests appeared to be from viewers acting independently.[8]

Advertising aimed at children has always been an area of great sensitivity, especially with parents. Children are very impressionable and prone to exploitation. Like the elderly, the young are vulnerable members of the community. If advertising is seen to exploit them, it exposes itself to a backlash from the community and increased regulation. In recent years there has been a call for more responsible child-oriented advertising, following discussions between the television networks and the Australian Broadcasting Authority. The standard of some children's programs has been a hot topic for some time now and there has been a recognisable shift by the advertising industry and companies to conform to an acceptable code of ethics in this area.

Public attitudes towards consumerism are likely to remain strong and, increasingly, consumers are willing to be active consumerists (i.e. join consumer groups). Traditionally, consumerism has been seen as the activities of government, industry, business, independent organisations and citizens that are designed to protect consumers' rights. Actual participation, however, often depends on the extent to which consumers feel that leaders of the relevant consumer groups are in touch with their needs. Among the strategies available to businesses to reduce the impact of consumer activism are:

- reducing the demand for consumerism by improving product quality, expanding services, lowering prices, modifying advertising claims and eliminating the causes of consumer dissatisfaction;
- participating in the consumerism movement by initiating an active consumer education program;
- cooperating with government agencies, non-profit organisations and consumer groups in their consumer education programs.[9]

For most businesses, the wisest approach is to create a corporate-wide and industry-wide environment that encourages ethical business practices. Many companies have found that industry-wide regulation is in every member's best interests; therefore an important function of industry trade associations today is to develop, police and, where possible, enforce an industry code of ethics. Since government regulation is often the result of public outcry about unethical practices, self-regulation wards off the likelihood of government intervention in an industry's practices. However, public outcry and the development of legislation to protect consumers is a major feature of the marketing environment.

➤ Public policy and its link to consumer protection

Public policy (or social policy, as it sometimes called) intersects the field of consumer behaviour when public policy makers believe that social intervention in the process or outcome of marketing exchanges (i.e. between marketers and consumers) will benefit society. The development of social policies that affect marketing are usually the outgrowth of marketplace abuses brought to the attention of policy makers through the media, consumer advocacy groups, professional or industry associations or consumers themselves, or *public recognition*. In relation to marketing and public policy, governments use five types of intervention. These include:

1. *Regulation:* policy makers can prohibit certain types of marketing practices (e.g. the sale of unsafe products), influence the nature of certain practices (e.g. the information provided on food labelling, standard weights and measures, a cooling-off period for door-to-door sales) and outlaw certain practices (e.g. misleading or deceptive advertising, privacy protection, selling hard drugs).[10]
2. *Consumer education:* e.g. the provision of booklets on such topics as the importance of breast-feeding or how to select a home-building contractor, and providing information on the dangers of certain consumption behaviours (e.g. smoking or drinking and driving).
3. *Encouragement of industry self-regulation:* e.g. endorsing industry codes in areas such as television advertising and professional practice.[11]
4. *Incentives:* to encourage desired behaviours such as tax deductions for charitable contributions, and the first home-owners' rebate to encourage home ownership.
5. *Complaints handling:* often as part of a self-regulatory system, but also involving government agencies.[12]

Marketing abuses have caused growing concerns among policy makers at every level of government (local, state and federal). Indeed, some critics complain that a knowledge of consumer behaviour simply enables marketers to exploit vulnerable and naive consumers more skilfully. This may in some cases be an acurate assessment. However, such practices are in reality a short-term focus of firms and generally firms engaging in such behaviours don't survive long or get away with it unnoticed.

Take, for example, the long-standing interest of many consumers in environmentalism.[13] Many marketers have sought the respect and loyalty of environmentally-aware consumers by reducing waste, recycling and reformulating products and packaging. The use of the dolphin logo on cans of tuna, for example, has focused world attention on humane fishing practices and the use of nets from which dolphins can readily escape. Other marketers, however, have targeted the same market niche for the same objectives by using misleading promotions and deceptive claims.[14]

Situations in which government agencies believe the marketing abuses to be substantial may warrant a ban on advertisements or a ban on the media outlets the advertiser uses. For example, there are bans on tobacco advertising on radio and television, at most sporting and cultural events, and in cinema and billboard advertising. The development of policies related to cigarette smoking has also seen government regulation being extended to health warnings on products such as cigarette packets.

Public policy and consumer behaviour has also seen a growing interest in nutritious foods and food labelling, especially in an era where busy lifestyles induce many consumers to buy take-away and pre-prepared foods. A number of food companies have made concerted efforts to address consumer concerns about nutrition and health by reducing the caloric content of foods, by eliminating fats and reducing sodium. Others have deceptively applied the terms 'light', 'low cholesterol' or 'fat-free' to their food labels in order to attract the same market segment, but without making the appropriate changes in their products.[15] Lately, genetically modified foods have aroused consumer uncertainty about their safety and prompted governments to start addressing consumer concerns.

Major marketplace abuses include misleading and deceptive advertising, unscrupulous sales practices,[16] false or misleading labelling, packaging-to-price deceptions, and exploitative advertising aimed at children. Database marketing practices have also raised a number of privacy issues. Abuses also include the inappropriate use of sex, language and violence in comics, television,[17] films, computer games and on the Internet. Legislators and government agencies have been spurred into action by the outcries of parents, teachers, and the consumer in general. As a consequence of community concerns, it has become accepted that a number of restrictions in the interests of community safety are required. Stricter gun laws and the classification and regulation of media content reflect the balancing of personal freedoms with community interests. The R-rating of some magazines, the illegality of selling X-rated videos in some Australian states and banning the purchase of certain products by minors (such as cigatettes and alcohol) are examples of these regulations.

In response to government and community pressure, many industry associations develop self-regulatory codes (e.g. the Market Research Society of Australia *Code of Professional Behaviour*) because they recognise that it is in their long-term best interests to do so. These codes aim to protect consumers while preserving the interests of association members.

➤ Consumer legislation and government

In Australia, the primary legislation that impacts on consumer-related marketing activities is the ***Trade Practices Act 1974***, administered by the **Australian Competition and Consumer Commission (ACCC)** (see <www.accc.gov.au>).[18] Numerous local and state government laws also exist that cover consumers and marketers. Trade policy is also affected by parts of the Australian Constitution, such as section 92 which guarantees free trade between the states. However, despite its small market size, Australia has as much regulatory legislation as larger countries like the United States.[19] Table 17.1 lists some of the major Commonwealth government and State and Territory legislation governing consumer affairs.[20]

The Australian *Trade Practices Act* has been amended many times since 1974, with major revisions in 1992 and 1997. The following areas of activity are covered:

- Anti-competitive practices
- Unconscionable conduct
- Consumer protection
- Product liability
- Product safety and product information
- Industry codes.

TABLE 17.1 Major Commonwealth, State and Territory Acts involving consumers

Commonwealth	State
Broadcasting Services Act 1992	*Consumer Affairs Act 1973* (ACT)
Commerce (Trade Descriptions) Act 1905	*Consumer Claims Tribunal Act 1987* (NSW)
Customs Act 1901	*Door-to-door Sales Act 1967* (NSW)
Freedom of Information Act 1982	*Fair Trading Act 1987* (NSW)
Insurance Act 1973	*Hire Purchase Act 1960* (NSW)
National Food Authority Act 1991	*Lay-by Sales Act 1943* (NSW)
National Health Act 1953	*Motor Car Traders Act 1974* (NSW)
Racial Discrimination Act 1975	*Weights and Measures Act 1915* (NSW)
Sex Discrimination Act 1984	*Consumer Credit Act 1994* (Qld)
Therapeutic Goods Act 1989	*Consumer Transaction Act 1972* (SA)
Trade Practices Act 1974	*Sale of Goods Act 1895* (WA)

The trade practices legislation seeks to prevent anti-competitive agreements[21] (e.g. cartels in the Queensland concrete industry and in Australian freight services) and to maintain competition (e.g. in 1999 the ACCC investigated whether the main tobacco companies in Australia could merge their operations). In 2002 judgments were made in relation to the Australian airline industry regarding proposed alliances between Qantas and Air New Zealand. From a consumer perspective, such action is intended to remove price fixing[22] and maintain the number of choices available. The Act also prohibits anti-competitive behaviour, such as predatory pricing (where an established company unfairly blocks a new market entrant by artificially lowering prices).

Unconscionable conduct involves trading where a stronger party deliberately takes unfair advantage of its superior position or bargaining power. Conduct deemed unconscionable includes the following:

- high-pressure sales techniques
- harassment
- use of standard form contracts that have no room for negotiation
- taking advantage of people who, due to a lack of skills in English or for some other reason, do not understand the documents involved.

The major thrust of the trade practices legislation, from a consumer perspective, comes from its **consumer protection** and product liability concerns.[23] It also monitors advertising that may be misleading and the sale of products that may be dangerous or that fail to follow mandatory Australian standards. It also provides for penalties for breaches of the Act.

Several other Commonwealth bodies also operate to protect consumers. Table 17.2 provides the details of some of the main bodies. The various States and Territories also have a variety of departments and agencies

TABLE 17.2 Selected Commonwealth and State bodies with consumer protection functions

Commonwealth body	Function
Australian Communications Authority	Telecommunications practices, service standards and pricing
Australian Broadcasting Authority[24]	Complaints, research, oversight of industry codes, regulates Australian content on Australian television and children's content on commercial television
Australian Competition and Consumer Commission (ACCC)	Fair trading, consumer safety, consumer education
Consumer Affairs Division (Treasury Department)[25]	Monitors product safety
Food Standards Australia New Zealand[26]	Monitors health claims, labelling, sets standards
Therapeutic Goods Administration[27]	Therapeutic drugs and devices, advertising
Ministerial Council on Consumer Affairs (MCCA)[28]	Coordinating Council of Commonwealth and State Ministers
Commonwealth Ombudsman	Complaints against Commonwealth government agencies, consumer education
State body	**Function**
Fair Trading Tribunal (NSW)	Consumer claims against providers, especially credit, building, leases and motor vehicle providers
Victorian Civil and Administrative Tribunal[29]	Disputes covering many government functions (e.g. freedom of information, taxation) and also private companies (e.g. discrimination, domestic building, guardianship, tenancies, travel agencies, motor traders)
Office of Consumer and Business Affairs (SA)[30]	Consumer affairs, tenancies, product safety
Fair Trading (WA)[31]	Trading, tenancies, auction sales, real estate, motor vehicles, product safety
Office of Consumer Affairs and Fair Trading (Tas)[32]	Consumer and business affairs
Office of Consumer Affairs (Qld)[33]	Consumer affairs

dealing with consumer protection. Like many Australian organisations, the names and structures of these agencies change frequently. In part, this has reflected the waxing and waning of the political value given to consumer and environmental affairs, depending on which government was in power. Similarly, the Howard Coalition government has sought to rationalise the overlap between state and commonwealth agencies, a move that led to changes in the late 1990s. Major types of state and territory Acts and agencies can be summarised as follows:

1. *Fair Trading or Sales of Goods Acts*. Each State and Territory has some form of this Act, which regulates particular marketing activities not covered at the Commonwealth level, such as the transfer of property, fraud, warranties and the rights of the seller. Many of these Acts originated over 100 years ago and in this respect consumer affairs and fair trading are not new public policy issues.
2. *Small Claims Tribunals*. These give consumers the right to take action against traders where there is a dispute about a product or service, where the value is below a threshold level.

3. *Other State legislation.* Typically, this covers areas such as weights and measures, auctions, trading hours, tenant and landlord rights, safety, motor traders, credit and food marketing (particularly dairy foods).

Local governments also have powers that affect the consumer, covering such matters as retail advertising, zoning and health and safety.

Credit and finance is an area that crosses state (and, for that matter, international) boundaries. The major Australian banks have established a Banking Industry Ombudsman to investigate consumer complaints, while State consumer credit Acts aim to give consumers detailed and specific information. For example, consumers seeking a loan should be provided with information about total repayments and effective interest rates to be charged, under the disclosure requirements of such Acts. Other industry groups have set up similar bodies, while governments have also established industry regulators and ombudsmen in cases where government-owned assets (such as telecommunications, electricity and gas) have been privatised (see Table 17.3). While consumer protection was a major issue of governments in the 1980s (particularly those of the non-ALP parties) they have recently moved to become more of a balance between consumer rights and business rights. Regulation and self-regulation imposes costs on business which may lead to higher consumer costs.

TABLE 17.3 Industry ombudsmen and regulators and industry self-regulation

Body	Function
Banking and Financial Services Ombudsman[34]	Resolves complaints against banks by consumers and very small (15 employees or less) businesses
Telecommunications Industry Ombudsman[35]	Handles unresolved complaints about telecommunications and Internet providers
Private Health Insurance Ombudsman[36]	Handles complaints against health funds and private hospitals involving health insurance matters
Office of the Regulator-General (Vic)	Enforces electricity industry standards and prices, reviews industry codes
Energy Industry Ombudsman (Victoria)	Complaints about electricity or gas companies
Advertising Standards Board (ASB)	Receives and evaluates consumer complaints about advertising
Advertising Claims Board (ACB)	Adjudicates primarily on competitor complaints about advertising involving questions of truth, accuracy and the law
Advertising Standards Bureau[37]	Administers the ASB and ACB, by reference to the Australian Association of National Advertisers' (AANA) *Advertiser Code of Ethics* and other industry codes
Market Research Society of Australia[38]	Administers *Code of Professional Behaviour*, protecting respondent rights
Australian Direct Marketing Association[39]	Administers *Code of Practice*
Internet Industry Association[40]	Fair trading practices, elimination of restricted material, payment security
Standards Australia[41]	Product standards, electrical safety, clothing sizes and labels, quality assurance. Administers about 6000 Australian Standards
Federation of Australian Television Stations (FACTS)	Produces and administers industry code covering program classifications, advertising time and advertising placement
Australian Securities and Investments Commission[42]	*Electronic Funds Transfer Code*, covers ATM and EFTPOS transactions

CONSUMER AVENUES TO SEEK REDRESS

The above discussion has highlighted the various regulatory bodies and the respective legislation and policies affecting marketers. There are numerous agencies consumers can turn to when injured by an unsafe product or feel unsatisfied by the marketers offering. There are specific agencies who decide (for example) when a product should be recalled or banned altogether. Usually, the Consumer Affairs Department or Office of Fair Trading within the States, or the Commonwealth Division of Consumer Affairs take responsibility for such actions. These bodies have the role of investigating individual complaints, reviewing product safety and suggesting changes to consumer laws (see Table 17.2).

The types of issues which tend to draw immediate attention and action from these bodies are 'widespread fraud, a string of victims, unconscionable or careless actions by a manufacturer, who is also seen as a standard setter, products which will hurt or endanger children, repeated offences, and blatant disregard for safety regulations'.[43] Not everything the consumer considers unsafe can be banned; for example, baby walkers that could result in high injury rates to babies when the walker tips down stairs or steps were not banned.[44] Although this type of accident may occur, it is more related to lack of supervision than product design.

Whilst most bans are appropriate, mistakes do occur. For example, a former New South Wales Minister for Consumer Affairs, in good faith, banned a toy gun as being exceedingly dangerous. When it was filled with water the gun fired ping-pong balls. The Minister had been told by the department's tester that the muzzle velocity of the gun was extremely high—a message the unfortunate Minister took to the people via television. In the meantime, the Defence Department conducted its own tests and concluded the New South Wales tester had put a decimal point in the wrong place. The gun was harmless, and the 60-day ban in NSW was quietly allowed to die.[45] Despite this example, there have been many incidents in which products have been banned or recalled by consumer affairs bodies. For example, a high-velocity catapult war toy, when tested, proved to be able to send a ball-bearing through the side of a steel filing cabinet. The then-Federal Bureau of Consumer Affairs banned it immediately. While the ACCC and State bodies have the right to set mandatory product standards and to initiate recalls, they mostly rely on manufacturers and distributors to make voluntary recalls of products found to be unsafe or unsatisfactory.[46]

Manufacturers and marketers need to be aware of the safety and fraud watchdogs and that they exist to promote and protect the best interests of the consumer. They should be used as such as an asset, because they eliminate unfair practices in their industry.

Because consumer legislation is so rarely based on empirical consumer research findings, the effectiveness of consumer legislation in safeguarding consumer rights has proved to be somewhat uneven. Consumer credit laws have been enacted in the States to ensure that consumers are aware of the true rates of interest they are charged for buying on credit (see Table 17.2). The law was intended to aid low-income consumers in particular, who often rely on credit purchases. However, research in the United States found that only a small percentage of those who had made a credit purchase after the passage of similar laws could report the true interest charges they had agreed to pay; moreover, low-income shoppers were among those who were the least aware of finance charges.[47] Further research discovered that low-income consumers were more concerned with the size and frequency of instalment repayments than with the amount of interest they were charged. These outcomes strongly suggested that research into consumer attitudes, habits and purchase behaviour should be a necessary precondition to the enactment of consumer legislation, and should be the requisite basis for remedying flaws in current laws.[48]

As we have seen, legislators enact much consumer-oriented legislation designed to deal with dishonest or unethical business practices, but this has not necessarily been as a result of research. The new laws have also established independent regulatory agencies, whose missions consist of policing a specific industry, enacting rules and regulations designed to prevent or eliminate abuses, and enforcing industry compliance with these regulations. Unfortunately, as business leaders have pointed out, the increased costs resulting from regulation are often reflected in higher retail prices. Because compliance costs are ultimately borne by the consumer, legislators and governments now actively weigh the costs and benefits of enacting and enforcing consumer legislation.[49] Such cost/benefit analyses are said to underlie the increasing trend in recent years toward deregulation and relaxed enforcement of existing statutes. Deregulation of the banking industry in the 1980s and telecommunications in the mid-1990s reflected this trend.

DEREGULATION, CORPORATISATION AND PRIVATISATION

Australia developed as a nation where the public ownership of basic infrastructure was taken for granted. Postal services (Australia Post) and telecommunications (Telstra), tertiary education (Bond or the Australian Catholic University), power (Hydro-Electric Commission), water and sewerage, roads (City Link), media (ABC, SBS), airlines (Qantas), banks (Commonwealth Bank, State banks), betting (Tabcorp) and railways (Connex trains) all originally had public ownership or a mixed model that saw a government operator up against one or more private sector companies. Public instrumentalities were assumed to protect the consumer in two ways. First, governments were seen to provide services that were either uneconomic or on too large a scale for private industry to finance. (Now the opposite is often true.) Second, because the utilities were in the public sector, they were assumed to be acting in the public interest.

Increasingly, governments of all political persuasions, of the left and the right, have come to question these assumptions. In addition, the financial lure of selling off assets was important to many governments and, from the mid-1980s, competition was introduced (such as Optus) and many instrumentalities were sold off. For example, the **privatisation** of electricity and gas authorities in Victoria occurred during 1995–99 and were promoted as offering greater efficiency, more services, lower prices and better customer service. Similar benefits have been claimed for the sale of major government corporations such as Qantas, the Commonwealth Bank and Telstra. Where public instrumentalities were privatised, governments often appointed regulators to police the industry (see Table 17.3). Where governments were unable or politically unwilling to sell assets, *corporatisation* (setting up utilities as government-owned trading corporations) was often employed, such as Pacific Power in New South Wales or Australia Post. Even traditional agencies have started to market their services, such as the Office for an Ageing Australia (see Figure 17.1) and Centrelink. Many government departments or government owned agencies now use notions of consumers, customers and the like to identify and market their services to the community. For example, Centrelink have a customer service charter (see <www.centrelink.gov.au/internet/internet.nsf/about_us/customer_charter.htm>) outlining how they deliver services and deal with customers.

At the same time, governments began to insist that *customer charters* be established by the newly-privatised utilities and their own service departments and agencies.[50] For example, Australia Post's Service Charter contains some general commitments and specific undertakings. Box 17.4 shows key extracts from their Charter. Telstra, United Energy, Yarra Valley Water and Federal government departments were among the organisations to establish service charters. Telstra, for example, have a charter for both mobile and standard telephone services (see Box 17.5, page 588).

FIGURE 17.1 The Office for an Ageing Australia markets its services

Source: Courtesy of Department of Health and Ageing, Office for an Ageing Australia.

BOX 17.4 Australia Post's service charter

Australia Post has introduced a customer service charter as an expression of our commitment to improving our service and communication.

Service Charter 2003

At Australia Post, we are constantly striving to improve our service and forge closer relationships with all our customers.

This Service Charter is an expression of our commitment to improving our service and communication with you. Our Service Charter sets out the standards you can expect from us, explains how you can obtain information and how to let us know if you have concerns, and offers advice on how you can help us to serve you better. The hallmark of our Service Charter is our promise to provide consistently professional and high-quality service. This means that at all times:

- you will be treated with courtesy and consideration and our staff will be helpful;
- your questions and needs will be attended to promptly;
- we will exercise the utmost integrity in providing services; and
- we will not disclose any information about you without your consent, except as permitted by law.

Our service commitment applies to everything we do, whether it is our letter service, or other services, provided by our own people or through licensees and contractors.

Community Service Obligation (CSOs)

We are required by law to provide a universal letter service which is accessible to all Australians and, in addition, to provide a standard letter service at a uniform price (currently 50 cents) from anywhere to anywhere in the country. This means our cost of delivering some letters can be many times higher than the postage charged. The CSO cost occurs when the real cost of delivery exceeds the charge for the service.

The cost of meeting our CSOs, currently estimated to be around $80 million each year, is funded by earnings from the reserved services (letters up to 250 grams) within Australia Post's letters business.

We do not receive any taxpayer money from the Government to meet the costs of CSOs.

The purpose of our Service Charter

The Service Charter sets out the standards you can expect from us, explains how you can obtain information, outlines how you can complain if the standards are not met and offers advice on how you can help us to serve you better.

Mail services

Australia Post is committed to making posting facilities easily accessible and to meet reasonable levels of local community demand.

Complaints

We believe that the fastest and most effective way to resolve a complaint and achieve customer satisfaction is to deal with the issue at the point of initial contact.

Making the most of Post

If we can enhance the service provided to you as a mail recipient, we will contact you personally to discuss our ideas for improvement and to seek your cooperation.

Performance reports

Australia Post reports on how well it lives up to its Service Charter in the Annual Report. This is available from the General Manager's office in each state.

Contact information

To request a copy of the Australia Post Customer Service Charter, or to find out more about the Customer Service Charter, use the following contact details in each state.

For full details of all aspects of the charter visit:

<www.australiapost.com.au/IXP/0,1083,CH2034%257EMO19,00.html>

<www.australiapost.com.au/GAC_File_Metafile/0,,2141_service_charter_dl1,00.pdf>

Within Australia, debates still exist politically about whether remaining state assets should be privatised, such as the complete privatisation of Telstra, the sale of electricity authorities in New South Wales and South Australia and the sale of water authorities. Arguments for and against deregulation and privatisation are in part economic, in part ideological and in part social. In the period after World War II, there was a trend towards *public enterprise*; the direction has now been reversed. Political trends change and nothing is inevitable, given debate over what the benefits are of either public or private enterprises and who benefits from their activities. Such debates will, in all likelihood, continue.

Summary

Public policy intersects the field of consumer behaviour when policy makers believe that intervention in the process or outcome of marketing exchanges will benefit society as a whole. The three types of interventions used by government include regulation, consumer education and information, and the provision of incentives to encourage marketing transactions that benefit society. Parliaments at the Commonwealth and State level have enacted consumer-oriented legislation in response to marketing abuses and public concerns. As a result, Australia has a mixture of public and private sector regulation, with the balance swinging to private sector self-regulation. At the same time, regulatory agencies such as the ACCC and the ACA have considerable power to influence the marketplace.

In addition to protective legislation, governments provide information and education to enable consumers to make wise buying decisions. Increasingly, government policy makers and consumer advocates recognise that they cannot protect consumers against all marketing abuses, and that the consumer's best defence is better product knowledge. Nutritional labels, monitored by ANZFA, are an important source of consumer information.

Because consumption is the most pervasive human activity, it is incumbent upon public policy makers to support, and academic consumer researchers to design and implement, consumer behaviour studies that identify and document areas in need of government intervention. Consumer behaviour research findings should provide the basis for consumption-related public policy.

Discussion questions

1. Evaluate the need for regulations and laws designed to protect the consumer. Have such laws been effective? Why or why not?
2. Describe the role of consumer research in developing consumer-oriented legislation.
3. A mouthwash marketer claims that its product eliminates 50% more plaque than other brands. In specific terms, however, the marketer's brand kills just 3% of the plaque on teeth while other brands kill only 2%. The marketer knows that most consumers are unaware of the fact that the 50% figure advertised represents only a 1% increase in the total plaque eliminated. The marketer also knows that dentists agree that a 1% increase in plaque reduction is insignificant. Does the marketer's advertising constitute an 'unconscionable lie', a 'claim/fact discrepancy', a 'claim/belief discrepancy', or none of these? Explain your answer. How would you use consumer research to decide into which of the above categories the marketer's claim belongs?
4. (a) 'Consumers need to be informed about products and services so that they can make better consumption decisions.' Discuss this statement in relation to (i) nutritional labelling, (ii) consumer use of nutritional information on labels.
   (b) Suggest ways to improve consumer education regarding the nutritional value of foods.
5. A well-known electronics company is introducing a new smoke detector with a special feature that makes the alarm beep once a minute when the detector's batteries are weak and need to be replaced. Assume that the company discovers that in many detectors the batteries can be too weak to operate the alarm properly for some time before the above feature is activated. Should the manufacturer:
   (a) recall and redesign the smoke detector?
   (b) stop making the alarm without recall and inform current owners of the problem by mail?
   (c) continue marketing the smoke detector while informing buyers of the need to change the batteries regularly?

   Explain your answer.
6. How can consumers make an informed choice about the use of genetically modified ingredients in foods? To what extent would labelling help consumers make their choice?
7. You are the marketing manager for a large company that manufactures and distributes chemicals. Would you prefer government (local, State or Federal) regulations or voluntary industry codes regarding:
   (a) acceptable levels of air and water pollution?
   (b) procedures for transporting hazardous chemicals?

   Explain your answers.

Exercises

1. Visit a supermarket and find examples of packaging-to-price deceptions. Present them in class and discuss the possible effectiveness of government regulation, industry self-regulation or consumer opinion in eliminating such practices.
2. Conduct a survey of 20 to 30 consumers regarding their use of nutritional, environmental or Australian owned–Australian made information on labels in deciding which household products they purchase. Identify the demographics, lifestyle characteristics and media habits that distinguish these consumers from the rest of the sample.
3. Visit a financial institution and obtain details of loan applications. What information is the consumer given about the loan, effective interest rates and total costs? What are the consumer's rights and obligations? Should governments provide more or less regulation of credit practices?
4. Compare the performance of a previous government corporation such as Qantas or the Commonwealth Bank before and after privatisation. In what ways are consumers better or worse off?

Key terms

Australian Competition and Consumer Commission (ACCC) *(p. 580)*
claim/belief discrepancies *(p. 589)*
claim/fact discrepancies *(p. 589)*
consumer education *(p. 600)*
consumer protection *(p. 581)*
consumer research priorities *(p. 601)*
corrective advertising *(p. 596)*
deceptive advertising *(p. 589)*
deceptive packaging *(p. 597)*
deceptive pricing *(p. 597)*
genetically modified *(p. 599)*
green advertising *(p. 593)*
marketing abuses *(p. 579)*
nutritional labelling *(p. 597)*
packaging-to-price deception *(p. 597)*
privatisation *(p. 585)*
public policy *(p. 579)*
self-regulation *(p. 577)*
Trade Practices Act 1974 *(p. 580)*
unconscionable lies *(p. 589)*

Endnotes

1. Immanuel Kant, *Groundwork of the Metaphysics of Morals*, translated by H.J. Paton (New York: Harper & Row, 1964).
2. Donald D. Robin and R. Eric Reidenback, 'Social responsibility, ethics, and marketing strategy: Closing the gap between concept and application', *Journal of Marketing*, 51, January 1987, pp. 44–53.
3. See, for example, Gene R. Laczniak and Patrick E. Murphy, *Marketing Ethics* (Lexington MA: Lexington Books, 1985), p. 36.
4. Ibid.
5. Ibid.
6. Dennis E. Garrett, 'The effectiveness of marketing policy boycotts: Environmental opposition to marketing', *Journal of Marketing*, 51, April 1987, pp. 46–57; Calvin Sims, 'The politics of dealing with the threat of boycott', *New York Times*, 14 March 1993, p. 2E; Arthur S. Hayes and Joseph Pereira, 'Facing a boycott, many companies bend', *Wall Street Journal*, 6 November 1990, p. B1.
7. Douglas C. McGill, 'Cosmetic companies quietly ending animal test', *New York Times*, 2 August 1989, p. A1.
8. Bill Carter, 'TV sponsors heed viewers who find shows too racy', *New York Times*, 23 April 1989, pp. 1, 22.
9. Paul N. Bloom and Stephen A. Greyser, 'The maturing of consumerism', *Harvard Business Review*, November–December 1981, pp. 130–139.
10. Bruce C. Clarke and Brendan J. Sweeney, *Marketing and the Law* (Sydney: Butterworths, 1997).
11. In 1997 the *Trade Practices Act* was specifically amended to deal with mandatory and voluntary industry codes. For a comprehensive overview of industry compliance, see <www.accc.gov.au/content/index.phtml/itemId/54418>.

12. Ibid.
13. Since the late 1980s, *Choice* magazine has continually raised environmental issues for consumers. See, for example, 'Supermarkets chase green glow', *Choice*, October 1991, pp. 16–21; 'Something in the air', *Choice*, July 1995, pp. 16–22; and 'Recycling in practice', *Choice*, April 1993, pp. 6–11.
14. 'Are you confused about plastics recycling?', *Choice*, June 1996, p. 27.
15. 'All dressed up', *Choice*, August 1998, pp. 9–14. The article evaluates health claims of 130 salad dressings.
16. 'Roof restoration—fact and fiction', *Choice*, March 1999, pp. 16–21.
17. Regulatory issues concerning content appear to resurface every few years. *An Investigation into the Content of On-line Services*, Australian Broadcasting Authority, 1997. Its predecessor, the Australian Broadcasting Tribunal, conducted a major study into television violence in the late 1980s. See *Television Violence in Australia* (Canberra: AGPS, 1990) (one of the book's authors conducted research for this study). See also *'Cool' or 'Gross': Children's Attitudes to Violence, Kissing and Swearing on Television*, ABA, 1994; and *Families and Electronic Entertainment*, ABA, 1996 <www.aba.gov.au/what/research/mono.htm>.
18. ACCC *Summary of the Trade Practices Act 1974* (Canberra: ACCC, 1999). See also <www.accc.gov.au>; 'ACCC cracks its whip', *Choice*, June 1996, p. 5; and 'To ban or not to ban', *Choice*, May 1993, pp. 30–33. For technical discussions of the operation of the trade practices legislation, see the *Competition & Consumer Law Journal*.
19. These include the Federal Trade Commission (FTC), the Food and Drug Administration (FDA), the Consumer Products Safety Commission (CPSC), the Federal Communications Commission (FCC), the Interstate Commerce Commission, the Federal Maritime Commission, the Securities and Exchange Commission (SEC), the Commodities Futures Trade Commission and the International Trade Commission.
20. Readers are warned that governments are constantly reorganising regulatory laws and the agencies covered by them. See <www.fed.gov.au> for a list of Australian federal government agencies.
21. 'Fels and the case of the $2 cookies', *Age*, 31 October 1998, p. B4.
22. '$1.25m fine for bread price-fixing', *Age*, 31 May 1997, p. A1.
23. Geoff Sirmai, *The Confident Consumer* (Sydney: Allen & Unwin, 1999).
24. See <www.aba.gov.au>.
25. See <www.consumersonline.gov.au>.
26. See <www.foodstandards.gov.au>.
27. See <www.tga.gov.au>.
28. See <www.consumer.gov.au>.
29. See <www.vcat.vic.gov.au>.
30. See <www.ocba.sa.gov.au>.
31. See <www.fairtrading.wa.gov.au>.
32. See <www.consumer.tas.gov.au>.
33. See <www.consumer.qld.gov.au>.
34. See <www.abio.org.au>.
35. See <www.tio.com.au>.
36. See <www.phio.org.au>.
37. See <www.advertisingstandardsbureau.com.au>. The AANA is located at <www.aana.com.au>.
38. See <www.mrsa.com.au>.
39. See <www.adma.com.au>.
40. See <www.iia.net.au>.
41. See <www.standards.com.au>.
42. See <www.asic.gov.au>.
43. 'To ban or not to ban', *Choice*, May 1993, pp. 30–33.
44. 'Baby walkers still under scrutiny', *Choice*, November 1993, p. 5.
45. Ibid., p. 30.
46. The Australian Treasury publishes an extensive list of product recalls. See <www.recalls.gov.au>.
47. George S. Day, 'Assessing the effects of information disclosure requirements', *Journal of Marketing*, 40, April 1976, p. 46; and Homer Kripke, 'Gesture and reality in consumer credit reform', in David A. Aaker and George S. Day (eds), *Consumerism: Search for the Consumer Interest*, 2nd edn (New York: Free Press, 1974), pp. 218–224.
48. Debra L. Scammon and Mary Jane Sheffet, 'Regulation in the 80s: What is the role of consumer researchers?', in Thomas C. Kinnear (ed.), *Advances in Consumer Research*, 11 (Chicago: Association for Consumer Research, 1983), pp. 463–465.
49. David McKenzie, 'Red tape worries small companies: Survey', *Age*, 12 June 1966, p. B1.
50. All Federal government departments, agencies and enterprises had established service charters by mid-1999. See <www.ctc.gov.au>.
51. Thomas J. Maronick, 'Copy tests in FTC deception cases: Guidelines for researchers', *Journal of Advertising Research*, 1991, p. 9.

52. David M. Gardner, 'Deception in advertising: A conceptual approach', *Journal of Marketing*, 39, January 1975, p. 42; and Australian Competition & Consumer Commission, News Release, Misleading air conditioner ducting advertising corrected, 12 December 2003, <www.accc.gov.au/content/index.phtml/itemId/420250/fromItemId/378016>.
53. 'Industry against fruit juice abuse', *Choice*, August 1994, p. 4; and 'Fathoming food facts', ibid, pp. 8–11.
54. Marian Burros, 'Labels on soups: Read with care', *New York Times*, 22 February 1986, p. 48. See also 'Vital signs', *Choice*, March 1992, pp. 7–9, for a discussion of Australian food labelling.
55. Laura Bird, 'Perrier's launch stalled again over health concerns', *Adweek's Marketing Week*, 30 April 1990, p. 5.
56. 'Made in Australia? Stuffed koalas?', *Choice*, January 1992, p. 5. See also 'Cook-On barbecue refunds', *Age*, 17 August 1996, p. A6. The manufacturers were required by the ACCC to advertise that their range of barbecues was not entirely Australian-made. The ACCC believed some consumers may have been misled by Cook-On advertising. *Choice* magazine has highlighted this issue on many occasions over the years. For example, see 'Is it true blue?', May 1992, p. 4; 'Buy Australian: Should you use this slogan as your shopping creed?', February 1994, pp. 6–12; 'Where do I come from?', May 1994, p. 4; and 'Labelling battle continues', January 1995, p. 5. See also Don Porritt, 'Buying into Australian made', *Australian Professional Marketing*, December 1993/January 1994, pp. 29–30; and Australian Competition & Consumer Commission, News Release, Egg Tick Logo Withdrawn After ACCC Concerns, 4 February 2004, <www.accc.gov.au/content/index.phtml/itemId/473321/fromItemId/2332>; and Australian Competition & Consumer Commission, News Release, ACCC warns suppliers of children's make-up, 27 December 2003, <www.accc.gov.au/content/index.phtml/itemId/420416/fromItemId/378016>.
57. See <www.afa.org.au>.
58. See <www.presscouncil.org.au>.
59. See <www.advertisingstandardsbureau.com.au> (June 2004).
60. See <www.tgacc.com.au> and <www.afa.org.au/WebStreamers?page_id=918> (June 2004).
61. See <www.aba.gov.au>.
62. Anne Davies and Christina Spurgeon, 'The Broadcasting Services Act: A reconciliation of public interest and market principles of regulation?', *Media Information Australia*, 66, November 1992, pp. 85–92; and Paul Chadwick, Sue Ferguson and Michelle McAuslan, 'Shackled: The story of a regulatory slave', *Media Information Australia*, 77, August 1995, pp. 65–72.
63. Federation of Australian Commercial Television Stations (FACTS), 1999, *Commercial Television Industry Code of Practice*, Sydney.
64. See *Review of Commercial Radio Codes of Practice*, <www.apra.com.au/member/pdfs/Review%20of%20Commercial%20radio%20Codes.pdf> (18 March 2004).
65. Ted Howes, 'Ad nauseam: Viewers voice outrage', *Sun*, 5 August 1991, pp. 12–13.
66. Megan Jones, 'Women speak out over sexist ads', *Age*, 27 October 1993, p. 2.
67. Caroline Milburn, 'Uproar over mother-to-be in Toyota ad', *Age*, 16 March 1993, p. 4.
68. Megan Jones, 'Complaints pouring in over commercial that taps revenge', *Age*, 3 November 1994.
69. 'Oh bugger! How crude commercialisation leaves our expletives depleted', *Sunday Age*, 18 April 1999, p. A7.
70. Advertising Standards Council, *Case Report: For the Months of April, May and June 1992*, References 9472–9473 (Commonwealth), 9475 (Westpac), 9476 (Metway).
71. Chuck Ross, 'What does it take to get a commercial on the air?', *New York Times*, 27 September 1992, p. F10.
72. Jeanne Saddler, 'FTC easing rules requiring firms to support ad claims', *Wall Street Journal*, 21 July 1983, p. 2
73. *Broadcasting in Australia* (Sydney: Australian Broadcasting Tribunal, 1990). The amount and placement of ads is now covered by the FACTS Code, op. cit.
74. Ted Howes, op. cit.
75. 'Into the mouth of babes', *Choice*, October 1990, pp. 4–7.
76. Reported in *Choice*, October 1990, op. cit. For the full report, see Heather Morton, 'Television food advertising: A challenge for the new public health in Australia', *Community Health Studies*, 1990, Vol. XIV(2). See also Jacinta Burke, Susanna Agardy, Maria Fricker and Jim Biles, *Children, Television and Food* (Melbourne: Australian Broadcasting Tribunal, 1982); David Bednall, P. Marzorini and R. Polglaze, *Television Advertising and Children: A Review of the Research Literature 1969–1979* (Melbourne: Australian Broadcasting

Tribunal, 1980); and David Bednall and M. Hannaford, *Television and Children: Children's Recall of Television Advertising and Programs* (Melbourne: Australian Broadcasting Tribunal, 1980).

77. Hillary Chura, 'McDonald's pulls further away from mass marketing', Adwatch: Outlook 2004, <www.adage.com/news.cms?newsld=40804> (June 2004).
78. See 'Fast bucks', *Choice*, April 1994, pp. 10–13.
79. *Fair Exposure: Guidelines for the Constructive and Positive Portrayal and Presentation of Women in the Media* (Canberra: Office of the Status of Women, 1983). See also Patricia Mann, 'Portrayal of women in advertising: Self-regulation and other options', *Media Information Australia* (1989), 51, pp. 50–55; there are relevant articles by Suzanne Keeler, Diana Wyndham and Bruce Cormack and Kate Henley in the same issue. See also Attracta Lagan, 'Demanding a female perspective', *B&T*, 6 August 1993, p. 16.
80. Katrina Strickland, 'Butt of ad jokes', *Australian*, 5 January 1995, p. 7.
81. Tony Burrett, 'Real women ads to be awarded by AFA', *Ad News*, 25 March 1994, p. 1. See also *New Woman*, November 1994.
82. *New Woman*, November 1994.
83. 'Advertising matter relating to cigarettes, cigarette tobacco or other tobacco products', *Australian Broadcasting Tribunal: Manual* (Sydney: ABT, 1992), pp. 88–91; Andy Biziorek, 'Tobacco ban spurs search for backers: Sports sponsorship faces $20m shakeup', *B&T*, 3 April 1992, p. 4.
84. 'Low tar cigarettes: The real story', *Choice*, August 1994, pp. 14–17.
85. Melissa Pearce, 'It's an alcohol induced moderation', *B&T*, 25 June 1993, p. 12.
86. *Environmental Claims in Marketing: A Guideline* (Canberra: Trade Practices Commission, 1992).
87. Advertising Standards Council, op. cit.
88. 'Fast food: Less waste', *Choice*, April 1994, p. 36.
89. 'Green laundry detergents', *Choice*, September 1991, pp. 42–44.
90. Gita Venkataramani Johasr, 'Consumer involvement and deception from implied advertising claims', *Journal of Marketing Research*, August 1995, pp. 267–279.
91. J. Edward Russo, Barbara L. Metcalf and Debra Stephens, 'Toward an empirical technology for identifying misleading advertising', in Richard J. Harris (ed.), *Information Processing Research in Advertising* (Hillsdale, NJ: Lawrence Erlbaum Associates, 1982), p. 15.
92. 'Corrective advertisement and apology', *Woman's Day*, 1 September 1997, p. 65.
93. 'Cook-on barbecue refunds', *Age*, 17 August 1996, p. A6.
94. James R. Taylor and Thomas C. Kinnear, 'Corrective advertising: An empirical tracking of residual effects', in Richard P. Bagozzi et al. (eds), *Marketing in the 80's: Changes and Challenges* (Chicago: American Marketing Association, 1980), pp. 416–418.
95. Alan R. Andreasen, 'Consumer behavior research and social policy', in Thomas S. Robertson and Harold H. Kassarjian (eds), *Handbook of Consumer Behavior* (New Jersey: Prentice Hall, 1991), p. 468.
96. Jacob Jacoby, Margaret C. Nelson, Waynes D. Hoyer and Hal G. Gueutal, 'Probing the locus of causation in the miscomprehension of remedial advertising statements', in Kinnear (ed.), op. cit., pp. 379–386.
97. William L. Wilke, Dennis L. McNell and Michael B. Mazis, 'Marketing's "scarlet letter": The theory and practice of corrective advertising', *Journal of Marketing*, 48, Spring 1984, pp. 11–31.
98. See Clarke and Sweeney, op. cit., pp. 203–204.
99. 'Bigger, not more', *Choice*, September 1993, p. 5. A manufacturer of infant formula changed to a larger can, but reduced the actual contents from 1 kg to 900 g.
100. 'Minimum Max Factors', *Choice*, April 1994, p. 6.
101. See *Food Standards Code* <www.foodstandards.gov.au/foodstandardcode> (June 2004).
102. See <www.afgc.org.au> (June 2004).
103. 'Food labels: What they reveal and conceal', *Choice*, April 1998, pp. 6–11.
104. Ibid.
105. William Mueller, 'Who reads the label?', *American Demographics*, January 1991, pp. 36–41.
106. Marian Burros, 'Health claims on food put FDA in a corner', *New York Times*, 19 February 1986, p. C1.
107. 'Keep it simple is the message from shoppers', in Sally James and Allan Sharp, *The Business of Health*, special advertising supplement prepared by the National Heart Foundation, 1992.
108. Burros, op. cit.
109. See A. Teade, 'Food terrorism', *Australian*, 15 February 1997, p. 23 (Arnotts); and E. Phillips, 'Kraft $6m loss is peanuts', *Daily Telegraph*, 27 December 1996.
110. See 'Genetically modified foods—the clock is ticking', *ANZFA News*, 10, March 1999, p. 1.
111. See <www.aca.com.au>.

112. Judith Waldrop, 'Educating the customer', *American Demographics*, September 1991, pp. 44–47.
113. See Australian Nutrition Foundation, <www.nutrition australia.org> (June 2004).
114. Jacinta Burke et al., op. cit.
115. Andreasen, op. cit.
116. Steven G. Lobello, 'Differences between blood donors and non-donors in AIDS-related attitudes', *Psychological Reports*, 66(3), Part 1, 1990, pp. 867–870; Robert M. Oswalt and Jennifer Gordon, 'Blood donor motivation: A survey of minority college students', *Psychological Reports*, 72, 1993, pp. 785–786.
117. Jane A. Pillavin, 'Why do they give the gift of life? A review of research on blood donors since 1977', *Transfusion*, 30(5), 1990, pp. 444–459.
118. Angela Lipsitz, Katherine Kallmeyer, Martha Ferguson and Andrew Abas, 'Counting on blood donors: Increasing the impact of reminder calls', *Journal of Applied Social Psychology*, 66, 1989, pp. 871–874.
119. Jean V. Linden, Dean I. Gregario and Richard I. Kalish, 'An estimation of blood donor eligibility in the general population', *Vox Sang*, 54, 1988, pp. 96–100.
120. Jeff Allen and Daniel D. Butler, 'Assessing the effects of donor knowledge and perceived risk on intentions to donate blood', *Journal of Health Care Marketing*, 13(3), 1993, pp. 26–33; and Raymond L. Horton and Patricia J. Horton, 'Knowledge regarding organ donation: Identifying and overcoming barriers to organ donation', *Social Science and Medicine*, 33(9), 1991, pp. 1037–1051.
121. Oswalt and Gordon 1993, op. cit.; Pillavin 1990, op. cit.
122. George P. Boe, 'Donor motivation in a volunteer blood program', *Laboratory Digest*, 36, 1973, p. 16; and John J. Burnett, 'Examining the profiles of the donor and non-donor through a multiple discriminant approach', *Transfusion*, 22, 1982, pp. 138–142.
123. Oswalt and Gordon 1993, op. cit.; and Robert M. Oswalt, 'A review of blood donor motivation and recruitment', *Transfusion*, 17(2), 1974, pp. 123–135; Pillavin 1990, op. cit.
124. Sarath A. Nonis, Charles W. Ford, Laddie Logan and Gail Hudson, 'College students' blood donation behavior: Relationship to demographics, perceived risk, and incentives', *Heath Marketing Quarterly*, 13(4), 1996, pp. 33–46.

Glossary

ABA Australian Broadcasting Authority.

ABS Australian Bureau of Statistics.

absent father syndrome Household where a father's activities (typically work) prevent him spending much time at home with his family.

absolute threshold The lowest level at which an individual can experience a sensation.

ACA Australian Consumers' Association (publishers of *Choice* magazine).

ACCC Australian Competition and Consumer Commission.

acculturation The learning of a new or 'foreign' culture.

achieved role A role expected of an individual as the result of some factor concerned with his or her personal attainment, such as level of education, income, occupational status or marital status.

achievement need The need for personal accomplishment as an end in itself.

acquired needs Needs that are learned in response to one's culture or environment (such as the need for esteem, prestige, affection or power). Also known as *psychogenic needs* or *secondary needs*.

activation Involves relating new data to old to make the material more meaningful.

activity relationship An interaction and coordination of activities between two businesses in a relationship, and one level of interaction that may constitute the relationship.

actor relationship An interaction of employees and roles between two businesses in a relationship, and one level of interaction that may constitute the relationship.

actual self-image The image that an individual has of himself or herself as a certain kind of person, with certain characteristic traits, habits, possessions, relationships and behaviour.

adaptation In the field of perception, the term refers specifically to 'getting used to' certain sensations or a certain level of stimulation, such as a hot bath.

ADMA Australian Direct Marketing Association.

adopter categories A sequence of categories which describes how early (or late) a consumer adopts a new product in relation to other adopters. The five typical adopter categories are: innovators, early adopters, early majority, late majority and laggards.

adoption process The stages through which an individual consumer passes in arriving at a decision to try (or not to try), or to continue using (or discontinue using) a new product. The five stages of the traditional adoption process are: awareness, interest, evaluation, trial and adoption.

advertising executions Different versions of an advertisement in the same campaign.

advertising tracking Response to ads (typically awareness and message comprehension) are measured repeatedly to see how they change in response to advertising

advertising wearout Overexposure to repetitive advertising that causes individuals to become satiated and their attention and retention to decline.

advertorial Advertisement in a newspaper or magazine that has the appearance of being an article. See also *infomercial*.

affect referral rule A simplified decision rule whereby consumers make a product choice on the basis of their previously established overall ratings of the brands considered, rather than on specific attributes.

affective component The part of the tricomponent attitude model that reflects a consumer's emotions or feelings (favourable or unfavourable) with respect to an idea or object.

affiliation need The need for friendship, acceptance and belonging.

affinity marketing Creating the view that the marketer and consumer hold similar values and have a good relationship.

affluent consumers Segment with high contestable income.

age effects Important purchase and consumption differences that occur with aging.

age subculture Social structure based on age.

aggressive individual One of three personality types identified by Karen Horney. The aggressive person is one who moves *against* others (e.g. competes with others).

AIDA model Theory of advertising effectiveness that assumes consumers move through the stages of Awareness, Interest, Desire and (purchase) Action.

aided recall measurement A technique used to measure advertising awareness in which respondents are asked if they remember seeing an advertisement for a specific product category.

AIOs Psychographic variables that focus on Activities, Interests and Opinions.

alternative medicine The practice of medicine using non-traditional approaches.

altruism Social behaviour carried out by an individual or organisation to benefit another without anticipation of rewards from external sources.

anthropology Study of people in their society, and the ways their language and culture develop.

APEC The Asia Pacific Economic Cooperation forum.

approach object Product, person, service, condition or other item which the consumer desires (e.g. physical fitness).

ascribed role A role expected of an individual as the result of factors over which he or she has no control, such as age, sex, family, race or religion.

ASEAN Association of Southeast Asian Nations.

aspiration level Goals that consumers desire to reach in key areas of their lives, such as wealth, education and sport.

aspirational group A group to which a non-member would like to belong.

assimilation effect An effect of the *social judgment theory* that suggests a highly involved person will interpret a message as more positive than it actually is, if the message is congruent with their own position.

assimilation-contrast theory A theory of attitude change that suggests that consumers are likely to accept only moderate attitude changes. If the change suggested is too extreme, the contrast with presently held attitudes will cause rejection of the entire message.

attitude A learned predisposition to respond in a consistently favourable or unfavourable manner with respect to a given object.

attitude consistency A characteristic of attitudes is their consistency, that is they are consistent in the behaviour they reflect.

attitude object Product, person, service, condition or other item that is the focus of a consumers' attitude.

attitude-toward-behaviour model A model that proposes that a consumer's attitude toward a specific behaviour is a function of how strongly he or she believes that the action will lead to a specific outcome (either favourable or unfavourable).

attitude-toward-object model A model that proposes that a consumer's attitude toward a product or brand is a function of the presence of certain attributes and the consumer's evaluation of those attributes.

attitude-toward-the-ad-model Consumers' cognitive and affective evaluation of advertising.

attribution theory A theory concerned with how people assign causality to events and form or alter their attitudes as an outcome of assessing their own or other people's behaviour.

audience profile The demographic or other characteristics of an audience.

autonomic (unilateral) decision Family purchase decision in which *either* the husband or the wife makes the final decision.

average person appeal Promotion that seeks to value a product or service because of its widespread, non-elitist appeal.

average person approach A reference group appeal that employs the testimonials of stereotypical satisfied consumers.

avoidance group A group with which a non-member does not identify and does not wish to be identified.

avoidance object Product, person, service, condition or other item that the consumer wants to avoid or prevent, for example, a fine for speeding.

awareness The first stage of the traditional adoption process.

baby boomers Members of the population born between the years 1946 and 1964.

back translation When a questionnaire is written in one language and translated into another by a translator and then translated back into the original by another translator.

balance theory An attitude-change theory that postulates that individuals avoid inconsistency and seek harmony (consistency) by changing the weaker conflicting attitude to agree with the stronger attitude.

behavioural learning theory Theory based on the premise that learning takes place as the result of observable responses to external stimuli. Also known as *stimulus-response theory*. See also *conditioned learning* and *instrumental (operant) conditioning*.

beliefs Mental or verbal statements that reflect a person's particular knowledge and assessment about some idea or thing.

benefits (or needs based) segmentation A form of psychological segmentation based on the kinds of benefits consumers seek in a product.

Bettman's information-processing model One of several comprehensive models of consumer behaviour.

brand attitude Summary of the mixture of consumer motivations in relation to a brand, some informational, some transformational.

brand awareness Consumer's knowledge of a brand, that may be measured by either recall or recognition.

brand equity The advantage that a brand, its name and symbol gives to a product in terms of increased sales or price.

brand loyalty Consistent preference and/or purchase of one brand in a specific product or service category.

brand personality An association of a brand whereby it is imbued with human-like personality traits.

brand personification Treating a brand as if it were a person.

brief See *request for tender (RFT)*.

broad categorisers Those who are more likely to risk a poor product choice in order to maximise their product options.

broadband services Pay television, online, interactive and home shopping services provided by a broadband cable or network.

broadcast media Radio, television and broadband services.

bundle pricing The marketing of two or more products in a single package for a special price.

buyer The person who undertakes the activities to procure or obtain the product or service.

BUYGRID Combining the buying categories with a more detailed analysis of the decision-making cycle.

buying centre The group of people in an organisation involved in decision making related to purchases.

CAMSA Council of Australian Marketing Services Associations.

CAPI (Computer Assisted Personal Interviewing) A technique where the questionnaire is displayed on the screen of a portable or handheld computer.

category width A cognitive personality scale that appears to be associated with the number of choices a person tends to consider when making product decisions.

CATI (Computer Assisted Telephone Interviewing) A technique which uses a computer screen to display the questionnaire and capture the answers recorded.

celebrity credibility The extent to which consumers believe that a celebrity is appropriate to promote a product or service in a particular category.

celebrity endorser A person of particular fame or recognition within society who is employed by companies to serve as a spokesperson for their product(s).

central route to persuasion Communication which focuses directly on the product or service benefits.

Chapin's social status scale Measure of status based on type of possessions and condition of housing.

claim/belief discrepancies Deceptive advertising where no factual error is made, but where a deceptive belief is created.

claim/fact discrepancies The omission of some relevant qualification of a claim, resulting in misrepresentation.

classical conditioning See *conditioned learning*.

classless society Social system that has equality of status and resources across all groups.

closure A principle of Gestalt psychology that stresses the individual's need for completion. This need is reflected in the individual's subconscious reorganisation and perception of incomplete stimuli as complete or whole pictures.

clutter The background noise provided by competing and other advertising that may prevent the marketer's message being noticed.

code of ethics A set of rules established and policed by a professional body or association that is designed to protect the rights of consumers, business clients and practitioners (e.g. the MRSA Code of Professional Behaviour).

cognition Knowledge that is acquired by a combination of direct experience and related information from various sources.

cognitive age An individual's perceived age (usually younger than their chronological age).

cognitive component A part of the tricomponent attitude model that represents the knowledge, perception and beliefs that a consumer has with respect to an idea or object.

cognitive dissonance theory A theory that holds that consumers experience some discomfort or concern about a purchase because of conflicting beliefs. It is based on the premise that purchase decisions often entail some compromise.

cognitive learning Learning based on mental activity such as problem solving.

cognitive learning theory A theory that holds that the kind of learning most characteristic of human beings is problem solving, based on mental information processing.

cognitive model of decision making A model that portrays consumers as active seekers of information that will enable them to make satisfactory purchase decisions.

cognitive personality trait *Need for cognition* and *visualisers* *vs verbalisers* are two cognitive personality traits that influence consumer behaviour.

cohort A group of people from a particular era who have significance as they develop or age, e.g. baby boomers.

cohort effects Unique purchase and consumption similarities that result from growing up or ageing in a particular chronological area.

Collection District (CD) Smallest unit of analysis in the Census conducted by ABS every five years. Typically consists of 200–300 homes.

commitment Strength of a consumer's relationship to a brand, service or product. Usually measured by the difficulty in getting a consumer to switch brands.

communication The process whereby individuals share meaning and establish a commonness of thought, achieved by the transmission of a message from a sender to a receiver by means of some kind of signal sent through a channel of some kind.

communication feedback Informing the originator of communication about the reaction to that communication; can be impersonal (such as market research into advertising effectiveness) or personal (such as a facial expression).

community languages Languages, including English, in common use in Australia today. Believed to include more than 100 languages, including aboriginal languages and the languages of NESB immigrant groups.

comparative advertising Advertising that explicitly names or identifies one or more competitors of the advertised brand for the purpose of claiming superiority either on an overall basis or in selected product attributes.

comparative reference group A group whose norms serve as a benchmark for highly specific or narrowly defined types of behaviour. See also *normative reference group*.

compatibility The degree to which potential consumers feel that a new product is consistent with their present needs, values and practices.

compensatory decision rule A type of decision rule in which consumers evaluate each brand in terms of each relevant attribute and then select the brand with the highest weighted score.

complexity The degree to which a new product is difficult to comprehend and/or use.

compliant individual One of three personality types identified by Karen Horney. The compliant person is one who moves *towards* others (e.g. one who desires to be loved, wanted and appreciated by others).

composite-variable index An index that combines a number of socioeconomic variables, such as education, income and occupation, to form one overall measure of social class standing. See also *single-variable index*.

compulsive consumption Addictive consumer behaviour, such as alcoholism.

Compulsory Competitive Tendering (CCT) A formal requirement for certain government bodies to tender out some or part of their activities.

conation The likelihood or tendency that an individual will undertake a specific action or behave in a particular way.

conative component A part of the tricomponent attitude model that reflects a consumer's likelihood or tendency to behave in a particular way with regard to an attitude object. Also referred to as *intention to buy*.

concentrated marketing Targeting a product or service to a single market segment with a unique marketing mix (price, product, promotion, method of distribution).

concept A mental image of an intangible trait, characteristic or idea.

conditioned learning According to Pavlovian theory, conditioned learning results when a stimulus paired with another stimulus that elicits a known response serves to produce the same response by itself.

conformity The extent to which individuals adopt attitudes and/or behaviour consistent with the norms of a group to which they belong or would like to belong.

conjunctive decision rule A non-compensatory decision rule in which consumers establish a minimally acceptable cut-off point for each attribute evaluated. Brands that fall below the cut-off point on any one attribute are eliminated from further consideration.

consequence evaluations A part of the theory of trying, where attitudes toward success, failure and process are partly determined by consequence evaluations.

consequence likelihood A part of the theory of trying, where attitudes toward success, failure and process are partly determined by consequence likelihoods.

conspicuous product A product that is particularly noticeable, either visually (i.e. that it stands out), or verbally (i.e. of a high degree of interest or easily described). These products are often bought in consideration of others' opinion.

construct A term that represents or symbolises an abstract trait or characteristic, such as motivation or aggression.

consumer A term used to describe two different kinds of consuming entities: *personal consumers* (who buy goods and services for their own or for household use) and *organisational consumers* (who buy products, equipment and services in order to run their organisations).

consumer-action group Type of group of consumers that organises to correct specific consumer abuse and then disband, or those that organise to address broader, more pervasive, problem areas and operate over an extended or indefinite period of time.

consumer behaviour The behaviour that consumers display in searching for, purchasing, using, evaluating and disposing of products, services and ideas.

consumer boycott Where consumers decide not to buy a product or service on the basis of a moral judgment, e.g. consumer boycotts of French goods and services during French nuclear testing in 1995 and 1996.

consumer conformity The willingness of consumers to adopt the norms, attitudes and behaviour of reference groups.

consumer decision rules Procedures adopted by consumers to reduce the complexity of making product and brand decisions.

consumer education Programs designed to help consumers make better buying decisions.

consumer ethnocentrism Suspicion of brands from other countries unrelated to characteristics of the product.

consumer heuristics See *consumer decision rules*.

consumer imagery Enduring perceptions or ideas that consumers have about a product, store or service.

consumer innovativeness The degree to which consumers are receptive to new products, new services or new practices.

consumer innovator See *innovator*.

consumer innovator profile Characteristics of consumers that identify the distinctions among the earliest purchasers of a new product that allow segments to be developed.

consumer involvement The extent to which consumers are concerned with a particular purchase decision and consider it to be important to them.

consumer learning The process by which individuals acquire the purchase and consumption knowledge and experience that they apply to future related behaviour.

consumer movement Groups of consumers and their organisations, such as the ACA, who focus on the rights of consumers and the ethical behaviour (or otherwise) of companies providing products and services.

consumer panel A sample of consumers who record their consumer behaviour over an extended period, e.g. AGB's Brandscan.

consumer profile Description of consumers in a target market.

consumer protection Consumer-oriented laws that attempt to correct any power imbalance that exists between buyers and sellers (e.g. misleading and deceptive conduct, product failures and dangerous products being sold).

consumer relevant groups Specific groups that have the potential to impact on consumer behaviour.

consumer research Methodology used to study consumer behaviour.

consumer research priorities Elements of consumer behaviour that require research in order to further satisfy both organisational and societal needs.

consumer sentiment Monthly measure of Australian consumers' views on where the national economy and their personal finances are heading.

consumer socialisation The process by which an individual first learns the skills and attitudes relevant to consumer purchase behaviour.

consumption process A process consisting of three stages: the input stage, which establishes the consumption set and consuming style; the process of consuming and possessing, which includes using, possessing, collecting and disposing of things and experiences; and the output stage, which includes changes in feelings, moods, attitudes and behaviour toward the product or service.

contactual group A formal or informal group with which a person has regular face-to-face contact and with whose values, attitudes and standards he or she tends to agree.

content analysis A method for systematically and quantitatively analysing the content of verbal and/or pictorial communication. The method is frequently used to determine prevailing social values of a society.

contestable income Household income which could be diverted to other spending.

continuous innovation A new product entry that is an improved or modified version of an existing product rather than a totally new product. A continuous innovation has the least disruptive influence on established consumption patterns.

contrast The difference between figure and ground.

contrast effect An effect of the *social judgment theory* that suggests a highly involved person will interpret a message as more negative than it actually is, if the message is not congruent with their position.

copy post-test A test to evaluate the effectiveness of an advertisement that has already appeared and to see which elements, if any, should be revised to improve the impact of the campaign or later advertising.

copy pre-test A preliminary test of an advertisement before it is run to determine which, if any, elements of the advertising message should be revised before major media expenses are incurred.

core values Values that are held by almost every person in a particular society.

corrective advertising Advertising designed to eliminate any residual effects of misleading advertising claims made by marketers.

counterargument A type of thought or cognitive response a consumer has that is counter or opposed to the position advocated in a message.

countersegmentation A strategy in which a company recombines two or more segments into a single segment to be targeted with an individually tailored product or promotional campaign.

credence product Product that the consumer finds hard to evaluate even after purchase and consumption.

credibility The consumer's perception of a celebrity's expertise and trustworthiness, thus providing strong referent power.

crisis communication plan A plan developed for emergency communications that marketers may have to make, e.g. when a product is found to be dangerous and has to be withdrawn from the market.

cross-cultural consumer analysis Research to determine the extent to which consumers of two or more nations are similar in relation to specific consumption behaviour.

cross-cultural consumer research Consumer research strategies designed to understand the similarities and differences between consumers of different cultures and countries.

cross-cultural psychographic segmentation Tailoring marketing strategies to the needs (psychological, social, cultural and functional) of specific segments.

cues Stimuli that give direction to consumer motives, i.e. that suggest a specific way to satisfy a salient motive.

cultural anthropology The study of human beings that traces the development of core beliefs, values and customs passed down to individuals from their parents and grandparents.

culturally diverse society A society in which each subculture has its own unique traits but still shares the dominant traits of the overall culture.

culture The sum total of learned beliefs, values and customs that serve to regulate the consumer behaviour of members of a particular society.

customer opportunity network A network designed to optimise customer opportunity. They are organised around groups or categories of need.

customer profiling Identifying the key characteristics of individual customers that are useful for marketing to them.

customs Overt modes of behaviour that constitute culturally acceptable ways of behaving in specific situations.

cut through The ability of advertising to be noticed, despite the clutter of competing advertising.

database marketing Use of systematic information on individual consumers to tailor marketing offers to them. See also *direct marketing*.

deceptive advertising Advertising that presents or implies false or misleading information to the consumer.

deceptive packaging A product strategy that misleads consumers, such as exaggerating package contents through design effects, not filling the content to the top, or over packaging.

deceptive pricing A pricing strategy that misleads consumers, such as deliberately promoting a price discount or reduction from a high price list.

decision A choice made from two or more alternatives.

decision time Within the context of the diffusion process, the amount of time required for an individual to adopt (or reject) a specific new product.

decoding Receivers' interpretation of the messages they receive on the basis of their personal experience and personal characteristics.

defence mechanism Method by which people mentally redefine frustrating situations to protect their self-image and self-esteem.

defensive attribution A principle that suggests consumers are likely to accept credit for success (internal attribution) and to blame others or outside events for failure (external attribution).

demarketing The marketing task of discouraging consumers or consumer segments from purchasing specific goods.

demographic segmentation The division of a total market into smaller subgroups on the basis of such objective characteristics as age, sex, marital status, income, occupation and education.

deontology An ethical philosophy that places greater weight on personal and social values than on economic values.

dependent variable A variable whose value changes as a result of a change in another (i.e. independent) variable. For example, consumer purchases are a dependent variable subject to level and quality of advertising (independent variables).

depth interview A research technique in which consumers are interviewed one at a time. It is designed to uncover a consumer's underlying attitudes and/or motivations through a lengthy and relatively unstructured interview.

detached personality One of three personality types identified by Karen Horney. The detached person is one who moves away from others (i.e. who desires independence, self-sufficiency and freedom from obligations).

differential threshold The minimal difference that can be detected between two stimuli. Also known as the *j.n.d. (just noticeable difference)*. See also *Weber's law*.

differentiated marketing Targeting a product or service to several segments, using a specifically tailored product, promotional appeal, price and/or method of distribution for each.

diffusion of innovations An area of research concerned with the diffusion and adoption of new products and services through a consumer market.

diffusion process The process by which the acceptance of an innovation is spread by communication to members of a social system over a period of time.

dinks Double income, no kids household, typically one consisting of a childless couple who are both working.

direct mail Advertising that is sent directly to the mailing address of a target consumer.

direct marketing A marketing technique that uses various media (mail, print, broadcast, telephone) to solicit a direct response from a consumer. See also *database marketing*.

disclaimant group A group in which a person holds membership, but of whose values, attitudes and behaviour he or she disapproves.

discontinuous innovation A dramatically new product entry that requires the establishment of new consumption patterns.

disguised question Market research question where the intent of the question is not revealed to the consumer.

disintermediation Business model characterised by the supply chain between original supplier and ultimate buyer being shortened.

disjunctive rule A non-compensatory decision rule in which consumers establish a minimally acceptable cut-off point for each relevant product attribute, so that any brand meeting or surpassing the cut-off point for any one attribute is considered an acceptable choice.

dissolution The final stage of the family life cycle with only one surviving spouse.

distributed learning Learning spaced over a period of time to increase consumer retention. See also *massed learning*.

dogmatism A personality trait that reflects the degree of rigidity a person displays towards the unfamiliar, and towards information that is contrary to his or her own established beliefs.

double jeopardy The situation where minor market share brands are at a disadvantage compared to major brands. Minor brands have fewer buyers and are purchased less frequently by these buyers and major brands have more buyers and are purchased more frequently.

downward mobility Consumers who are losing affluence, relative to the rest of the community.

drip-feed advertising Advertising shown over a long period but with a low to medium weight.

drive An internal force that impels a person to engage in an action designed to satisfy a specific need.

dyad A grouping of two parties (consumer–producer or supplier–manufacturer) interacting.

dynamically continuous innovation A new product entry that is sufficiently innovative to have some disruptive effects on established consumption patterns.

early adopters People who are among the first to sample a new product or service.

early majority The bulk of the first half of the population of adopters.

economic decision-making model A model that depicts the consumer as a perfectly rational being who objectively evaluates and ranks each product alternative and selects the alternative that gives the best value.

effective reach The number of people in an advertising target group who have received three or more confirmed exposures to an ad or program. See also *TARP*.

ego In Freudian theory, the part of the personality that serves as the individual's conscious control. It functions as an internal monitor that balances the impulsive demands of the *id* and the sociocultural constraints of the *superego*.

ego-defensive function A component of the functional approach to attitude change that suggests that consumers want to protect their self-concept from inner feelings of doubt.

elaboration likelihood model A theory that suggests that a person's level of involvement during message processing is a critical factor in determining which route to persuasion is likely to be effective. See *central route to persuasion* and *peripheral route to persuasion*.

elderly consumers Consumers who are 65 years old and over.

electronic shopping Direct marketing approach to shopping through home-shopping channels or programs.

elimination-by-aspects rule Consumers rate attributes in order of importance and set minimum cut-off values. The most important attribute is considered first and any brand that does not have the minimum acceptable amount of the attribute is eliminated. Then the second most important attribute is considered and any brand that does not have the minimum acceptable amount of the attribute is eliminated. This process continues through the attributes until there is only one brand remaining.

embeddedness Where the boundaries between organisations become permeable, and with greater embeddedness the greater the cooperation.

embeds Disguised stimuli (often sexual in nature) that are planted in ads in an attempt to influence consumers subconsciously to buy the product.

emotional arousal Motives aroused through emotional factors (e.g. anger).

emotional decision-making model A model that suggests consumers make decisions based on subjective criteria, such as love, pride, fear, affection and self-esteem, rather than objective evaluation.

emotional motive An approach to a person, object, condition, product or service that is based on subjective criteria. For example, consumers may purchase a perfume on the basis of the feelings (mood, emotion, memories) it represents to them.

empty-nest stage Stage of the family life cycle that is categorised by children no longer living at home, and by parents being financially comfortable and in consideration of retirement.

empty nesters People who live in households where their children have left home.

encoding The process by which individuals select and assign a word or visual image to represent a perceived object.

enculturation The learning of the culture of one's own society.

end-states of existence Personal goals that individuals work toward attaining or developing as part of their values.

end-use consumption The actual consumption or use of a product by a consumer, who is not necessarily the buyer.

end user Person who actually consumes a product or service, as opposed to the producer, wholesaler, retailer or buyer.

endorsement Celebrities, who may or may not be users of a particular product or service, lending their names to advertisements for such products or services for a fee.

Engel-Kollat-Blackwell (Engel-Blackwell-Miniard) model One of several comprehensive models of consumer behaviour.

environmental arousal Motives activated at a particular time by specific cues in the environment.

environmental marketing Advertising targeted to ecologically concerned consumers.

ESB English-speaking background.

established families Families who have built up a relatively secure financial position and whose family life is intact.

ethnic subculture People who identify with a particular distinct cultural group that is a segment within a larger society.

ethnography Study of consumers in their natural habitats, their social behaviours and beliefs. Case studies and participant observation are typical methods.

European Union (EU) Membership of European countries that allows freer cross-country investment and trade. Currently there are 15 member nations – Austria, Belgium, Denmark, Finland, France, Germany, Greece, Ireland, Italy, Luxembourg, the Netherlands, Portugal, Spain, Sweden, and the United Kingdom.

evaluation The third stage of the traditional adoption process, in which the consumer either draws conclusions about a product innovation or determines if further information is needed.

evaluation of alternatives A stage in the consumer decision-making process in which the consumer appraises the benefits to be derived from each of the product alternatives being considered.

evoked set The specific brands a consumer considers in making a purchase choice in a particular product category.

executions See *advertising executions*.

expectation Anticipation of product or service, often affected by advertising.

expected self-image How individuals expect to see themselves at some specified future time.

experience product A product whose attributes can only be discerned after purchase or during consumption.

experientialism An approach to the study of consumer behaviour that focuses on the consumption experience. See also *interpretivist* and *postmodernism*.

expert appeal The promotional use of a person who, because of his or her occupation, special training or experience, is able to speak knowledgeably to the consumer about the product or service being advertised.

exploratory qualitative phase The phase of an in-depth segmentation study in which usage patterns, buying habits, benefits sought and consumer attitudes about a product class are examined.

exploratory quantitative phase The phase of an in-depth segmentation study in which brand similarities, consumer attitudes, perceptions of brand images and preferences are measured.

extended family A household consisting of a husband, wife, offspring, and at least one other blood relative.

extended self Enhancement of people's view of themselves on the basis of their possessions.

extensive problem solving A search by the consumer to establish the necessary product criteria to evaluate knowledgeably the most suitable product to fulfil a need.

external attribution A principle that suggests that consumers are likely to credit their success in using a product to outside sources.

extinction The point at which a learned response ceases to occur because of lack of reinforcement.

extrinsic cues Cues external to the product, such as price, store image or brand image, that serve to influence the consumer's perception of a product's quality.

factor analysis Statistical data reduction technique. Used to identify a small group of dimensions underlying responses to a set of attitudes in a survey, or to cluster consumers into groups, according to their responses on a survey.

family Two or more people related by blood, marriage or adoption who reside together.

family branding The practice of marketing several company products under the same brand name.

family gatekeeper A family member who controls the flow of information to the family about products and services, thereby regulating the related consumption decisions of other family members.

family influencer A family member who provides product-related information and advice to other members of the family, thereby influencing related consumption decisions.

family life cycle (FLC) Classification of families into significant stages. The five traditional FLC stages are young singles, young marrieds, parenthood, post-parenthood and dissolution.

family role structure orientation Patterns of decision making in families, based on the roles given to groups such as women or fathers.

feedback See *communication feedback*.

field observation A cultural measurement technique that takes place within a natural environment (sometimes without the subject's awareness—see *shadow shopping*) and focuses on observing behaviour.

figure and ground A Gestalt principle of perceptual organisation that focuses on contrast. Figure is usually perceived clearly because, in contrast to (back)ground, it appears to be well-defined, solid and in the forefront, while the ground is usually perceived as indefinite, hazy and continuous. Music can be figure or (back)ground.

financial risk The perceived risk that the product will not be worth the cost.

firmagraphics Broad characteristics of business, including business size, customer base, sole versus multiple location(s), geographical location and industry type.

fixated consumers Those who have a passionate interest in a specific product category.

fixated consumption behaviour The normal and socially acceptable consumption behaviour whereby individuals possess a deep interest in a particular object or product category, a willingness to go to considerable lengths to secure additional examples of the object or product of interest, and a dedication of a considerable amount of discretionary time and money to searching out the object or product.

focus group A qualitative research method in which 8–10 people participate in an unstructured group interview about a product or service concept.

foot-in-the-door technique A theory of attitude change that suggests individuals form attitudes that are consistent with their own prior behaviour.

formal group A group that has a clearly defined structure, specific roles and authority levels, and specific goals (e.g. a political party).

formal learning of culture Cultural values taught in a formal way (e.g. at school or in church).

formal source Direct communication between a person representing a profit or non-profit organisation and one or more others (e.g. a discussion between a salesperson and a prospect).

four-way categorisation of interpersonal communication Classification of individuals on the basis of opinion leadership scores, such as socially integrated, socially independent, socially dependent and socially isolated.

framing The process whereby consumers assign losses and gains.

frequency How often advertisements are run during a specified period of time.

Freud's stages of personality development Freud postulated that the personality is formed as the individual passes through the following stages of infant and childhood development: oral, anal, phallic, latent and genital.

Freudian theory A theory of personality and motivation developed by the psychoanalyst Sigmund Freud. See also *psychoanalytic theory of personality*.

friendship group Generally an informal group that is unstructured and lacks specific authority levels – the most influential group after family.

frustration Emotional state that occurs when something blocks consumers from expressing their wants or desires.

functional approach An attitude-change theory that classifies attitudes in terms of four functions: utilitarian, ego-defensive, value expressive and knowledge.

functional risk The perceived risk that a product or service will not perform as expected.

gatekeeper Person who controls whether a piece of communication is passed on to other people.

gay subculture A distinct cultural group that exists on the basis of homosexuality as an identifiable segment within our larger more complex society.

gender subculture A type of subcultural category based on sex, roles and identity of a particular gender.

Generation X Members of the population born between the years 1965 and 1979 (also referred to as Xers or busters).

Generation Y Members of the population born between the years 1980 and 1994.

generic goals The general classes or categories of goals that individuals select to fulfil their needs. See also *product-specific goals*.

genetically modified Containing genetic material from other organisms, modified genetic materials etc.

geodemographic clustering See *geodemographic segmentation*.

geodemographic segmentation A composite segmentation strategy that uses both geographic variables (ABS Collectors Districts, postcodes, local government areas) and demographic variables (income, occupation, value of residence) to identify target markets.

geographic segmentation The division of a market by location such as geographic variables (e.g. region, state or city).

Gestalt A German term meaning 'pattern' or 'configuration' which has come to represent various principles of perceptual organisation. See also *perceptual organisation*.

Gestalt psychology School of psychology that developed specific principles underlying perceptual organisation and the understanding of stimuli.

global advertising The advertising of a brand throughout the world with the same campaign.

global advertising strategy Marketing strategy that focuses on creating a world brand that appeals to markets across international borders.

global brand A brand which is marketed in numerous countries.

goal The sought-after result of motivated behaviour. A person fulfils a need through achievement of a goal.

granfalloon Term coined by novelist Kurt Vonnegut to mean a false and arbitrary sense of belonging to a group.

green advertising A marketing strategy with a strong emphasis on protecting the environment.

group Two or more people who interact on a regular or irregular basis in their pursuit of individual or common goals.

group cohesiveness The extent to which group members tend to 'stick together' and follow group norms.

group norms The implicit rules of conduct or standards of behaviour which members of a group are expected to observe.

grouping Gestalt principle by which people organise stimuli into groups.

habit A consistent pattern of behaviour performed without considered thought. Consistent repetition is the hallmark of habit.

habituation The mechanism by which an individual systematically ignores those stimuli (e.g. products or advertising messages) that are predictable or readily recognisable because of excessive repetition. See also *wearout*.

halo effect A situation in which the perception of a person on a multitude of dimensions is based on the evaluation of just one (or a few) dimensions (e.g. he is trustworthy, fine and noble because he looks you in the eye when he speaks). Also describes the action of people who respond in a similar way to a long list of statements testing attitudes.

hemispheral lateralisation Learning theory in which the basic premise is that the right and left hemispheres of the brain specialise in the way they process information. Also known as *split brain theory*.

heuristics See *consumer decision rules*.

hierarchy of human needs See *Maslow's need hierarchy*

hierarchy of needs See *Maslow's need hierarchy*.

high involvement A situation where consumers judge a purchase decision to be important enough to engage in extensive information search prior to making a decision.

high-tech positioning Marketing that represents a product in terms of its technological features.

household The family is one type of household. Another type comprises those living together who are not related by blood, marriage or adoption – often termed 'group households'.

Howard-Sheth model One of several comprehensive models of consumer behaviour.

husband-dominated Households where the husband makes a disproportionate number of purchase decisions.

hypothesis A tentative statement of a relationship between two or more variables.

hypothetical construct See *construct*.

id In Freudian theory, the part of the personality that consists of primitive and impulsive drives that the individual strives to satisfy.

ideal age The age a person would like to be.

ideal self-image How individuals would *like* others to perceive them.

ideal social self-image Element of the self construct that is the way consumers would like others to perceive them.

imagery The forming of mental images by consumers.

imitative purchasers People who follow the lead of early adopters of a new product or service.

independent variable A variable that can be manipulated to effect a change in the value of a second (i.e. dependent) variable. For example, price is an independent variable that often affects sales (the dependent variable).

index of status characteristics (ISC) A measure of social class that combines occupation, *source* of income (not amount), house type and dwelling area into a single weighted index of social class standing. Also known as *Warner's ISC*.

indirect reference group Individuals or groups with whom a person identifies but does not have face-to-face contact, such as TV personalities, sports heroes, political leaders or humanitarians.

inept set Brands that a consumer excludes from purchase consideration.

inert set Brands that a consumer is indifferent towards because they are perceived as having no particular advantage.

influence strategies Planned promotions designed to change consumer behaviour or attitudes.

infomercial Thirty-minute commercials that appear to the average consumer to be documentaries and thus receive more attentive viewing than obvious commercials would receive. Usually they contain direct marketing advertisements for the products featured. See also *advertorial*.

informal group A group of people who see each other frequently on an informal basis, such as weekly poker players or social acquaintances.

informal learning of culture Situations in which a child learns primarily by imitating the behaviour of selected others (family, friends, television characters).

informal source Direct communication between two or more people who are friends, neighbours, relatives or co-workers.

information overload A dysfunctional situation in which the consumer is presented with too much product- or brand-related information.

information processing A cognitive theory of human learning patterned after computer information processing which focuses on how information is stored in human memory and how it is retrieved.

informational motivation Describes negative motivation that advertising uses when it removes a problem, prevents a problem, provides a solution for lack of satisfaction, involves a product with positive and negative features or describes a product where the consumer has need of further supplies.

innate needs Physiological needs for food, water, air, clothing, shelter and sex. Also known as biogenic needs or *primary needs*.

inner-directed consumers Consumers who tend to rely on their own inner values or standards when evaluating new products and who are likely to be consumer innovators.

innovation Any new product, service, idea or practice.

innovation decision process An update of the traditional *adoption process* model, consisting of the following four stages: knowledge, persuasion, decision and confirmation.

innovativeness A measure of a consumer's willingness to try new products.

innovator An individual who is among the earliest purchasers of a new product.

institutional advertising Advertising designed to promote a favourable company image rather than to promote specific products.

instrumental (operant) conditioning A form of learning based on a trial-and-error process, with habits formed as the result of positive experiences resulting from certain responses or behaviours. See also *conditioned learning*.

instrumental values Values which are a means to an end, i.e. to help people fulfil their ultimate values.

intention to buy Consumer state where a decision has been made to purchase, but purchase has not occurred.

interactive marketing messages Advertising that uses a medium in which the consumer can be in dialogue with the marketer (e.g. on the Internet or in using interactive broadband services).

interactivity The process of getting consumers involved in advertising, where marketers indulge in a two-way communication with customers. Telstra's broadband services, such as home banking, provide communication of this type.

interest The stage of the traditional adoption process in which the consumer actively seeks out information concerning a new product innovation. See also *AIDA model*.

interference Where previous learning disrupts new learning (e.g. an advertisement for a new brand is mistaken for the main brand).

intermarket organisation A network designed to exploit intermarket synergies.

intermediary audience Wholesalers, distributors and retailers who are targeted with trade advertising designed to persuade them to order and stock merchandise, and relevant *specifiers*, such as architects and doctors, who are sent advertising and samples in the hope that they will select them on behalf of their customers.

internal attributions A principle that suggests that consumers are likely to credit their success in using a product to their own skill.

interpersonal communication Communication that occurs directly between two or more people by mail, telephone or in person.

interpretivist A researcher who seeks to find common patterns of operative values, meaning and behaviour across consumption situations.

intrinsic cues Physical characteristics of the product (such as size, colour, flavour or aroma) that serve to influence the consumer's perceptions of product quality.

involvement theory A theory of consumer learning which

postulates that consumers engage in a range of information-processing activity, from extensive to limited problem solving, depending on the relevance of the purchase.

Jungian personality types Carl Jung's theories and insights concerning personality types that are specifically relevant to consumer behaviour, particularly the dimensions of sensing–intuiting, thinking–feeling, extroversion–introversion and judging–perceiving. See also *MBTI*.

just noticeable difference (j.n.d.) The minimal difference that can be detected between two stimuli. See also *differential threshold* and *Weber's law*.

keiretsu A coalition of Japanese firms that do business with each other on the basis of historical, organisational and personal ties between the management of the companies.

key informant A person who is keenly aware or knowledgeable about the nature of social communication among members of a specific group.

key informant method A method of measuring various aspects of consumer behaviour (such as opinion leadership or social class) whereby a knowledgeable person is asked to classify individuals with whom he or she is familiar into specific categories.

knowledge function A component of the functional approach to attitude-change theory that suggests consumers have a strong need to know and understand the people and things they come into contact with.

laggards People who are among the last to adopt a new product or service.

latchkey children Children who arrive home when there are no adults present.

late majority The bulk of the last half of the population to adopt a new product or service.

leading indicator A social measure that provides good evidence of a coming change in economic conditions.

learning The process by which individuals acquire the knowledge and experience they apply to future purchase and consumption behaviour.

level of aspiration The personal goals that an individual may set for themselves and strive towards.

lexicographic decision rule A non-compensatory decision rule in which consumers first rank product attributes in terms of their importance, then compare brands in terms of the attribute considered most important. If one brand scores sufficiently high, it is selected; if not, the process is continued with the second-ranked attribute, and so on.

licensing The use by manufacturers and retailers (for a fee) of well-known celebrity or designer names to acquire instant recognition and status for their products.

lifestyle See *psychographics*.

lifestyle profiles of social classes A constellation of specific lifestyle factors (shared beliefs, attitudes and behaviours) that tend to distinguish the members of particular social classes.

Likert scale Scale for measuring attitudes. Based on a balance of positive and negative response codes (e.g. levels of agreement) that can be treated as interval data and hence summated.

limited problem solving A limited search by a consumer for a product that will satisfy his or her basic criteria from among a selected group of brands.

List of Values (LOV) A values scale designed to be used in surveying consumers' personal values. It contains nine value items based on the terminal values of Rokeach.

localised marketing Marketing tailored to the special circumstances, consumers and advertising media in particular national or sub-national markets.

long-term store In information-processing theory, the stage of real memory where information is organised, reorganised and retained for relatively extended periods of time.

low involvement A situation where consumers judge a purchase decision to be so unimportant or routine that they engage in little information search prior to making a decision.

loyalty The commitment of a consumer to a product or service, measured by repeat purchase or attitudinal commitment.

mail survey Survey using self-completion questionnaires mailed to respondents.

manufacturer's image The way in which consumers view (i.e. perceive) the 'personality' of the firm that produces a specific product.

market maven Individual whose influence stems from a general knowledge or expertise in specific areas that leads to an early awareness of new products and services.

market-oriented definition of innovativeness Judges the newness of a product in terms of how much exposure consumers have to the new product.

market segment A segment of a market which is homogeneous in terms of one or more relevant characteristics.

market segmentation The process of dividing a potential market into distinct subsets of consumers and selecting one or more segments as a target market to be reached with a distinct marketing mix.

marketing abuses Misconduct or behaviour that exploits consumers, engaged in by companies in the marketing of their products.

marketing activities Strategies designed to enhance the flow of goods, services and ideas from producers to consumers in order to satisfy consumer needs and wants.

marketing concept A consumer-oriented philosophy that suggests that the satisfaction of consumer needs provides the focus for product development and marketing strategy to enable the firm to meet its own organisational goals.

marketing ethics Designing, packaging, pricing, advertising and distributing products in such a way that negative consequences to consumers, employees and society in general are avoided.

marketing mix The unique configuration of the four basic marketing variables (product, promotion, price and channels of distribution) that a marketing organisation controls in product marketing (the 4 Ps). Service marketers usually add physical facilities, procedures and personnel to this list.

marketing myopia Focus on the product rather than on the consumer need it is supposed to satisfy.

marketing of social causes Advertising campaigns designed to promote socially desirable behaviour.

Maslow's need hierarchy A theory of motivation that postulates that individuals strive to satisfy their needs according to a basic hierarchical structure, starting with physiological needs, then moving to safety needs, social needs, egoistic needs and, finally, self-actualisation needs.

mass (impersonal) communication Communication directed to a large and diffuse audience, with no direct communication between source and receiver.

mass customisation Products and services specially customised to individual customers using a database. To do this requires customer profiling.

mass marketing The practice of offering a single product and marketing mix to the whole potential market.

mass media Form of communication that does not involve direct person to person contact, and can include print (magazines, newspapers, billboards), broadcast (radio and television), and electronic media (the Internet).

massed learning Compressing the learning schedule into a short time span to accelerate consumer learning. See also *distributed learning*.

materialism Distinguishes between individuals who regard possessions as essential to their identities and lives and those who regard possessions as secondary.

materialistic consumers Consumers who value the acquisition and display of more and more possessions.

MBTI Myers-Briggs Type Indicator. Personality test based on Jungian personality types.

means-end chain Gutman describes the interface between culture and consumer behaviour as a means-end chain. The means are the vehicle for attaining personal values with the consumption goals as an intermediary between them.

media demassification Publishers shifting their focus from large, general interest audiences to smaller, more specialised audiences (e.g. women's magazines, broadband television services).

media strategy An essential component of a communication plan which calls for the placement of advertisements in the specific media used by selected segments in order to achieve a desired reach and frequency. See also *TARP*.

medium A channel through which a message is transmitted (e.g. TV commercial, newspaper advertisement or personal letter).

mega-brand Major brand, usually with international recognition (e.g. Coca-Cola).

membership group A group to which a person either belongs or qualifies for membership.

message The thought, idea, attitude, image or other information that a sender conveys to an intended audience.

message comprehension The extent of meaning derived from the message.

message framing Positively constructed messages (those that specify benefits to be *gained* by using a product) are more persuasive than negatively constructed messages (that specify benefits *lost* by not using a product).

micromarketing Marketing strategies directed to small segments (e.g. regions) that are specially geared to their needs and conditions.

misleading advertising Advertising which makes or implies untrue statements about product or service benefits.

model A simplified representation of reality designed to show the relationships between the various elements of a system or process under investigation.

modelling A way of learning in which individuals observe the behaviour of others, remember it and imitate it.

modified rebuy A buying decision where there is either some change in a firm's requirements or in what the market has to offer.

mood Feelings or affect experienced by a consumer at a particular point of time.

MOSAIC A geodemographic classification of Australians developed by Pacific Micromarketing.

mossers Acronym for middle-aged, overstressed, semi-affluent suburbanites.

motivation The driving force within individuals that impels them to action.

motivational research Qualitative research designed to uncover consumers' subconscious or hidden motivations. The basic premise of motivational research is that consumers are not always aware of, or may not wish to reveal, the basic reasons underlying their actions.

MRQA Inc Market Research Quality Australia. Organisation that audits the quality of market research fieldwork under the Interviewer Quality Control Australia scheme.

MRSA Market Research Society of Australia.

multi-attribute attitude models Attitude models that examine the composition of consumer attitudes in terms of selected product attributes or beliefs.

multicultural society Society which encourages diversity in cultural values and practices, within an agreed legal system.

multinational strategy Any strategy that aids a multinational organisation to compete effectively in diverse target markets throughout an international market.

multiple self Concept that recognises that consumers will vary their behaviour depending on the people they are with and the situation they are experiencing.

multi-step flow of communication theory A revision of the traditional two-step theory that shows multiple communication flows: from the mass media simultaneously to opinion leaders, opinion receivers and information receivers (who neither influence nor are influenced by others); from opinion leaders to opinion receivers; and from opinion receivers to opinion leaders.

narrow categorisers Those who prefer to limit their purchase decisions to known and safe choices.

national brands Brands which are promoted and distributed in all the main markets.

need for cognition The personality trait that measures a person's desire for or enjoyment of thinking.

need recognition The realisation by the consumer that there is a difference between 'what is' and 'what should be'.

negative influence The effect of a particular reference group whose values are not shared by those of the consumer.

negative motivation A driving force away from some object or condition, for example, drink-driving advertisements aimed at getting drivers not to drink and drive.

negative reinforcement An unpleasant or negative outcome that serves to discourage repetition of a specific behaviour.

neo-Freudian personality theory A school of psychology that stresses the fundamental role of social relationships in the formation and development of personality.

neo-Pavlovian theory Consumers can be viewed as information seekers who use logical and perceptual relations among events, together with their own preconceptions, to form a sophisticated representation of the world.

NESB Non-English-speaking background. Describes a person whose first language is not English.

network A way of representing intra- and inter-business relationships.

network integrator A supply chain in which a network of firms have joint ownership.

network structure The pattern of relationships that individuals have with other people in their organisation or virtual organisation.

new-age elderly Older consumers whose lifestyles and values are atypical of most elderly.

new buy (task) A decision to acquire a new item that has never been purchased before by the firm.

niche marketing See *micromarketing*.

Nicosia model One of several comprehensive models of consumer behaviour.

non-compensatory decision rule A type of consumer decision rule whereby positive evaluation of a brand attribute does not compensate for (i.e. is not balanced against) a negative evaluation of the same brand on some other attribute.

non-probability sample Where relationship between sample and population is not known (i.e. convenience, judgment, quota or snowball samples).

non-profit marketing The use of marketing concepts and techniques by not-for-profit organisations (such as museums or government agencies) to impart information, ideas, fund-raising products or attitudes to various segments of the public.

non-traditional FLC stages An FLC schema that includes non-traditional household types (e.g. gay couples, divorced young adults).

normative reference group A group that influences the general values or behaviour of an individual. See also *comparative reference group*.

North American Free Trade Agreement (NAFTA) Trade bloc formed by the USA, Canada and Mexico.

not-for-profit marketing See *non-profit marketing*.

nuclear family A household consisting of a husband and wife and at least one offspring.

nutritional labelling The placement on processed foods of labels to reveal the ingredients, health claims and dates marks etc.

objective measurement of social class A method of measuring social class whereby individuals are asked specific socioeconomic questions concerning themselves or their families. On the basis of their answers, people are placed within specific social class groupings.

objective method Method for measuring opinion leadership by putting consumers in an artificial leadership situation and measuring how they behave.

objective price claims Provide a single discount level.

observability The ease with which a product's benefits or attributes can be observed, visualised or described to potential customers.

observational research A research procedure which examines the actual behaviour of consumers in the marketplace.

occupational status The measure of a person's social standing on the basis of his or her occupation.

one-sided (supportive) message A message that tells only the benefits of a product or service.

open-ended question Survey question where the answers are not pre-coded. Normally used where the researcher needs further information (e.g. 'Why do you say that?').

opinion leader A person who informally influences the attitudes or behaviour of others.

opinion leadership The process by which one person (the *opinion leader*) informally influences the actions or attitudes of others, who may be *opinion seekers* or *opinion recipients*.

opinion leadership overlap The degree to which people who are opinion leaders in one product category are also opinion leaders in one or more other categories.

opinion receiver/recipient Individual who either actively seeks product information from others or receives unsolicited information.

opinion seekers Consumers who actively seek information about a product or service they are considering.

optimising decision strategy A strategy whereby a consumer evaluates each brand in terms of significant product criteria. See also *simplifying decision strategy*.

optimum stimulation level (OSL) The level or amount of novelty or complexity that individuals seek in their personal experiences. High OSL consumers tend to accept risky and novel products more readily than low OSL consumers.

ordered protection motivation (OPM) model Proposes that individuals cognitively appraise the available information regarding the severity of the threat, then they appraise the likelihood that the threat will occur; they evaluate whether coping behaviour can eliminate the threat's danger and, if so, whether they have the ability to perform the coping behaviour.

organisational consumer A purchasing agent (or group) employed by a business, government agency or other institution, profit or non-profit, that buys the goods, services or equipment necessary for the organisation to function.

other-directed consumers Consumers who look to others for direction and approval.

outsourcing Practice by which organisations arrange for suppliers to conduct an activity (such as marketing) previously conducted within the organisation.

packaging-to-price deception Maintaining the price and size of a package while reducing the contents.

parenthood The stage in the family life cycle where a married couple has at least one child living at home.

participant observer A researcher who becomes an active member of the environment he or she is studying.

passive decision-making model A theory that depicts the consumer as a submissive recipient of the promotional efforts of marketers.

payer The person who provides the money or other object of value to obtain the product or service.

penetration policy Strategy of a low price for a new product in order to encourage widespread adoption.

perceived age See *cognitive age*.

perceived quality The quality attributed to a product by the consumer on the basis of various informational cues associated with the product; some cues are intrinsic to the product or service, others are extrinsic (e.g. price, store image, service environment, brand image and promotional messages).

perceived risk The degree of uncertainty perceived by the consumer as to the consequences (outcomes) of a specific purchase decision.

perception The process by which an individual selects, organises and interprets stimuli into a meaningful and coherent picture of the world.

perceptual bias Occurs when a consumer's expectation or previous experience distorts what they perceive. See also *selective attention*.

perceptual blocking The subconscious 'screening out' of stimuli that are threatening or inconsistent with one's needs, values, beliefs or attitudes.

perceptual defence The process of subconsciously distorting stimuli to render them less threatening or inconsistent with one's needs, values, beliefs or attitudes.

perceptual interpretation The individual interpretation of stimuli based on expectations in light of previous experiences, on the number of plausible explanations that they can envision, and on their motives and interests at the time of perception.

perceptual mapping A research technique that enables marketers to plot graphically consumers' perceptions concerning product attributes of specific brands.

perceptual organisation The subconscious ordering and perception of stimuli into groups or configurations according to certain principles of Gestalt psychology.

perfect decision A rational choice made on the basis of complete information.

peripheral route to persuasion Communication taking an indirect approach to persuasive communication, usually for low-involvement products or services.

permission marketing Marketing communications strategy whereby a consumer gives permission to a marketer to communicate promotional information.

personal consumer The individual who buys goods and services for his or her own use, for household use, for the use of a family member, or for a friend. Sometimes referred to as the ultimate consumer or *end user*.

personal interview Interview conducted face-to-face.

personality The inner psychological characteristics that both determine and reflect how people respond to their environment.

personality scale A series of questions or statements designed to measure a single personality trait.

personality test A pencil-and-paper test designed to measure an individual's personality in terms of one or more traits or inner characteristics.

physical risk The perceived risk to self and others that the product may pose.

physiological needs Innate needs (e.g. biogenic) including the needs for food, water, air, clothing, shelter and sex. Also known as *primary needs*.

political marketing The use of marketing concepts and techniques by candidates for political office and by those interested in promoting political causes.

political persuasion The process of using various techniques to influence the voting decisions of individuals.

positioning Establishing a specific image for a brand in relation to competing brands. See also *product positioning*.

positive motivation A driving force towards an object, condition, product or service (e.g. Hoyts promoting a film so consumers will come to see it). See also *transformational motivation*.

positive reinforcement A favourable outcome to a specific behaviour that strengthens the likelihood that the behaviour will be repeated.

positivist A researcher who uses rigorous empirical techniques to discover generalised explanations and laws.

post-campaign research The third stage of market research into the effectiveness of mass communication and advertising, designed to measure the awareness, recall and accuracy of the message.

postmaterialism A social perspective that suggests a back-to-basics lifestyle is more enjoyable and socially responsible than an obsession with ever-increasing material goods.

postmodernism Philosophical approach which is interested in going beyond what consumers do and the stimuli that bombard them to an understanding of how they construct and interpret the world in which they live and consume.

post-parenthood The stage in the family life cycle when a married couple has all children living permanently apart from them.

post-purchase cognitive dissonance The discomfort or dissonance that consumers experience as a result of conflicting information. See *balance theory*.

post-purchase dissonance Cognitive dissonance that occurs after a consumer has made a purchase commitment. Consumers resolve this dissonance through a variety of strategies designed to confirm the wisdom of their choice. See also *cognitive dissonance theory*.

post-purchase evaluation An assessment of a product based on actual trial after purchase.

power group When consumers are primarily concerned with the power that a group can exert over them, they might choose products or services that conform to the norms of that group in order to avoid ridicule or punishment.

power imbalance A one-sided commercial advantage for a supplier or buyer.

power need The need to exercise control over one's environment, including other people.

precision targeting Advertising campaign that efficiently reaches most of the target audience, but few other people.

preconceptions Ideas, expectations and beliefs that consumers take into a buying situation.

predatory pricing Anti-competitive behaviour by an established company which temporarily drops prices to prevent a competitor gaining a viable place in the market.

prepotent need An overriding need, from among several needs, that serves to initiate goal-directed behaviour.

pre-purchase search A stage in the consumer decision-making process in which the consumer perceives a need and actively seeks out information concerning products that will help satisfy that need.

pre-testing The first stage of market research into the effectiveness of new communication and advertising, which is presented to a sample audience and designed to measure the overall effect of the advertisement on consumers. The results of this research can reshape or remake the particular advertisement.

price-quality relationship The perception of price as an indicator of product quality (i.e. the higher the price, the higher the perceived quality of the product).

price-sensitive consumers Consumers who buy a product mainly on the basis of price.

primacy effect A theory that proposes that the first (i.e. the earliest) message presented in a sequential series of messages tends to produce the greatest impact on the receiver. See also *recency effect*.

primary data Information that is collected through surveys, interviews, questionnaires, observation or experimentation for a specific research project.

primary group A group of people who interact (e.g. meet and talk) on a regular basis, such as members of a family, neighbours or co-workers.

primary needs See *innate needs*.

primary research Research that is collected for a specific purpose by or on behalf of the marketer who uses that research. Most market research is of this type. See *secondary research*.

print media Mainly newspapers, magazines and letterbox advertising.

private label brand A major manufacturer will prepare a special brand for a retailer (e.g. Australia's Choice brand for Kmart).

privatisation The selling of government owned/controlled enterprises to private business.

PRIZM Potential Rating Index by Zip Market. A composite US index of geographic and socioeconomic factors expressed in residential zip code neighbourhoods from which consumer segments are formed.

probability sample Sample where there is a known probabilistic relationship between the sample and the population (i.e. simple random, systematic random, cluster and stratified samples).

product adaptation Small changes in a global product to adapt it to a local market.

product conspicuousness The degree to which a product stands out and is noticed.

product image The 'personality' that consumers attribute to a product or brand.

product life cycle The changing phases of new product adoption, widespread diffusion and replacement.

product line extension A marketing strategy of adding related products to an already established brand (based on the *stimulus generalisation* theory).

product positioning A marketing strategy designed to project a specific image for a product.

product-specific goals The specifically branded or labelled products that consumers select to fulfil their needs. See also *generic goals*.

product standardisation Making products uniform across all markets.

Professional Dynametric Programs (PDP) A multiple trait personality test used to profile predictable behaviour.

projective techniques Research procedures designed to identify consumers' subconscious feelings and motivations. These tests often require consumers to interpret ambiguous stimuli such as incomplete sentences, cartoons or ink blots.

proletariat Those people with limited ownership, organisational or skills assets.

prospect theory All choices are evaluated in two stages: editing and evaluation stage. All transactions involve a form of risk and can be seen as a balance of losses and gains.

psychoanalytic theory of personality Popular theory developed by Sigmund Freud, which holds that unconscious needs and drives can determine human personality and behaviour.

psychogenic needs See *acquired needs*.

psychographic inventory A series of written statements designed to capture relevant aspects of a consumer's personality based on their responses to statements about their activities, interests, and opinions.

psychographic segmentation Identifying segments of consumers based on their responses to statements about their activities, interests, and opinions.

psychographics Intrinsic psychological, sociocultural and behavioural characteristics that reflect how an individual is likely to act in relation to consumption decisions; also referred to as *lifestyle* or *AIOs*.

psychological field Represents the internal influences that affect consumers' decision-making processes.

psychological noise A barrier to message reception (e.g. competing advertising messages or distracting thoughts). See also *cut through*.

psychological segmentation The division of a total potential market into smaller subgroups on the basis of intrinsic characteristics of the individual, such as personality, buying motives, lifestyle, attitudes or interests.

psychology The study of the intrinsic qualities of individuals, such as their motivations, perception, personality and learning patterns.

public policy A systematic view about how government and non-government bodies should handle major social issues, such as regulation, safety, food labelling and communications.

purchase behaviour Behaviour of two types: *trial* (the exploratory phase in which consumers evaluate a product through use) and *repeat purchase* (in which consumers demonstrate some loyalty to the product or service).

purchase cycle The average time between purchases of a product.

purchase time The amount of time that elapses between consumer awareness of a new product or service and the point at which they either purchase or reject it.

purchaser The person who undertakes the activities to procure or obtain the product or service.

qualitative research Research based on describing markets in a way that captures their meaning and significance, typically generated by in-depth interviews and group discussions.

quantitative probability phase The phase of an in-depth segmentation study that identifies the prime segments to be pursued in such terms as members' behaviour, attitude, demographic characteristics and media habits.

quantitative research Research based on describing the market by the use of scales and other questions which produce numeric data using surveys or experimental methods.

quintile One-fifth of a distribution (e.g. the upper quintile of income earners would comprise the top 20% of income earners).

racial subculture A subculture categorised by race.

rank-order scale An attitude scale in which consumers are asked to rank items, products, stores or services along a dimension such as value for money.

rate of adoption The percentage of potential adopters within a specific social system who have adopted a new product within a given period of time.

rate of usage The frequency of use and repurchase of a particular product.

rational motive Motive or goal based on economic or objective criteria, such as price, size, weight or km/litre.

rationalisation When individuals redefine a frustrating situation by inventing plausible reasons for not being able to attain their goals.

reach The number of people, households or decision makers who have seen a particular advertisement at least once.

reactance theory The theory that when a person's freedom to engage in a particular behaviour is threatened, the behaviour becomes more attractive.

recall and recognition post-test Conducted to determine whether consumers remember seeing a commercial and whether they recall its content.

recency effect A theory that proposes that the last (i.e. most recent) message presented in a sequential series of messages tends to be remembered longest. See also *primacy effect*.

recognition measure A research technique in which the consumer is shown a specific advertisement and asked whether he or she remembers having seen it.

redundancy Repeated information.

reference group A person or group that serves as a point of comparison (or reference) for an individual in the formation of either general or specific values, attitudes or behaviour.

reference price Any price that a consumer uses as a basis for comparison in judging another price.

referents Prominent people or groups that consumers look to, having an effect on their consumption.

regional subculture Type of subculture according to the geographical area a person lives in.

rehearsal The silent, mental repetition of material. Also, the relating of new data to old data to make the former more meaningful.

reinforcement A positive or negative outcome that influences the likelihood that a specific behaviour will be repeated in the future in response to a particular cue or stimulus.

reinforcing A desired outcome of certain communication messages, of which the intention is to strengthen particular beliefs (relating to a product).

relationship marketing Marketing aimed at creating strong, lasting relationships with core groups of customers in order to strengthen their commitment to the marketing supplier and its products and services.

relative advantage The degree to which potential customers perceive a new product to be superior to existing alternatives.

reliability The degree to which a measurement instrument is consistent in what it measures.

religious subculture Type of subculture based upon religious affiliation.

repeat purchase The act of repurchasing the same product or brand purchased earlier.

repertoire of brands Group of brands bought in a particular product category, over a period of time.

repetition Some overlearning (repetition of information) increases the strength of the association between a conditioned stimulus and unconditioned stimulus.

repositioning Strategy used by marketers to change the attributes consumers associate with a brand.

reputational measures One of three approaches to measure social class, whereby community members are asked to judge the social class membership of other members in their community. See also *key informant method*.

request for tender (RFT) A formal process for buying products by organisations. They make explicit the requirements for products and services and how they should be delivered.

resonance The emotional fit between the theme of a message and the feelings of the consumer.

response The reaction of an individual to a specific stimulus or cue.

response style The way consumers respond to market research questions (e.g. in forming categories, or in estimating quantities and periods of time).

retention Remembering of information; maintaining a customer.

retrieval The stage of information processing in which individuals recover information from long-term storage.

ritual A type of symbolic activity consisting of a series of steps (multiple behaviours) occurring in a fixed sequence and repeated over time.

ritualistic behaviour Any behaviour that a person has made into a ritual.

roadblocking An element of communication that prevents the consumer accepting the persuasive message.

Rokeach Value Survey A self-administered inventory consisting of 18 terminal values (i.e. personal goals) and 18 instrumental values (i.e. ways of reaching personal goals).

role A pattern of behaviour expected of an individual in a specific social position, such as the role of a mother, daughter, teacher or lawyer. One person may have a number of different roles, each of which is relevant in the context of a specific social situation.

routinised response behaviour A habitual purchase response based on predetermined criteria.

Roy Morgan Values Segments Ten values segments developed for Roy Morgan Research by the Horizons Network.

salience Degree to which a stimulus (e.g. an advertisement) attracts attention.

schema The total package of associations brought to mind when a cue is activated.

seal of approval A product or service rating that serves as a positive endorsement to encourage consumers to act favourably to the product or service featured (e.g. Australian Direct Marketing Association Seal).

secondary data Data that have been collected for reasons other than the specific research project at hand.

secondary group A group of people who interact infrequently or irregularly, such as two women who meet occasionally in the supermarket.

secondary needs See *acquired needs*.

secondary research Research information collected elsewhere or for another purpose which a marketer finds useful. See *primary research*.

segmentation criteria Nine category types that are the most common bases for segmentation: geographic, demographic, psychological, psychographic, sociocultural, use-related, use-situation, benefit sought and hybrid.

selective attention A heightened awareness of stimuli relevant to one's needs or interests. Also called *selective perception*.

selective binding A technique that enables publishers to narrowly segment their subscription bases.

selective exposure Conscious or subconscious exposure of the consumer to certain media or messages, and the subconscious or active avoidance of others.

selective perception See *selective attention*.

self-concept See *self-image*.

self-designating method A method of measuring some aspect of consumer behaviour (such as opinion leadership) in which a person is asked to evaluate or describe his or her own attitudes or actions.

self-gifts Gifts or treats a consumer will buy for himself or herself.

self-identification People's perception of the group or groups to which they belong (e.g. people who identify with their parents' ethnic group).

self-image The image a person has of himself or herself as a certain kind of person with certain characteristic traits, habits, possessions, relationships and behaviour.

self-organising A business network that learns to grow, die or adapt within a broad framework that is flexible, multilevel and under constant review.

self-perception theory A theory that suggests that consumers develop attitudes by reflecting on their own behaviour.

self-regulation Where an industry body, such as ADMA, develops and polices a code of ethics that its members agree to follow.

self-report attitude scales The measurement of consumer attitudes by self-scoring procedures, such as Likert scales, semantic differential scales or rank-order scales.

self-reports Pen-and-pencil 'tests' completed by individuals concerning their own actions, attitudes or motivations in regard to a subject or product under study.

semantic differential scale A series of bipolar adjectives (such as good–bad, hot–cold) that are anchored at the end of an odd-numbered (e.g. 5 or 7) set of points. Respondents are asked to rate an object (e.g. brand, company, service) on the basis of each attribute (i.e. bipolar pair) by choosing a scale point that best describes it. Treated as interval data.

semiotics The study of symbols and the social meanings they convey. Often used to analyse the meanings of various consumption behaviours, rituals and advertising.

sensation The immediate and direct response of the sensory organs to simple stimuli (e.g. colour, brightness, loudness, smoothness).

sensory adaptation Accommodating (i.e. 'getting used to') certain repeated sensations, such as a loud noise, a bright light or a novel advertisement.

sensory receptors The human organs (eyes, ears, nose, mouth, skin) that receive sensory inputs.

sensory store According to information-processing theory, the place in which all sensory inputs are housed very briefly before passing into the short-term store.

sex roles The roles assigned to males and females within the society in which they live.

shadow shopping Market research technique in which the researcher acts like an ordinary shopper, in order to evaluate the service actually delivered.

Sheth family decision-making model One of several comprehensive models of consumer behaviour.

Sheth-Newman-Gross model of consumption values One of several comprehensive models of consumer behaviour.

shopping group Two or more people who shop together.

short-term store In information-processing theory, the stage of real memory in which information received from the sensory store for processing is retained briefly before passing into the long-term store or being forgotten.

simplifying decision strategy A strategy whereby the consumer evaluates alternative brands in terms of one relevant criterion. See also *optimising decision strategy*.

simulation A promotional tactic that suggests to the target audience that it is appropriate to discuss a particular subject or product.

single-component attitude model An attitude model consisting of just one overall *affective*, or 'feeling', *component*.

single parent family Households consisting of one parent and at least one child.

single-trait personality tests Measure just one trait, such as self-confidence.

single-variable index The use of a single socioeconomic variable (such as income) to estimate an individual's relative social class. See also *composite-variable index*.

skimming policy Strategy of charging high prices for a new product for a quick return on development costs.

sleeper effect The tendency for persuasive communication to lose the impact of source credibility over time (i.e. the influence of a message from a high-credibility source tends to decrease over time; the influence of a message from a low-credibility source tends to increase over time).

slice-of-life commercial Television commercial that depicts a typical person or family solving a problem by using the advertised product or service. It focuses on 'real-life' situations with which the viewer can identify.

social character In the context of consumer behaviour, a personality trait that ranges on a continuum from inner-directedness (reliance on one's own inner values or standards) to other-directedness (reliance on others for direction).

social class The division of members of a society into a hierarchy of distinct status classes, so that members of each class have relatively the same status and members of all other classes have either higher or lower status.

social judgment theory An individual's processing of information about an issue is determined by his or her involvement with the issue.

social marketing The use of marketing concepts and techniques to win adoption of socially beneficial ideas.

social prestige The status an individual has in society.

social psychology The study of how individuals operate in a group.

social risk The perceived risk that a poor product choice may result in social embarrassment.

social self-image How consumers feel others see them.

social status See *social prestige*.

social system A physical, social or cultural environment to which people belong and within which they function.

socialisation A process that includes imparting the basic values and modes of behaviour consistent with the culture.

societal marketing concept A revision of the traditional marketing concept, suggesting that marketers should adhere to principles of social responsibility in the marketing of their goods and services, i.e. they must try to satisfy the needs and wants of their target markets in ways that preserve and enhance the well-being of consumers and society as a whole.

sociocultural environment Consists of a wide range of non-commercial influences, such as comments of a friend, an editorial in the newspaper, usage by a family member etc.

sociocultural segmentation variables Sociological or cultural variables such as social class, stage in the family life cycle, religion, race, nationality, values, beliefs or customs.

socioeconomic profiles Target market profiles developed using family income, occupation and education that allow segments to be developed.

socioeconomic status score (SES) A multi-variable social class measure used by research companies that combines occupational status, family income and educational attainment into one measure of social class standing.

sociology An understanding of society and how it functions.

sociometric method A method of measuring opinion leadership whereby the actual pattern or web of person-to-person informal communication is traced.

source The initiator of a message.

source credibility The perceived honesty and objectivity of the source of communication.

specifiers Professionals such as architects or doctors who decide product or service choice on behalf of consumers.

spin-doctor Public relations person whose job it is to make the best out of any political, business or environmental controversy.

split brain theory See *hemispheral lateralisation*.

spokesperson A celebrity who represents a brand or

company over an extended period of time, often in print, television and personal appearances. Usually called a company (or corporate) spokesperson.

SRI Values and Lifestyle Program (VALS2™) A research service that tracks marketing-relevant shifts in the beliefs, values and lifestyles of a sample of the population that has been divided into a small number of consumer segments.

stages in the adoption process A five-stage process through which the consumer passes in making a decision of whether to try or not to try, or to continue or discontinue use of a product. The five stages are: awareness, interest, evaluation, trial, and adoption or rejection.

standardised product A product (brand) sold in multiple (global) markets without any changes or modifications.

Starch Readership Service A syndicated service that evaluates the effectiveness of magazine advertisements.

status The relative prestige accorded to an individual within a specific group or social system.

stereotypes Individuals tend to construct images in their minds of the meaning of different kinds of stimuli. These stereotypes serve as expectations of what specific situations or people or events will be like and are important determinants of how such stimuli are subsequently perceived.

stimulation Promotional strategy that is sufficiently interesting and informative enough to provoke consumers into discussing the benefits of the product with others.

stimulus Any unit of input to any of the senses. Examples of consumer stimuli include products, packages, brand names, advertisements and commercials. Also known as *sensory input*.

stimulus ambiguity Where consumers are unsure of the meaning of information they receive in the environment (e.g. an unfamiliar icon in a computer package or an unfamiliar symbol on a product pack).

stimulus discrimination The ability to select a specific stimulus from among similar stimuli because of perceived differences.

stimulus generalisation The inability to perceive differences between slightly dissimilar stimuli.

stimulus-response theory Theory which focuses on the observational study of what consumers do in response to the stimuli that impinge on them, rather than being concerned with mental processes such as cognition and emotion. See also *positivist*.

storage The stage in information processing in which individuals organise and reorganise information in long-term memory received from the short-term store.

store image Consumers' perceptions of the 'personality' of a store and the products it carries.

straight rebuy A simple decision-making process, as in repeated purchase of items over time.

strata A division or grouping of social class into discrete levels ordered hierarchically.

subcultural interaction Because consumers are simultaneously members of several subcultural groups, marketers must determine how consumers' specific subcultural memberships interact to influence the consumer's purchase decisions.

subculture A distinct cultural group that exists as an identifiable segment within a larger, more complex society.

subjective measurement of social class A method of measuring social class whereby people are asked to estimate their own social class position.

subjective norm A consumer's perception of whether other people want them to engage in that behaviour.

sublimation The manifestation of repressed needs in a socially acceptable form of behaviour; a type of defence mechanism.

subliminal embeds Symbols implanted in print advertisements, presumed to appeal to consumers below the level of their conscious awareness.

subliminal perception Perception of very weak or rapid stimuli received below the level of conscious awareness.

substitute goal A goal that replaces an individual's primary goal when that goal becomes unattainable.

superego In Freudian theory, the part of the personality that reflects society's moral and ethical codes of conduct. See also *id* and *ego*.

supply chain A network of organisations from initial producer of raw materials to end user.

supraliminal perception Perception of stimuli at or above the level of conscious awareness.

surrogate cues Evidence that consumers use to make judgments about a product or service where they lack direct information (e.g. a consumer can estimate the quality of an unfamiliar product by its price).

symbol Anything that stands for something else.

symbolic adopters Consumers who believe the product is for them but have yet to adopt it.

symbolic group A group with which an individual identifies by adopting its values, attitudes or behaviour, despite the unlikelihood of future membership.

symbolic rejectors Consumers who know of the product but have decided that it is not for them.

syncratic (joint) decision A purchase decision that is made jointly by both spouses.

tachistoscope Device for showing a picture, product or advertisement for a very brief period. Marketers have used it to study product and pack recognition.

targeting The selection of a distinct market segment at which to direct a marketing strategy.

TARP (target audience rating point) The average proportion of the target audience who have been exposed to an ad. A TARP of 100 would mean that, on average, each member of the target audience has seen an ad once.

technical learning of culture Learning in which teachers instruct the child in an educational environment about *what* should be done, *how* it should be done and *why* it should be done.

teleology An ethical philosophy which considers the moral worth of a behaviour as determined by its consequences. See also *utilitarianism*.

telephone survey A method of collecting data via the telephone.

tensile price claims Specific phrases that are used to promote a range of price discounts.

testimonial A promotional technique in which a celebrity who has used a product or service speaks highly of its benefits in order to influence consumers to buy.

theory A hypothesis (or group of hypotheses) that offers an explanation of behaviour.

theory of reasoned action A comprehensive theory of the interrelationships among attitudes, intentions and behaviour.

theory of trying Recasts the theory of reasoned action model by replacing *behaviour* with *trying to behave* (i.e. consume) as the variable to be explained or predicted.

three-hit theory A theory that proposes that the optimum number of exposures to an advertisement to induce learning is three: one to gain consumers' awareness, a second to show the relevance of the product, and a third to show its benefits.

time risk The perceived risk that the time spent in product search may be wasted if the product does not perform as expected.

Trade Practices Act 1974 A legislative Act of parliament that was passed to regulate business in its dealings with consumers and business.

trait Any distinguishing, relatively enduring way in which one individual differs from another.

trait theory A theory of personality that focuses on the measurement of specific psychological characteristics.

transformational motivation Describes the positive motivation generated by advertising that provides sensory gratification, intellectual stimulation or social approval.

trial The fourth stage of the traditional adoption process in which the consumer tries the product innovation on a limited basis.

trial adopters Consumers who have tried the product but have not made an actual purchase.

trial purchase A type of purchase behaviour in which the consumer purchases a product (usually in a small size) in order to evaluate it.

trial rejectors Consumers who try a product but find it to be lacking.

trialability The degree to which a new product is capable of being tried by consumers on a limited basis (e.g. through free samples or small-size packages).

tricomponent attitude model An attitude model consisting of three parts: a cognitive (knowledge) component, an affective (feeling) component, and a conative (doing) component.

two-sided (refutational) message A two-sided message also includes some negatives, thereby enhancing the credibility of the message.

two-step flow of communication theory A communication model that portrays opinion leaders as direct receivers of information from mass media sources who then interpret and transmit this information to the general public.

unaided recall An advertising measurement technique in which respondents are asked to recall advertisements they have seen, with no cues as to the identity or product class of the advertisements to be recalled. Often used to measure the influence of timing on learning schedules.

unaware group Consumers who do not know about the innovation or do not have enough information to make a decision about the product yet.

unconditioned stimulus Stimulus that consumers react to without learning.

unconscionable lies Deceptive advertisements in which completely false claims are made intentionally.

unconscious needs Hidden, deep-seated drives or motivations which consumers have.

unfair advertising Advertising in which the advertiser withholds information that could result in damage to consumers.

unfounded rumours Negative comments that are untrue and which can sweep through the marketplace to the detriment of a product or service.

unintended audiences Includes everyone who is exposed to an advertising message, but who is not specifically targeted by the source.

upward mobility Displayed by people whose affluence is increasing, relative to the rest of society.

use-related segmentation Popular and effective form of segmentation that categorises consumers in terms of product, service or brand usage characteristics, such as usage rate, awareness status and degree of brand loyalty.

user-situation segmentation Based on the idea that the occasion or situation often determines what consumers will purchase or consume (i.e. special usage situations, certain products for certain situations, such as bridal wear).

utilitarian function A component of the functional approach to attitude-change theory that suggests consumers hold certain attitudes partly because of the brand's utility.

utilitarianism A teleological theory best summarised by the idea of 'the greatest good for the greatest number'.

validity The degree to which a measurement instrument accurately reflects what it is designed to measure.

VALS2™ See *SRI Values and Lifestyle Program*.

value-expressive function A component of the functional approach to attitude-change theory, suggesting that attitudes express consumers' general values, lifestyle and outlook.

value pricing Based on products of high quality in their product class that are marketed at the lowest possible price.

values Relatively enduring beliefs that serve as guides for what is considered 'appropriate' behaviour and are widely accepted by the members of a society.

values instruments Data collection instruments used to ask people how they feel about basic personal and social concepts such as freedom, comfort, national security and peace.

variable A thing or idea that may vary (i.e. assume a succession of values).

variety seeking A personality trait, similar to OSL, that measures a consumer's degree of variety seeking, related to exploratory purchase behaviour, vicarious exploration and/or use innovativeness.

venturesomeness A personality trait that measures a consumer's willingness to accept the risk of purchasing innovative products.

verbal communication A message based on the spoken or written word.

verbalisers Consumers who prefer verbal information and products, such as membership in CD or book clubs. See also *visualisers*.

viral marketing A marketing strategy that encourages consumers to pass on a marketing message to other consumers, such that the potential for awareness and influence growth of that message is exponential (the spread of the message is akin to a virus).

virtual organisation Comes from one or more organisations working closely together so that they mostly behave like a single organisation.

visual communication Non-verbal stimuli such as photographs or illustrations commonly used in advertising to convey or add meaning to a message or to reinforce message arguments.

visualisers Consumers who prefer information and products that stress the visual, such as membership in a videotape club. See also *verbalisers*.

visualisers vs verbalisers Type of cognitive personality trait that can influence consumer behaviour. See also *visualisers* and *verbalisers*.

voluntary simplifiers A segment of consumers who select uncomplicated lifestyles designed to maximise the amount of control they have over their own lives.

voter behaviour The activities of individuals prior to or during an election campaign (see *consumer behaviour*).

WAPI (Web Assisted Personal Interviewing) A method of interviewing respondents via the Web.

Warner's ISC See *index of status characteristics (ISC)*.

wearout The point at which repeated exposure to a stimulus, such as an advertising message, no longer has a positive or reinforcing influence on attitudes or behaviour.

Weber's law A theory concerning the perceived differentiation of similar stimuli of varying intensities (i.e. the stronger the initial stimulus, the greater the additional intensity needed for the second stimulus to be perceived as different).

wife-dominated Households where the wife makes a disproportionate number of purchase decisions.

word-of-mouth (WOM) Informal conversations concerning a product or service.

work group A group formed and sustained on the basis of work/employment interactions.

world brand Product that is manufactured, packaged and distributed in the same way, regardless of the country in which it is sold.

Yankelovich MONITOR® A research service that tracks over 50 social trends, and provides information as to shifts in size and direction, and resulting marketing implications.

young achievers People who have achieved visible success at an early age.

young marrieds A young married couple; the second stage of the family life cycle.

young singles The first stage in the family life cycle, where young single adults live apart from their parents.

zapping Avoiding advertisements on TV by changing channels.

zipping Fast forwarding through advertising material on a videotape.

Index

Page numbers followed by fig indicate figures; those followed by tab indicate tables.